# INTO THE NINETIES

This book is dedicated to

Oodgeroo of the tribe Noonuccal – 1920-1993

and

Barbara Hanrahan – 1939-1991

# INTO THE NINETIES
## Post-Colonial Women's Writing

Edited by

Anna Rutherford, Lars Jensen, Shirley Chew

Dangaroo Press

# ACKNOWLEDGEMENTS

We wish to thank all contributors to this book and to acknowledge the writers and publishers for permission to reprint extracts from the following books: Heinemann Australia for the extract from Thea Astley's *Coda*; Penguin India for Githa Hariharan's 'The Remains of the Feast'; Chatto and Windus for Marina Warner's story 'Salvage' from *The Mermaids in the Basement*; Penguin Australia for Beverley Farmer's story 'The Woman with Black Hair' from *Home Time*; Alfred A. Knoph for the extract from Bharati Mukherjee's *The Holder of the World*; Syballa Co-operative for the extract from Mary Fallon's *Working Hot*; Macmillan Australia and UK, and Harcourt Brace USA for the extract from Kate Grenville's *Dark Places*, to be published in the USA under the title *Albion's Story*; Century Hutchinson for the extract from Meira Chand's *House of the Sun*; Penguin New Zealand for permission to use Patricia Grace's story 'Flower Girls' from her recently published short story collection; Bloodaxe UK for Jackie Kay's poems from *The Adoption Papers*. Jo Steele and Kensington Galleries for permission to use Barbara Hanrahan's work for the cover.

We would also like to thank the following publishers for providing photographs of the authors: Bloodaxe, Chatto and Windus, New Beacon, Virago, The Women's Press and Kensington Galleries. The photography credits appear at the end of the book.

Thanks also to Grethe Kirkebye Poulsen and Anne Mette Finderup for their help with the proofing. We have done our best to ensure that we have included all the people and publishers who should be thanked. If we have inadvertently left anyone out we apologize.

Cover: 'Angel' by Barbara Hanrahan, 1976.

*Kunapipi* is published with assistance from the Literature Board of the Australian Council, the Federal Government's arts funding and advisory body and the European branch of the Association for Commonwealth Literature and Language Studies.

Australia Council
for the Arts

First published by Kunapipi in 1994

This edition first published by Dangaroo Press 1994
Australia: P.O. Box 1176, Armidale, New South Wales 2350
Denmark: Pinds Hus, Geding Søvej 21, 8381 Mundelstrup
U.K.: P.O. Box 20, Hebden Bridge, West Yorkshire HX7 5UZ

ISBN: 1-871049 52 0

Printed in Great Britain by Villiers Publications, London N3

# Contents

ANNA RUTHERFORD

# Foreword

This book had its genesis around 1989-90. One of my joys is to travel and when I do I tend to meet the literary community and start talking about writers. And one of the things that always strikes me – if I'm honest, irritates/depresses me – is the almost total ignorance of the people I speak to about writers who are not only well known but famous in their own country but totally unknown outside it. When these unknown names are mentioned, one feels as one does when one looks in the fishmonger's window and sees the glassy look in the eyes of the fish! This, I must hasten to add, is not the fault of the people to whom I am speaking. The fault lies in the fact, as Rosemary Sørensen, editor of *Australian Book Review*, pointed out in her report on the Commonwealth Writers Prize, that we are faced with a publishing culture threatened with increasing banality, as multinational conglomerates 'rationalize' the market (*Australian Book Review*, December 1993/January 1994). Rosemary had just been present at the judging of the Commonwealth Writers Prize in Singapore, a prize sponsored by the Commonwealth Foundation. The Foundation is not only one of the few, it is the only major body to try to bring to the attention of the rest of the world the wealth of writing to be found in the Commonwealth countries, and we all owe it a great debt.

Also present in Singapore was Michael Ondaatje and he, too, brought up the problem of writers getting their stories told – an issue that is raised again and again in this book. His solution was the small presses, but the economic climate is slowly, but surely, eliminating those small presses. As a director of a small press, with a staff of one, I can speak with conviction and experience. BUT I come from a family which, if you're kind, you can say are strong-minded, and if you're Australian and honest you can say are 'bloody-minded'. Indeed, it was said of my relatives, the Bradys, 'if any one of them drowned in the river, one shouldn't bother to look for the body downstream because it was sure to go upstream'.

And so I decided to try in a small way to rectify this situation and put out a special women's issue of *Kunapipi* (the journal I edit, which goes to most countries in the world, including the island St Helena). My aim is to present as many different voices as possible, and to introduce to a wide audience, those different voices and their concerns.

It set out to be a single issue of *Kunapipi*, but it just grew and grew so now there are nearly seven hundred pages, and what was first known as

'The Women's Issue' is now rather sarcastically referred to by some of my 'friends' as 'The Women's Encyclopedia'. For the lucky people who subscribe to *Kunapipi* it still remains a single issue, because the Literature Board of the Australia Council insists that you can only have single issues, no matter what the size. It is a decision I accept and respect because without the aid of the Literature Board *Kunapipi* would have ceased to exist long ago. However, I am also issuing it as a book – a great book, I believe, and I hope you, the readers, think so too.

I might say it hasn't been an easy book to put together. I have discovered that I'm not the only person who likes to travel – writers do as well, and they are rarely where they are supposed to be.

I am also aware that it is uneven in its contents. Africa is a huge continent, but the African section is small. However, this is due essentially to circumstances quite outside my control. To give one example: The only way I could get in contact with Kanchana Ugbabe was via Ralph Elliott in Canberra who had a friend in the Nigerian High Commission. The letter was sent by diplomatic bag to Nigeria, car to Jos and back to Lagos, diplomatic bag to Canberra and faxed to me in Denmark.

In another book I edited, *From Commonwealth to Post-Colonial*, in my note *to* contributors I suggested that they believed I had a secret urge to be a sleuth. At that time I denied it. But now, after putting this book together and tracking down so many people, I'm not so sure!

My aim, and the aim of this book, is to bring a rich, variegated world of women writers to you. Being women they have certain things in common, *but* living in different social, political and cultural worlds, their concerns must almost of necessity be different. True, they have much in common, but true also is the fact, as Jamaica Kincaid pointed out in her novel *Lucy*, that what might for one woman symbolize one of the most beautiful things in the world can for another woman, from another section of the world, symbolize 'a scene of conquered and conquests'. I am referring to the scene where Mariah (American) presents Lucy (West Indian) with her first view of daffodils. Mariah is upset about Lucy's negative reaction, and as the two women walk away in silence, Lucy contemplates the situation:

> It wasn't her fault. It wasn't my fault. But nothing could change the fact that where she saw beautiful flowers I saw sorrow and bitterness. The same thing could cause us to shed tears, but those tears would not taste the same. (*Lucy*, p. 30)

This volume contains both the tears, laughter and thoughts of women from around the world. Some of it you will recognize and share, and some of it will, I hope, surprise you and add to your understanding of women's tears, laughter and thoughts in faraway or unknown places and situations.

# AUSTRALIA

# Oodgeroo (Kath Walker)

## THE PAST

Let no one say the past is dead.
The past is all about us and within.
Haunted by tribal memories, I know
This little now, this accidental present
Is not the all of me, whose long making
Is so much of the past.

Tonight here in suburbia as I sit
In easy chair before electric heater,
Warmed by the red glow, I fall into dream:
I am away
At the camp fire in the bush, among
My own people, sitting on the ground,
No walls about me,
The stars over me,
The tall surrounding trees that stir in the wind
Making their own music,
Soft cries of the night coming to us, there
Where we are one with all old Nature's lives
Known and unknown,
In scenes where we belong but have now forsaken.
Deep chair and electric radiator
Are but since yesterday,
But a thousand thousand camp fires in the forest
Are in my blood.
Let none tell me the past is wholly gone.
Now is so small a part of time, so small a part
Of all the race years that have moulded me.

Oodgeroo

DI YERBURY

# A Tribute to Oodgeroo of the Tribe Noonuccal

I was proud and privileged to know Oodgeroo of the Tribe Noonuccal (formerly Kath Walker), poet, artist, political activist and teacher, in the last years of her life.

Like many Australians I had heard much of Oodgeroo and read her work, but it was not until 1988, when she agreed to accept an Honorary Doctorate of Letters from Macquarie University, that I came to know her personally.

That experience had a profound effect on me. Oodgeroo was a woman filled with a creative and positive spirit which, combined with her sensitivity to and deep knowledge of the Aboriginal tradition and her immense store of wisdom, gave Australians, both Aboriginal and non-Aboriginal, a new dimension to their heritage. She was also a woman with deep reserves of warmth and personal strength, who gave of herself unstintingly.

As a poet and artist her work was not just distinguished and original, but also popular. She became the best-selling poet in Australia after C.J. Dennis. She was mainly self-educated through her love of reading, going on in later life to be invited to lecture at universities throughout the world.

From the early 1970s Oodgeroo lived a simple life on North Stradbroke Island in Queensland, the locus of her tribal roots, running an education cultural centre, and spent much of her time teaching thousands of children of all racial backgrounds about Aboriginal heritage and the natural wonders of the places, flora and fauna she knew so well. It was there, I believe, that she was happiest.

I'm delighted to be part of a tribute to this remarkable woman of vision, talent, courage and dedication to her people, and to place on record again my admiration of her life and achievements.

Di Yerbury is Vice-Chancellor at Macquarie University.

OODGEROO

# Acceptance Speech

Allow me to begin this address by expressing my sincere gratitude to Macquarie University for bestowing such an honour upon me. It represents a milestone in the history of this land now known as Australia, for it recognizes, belated though it be, the value of a most ancient earth culture to modern society for us who came late to 'civilization', missing the gap of centuries. When you came we admired and marvelled, but with foreboding. We had so little, but we had happiness, each day was a holiday. For we were people before we were citizens, people before we were ratepayers, tenants, customers, employees, parishioners. We could not understand white man's gradings, rigid and unquestioning. Your sacred tokens of lord and lady, highness and holiness, eminence, majesty. We could not understand your strange cult of uniformity, this mass obedience to clocks, timetables. Puzzled, we wondered at the importance to you of ties, gloves, uniforms and shoes. New to us were gaols and orphanages, rents and taxes, banks and mortgages. We, who had so few things, had the prime things. We had no policemen, lawyers, middlemen, brokers, financiers, millionaires. So, the new 'wonders', stocks and shares, real estate, compound interests, sales and investments, had bewildered us all. Oh, we have benefited, we have been gifted with new knowledge, a new world opened. Suddenly caught up in the white man's ways, gladly and gratefully we accept, for this is necessity. But remember white man, if life is for happiness you too surely have much to change. In summing up I would like to restate that a multicultural society can only successfully occur in this country when seventh generation Australians recognize the Aboriginal culture. No change can, or will occur, until the theft of Aboriginal land and the slaughter and enslaving are redeemed and compensated. This Aboriginal land will never accept and will always be alien to any race who dares try to enslave her. Aboriginals will always be the custodian of the traditional lands, regardless of any other enforced law system. For ladies and gentlemen, my friends, the land is our mother. Aborigines cannot own her for she owns us. Thank you.

At the conclusion of the ceremony Oodgeroo recited the Aboriginal Charter of Rights:

We want hope not racialism,
Brotherhood not ostracism.
Black advance
Not white ascendence.
Make us equal not dependent.
We need help not exploitation.
We want freedom not frustration.
Not control but self-reliance
Independence not compliance.
Not rebuff but education
Self-respect not resignation.
Free us from a mean subjection
From a bureaucrat protection.
Let's forget the old time slavers,
Give us fellowship not favours,
Encouragement not prohibitions
Houses, not settlements and missions.
We need love, not overlordship
Grip of hand, not whip hand wardship.
Opportunity that places
White and Black on equal basis.
You dishearten, not defend us,
Circumscribe, who should befriend us.
Give us us welcome, not aversion,
Give us choice, not cold cohesion.
Status, not discrimination
Human rights, not segregation.
View the law like Roman Pontius,
Make us proud, not colour conscious.
Give the deal you still deny us,
Give goodwill not bigot bias.
Give ambition, not prevention,
Confidence, not condescension,
Give incentive, not restriction,
Give us Christ, not cruxifiction.
Though baptized and blessed and bibled,
We are still tabooed and libelled.
You devout salvation-sellers
Make us neighbours, not fringe dwellers.
Make us mates, not poor relations,
Citizens, not serfs on stations.
Must we native old Australians,
In our own land rank as aliens.
Banish, ban, and conquer caste.
Then we'll win our own at last.

# An Interview with Oodgeroo

This interview took place prior to the awarding of the honorary degree.

*In 1987 you chose to give up the name of Kath Walker and choose the Aboriginal name. Can you tell us about that decision?*

Pastor Don Brady, who is now dead, was quite surprised at the way my poems were accepted into the White Australian scene and that White Australians were buying them and he said, 'Kathy you know if we didn't have the white people dictating terms to us, and if we still had our own way of life, our own Aboriginal laws to uphold, the tribal elders would have given you the name of Oodgeroo, that's the paperbark tree, because without the paperbark you could not have done it.' And it's from then that I started thinking, 'Why should I carry the English name? Why should I not go back to my own identity and my own name?' And I thought, 'I think the time is now for me to strike a blow in the interest of the cruelty that was inflicted upon the Aboriginals.' And I did it as a protest against that.

*When you gave up that name and took on the name Oodgeroo, you also gave up your M.B.E. Did you have any problems in your own mind about accepting the honorary doctorate having given back the M.B.E.?*

Well as far as the M.B.E. was concerned, as I'd rejected the English name it would have been hypocritical of me to hold the M.B.E. I would have been a hypocrite to do it. On the other hand, when the Chancellor of Macquarie University wrote to me asking if I would accept this great honour that they had bestowed on me, the doctorate of letters, I felt I had really earned it and that the offer was sent to me with all good faith and in all sincerity, without any tokenism whatsoever, and for that reason it was my pleasure to accept it.

In her colourful and vital life, Oodgeroo has won international recognition as a writer and poet, a teacher, an artist and an Aboriginal activist.
    Born in Brisbane in 1920, her formal education concluded when she left school at the age of 13 to work in domestic service. Through a life-long love of reading Oodgeroo is self-educated and notes the irony that she is

now invited to lecture at universities around the world. She began writing for the entertainment of her friends and her own interest. Through contact with an Australian writers' group she was encouraged to continue her writing. Her poetry came to the attention of Mary Gilmore who recognized the merit of her work and urged her to share her poems by publishing them. With the support of Judith Wright, Oodgeroo received a grant from the Commonwealth Literary Fund to publish her first book and her career in the writing world began. She has five books of poetry to her credit and another, written during her visit to China in 1985, was published both in Chinese and Mandarin.

Her achievements as a writer have been recognized by many awards, including the Jesse Litchfield medal, the M.G. medal and a fellowship of the Writers' Guild. She has been an official representative at many overseas festivals and arts conferences. She toured the United States as a Fulbright scholar.

Oodgeroo has always painted for her own personal fulfilment. Again her talent as an artist was recognized by chance and she was persuaded to exhibit, attracting considerable acclaim. A book of her paintings was published by the Aboriginal Arts Board in 1986. A short film biography of her life made in 1977 resulted in an international prize for acting and a place in the U.S. Black Hall of Fame. She also appeared and served as script consultant in Bruce Beresford's film, *The Fringedwellers* in 1986.

# EVA JOHNSON

Eva Johnson was born at Daly River in the Northern Territory. She moved to Adelaide in the 50's and in 1979 wrote her first play. Her third play *Voices* was performed as part of the Hiroshimo Arts Festival in Japan in 1990. Eva's writing has taken her to many parts of the world. In 1988 she was invited to the first International Women's Playwrights Conference in Buffalo, New York, was writer in residence at the Native American Community School in Minnesota, and has spoken at several universities throughout America including the Massachusetts Institute of Technology; Rollins College Florida, and the University of Minnesota. In 1991, Eva was a speaker at the 3rd International Feminist Book Fair in Barcelona, Spain. Her most recent play *Heartbeat of the Earth* had its world premier performance as part of the 1993 2nd World Indigenous Youth Conference in Darwin. In 1993 Eva was awarded the Australia Council inaugural Red Ochre Award in recognition of her outstanding contribution to Aboriginal and Torres Strait Islander Arts culture. Her published works include – plays ('Murras' – in *Plays from Black Australia*; and 'What do they Call Med' in *Heroines*) and poetry (*Inside Black Australia* and *Spirit Song*).

EVA JOHNSON

# On the Line

The biggest question that lies important in my life at the moment is, what is my role in this country, as a writer, a woman, a mother and most importantly, as an Aborigine?

My sense of responsibility comes from a place where, as a writer, the knowledge that I have acquired is the tool that connects both traditional and contemporary Aboriginal concepts. Aboriginal writing includes society as the focus of our Art.

My writing is specifically Aboriginal because it deals with my life experiences as an Aborigine and those of other Aborigines. Writing for me, as an Indigenous Australian, is about the will to survive. I try to work towards the accomplishment of the ideal of freedom through writing plays which seek to eliminate the many confusions that hinder Aboriginal people and I deal with questions that are crucial to Aboriginal people and our experiences.

Aboriginality is a major part of the texture and meaning of all important works by Aboriginal writers. Writings of protest, resistance and cultural revolution have typified Aboriginal literature.

My writing allows me to speak. The characters in my plays are real; they are living a life on stage, perhaps their lives, perhaps that of another Aborigine and their experiences. I write about people who have been under prescribed treatment for over two hundred years, who have endured the harshness, the traumas, of a hostile racial history in their own country. These historical events are different configurations of racism but these are lived experiences. My writing exemplifies these experiences. My writing is often triggered by childhood memories...

I remember my mother running through the bushes
with me on her back,
her screams deafened my ears.
Other women were running too.
She placed me in the bushes on the ground,
covered me with leaves.
The sound of hooves galloping
pounded my heart
my screams of fear burst my lungs
exposed my camouflage.
Strange hands brushed away the leaves

picked me up, placed something sweet in my mouth
I spat it out
put me on the back of a horse.
The bush became deadly silent.
That was the last time I saw my mother.

from the play *Tjindarella*, 1984

I began writing in the late 1970's when Aboriginal people were no longer content to remain invisible. From 1967 when Aborigines were honoured with citizenship rights in their own country, when we were no longer seen as part of the flora and fauna, the first moves began towards constituting a black consciousness, a black social force in this country.

Writing became one of the most powerful tools of protest. Thus began the resurrection of a new kind of writer, beginning with such well-respected Aboriginal writers as Kevin Gilbert, Oodgeroo Noonuccal and Hyllus Maris. These writers are part of Aboriginal history and indeed the history of establishing Aboriginal Literature within the context of Australian literature.

My whole focus as a writer is to deal with history. The Land Rights struggle brought to light a particular political concept for me. I began to write poetry about the land, the people and the living spirits that are part of Aboriginal culture. Through the genre of land, black consciousness, I sieved through the events of history, especially the treatment of Aborigines, and drew a clear conclusion of how immense the future struggle for Aborigines would be. My initial response was that of anger.

The realisation for me was that while struggling for acceptance in this country, the enemy seen by those in power was in fact my own Aboriginality, my own blackness. It was used against me by a manipulative structure that would inevitably use as its tool restrictive policies, with a view to destroying any sense of self-worth and most importantly, cultural identity.

So initially, anger became a catalyst for my writing. Anger became a valuable political tool for analysis, confrontation, redress, and in fact acted as a neon repellant against any notion of serving the government in the very institutions that moulds Aboriginality into useless captive tokens.

Writing became my partner in the war against injustice. Writing became a therapeutic balm, using works of creative expression to expel negative thought, writing words of self-affirmation, love and wisdom. Writing became a part of my spirit, the very core of my being. Writing brought me to understanding the true concepts of Aboriginality, Identity and most importantly, a sense of humour. Writing about our oppression through humour is for me one of the most poignant interactions with reality.

Weavilly porrige I'm going insane
weavilly porrige gonna wreck my brain
H,mmm, mission food

send'm from heaben
must be good
bless'em little weavill
bless'em little me
I been lungga trick'em
just you see
catch'em little weavill
put'em in the tea
only fulla drink'em up
MISSIONARY!!!!!

I am often asked if my work is autobiographical. For the most part it is.
So many things have happened to me in my lifetime that it is important
for me to retrace, to record some of the events. My children grew up in
an era that had no relation to any of the childhood experiences that I had.
They want to learn of my past, our past, Australia's history in the past.

I also have an inherent interest in all that is Aboriginal. Thus anything
that hinders or threatens the progress of Aboriginal survival forces me to
respond. Every day I deal with the notion of superiority/inferiority and
that is unsettling to me as it brings with it the sense of imbalance in this
society. Does my writing sabotage the notion of white racial superiority
and bring to reality the power of my existence?

Writing has the power to unveil almost any conscious or unconscious
thought. I write to that consciousness, the conscious demon that arrived
in this country two hundred years ago.

I'm not sure whether I take my writing seriously enough. The process of
my writing is erratic and at most times steered by time deadlines. Pro-
crastination is my greatest enemy. I detest being 'organised' and much
prefer to do things in my own time. But I am no longer afraid of what I
write, nor do I allow any room for self-censoring. MY writing has to be
attuned to my philosophical and spiritual beliefs, in that whenever I write,
the contents must come from that part of me which is the conscious
source of my being.

Writing is the most daring thing I have ever done and the most rewarding. The rewards of my writing are reflected by those who acknowledge
my work, particularly Aboriginal people. For me this acknowledgement
is an affirmation that the audience for whom I specifically write endorses
the worth of my work.

There are other Aboriginal writers who have forged the way for writers
such as I, writers whom I acknowledge as our heroes of the pen. To them
I dedicate this poem. As someone once said... Speak loud, speak unsettling
things and be dangerous.

# Eva Johnson

## THE BLACK PEN.

The Black Pen that traced our history,
the unspoken words silenced by fear
that brought to life the power of truths,
coloured red,
carved indelibly in blood along journeys
that knew the anguish of the land.
The Black Pen that witnessed the tortures of slavery
and abduction of a people hurled against the face of 'civilization'
their flesh throbbing with the winds and the waters.

The Black Pen that fights against injustice,
coloured red,
carved indelibly in blood on walls
of prison cells, in words that resist the silence of genocide,
that expose the curse of the ignorant, the sentences of death.
The Black Pen echoes the cries of Women,
whose children were captured tokens of servility,
their future sabotaged by institutions,
fractured by displaced identity.

The Black Pen that speaks with courage,
coloured red,
carved indelibly in blood,
searches for new visions along the paths of our Ancestors,
that return us to the meeting places
of the winds and the undrained beds of the waters.
The Black Pen celebrates our defiance,
our resistance, our survival, our unity,
sets our spirits free,
and honours the memory of those
read on pages
where blood red flows no more,
where indelible black ink vanishes,
No More.......

ELAINE LINDSAY

# Women Rising: Spirituality in the Writings of Barbara Hanrahan

Pink roses everywhere, roses raining from a blue summer sky, and a green beanstalk man reaching down with his leafy green fingers and snatching my grandmother away. Puffballs of Father Christmas thistles, poppies spilling their black birth dust. My grandmother's legs float higher; they're patterned with veins and the stems of an unnatural garden: witch bell, star flower. She is a giant earth mother in the sky; she is the girl she used to be. Black shiny hair full of diamond-bright sun sparks, threaded with satin ribbon; sleepy almond eyes, forget-me-not blue; all the wrinkles gone away and she's the goddess of the rainbow. She floats, she dissolves. She is just a great white cloud spread across the sky. Iris floating free over all the gardens of Rose Street.[1]

When discussing spirituality and the religious impulse in Australian literature, literary critics and theologians draw their illustrations from the writings of male poets and fiction writers, virtually ignoring the work of women writers. There are occasional exceptions, references to poets such as Judith Wright and Rosemary Dobson, but scant attention has been paid to the spiritual and theological content of novels and stories by contemporary women writers. Until recently, too, most Australian feminists with an interest in theology have looked elsewhere for expressions of women's experience of the divine, to American writers such as Adrienne Rich, Alice Walker and Denise Levertov. This lack of acknowledgement given to local women writers deserves comment, especially as there are in circulation many books by Australian women which reflect seriously upon matters moral, religious and spiritual.

My purpose here is to uncover the spiritual and religious dimensions of the writings of Barbara Hanrahan (1939-1991) whose visions, all be they idiosyncratic, are also emblematic of the approaches many women are adopting when they address the divine. The fact that these approaches differ markedly from the Christian 'malestream' spirituality which is often regarded as Australian spirituality incarnate may account in large part for society's inability to interpret the words of women. For these women refuse to celebrate a desert spirituality which locates meaning in a distant emptiness or to laud the male pilgrim who sacrifices all in search of the divine, preferring instead to portray the world as a paradise garden where the divine is present in all things and in all people and where creativity,

Barbara Hanrahan

loving kindness and joy are the ways to God. Typically, 'malestream' spirituality encourages a turning towards a transcendent God, away from the fallenness of creation as epitomized by the ravenous maw of mother nature, while women's spirituality revels in the goodness of creation and finds in it evidence of an immanent God. Women have learnt to empathize with desert spirituality but men – and this is to generalize – have failed to recognize the spirituality of the settled areas and have dismissed women fiction writers as having nothing to say that is of theological importance.

I have chosen the writings of Barbara Hanrahan to illustrate aspects of women's spirituality because of their richness and diversity; her prints and paintings, while they have informed this reading, are not the subject of the discussion which follows and still await informed exposition. A prolific writer as well as a prolific artist, Hanrahan wrote fifteen books, of which five may be described as 'autobiographical fictions', five as 'fantastic fictions' and five as 'biographical fictions'. The three categories of books are quite different from one another: the autobiographical fictions published between 1973-1992 record their narrator's coming into creativity and her recognition of the divine spark within, the fantastic fictions (1977-82) are meditations upon evil, and the biographical fictions (1985-92) are celebrations of the sacredness of the everyday, the spirituality of the humble. While it is beyond the scope of this paper to address these books singly it is possible, by concentrating on the three categories, to offer a perspective which will encourage the reading of each book as a spiritual, moral and religious document and as a refreshing alternative to the desert spirituality that holds sway in Australian critical and theological commentaries.

## AUTOBIOGRAPHICAL FICTIONS AND INNER SPIRITUALITY

Barbara Hanrahan made no bones about the religious nature of her calling as an artist and writer:

> I have always felt close to God. I have a strong belief in what I do – I have always known I was meant to live the life that I do. It would have been wicked – evil – if I had tried to do otherwise, to escape my responsibility to my talents.[2]

For Hanrahan, writing and print-making were as religion to her;[3] it was the creative act which brought her into contact with 'something so much greater than oneself'.[4] The formal practice of religion, however, was of little interest to her, critical as she was of the narrowness of mind and lack of humanity which often lurks behind the espousal of doctrine and dogma. Hanrahan's wish seems to have been to live the life of the spirit, a hope she described with reference to William Blake:

When I read something of Blake's or look at his engravings, I find a world I feel at
ease in: his spiritual world was with him all the time, there wasn't any difference
between that world and this. That to me is an ideal state.[5]

It is always tempting to conflate a writer's life with the lives of her (or
his) characters and the temptation with Hanrahan is strong, particularly
in the autobiographical fictions, *The Scent of Eucalyptus*, *Sea-Green*, *Kewpie
Doll*, *Iris in Her Garden* and *Michael and Me and the Sun*. Of these books *Sea-
Green* is the most consciously fictionalized, but all share the same narrator,
most often unnamed, who grows up in Adelaide, who is torn between society's expectations of her as a woman who will marry and bear children
and her own creative aspirations, and who leaves Australia to study art
in England. To what extent the recurring figures of Bob, Ronda, Iris and
Reece can be equated with Hanrahan's similarly named 'real' father,
mother, grandmother and great-aunt is not an issue here, for the focus of
attention is on the narrator's journey of self-discovery, much of which, on
the evidence of interviews and frankly autobiographical material, can be
regarded as Hanrahan's own journey.

Hanrahan's writings invite a variety of readings. The autobiographical
fictions might be regarded as an account of a young person's journey to
psychological maturity or to artistic fulfilment, as comment upon a
woman's struggle to overturn the dominant patriarchal and imperial
order, or as a search for an Australian identity, the exploration of an
Australian consciousness. In the context of this article they could also be
read as a journey into spiritual wholeness, an attempt to reconcile the
contradictions between the social and real selves and to nourish the child
within, the spark of divine creativity. Instead of seeking God in what are
often described as the waste places of the desert, Hanrahan finds God
within herself and within the suburban hills, gardens and homes of
Adelaide, the sacredness of daily life expressed in the rituals of women
and family, in their care for nature and each other.

This understanding did not come easily, as witnessed in *The Scent of
Eucalyptus* where the narrator records that

it was in the wild night garden that I discovered I did not fit into the snug electric
world as others did – as they thought they did. I discovered I was different, yet I
did not know where the real world lay (I was still too blinkered to know its face;
I was not yet simple enough to know that it dwelt inside me, waiting to be
reclaimed).[6]

The importance to Hanrahan of the search for a unified self which would
be at peace with the physical and spiritual worlds can be gauged by the
fact that she returned again and again in her books to the period 1939 to
the mid-1960s, when this search was most painful and intense. Significantly, she felt no need to write publicly of her life as a successful artist
and writer - her autobiographical fictions do not go beyond the point at

which she realized the possibility of living a life dedicated to and permeated by the art she likened to a religious quest. One must assume that, once Hanrahan had accepted her vocation, her inner tensions receded and she was able to focus her energies on more creative work. It may not be too far-fetched to liken Hanrahan's life to that of a mystic, noting in particular her withdrawal from the more commercial aspects of literary and artistic life, her refusal to compromise her work in order to achieve wider recognition, her abiding sense of the presence of God, her delight in the unity and sacredness of created things and her longing to be absorbed into the mystery, the perfection of it all.

## FANTASTIC FICTIONS: CORRUPTION AND THE VANITIES

Hanrahan's brace of fantastic fictions, *The Albatross Muff*, *Where the Queens all Strayed*, *The Peach Groves*, *The Frangipani Gardens* and *Dove*, have roused a variety of reactions amongst literary critics, ranging from discomfort to appreciation. It is men who appear the most uneasy, overwhelmed by 'the author's characteristic preoccupations ... with physical ugliness and maiming, sexual perversion and obsession, the processes of the body and grotesquerie of various kinds',[7] but they seem incapable of asking why Hanrahan chose to use such material. Women, in comparison, have been generally more receptive, recognizing the seriousness of Hanrahan's explorations of good and evil, reality and illusion, innocence and experience. I would suggest that in these books Hanrahan is offering a series of meditations upon all that can happen when evil, carnality and greed are allowed to run unchecked in isolated societies. In doing so she addresses subjects as diverse as the individual's search for wholeness; the innocence of children and the debilitating effects of sexuality and society, especially upon women; the feebleness and hypocrisy of conventional religion; the life-denying qualities of avarice, materialism and witchcraft; the healing powers of nature; the relationship between secular and sacred time; the loveliness of death which will make us whole; and the potential of art to transcend the mundane, to endure, and to enter into the mystery of being.

Given Hanrahan's distrust of formal religion, it should be expected that these meditations will have nothing of conventional piety about them. At best religious formulae are portrayed as hindering independent speculation into the meaning of life and the possibility of salvation, at worst religion is a smoke screen hiding the immorality and falseness of those who practise it. For people who would come to terms with their true selves, their best recourse is not belief in a 'Willy-wetleg Jesus'[8] but dedication to the arts; thus it is that Edith/Dissy, the one character of *The Albatross Muff* who does achieve a sense of Oneness, of purpose, meaning and future does so through her writing, not through religious adherence. But this is not to deny the possibility that God inspires artists, true artists

rather than maidenly daylight daubers. Doll Strawbridge's night-time in-
carnation in *The Frangipani Gardens* might well be regarded as a model of
the artist as prophet, freed from all inhibitions:

> The stars shone brightly, and the moon somehow swooped, and the quinces hung
> like dusty yellow lanterns. There was light all about her, and Tom saw she wasn't
> Auntie but a stranger. She wasn't timid and ladylike; she was still the bold artist
> who'd painted in the dark without a fumble, as if she were guided by God. Her
> blind eyes were shining, she'd left off her spectacles, her hair shed its pins to float
> loose. She had paint all over her fingers and it was smeared on her face – she was
> a painted queen jumped free of a portrait, though her dress swirled as Queen
> Mary's never would. Tom ran down the crazy path behind her. Where was she
> going, what did she seek?[9]

In these books Hanrahan captures well the sense of mystery which permeates the everyday, intimating that behind the material world is a spirit
world which must be confronted unless life is to remain a mean and
shallow thing.

While the books canvas a range of preoccupations, one is left with the
impression that it is the nature and necessity of evil which most fascinates
Hanrahan at this time of her life. Again she offers a distinctive perspective, suggesting not that evil must be fought and overcome by goodness,
but that evil and good must be kept in check for both are parts of the one
whole. When evil does run rampant it collapses under its own weight, in
the same way that those who call down evil upon others eventually become evil's prey. Hanrahan reminds her readers how thin is the veneer of
civilization behind which we shelter from the dark forces.

It is fitting that *Dove*, the last novel in this sequence, concludes with a
massive conflagration which, whether or not it promises the establishment
of a new, less exploitative society in Depression Adelaide, does mark the
end of Hanrahan's meditations on the vanities, the sins to which the flesh
is heir. As *The Albatross Muff* was a transitional novel, still working out
some of the concerns of the autobiographical fictions, particularly the
development of the self as artist, so *Dove* clears the way for the biographical fictions, burning away hypocrisy and false values to enable a
celebration of endurance, patience and loving kindness within the most
ordinary of lives.


BIOGRAPHICAL FICTIONS: THE SACREDNESS OF THE EVERYDAY

Perhaps Hanrahan's greatest contribution to the development of Australian women's spirituality can be found in her biographical fictions,
*Annie Magdalene, Dream People, A Chelsea Girl, Flawless Jade* and *Good Night,
Mr Moon*, most of which are monologues or stories based on the lives of
people known to her but unremarked by the world. It is here that

Hanrahan turns outwards to acknowledge the heroic qualities of those who quietly go about the task of living and caring for family and neighbours. These people do not need to cast off attachments and responsibilities to enter into a search for a distant God because they already enjoy the comfort of a present God. They may endure loss and hardship but they do not need to rationalize it in terms of mortification of the flesh, the ego. They do not rail against their circumstances but take life as it comes, accommodating to it but not compromising themselves, buoyed up by a simple trust that eventually all will be well:

> I thought there was Somebody looking over us. I believed in Heaven, I believed there was an Almighty above – though a lot of people didn't think so and said it was a lot of rubbish. I never laid my head down any night without I didn't say a prayer and thank the Almighty for seeing me safely through another day.[10]

It should be noted that, in comparison with the characters who populate Hanrahan's other books, the heroines of these novels, as well as most of the Dream People, are 'whole' people, untroubled by the tensions of a divided self. This may be because they are older people who have come to reflect that, whatever has befallen them, they have survived. But perhaps there is also an optimism that, when the curtains are drawn back, a new form of life will begin. Sarah Hodge in *A Chelsea Girl*, for example, is already half out of this troublesome world and has turned her gaze towards another existence in the life of the spirit. The gift that Hanrahan offers her readers through these characters is the opportunity to advance prematurely to the end of physical life, to reflect upon its meaning, to distinguish what is true and necessary from what is worthless, and to bring that knowledge back into their own reality.

In creating archetypal life-giving figures such as Annie Magdalene, Sarah Hodge, Alexandra Rodda and, in her autobiographical fictions, Iris Goodridge, Hanrahan not only offers a vastly different set of heroes to those favoured by malestream spirituality – the explorer, the digger, the bushranger, the soldier and the sportsman – but also insists upon the sacredness of the suburbs, the cities and the cultivated areas, the areas traditionally associated with women and children. The values she upholds are those which, like loving kindness, facilitate relations between people and make it easier for them to find God where they are, in the midst of life. In her love for all creation she offers a positive antidote to that distrust – if not fear – of nature so often evinced by Australian male theologians and cultural commentators. In Hanrahan, in place of the whore/temptress/bitch land which lures men to their downfall we have the figure of Annie Magdalene in her garden, the earth goddess herself as she tends to the smallest creatures of creation:

In summer, when I have short sleeves, the bees sit on my arm. They don't worry me at all, I think they love me; I just let them stay (if you brush them off they get cross), they're only sitting there to have a rest. The bees often come and sit beside me to die - such a lot do that and I dig a little hole, drop them in and cover them up, rather than let the ants eat them. When I pick off the dead flowers from the daisy bushes, I tell the bees they have to put up with me. But you must never talk loud to the bees, you must talk softly.[11]

In these books, as in all of Hanrahan's books, God is intimately linked with images of the garden and the fecundity of nature – the waterless desert and the patriarchal Father God are nowhere to be found. If one were to encapsulate Hanrahan's expression of the divine one could not go past her several Eye of God prints where the genderless and open eye of God, flanked by a smiling sun and moon, gazes out of a treasury of birds, stars, animals, flowers, insects and humans. Symbols of power and authority are eschewed in these celebrations of bountifulness, joy and the co-existence of this world and the spiritual world.[12]

CONCLUSION

I am suggesting that, however one wishes to read Barbara Hanrahan, she should be considered first as a spiritual writer working out of a contemplative – if not mystical – awareness of the divine and the role of love in the world. As she wrote in her diary:

The only way I can influence the 'world' is by being small, by being true to me and the real world of nature about me. Like a monk, like a hermit who works through prayer. By praying, by working, by *loving* the sea and the trees and the sky. By knowing God in the goodness of it all. By making my own peace. Not by dwelling on the evil, adding to it.[13]

What would such a reading achieve? Specifically, it would draw Hanrahan's writing, art and life together into a whole which is greater than the sum of its parts. The repetitions, obsessions, details and apparent banalities which have troubled some critics would be seen as serving Hanrahan's overall purpose of challenging stereotypes of Australian belief and behaviour and of offering instead the truths of lives honestly led, of insights gained by those who are close to nature and the divine. Such a reading would concentrate attention on Hanrahan's particular contribution to Australian self-understanding, her critique of the masculinist spirituality which still dominates cultural and theological discourse and her visioning of an alternative spirituality, one which is based on the fact that women have walked in the paradise garden and found it very good.

NOTES

1. Barbara Hanrahan, 'Iris in Her Garden', *Iris in Her Garden* (Deakin: Officina Brindabella, 1991) pp. 58-59.
2. Barbara Hanrahan, personal papers, undated. Thanks to Jo Steele for making this material available.
3. Recorded in Elsebeth Gabel Austin's interview with Barbara Hanrahan, April 1985, *Kunapipi*, 7, 2 and 3 (1985), p. 159.
4. Interview with Julie Mott, 28 August 1980, *Australian Literary Studies*, 11, 3 (May 1983), p. 44.
5. Ibid. p. 158.
6. Barbara Hanrahan, *The Scent of Eucalyptus* (London: Chatto and Windus, 1973), p. 162.
7. Laurie Clancy, 'The full circle before the world', *Australian Book Review* , 63 (August 1984), p. 20.
8. Barbara Hanrahan, *The Peach Groves* (St. Lucia: University of Queensland Press, 1979), p. 47.
9. Barbara Hanrahan, *The Frangipani Gardens* (St. Lucia: University of Queensland Press, 1980), p. 212.
10. Barbara Hanrahan, *A Chelsea Girl* (London: Grafton, 1988), p. 208.
11. Barbara Hanrahan, *Annie Magdalene* (London: Chatto and Windus, 1985), p. 121.
12. See for instance 'The Eye of God' lithograph 1964; 'The Eye of God' linocut 1974; 'Sun and Moon and the Eye of God' linocut 1988; and an untitled work reproduced on the cover of *Antipodes*, 6, 2 (December 1992). The appearance of the sun and sunflowers in many other prints is also reminiscent of the Eye of God.
13. Barbara Hanrahan, diary entry, 11 May 1986, Barbara Hanrahan Papers, National Library of Australia, Canberra.

# THEA ASTLEY

Thea Astley was born in Queensland in 1925. She is without doubt one of Australia's major writers and has won, on more than one occasion, most of Australia's most prestigious literary awards. She is a lively social satirist and very often she has directed her satirical, sometimes moralistic gaze at the pettiness of small-town philistinism. Very often her works, e.g. *The Acolyte* and *A Kindness Cup*, take opposite tacks in their exploration of conscience muscled away by mob-mentality and the resultant horror of that sacrifice. One of her latest novels, and I personally find one of her best is *It's Raining in Mango* in which she, focusing on four generations of her own personal history also focuses on Australia's own history. *Coda* is an extract from her latest novel published in 1994.

THEA ASTLEY

# Why I Write

Throughout all my writing years I have been aware of one intention only, I suppose, and that is to try to recapture for myself certain moments, incidents, events that have at the time acted as some kind of emotional impetus. Writing about them seemed to give a permanence. Others might read what I had seen or felt and be affected too. This is what I hoped. But primarily writing is a form of self-indulgence. I admit readily that as I wrote, the shape or outline of the captive moment changed. There's the pity! Never was I able to recapture in its first innocence that primary stimulus. The very nature of fiction writing affected whatever I touched. Other characters intruded. Dialogue sharpened or blunted what had appeared to me as entire in itself.

I have always been interested in the misfit, the outsider, the less than successful. That is why several of my novels or stories deal with blacks or half-castes, with adolescents or 'failures' in the world's sense of the term. When I was writing *Beachmasters* about the Jimmy Steven's revolution in Santo, the most northern island of the then New Hebrides, I was moved more by Steven's failure to secede than the plight of 'colour' inside the stuffy rituals of white colonialism. When I wrote about the blacks of north Queensland in *Hunting the White Pineapple* and *It's Raining in Mango* I drew on those whom I had known living in the tiny settlement across the river from our house. But what the non-writer cannot seem to understand is that my stories were not photographs of people as I knew them in deadly accuracy, but sketches of an aggregate of what I had read of local history, of what I saw and what I heard: writing is an exercise in photography – but the developing fluid is feeling.

THEA ASTLEY

# CODA
(an extract)

Take five!
Take longer if you feel like it.
Here's this crazy, this wacker, this...this...whatever you feel like calling the poor coot, obsessed, so riddled with this maggot to sing, golden-throated, golden-tongued, Tosti's last song, the ultimate lament, from a bridge in Venice, a bridge spanning one of the smaller canals leading into the bassino.
Ah well.
For a once-off?
To frighten the gondoliers? The tourists? Send sonic but useless messages to a lost love?
Well, maybe.
Nothing but water and bells, he imagined, and his voice, rapturous with resonance, rocking the bassino into wavelets.
He lifted his head into dawn air, inhaled deeply, opened his mouth wide, wider, and launched into the opening bars of *L'ultima canzone: M'han detto che domani, Nina vi fate sposa,* he sang. Full. Loud. Louder. Resonance.
Rez-o-nance!
Workmen going by hesitated, grinned widely, leaned against the bridge railing and eyed him from under their caps with pleasure. One joined in. They sang *duetto,* allowing their voices to melt into curves that floated up and over the water, dominating the liquidity of bells, curling into the wisps of cirrus teasing church spires across that glinting world. His song was a gondola of grief on which he poled away from the watchers, even his singing partner, oblivious to their surprise of delight, sensing only the rotundity of sound as it left his throat, curvilinear.
When he reached the last throbbing note – and he allowed it to throb in the finest Italianate style – there was a burst of applause, ragged, fragmented, from the loiterers. '*Grazie,*' he said with a self-mocking bow. '*Grazie. Molte grazie.*'
Without looking into their smiles, their curiosity, he turned and began walking away quickly, losing himself in a network of alleys and lanes, crossing market squares, moving ever farther and farther from the hotel where his wife was now unpacking in the too expensive room their travel agent had booked. Leaving now before the old routine set in, the museum

trudging, gallery goggling, piazza dining turning each day into its organ-ised monetary orgasm. Bells reached a climax of slashed air about him, cutting small winds to streamers from a tower across the square; and he chased after their summons and entered a world filled with the cobwebs of ancient prayers.

He was, is, interested in the processes of goodness, the abstractions of duty, self-sacrifice, the sheer purity of the unladen soul. On this morning of early March, striding across the endless skies, as it were, of Venice's floating floor, the sole-heel-toe of him felt no paving, no grit and agonised clutch to earth. As if involved in chicane, in subterfuge, he had whizzed from that hotel room scooting across arpeggios of bellringers, silently ex-horting steeples, workmen, cringing cats, sly before-times moneychangers, insomniac tourists, in order to utter the briefest aspiration of God-directed gratitude.

So long, Bosie!

So long, Bimbo and Chaps!

Bimbo and Chaps now not quite completing academic courses, not quite dropping out.

Bosie unpacking the drip-dry and hanging it carefully on racks in the monstrous wardrobe that threatened the bed.

So long! *Arrivederci!*

A mass was half-completed, the sanctuary bell ringing at the elevation of the Host, the saddened weathered cunning simple duplicate human discs raised, lowered, raised, the prayers pressed like everlastings between hands draped with rosaries, rings and the tiredest of tired skins.

Kneeling with chin on knuckled hands he thought of Bosie. Why didn't she laugh? Ever? Once, listening to a political leader gabbling idiotically away on television, he had commented, 'They've left the scrambler on.' Not a smile. Not a glimmer of a smile. She was unmoved by most things of the spirit. And another once when he played her Te Kanawa singing Strauss's *Vier Letzte Lieder* with that effortless floating, effortless buoyancy of the heart out of sight, a bird – out – of – sight, ah, she had switched on the Hoover and worked around his scuffed running shoes.

There was nothing like the Romantics, he had informed her, talking to air. The hell, he had told her, with Victorian schmalz and tenors, me dear, one hand lightly placed on the grand, moustache always blond down-drooping, thrumming to the tentative occasionally wrong notes struck by an hour-glass garbed woman-fashion, swaying on the piano stool. She had kept on Hoovering. But Tosti! Brain had begun to shout above the racket. Who could resist him? He couldn't. Partly for the thought of that ingrati-ating Latin giving music lessons to the royal toad and the toad's children in the soot and gas lamps of London.

His own eyes were stained with the sea as he explained.

Jesus God! *L'ultima canzone!* He would try not to remember that it was written at Folkestone.

He flicked off the player and began singing to his Hoovering wife.
The last song.
Over
and
over.
'For Chrissake!' Bosie had screamed, going out to the pool and an
aureole stench of guinea flower. 'Will you give up on that goddam song!
That bloody song!'
'Mother,' he had reprimanded, following his wife and breaking from
lyric mode to speech mid-note, 'played it for father.'
'I don't,' Bosie shouted, her small acquisitive face screwed up into what
Brain recognised as the first honest resentment in twenty years of marriage, 'give a stuff if she played it for the president of the Yew Ess of Ay
or Yasser Arafat.' A leaf dropped its exclamation point, tested her hair
briefly and fluttered away to the terrace.
That vignette he offers now to his raw and guilty soul. Or had he
screamed slut? He couldn't remember.
He was hugging his personal alto rhapsody to himself like a comforter,
a warmer, a cuddle-bunny of escape into unachieved but dreamt-of contacts, say: girl crossing landscape – serious, gawky – on a lonely beach on
Magnetic; girl swinging into bus-stumble, his quickly gallant hand sup-
porting a succulence of flesh, wanting, oh God, wanting what? He could
accept the lust in either vignette with the figure erased from landscape.
Was he a queer?
Years ago – three? four? – Nina Waterman had knelt literally at his feet
on a pool scootway flooded by the splashings of yoicks, polluted by
arcadian flat-chested nymphs and lugger shepherd boozers, and bowed
her magnificent head as his party song climaxed – *honey, did yo' hear dat
mockin' bird sing las' night?* To lager and stubby wash of the good ship
Hackendorf, Brain Hackendorf sang.
When he left the church the gondolas on the canal swung by with barely
a glance from boatered polesters under the thin wash of early sun damped
down by mist, pollution and the rags of sea-dragging cloud.
So long, Bosie, now rinsing out her underwear to hang on a neat pack-
away traveller's clothesline hooked across bathtub or shower screen.
In a room whose ceiling was cluttered with *putti.*
Something nagged.
Guilt.
Impulsively he rang Kathleen from a pay phone at an *ufficio postale,*
ignoring the thought that it was now nearly midnight in Brisbane.
'Mother,' he said without preamble, 'I've left Bosie.'
'Where, dear?' his mother asked. Her voice came through as strongly as
if she were in the next phone booth.
'In Venice.'
'Darling,' Kathleen said, 'what a lovely place to leave her.'

JOAN KIRKBY

# 'The Vertigris of Glory': The Lure of Abjection in Thea Astley's *The Acolyte*

Yes, *The Acolyte*'s the one I like best ... I was working at Macquarie University at the time, and the corridors were ringing with the sound of symbols, and I wanted to write an anti-symbol novel. I always remember the time someone rushed down the corridor and said, '*Moby Dick* is actually a giant penis.' I got tired of this extrapolation of symbols from novels and I thought, I'll write an anti-symbolic novel and I'll use as many symbols as I can, and send them up. That's why Vesper built a gigantic sling – it was really a giant phallus.[1]

The thing was that I grew up in an era where I was completely neutered by my upbringing ... when I was eighteen or nineteen I thought to myself that the only way one could have any sort of validity was to write as a male ... I don't even know how women in general think. I've been neutered by society so I write as a neuter.[2]

About a third of the way into the *The Acolyte*, the blind artist Holberg 'crushed every bone and severed the tendons' of his right hand, making Paul Vesper indispensable to him as amanuenses, gardener, grocery boy and wife comforter. Vesper says this about the decisive incident:

For the moment I couldn't see beyond the immediacy of the event. I've never been one of your symbol hunters. I'm hopeless at chess despite my play with mathematics. It's only since I've been absorbed by the arty parasites that nudge their tiny proboscises into the skin of Holberg's talent that I realize my deficiency in a whole world of experience. Doc, what's up with me? I simply don't see trees as dicks thrusting into the gaping uterus of the sky. I see them as trees. I need help. Here's a whole acre of people who live in a world of phalli ('Sockets and spigots!' says rough-hewn Slocombe. I love you Nev –), of gulping labiae, of fourth-form interpretations of cars, whales, telegraph poles and mammalian light-bulbs. Look, doc, there are only two possible continuous lines – straight and curved. Do I *have* to see them as genital substitutes? Do I? It makes eating an ice-cream cone difficult. You take my point, doc? My low-grained sensibilia apprehend cars, whales, telegraph poles and light-bulbs. I lick *ice-cream*, feller. I munch a flour-and-water wafer cone. I am not homosexual. I like girls in moderation. I don't want to bite off anyone's tool or switch on a breast or impregnate the Pacific. I am still the clean-cut fifteen-year-old now lumbered with twice that number of years who won two cups for running and I can't get into the team. I can't cry along with my pouched debilitated mate suh-hex! suh-hex! I don't want to. doc, am I normal? I want tea-pots to *be* tea-pots and cups to be cups.[3]

Passages like this, together with references throughout the novel to those who write about art as 'the devious flies of art' (100), parasites on the ecology of culture (74) – 'their names are wrapped round the meat' (76) – must give pause to anyone who would wish to do more than examine the brilliant surface of Astley's prose. However, as *The Acolyte* is one of the most powerful critiques of the pattern of domination and subjugation which runs throughout Australian literature, it is important to risk the artist's ire in order to explore the source of the peculiar anger and aggression of the text. And since I am probably the person alluded to – the one who rushed down the corridor and said, '*Moby Dick* is actually a giant penis' – it is appropriate that I should risk this foolhardy enterprise. However I must point out that it was actually D.H. Lawrence who said that Moby Dick is 'the last phallic being of the white man', 'hunted by the maniacal fanaticism of our white mental consciousness'[4] and that he took his cue from Melville himself who makes enough puns about the sperm and foreskin and erections of the whale to inspire even the resistant symbol hunter.

Without making too much of symbolism, I believe with Cassirer that the human animal is both 'animal rationale' and 'animal symbolicum': 'to know is to symbolize in one way or another.' As Charles Feidelson writes in his classic study of symbolism in American literature: 'To consider the literary work as a piece of language is to regard it as a symbol, autonomous in the sense that it is quite distinct both from the personality of its author and from any world of pure objects.'[5]

> A poem delivers a version of the world; it is the world for the moment. And just as the language of a poem is a plastic symbolic medium in which subjective and objective elements are presented as an integral whole, so within the poem each word is potentially a standpoint, a symbolic crossroad, from which the whole poem may be viewed. (56)

> Moreover, the exercise of the alogical language of poetry is necessarily anti-logical. Existing in the same medium, literature supersedes, manipulates, and recasts logical structure. Figures of speech fly in the face of logic; their structure is ordered on a different plan. They cast through the body of language a light that erases the lines drawn by logical discourse and creates new contours in the same stuff. (58)

That symbolism involves alogical structures of multiple meaning may have something to do with the resistance of Australian writers to the idea of symbolism. The refusal of any meaning or resonance that was not consciously intended is perhaps part of a resistance to the idea of the unconscious – as well as the non-conscious, that is 'the domain not subject to repression but not within the reach of consciousness either' – 'the whole system of myths and images that gives our view of society and of our place in it a specific orientation'.[6] However, twentieth century interest in symbolism has been 'part of the reaction against the nineteenth century's rationalism, positivism and scientism' and Mircea Eliade has argued that 'we have not even the right to restrict ourselves to what the authors thought about their own creations': 'Archaic symbolisms reappear spontaneously, even in the works of "realist" authors who know nothing about such symbols.'[7]

For all her resistance to the idea of symbolism Astley herself acknowledges that 'I can't resist using imagistic language'. She speaks of her own moments of epiphany: 'There's a sudden sort of formless knowledge. And you see those as distinct happenings. I suppose they're epiphanies, whatever that word means in the literary sense.'[8] This sense of the evocation of one plane in terms of another sounds curiously like symbolism.[9]

What I would like to do in this paper is simply to examine some of the recurring images that occur in *The Acolyte*, in particular the imagery of pollution and defilement, in the context of contemporary theories of carnival, liminality, and abjection. *The Acolyte* is a key text in the Australian literary canon (*The Man Who Loved Children* is another) as an exemplar of the literature of abjection which Julia Kristeva has argued represents 'the ultimate coding of our crises, of our most intimate and most serious apocalypses'.[10]

> But not until the advent of twentieth-century 'abject' literature (the sort that takes up where apocalypse and carnival left off) did one realize that the narrative web is a thin film constantly threatened with bursting. For, when narrated identity is unbearable, when the boundary between subject and object is shaken, and when even the limit between inside and outside becomes uncertain, the narrative is what is challenged first ... the unbearable identity of the narrator and of the surroundings that are supposed to sustain him can no longer be *narrated* but *cries out* or is described with maximum stylistic intensity (language of violence, of obscenity, or of a rhetoric that relates the text to poetry). The narrative yields to a *crying-out theme* that when it tends to coincide with the incandescent states of a boundary-subjectivity that I have called abjection, is the crying-out theme of suffering-horror. In other words, the theme of suffering-horror is the ultimate evidence of such states of abjection within a narrative representation. If one wished to proceed farther still along the approaches to abjection, one would find neither narrative nor theme but a recasting of syntax and vocabulary – the violence of poetry, and silence. (141)

The literature of the abject exposes 'under the cunning orderly surface of civilizations, the nurturing horror that they attend to pushing aside by purifying, systematizing, thinking' (210). Kristeva's theories have a particular resonance in relation to Astley's novel, in its conceptualisation of the acolyte, the lush imagery of abjection and the language of violence in which it is articulated. Reading *The Acolyte* is similar to Julia Kristeva's description of reading Celine: 'A universe of borders, see-saws, fragile and mingled identities, wanderings of the subject and its object, fears and struggles, abjections and lyricisms. At the turning point between social and asocial, familial and delinquent, feminine and masculine, fondness and murder' (135).

Abjection, writes Kristeva, is that which 'disturbs identity, system, order' – 'what does not respect borders, positions rules. The in-between, the ambiguous, the composite' (4). A concern with borders and their violation, with the unclear and undifferentiated permeates *The Acolyte*; indeed the acolyte is one for whom the borders between self and other have disintegrated. Astley's exploration of her 'rubbish tip saint' (104) and the 'mess', the 'garbage tip of relationships' (93), is set amidst 'the stink of summer' and the 'subtropical smudginess' of Queensland. Grogbusters itself is 'a border town' where trams jerk 'like cripples to predestined ends' (35). The town of Dingo is 'a hideous little outcrop of houses ... so ugly its demands for love eat out the observing heart':

> The pub totters on the brink of every known disaster and smells permanently of beer and mangoes. We slumped our failure at a crippled table on the veranda in the moist dark and steadily drank our way through commiseration (false), friendship (temporary) and a distanced state where each of us observed two of the other with disgusted appraisal... Mangoes rotted. (35)

In addition to the imagery of rankness and rot, animals and acts which break down borders between human and animal, inside and outside, permeate the novel. There are numerous parasitic creatures who violate the border of the living subject they feed off, like 'the arty parasites who nudge their tiny proboscises into the skin of Holberg's talent' and 'the devious flies' on the meat of art referred to earlier. Vesper repeatedly refers to himself as a thrip, a small, destructive, usually winged insect that sucks the juices of plants. The blindness of Holberg – 'the great man crabbing his way along the fly-walk score of a negligible quartet' (3) – is a result of fly-strike, 'one eye entirely closed – no eyeball ... and the other permanently opened on a yellow clotted muscle with a faint smear of blue where the iris had once been' (7).

Crustaceans of various sorts – crabs, prawns, crayfish and lobsters – also permeate the text, both as meal and as analogy. 'Shrimped out, the lot of us, beside the pool' (75). Vesper rarely mentions Hilda without referring to 'the prawn sheen on Hilda's lip' (49); Ilse wins a lobster and 'There we are with this large crustacean in a bag on the floor beside us, listening to its pitiful assays to escape as it feels round and round the wet sacking. Slow, blind, unending, it fumbles and fumbles ...' (39) Holberg's thickening body is 'now swaddled in tropic carapace' (25) – the upper shell of a tortoise or crustacean.

> 'Have you ever seen crabs eating each other?' something made me ask. 'Alive. If one has the bad luck to fall on its back, the rest pounce in a flash. Nibble nibble. With the utmost delicacy, of course, getting their proteins live. On the claw, as it were. Let's eat each other. Everyone does.'

Their mouths all curved into disgusted crescents, then they ignored me. Rightly. We listen to it nightly on the news – political state smorgasbord, racial dinings, organized meat cubing called the glory of war, small private enterprise attacks on old ladies, petrolled and fired gentlemen in bush-sheds, children dawdlers on the way to school. They're all at it everywhere, and we ignore it and go on munching our own vegetarian servings while outside the carnivores pause for a minute and smack their lips. 41)

The imagery of sucking, swarming, crawling creatures inevitably evokes the abominations of Leviticus and its prohibition against certain 'creatures that cannot be unambiguously classified in terms of traditional criteria'.[11]

Whatsoever hath no fins nor scales in the waters, that shall be an abomination to you ... neither shall ye defile yourselves with any manner of creeping thing that creepeth upon the earth ... To make a difference between the unclean and the clean ... (Leviticus, 11: 11, 43, 47)

Mary Douglas has argued that the concept of pollution is an attempt 'to protect cherished principles and categories form contradiction': 'What is unclear and contradictory (from the perspective of social definition) tends to be regarded as unclean.' 'Holiness,' she writes, 'means keeping distinct the categories of creation. It therefore involves correct definition, discrimination and order.'[12]

In the midst of this imagery of fecundity and abomination, Paul Vesper is presented as the epitome of the bourgeois subject defined in contradistinction to all that is gross and animal. He repeatedly affirms 'his appalling normalcy' (3) and 'the savagery of conformism' of his culture (63).

I want to assure you from the beginning, now that I am absorbed by my revolutionary climacteric, that I had all the properties of a suitably structured childhood. Fruit-juiced, three-mealed, educationally toyed, disciplined with all the footballer logic (tempered by a scatter-brained intellectualism in my mother) that a middle-class dad with a company car and conservative expense account could display. It was intensive gardening and my tiny shrub grew into the sort of sapling they felt they deserved, just a touch of thrips on the leaves at the right time, a non-dangerous performance at examinations and two cups for running. (2)

He takes 'an undistinguished degree' in one of 'the secure faculties like engineering' (9). An obsession with order characterises all his activities, 'everything clean, every product of my horrible clockwork mind' (18). He practices musical composition with 'a mathematical sweetness like knitting for old ladies' (13) and possesses just 'the sensitivity to regret the need to use other people' (4).

Vesper is the acolyte of the title of the novel, who has surrendered his own autonomy and selfhood ostensibly out of his love for the blind artist Holberg but as much to resist the fierce struggle for autonomy that besets us all: 'I am a natural assistant' (19). He shares his girlfriend Freckles as he later shares Hilda: 'We were just one big happy incestuous family.' He seems a paradigm of the negative selfhood articulated by Graeme Turner in *National Fictions*:

> The version of the individual which emerges has the Australian protagonist responding to a secularised and alienated environment by admitting the withdrawal of meaning and value, but without inventing a replacement for which he may accept responsibility. Behind this metaphysic there is an ideological proposition that negates the value of individual action and legitimates powerlessness and subjection.[13]

Vesper says of himself:

> I was like a dog in many of my responses. Beg! I begged. Sit! There I was slavering and grinning with my front paws paddling. Heel! I wheeled back to the sniff-rear of ankle in a second. Play dead! Down on my back in a flash, eyes checking, rolling in their whites, to gather the response. (23)

Relentlessly he chronicles his servitude: 'I am the gauche butler when the curtain rises, the dusting maid, the harem eunuch' (31); 'I'm a born limpet' (47); 'I feel like a parasite. And the more I feed the emptier I become' (150). He is 'Holberg's eunuch' (86), a baronial retainer (94), 'the more than general factotum' managing his master's affairs' (97), 'a grocer's gardener's stud boy' (109), 'the dumb servitor', 'the harem pander', 'the dusting maid' (115). 'I have a pregnant bank-book, no talent, a tin tray, a Burne-Jones print, no talent, two glowing letters of reference from the old firm, an unused clarinet, no talent and a dinner suit' (121).

Content to sit in the shadow of another, whether Slocombe or Holberg, he muses:

> ...I am Holberg's other self, his seeing self, and while I store up, programming my giant Cyclops eye like a slave computer, he expends all his heart-pulse on interpretation. It could explain my bondage, which has all the transparency of cellophane but is a thousand times tougher ... May I crampon up the rocks of your indifference? I may? Pitch camp on the shallow ledges of your eyes and sit out the blizzard? ... I am filled also with self-loathing. (39)

> Holberg is my cross and I'm nailed to him and you wonder why it is I don't wriggle off and walk away? The rips in the soft pads of my pander hands, perhaps. The rags of feet. I'm the mini-Jesus!' (70)

> I am the schoolboy fag for the hero of the sixth, God love us, and I will do anything at all, anything, lick your boots, replay and replay your phrases, cart your beer, accommodate your wife give me half the chance. The lot. (82)

> Mawkish Vesper! Mystically I have outdistanced myself and across the uneasy landscape of my nullified dreams, plans, ambitions, spot this tiny figure that is me stumbling between the cratered dunghills of my achievements ... Mother, father, you would not be proud of me. There is nothing my tepid personality has contributed ... A shapeless aggregate of forty-odd years who has rendered only a menial apostleship ... my choir-boy seed sprouting my own choirboy face. (111)

In Kristeva's terms, Vesper is a stray; a subject who 'presents himself with his own body and ego as the most precious non-objects; they are no longer seen in their own right, but forfeited abject': 'Such are the pangs and delights of masochism' (5). He is one for whom the other – the negative selfhood articulated by his society – has become alter ego; he leads a forfeited existence. Though he is able to establish a defensive position he lacks a secure differentiation between subject and object (7). He is not at all unaware of his abjection and not without laughter – since laughing is a way of placing or displacing abjection (8). The experience of abjection is specifically related by Kristeva to '*Too much strictness on the part of the other*, confused with the One and the Law': 'I experience abjection only if an Other has settled in place of what will be me – a being there of the symbolic that a father might embody' (10). There is much evidence in the novel, as the above passages suggest, that Vesper's individuality and self-hood have been forfeited to the savage conformism of his suitably structured society. Like the young Hal Porter he feels impelled to be 'the practised participant in other people's lives'. He is 'the solid citizen arriving at the job on time, reading my books, wiping down the draining-board, pruning the mandevillea, camouflaged with stratagems that can only reaffirm my essential dullness' (37). 'Your trouble,' Hilda suggested, 'is the fact that you're so old. I mean you're not young' (15). Hence as he says to his parents on his 'betrothal of sorts': 'I love you with every oedipal pore of my entire body. Having been moulded into what I am, a colourless mechanic. I feel the least I can do is make you two happy. I feel that's all I'm expected to do. I don't come into it' (16).

The musician Holberg is the antithesis of Vesper; in both life and art he transgresses the boundaries of order and taste – his 'racy diminished sevenths ... ram, bomb-crude, into a knees-together prissiness of formal composition' (38). He and his musicians 'indulge in the horsing about of rape-packs – the uh one uh two uh three uh four' (51). He explores 'the entrails of every possible harmonic combination' (65). Set apart by his blindness and his genius, and allowed a license not extended to other members of the culture, Holberg with his 'meaty face' and fly-struck eyes and his sexual cannibalism, represent all that is excluded by yet fascinates the dominant culture:

> They enjoyed guiding his uncertain feet around homestead verandas until it bored them or watching him eat with his fingers more difficult chops, repulsed and fascinated, and tolerated his drunken jazz assaults on their untuned pianos because his affliction was so outrageous and so total. (4)

People are drawn to his outrage, his brutal selfishness, 'his complete involvement in his own darkness, as if he loved the cage with the cover' (12). 'His life wound was smiting us, I see now, I see now, but we thumped our feet and walloped our hands into painful redness' (26). Women are attracted to his vulnerability (125). '"He's like a primitive god, groans sordid Ilse, head down, among the egg-shells and the toast crusts. He wants everything he's touched ... He's taken the lot and ruined the lot and all we've done is sit around and wait to be ruined."' (129) 'He is the centre of chaos. All round us are dancers, screamers. I sense tribal copulation but he is blind and unaware, rising as the players slam into the terminus' (133).

Amidst 'gullies clotted with subtropical rain-forest', Holberg builds his house, 'a massive set of linked glass boxes set along the plateau rim in a shaggy garden where Holberg has had placed in surprising secretnesses classically naked statues of half a dozen women whose plaster hands modestly shield their pudenda' and with whom Vesper finds him copulating animal fashion (67, 25). There he holds his court to his 'hideous Greek chorus of yes-men who can't do a thing ourselves' (71): 'And I look across the drink swirling room at Hilda and see us both as ancients, servitors sucked dry of youth while Holberg, self-regenerating with every bar he writes, grows fat with procreation' (71).

There Holberg humiliates his guests, the 'jackals' of culture. And in his rage he transgresses the limits of their pretensions and prohibitions. This is his attraction and his power. Holberg rages against the would-be playwright Shumway, 'What stinks is your dishonesty.'

> (Holberg, there's gravy dribbling down your coat, you are facing the wrong way, your elbow is on Bonnie Coover's bread roll, but there is a magnificence about you.) 'If you want total theatre, matey, then I'm with you. But I want urination and defecation and vomiting and nose-blowing. The lot.' People stopped poking at their doubtful brown servings. 'I want diarrhoea and spewing and mucus and none of your bloody plastic turds, matey. If that actor can't turn on a good crap at ten past nine *every* night in Act Two then I want him drummed out of Equity. I want stench and fartings and blokes blowing their noses between their fingers and spitting great gobbets into the orchestra pit and then I'll be with you. Then I'll subscribe. Then Ill deliver you some incidental music that you'll be incapable of assessing anyway. But I'll respect your motives. You funny man! You seem to think the cerebellum is located in the scrotum.' ... We should have lost a lot of friends that way. These things work in reverse for sucking fish, however, and Holberg's social monstrousness brought out the masochist flagellant in all of them. (82-83)

As this passage suggests, Holberg offers a world of carnival, of profanation and excess – all that is relegated to the margins of Vesper and his culture's 'appalling normalcy'. All the major motifs of carnival are exhibited – the transgression of boundaries, the opening of orifices usually closed in the interest of social order, the comic privileging of the lower half of the body – in Bakhtin's words, 'Eating, drinking, defecating and other elimination (sweating, blowing the nose, sneezing).'[14] Carnival provides a space for 'symbolic inversion', 'any act of expressive behaviour which inverts, contradicts, abrogates, or in some fashion presents an alternative to commonly held cultural codes, values and norms be they linguistic, literary or artistic, religious, social and political'.[15]

In *The Politics and Poetics of Transgression*, Peter Stallybrass and Allon White describe the way that carnival 'attacks the authority of the ego (by rituals of degradation and by the use of masks and costume)'; it 'denies with a laugh the hierarchical arrangements of the symbolic at the same moment as it re-opens the body-boundary, the closed orifices of which normally guarantee the repressive mechanism itself'.[16] It provides 'a temporary liberation from the prevailing truth of the established order' (7). They go on to argue that 'the bourgeois subject defined and re-defined itself through the exclusion of what it marked out as "low" – as dirty, repulsive, noisy, contaminating' (191). However, precisely because 'the grotesque physical body' is suppressed and distanced as the very sign of rationality and bourgeois subjectivity, it exists as 'what Macherry calls "a determining absent presence"' (105). It is this 'determining absent presence' which shapes Vesper's world and explains the dynamics of his attraction to Holberg. Disgust turns to desire; what has been violently excluded emits an irresistible fascination. Holberg's fascination is the fascination of abjection itself; he represents, in Kristeva's terms, 'a conjunction of waste and object of desire, of corpse and life, fecality and pleasure, murderous aggressivity and the most neutralizing power'. Holberg is 'the impaired master': 'And I who identify with him, who desire to share with him a brotherly, mortal embrace in which I lose my own limits, I find myself reduced to the same abjection, a fecalised, feminized, passivated rot.'[17]

Astley's acolytes long for the ritual debasement of carnival – all that has been culturally excluded from their lives. As Vesper says, 'Do I have to confess bless me father to a sneaking liking for the verdigris of glory that rubs off on me? (I am all greenish stain!) ... I'm the natural tick parasite necessary for preserving the ecology of culture' (74). At the performance of Holberg's 'Gold Coast Sinfonia', the acolytes find themselves 'sitting on the edge of some deformed revelation'; they find themselves exposed without transfiguration in Holberg's composition: 'The ruined people. After those lyrics, how can I (or he) achieve redemption? Is it only to scrape up a little of Holberg's exuded genius, like slime, I tell myself now? Like slime?' (106).

This 'edge' is what Victor Turner describes as 'liminality', a liminal phase being one where novices are 'temporarily undefined', beyond the normative social structures and obligations. They experience 'a close connection with the non-social or asocial powers of life and death'.[18] There is in these liminal moments the potential for liberation; these moments may become the space in which hybridization occurs, providing new combinations that might shift the terms of the system (14, 58). Certainly the excesses of Holberg and his entourage suggest a desire for the dissolution of the inadequately constituted bourgeois subject in Australian society, a desire to dissolve rigid categorical structures that stifle and destroy even as they sustain and protect.

However, whereas liminal situations may provide a space in which new models, symbols and paradigms might arise, they may function simply as an inversion, a temporary release that makes ordinary confinement more bearable. Turner emphasises that liminal phases invert but do not necessarily subvert the status quo. The reversal may simply underline to the community that chaos is the alternative to cosmos (40-41). Moreover, as Stallybrass and White point out, carnival often abuses and demonizes the weaker not the stronger social groups in a process of displaced abjection whereby a low social group turns gainst a lower (19). Certainly in Holberg's carnivalesque world, abjection is displaced on to woman. In that respect Holberg's carnival turns out to be an intensification rather than an inversion of the dynamics of the outside world.

Within the world of *The Acolyte*, it is 'woman' who carries the force of the images of abjection and readers often remark the 'feminine' qualities of Vesper. The narrative abuse is relentless. Holberg tells his wife: 'Nothing satisfies your sex but the inside turned out, the glistening bowels of me and the small white pip of a soul. And then you'd want to carve your name on the pip, even, no matter now tiny' (94). Like Kristeva in *Powers of Horror*, Astley in this novel, and the genuinely horrifying short story 'Ladies Need Only Apply', is working with some of the more grotesque cultural stereotypes of women and this is one of the most discomfiting aspects of her work. However, both writers expose the vicious inadequacy of these images. Grogbuster socialites are 'the sort of women who collected amusing oddities to stave off boredom – shrunken heads, the preserved genitals of native hillsmen, shark-tooth cigarette holders ... oh, anything that might provide pseudo-artistic talking-point at Grogbusters folk evenings' (4). There are the women who pander to Holberg, 'thick bosoms and chests desperate to claim suckledom' (27).

> They would swoop on him like social rocs carting him off to mongrel gatherings of the rich and influential; race across home-coming tarmacs to greet him with casseroles ... drive all the dedicated miles to Plateautop to air the shrine when the idol was absent for a stretch, performing menial domesticities with the joyous dedication of Carthusians ... Bonnie Coover was one of these. She was a spectacularly plain woman, wrestler-shaped, whose skin had been varnished by too much sun and too much liquor. A place-dropper of distinction with a passion for headwaiters, she also dropped names. These stale dung-pads littered her conversation. (69)

There is 'Slum Chum' Freckles whom Vesper shares with his boss Slocombe:

> 'You look' – struggling with her basic English vocabulary for a word – 'fagged', she brought out with a mighty semantic effort ... She had North Queensland peasant legs and my present revulsion was largely sympathy, I swear ... She sat there with the stoicism of her legs, drinking tea with me and trying not to listen. (21)

Freckles, who 'pregnant at last', is 'found strangled in her cheeky red car beached in a tangled bay of sunless tea-tree in the hills outside town' (53). There is Bathgate's friend who 'hanged herself on the rotary clothes-hoist among eight of her husband's drip dry shirts' (48), Bathgate's dying wife Emmie – a chrysalis-frail woman whose limbs are gradually turning to chalk: 'Smudged words were padding the air – Emmie's disease had affected her speech ("She can only nag me in glottal stops now," ... and there he was sponging her down with the gentleness of a martyr...' (59). There is Holberg's indomitable 'sickly yellow', 'macaw eyed' Aunt Sadie, 'a grotesque baby in a cow-girl outfit and a stetson' (64), 'a tiny glutton who drools through the hours between meals' (96). Holberg fondly strokes her 'near-bald unwigleted head' (106).

There are 'the goose-girls', Ilse all 'fragility of bone and diffident flesh' (7), 'the mothering bitch' with 'her food-wrecking paws' (44), and her younger sister Hilda, 'a cream cheese Teuton' (24) with a mouth 'the colour of prawn' (31). Hilda's wifely abjection to Holberg surpasses even Vesper's: 'Hapless Hilda. She suddenly looked incredibly weary, her features smudged in across her face as though Holberg were gradually painting her out' (56). As Holberg succumbs to the groupies who flock to his bed – 'the raped child', a librettist, 'a contralto', a cellist, 'a mournful swamp creature' – 'poor cream cheese' in paroxisms of abjection feigns blindness, crashing through kitchen and garden, serving sugared steak and salted puddings for 'sacrificial periods' each day (98). Holberg beats her for her 'gutless snivelling', punching her 'again and again on the side of her pliant face, while her torn leg bled redly into the bracken' (117). Vesper 'comforts' her: 'in the shelter of some rocks where we once scraped our climbing shins I worry her frantic flesh into a temporary forgetfulness' (100).

Ilse, devastated when Holberg marries Hilda, had 'played a mini-Greek tragedy of devoted sister ministering, ministering'.

> Her kitchen was choking on the stench of burned vegetable. A blackened pot was askew in the sink. And now eyelids like swollen pink prawn bulging over grievance ... insect din quivered its ragged patterns. Oh, this slatternly cave of her being, a slum of stained hopsack and smoke-filled curtain-weave and wine-blessed carpet across which several cushions had crept in a piteous attempt to escape. Inside her weeping house-coat she had shrunk to nothing and the corn tassels of her hair simply hung.
> 'He's taking legal action to get Jamie.'
> I sipped Ilse's version of tea. My days were brown enough. This is woman's magazine stuff with a stinking vengeance. (129)

Ultimately, at the pop concert of the 'hoodlum cult where every singer projects like a pack-rapist', amid 'hyena howls flying drink cans and the girl abandoning the last scrupulous preserves of self' – Ilse is raped:

Ilse has been discovered, bedraggled nereid, in the mud body-hollowed parking lot
alongside the creek. The five louts had screamed back into the mob. It could have
been anyone at all. It was Jamie who had found her ... just as they were finishing
with her ... Her face was gummed with grass and leaves that acted as a benign
plaster to the already swelling and lop-sided cheek-bone, the purplish darkening
tegument around the eyes. One arm had been bent viciously back under her and
when Hilda drew it gently out the wrist hung grotesque and useless. (134)

However, Ilse is to be further abjected: 'But oh my god, what will have
happened to him' (136) is Holberg's response; 'Jamie, I thought, I wish
you hadn't seen what you did' (144) is Vesper's. Jamie himself wants nothing more to do with his mother. When she is released from hospital she
comes to live at Holberg's mansion, 'a shadow goose-girl pecking gently
round the edges of our pond' (47).

'You? Well, you are the genuine masochist goose-girl, aren't you, eh? Your wounds
bleed profusely and you display them with pride. The Holberg stigmata, that's
what you've got. Maybe you are a genuine saint. What you're really trying to tell
me is that I don't love my dunghill, isn't that it? I don't love the crap and the
stink?' (150)

There are various 'readings' that might be given to this abjection of
woman in the text; an older style feminism might argue that the author
has internalised the woman-hatred of the dominant social order. Astley
gives weight to this reading in her remark: 'I grew up in an era where I
was completely neutered by my upbringing ... when I was eighteen or
nineteen I thought to myself that the only way one could have any sort of
validity was to write as a male ... I don't even know how women in
general think. I've been neutered by society so I write as a neuter.'[19] A
somewhat later feminist reading, on the model of Kaja Silverman's reading
of 'the masochistic excess' of King Vidor's *Gilda*, might argue that Astley
pushes the social definition of woman as abject to breaking point, thereby
exposing the inadequacy of subject positions available to woman in the
social order. Silverman, for instance, argues that Gilda's ritual self-
humiliation highlights 'the degree to which her masochism is culturally
inherited and written and represents a point of female resistance within
the very system which defines woman as powerless and lacking'; it can be
understood as 'the process whereby the inadequacy of the subject's position is exposed in order to facilitate (i.e. create the desire for) new
insertions into a cultural discourse which promises to make good that
lack'.[20] Or one might use Kristeva's articulation of abjection as having to
do with feminine POWER and see the language of the novel as subversive
in disrupting the border of the social order – literally exposing its
limitations as well as embodying the potential force that might transfigure
it.

Kristeva's particular contribution to theories of pollution and defilement
is her insight that the loathing of defilement is a protection against what

is seen as 'the poorly controlled power of mothers' (77). Indeed Kristeva argues that 'The power of pollution thus transposes on the symbolic level the permanent conflict resulting from an unsettled separation between masculine and feminine power at the level of social institutions. Non-separation would threaten the whole society with disintegration' (78). Abjection, the weight of meaninglessness 'on the edge of monexistence and hallucination, of a reality that, if I acknowledge it, annihilates me', is first experienced when the child attempts to establish autonomy by separating itself from the mother.

> The abject confronts us ... with our earliest attempts to release the hold of maternal entity even before existing outside of her, thanks to the autonomy of language. It is a violent, clumsy breaking away, with the constant risk of falling back under the sway of a power as securing as it is stifling. (13)

Abjection is related to the logic of separation, the attempt of a subject who is not yet a subject to separate itself from the mother whom it is not yet able to see as an object. Because the mother effects the original mapping of the body into clean and unclean, she is associated with excrement and its equivalents – decay, infection, disease, blood, in short with defilement and pollution. Paternal law – the order of language and culture – represses maternal authority and the corporeal mapping of the body (72). Kristeva argues that just as there is on the part of the subject a fear of her/his own identity sinking into the mother, the symbolic order has a violent need to subordinate the maternal: 'the masculine, apparently victorious, confesses through its very relentlessness against the other, the feminine, that it is threatened by an asymmetrical, irrational wily, uncontrollable power' (70). There is a fear of 'a phantasmatic mother who also constitutes, in the specific history of each person, the abyss that must be established as an autonomous (and not encroaching) place and distinct object, meaning a signifiable one, so that such a person might learn to speak' (100). Abjection, signified by corporeal waste – menstrual blood, excrement, nail parings, decay – evokes the pre-symbolic maternal fusion and suggests the frailty of the symbolic order in its attempts to repress the mother (70).

However, Kristeva maintains that within the symbolic order there remains a trace of the maternal in a space that she calls the semiotic which exists simultaneously. The semiotic, in Kristeva's version of Lacan's imaginary, is the pre-oedipal space of polymorphous drives, rhythms, impulses, – body energy before arranged by the constraints placed on the body by family and social structures. It is a kinetic rhythm that precedes and underlies figuration.[21] It precedes the symbolic order and has the potential to undermine and threaten it. It is 'a maternal space, the space where the child's body and the mother's body occupy a mutual space ... a threshold' where first vocalisation and later naming and language can take a hold. Kristeva contends, as Toril Moi points out, that 'any strengthening of the semiotic, which knows no sexual difference, must therefore lead to a weakening of traditional gender division'.[22] Kristeva's theory of the semiotic, as Jacqueline Rose has written, is an attempt 'to confront language at the point where it undoes itself' and the attraction of the theory is that it suggests 'aspects of language which escape the strait-jacket of social norms'.[23]

In artistic practice, the irruption of the semiotic within a text – signalled by maximum stylistic intensity, energy, violence, a rhetoric that relates the text to poetry – represents an overthrow of the social order, an undoing of the violence previously done to the body in the acquisition of language and culture. As Kristeva writes,

> semiotic violence breaks through the symbolic border and tends to dissolve the logical order which, is in short the outer limit founding the human and the social ... the subject crosses the border of the symbolic and reaches the semiotic chora, which is on the other side of the social frontier. The re-enacting of the signifying path taken from the symbolic unfolds the symbolic itself and ... opens it up to the motility where all meaning is erased. (79)

In this context Astley's idiosyncratic style has particular relevance. Adrian Mitchell has argued of Astley's 'arch mannerisms' and 'Gothic splendours' that 'the substance of her fiction tends to be diminished by the playful intelligence of the narration and more critically that the liveliness is separate from the imaginative centre of the narrative'.[24] However, Kristeva provides a framework in which the opposite could be said to be true. In this novel of abjection, in which abjection is so violently displaced on to woman, the style powerfully evokes the suppressed pre-Oedipal maternal rhythms. The novel is characterised by the disruptive aspects of language which Kristeva identifies with 'the discourse of the mother' – 'something that evades the repressive aspects of signification in language, something that's on the edge, on the border, beyond signification'.[25] There is in Astley's style, to borrow Kristeva's words again, 'a deluge of the signifier which so inundates the symbolic order that it portends the latter's dissolution in a dancing, singing and poetic animality' (79). In cracking the socio-symbolic order, splitting it open, changing its vocabulary and syntax, the word itself, and releasing from beneath them the drives, poetic language confronts order at its most fundamental level, the logic of language and the principle of the state (80). In Kristeva's terms, Astley's novel is highly ethical in that it 'pluralizes, pulverizes, musicates' and disrupts the symbolic order (233).

Kristeva's theory provides a model for reading the excess of abjection in Astley's text as a representation of what Josephine Feral calls 'the spasmodic force of woman':

> Having remained close to the maternal body in spite of the repression which society forces upon her, she inscribes herself naturally within the semiotic and occupies a

> privileged position within it ... This is an a-symbolic force which allows the subject to renew the bonds with what is repressed within her, with the repressed that is always the mother, in order to make it reappear in the form of insolence ... Taken to the extreme, the spasmodic force can lead to the subject's disintegration and death, and at the same time, to a total rupture of the state's order, to the subversion of the laws, to the incoherence of all discourse, to the foreclosure of communication. (27)

The excess of abjection and the baroque style in *The Acolyte* are the mark of anger and resistance to the dominant paradigms of the text, a dynamic made explicit in the last chapter of the book when Vesper turns the 'steel member' of Taurus, Astley's explicit phallic symbol, against the demonized Holberg:

> What is there left for a servant of the lord who has discovered that the idol's hands never move towards the slowly spoiling offerings unless it be to stroke its own stone thighs ... The swaying, chanting throngs bearing the garlanded monstrosity through summer streets will be crushed by their own abasement and still nothing will shower down upon them.

> Get up off your bloody plinth! I shriek right through the bored-out channels of my empty self...

> What bound us together was our religion, our unstinted worship of the love-object who was indeed one of ourselves. God and man. (147-149)

> I want to break into obscene cries about his half-baked genius, his gluttony for worship, my pity for him, my latest understanding, my own dismemberment. (154)

However, this chapter is also redolent with maternal imagery. Vesper longs for his lost Paradise, Huahine – 'my days there will be so fluid there will be reversals of earth and water' (144) – and putting into his mouth the resin of a blue gum 'that held memories of the wife' he thinks of 'the nature-rape child years': 'knowing, carnally this roly-poly slope, wallowing in it, down it, learning its curves by heart ... squatting on it, balancing, feeling the salt-scars; conning trees, branch by branch, climbing, hanging ... I chewed ...' (152). Though he still longs to 'lie stretched full length in the chaotic undergrowth and weep for the lot of us' (154) he finds he can no longer swallow the communion bread which 'rises in my gorge': 'I chew it again with my blunted irreverent teeth, but it refuses to be swallowed ... And I am cut in half' (154). In psychoanalytic terms the child's refusal to ingest food marks the beginning of separation; in the expulsion of food s/he discloses a space between self and other. Subsequently Vesper shatters the glass walls of his imprisonment, blood 'pours its protest without staunch', another Kristevan emblem of the breaking down of the separations on which the social order is based, and 'Outside rain releases a haemorrhage of water and whole landscapes are wiped out in an instant ... I cannot speak but their voices go on and become wordless'. The motifs of blood and rain, the dissolution of walls and boundaries, the intermingling of that which is usually separate, the dissolution of speech into wordlessness, all suggest a return to the energies of the undifferentiated semiotic which underlies the symbolic order. Although David Tacey has recently argued a negative reading for the dissolution in Patrick White's fiction,[27] in the rigidly authoritarian society Astley portrays in *The Acolyte* – one with alarming similarities to the prison state outlined by Foucault in *Discipline and Punish* and indeed Graeme Turner argues for the appropriateness of this model to Australia – dissolution may be heralded as a positive force. It is the mark of resistance to social structures experienced as oppressive and insufficient. It suggests a longing for oppressive forms to be dissolved and returned to a fluid state, thus liberating the elements to be recombined into new patterns. Astley's great power as a novelist is her ability to identify these so-called private terrors as cultural terrors. The acolyte does not represent a private dilemma; in Astley's cultural analysis, the acolyte is a manifestation of a particular cultural terror of a troubled social group. To cite Turner again, 'the Australian myth accommodates us to the inevitability of subjection': 'Granted that meaning is socially constructed, then the function of the thematic model which I have outlined clearly is to naturalise a position that undermines the individual's prospects of playing any active, individualised role within society' (76).

NOTES

1. Thea Astley, in *Rooms of Their Own*, interviewed by Jennifer Ellison (Melbourne: Penguin, 1986), p. 54.
2. Thea Astley, in *Yacker: Australian Writers Talk About Their Work*, interviewed by Candida Baker (Sydney and London: Picador, 1986), pp. 42-43.
3. Thea Astley, *The Acolyte* (Sydney: Angus and Robertson, 1972), pp. 63-64. All further references are to this edition and will be included in the text.
4. D.H. Lawrence, *Studies in Classic American Literature* (London: Mercury, 1965), p. 152.
5. Charles Feidelson, *Symbolism and American Literature* (Chicago and London: The University of Chicago Press, 1953), p. 55.
6. Leon Roudiez, 'Introduction' to *Revolution in Poetic Language* by Julia Kristeva (New York: Columbia University Press, 1984), p. 8.
7. Mircea Eliade, *Images and Symbols* (London: Harvill Press, 1961), pp. 9, 25.
8. Thea Astley, *Yacker*, op.cit., pp. 47, 53.
9. Kathleen Raine, 'On the Symbol', *Defending Ancient Springs* (Ipswich, Suffolk: Golgonooza Press, 1985), p. 108.
10. Julia Kristeva, *Powers of Horror: An Essay on Abjection* (New York: Columbia University Press, 1982), p. 208. Subsequent page numbers will be incorporated into the text.
11. Victor Turner, 'Betwixt and Between: The Liminal Period in *Rites de Passage*, *The Forest of Symbols* (Ithaca: Cornell University Press, 1967), p. 98.

12. Mary Douglas, *Purity and Danger: An Analysis of the Concepts of Pollution and Taboo* (London, Boston, Melbourne and Henley: Ark, 1984), p. 53.
13. Graeme Turner, *National Fictions* (Sydney, London and Boston: Allen and Unwin, 1986), pp. 9-10
14. M. Bakhtin cited in *The Politics and Poetics of Transgression* by Peter Stallybrass and Allon White (London: Methuen, 1986), p. 65.
15. Barbara Babcock, *The Reversible world: Symbolic Inversion in Art and Society*, edited by Barbara Babcock (Ithaca and London: Cornell University Press, 1978), p. 14.
16. Peter Stallybrass and Allon White, op.cit., pp. 183-184.
17. Julia Kristeva, op.cit., p. 185.
18. Victor Turner, *From Ritual to Theatre: The Human Seriousness of Play* (New York: PAJ Publications, 1982), pp. 27-28.
19. Thea Astley, *Yacker*, op.cit., pp. 42-43.
20. Kaja Silverman, *The Subject of Semiotics* (New York and Oxford: Oxford University Press, 1983), p. 231.
21. Julia Kristeva, *Revolution in Poetic Language*, op.cit., pp. 25-27
22. Toril Moi, *Sexual/Textual Politics* (London and New York: Methuen, 1985), p. 165.
23. Mary Jacobus, 'Interview with Beate Josephi' in *Australian Feminist Studies*, No. 2 (Autumn, 1986), pp. 47, 49.
24. Jacqueline Rose, *Sexuality in the Field of Vision* (London: Verso, 1986), pp. 143, 151.
25. Adrian Mitchell, 'Fiction', *The Oxford History of Australian Literature*, edited by Leonie Kramer (Melbourne: Oxford University Press, 1981), p. 166.
26. Josette Feral, 'Antigone or the Irony of the Tribe', *Diacritics*, Vol. 8 (September 1978), p. 10-11.
27. David Tacey, *Patrick White: Fiction and the Unconscious* (Melbourne: Oxford University Press, 1988).

# GILLIAN MEARS

Gillian Mears was born in 1964 and apart from four years in Sydney where she completed a Bachelor of Arts in Communications, has lived most of her life in the NSW country town of Grafton. Her first collection of stories, *Ride a Cock Horse*, won a regional section of the Commonwealth Writers Prize First Book prize. Since then, she has been awarded a Fellowship B from the Literature Board of Australia, The Marten Bequest Travelling Scholarship for Prose, 1990, and is the current recipient of the NSW Ministry of Arts Writing Fellowship. University of Queensland Press are publishing a second collection of stories, *Fineflour*, later in 1990. Her first novel, *The Mint Lawn*, a novel reflecting on the dual processes of infidelity and memory, won the 1990 Australian Vogel Literary Award.

GILLIAN MEARS

# Why I Write

Although I only began to contemplate my fiction writing as something to be taken seriously when I was a writing student at the (then) NSW Institute of Technology, I began writing stories from an early age. Even these earliest stories reveal an intensive interest in regional idiosyncracies and sadnesses. My shorter fiction continues to try to make sense of country-town childhood and the accompanying eccentricities, guilts, pleasures, underlying disturbances. A sense of sadness seems to underline much of my fiction. Often this sadness has a direct link to the unbalanced relationship between women and men that flourishes in NSW country towns. Only rarely can my writing alleviate this sadness but I am glad it highlights it. More recently I think my writing has been exploring notions of female guilt, as evidenced in mothers who for some reason must abandon their children or their homes: women whose domestic and emotionally starved lives have brought them to the brink. I often write about the idea of Absent Mothers. My novel, *The Mint Lawn*, works towards an understanding of, and a sympathy, for the often unacknowledged plights that confront Australian women in small country towns: the trap-like nature of unequal marriage and desire.

GILLIAN MEARS

# Who Kissed my Posy Rash?

We were women with very white teeth. One day Beatrice said it was as
if we'd been cleaning them with small burnt twigs in Africa or in
Katherine, since childhood. Really it was because it was a blistering
Sydney summer and though we wore hats and creams, the sun and the
wine burnt us all except for Pepe Botero, the Mexican who said he was a
writer. Our teeth were white, our skins only imperceptibly older unless
you suddenly saw someone or yourself in Lena's mirrors, in afternoon
light. Beatrice had bought the terrace next door when I was away but I
met her dog first. On certain hot nights the Great Dane would somehow
find his way across the roof and poke his head into my bedroom window.
From the first night, despite the dog's size, the effect was comical not
frightening. The registration tag told me his name was Lace. And I imagined then that she must be romantic, my new neighbour, whose dresses
I had been watching on the line, whose dog's black coat was full of torn
white threads that made you think of fine point serviettes in a grandmother's bottom drawer or the laceiness of the sea at night after a big
wave has broken.

   I was just back from nearly a year away and sat at my window imagining whimsical and innocent pastimes. Perhaps my new neighbour was a
cross-dressing boy who would entertain me endlessly with stories of his
romances, I thought. Or maybe I'd become good at sketching street
pigeons flirting and fucking under my tamarisk tree. But I'd come home
the month before Christmas and already, before I'd met Beatrice, there
seemed to be a momentum to the parties and a convergence of the same
people.

   Each morning at about nine o'clock, a wind would knock over the screen
I'd brought home. It was far too fragile for the strength of an Australian
summer and whereas in Europe it had cut out the midwinter light and un-
leashed the tongues of people sleeping in my room on the other side of it,
here the screen was almost transparent. No one could be hidden behind
it, let alone feel safe enough to tell any of their secrets. The morning
winds preceded brief storms and instead of pigeons or dogs or com-
mencing the sketches for Eva, I drew the rain wetting the sundresses of
my new and unseen neighbour. I drew the dresses the same miniature
size as cut-out costumes from childhood. Cutting out the dresses was a
pleasant task to nurse away the mild hangovers which I persuaded myself

were as much to do with my eyes adjusting to the blast of Australian colours, as alcohol. I couldn't get used to Australia. Australian voices again. And air so rich it felt to me that it or I would begin to rot out from our edges. My sweat seemed to smell of grass.

'Even the mangoes have sunburn,' I said to Lena, my voice full of disbelief. 'The colours. Like I've woken up in Kindergarten. And this elbow! So burnt after yesterday's drive to South Head.'

'Your skin will adjust soon,' she said and cut another piece of mango into a grid for me. 'Soon, you'll notice nothing.' She put a piece of mango onto the bone of my elbow with her tongue. 'You were like this last time you came back from London.'

Beyond the line of Beatrice's dresses four children pushed their dog up the steps of the slippery dip at the park and sent him down. Lena was moving the yellow square of fruit in small circles inside my elbow but it was no use. I felt more care for the dog on the hot slippery dip. Lena's sweat also smelt of grass and I wanted to ask why she was bothering with what had after all died between us before I went away.

'Sorry to be so obvious, but once you start working again, you'll feel like you were never anywhere else except Riley Street.' Lena suddenly stopped trying to make love and picked up five of my paper cut-outs instead. She dressed them on each finger of her left hand. We tried to remember the last real dresses we'd ever worn. I thought it was when I was still married and had had to accompany him to a garden party in London. It was pink and ankle-length and made me look like I should've been selling ice creams to the tourists outside the black and gold-gilt gates. Lena couldn't remember her last dress. She dipped one of the paper finger dresses into her glass of water. For a moment I watched as the dress clung as real cloth would to my girlfriend's finger.

My table began to seem too round for us to do anything constructive. We couldn't be comfortable. Lena had asked me to help with the design of her Christmas Street party invitation. We moved everything to the next seat and then round again, or pulled the curtains back even further along the rail, expecting at any moment for my neighbour to come rushing out to bring in her dresses from the storm.

'Are you going to invite her,' I asked.

'Of course. Silly.'

We were already a bit repulsed by each other. I wished Lena would put on a t-shirt so that I didn't have to observe her swollen veins.

There's no smell quite as reassuring as freshly sharpened pencils. I find that to have my box of Derwents open comforts me more than any other thing. Lace sits on my feet under the table. Sometimes I chide him: you shouldn't have trusted him darling, and the regret in my voice makes me cry all over again, for I'd also placed at least a kind of trust in Pepe Botero. Two weeks before Beatrice died he pushed me into a dark room to try to frighten and kiss me. Everything might've happened differently if only I'd told her about this. His tongue seemed to belong to an animal seeking a secret breeding place in my throat.

As planned we first met Beatrice at the Christmas Street party. For the invitation Lena had taken a photograph of local graffiti which said No laughing, do not Frolic. Very droll, very wonderful, very Lena-esque, people said, kissing her. So that before it was dark she appeared to have been purposely seeking the kisses of women wearing only the gaudiest shades of lipstick. But the party also had a sense of a family Christmas in that many of the people in Riley Street knew each other. There were picnic rugs and trestles in front of the canal and quite a few children much older already than I remembered. Beatrice arrived at a moment when the sky was so mauve it could've been Paris. The big dog progressed in loops around her. It was impossible not to notice and the entire party seemed to pause and watch. She was taller than I'd imagined, darker and there was something almost military in the way she held her head. Yet if you had to describe her to a perfect stranger you would've had to use words applicable to her dresses – flimsy, vulnerable. The type of woman I thought, who'd always have many mysterious garments, too delicate for the sun, drying in her bathroom. Her neck was long but her face reminded me of a Paula Becker painting of a girl. A translucent quality. I thought she was about thirty but Lena told me later her true age of forty three. The other thing I noticed immediately, once Lena had introduced us, was how sad Beatrice's eyes were and how flecked, as if for elaborate camouflage in a yellow and green forest. So that even though we were laughing within the first few seconds of having met – over my story of her dog's late-night forays to my bedroom window – and leaning down together to pat Lace, my overwhelming impression was of sadness.

'She's truly the worst watchdog in the world,' Beatrice said. My only chance would be that Lace lick them to their death. Wouldn't it Lovely?' Putting her small hand with its small fingers onto the dog's gigantic face.

I also noticed that Beatrice was looking at Lena's forearms, which were very hairy and strange against the sleekness of the dog's coat. Later, during the downpour, when everyone ran for cover under the viaduct and we were all a little bit drunker, Beatrice whispered that she found the hairiness of Lena's wrists very enticing. She surprised me, putting her hand towards my breasts. 'Look,' she said. From running, beaujolais had sprayed my shirt with the shape of a delicate pink fan.

I told Beatrice I'd never really liked the hairiness of my lover's arms to which she replied she'd always loved such small aberrations in hers.

Although from the first I had the feeling Beatrice had had some lesbian experience, the man who became her lover didn't arrive at the Christmas Street party until much later in the night. His teeth were brown with a grey band through the middle of them. You can't condemn a man for that;

I remember defending Pepe Botero's teeth and other things to Lena, but she said he made her feel slightly sullied. Whether it was his teeth or his eyes, or his lies about publication in eminent overseas literary journals, Lena wasn't sure.

Though I secretly agreed with Lena, I went on to tell her the story about the brown scars running in his eyes. When Pepe Botero was eleven years old a wild Mexican pony bolted with him through a barbed wire fence, strung at that height to stop paupers stealing lemons from his mother's orchard. During the following time of blindness, when he had to wear gauze guards over his eyes, Pepe began to learn the shreds of other languages known to his mother. She would brush his hair until blue sparks flew out of its ends, speaking all the while to him first in this language, then in that. To begin with their lessons concentrated on making up sentences about the pony gelding who still roamed at will in the orchard, eating up the fruit. His mother would use the terrible swear words of foreign languages to describe the pony. Or muddle them together. What a dangerous boy slut the pony was, she told Pepe. But at other times she'd make fairytales up about another quite magical little horse who ate only oranges and lemons and then slaked his thirst on buckets full of home-made lemonade. It was only because the lazy maid had made half the normal quantity of lemonade one afternoon, that the pony's wings failed to grow properly. So that instead of the pony and his boy clearing the fence around their palace, they crashed.

One day when Pepe asked why it was they hadn't killed or sold the real pony that had nearly blinded him, his mother replied that an extra gardener would have then had to be employed. Such levels the windfall fruit would quickly reach, a man could spend half a day, wheeling it away in a barrow. She ran her fingers through her son's long hair and tugged at it until he said ouch. Where else, she asked him, would they find such a little horse who genuinely liked to eat mouldy fruit. And what could Pepe Botero expect but to be hurt if he ever again tried to jump onto a sleeping unbroken pony's back?

When it occurred to him to say but Mama why didn't they give the fruit to the poor people who sometimes tried to climb into the orchard on the dark nights before new moon, his mother said that it was only old alcoholics who were after the lemons. To flavour their methylated spirits or whatever other concoctions they might have made out of the boot polish stolen from hard working shoe shine boys. Or the sugar-cane sticks thieved from the oldest women at the markets.

According to Beatrice, it was at this early age that Pepe became a socialist, eventually to be disinherited by his wealthy parents. She told us this as if we must love him too, for his political ideology if not himself. As a twelve year old he had given away a whole box full of pink marzipan piglets to a dusty beggar, knowing that when he told his mother she would have his father whip him with the belt full of lucky silver horseshoes.

'He's so full of bulldust,' said Lena, 'that even if you tapped him with your little finger out it would all belch.' Pepe Botero reminded us of an engraving at the large and showy Face exhibition Julia Mento had curated to such complex acclaim. In the engraving the man's face was halfway through its transformation into an alligator. We went all together but Beatrice and Pepe travelled around the show separately from us, so that often it felt to Lena and I that we were being as secretively attentive to their affectionate indiscretions, as to the hangings. 'What I keep thinking,' Lena said, 'is all that hair when they're in bed.' I too had thought that, I admitted and Beatrice's laughter, even though she didn't know what we were laughing about, was as sumptuous as the gallery. I thought it sounded like fruit being unpeeled in one long lovely curl and held Lena's little finger in my own. I thought of the inappropriate memories Beatrice was prone to telling me: about the shape of her mother's lips dripping down through a fringe of pubic hair: how long and ragged and mauve. Quite unattractive compared, Beatrice said, to the neat shape and pinkness she'd been blessed with. She said things like this to me. Or would return again and again to the memory of climaxing with kittens on her clitoris; how no orgasm had ever been quite so sweet. Then there was a day in later adolescence, when she pushed the tip of her paintbrush into her siamese's vulva and gave an orgasm back. 'Even now, when I see a kitten,' she confessed during one of these conversations in my kitchen,' I think of that almost fake feel of cat fur on my own little twelve year old body.'

I could only think of some pale, subtle European detail in exchange: how the skylights of Laon smelt of the folds of the freshly washed sex of a mature woman.


Only at one point at the exhibition was Beatrice able to stand alone in front of a picture. This was a kind of illuminated perspex screen of a mare's face, life size, half from the side. Lights shone through the horses eyes. The artist had also let light stream down one line of long jaw bone. The overall effect was quite eerie and beautiful. 'We might be standing in front of the Demeter horse goddess, mightn't we?' Beatrice said, when we came up to her. 'Or the goose girl's talking horse who lost his life. O du Falada da du hangest...' So that I hung my own head for a moment to remember a girl from a long time ago slipping her hands under my white horse's neck to say oh the sad, dark smell of horses. So that I tried to kiss her better, putting the horse's shoulder between us and the wind off the river. And Beatrice told us for the first time that her father was a NSW government tickie. All through her childhood, she said, shambolic ex-racehorses had roamed around the paddocks of their farm near Green Pigeon, because her father couldn't bear to see horses who'd once been the finest and glossiest going through the tickgates in expensive horse floats, going to the abattoirs. 'I'm sure you and my Dad would really get on,' she said to me.

'Why?'

'I just know. He is such an old sweetheart. The same kind of kindness that you have.'

Lena snorted.

Pepe came back from having a drink from the steel refrigerated bubbler in the corner. He put his face underneath Beatrice's dark pony tail until his cold red lips just touched the back of her neck. He said something to her in some other language. Lena thought he said, Je t'adore, but I argued it had been something far lewder in a language unknown.

In the lift, he undid his ponytail and began to conduct an invisible orchestra. This wasn't very funny but we laughed because we liked Beatrice. He continued conducting long after the laughter could go on and Beatrice alleviated the awkwardness by fixing up her face and taking the attention from him. She took out her lipstick and used the lift mirror. She knew, she apologised, that the lipstick she wore was very red, because children on public transport always stared at her mouth. I didn't know Beatrice very well at that point but felt already the familiar feeling of a summer flirt beginning between us. There was just that certain feeling that Beatrice had had at least one woman lover. Pepe held the lift door open with his body while Lena tried Beatrice's lipstick.

'Oh look at my wine rash,' I groaned, seeing under the lift-light all the broken blood vessels on my cheeks. 'I look like I have the pox.'

'No, it's posy,' said Beatrice.

'Poxy.' I made a face at myself.

Lena kissed the mirror. Beatrice kissed Pepe who was immediately worried that she'd left lipstick on the skin around his mouth. 'As if I'd do that to you dahlink,' said Beatrice.

'Isn't she bewtifool. A bewtifool personne,' and he held the inside of her wrist out to us, as if it was a long stemmed, cut freesia for us to appreciate.

The power any reasonably intelligent but monolingual Australian gives to people who speak more than one language, with at least an air of fluency, was never more apparent than this summer. Even Lena, who unfailingly called him Pea Beau in a conscious mockery of Beatrice calling him PB or Peps, was half taken in. And no matter how precarious or jealous Pepe's moods grew, Beatrice was able to cite his intelligence and sensitivity, with no proof other than that he said he possessed seven languages. He was meant to have honed his French and his socialism at the Sorbonne but couldn't remember the name of the street the university ran alongside.

Although he was this unconvincing, Lena asked me one day had I noticed how we'd all begun to talk a peculiar kind of broken English around him. Fractured voice patterns and the misuse of ordinary verbs had become our way of putting him at ease. For instance if something amusing happened we'd say – And it is making me laughing – as if butchering our sentences was the equivalent of speaking in a voice more exotic than our own Australian ones. On the night he phoned at 2am to tell me he and Beatrice had had a terrible fight, I heard my own voice like some kind of French, tin monkey wind-up, saying oh non, non, non. As if it were inconceivable, as if at the sound of his voice I had learnt to assume another one, even at a moment of crisis.

She was in the bathroom, with the taps on so that it sounded like a suicide not a murder. She'd managed to lock herself away from him. Or maybe he fled. Then she crawled. When he came back and phoned me, she was paradoxically safe from him but not from herself. She'd bitten his lip and possibly punched him twice. 'Look,' he said. 'Why she do this to me? Last night she was horrible.'

I stood beside him wheedling with an accent that wasn't my own, at the locked door. The hiss of the bath and the shower running at once. The look of her teeth marks on his mouth where he said she'd bitten him. Before I called the police, before he left the house, scared there would be problems regarding his expired visa, I asked had he finished with the Thomas Bernhardt stories I'd lent him, as if I knew I wouldn't see him again. I had purchased a poor translation, he said and handed me the stories from his satchel. We did this at the front door, perhaps at the actual moment that she died.

I think it's possible to believe that what lead to Beatrice's death, as much as the pills she swallowed after the bashing she received, was her own desire for something more exotic than Australia. I think her father might understand this explanation in that he first instilled it. In between spraying horses and manning the tickgates, all Beatrice's father would do was read. Other tickies gardened or drank or learnt how to crochet but he read French classics and Hemingway. Beatrice would never forget his joy, she said, if ever he came across a horse person or a cattle truck driver who shared the same reading passion. When I met him in the bar of the Southern Cross on Broadway where country people stayed, Beatrice's father cried like a young man. So that his hair seemed like the costume shop from across the road had placed an incongruous nest of white hair above his almost unlined, olive skinned face. And what am I to say to him, I keep wondering, what can I tell, when he comes to see me this afternoon, when he catches the 426, 422 or 423 as I told him to and walks down Riley Street as we arranged yesterday he would do.

How was it, he asked me sipping his beer, that *his* daughter, had let a lunatic from Mexico do that to her. When in only another three days she'd promised him she was coming north with Lace and I to do some of the walks they hadn't done since she was small, before the weather cooled down, before his knee operations. Her letters had often mentioned me, he said.

'I know,' I looked away from him. 'I don't know. We were so looking forward to it all.' And in the smokey air of the Great Southern, we were struggling with tenses, with whether or not to refer to Beatrice in the past or in the present and muddling them up so much that this curious feeling grew in me that she was neither dead nor alive but merely dislocated from us because of our clumsy use of the English language.

'I want to know why,' he said.

His eyes are like a whippet puppy's eyes, very clear, very *clean* eyes, just as Beatrice's were only without the flecks. They make me fear that when he arrives I will immediately want only to cradle his head in my arms as I cradled hers. I'd like to pour myself just one glass of beaujolais, in preparation for the shock of her eyes in his face, but have been resisting this urge since lunchtime.

When I take out the packets of photographs taken over the summer, of parties and trips to Balmoral or Bondi I'm not looking for anything in particular, except perhaps what shouldn't be shown to a father. As my fingers find something rough on one of the photos, I don't remember what I've done until I look down. At first I think someone else has defaced the photo of Pepe Botero. Perhaps even a child, for it has the superficial look of say a moustache scribbled onto a Mona Lisa in a magazine. But there is handwriting too and it's just recognizable as mine. Die, it says, and then some swear words. I must've been very drunk. I have no memory of poking him so full of holes. I was selective, only pushing pins into his throat and tongue. Then one in his belly, one under his ear. I remember now. The roar of Chivas Regal in my throat. I remember too when the police came to Beatrice's house, to batter down the bathroom door, how they found many photographs of Beatrice and Pepe Botero half burnt and melted in the kitchen sink. But thrown under the tap before their faces had totally gone. The burns had pushed out or disintegrated their cheeks and made bubbles in their foreheads. I imagine it was Beatrice who burnt them but perhaps I'm wrong.

Held to the light, the photo I have attacked isn't dissimilar to the horse head at the exhibition. But whereas in that picture, the holes of light lent the mare a soulful, sad wisdom, the holes I punched in Botero make him look afraid. His arm's up; against the taking of the photo which he always hated but now it looks as if he is fending off my own savage stabbing. The photo shows a crust of red wine on his lips like an old man's secret lipstick. He is wearing Beatrice's crimson shot silk jacket. He was always borrowing from her. We'd only ever seen him in two of his own shirts.

Why did Pepe Botero appear at Lena's party? No one seems to know very clearly but I remember he came in his red and white shirt with his hair braided and tucked under into a club. He didn't live in the street. Perhaps he was vaguely known to the girl right at the end. 'But so what,' Beatrice would say, 'that I don't know much about him.'

He kissed her a few hours after arriving, standing on a root of a fig tree
to be as tall. 'You're drunk!' A blonde prepubescent boy said to me in a
voice full of disdain.
'No. I'm not.'
'You are so.'
But if he was right, I was a very watchful drunk. I was watching their
first kiss.
I remember now lots of hair like something full of foreboding. Loosened
from its plait his was long and black and began to cover her face from my
view. If only she'd cut off her hair and worn boots not strappy sandals.
As he punched her, he must also have trodden all over her feet. At first
the police doctor thought he might've tortured her, the injuries on her feet
were so much more profound than was usual in usual cases of assault. If
only I'd told her that one night, at one party, he pulled my elbow behind
my back and pushed me into a dark and unknown room. In there he
squeezed my cheek and said, you are very bewtifool personne, the way
he did to Beatrice. As if somehow the fact he perceived you like this after
he'd had two bottles of wine to drink was something wonderful.
'You're a bewtifill personne but I'm so jealous. I not like it when you
two laugh together like that. You've been together haven't you.'
'No. No we haven't.'
'She told me you have.'
'No.' But it was totally black in the unknown room when he tried to kiss
me with his long tongue. 'This will be our secret,' he said and moved out
of the room. Then only a week later, he had headbutted Sasha Marchant,
the delicate and funny performance poet from Melbourne, who'd know
Lena for years. Sasha had said something mildly derogatory about Pepe
Botero, enfolded in a joke.
'The trouble is,' said Beatrice in the taxi we took home, 'that he makes
me feel so beautiful. Even though he's smaller than I am, and it's so
awkward sometimes we laugh. I'm like that salmon hibiscus on your
verandah, I just come and come and come.'
But in the taxi she was trembling. Had I seen how fast he had moved in
on Sasha, she wanted to know. And tried to show me bruises from the last
weekend, when after seeing her laughing with another man he'd grabbed
her arm. I just sat there, saying nothing, listening to her listing other
things about him that contradicted his bad behaviour and meant they
were meant. Fragile coincidences such as their birthdays being on the
same days in April. Or did I know their handwriting was interchangeable?
Not even Lena had been able to tell it apart.
'But, isn't it true,' I asked, 'that when you stay at his place, you have to
leave by dawn?'
'Oh yes but that's just because of who he's sharing the house with. It's
easier.'
'Sounds like horrible heterosexual behaviour to me,' I said.

'Sometimes it's nice for me too, waking up on my own. Last night, for instance, I was dreaming that someone kissed *your* posy rash.'

'My poxy rash.'

She took my hand. 'No, posy. In the dream, as in real life, it was shaped like the curve of old verse people used to place inside romantic rings for their lovers to wear.'

'So who kissed my posy rash?'

She wouldn't say but that was how she flirted. Alcoholically, she was more resilient. When we reached my place she said we must have just one more drink to make sure we slept. And when I refused took the same roof route as her dog, to climb into my bedroom window carrying a bottle of champagne. She was paying one hundred and fifty dollars an hour to have the broken blood vessels of her cheeks removed by laser so why shouldn't we drink a sixty dollar bottle of champagne. Her toes were as cold as the bottle. She was kissing my cheeks or I was kissing hers.

I sit looking at photographs. They are all slightly out of focus, the lens always focused more on the objects or paintings beyond the people. He is so out of focus his face is like a rotting moon on a white stalk above the crimson coat. The print behind him is of some kind of procession where animals on their hind legs and people on all fours are progressing towards the sea.

I make myself a pot of fresh spearmint tea and sit watching the leaves float. The green of a pistachio nut lying half out of its shell matches the leaves. This is how it has been since Beatrice died. As if everything I look at is a still life painting: every object on my table weighted and profound. One day in front of a Cezanne in the Musee d'Orsay, Beatrice said, tears had sort of leapt from her father's eyes. When he retired he'd fulfilled a lifelong wish to see Paris by taking a 14 day coach tour. It was the way the ripe fruit were sitting, he wrote on the back of the postcard of the same picture. Almost ready to rot but not. Lush.

And I thought he might almost have been writing about Beatrice. For once Lena had told me Beatrice's age it was apparent if you looked, or when she had a hangover. He too was on the point of turn. He was like the patches on an autumn frangipani flower, the brown spreading into the yellow, but when he arrived at the door, she shed about thirty years to become uncertain and skittish. She'd light a long cigarette to hide her confusion. She'd smell his neck.

I walk up the stairs to see from the second floor front verandah any sign of her father in the street. Lacey walks behind me on her big paws. I used to stand here on some nights, my window a perfect frame of Pepe Botero and Beatrice beginning their drunken wind home from the top of the street. Riley Street at the city end had been closed to traffic for years, so the taxis could never take you right to your door.

The bruise on my nipple looks like cancer, I cannot tell anyone and already have had to stop Lena who still wanted to playfully lift up my t-shirt. I press the bruise until it hurts. Only after Beatrice had actually died did all the bites on my neck and chin turn yellow and obvious.

'Who on earth has been kissing *you*?,' Lena said to me so strangely yesterday I wondered had she guessed as well as fearing that she'd guessed wrong and thought Pepe Botero had left them there. She wouldn't touch me and went away crying when I said I just couldn't say.

'I'd never do that to you,' Beatrice always said to him, wiping the red lipstick off his cheek or chin. For my birthday, elaborately wrapped, she gave me her favourite French novel. On every page where there was mention of love, she put a kiss. My memories make me feel like sicking up. I remember saying she must bite me and that she didn't want to. Bite me, put in all your hand, I think I kept saying. And maybe I made her and if so, against her will. She crept out early in the morning, first downstairs, but the door was deadlocked, so then back up into my room and like a frightened child out of my window. I remember that she'd looked afraid. Of me. So that I can't tell her father about how his daughter was the last time I saw her.

Pepe Botero only had a hand like a small olive glove. They said he must have punched her when she was down, for quite a long time, for such injuries. Or kicked with the court shoes on, always so highly polished, that she'd adored. How she'd managed to lock him out wasn't yet known, or whether she had died from head injuries or all the pills she'd begun to take once safely inside her bathroom.

My last lover before I came home to Australia was a thirty-six-year-old writer who survived by translating Harlequin romances into French. Her own novel in progress lived in the bottom drawer of a black desk, underneath a haphazard array of the faces and breasts of other girls. The novel was to be about her grandmother who'd been a bean farmer in the South, whose portrait had fallen to the bottom of a frame on a cluttered bookshelf. Monique said look at the size of her hands. Ouf! She was a giantess, yes? Holding her own delicate fingers up to the broad photo hand before snapping off small dark pieces of George Sand's chocolate face from the patisserie on rue du Cherche-Midi.

There are things I won't be able to tell you, should I say to her father? So many misapprehensions. Only last night for instance, did I realize the call Beatrice and I always thought was some kind of strange night bird, was the sound of children winding up and down their garden's hills hoist. If I open the window things are momentarily much clearer. The children wind it down and then hang themselves from it to fly around through the air. A peculiarly Australian kind of carousel, I can imagine turning around to say to Beatrice who'd be holding ice cubes over her swollen eyes, in my sun chair, in preparation for her first glass of white wine for the day; her dog's head in her lap; her stories of Pepe Botero rolling indiscriminately from her tongue so that I came to know exactly how he kissed the top of her very round forehead. I remember how the top of its dome was even in death like a detail from a Paula Becker portrait postcard I've found to show her father if the moment arises.

The children are tearing around with barely any clothes on and will be itchy and tearful when they are called inside. Beatrice always said that the church we could see had a steeple with bits at the top like antlers. When it rings its bells the children drop off the hoist.

Sometimes I'd think Beatrice would be unfriendly. Say if I caught sight of her in the mornings, in the street, but really she was taking into her house, hangovers too monstrous for my cures let alone conversation.

When I lift up my shirt again, the cloth seems so old it looks dark green not black. If possible, or is it just the late afternoon light, the yellow bruise is deeper and I can make our the exact imprint left from her little teeth. Some cars have their lights on, some don't but thank goodness it will soon be dark. Beatrice and I used to agree it is much easier to lie in the semi-light of evening, when if your skin blushes in a line beneath your posy rash, it only looks to the person deceived like the attractive flush from lunchtime's sun.

In my sitting room, her father's hair is like a thick white mane once hogged for pony club now left to go wild. I tell him how my father used to trick the tickies going through the gates at dusk with a fake padlock tied to the back of the float. Beatrice's father responds by describing Beatrice as an eleven year old who was dead keen on a collection of bottle ticks in glass jars on her window ledge, waiting to see if they ever became less bloated.

To dive into small eastern NSW histories like this, is a mutual decision. I feel our stories bumping and parting and moving on. Every memory of even the smallest itch from a coastal tick must be told or invented, any precarious personal detail will do, as long as it isn't the immediate past. And when we have exhausted this it is Beatrice's father who moves the conversation to France and art. He tells me of his disappointment to find so few Chagall pictures in Paris but that the postcard shops sold reproductions ten times better than those he had found here in Sydney. The colours of these reminded him of the lantanas in flower. Did I know what he meant? The greens against the pinks: the particularly lyrical shades that weed reaches in spring, on the back road to the town of Green Pigeon. Did I ever hear Beatrice describing the remarkable soil? he wants to know.

'So fertile it could grow babies?'

He beams. I have remembered. I have looked slightly to the left of him. I can only see the outline of my face reflected in the glass of a picture frame and would have to move closer to try to make out the features within.

# MARION HALLIGAN

Marion Halligan was born in Newcastle on the east coast of Australia and grew up by the sea. She now lives in Canberra, with her husband and occasionally two children, and has spent some time in France. Her books have been nominated for most of the major literary prizes and have won several, including the Steele Rudd Award (for the best collection of short stories in its year), the Braille Book of the Year for *The Living Hothouse* in 1989, and the Geraldine Pascall Prize for critical writing in 1990. Her latest novel, *Lovers' Knots* (Heinemann, 1992; Minerva, 1993) won The Age Book of the Year Award 1992, the ACT Book of the Year Award for 1993 (shared with the poet A.D. Hope) and the 3M Talking Book of the Year award. Her other books are the novels *Self-Possession* (UQP, 1987 & 1992), *Spider Cup* (Penguin, 1990), two more collections of short stories, *The Hanged Man in the Garden* (Penguin, 1991) and *The Worry Box* (Minerva, 1993), and *Eat My Words*, a collection of essays about food and other things.

She is currently Chairperson of the Australian Literature Board.

MARION HALLIGAN

# Why I Write

I write in order to put the world into words. I've always done that in my head. I can't perceive anything without trying to find words for it. When I began to put the words down on paper and work at getting them exactly right I became a writer. I do this with a pen; I enjoy the physical pleasure of forming the letters, the ink flowing. The way words look is important, and so is the way they sound. I'm interested in the way that getting the sound right, in terms of their music, the rhythm, the variations and repetitions of syllables, makes the words mean what you want them to say, so that sometimes finding the way things should sound achieves the meaning that you are looking for. Sometimes I think the words are more important than the things. When I find the words I'll know what the things are.

This is the way my imagination works. Anything that it lights on is material to it. It has its own honesty. Looking at the words on the page I can see whether they're true or not; if they're not I have to work at them until they are. Writing for me doesn't start with a subject, it's always words, and I've learned to trust them. It's pleasure and effort. I hope my readers will reverse the process, will get my words into their imaginations, and get pleasure from this effort; the pleasure of knowing or seeing or feeling the world I've got into words.

MARION HALLIGAN

# I Love You

Yes, that's her. She's gorgeous, isn't she. Those long legs. I love a woman with long legs. Like a young horse. They have nervous legs, delicate, full of energy. You can tell, she's just arrived, come galloping up the hill and skittered to a stop when she saw the writing on the car. We'd had a pretty grotty trip, dust and rain and mud. There was a good thick coating to make the marks in.

True? Of course. Yes, I did love her. She knew that. Came up the hill, saw the writing, turned round, and I took the shot just as she stood, poised, with that sexy pleased look. She was photogenic, you didn't need to pose her, any fleeting moment you caught her she looked good.

Of course shooting her wasn't the object of the outing. Shooting any-thing, although I had my camera along and got some nice photographs of the lake. There was a kind of silver light that day, and I thought, this is peace, and I photographed it. I thought I am actually photographing peace. There was nobody around, no human noises. It's hard to get away from human noises. There's always our machinery cutting the silence into shreds. Lawn mowers or cars or chain saws, even those screaming little things for beating up cakes. She didn't talk much, and anyway she had a soft voice, husky and slow, she'd always talk in a murmur, and there was the water making a liquid lapping sound against the pebbles, and no wind to rustle the leaves. No sun, either. Have you noticed how noisy the sun makes things when it shines? The bright light and the bright noise. I liked the greyness and calmness.

We walked around the shore for quite a bit. She didn't have any shoes on, she liked to travel light, that bird. It was rocky, but she picked her way, the rockiness didn't bother her. There were little sandy coves and thick mats of reeds washed up and sometimes shingle; she said she liked the feel of all the different surfaces of the earth under her feet. In amongst the rocks there were these small patches of grass, the kind that grows around lakes, thick and lush with little soft blades that don't prickle at all when you lie on them, even with no clothes on.

Yeah, we made love. I'm not always ... I mean, I can sometimes. I sup-pose it was the peacefulness, all that quiet emptiness, the silvery grey lake and the sky and the water lapping. It worked in the straight way, normal, her on her back and those legs around me and it was slow and sort of kind and afterwards we just lay on the grass and yes I did love her and she loved me. She had a tattoo on her bottom, on the left side, a dragonfly she said it was. I thought its wings shimmered when she moved. You know, she'd twitch her bum and the different colours of its wings'd shimmer. I thought it just suited her, a dragonfly, because of them being long and slender and big-eyed. I haven't got wings, she said, and I said where's your imagination girl. I see wings.

It was cool there, not cold, we didn't feel cold, but the air was cool and sort of dry. There was this faint watery breeze off the lake, but it wasn't humid, not that jungle humid where your skin can't breathe, when you're sweating and the atmosphere's sweating and there's nowhere for it to go. And for a bit I thought, I could stay here forever, but of course you never can. Not in the good places. We put our clothes on and walked back around the shoreline. There weren't even any boats pulled up. I wished I had one of those old wooden boats that people used to go fishing in. I could see myself carrying down the oars and setting off in the dawn, that's what it felt like, without the sun, the light all clear and grey like that, it felt like a dawn, the day not begun yet. And you push the boat out, you're wearing old sneakers in case of oyster shells or sharp rocks on the bottom, and you crawl in, and the oars make a quiet splash as they pull you through the water. You know the right places for the fish, and drop the anchor over, and bait your hooks with pongy old bits of green prawn, and throw the lines in, and you sit and wait for the fish to bite.

Of course it was the afternoon then, and too late in the day for fishing, even if we'd had a boat, with oars in it, and lines, and bait. We walked back to where we started, where the hill came down from the road. We didn't walk up the slope together. I felt good, I didn't need her right beside me at that moment. She'd stopped to look at something growing, the hillside had little scrubby plants with flowers on, she liked to look at things like that. Not pick. As I said she travelled light, she just looked Well, when I say she travelled light, I don't know about in her head. Who knows what's in people's heads? And maybe she didn't carry much baggage with her because of what she took along in her head. Stuff you'd like to chuck away, but you can't. If you could pack it all up in a port and leave it behind in a motel, with a false name and lost property never catching up with you. Lost property: I should be so lucky.

So I walked up the hill on my own, her mooning over some plant, and the choppers went over. You can't even see their blades whirling, just the air disturbed. The choppers went over and they chopped the sky in pieces and it fell down in chunks around me and I raced up the hill but still there was this noisy sky falling in chunks all round me. I couldn't get away. I got in the car but it didn't help. I got out and waited for her and that was when I wrote the words in the dirt on the side of the car. The choppers were gone by then but the quiet was still falling in pieces around us. Sharp pieces, heavy, that do damage.

She wasn't hurrying, it was the plants she cared about, bending and touching them as though it would make them feel better, but finally she stopped that and came galloping up the last bit of hill to the top and saw the words and skittered round and leaned and stood the way you see her there, poised on her toes lifting her head back offering her throat with that slow pleased smile and pulling her shirt down in her rather shy way with her big kind knuckly hands so careful of the flowers and that was when I shot her, first with the camera and then with the gun and then the camera again. You can see what the camera is about to pick up, just there in the corners of her mouth, the doubt that will turn into amazement, here, in this one, when she sees I've got the gun, the amazement already sliding into fear as she realizes what I'm going to do, here, and when I've done it, when I've pulled the trigger, haven't I, there's the writing on the car smudged where she fell across it.

It's a good camera, you see you only need one hand. I wanted a good camera, I wanted to take good pictures, you have to try to do things well. These pictures turned out well, even using only one hand. The gun behaved well too. The noise of the gun isn't like the noise of the choppers, it doesn't chop the sky into pieces falling on your head, it's an orderly sound, that puts things back. The noise of the gun rings like a bell and all the sky is back in place again and everything is very very quiet.

The writing? I used the gun. I guess it scratched the duco. It didn't seem to matter at the time.

# BEVERLEY FARMER

Beverley Farmer was born in Melbourne in 1941 and educated at MacRobertson's Girls' High School and Melbourne University. Except for six years of secondary teaching, she has supported herself mainly by hotel and restaurant work in Australia and overseas. In 1965 she married a Greek migrant and for some years, during which she wrote her first book, *Alone* (1980), they lived with his family in the village house where he was born. The stories that came out of this experience are collected in *Milk* (1983), winner of the 1984 NSW Premier's Prize for Fiction, and in *Home Time* (1985). *A Body of Water* (UQP) 1990), journal and writer's notebook interspersed with poems and stories, was shortlisted for the National Book Council Non-Fiction Banjo *Award* and for the NSW Douglas Stewart Prize for non-fiction. Her most recent novel is *The Seal Woman* set both in Australia and Denmark.

Beverley Farmer has one son, born in Australia in 1972.

BEVERLEY FARMER

# Why I Write

I write in fragments, cutting and polishing until each one seems ready to be put in place – here? or there? – in the mosaic. As the work fills out and the pattern begins to show, it becomes easier to stand back and judge the effect. I look for the illusion of depth and of movement in time and space within the frame of the thing – story, poem, novel – and a symmetry set up by its resonances and correspondences. Towards the end, it seems to be writing itself, fulfilling its own demands. The whole should have the feel of a lived experience, and seem to come together naturally.

Writing for me is a matter of fits and starts, any number of false starts. I work my way by instinct towards making what is on the page fit in with my sense of the whole work-to-be. The process is like getting to know someone intimately. We go on limited knowledge, fumbling our way to a greater knowledge, or to rupture. Works fail, come apart.

I try to make whatever I write as airy and spare a structure of words as will bear the weight. Through phase after phase I find more that can be left out. I strive for clarity.

BEVERLEY FARMER

# A Woman with Black Hair

Her front door locks, but not her back door. Like the doors on many houses in her suburb, they are panelled and stained old pine ones, doors solid enough for a fortress: but the back one opens with a push straight into her wooden kitchen. Moonlight coats in icy shapes and shadows the floor and walls which I know to be golden pine, knotted and scuffed, having seen them in sunlight and cloudlight as often as I have needed to; having seen them lamplit too, cut into small gold pictures by the wooden frames of the window, thirty small panes, while I stood unseen on the back verandah. (The lampshades are lacy baskets and sway in draughts, rocking the room as if it were a ship's cabin and the light off waves at sunset or sunrise washed lacily inside it. Trails like smoke wavering their shadows over the ceiling are not smoke, but cobwebs blowing loose.) These autumn nights she has a log fire burning, and another in her front room just beyond. With the lights all off, the embers shine like glass. They fill the house all night with a warm breath of fire.

An old clock over the kitchen fire chimes the hours. One. Two.

Off the passage from her front room is a wooden staircase. Her two small daughters sleep upstairs, soundly all night. Beyond the staircase a thick door is left half-open: this is her room. In its white walls the three thin windows are slits of green light by day, their curtains of red velvet drawn apart like lips. There is a fireplace, never used; hardly any furniture. A worn rug, one cane armchair, a desk with a lamp stooped over books and papers (children's essays and poems drawn over in coloured pencil, marked in red ink); old books on dark shelves; a bed with a puffed red quilt where she sleeps. Alone, her hair lying in black ripples on the pillow. For me a woman has to have black hair.

This one's hair is long and she is richly fleshed, the colour of warm milk with honey. Her eyes are thicklidded: I have never been sure what colour they are. (She is mostly reading when I can watch her.) They seem now pale, now dark, as if they changed like water. On fine mornings she lies and reads the paper on the cane sofa under her shaggy green grapevine. She is out a lot during the day. She and the children eat dinner by the kitchen fire – her glass of wine glitters and throws red reflections – and then watch television for an hour or two in the front room. After the children go up to bed, she sits on and reads until long past midnight, the lamplight shifting over her. Some evenings visitors come – couples, the children's father but no one stays the night. And she has a dog: an aged blond labrador, half-blind, that grins and dribbles when it hears me coming and nuzzles for the steak I bring. It has lolloped after me in and around the house, its tail sweeping and its nails clicking on the boards. It spends the night on the back verandah, snoring and farting in its sleep.

The little girls – I think the smaller is five or six, the other not more than two years older – have blond hair tied high in a sheaf, like pampas grass. (The father is also blond.)

Tonight, though the moon is nearly full, it is misted over. I may not even really need the black silk balaclava, stitched in red, that I bought for these visits, though I am wearing it anyway, since it has become part of the ritual. I am stripped to a slit black tracksuit – slit, because it had no fly – from which I unpicked all the labels. I have the knife safe in its sheath, and my regular tracksuit folded in my haversack ready for my morning jog when I leave the house.

Tonight when the clock chimed one she turned all the lights out. When it chimed two I came in, sat by the breathing fire, and waited. There is no hurry. I nibble one by one the small brown grapes I picked, throwing the skins and the wet pips into its flames of glass, making them hiss. Nothing moves in the house.

When the clock chimes three I creep into her room – one curtain is half-open, as it always has been – to stand watching the puddle of dimness that is her pillow; the dark hair over it.

I saw her once out in the sun untangling her wet hair with her fingers. It flowed over her face and over her naked shoulders like heavy dark water over sandstone. The grass around her was all shafts of green light, each leaf of clover held light. There were clambering bees.

There is a creek a couple of streets down the hill from here. I wish I could take her there. It reminds me of a creek I used to fish in when I was a boy. There were round speckled rocks swathed with green-yellow silky weed, like so many wet blond heads combed by the fingers of the water. (My hair was – is still – blond.) I used to wish I could live a water life and leave my human one: I would live in the creek and be speckled, weedy-haired, never coming out except in rain. I lay on the bank in spools and flutters of water light. A maternal ant dragged a seed over my foot; a dragon-fly hung in the blurred air; a small dusty lizard propped, tilted its head to take me in, and hid in the grass under my shadow.

Over the weeks since I found this woman I have given her hints, clues, signs that she has been chosen. First I took her white nightgown – old ivory satin, not white, but paler than her skin – and pulled it on and lay in her bed one day. It smelled of hair and roses. I left it torn at the seams on the sofa under the grapevine that shades her back verandah. I suppose she found it that night and was puzzled, perhaps alarmed, but thought the dog had done it; anyone might think so. Another day I left an ivory rose, edged with red, in a bowl on her kitchen table. She picked it up, surprised, and put it in a glass of water. She accused her daughters of picking it, I could tell from where I was standing by the kitchen window (though of course what she was saying was inaudible), and they shook their heads. Their denials made her angry; the older girl burst into loud sobs. Another frilled rose was waiting on the pillow in the room with the three red-lipped windows. I wonder what she made of that. They looked as if they were crumpled up, then dipped in blood.

I drop a hint now. I sit down in the cane armchair, which creaks, and utter a soft sigh. Her breathing stops. She is transfixed. When it starts again, it is almost as slow as it was when she was asleep, but deeper: in spite of her efforts, harsher. Her heart shudders. For long minutes I take care not to let my breathing overlap hers; I keep to her rhythm. She does not dare to stop breathing for a moment to listen, warning whoever is there, if anyone is, that she is awake. And at last – the kitchen clock chimes four – she starts to fall asleep again, having made herself believe what she must believe. There is no one there, the noise was outside, it was a dream, she is only being silly.

I make the chair creak again.

She breathes sharply, softly now, and with a moan as if in her sleep – this is how she hopes to deceive whoever is there, because someone is, someone *is* – she turns slowly over to lie and face the chair. Her eyes are all shadow. Certainly she opens them now, staring until they water, those eyes the colours of water. But I am too deep in the dark for her to see me: too far from the grey glow at the only tall window with its curtains left apart.

This time it takes longer for her to convince herself that there is nothing here to be afraid of. I wait until I hear her breathing slow down. Then, as lightly as the drizzle that is just starting to hiss in the tree by her window, I let her hear me breathing faster.

'Who is it?' she whispers. They all whisper.

'Quiet.' I kneel by her head with the grey knife out.

'Please.'

'Quiet.'

The clock chimes. We both jump like rabbits. One. Two. Three. Four. Five. I hold the knife to her throat and watch her eyes sink and her mouth gape open. Terror makes her face a skull. 'Going to keep quiet?' I whisper, and she makes a clicking in her throat and nods a little, as much as she dares to move. 'Yes or no?'

She clicks.

'It's sharp. Watch this. 'I slice off a lock of her black hair and stuff it in my pocket. 'Well?'

Click.

'Well?'

'Yesss.'

When I hold her head clear of the quilt by her hair and stroke the knife down the side of her throat, black drops swell along the line it makes, like buds on a twig.

'Good. We wouldn't want to wake the girls up, would we?' I say. I let that sink in, let her imagine those two little girls running in moonlit gowns to snap on the light in the doorway. Then I say their names. That really makes the pulse thump in her throat. 'They *won't* wake up, will they?'

'No,' she whispers.

'*Good.*'

I press my lips on hers. My mouth tastes of the grapes I ate by her still fire, both our mouths slither and taste of the brown sweet grapes. I keep my tight grip of my knife and her hair. She has to stay humble. I am still the master.

'I love you,' I say. Her tongue touches mine. 'I want you.' Terror stiffens and swells in her at that. 'Say it,' I say.

'I – love you,' she whispers. I wait. 'I – want you.'

Now there is not another minute to wait. I throw the quilt off and lift her nightgown. She moves her heavy thighs and the slit nest above them of curled black hair.

There is a hot smell of roses and summer grasses. I lie on top of her. 'Put it in,' I say, and she slips me in as a child's mouth takes the nipple. 'Move,' I say. She makes a jerky thrust. 'No, no. Make it nice.' Her eyes twitch; panting, she rocks and sways under me.

I have to close her labouring mouth with my hand now; in case the knife at her throat slips, I put it by her head on the pillow (its steel not cold, as hot as we are), and it makes a smear where the frilled rose was. Her nightgown tears over her breasts, black strands of her hair scrawl in red over the smooth mounds of them, warm wet breasts that I drink. Is this the nightgown? Yes. Yes. Then we are throbbing and convulsing and our blood beats like waves crashing on waves.

None of these women ever says to me, How is your little grub enjoying itself? Is it in yet? Are you sure? Can it feel anything? Oh, well, that's all right. Mind if I go back to sleep now? No, move, I say, and they move. Move nicely. Now keep still. And they do.

'Now keep still,' I say, picking up the knife again. She lies rigid. The clatter of the first train tells me it is time. Day is breaking. Already the grey light in the window is too strong to be still moonlight, and the dark tree has started to shrink, though not yet to be green and brown. 'I have to go. I'll come again,' I say as I get up. She nods. 'You want me to. Don't you.' She nods, her eyes on the hand with the knife.

I never will. I never do. Once is all I want. At night she will lie awake thinking I will come to her again. Just as she thinks I might cut her throat and not just slit the skin; and so I might. But their death is not part of the ritual. The knife is like a lion-tamer's whip: the threat is enough. Of course if the threat fails, I will have to kill her. She, for that matter, would turn the knife on me if she could. Chance would then make her a killer. Chance, which has made me the man I am, might yet make me a killer: I squat stroking the knife.

'Well, say it,' I say.

'Yes.'

'You won't call the police.' She shakes her head. 'Or will you? Of course you will.' My smile cracks a glaze of blood and spittle around my mouth. In the grey mass on the pillow I watch her eyes roll, bloodshot, bruised, still colourless. 'I want you to wait, though. I know: wait till the bird hits the window.' A bird flies at her window every morning. I see her realize that I even know that; I see her thinking, Oh God, what doesn't he know? 'That's if you love your little girls.' Her eyes writhe. 'You do, don't you. Anyone would.' Girls with hair like pampas grass. 'So you will wait, won't you.' She nods. 'Well?'

'Yes.'

Her coils of dark hair are ropy with her sweat and her red slobber, and so is her torn gown, the torn ivory gown that I put on once, that she never even bothered to mend. A puddle of yellow haloes her on the sheet. She is nothing but a cringing sack of stained skin, this black-haired woman who for weeks has been an idol that I worshipped, my life's centre. The knowledge that I have got of her just sickens me now. Let them get a good look at what their mother really is – what women all are – today when they come running down to breakfast, her little girls in their sunlit gowns. 'You slut,' I say, and rip her rags off her. 'You foul slut.' Just having to gag her, turn her and tie her wrists behind her and then tie her ankles together makes me want to retch aloud. Having to touch her. But I stop myself. Turning her over to face the wall, I pull the quilt up over the nakedness and the  stink of her. I wipe my face and hands, drop the knife and the balaclava into my haversack, and get dressed quickly.

The dark rooms smell of ash. Light glows in their panes, red glass in their fireplaces. The heavy door closes with a jolt. I break off a bunch of brown grapes with the gloss of the rain still on them. The dog snuffles. Blinking one eye, it bats its sleepy tail once or twice on the verandah.

I have made a study of how to lose myself in these hushed suburban mornings. (The drizzle stopped long ago. Now a loose mist is rising in tufts, and the rolled clouds are bright-rimmed.) I am as much at home in her suburb as I am in her house, or in my own for that matter, though I will never go near the house or the suburb, or the woman, again. (I will find other women in other houses and suburbs when the time comes. Move, I will say, and they will move. Move nicely. They will. Keep still. Then they will keep still.) And when the sirens whoop out, as of course they will soon, I will be out of the way. I will wash myself clean.

I am a solitary jogger over yellow leaves on the echoing footpaths. No one sees me. I cram the grapes in my haversack for later.

I know that soon after sunrise every morning a small brown bird dashes itself like brown bunched grapes, like clodded earth, at the bare window of her room, the one with its red curtains agape. Again and again it launches itself from a twig that is still shaking when the bird has fallen into the long dry grass and is panting there unseen, gathering its strength for another dash. (The garden slopes away under her room: no one can stand and look in at her window.) It thuds in a brown flurry on to its own image shaken in the glass. It startled me, in the garden the first morning. I think of her half-waking, those other mornings, thinking, It's the bird, as the brown mass thudded and fell and fluttered up to clutch at the twig again: thinking, only the bird, and turning over slowly into her safe sleep.

But she is awake this morning. She is awake thinking, Oh God, the bird, when will the bird? Twisting to free her hands and turn over: Please, the bird. Her shoulders and her breasts and throat are all ravelled with red lace. Her hair falling over them is like dark water.

# Beverley Farmer

## PADDLE

We three women walked to the cove.
>   Silver, the long light, swans drifting, pied
>   >   cormorants on guard

and three gulls, restless
>   as we tipped over the yellow rowboat
>   >   stranded on the sea grass

its gathered leaves and rain
>   water spilling in thin air.
>   Shoes under one arm and trousers rolled

we made our way back

we three, planting each foot
>   on clear dry sandstone
>   >   studded with sharp winkles –

look, here's a starfish! – and a flowering
>   here red, here gold
>   >   of lichen

here a fan, here a broad
>   charcoal heap and fire blister of rock
>   >   and here a crinkling of white comb

>   fine as an abalone mushroom

and sinking to our knees on to deep rocks
>   the clearer for being immersed
>   >   in that pure density and weight

more like the lees of the afternoon
>   light, grey and leaf yellow
>   >   and autumn cold, than

water. By then the hull
    was a lemon shell among shells
        on the edge of trees glassed

        in shadow, and still

one or other of the gulls was lifting
    off in a hush of feathers and red
        feet, to settle back

down, fold and flourish of wing spray
    close by another who
        lifting, swept past, and so on

in slow sequences of approach
    and veer, those same three
        keeping the space of water and air

    between them constant.

XAVIER PONS

# Blood and Water:
# Feminine Writing in
# Beverley Farmer's *The Seal Woman*

Using the phrase 'feminine writing' in the title of a paper would seem to take it for granted that there is indeed such a thing, that women do write – or at least can write – in a specifically feminine way which it is possible to identify, describe and comment upon. The idea remains hotly debated even though many critics, not all of them radical feminists, have asserted that indeed this is so, and have proceeded to point out what they re- garded as the characteristic features – with regard to content and/or style – of this type of writing. The exercise has not always turned out to be very liberating for women writers, who were sometimes consigned to the ren- dering of a certain type of experience which, in the eyes of men, simply went to show that women were hysterical creatures who could only on rare occasions rise above the emotional quagmire to which their sex con- signed them.

Thus, at the turn of the century, Henry Lawson wrote a preface to Miles Franklin's *My Brilliant Career* in which he said: 'I hadn't read three pages when I saw what you will no doubt see at once – that the story had been written by a girl.' This was a back-handed compliment. Lawson meant to praise the novel, one of whose merits was a realism which occasionally transcended the defects inherent in women's writing, and to which Law- son referred obliquely by saying: 'I don't know about the girlishly emo- tional parts of the book – I leave that to girl readers to judge.'[1] The novel, written under a man's name, was a fine one on the whole but, Lawson im- plied, was marred by unmistakable traces of femininity. Although Miles Franklin was a crafty counterfeiter,[2] her real nature shone through her attempted disguise – she was the victim of an emotionality which is char- acteristic of women's nature. Women's writing, in this perspective, means the unbecoming predominance of emotion over reason. Compared with men's writing, it is simply immature. This sexist perspective rightly infuriates feminists, although they are divided on the question of whether a truly feminine sort of writing exists. While Virginia Woolf suggested that there is such a thing as a 'woman's sentence', Shosana Felman held that women still had to reinvent language in order to be free of what she termed 'the phallacy of masculine meaning'.[3] As for Hélène Cixous, she prefers to speak of a 'decipherable libidinal femininity'[4] which can be penned by either men or women. The problem is at once one of content and style, with feminine characteristics – whether assumed or genuine – envisaged in a rather different perspective in each case. Male critics have always acknowledged that women were good at writing about certain, mostly 'domestic' subject matters, with the result that women writers were not encouraged to venture beyond this traditional territory – their castle was also their prison. The purely stylistic character of 'écriture féminine', on the other hand, is regarded as far more elusive, and is sometimes dismissed out of hand as a feminist myth. The links between style, gender and an authenticity of female experience remain controversial.

I make no claim, obviously, to have found a definitive answer to this difficult literary – and more than literary – problem. My ambition is solely to look at a contemporary novel, Beverley Farmer's *The Seal Woman*,[5] which I found stunningly beautiful and which, it seemed to me, only a woman could have written – by which, and unlike Lawson, I mean that its literary qualities rather than its shortcomings are somehow uniquely feminine. What defines the femininity of the type of writing which is embodied by this novel? It is not for the most part a question of subject matter, of vocabulary, of syntax or of narrative mode – and yet it is all of these at once. Taken separately, the various ingredients which go into the writing of feminine fiction do not perhaps matter very greatly, or at least they matter less than the overall effect produced by their meaningful and deliberate combination into a kind of substance which is feminine writing – or at any rate an instance of it.

The French novelist Christiane Rochefort said women were supposed 'to write about certain things: house, children, love'.[6] Feminine writing thus reflects the social experience of women, whom the ruling patriarchal order circumscribes to so-called 'feminine' activities, places and emotions. In *The Seal Woman* a great deal of attention is paid to those traditional areas. Consider how the novel's protagonist, Dagmar (she's a Danish woman whose husband has been lost at sea and who revisits Australia, where she spent her honeymoon twenty-two years earlier) describes her activities: 'I chopped crisp, snowy leeks and potatoes for soup. I gathered up a sprawl of washing and switched the machine on, in the hope that this would restore me to calm, or at least let me ride out the storm' (p. 18). Here is a woman doing what women do traditionally – cooking, doing the washing – and coping with disturbingly strong emotions. Like any other male chauvinist, Henry Lawson would have understood this kind of feminine writing. But he would have been disconcerted by other accounts of female behaviour, such as the following: 'First thing in the morning of one of my first days here I got up on a ladder and swept down all the cobwebs, under the sway of the nesting urge that still takes over for a day or two near the full moon when my blood flow used to start' (p. 33). More housework – but not performed as the result of some social conditioning. The passage suggests an interaction between the natural world – both inanimate ('the full moon') and animate ('nesting urge' suggests birds) – biology (menstruation), and female behaviour. A male chauvinist would say that women are the victims of anatomy, almost of instinct. Indeed Dagmar's behaviour seems determined by factors beyond her control. But the implication is that this results from women being in touch with or attuned to realities to which men are simply blind. The source of their behaviour is far deeper than the tyranny of a patriarchal order. Women are in and of the world, not detached on-lookers like men: they participate in its rhythms; their experience is almost necessarily cosmic.

Beverley Farmer's writing shows features which have been traditionally regarded as feminine, such as a particular and somewhat romantic attention paid to nature, flowers, animals, etc., as in the following passage:

> Bananas are so cheap, and there are all the tropical fruits I knew – pineapples, papaya and kiwi and passion fruits all purple and gold, eaten with a spoon, and wary custard apples with their leaves of sandy pearflesh – and other new ones. There is a sleek red-skinned egg with blood-red seeds coiled in gold flesh around the shape of a Byzantine cross when cut through its equator... (p. 50)

More than thirty lines are thus devoted to a description of the fruits Dagmar loves to eat in Australia – a typical feminine conceit, one might be tempted to think. But these descriptions are not meant to prettify the text, nor are they a sign that the author cannot stick to a narrative thread and is constantly getting side-tracked into irrelevant details. The fruits are not just beautiful to look at – they're nice to eat, and eating is part of living. The passage is in fact a celebration of living: it is a glory of colours ('purple and gold'; 'blood red') and those colours, as we shall see, are a symbol of life. Nor is it by accident that the narrator refers to the fruits in metaphorical terms of the earth ('its equator') and of people ('flesh'). These fruits, which sustain life, testify to the fertility of the earth, its bounteousness; they suggest harmonious and abundant living. The passage has directly to do with the major preoccupations of the novel, which concern living and dying, creating and destroying, fertility and barrenness, and which strike me as being especially feminine.

Dagmar, the heroine, is a frustrated and unhappy woman: she has lost her husband Finn prematurely – the novel accepts death as part of nature; what is not acceptable is when death is premature or unnecessary – she has no children and believes herself no longer fertile – apparently, she is experiencing an early winter of life.[7] Her mind is on destruction and on death – 'In a way I am a grave' she says (p. 188) and she comes to Australia to work through her mourning, even though she doesn't think she can do it: 'What does it matter, after all, where I am? I am a vessel, and my cargo is the death of Finn wherever I am, bequeathed to me, and I live in a net of shadows' (p. 188). However, Australia will regenerate her, effect a cure, almost in the psychoanalytic sense, and in the end she will go back to Denmark, pregnant by her reluctant lover Martin, ready to carry on living.

Her odyssey is not simply an individual one – it has something archetypal about it. It is a paradigm of the eternal fight between the forces of death and the forces of life which involves the entire planet. Dagmar is a concerned environmentalist; she worries about the future of the earth which is threatened by man's thoughtless activities – pollution, hunting and fishing in particular. Soon, she says, 'only the submarines of the great powers will be left alive in the sea' (p. 61), and then she adds, 'The earth is one great graveyard, as we all know too well' (p. 65).

In the fictionalising of these preoccupations, it is Beverley Farmer's method, even more than the preoccupations themselves perhaps, which shows an unmistakable feminine touch. Under a man's pen, it is likely that these preoccupations would have taken the form of an allegory or of an intellectual discourse; Farmer's manner is far more subtle – and a good deal more effective as well.

In their studies of women's autobiographies, Suzanne Juhasz[8] and Rebecca Hogan[9] have insisted on the diarists' immersion in a profusion of details, resulting in a seeming loss of perspective which is in fact a non-hierarchical perspective and which has variously been described as 'verbal quilt' or 'radical parataxis': 'immersion in the horizontal, non-hierarchical flow of events and details – in other words, radical parataxis – seems to be one of the striking features of the diary as a form,' Hogan observed.[10] 'Diaries are not so much inclusive because they contain everything from a given day, as they are inclusive in the sense that they do not privilege "amazing" over "ordinary" events in terms of scope, space or selection.' Much of this applies to the narrative mode Beverley Farmer uses in *The Seal Woman*.

The novel is a homodiegetic narration, and often takes the form of a diary in which Dagmar writes down her experiences of the day – thus: 'At night the rooms next door cast light into the trees. Now and then I hear voices or the radio or TV' (p. 76) or 'At the surf beach at sunset the waves cover my footprints and run back' (p. 272). This narrative mode is inherently parataxic: the juxtaposition of fragments and the use of the present tense prevent a perspective from emerging clearly; perceptions and sensations are jumbled, chaotic. This reflects Dagmar's confusion, her struggle with depression. The present, however, does not predominate. Most of the narrative is written in the past tense and, were it not for its fragmentary character, would appear rather more conventional. The interplay between past and present – in the grammatical as well as in the psychological senses – is an essential aspect of the narrative. Dagmar, overwintering in Australia, is taking stock, and trying to make sense of her past. The alternance of past and present tenses convey this attempt. Passages written in the past tense are truly narrative: they recount the activities of Dagmar and her acquaintances with a sense that they are inserted in the inescapable flow of time. Passages written in the present tense, on the other hand, are removed from this flow: they are moments of reflexion and interpretation, of nightmares and fantasies too. They transcend events and thus provide a perspective on them. The past – in so far as it is a source of alienation and depression – is thus gradually exorcized, which paves the way for a preoccupation with the future which shows Dagmar to be a free agent again.

This effect is reinforced by the collage technique which Beverley Farmer uses abundantly. Information is supplied in a fragmentary, apparently random manner – a snippet here and a snippet there – and the reader has to piece the fragments together. Finn's death when his ship was rammed by a tanker, for instance, is introduced cryptically: 'Martin said to me once, his mouth against the nape of my neck: "There was no doubt they went – in the water, then? They couldn't have burnt to death?"' (p. 7). The significance of the question is revealed only later, thanks to other fragments such as: 'I am Dagmar, a Dane. I am here now as Finn's widow where I came once as his bride' (p. 9). Her odyssey unfolds slowly and gradually, interrupted at intervals – as it seems – by what Murray Bail would call 'intrusions from real life'.[11] Those intrusions consist in quotations, some of them almost a page long, from a variety of sources: poems, songs and ballads, folk tales, newspaper cuttings (cf. p. 15), excerpts from the Bible (cf. pp. 153 & 177), from Coleridge (cf. p. 145), from Mircea Eliade's *Shamanism* (cf. p. 116), from Rowena Farre's *Seal Morning* (cf. p. 208), from Robert Graves's *The White Goddess* (cf. p. 209), etc. These interruptions or asides often act as instances of lateral narratives, in the sense in which one speaks of lateral thinking, criss-crossing the main story line, opening it up, infusing it with other yet related preoccupations. What happens to Dagmar, in other words – her fears, her joys, her attitudes – is not something apart, purely individual, but part of a bigger, perhaps cosmic pattern. This dismantling of closures and boundaries – between the fictional, the mythical and the historical, between the past and the present – is in a sense peculiarly feminine. Woman, Hélène Cixous said, must 'write from the body': 'Her libido is cosmic, just as her unconscious is worldwide. Her writing can only keep going, without ever inscribing or discerning contours.'[12]

Dagmar, the narrator, indeed writes from the body – a dispirited and forlorn body at first, and then a serene, almost triumphant one, but always a very concrete one with strong life-asserting urges and cravings.

This gives Beverley Farmer's writing a paradoxically feminine earthiness. The feminine, as lady-like, is often associated with daintiness or prettiness, that is, a remoteness from the grosser aspects of existence. This is of course an alienated and mutilated version of femininity rather than the real thing. Farmer's narrator does not flinch from reporting, mostly in a matter-of-fact way, facts of life which are often regarded, especially by women writers, as too coarse to mention. Thus: 'I went to piss, I brought in the bicycle, already wet with dew. Then I undressed and slid into his bed which smelled of him, his strong sweat [...] I filled the bed with their shadows and ghosts, Martin and Tess, Finn, and Janni and my good hands that were wet when I came' (p. 233). Such passages might seem to be a long way from more traditionally feminine lyrical descriptions of flowers or animals, which also abound in the novel. But in fact they underline the novel's *inclusiveness*, its refusal to consider certain things as irrelevant, coarse, unworthy of attention. When Dagmar, pregnant, is planning her return to Denmark, she thinks: 'And now I will have flesh and blood to grapple with also, and be anchored, earthed' (p. 298). The novel's occasional earthiness is a way of being earthed, in touch with global reality. It also underlines the fundamental role of the body in the process of living: to some delicate souls, micturition, smells and masturbation have no place in fiction; yet no one can deny they are part of living. Farmer refers to them in a matter-of-fact way which is anything but titillating or perverse: the body has its own way of speaking or writing, and can only be denied at the price of mutilation and alienation.

Farmer's conception of writing is nothing if not holistic. It is imbued with a sense of the connectedness of things, with the intuition or conviction that human beings are not so much discrete individuals as elements in a wider, cosmic, scheme. This is reinforced by the novel's mythopoetic dimension, and in particular by the numerous references to other cultures with which the narrative is studded. Dagmar would seem to be a frustrated anthropologist, with an enormous curiosity about folk tales, the legends and myths of remote civilisations – whether the Aborigines, the Inuit, the Celts or the Vikings. Her mind is constantly drawn to those alien yet familiar cultures because they have answers to the fundamental questions by which she is obsessed – especially those that have to do with life and death. The following passage is a good instance. Dagmar has planted some beans:

> how strange that the bean, no less than the bee and fly and butterfly, was thought of as a vessel for the soul. In Greece and Rome you could drive a ghost away if you spat beans at it. They had air in them, breath, or why else would you fart after you ate them, and the breath and the soul are one and the same: that seems to have been the train of thought. (p. 79)

The most trivial everyday activity – like gardening – can be the starting point of a meditation on the mysteries of life, to which even farting is not irrelevant.

The cosmos is both one and multiple, and everything is connected with everything else. Ancient and modern mythologies converge to assert this. The author's intuitive sense of the affinities which cultures have with one another, and which beings of this or that order have with beings of other orders, this refusal of rigid boundaries, this plasticity, has something especially feminine about it. It does not, however, degenerate into syncretism. Boundaries can be crossed temporarily but not abolished: all creatures belong in a certain environment which they cannot leave permanently – this is illustrated by the tale of the seal woman, which Dagmar transcribes for her lover's daughter and appends to her diary. Dagmar herself, by the same token, has to go back where she came from, where she belongs, in order to be whole – Australia can only be a place of transition for her. Nature is flexible, but its laws must not be transgressed.

Beverley Farmer's preoccupation with living and dying is not expressed in an abstract, philosophical fashion. She eschews intellectual discourse and allegory alike and relies instead on clusters of images to let significance emerge. One very basic function of her metaphors is to establish the invisible kinship which unites all creatures of nature: human beings, animals, plants, the earth itself are a whole: 'the whole land, when you think of it, is a vast body,' Dagmar exclaims (p. 185), and to her the Nullarbor caves are 'the lungs of the earth' (p. 247). Elsewhere she writes of 'the dry rough skin of the rock' (p. 4) or of the 'fleshy smell' (p. 1) which a beach has in its salt, thereby emphasizing the links between humanity and the inanimate world. Metaphors also suggest links between humanity and the vegetable and animal kingdom. The pubic hair of Dagmar's lover is 'damp and warm like seaweed' (p. 1); the sounds made by children running on the wooden floor suggest 'a swan leaving the water, a pelican, slow beats of a paddle' (p. 1). The linkage between the various worlds is also expressed, with particular insistence, by the legend of the seal woman and the silkie – mythical creatures who are human beings upon the land and animals in the water.

What unites all creatures – even inanimate ones – is the fact that they are subjected to the processes of living and dying – mostly the latter. The characters feel very concerned about destruction, ecological disasters, etc. of which Australia appears to be an awful example: 'The desert is growing fast,' the protagonist writes; 'soon all that grows here will be the desert which is dead land... From horizon to horizon vast lands are already bone dry dust under a white shimmer like ice, the death mask of the salt' (p. 23). The major paradigm of destruction, which is referred to at regular intervals throughout the novel, is the mysterious sickness which in the late 1980s killed thousands of seals in the North Sea.[13] This sickness appeared to derive from high pollution levels, and was thus man-made. Since the seal is presented by Dagmar as a semi-human creature, its destruction is symptomatic of mankind's self-destructive drive.

This preoccupation with death and destruction, once again, is mostly expressed through a series of related images which cluster around the twin poles of blood and water. It is not that either liquid stands for either life or death: each has dual, ambiguous connotations, and intermingles with the other to create a vision of great complexity and of compelling concreteness.

Blood suggests carnage, and is something of an obsession with Dagmar: 'The bloodbath, I say, always the blood bath', she repeats on various occasions (cf. pp. 34, 284 & 296). Blood stands for the urge to destroy, as in the documentary she watches in which piranhas eat a small calf of some native species:

> In close-up the swarm gnashes and frays and crunches his still-living meat, bones and all, while the blood swirls over their gold eyes and the screen, the lens, and a soothing teacherly voice calls attention to the savagery of their bloodlust. But how, I wonder, could this have happened precisely in front of his camera unless the gallant little calf were trapped and offered up? And for what if not to slake our savagery, our bloodlust? (p. 177)

Blood is life slipping away, to be gone forever, as when Dagmar had a backstreet abortion to get rid of the bastard child Janni has fathered: 'I bled for two weeks, bedridden, but I covered my tracks... I had thrown overboard the only hope that I might have a child... I had blood on my hands' (p. 197).

By the same token, however, blood means life too. Blood, as one of the characters, the painter Olwen, asserts, is a symbol of life in many mythologies: 'The [Aborigines'] red ochre, the Holy Grail, the Cauldron of Regeneration, even your Odin's mead, if I remember rightly,' she tells Dagmar. 'The blood was life everlasting. They mixed it with honey, menstrual blood, and drank it' (p. 287). Dagmar is aware of the religious and creative, or redemptive, significance of blood, as is shown by her atttitude when she bangs her head in a cave in the Nullarbor: 'I sat and held my stung scalp. Red in the torchlight, my left hand, bright with blood and water, and I pressed it on the wall. Make an offering of blood, they say, and the dead tongues come alive' (p. 249). The life-giving power of blood is illustrated in particular by menstrual bleeding. For Dagmar, who is forty-one at the time of her second visit to Australia, an apparent early menopause signifies the approach of death, and reinforces her depression: her life is sterile, pointless. But one day her period returns unexpectedly and she feels joyful, rejuvenated. This is narrated in a matter-of-fact way which may disturb queasy readers (whether male or female) but which enhances the life-affirming aspect of the experience: 'A red sheen shone on the lino where I had stood to make tea. I bent and peered: it was wet blood. I dipped a finger in my fanny and brought it out glossy with bright blood. It was rich and not so salty as I remembered nor so fishy, and sweeter, the red honey as it oozed from my combs' (p. 234).[14] The potential to create is necessarily sweet and satisfying. Hence Dagmar's intense disappointment when, a little later, her period stops again: 'All this month, all November, no blood came: not a drop of blood. No heaviness and bloat, no clench of the belly, no bloodflow. Nothing flowed from me or into me any more. I never knew until it vanished again how glad of it I was, how proud. It was all of a piece with the loss of Martin [the lover

who has rejected her], both to be mourned for without distinction. So soon
after I had got it back, to have dried up again, and be barren, that was
hard to bear' (p. 290). The metaphor of the vessel ('Nothing flowed from
me or into me any more'), like that of the cauldron (cf. p. 297), which both
express female creativeness, suggests an answer to the question raised by
feminist critics Gilbert and Gubar: 'If the pen is a metaphorical penis, from
what organ can females generate texts?'[15] Soon afterwards Dagmar realises
that her period stopped because, against all odds, she is pregnant. 'I am
flesh and blood,' she exults, 'heavy flesh, thick blood. Everything I see is
solid' (p. 296). Her creativity is vindicated and depression lifts. She is
whole again, ready to go home.

Blood imagery is complemented by water imagery. The two kinds share
a common liquidity, and as well both are associated with femininity: menstrual blood is of course uniquely feminine, and water is also a feminine
element, as a quotation from Rowena Farre's *Seal Morning* underlines: 'In
Scotland, as in most other countries, the female sex is symbolized by water
and the male by fire' (p. 208). The affinity of woman with water is also
asserted by Martin: '"Years ago," he said, "some bloke, I'm pretty sure it
was a bloke, wrote a book about woman having been semi-aquatic back
in pre-history. Woman as opposed to man"' (p. 141). Aboriginal customs
seem to confirm this affinity: 'The sea was the women's domain, the men
were banned' (p. 58). Water and blood are often associated rather than
opposed, as in Dagmar's pet phrase 'the blood bath' or the quotation from
a Norse saga, Snorri's *Edda*: 'How shall sea be referred to? By calling it
Ymir's blood...' (p. 228). The painter Olwen also refers to 'the sea as the
mother of life. Salt water as the mother of our blood' (p. 287). Like blood,
water also symbolizes creativity and fecundity. This is suggested by a
quotation from Genesis: 'And God created great whales, and every living
creature that moveth, which the waters brought forth abundantly' (p. 78).
The association of femininity and fecundity is of course not accidental –
it is very much part of the feminine character of the novel.

But, like blood, water can also be synonymous with destruction, with
death. Finn drowns with his fellow-sailors: 'A hole opened in the sea and
swallowed them,' Dagmar remembers only too clearly. 'Well might they
bury the drowned in the between-tide sand, those that are washed up, as
was the way of things in old Jutland, and not in the churchyard for fear
that the sea would rise up after her own and take the living as well'
(p. 17). One might be tempted to see the drownings referred to in the
novel – there is Finn, and two young surfers (cf. p. 212) – as a sign that
the sea's association with femininity makes it hostile to the male sex, were
it not that Martin's sister, then a seven-year-old girl, also drowned (cf.
p. 239). For all its femininity, the novel does not posit such stark oppositions between the sexes.

It is above all in the form of ice that water is a destructive force. The
novel abounds in references to the Antarctic – the animals that live there

and the men who died there. Dagmar has a curious memory of being, as it were, debarred from her almost-natural element, water: 'It seemed to me that more than anyone I was bound to this water, belonged there, and yet I alone could not go in, however hard I tried. I walked in it up to my thighs, but could no more move one step forward than if it were solid ice' (p. 7). The hostility or deadliness of ice is also suggested by references to the Norwegian film *The Ice Palace*, in which a little girl gets lost inside a frozen waterfall. Ice figures prominently in Dagmar's nightmares: 'The walls are ice. Nowhere dark to turn my face. Everywhere is radiant white' (p. 67). It also becomes a metaphor of grief: 'Is there a figure of speech, to be *frozen with grief*? He in his grief was like a river clotted with slurries of ice...' (p. 218).

The colour white, which is of course associated with ice, also comes to represent sterility and death. Evoking the progress of desertification in Australia, Dagmar remarks: 'From horizon to horizon vast lands are already bone dry dust under a white shimmer like ice, the death mask of the salt... Now there is a curse on our land and it is a white curse' (p. 23).[16] Traditional Aboriginal beliefs point in the same direction: 'They thought a white skin meant death. They weren't far wrong', Martin remarks (p. 97). Dagmar herself, who has come to Australia to mourn and who is obsessed by death, stands out because of her pallor: 'How can anyone who spends so much time on the beach be so white? I was once asked' (p. 39). The fact that she spends most of her time in the water rather than actually on the beach only partly explains the oddity. However, the association between white and death is not unambiguous. As usual in *The Seal Woman*, symbolic meanings are apt to shift from one pole to the other, or at least to be complemented with opposite associations. Thus Dagmar's husband Finn is associated with red, which is the colour of blood, and therefore of life – he is described as 'shy, burly, sunburnt as red as the hull of his ship' (10). But we are told that the name Finn 'meant the "fair" or the "white" in old gaelic' (p. 53). Finn thus comes to signify both life and death – the life that was and which is no more. This paradox is apparent in a vision which Dagmar has of her dead husband: 'It is Finn trapped not in ice but in fire, his hair on fire, a lamp burning the wall yellow. His face is still as stone, as red stone. He is the Red Man who does not know he is dead' (p. 275). To the life giving elements (fire, burning, red) stand opposed those elements which signify death (ice, still, stone) resulting in a ghost-like creature, a man who does not know he is dead.

What, in conclusion, can *The Seal Woman* tell us about feminine writing? It shows that this is a kind of writing which, as male critics suspected, is not placed under the primacy of the intellect. The critics concluded that this made it inferior but I would argue that it makes it simply different. There is of course no lack of intelligence or subtlety in this writing, quite the reverse, but its intelligence is as it were made flesh. It has a sensuous, organic quality about it which male writing seldom attains, and which appears for instance in the loving attention paid to visual details.[17] Much of it has to do with the use of imagery. It is not just that some images are unmistakably feminine, as when Dagmar speaks of 'my shadow about my feet like a skirt I had undone' (p. 157). More importantly, recurrent, almost obsessive imagery – especially blood and water imagery – gives the writing a distinctive texture which is at once exquisitely concrete and remarkably imaginative. It works on a variety of levels, literal and metaphorical, realistic and mythopoetic, and is full of a sense that each level is intimately connected with the others. This all-inclusiveness, this refusal to regard anything as beyond the pale, this openness, is feminine to the extent that the masculine often means discrimination and exclusion, rigid compartments with little or no communication between them. Beverley Farmer's writing flows like a strong, winding stream whose waters are the very substance of life. It seems to invite comparison with Hélène Cixous' own writing, especially as far as biblical and mythological imagery are concerned. Cixous' mythical and biblical allusions, critic Toril Moi asserted, 'are often accompanied by – or interspersed with – "oceanic" water imagery, evoking the endless pleasures of the polymorphous perverse child.' She went on to say that 'For Cixous, as for countless mythologies, water is the feminine element *par excellence:* the closure of the mythical world contains and reflects the comforting security of the mother's womb. It is within this space that Cixous' speaking subject is free to move from one subject position to another, or to merge oceanically with the world. Her vision of female writing is in this sense firmly located within the closure of the Lacanian Imaginary: a space in which all difference has been abolished.'[18] As far as Beverley Farmer is concerned, however, we have seen that the plasticity of her vision did not extend to the abolition of differences. As the tale of the seal woman indicates, this attempted abolition is a sterile transgression.[19] Her heroine does feel the temptation of closure – she says at one point 'All I wanted was a head pricked and blown clear like a goose egg, polished walls enclosing nothing' (p. 220) – but this is a pathological symptom which shows how close to mental breakdown Dagmar is then. What saves her is that she has in fact the strength to reach out and engage the world around her instead of remaining enclosed within her own grief. Closure is all right as long as it is provisional: the egg – to go back to the image Farmer used – must eventually break open to let life emerge. Perhaps the most feminine trait in Beverley Farmer's writing is its constant opening onto ever different planes, with pulsations which are the very rhythm of life.

It was brought to my attention that the two adjectives 'holistic' and 'mythopoetic', which I use to describe Beverley Farmer's writing, are often applied to the writings of Nigerian playwright Wole Soyinka.[20] And there is little doubt that they could be applied to the writings of other men too. This is not surprising – Hélène Cixous has been saying all along that 'écriture féminine' was not the exclusive preserve of women. Besides,

Farmer's mode of writing is simply one paradigm of feminine writing among others. All the same, the fact that Soyinka's writing can also be described as holistic and mythopoetic is not without interest: it suggests a common deviance from a norm which is perhaps less masculine *per se* than Occidental. The dominance of reason and logic, of linearity, which is an attempt to impose order on seemingly chaotic reality in order to understand it and therefore master it, the privileging of a single type of connection between events – chronological, cause and effect – at the expense of the many others which are no less real – those features of 'masculine writing' are perhaps associated with Western imperialism rather than with masculine 'nature' as such. In this perspective, there is no contradiction when both women and post-colonial male writers practise a type of 'écriture' which rejects those constrictive conventions in order to open new doors and release new energies. Feminine writing, then, could very well be another name for creativity.

NOTES

1. Henry Lawson, *Autobiographical and Other Writings 1887-1922*, ed. by Colin Roderick (Sydney: A&R, 1972), p. 118.
2. Cf. the implication of guilt in Lawson's sentence 'I wrote to Miles Franklin, and she *confessed* that she was a girl' (ibid., p. 119).
3. S. Felman, 'Women and madness; the critical Phallacy', *Diacritics* 5, Winter 1975, p. 10.
4. Cf. V.A. Conley, *Hélène Cixous: Writing the Feminine* (Lincoln: University of Nebraska Press, 1984), p. 129.
5. Beverley Farmer, *The Seal Woman* (St Lucia: UQP, 1992). All further references are to this edition and are included in the text.
6. Christiane Rochefort, 'Are Women Writers Still Monsters?' in *New French Feminisms* (Amherst: University of Massachusetts Press, 1979), p. 186.
7. Cf; p. 19: 'Even the bloodflow which always came at around the full moon for thirty years, stopped. Now I no longer bled. Most likely the menopause, the doctor said: I had no sign of cancer. It was a small matter; only right and proper, in a way: all of a piece with the death of Finn, of my youth, an early winter.'
8. S. Juhasz, 'Towards a Theory of Form in Feminine Autobiography', in Estelle C. Jelinek, ed., *Women's Autobiography: Essays in Criticism* (Bloomington: Indiana University Press, 1980).
9. R. Hogan, 'Engendered Autobiographies: The Diary as a Feminine Form' in Shirley Neuman, ed., *Autobiography and Questions of Gender* (Portland, Oregon: Frank Cass, 1991).
10. Ibid., p. 103.
11. Cf. Murray Bail, 'A,B,C,D,...' in *The Drover's Wife and other stories* (St Lucia: UQP, 1980 (first published 1975)), p. 178.
12. Quoted in Janet Wolff, *Feminine Sentences* (Cambridge: Polity Press, 1990), p. 133.
13. Cf. pp. 15 & 96.
14. Dagmar's attitude should perhaps be seen in the context of the sense of shame menstruation still evokes in a number of women, and which was stigmatized as

follows by Germaine Greer: 'If you think you are emancipated, you might consider the idea of tasting your mentrual blood – if it makes you sick, you've got a long way to go, baby' (G. Greer, *The Female Eunuch* (London: Paladin, 1971), p. 51). Interestingly enough, the comparison between menstrual blood and honey also occurs in a masculine novel in which a girl who has only just started menstruating finds herself covered in bees: 'Ah, so that is it! They have smelled the sticky blood-flow. They think it is honey. It is' (David Malouf, *Remembering Babylon* (London: Chatto & Windus, 1993), p. 142). In Malouf's novel – which by what might seem a remarkable coincidence also refers to silkies and seal women (cf. p. 154) – however, blood does not play the essential, and particularly feminine, part it does in Beverley Farmer's.

15. Sandra M. Gilbert & Susan Gubar, *The Madwoman in the Attic: The Woman Writer and the Nineteenth Century Literary Imagination* (New Haven: Yale University Press, 1979), p. 7.

16. Another association of ice with death is the fear of a new Ice Age which will obliterate most living creatures – cf. p. 182.

17. Cf. for instance this description of fish: 'Three were pale with only a glimmer of blue, all their fins beige, but the other was daubed with a tropical blue so intense that around the red eye it throbbed and made the fawn lacework along the skull seem an after-image. This same blue, diamond crossed with green, spread along each flank to the blue fan tail. But the side fins were grass green. Its ridge of back was mottled, a dark rock; and its flattened dorsal fin – I spread it out – was a deeper blue. Even the flesh in its vault of ribs was blue, spotted with blood, of a milk-and-water transparency' (pp. 52-53).

18. Toril Moi, *Sexual/Textual Politics* (London: Routledge, 1985), pp. 116 & 117.

19. Dagmar is robustly heterosexual, and in this respect too her story suggests that difference has to be accepted.

20. I would like to thank my colleague Prof. Christiane Fioupou for making this helpful remark.

# Rebuilding Lifeworlds: Marylynn Scott Interviews Beverley Farmer

*You have written a substantial amount since the publication of* Alone *in 1980, including* A Body of Water, *a work which figures as a watershed in your oeuvre. In the opening pages, you refer to the book as 'my new departure.' In what way was it a departure for you?*

At the time I wrote that, I didn't have any more than a sense of it being a departure. I had a vague hope of it, if anything. I started touching base with everything that matters to me emotionally and intellectually, including the past because you don't just wipe it out; you have to find what its place should be in a new life. The book was a way of establishing the foundations for the future. Looking back now, I can see that without having written it I couldn't have written my novel, *The Seal Woman*.

A Body of Water *reads like a taking-stock of things both personally and in terms of the creative process. Was writing it a means of consolidating different parts of yourself?*

I think so. I'd come to a new home, this house, and that was an important step. I'd started writing it in my first summer in this house after coming here in the spring of 1986. I began it in late summer on my birthday. I'd lived in Lorne before that for thirteen years where my marriage had been. My husband (who became my ex-husband) and I ran a restaurant there. My mother had bought a house down there to be near us which I took over when she died. I was living more or less in the wreckage of a marriage, and my reason for living in Lorne no longer applied. It was an important step for me to come and have a new house and a new life somewhere else.

*You imply in* A Body of Water *that you had reached a block in your writing.*

I hadn't written anything for a long time. Worse than that, I'd written 15,000 words of something which had then died. It had just turned brittle and dead on me. I could see when I reread it that it was worthless. I had worked for months on it without seeing that, which is a very unnerving experience, not so much because it shouldn't disintegrate, but because I didn't know for all that time that it wasn't any good.

*What brought you to that point?*

I wasn't working close enough to the bone; I was being too careful not to expose my secret life. All that could have been a psychological explanations.

*In* A Body of Water, *you foreground your practice of shaping stories out of fragments of the everyday by recording experiences in the journal as you were living them. Were you actually trying to capture the transformation of life into art?*

I was while editing it, but not while I was writing it. There weren't a lot of revisions in the journal. It was meant to be a writing journal, so there were things cut out which didn't have anything to do with writing. I'm not so meticulous and systematic at keeping notebooks t.hat only diary material goes into the diary. It's not like *The Golden Notebook* where everything is separate and different. I didn't write anything for the diary, so there are things that were momentous in my personal life which didn't come into any of the stories or poems and, therefore, they were cut out. It was long enough already with things that did have a bearing, so I cut out the materials that just obscured the process. I think it was Elizabeth Bowen who said, 'If something doesn't contribute to it, then it takes away from it.'

*What do you mean in* A Body of Water *when you refer to 'beginning my new phase of writing'?*

I didn't want to write that book in the old way, with the old sort of clarity and meticulousness that Blanche D'Alpuget, among others, has said characterizes my earlier work. I felt that no longer corresponded to how my impressions of life and of other people were coming to me. I realized that while you can deal with human experience like that, there are other ways of getting closer to it, and fiction is uniquely privileged to do this. I had been neglecting those ways, writing things that were like plays or film in being external, and I wanted to write something more internalized.

*Does this development carry over from* A Body of Water *to your new novel?*

Yes, *The Seal Woman* springs directly from it, although it's fictional. I'm not in it. How it springs out of A *Body of Water is* hard to say without recapitulating the book, but it has much greater looseness and freedom than I've ever been able to allow myself before, not with regard to style or structure, but rather to the development of character. I can allow a character to materialize in the reader's mind without feeling I have to direct it like a puppet from here to there, as if it were a film I was directing and the character was only real when on the screen. Now I've got an idea of how to have characters live on when they're out of sight, so there's more depth to them than there was. They're not all surface, as I think of my past work as being.

*Does this mean, for instance, that the creation of Shirley in* Alone *differs from that of Dagmar in* The Seal Woman?

I think of *Alone* as a dramatic monologue in that it is written largely in the present tense, and, as a reader, you're only presented with what you're told; you're not given the liberty to weave the character of Shirley. She's presented like a character on a stage, whereas I didn't do that with Dagmar, who, like Shirley, also narrates the story. Dagmar takes a lot more for granted from the reader than Shirley does in matters having to do with beliefs and experiences in common, as well as with things she can just touch on knowing that the reader knows what isn't being said. I couldn't do that with Shirley because I didn't know enough about readers' responses. I don't know that it's a matter of technique so much as letting go, as not being so uptight about making sure I get across what I want to. I'm freer now; if something doesn't reach everyone, I don't worry so much anymore.

*You have said that Shirley is a character based largely on yourself. Can you talk about the autobiographical underpinnings of* Alone? *Would you call it a lesbian novel?*

*Alone* is very much a contemplative novel, if it is a novel. It was meant to be a projection of adolescence. When I was that age, I didn't want to live anymore. I *did* want to kill myself because I thought there was nothing to live for. I started writing the story in 1969, ten years after the experience, but it was still very clear to me how it had been because, when you want to die, it really does concentrate you.

The lesbian experience on which *Alone is* based happened in College, that is in residence, while I was at the University of Melbourne, not in that boarding house where the story is set, although I did live there later when I was twenty. Shirley is eighteen in the story, but I was twenty. It was the cheapest place in Melbourne; I think it was two pounds a week. I did live on bread and milk and go to the market and get fish that were being thrown out; there was a pile of shit by the gully trap. All those physical details were true except for the chooks; they came from somewhere else. There wasn't a henhouse, but everything else was there. The boarding house has been tarted up now, but a whole lot of 'derros' still live there.

As you will have guessed, May O'Toole is meant to be a sort of mother substitute because Shirley's own mother and father have failed her. She sees May as a possible mother and the funny old bloke, the one who lends the bike, as a sort of father figure. She's conscious of their parental care for her in their rough and ready way, but that's all she can bear too. She can't let them closer than that, but that's what she needs from them.

*How much did you change your own lifeworld in writing the story?*

There were things I transposed and heightened. I began it as a love affair between a man and a woman because what sort of love affair it involved seemed unimportant at the time. The story is about a suicide, so the focus was on the failure of the relationship and the young woman's wish to kill herself. I thought it would be a lot easier for people to accept the story if the love affair were with a man. My parents were still living and they didn't know about my relationship. As it happened, I didn't publish it until after they died.

The story that *Alone* grew out of was published earlier, in 1968, and, in that story, it was a man who dumped her. I could carry something like that off in a short story, but, in fact, I felt it was inauthentic. I had rot experienced first love as love with a man and I couldn't fake it to that degree. I hadn't even seen the male genitalia at that point. I wasn't interested in writing the story if I had to fake it that much; I lost any interest in doing it at all.

*Is Dagmar a version of yourself as well?*

No, she grew out of my imagining what a Danish woman, whom I met 25 years ago while she was visiting Australia, might be like now. It never occurred to me then that she might ever have a novel centred around her, although I was interested in her experience. Various sets of circumstances make me want to centre something on a fictional character based on her. Because it is so difficult to write as a Dane when I'm not and r don't know any Danes, I tried to make her Australian to save myself a lot of trouble and anxiety, but it didn't work. For some reason or other, this woman insisted on being a Dane, and there was no way around it.

Sometimes authors who haven't been important to you for a long time suddenly resurrect in a new light because of some problem you're tackling. That's what happened here. I went back to Karen Blixen because of a Dane being the voice in this novel. The particular cast of Dagmar's voice, which is a very definite voice different from my own, has something of Karen Blixen in it.

*Do you get tired of readers confusing you with your narrators?*

That's an interesting question. It's not something I get tired of, but sometimes it can be irritating. For example, the assumption that Shirley is me in *Alone* can be very irritating.

I'm not surprised by people making this connection, but I feel invaded by it. On the other hand, it's a risk any writer takes because the illusion you're trying to create is that this is a real woman speaking to you from her real self. When some people read, they need to feel that they're being addressed by a sort of puppet with a real writer behind it; that's just the way they read.

*This connection must be easy to make when a writer's life experiences parallel the ones described in the art.*

Well, I think most writers' lives do parallel their art. It's just that we know less about some writers' lives than others. But the more biographies I read – and biography is one of my favourite genres – the more the lives seem close-knitted with everything they've written.

*You've said before that you think the writer should move back into the shadows so that the work can stand alone.*

Yes, sometimes I think that, but when I read *A Portrait of the Artist as a Young Man*, I'm very conscious of James Joyce. I read every page of Richard Ellmann's biography of Joyce (and there are so many pages) with fascination and I think that most of the interest in Joyce is from knowing that this is a real man telling you what he knows about life, both about other people and about himself.

*It follows that a reader of your work might be interested in you as a person as well.*

Maybe, but it's all very well to feel like this about someone else and not about yourself!

*Are you conscious of an ideal reader when you write?*

I'm not conscious of a personality. I'm conscious of an eye, like a camera eye. I'm in a double role when I'm writing.

I'm creating something for a reader, but I'm also reading. When I add something to a piece, I try to see it from the double perspective of what it gives the reader to add to what she already has. It's almost instinctive; at a certain point, I realize I haven't given enough information that something is missing. It's the reader part of me, not the writer, that tells me this, so I have to go back and supply that missing clue.

The piece is only written so that a reader can go through it from beginning to end and resurrect in her mind at least an approximation of what I had in mine when I wrote it. The closer those correspond the better; the more skilful the writing has been.

*How would you characterize your ideal reader?*

That would be someone exactly like me probably because I'm my own first reader looking over my shoulder. I more or less assume that people are going to see things in the same way as I do! But jokes aside, an ideal reader would be someone who is intuitive and perceptive.

*Do writers have a 'third eye' that sets them apart from the rest of us?*

I think *good* readers have the same eye as writers. The difference with writers is that they actually sit down and get it done. There are millions of potential writers walking around out there who don't write, but they could if they sat down and put in the hours every day. It's important for readers to feel an affinity with a writerly mind, which they certainly do if they're ideal readers.

*When you appropriate material alien to your own experience, as is the case with Dagmar or with your male narrators, do you seek what is other in order to distance yourself from the narrative?*

It starts that way, but, as Flaubert said, the more you write about someone, the more you make them like yourself. So Madame Bovary started off being utterly different from Flaubert, but in the end they were one and the same: *'Madame Bovary, c'est moi!'* Peter, the narrator in 'Fire and Flood,' for example, is very like me in some respects; the psychological paralysis and sterility that I mention at the beginning of *A Body of Water* is the state of mind Peter is in too, although he's catatonic as well. If I hadn't felt at least part of what he is feeling, I wouldn't have been able to put the words in his mouth.

*How do you connect with a narrator like the rapist in 'A Woman with Black Hair'?*

That's a projection, of course. He's an extreme version of men I've known, a variation on the type whose attitude towards women is a combination of the romantic with the bitter and sadistic, and who boasts about his sexual conquests. The story grew out of an experience I had in the house where the story is set: I awoke and imagined there was a man sitting in a chair in the room. I stared in terror at the chair for at least an hour before it became light enough for me to realize that it was empty.

*Have you been accused of appropriating the territory of male writers?*

No, actually my fascination with rape has been the one thing that has attracted most comment. For example, in a competition that was anonymous, somebody mentioned that I'd submitted an entry. 'Oh,' said one of the judges, 'that's funny, I don't remember a story about rape,' as if to say that if I had written a story it had to be about rape.

*How do feminist readers react to your work?*

I've been accused of writing from a pre- or post-feminist perspective or from a reactionary perspective because my women are victims. However, my men are victims too, at times, and in a story like 'Maria's Girl,' the man and the woman are fully victims, if victim is relevant at all to a situation like that. In a story like 'Milk,' you have to ignore... Wait! I don't even know why I'm answering this accusation. It seems to me to pick on a side issue to talk about victims in my work.

*By writing about feminist concerns such as rape, gender and relationships (whether heterosexual, lesbian or even incestuous anti-relationships) as well as from a male perspective at times, you invite, if unintentionally, the appraisal of feminists.*

Ideally, people would read those stories without knowing who had written them. It seem, a pity that one's idea of the writer contaminates the content of the story when it isn't meant to. There are some stories when it *is* meant to as with 'Black Genoa' in *A Body of* Water, but that's not always the case. If something has been written as if it were a film script, for example, where the writer's character or personality isn't part of the content, to introduce it skews the balance of the story.

*Have you been attacked by feminist critics in Australia?*

Yes, I have been attacked by critics saying that my women aren't strong, that they're not role models. I reply by saying that they were never intended to be.

*Your male characters often express frustration and become aggressive and violent. They're isolated in their relationships with others and from the world around them. These are characteristics one might associate with an essentialist view of male behaviour. Is this your view?*

I don't have a fixed view of what's male or female. I don't know that anyone is fixed; people fluctuate throughout their lives and vary from one to another. Those adjectives and characteristics apply equally to a lot of my female characters too, so you could say the same about them. For example, there's the woman figure living in a Greek culture who feels that she's inadequate compared to some of the women around her and unable to live up to what's expected of her. She falls short all the time because she feels she's either not in tune, not as good a wife or a mother, or not as beautiful as others. That's Barbara's experience in 'White Friday" and 'Our Lady of the Beehives' or Bell's in 'Place of Birth.' Bell is only really reconciled with her mother-in-law when they meet again after the divorce. When she goes back to the village in 'Pomegranates,' she is accepted on her own terms by her mother-in-law rather than as a daughter-in-law. She can see clearly everything she found repellant about the Greek culture as well as everything she found magical and still loves about it.

*Why don't you acknowledge in your characterizations that there are differences between men and women resulting from their gender conditioning?*

I think it's because I'm only really conscious of the men at the moment when they're in conflict with the women in their lives. In a sense, the men are almost dummies.

*Do you mean that they serve as foils for the women?*

I mean they might seem to the reader to be dummies. It's not my intention to depict them that way, but, instead of getting the male character's thoughts, his internal monologue, what you usually get are the woman's thoughts about him. Occasionally I've tried to redress this by using a male narrator, but in the stories where there's conflict between men and women, I've always taken the woman's point of view as far as I can recall. Because the man's perspective remains external whereas the woman's thoughts are revealed, she is privileged in those scenes. But I don't deliberately tell you what the woman is thinking, while withholding the man's thoughts, in order to create a particular perspective. It's not as conscious as that.

*Your characters often find themselves in conflict with the culturally conditioned codes of behaviour associated with gender, say, or romantic love. Peter in 'Fire and Flood' admits that 'At the best of times I was – am – far from being a man of action.' The story turns on his not living up to others' expectations of him as a male. After watching the movie* Casablanca, *the women in 'Home Time' compare the inadequacies in their relationships with what they've just seen on the screen. Do you reject codes such as the one connected with romantic love?*

I don't reject romance with a capital 'R' or with a small 'r,' but the stuff Mills & Boon publishes is corrupt romance, and, of course, I reject that. It's corrupt and commercial, venal and disgusting: it's a lie. But romance doesn't have to be a degraded version. There are other types as well, such as true romance. I don't mean the *Casablanca* sort of romance. 'Home Time' is more about the non-meeting of minds and the impossibility of communication that mirrored the true event in my life which it was based upon. It's not necessarily meant to be about all human relationships; it's just showing the pattern as it applied to those particular lives.

*But what we see here seems to be true of the relationships that many of your other characters experience. Is it not possible to extrapolate some general truths regarding relationships from these particular lives?*

There is a large element of cruelty in those relationships. Even though the young man cries along with his girlfriend while watching *Casablanca*, later he quite brutally accuses her of scavenging her story materials and forbids her to ever write about him: 'Perhaps if you wore a badge, a brand on your forehead that meant: *Beware of the scavenger?* Then people would know they were fair game.' But the man, for example, in 'Vase with Red Fishes' from *A Body of Water is* not cruel. He preserves his singularity; he doesn't respond to his girlfriend, but he doesn't hurt her either and he retreats gracefully. She's not surprised by the outcome of the relationship. He hasn't tried to destroy her as some of the other men have tried to destroy their women.

*Do you distinguish between male and female modes of discourse?*

I'm sure there are differences between these modes of discourse, but I haven't had time to pursue them very fully. The threshold is a very female way of writing, which is what fascinates me about Peter Handke. In fact, all the writers who interest me most have a very strong element of the androgyne about them. They are writers who embrace the whole of humanity, the two halves, such as Handke, Virginia Woolf and D. H. Lawrence. It's there as luminality in A. S. Byatt's *Poscession*. I thought maybe she had made it up and was satirizing the Romantic movement, but it seems that there is such a field. It is the study of thresholds and the mystical interfaces, the fluidity of borders, between two worlds or modes of existence. That struck me with tremendous force because *A Body of Water is* all about the writer being a thresholdologist, that is 'a seeker after thresholds,' as Andreas Loser says in *Across*. That's what fascinates me most at the moment.

*In 'Vase with Red Fishes', the woman who's arguing with the man about Narcissus says, 'I think it's an illusion...that human beings can transcend gender.' Can you comment on this statement from your own perspective?*

I've never thought about it from my perspective. That seemed to me something she would say to get some response from him, and, in his case, to keep her at arm's length. It's part of the struggle that these two people are engaged in, which is a sexual battle as well; there's no meeting in their sexual intercourse. It wasn't something coming from deep within myself necessarily, but, even though there are no absolute truths, I'm certain there's a lot of truth in it. I was brought up – or rather I brought myself up – on *The Second Sex* and how one becomes a woman by being made a woman; the same goes for men too, of course. I suppose my characters, both male and female, tend to come up against a situation which is a stone wall for them and they know it. It isn't gender, but something else in their own characters, in their lack of particular strengths, or in their circumstances. It happens to all of them; they reach their limitation or something that they can't transcend. The realization of this, the moment of truth, is the crux of the story. I think that is the basic situation for a lot of those stories.

*Do the characters experience moments of epiphany then?*

I think of epiphany as something optimistic and joyful: in that respect, not necessarily so.

*Think of epiphany in the Joycean sense of it being an awakening, a realization.*

Yes, I suppose it's an illumination, in the sense that they see more clearly.

*You've said that you don't try to achieve psychological realism in your male characters.*

Nor in the female characters. That isn't really the point of what I'm trying to do so much as to create impressions of a situation as it takes place. I emphasize certain things and not others; for example, a painter of portraits might leave out a subject's nose without the viewer noticing because enough other details are included in the picture to achieve the desired impression.

*Which things do you emphasize?*

It varies. Sometimes, for instance, I actually do a bit of drawing just as a memory aid and as a way of concentrating my attention on something that I want to describe, such as a jelly fish. I sketch its shape, and the features that I pick out first to sketch are the ones I emphasize when I write about it; that helps me to decide how to describe it.

*Do you imagine the reader filling in the noses, filling in the missing details?*

Yes, or at least subliminally knowing where the nose should go. I think my men and women are recognizable people one might meet.

*Yes, certainly, they are which suggests that the artist, painter or writer, must master the details before she can confidently omit some of them. Are you interested in psychology even though you don't foreground it in your writing?*

Yes, I am and I am defensive about it as well. The science of psychology, including psychoanalysis and all the other different schools of thought attached to it, seems enormously dogmatic to me. The human psyche is much less definable than many theorists believe. So I'm wary and suspicious of psychology, but very interested in it nonetheless.

Its influence on literature hasn't always been a good one. If you look back before psychology became such a dominant force, at the nineteenth century novel, for instance, you find that the characters were as vivid and intense then, if not more so, than they are now. What did Chaucer know about 'psychology,' but the precision of his psychology in a work like 'Troilus and Criseyde' is just wonderful. Psychology needs to be kept at arm's length by an artist, otherwise it can take over and wreck something very easily. You can analyze something to death or explain characters away instead of letting them just exist there on the page or having them tell you what they are thinking or feeling. There are quicker, sharper, more economical ways of revealing character such as through body language. The more economical the means, the better the art; it all comes down to an economy of means.

*Even though you talk about being distanced from the experiences you write about, we keep coming back to the close connection between life and art.*

Oh, I think *A Body of Water is* all about the way they interrelate. Quite obviously, there is nothing that can feed art except life and other reading, so the work fruits out of these. It helps me not to be too conscious of the process or aspects of it, such as why I choose this rather than that, but many characters and events are rooted in experience.

Even with a story like 'Snake,' where it's hard not to think of D. H. Lawrence's poem being in the background, a personal experience underlies it. The genesis of that story was a real snake in Greece which I had tried to kill, then repented of trying to kill and let escape as Manya does. Manya, herself, is a snake too in the sense that pride is her downfall and she's too proud even to recognize or to care that this is the case.

Jimmy/Dimitri, the narrator in 'A Girl on the Sand,' is based partly on my husband and partly on a couple of other Greeks whom we knew in the group we moved around with when we lived in the Greek ghetto in Melbourne. There, again, these parts were fused with myself in some respects. My husband told me about the incident of the girl in the sand.

There was a girl discovered like that on the beach at Kennett River while we had our restaurant there. So the raw materials were there, but separate from each other; in fact, the connection was not made by him, but by me in the story. Dimitri's emotional dominance by his mother is something I've noticed a lot in Greek sons, and I think there's something quite feminine about him.

'Fire and Flood' was actually set in the flat that I lived in at that time – those trees, all that was there. The fire on Ash Wednesday in 1983 burnt Lorne and destroyed over 300 houses at Aireys Inlet at Anglesea. It was terrifying in Aireys because no direct access to the beach, so people were fleeing along the road through the tea-trees to get to the lighthouse, to the one the locals call 'The White Queen,' and to the water before they were taken over by the fire. There were a lot of cases like Peter, who's suffering almost paralytic neurosis. People came up to me after reading the story and said, 'You're one of the few who seem to realize how long the effects of Ash Wednesday have lasted.'

*Kate Grenville talks about there being two levels of place: the one you inhabit physically and the one you can inhabit imaginatively. Do you move back and forth between these two senses of place or are you more concerned with the place that you're settled in and how you can translate that into a reflection of your own preoccupations?*

Being concerned with the place I am living in is fairly recent in my case. *Alone* was set in Melbourne and written in Greece, so the high colour and overwhelming nostalgia of place in that story came from my not being in the spot, but from the radiance of memory. *Milk* was largely about Greece written in Australia after my divorce, after the Greek experience was closed off in time and place and quite remote for me. *Home Time* was partly Greek and partly American, with episodes that again were closed off to me. *A Body of Water* was really the first book in which I was open to the place I was writing in and writing from that place and about it at the same time as I was living in it. It was more or less an experiment in being present in the here and now and letting the writing come out of that.

Before *A Body of Water*, I relied heavily on photographs and on images that I remembered, whereas all the rest of the experience was washed away. Only the vivid memories and moments came through, so I was writing short stories based around those moments. When I was writing *The Seal Woman*, which is set here in Australia, I wanted to avoid photographs and depend instead on emotion and fleeting impression. I didn't want things to be cut and dried up, either by memory or by a camera or by any device like that, but to be more or less straight from life onto the page, as in what D. H. Lawrence called 'the living plasm.'

*Can you compare your use of place in the novel with that in your writer's notebook?*

I used the landscape near my home at Point Lonsdale as a setting for *The Seal Woman*, although I gave myself the liberty to change a few things. I used it in a quite different way than in *A Body of Water* because Dagmar is a visitor, a transient, not planting herself by definition. Her sensations are fleeting; her experiences are a sort of time out of time for her, not part of her real life, whatever that is. She has been here before, so there's that double image or blur, the mirror image in which the past is juxtaposed with the present. Tension exists between who she was then and who she is going to be. This is her hiatus between that old life, which is closed off to her now by her husband's death, and the new life.

*Dagmar is reminiscent of many of your characters in having reached a hiatus in her life. Is* The Seal Woman *a continuation of what is one of your major preoccupations as a writer?*

Yes, as I said, what I'm most interested in are transitional moments or moments of crisis in somebody's life, changing points or revelations. I don't know that a subject interests me unless it has an element of that in it. Dagmar is making the journey to the land of the dead because she has just been widowed. She has come south to Queenscliffe, in fact, although it's called Swanhaven. She spent her honeymoon there because her husband, who was a seaman, went to Antartica. Now that he's dead, she has gone back to where they were first together.

Her experiences take place in a sort of underworld because Australia *is* the underworld in that sense, a return to the past, a way of purging herself of all unfinished business because he has died as a middle-aged man in an accident at sea. The story is set in 1988 when the *Nella Dan* crashed onto rocks at McQuarrie Island and was scuttled and burnt.

She knows all the tales of visits to the land of the dead such as the myth of Orpheus and Eurydice and the story of the Eskimo shaman and his voyage under the ice to speak to the Goddess of the sea beasts; and about Norse mythology as well as about the Bog people in Denmark whose bodies were supposedly resurrected from the bogs looking as if they died yesterday, although they were 2000 years old. I make her conscious of all this without weaving it in too closely or making it too obvious, I hope. She deals with her bereavement basically through these tales, although there are people she meets there, a woman, a man. She relives the past in her memory and creates a new life in Swanhaven for the time she is there until she overcomes the grieving process.

*Often your characters write poems or stories within the story in which they appear, beginning with* Alone *and extending through to* A Body of Water, *where you reveal the day-to-day ideas and influences that nourish your creativity. How does this metafictional feature, this foregrounding of the writing process, figure in* The Seal Woman?

Dagmar isn't a writer in this story. Hang-on, she's a writer in the sense that she might be a writer of children's stories. She grew up on Hans Christian Anderson. She isn't writing her own story yet. Maybe she will, but not as a writer, as a diarist, if anything. At this stage, anyway, she's not conscious of any wish to be a writer, but she's making notes on books she reads. What you're given now are just seeds of what might possibly turn into material for a writer.

*Did your use of narrative techniques change at all in* The Seal Woman?

Conversations are more important in this book than they have been before. The characters more or less created themselves through their conversations. At one point, for example, I discovered that Tess, a woman who had been in the book for several weeks, is partly Greek, that her father is Greek. She lives in Swanhaven in the story and she wasn't going to be partly Greek, but then there developed a logical necessity that she should be, and I'm glad of that.

*If your characters are conversing more, does it mean that they are becoming better able to communicate with each other?*

I think so. Cruelty, as I said, is a large element in many of the relationships between my male and female characters in the earlier works. In this book, there is at last a real warmth, a feeling of security and mutual generosity, between a man and a woman where there hasn't been before.

*Was this made possible by* A Body of Water *and the experiences underlying it?*

Yes, and it is also a matter of age and experience as well. As May O'Toole says in *Alone* 'What wouldun I give ter be eighteen all over again! The best a life all still ter come. But knowun what I know now.'

# DIANE FAHEY

Diane Fahey grew up in Melbourne, lived for some years in Britain, moved to Adelaide in 1986. She is at present Writer in Residence at Ormond College at the University of Melbourne. Her collections of poetry are: *Voices from the Honeycomb* (Jacaranda, 1986), *Metamorphoses* and *Turning the Hourglass* (Dangaroo, 1988 and 1990), and *Mayflies in Amber* (A & R/Harper-Collins, 1992). She has won various awards including the Mattara Poetry Prize, and has received three Writer's Fellowships from the Literature Board of the Australia Council, and two from the South Australian government. In 1993 she was a fellow at Hawthornden International Writers' Retreat.

DIANE FAHEY

# Why I Write

I write, in the first instance, to sort myself out, to further my discovery of who I am. This means often positioning myself at edges, thresholds. It also means attending to patterns of continuity within experience: self as story.

Secondly, I write as an act of engagement with the human world in which I find myself. In *Metamorphoses*, my focus was on exposing the distortions of image and perception which underlie sexism - the arena of emotional and physical violence which has most impinged on my life and awareness.

I believe it is ultimately impossible to separate sexism from the other imbalances and oppressions which are also the subject of an ever-growing movement of human consciousness: race, sexual identity, economic status, political freedom... A feature of all such oppression is the imposition of negative projections on to the feared other. Within that fear, and fuelling it, is, so I understand, the fear of being and becoming – of accepting mortality, working with boundaries and difference, and the unknown or unborn parts of oneself.

The degree of integrity I have in owning and clarifying my own projections determines the firmness of the ground on which I stand in this wider personal-political process. Thus the process I began by describing is the basis for all else. Ask the hard questions of oneself first – so I remind myself, often.

How can one sustain oneself in the work of facing so many difficult realities? If I were to try to imagine 'kingdom of heaven' as an immanent reality, I would think of what is known and experienced in moments of communion – with the self, the loved other, the natural world; with poetry itself along with all the arts; and perhaps, one could say, with time itself...

The dance of connection between the elements of creation is both glimpsed and amplified at such moments. In my work as a poet, I've attempted to record some of those moments, occasions, glimpses, as they've been available to me. So this is the third reason why I write – the search for a vision of paradise. That search involves forms of meditation, and play...the play out of which new configurations arise, thus subtly transforming the whole.

In particular, the world of nature has become an increasingly powerful magnet for me. This is the fourth reason why I write: to witness to, celebrate, and – since this is the century of the death of nature –

commemorate, the natural world. Even the most successful order of creatures on earth, the insects, of which I have written in *Mayflies in Amber*, is not invulnerable to the contagion of extinction – it too composes a picture with specks and  larger areas slowly fading and becoming invisible.

Presently my creative attention is on sea creatures, for a future book, *In Praise of Sea Horses*. I can only say I am connected to such work by a compelling psychic energy. Believing as I do that all created beings and things are expressions of an energy that has an imaginal counterpart in the human psyche, I see the latter as not only a microcosm of the world, but as holding a potential for healing and restoring some of the human damage done to the world through work on images. The world is both real and symbolic, and if human consciousness can re-enter creation with fresh vision – re-see it – then the symbolic order has some power to transmute the realm of fact.

I do not and cannot separate body and psyche; the personal and the political; the ethical and the religious; the symbolic and the real. Working as a poet helps me to explore the relationship between all these dimensions of human life, resonances of the world.

Poetry has been for me a great learning experience, a journey into body and psyche and the interconnected life of this planet. As one defines, through moments of gift and clarity, one's place on a map, the map itself grows larger, becomes more unknowable...more challenging.

In the very physical maze of language, one searches for connection with one's origins, and a grounding experience of home, in this place of so much tragic dislocation. For the poet, words are the trail of seeds one leaves behind as one enters one's own and the world's darkness – seeds that are also beads of amber, arisen from the depths and therefore able to hold and refract light.

# Diane Fahey

## THE POOL

He has given her this room of mirrors, in which she is bored;
she may speak to him only when he speaks to her.

He spends most of his time by the pool. What is it he sees,
staring down at its tiled floor – some classical coin

with shimering bronze face? He is as beautiful as a dolphin
but never swims. She often does. She likes the splashing cry

of the water as her long arms slice through vivid green.
Why does he never look at her? He is always looking down –

even into his glass as they sit in the evening by the pool.
'Have you had a nice day?' (he stirs and pokes his ice);

'...a nice day?' she echoes, desolate.
                              Oh, but she loves him!
Once she swam the pool's whole length to surprise him,

curving up to where he gazed soulfully, teardrops pocking
the chlorine. At first he did not see her face, then,

when she was almost out of breath – but still smiling –
those clear eyes glazed with shock and he looked away.

She did not hear the slapping of her feet on concrete
as she walked inside then dripped up the long, soft stairs

to her room. 'With only mirrors to keep me company
I shall waste away, waste away...' she thought,

but could not say – as usual, the words stuck in her throat.
And she curled into herself, hiding from all those faces.

Stretched out flat by the pool, he too loved and wasted,
had not even sensed her walking away, her stifled sigh.

## DANAE

Pennies from heaven –
a celestial dew!

Artists show your garments
conveniently askew...

With immaculate conceptions
there's so little to do –

you just lie there pretending
you're looking at the view.

Not being raped but being rained on,
it's difficult to sue.

Should you sleep with an umbrella
in case he tries to renew

your acqaintance with a brief
shower or two?


## CICADAS

Holes pock the ground;
husks cling to stucco,
spine the lilac trunk;

in a whirr of cellophane
small zeppelins veer up
towards the tops of trees.

Sometimes their song
is a razor strop rasp
back and forth over the mind,

at others, patience
in tension with longing.
In mid-spring, their

climbing voices
promise heat, sex, death –

an iridescent throb

like a benign nerve;
an image beyond reach
provoking memory.

Befriending me, one covers
cheek, nose, ear
with ticklish tracks,

invades my hair.
three amber gems stud
the velvet between its eyes,

so mildly red. Close up,
I see the light they hold
and two black pinpoints,

then lift the cicada
back to earth and slip indoors –
enveloped still by that

high-pitched chant once
nurtured at the roots.


## MOTHS

Soft, almost unseeing sentinels,
they wait without purpose on walls,
in cupboards, ready to be disembodied,
like candle flames, by a finger-pinch.

As cupped hands open to outer air,
they fidget, cling – do they know
how to be saved? Some prefer
to grow brittle on curtains, silk fringes.

Yet, multiplying as if by thought,
they have their future strategies:
pupae wreathed inside lids, buff wrigglers
chiselling rice to webbed clumps.

Most are radiantly nondescript,

somewhere between a sheen
and a colour; others, bark paintings:
a geometric opulence.

Tonight, one climbs the shadow
of the lamp, flirts with
the twisted gold nerve that draws
dull mysteries to fulfilment.


## WEEDY SEA-DRAGON

With something of a race-horse's
vigilance of eye, taut slenderness,

it moves just faster than
the speed of stagnation –

by drift, out of sheer necessity –
sips plankton through a straw,

sports outcrops of kelp
that ripple like tourney flags

as it flows nowhere – at one
with its milieu (how we know

that which we hide amongst);
subliminal flares of violet,

yellow, red, help it stay unseen...
Light fills a weightless body

found, sea-stripped, near sandy feet.
Ants circle eye-sockets, work at

a final cleansing: this innocent bone
patched with fish-skin,

its shape rhythmed in an upbeat –
a gracefully complicated wave

poised between quietism
and a quirky valour.

# CLOCK MUSEUM

Long-case clocks line ancient walls:
transformed trees; survivors proving time's
errant constancy. One strikes seven at four o'clock
with the certainty of tone that poets crave:
words dissolving in a sea of resonance.

Seismograph of oak; split Rorschach of walnut;
the honeyed shine of elm, crudely planed...
In leaf shapes, black traceries
track shadows over silver, point to
three straight cyphers that translate all hours.

Old clockmakers wished time to be
present to us, stand in drawing room or hall
breathing the air of our dramas – lofty yet
patient companions, benevolent totems,
whose faces can hold our gaze, take our measure.

The sombre ticking off of lives... As these
shapers of it knew, time works on weight –
gravitas of flesh and wood and metal,
all culled from earth to be embraced by light,
fall towards the darkness of new origins.

# — KATHLEEN MARY FALLON —

Kathleen Mary Fallon was born in Brisbane in 1951. She moved to Sydney in her early twenties and since then has lived in Hobart, London, Paris (briefly) and Melbourne where she now resides. She self-published two books, *Explosion/Implosion* and *Sexuality of Illusion*, in the early eighties; wrote the text for *Spill*, a play performed in Sydney's Bay Street Theatre in 1987; published the novel *Working Hot* in 1989; and wrote and performed a one-woman show on the Gulf War called *Credibility Gulf*.

Fallon is currently working on another novel *The Staff of Life* as well as writing an opera/voice piece for Chamber Made Opera. She is also writing a two-act play on interracial relations and violence in the suburban Australian home, *Three Boongs in the Kitchen*, and a piece for adult puppet/object theatre for Terrapin Puppet Theatre called *Royal Commission into Black Deaths in Custody – A Contact Event* based on her relationship with her Torres Strait Island foster son and what that has taught her about racism in Australia, motherhood and foster motherhood during the years spent with him.

KATHLEEN MARY FALLON

# Why I Write

1. Trying to salvage from those great oceans – Silence, Forgetfulness, Numbness.

2. Because everything operates to make you stay silent, remain forgetful, maintain numbness to that which is not culturally coded. To exist I have to insist on the other tracks that my life runs down. I don't want to betray these other realities.

3. Because I want to leave a trace of where I've been.

4. Because sometimes I can't speak.

5. And I must speak to exist. Sometimes I feel culture, representation, as a huge brick wall that suffocates and imprisons and limits me and I want to smash into it, smash into it with my words, ideas, existence.

6. It is the only hold I have on the reality of my life.

7. Because more and more by writing I am making something out of the pain, loss, detritus, unacceptable, reprehensible or ugly times of my life. Making a silk purse out of the sow's ear.

8. I write because I really don't know what I'm doing or thinking or what's what but when you write something down, make sentences, make words, make structure, make some kind of sense to yourself and you go back a week later, a month later, you find another pattern, another meaning altogether than the one you thought you were making - It gives you some access to your unconscious, or patterns and movements and drives in your life that would otherwise remain obscure to you.

9. I think I was deeply offended and hurt as a child, as an adolescent, then as a woman that I wasn't noticed. Sometimes I felt (feel) invisible. (It's probably gender based.) I write to make people take notice of me.

10. To make mummy love me, to make daddy love me? No! To knock off both of the bastards and vamoose out of the ghastly Oedipal triangle once and for all.

KATHLEEN MARY FALLON

# Extract from *Working Hot*

ETVOITEO
OR
DEAD WOMEN TELLING
THEIR OWN LIES

*Rough notes for a movie script – some scene breakdown*

It won't be a long movie – fifteen to twenty minutes.
Shot in a combination of black-and-white and colour.

It begins with two women – Evie and Toto – meeting in a Paris cafe at
night. They are both in their early thirties.
They were lovers for six years but have not seen each other for ages after
a fairly disastrous break-up which left them both bitter and damaged –
Evie just walked out one night to go and live with another woman.
Despite everything, there is still some deep attraction between them. They
meet and talk. Evie says, with deep satisfaction, 'You were wrong about
a lot of things'. Toto says, 'What happened with us? I still don't
understand. Did you ever love me? How could you have stayed with me
so long if you didn't and how could you have left me like that if you did?
I still don't understand'.
    'Oh god, really Toto, you're not still harping on about all that are you?
Honestly, it was all so long ago.' Toto, cursed with her trap-door heart.
'My heart is like a trap-door spider-once you get in, you never get out.'

SCENE FIVE
*[Black and white]*
Toto imagines herself.
There is an image of Toto fishing around in the fluff of her pockets,
fumbling for the bit of a question, forever and for ever going on, asking
of occasional lovers,asking it desperately of occasional lovers. She believes
'if only someone would give me a straight answer' she could take stock
of herself.
    As Toto and Envie talk there are shots of an exhibition of Toto's work
and as the shots of various paintings and sculptural pieces are shown, the

catalogue is read out in the voice of Archangel Mademoiselle Montgolfier [*See Appendix*]

SCENE EIGHT
[*Colour*]

Backyards of derelict terrace Squats in London – rubble and rubbish everywhere except for one back garden which is wild with hundreds of different kinds of roses. Toto is climbing along the broken stone-fence, cutting dozens of roses with a long pair of silver scissors. She filling a green gladbag with roses.

SCENE NINE
[*Colour*]
There is a big Jamaican practising his flame throwing and she has to keep ducking as he belches his flames over the rose garden.
There is also another old black guy stoned out of his mind leaning up against the back of the Mecca gambling house crying out like a muezzin from a minaret, 'ohgodjesusrasta-why-is-life-so-hard'. Over and over he wails to the sound of the rapid clicking of dominoes being played in the gambling house and glass being broken by kids throwing stones through windows.

SCENE TEN
[*Colour – there is a pervasive rose-gold colour in these shots*]
Toto emptying hundreds of roses out of the gladbag onto Evie's bed.

SCENE ELEVEN
[*Colour*]
Evie standing in front of Toto in a pub screaming angrily, 'Yes, but roses have thorns. You know they do'.

[*Black and white*]
All this is interspersed with shots and bits of conversation in the café while they drink.

SCENE FIFTEEN
[*Black and white*]
They leave the café and walk through the dark Paris streets.
There is a full moon and deep cloud creating a sharply chiaroscuro effect. They walk beside the Seine.

Superimposed and reversed footage creating a mirror/doppel-gänger effect. They are walking toward and through each other. This is all a bit skewiff, hologrammed as they walk arm in arm, talking intimately. They

walk beside the Seine along cobbled walkways. The water is bright and dark. Sometimes they seem to be walking down stone steps. They eventually go into one of the stone grottoes let into the stone wall beside the river and they make love.
The lovemaking denies nothing.
They realise what has been lost.
Toto is left sitting on the stone ground.
Evie lies behind her on the bench, naked.
Toto only has her jeans on.
Evie has a leg draped over Toto's shoulders.
Toto turns to look at her.
This turn is repeated a number of times and each time it is a falling together, a falling into each other's eyes.
There is an inevitable course of action.
It has been thwarted for years.
THE erotic act.
THE course of action.
Toto lifts the long, silver knife above her head.
It is a totally satisfying act.
It is all understood between them.
She falls forward onto the other and the blade comes up red.
Something has been accomplished.
The final act between the assassin and the assassinated and the vice versa.
They have wiped their hands of each other forever.
Now they are both free
It is the orgasm in which both are sated.
It is the end.

SCENE TWENTY-FOUR
[ *Colour – but still only yellow night lights on water and, of course, the full white moon*]
Toto thinks 'falling into eachother's vacuum, falling into each others eyes'. As they cross the Pont Neuf, Toto says to Evie 'See that seat down there. I dreamt I stabbed you there. We'd just fucked and I killed you, stabbed you with a lovely long blade. I dreamt it before I came to Paris or even knew I was coming. I dreamt about that place right there. Imagine how freaked out I was when I saw I was living just across the road from the place.'
'Oh, honestly', said Evie, 'You talk nonsense. Are you trying to scare me or something?'

SCENE TWENTY-FIVE
[*Black and white*]
The full moon is the sad moon face of poor old Oscar Wilde reciting pompously a verse from his *Ballad of Reading Gaol* –

'Yet each man kills the thing he loves,
By each let this be heard,
Some do it with a bitter look,
Some with a flattering word,
The coward does it with a kiss,
The brave man with a sword.'

SCENE TWENTY-SIX
Toto laughs, 'Sorry, I'm a bit pissed. I didn't mean to scare you. Honestly'.
Evie: 'You've always thought that was enough. Just saying you were pissed was excuse enough for everything'.

SCENE TWENTY-SEVEN
Evie writing on a postcard to a friend, 'What did I ever see in her?'

SCENE TWENTY-EIGHT
Toto talking to a friend on the phone. 'I suddenly realised that the whole purpose of the meeting was to prove to ourselves that the other was a deadshit to justify vindicate ourselves and yet she was fishing around for something and you know what I think it was I think she expected me to tell her I still loved her I think she came all this way for what she has always considered was her due her entitlement I think she wanted me to tell her I still loved her and would always love her ... and everytime I'd try to talk about our past just mention things we'd done she'd say I don't remember did we or I can't remember would we ...'

SCENE TWENTY-NINE
Toto's bedroom

'She has been granted the gift
of forgetfulness' soothed
Archangel Mademoiselle Montgolfier
'It's a sickness', Toto woke up yelling.

SCENE THIRTY-FOUR
Images of Toto asleep in Paris and Evie asleep in London are superimposed. Evie's head and torso at one end, facing right. Toto's head and torso the other end, facing left. Joined at the genitals. The effect created is reminiscent of the royals in a card pack. The move ends with the following poem read by Archangel Mademoiselle Montgolfier.

**a bad patch**
**target area**

do
we
know when death enters us
like a dart
sinks
into cork board
. and
is
all this flailing of arms
the manic
activity
around the knowledge
of the black flight feathers

I can touch no place
I have been loved
gently
but I can put my finger
on the sore spot
of entry

APPENDIX

**Catalogue**
**No 1 *Rosegold Afterglow***
This painting almost creates a scent, a perfume – the perfume of flesh after
lovesex. The transparent layers of pastel watcrcolour blur the surface
between skin, sheet, duvet, sky.

**No 2 *The World Drained of Colour***
A huge serpent stretches into the foreground from a green point of light
at the other end of the universe from which tremendous arrows of light
plunge toward you. A pale corpse of a woman floats upside down in
space. The serpent bites her in half and as its jaws close, a pale blue
cherub flies up into cyan-blue space. It metamorphoses into a magnificent
Aztec-type stylised bird with a red and blue body, black and white wings,
gold and black head. It lowers its wings at a forty-five degree angle and
speeds off.

'I painted this and the next morning when I woke up the whole world
seemed to be drained of colour and my first thought was that all the

colour had drained between my legs. The whole world had gone grey over night. When I was fully awake I realised we had had our first snow of the season. Later that morning I heard that a neighbour's son had been killed when his bike smashed through a plate glass window. His mother had to identify the body and apparently his hair was completely white. I had already sent Evie a chunk of my white pubic hair'

### No 3 *Medusa Head*
Medusa head showing the shadows of the wings of death— only the shadows, mind you - and the arrow head of determination containing the bud of potential and the triangle of protection.

### No 4 *Peace*
Completely different to the rest of the exhibition, this abstract expressionist painting occurred to me one day in Edinburgh at a Kandinsky exhibition and I could not rest until it was painted and when it was I felt peace for the first time in my life. [Red, yellow and black geometric shapes on a gold-ochre background]

### No 5 *Lesbian Punk Love*
The Kundalini serpent goes the wrong way.

### No 6 *Sheila na gigs*
I painted this after I'd seen photographs of Celtic rock carvings of female figures called Sheila na gigs.

### No 7 *Big Grey Mother*
With her barbed wire fanny.

### No 8 *Beyond the birth trauma*
There is a Prussian Blue figure ascending the bone white steps in my head.
It was the vision I had the night I went – holy hell and hang onto your hats for this one – beyond the birth trauma. It all started happening and I thought 'OK OK fine I've read about this' but it all kept happening and I wasn't out of it on anything either and, shit a brick, there I was – become the bloody egg and this bloody sperm stuck in me
'Rape' I screamed but apparently it's best to yell 'Fire'

### No 9 *The Beautiful and Shining Flower Woman of Spring*
Outside in the derelict yards, bits of green were starting to show after a particularly bitter winter. It had been one of those terrible London winters and I saw her one day growing in moss and lichen and small flower colours on our backyard brick wall.

*Horse Chestnut*
I am as vast as grass
I am as gay as a nasturtium
I am as complex as an iris
I am as hammered home as a rook's nesting tree.

**No 10** *Pansies*
A sculptural piece of a doll on its back in the garden with a hole cut in its
stomach from which sprouts a cluster of pansies.

'I lay at night upon the ground
my body stretched with tension
I lay and my tension became the tension of
I closed my eyes – I covered all the hill
I put my fingers in my ears – my head burst
into a flush of flowers
and trees grew out of my belly
and bowels
my breasts split
and under the moon water holes glistened
rooted to the earth I became earth
my eyes glistened upwards with thanks.'

MELISSA BOYDE and AMANDA LAWSON

# Diving for the Red Pearl: Surfacing and Setting the Centre in *Working Hot.*

Between the inclusion of works with a lesbian presence in the 1982 anthology *Frictions* and the publication of two specifically lesbian anthologies a decade later – *The Exploding Frangipani* in 1990 and *Falling For Grace* in 1993 – several writers have emerged in Australia who have produced lesbian texts. While these writers should not be restricted by categorisation as 'lesbian writers', the collection *Surly Girls* by Susan Hampton (which won the Steele Rudd award for short fiction in 1990) and the novels *Remember the Tarantella* by Finola Moorhead and *Working Hot* by Mary Fallon (awarded the 1989 Victorian Premier's Literary Award for New Writing) are notable because they centre on the figure of the lesbian while experimenting with conventions of realist narrative.[1]

In her collection of short stories and prose poems, *Surly Girls*, Hampton extends, and questions the nature of, boundaries around gender and sexuality by crossing genre boundaries. *Back Cover Blurb* plays with both genre and techniques of compression to establish a text which interrogates the construction of homosexual subjectivity as well as the packaging of the book trade: Back Cover Blurb.

> What is heterosexuality? Why does a certain percentage of the population feel attracted to the opposite sex? Is it curable? Experts in the field file their reports. (p. 61)

In writing *Remember the Tarantella* Moorhead takes up a challenge from Christina Stead: 'its very difficult to make an interesting novel with no men in it at all' (p. ix). She develops an 'Alphabet of Characters' from Arachne to Zorro to explore the ways in which female myth is created and transmitted between various groups of women. Strategies such as dispensing with the patronymic and a mathematically formulaic plot structure reveal and experiment with how both masculinist narrative and female and lesbian subjectivities are constructed.

In discussion of 'lesbian' writing it is important to recognize that the use of the term lesbian is not intended to locate the lesbian outside societal negotiations of power and gender but rather attempts to take into account historical and cultural specificities. When no qualifier is attached to a term such as text or novel it is most likely to be assumed that it is heterocentric. Eve Kosofsky Sedgwick in *Epistemology of the Closet* points out that the development at the turn of the nineteenth century of a homosexual/heterosexual binarized identity has 'left no space in the culture exempt from the potent incoherences of homo/heterosexual definition'.[2] The relationship between gender and literary experimentation and innovation has been mapped to some extent, from Virginia Woolf's *A Room of One's Own* to more recent critical work such as *Breaking the Sequence,* edited by Ellen Friedman and Miriam Fuchs. Constructing readings of experimental texts, and specifically naming them as lesbian, attempts to instate an anti-homophobic analysis which raises the possibility of undoing the determinacy of the homo/hetero polarization. It also raises the possibility that inscriptions of what has hitherto been determined non-normative sexuality expose and disrupt textual conventions and destabilise the hegemonic investment in those conventions. In a conference paper entitled 'Experimental Desire: Bodies and Pleasures in Queer Theory' Elizabeth Grosz proposes a link between innovation and queer sexuality.

> In each of us there are elements and impulses that strive for conformity and elements which seek instability and change: this is as possible for heterosexuals as it is for queers of whatever type, although it may well be less enacted, it may well be that there is less impetus for expansion, development and change for those who reap the rewards and benefits of functioning according to social norms ... certain types of queer theory end up outlining and analyzing the paradoxical strangeness of heterosexuality and its norms.[3]

Queer as a discourse of radicalism raises some interesting issues for the critiquing and contextualising of lesbian texts, which, in Sydney in 1993 and 1994 at least, seem to be inescapably near to, if not elided with, queer writing.[4] Despite or indeed because of its subversive or avant-gardist stance, queer provides a space for interrogating hitherto assumed centres.

It is interesting to note in this connection that the title of Fallon's novel *Working Hot* is contextualized in the under(Other)world of the sex worker:

> 'when I worked at the Pink Pussycat they'd let the guys touch you were always out of it and the guys could touch you or lick you or whatever you know it's called working hot that's how I like to work I like to work hot' that's Kinky Trinkets. (p. 7)

Fallon disrupts and disturbs notions of the normal when she exhibits a line-up of sexual deviants and deviations: sex workers, johns, pimps, and sadomasochistic practice. The interactions of Kinky Trinkets, her clients and Gizmo the Pimp; the voyeuristic presences of men who fantasise about sleeping with lesbians; and the textually fleeting appearances in the novel's opening pages of characters such as a 'Greek or Italian' man who picks up a hitchhiker outside Cairns who reports he was 'wearing a skirt I thought was his national costume until I noticed the frilly undies and the machete on the floor' or 'a fourteen-year-old girl who had had an abnormally large clitoris removed' in a Sydney hospital formulate a collage of deviance which locates the novel in the interrogatory discourse of queer.

Set within this milieu, yet distant from it, is Toto Caelo's emotional and erotic journeying through her intense relationships with her lovers, Freda Peach, Top Value, and Evie. At times streetwise, comic speech like 'I don't want to get into any ashram honey except the one between your legs' is used, simultaneously satirising a specific (Sydney) lesbian fad for Eastern religions and exposing Toto's sexualized obsession with Freda. The erotic exploration described in part two of the novel entitled 'Sextec', gives lesbian sexuality a central place in the text, signalled by the metaphor of diving for the red pearl:

> 'I am anxious for the red pearl' said the ABALONE DIVER
> fishing around in the aquarium of her mind
> with a pretty finger (p. 37)

The metaphor suggests entry into a fluid realm, the symbolic feminine associated in literary myth with monstrous females like Grendel's sea-cave dwelling mother in *Beowulf*. Instead of the female figuring as an eruptive, extraneous monster to be destroyed, the lesbian body in *Working Hot* is metaphorised into an underwater seascape:

> ...your hands I
> tell you are waves of water my cells I tell you are
> barnacles they open with tide-and-wave action...
> inside you (as far as I went that is) was that wet cave
> was that grotto and there was moisture running down
> the walls – rising damp (pp. 44/45)

At the centre of *Working Hot* is a process of both locating and bringing to the surface a reimagined lesbian sexuality, one in which the phallus is displaced by the pearl at the heart of the oyster.

This reimagining is intimately linked both to the form as well as the content of the novel. Strategies of appropriation and allusion combine with a fragmented structure in layers of self-reflexivity which accumulate to undo the authority of the singular narrative voice often found in the realist novel. Point of view shifts between many exotic characters, Toto Caelo, Freda Peach, One Iota and Kinky Trinkets. Lists of quotations from literary texts and popular culture appear throughout, interspersed with quotations attributed to characters in the novel, or to the author herself under one of her other names, Kathleen Denman. The final lines of the novel –

*and I walked for days until I reached that plateau of*
*thwarted desires and dead dreams called Maturity* (p. 289)

satirise the narrative culmination as a process of linear development so familiar from *Bildungsroman* and *Kunstlerroman*.

Narrative in *Working Hot* is interspersed with performative episodes. Genres such as song, radio play, film script and opera libretto are used, for example: 'To Resort to the Sandy-Beached Tourist Resort of the Body: An Opera for Three Voices and a Choir of Five Hundred'; 'Honeymoon in Crazy Springs: A Radio Play'; and the 'cashchorus' which repeatedly parodies suburban normalcy:

...where there's life there's hope with a TV and a heater
and a couple of catcatcats
we'll have to get out of these pyjamas first
and where can we borrow oh where can we borrow oh
where can we borrow the cashcashcash
the cashchorus (p. 236)

In *Unmarked: the Politics of Performance*, Peggy Phelan examines the relationship between visibility and representation, arguing that:

Representation reproduces the Other as the Same. Performance, insofar as it can be defined as representation without reproduction, can be seen as a model for another representational economy, one in which the reproduction of the Other as the Same is not assured.[5]

In its performative aspect, *Working Hot* gestures towards a representation which is not easily assimilable within realist concepts of mimesis. It makes the sexuality 'constituted as secrecy'[6] visible, but within endlessly varied performances. Sedgwick discusses how the secrecy around homosexuality brings about a continual negotiation of the closet, rather than a singular 'coming out'. *Working Hot* reflects this process, which is never fixed.

Fallon's novel discloses its debt to modernist experimental writing, particularly by writers who explore transgressive or lesbian sexuality, such as Gertrude Stein and Djuna Barnes. Stein's codification of lesbian eroticism where words such as butter and 'lifting belly' stand for a range of sexual activities is played on by Fallon in the following sequence:

TOTO: ya wannabit a the old mons venis hey
abituvataste uv the old monso veneseo she's a nice
drop hey wanme ta go fa a bit uv a tit a tit wiv ya
clit hey a bit atheoldbluetongue between the
leggings lass want a bituv a tonguin where it counts

do ya sheila
aw playin possum are we...
TOP VALUE: you turn me to butter
TOTO: well Gertie did maintain that the fact that butter
melts is one of the important facts
here I'll whip that cream for you

Any idea of secrecy around sex collapses in *Working Hot*.
Two of Fallon's narrators, Inside Information and E.C.R. Saidthandone
provide an ironic commentary on the sidelines, reminiscent of the Doctor
in *Nightwood* by Barnes while Archangel Mademoiselle Montgolfier in
*Working Hot* recalls Dame Evangeline Mousset in Barnes' *Ladies' Almanack*.
Fallon uses the experimental device noted by Friedman and Fuchs in
which 'the reader is invited into the frame of the narrative to participate
in its complexities'.[7] In the passage in *Working Hot* 'Close Enough to the
Heart of the Matter' – typeset to resemble the design of *Ladies' Almanack*
(which in turn resembles a sixteenth century book of days) – Montgolfier
is engaged in the excavatory process that the reader encounters in *Working
Hot*:

Of course, she knew that the transcription of this palimpsest was a massive and
quite mad undertaking (perhaps even dangerous) and yet Montgolfier worked
obsessively and eventually began to make headway in the translation and
comprehension of this mass of often contradictory and always paradoxical material
(p. 97)

The reading process is signified in terms of dissecting the human body to
extract 'a heart mass', an 'accumulation' likened to 'the development of
the pearl'. The doubling of the image of the pearl, as the 'red pearl' of the
clitoris and as the pearl of wisdom, sets lesbian sexuality at the discursive
centre of Fallon's experimental text. Like the gritty, irritant process of
developing a pearl, the reader engages simultaneously in uncovering the
text and lesbian sexuality. When Fallon invites the reader to:

lingalonga over lingua
you leave me reader working on the body of my new
lover Trixi oh sorry what was it again Lexi yes Lexi Con
holding her spine in the palm of my hand
ah and ohyes the body of language (p. 32)

the relation of language to knowledge, and sexuality to both, is inextricably asserted.

In tracing developments in lesbian experimental writing in Australia,
Fallon's novel *Working Hot* is a pivotal text. The breadth of experimentation, the complex, uncompromising eroticism of the language and the
novel's lesbian textuality and intertextuality place it in an international
tradition and context of lesbian experimental writing. *Working Hot*

traverses various sites, including contemporary Australia and the modernist centre of lesbian textual production, Paris. Like *Ladies Almanack*, Fallon's text centres on lesbian lives but in *Working Hot* the location is inner-city Sydney, the idiom Australian 'queer' and the imagery aquatic and fluid, anchoring the text offshore in the clear waters which surround the mainland. As a 'coral bowl with all kinds of juicy fruits in it' and a 'sandy-beached tourist resort', the lesbian body is undeniably posited as both a site of desire and a desirable site.

## Notes

1. Anna Gibbs and Alison Tilson (eds.), *Frictions: An Anthology of Fiction by Women* (Melbourne: Sybylla, 1982); Cathie Dunsford and Susan Hawthorne (eds.), *The Exploding Frangipani* (Auckland: New Women's Press, 1990); Roberta Snow and Jill Taylor (eds.), *Falling For Grace: An Anthology of Australian Lesbian Fiction* (Sydney: Blackwattle Press, 1993); Susan Hampton, *Surly Girls* (Sydney: William Collins Press, 1989); Finola Moorhead, *Remember the Tarantella* (Sydney: Primavera Press, 1987); Mary Fallon, *Working Hot* (Fitzroy, Vic: Sybylla Press, 1989). All subsequent references are to these editions.
2. Eve Kosofsky Sedgwick, *Epistemology of the Closet* (Hemel Hempstead, UK: Harvester & Wheatsheaf, 1990), p. 2.
3. Elizabeth Grosz, 'Experimental Desire: Bodies and Pleasures in Queer Theory', Forces of Desire Conference, Humanities Research Centre, Australian National University, August 1993.
4. *Falling For Grace* was launched at the inaugural QueerLit conference in Sydney, July 1993; the gay and lesbian coalitionist movement which led to the inclusion of Lesbian in the Sydney Lesbian and Gay Mardi Gras has had the effect of making the Mardi Gras Festival a major cultural event, which features lesbian writing groups such as the Bluetongues in its calendar; publishing opportunities offered by magazines such as *Burn* (now defunct) and *Cargo* also resulted from this move.
5. Peggy Phelan, *Unmarked: The Politics of Performance* (London, New York: Routledge, 1993), p. 3.
6. Sedgwick, p. 73.
7. Ellen Friedman and Miriam Fuchs, *Breaking the Sequence* (Princeton, New Jersey: Princeton University Press, 1989), p. 39.

# —JANETTE TURNER HOSPITAL—

Janette Turner Hospital was born in Melbourne in 1942, but moved to Brisbane at the age of 7. By education and emotional allegiance, she is a Queenslander, with a particular attachment to the tropical far north where she used to teach high school and where she returns every year.

She is a regular reviewer for the *New York Times*, the *Los Angeles Times*, the *Boston Globe*, and the *TLS*.

She has published five novels and two collections of short stories. Her first novel *The Ivory Swing*, 1982, won Canada's Seal Award. This was followed by *The Tiger in the Tiger Pit* (1983); *Borderline* (1985), runner up for the Adelaide Festival's Fiction Award; *Dislocations* (short stories; 1987; winner of Fellowship of Australian Writers' Fiction Award); *Charades* (1988), a finalist for both the Miles Franklin and the National Book Award in Australia, and also cited by the New York Times as one of the 'Most Notable Books of 1988'; *Isobars* (short stories; 1990), shortlisted for Canada's Trillium Award; *The Last Magician* (1992), was shortlisted for Australia's Miles Franklin Award and Canada's Trillium Award, was listed in the *New York Times'* 'Most Notable Books of 1992'.

JANETTE TURNER HOSPITAL

# Why I Write?

Why do I write? This is like being asked why do I breathe, eat, sleep; and the short answer is because it is impossible to do otherwise. Even before the first geographical dislocation in my life (the 1000 mile move, at the age of 7, from Melbourne to Brisbane which are two different countries), I found it necessary to tell myself stories – and indeed to write them down in little notebooks – to explore the meaning of the bewildering contradictions I kept bumping into. From my first day at school, I felt like a space voyager, travelling daily between alien planets whose languages and customs were incomprehensible to each other. (This turned out to be good training for the rest of my life.)

I grew up in a micro-culture radically different from the macro-culture I encountered at school. My home life existed within that particular pocket of lower working class culture which, instead of finding meaning in pub, racetrack, violence, and sport (the usual Australian sources of working-class cohesion), found consolation and validation for a marginalized existence in fundamentalist evangelical religious fervour. My home life was severely circumscribed (quaintly and richly, it seems to me now). I was, for example, 20 years old before I had seen a movie, watched television, been to a doctor, or tasted alcohol. But also – and this was what people on the other planet I visited could never comprehend – family life was warm, rollicking, rich in love and hilarity. Indeed, my first experience of intolerance and the terrible cruelties which attend it came not from fundamentalists (the designated 'bigots'), but from school: and not only from bullying kids both fearful and scornful of difference, but from teachers, those symbols of liberal enlightenment. This has given me a lifelong fascination with the prejudices and incipient fascisms of the 'radical' and the 'enlightened'.

Though I've put a great deal of distance (in all senses) between me and my fundamentalist background, I am nevertheless constantly amazed by the unwarranted, unearned, and deeply uninformed glibness and bigotry of intellectuals toward non-intellectual sub-cultures (or, more accurately: toward non-standard-intellectual sub-cultures, for the appropriating and privileging of one small facet of the intelligence by western academics and 'rationalists' is in itself an act of aggressive intolerance.) The demonizing of the Other goes both ways; it is by no means the exclusive preserve of the intellectually primitive; and the etiology of this phenomenon is part of my subject matter.

In my writing, I often prod at the ironies, discrepancies, contradictions, and hypocrisies that arise from the clash of belief systems. I harbour, I confess, a deep-seated cynicism about the blustering prophets of polemic, and also about the quiet well-bred tyranny of academic specialists. I observe such foci of authority very closely indeed, particularly when they are not hiding behind the masks of lectern or text. I am extremely interested, for example, in how they speak to taxi drivers and waitresses. 'Marginal' comments and events have always grabbed me. I listen hardest to what people don't say.

My urgent childhood need to decode a bewildering sign system in order to make sense of and to function at school has made me an instinctive semiotician. Dislocation (of belief systems, of geography, of culture, of trauma) and the ways in which characters mediate for themselves massive disruptions in their lives are my constant subject matter, but in exploring these issues, my attention is always focused at the edge of the stage, in the margins, on the 'bit players' and the 'extras'. I prefer to listen to the people no one listens to.

Silences and absences haunt me. I am absorbed by the ways in which silence, for the radically marginalized and disempowered, can be a form of protection, dignity, and survival.

My writing, I suppose, is a kind of map making (always provisional) of the potent unseen and unheard.

JANETTE TURNER HOSPITAL

# Our Own Little Kakadu

There must be, by Maggie's reckoning, upwards of fifty chooks running loose, but who would know? When she steps carefully between pineapple rows to test the fruit cones, she puts her foot on at least a dozen eggs. First comes the soft crunch, then the streaky corona-squirt of ochre and snot, then the ooze between her toes. The soles of her feet squelch against her sandals, she is practically skating on slick. Hah, she thinks. Walking on water, tiptoeing on eggshells, what's new?

'He took an axe to the chook house months ago,' her mother said on the drive from the airport. At the stop light, her mother had lifted both hands from the wheel, palms up, and raised them toward the roof of the car, beseeching someone, something, to bear witness.

'Jug's violent again?' Maggie was startled. 'I mean, *physically* violent?'

'Not toward me, no, no. Not at people. Not even at your brother. But there's something... he *feels* violent, yes. He's against anything being penned in now. Against pruning. You should just see the passionfruit. I could rip miles of it off the laundry shed if I thought I'd get away with it. It's taking up all the clothesline space, I have to hang half our underwear on trees.' She clasped her hands together, the interlaced fingers pressing the knuckles white. 'Well, he's never done anything by halves, has he?'

'Juggernaut by name,' Maggie said.

'You can say that again. I never know what it's going to be next. I'm terrified he'll decide *mowing's* forbidden. We've had two pythons on the verandah already, and God knows what's living out there in the bus with him.'

'Mum, the light's green.'

'What? Oh.' The car leaped forward, stalled, rallied. 'You don't know what it's been like, Maggie. Chooks roosting in the laundry, in the bananas, in the vegetables, in the—'

'Mum, mind the—! Would you like me to drive?'

'I had a smashed egg in my *hair* last week. They're laying on the rafters in all the sheds, you never know what's going to fall on you. Not to mention chicks hatching wherever you happen—'

'Mum, pull over. You're upset. Let me drive.'

'I'm not upset, I'm scared. He won't talk to me, he won't talk to your brother, he's started drinking again, he does say things to his mates at the pub when he's pissed, and there's *talk*, there's plenty of talk, but nobody

can make sense of it. Nobody knows what happened. That's why you had
to come back, I'm counting on you.'
'Oh yes,' Maggie said drily. 'We're famous for getting on famously, me
and Jug.'
'That's the point. You'll strike sparks. If he gets mad enough, he might
blurt out some clue.'
'Doesn't Ben strike enough sparks?'
'It's weird. They're totally silent with each other. Anyway I can't get
your brother near the place now, I have to go to him and Liz. And this is
a taboo subject with them. Look, I wouldn't have dragged you back from
Melbourne for nothing.'
'I think I was looking for an excuse to come back anyway.'
'Yeah? The girl who couldn't wait to get out, couldn't wait to shake the
dust—'
'Yeah, well.'
'Melbourne people are so up themselves, I did warn you.'
'Yeah.' Maggie laughed. 'Made a bet with myself you'd say "I told you
so" before we got home.'
'And wasn't I right? Didn't they give you the pip?'
'Yeah. Well, you know, there's all kinds. I've got some good friends. It's
just... I don't know... You can't even talk about Darwin down there. You
might as well announce you've come from Mars.'
'They give me the pip.'
'Whew, I'd forgotten how sticky—' Maggie eased her damp shirt away
from her skin and leaned out the window. She wouldn't forgive her body
if it had switched allegiance, adjusted to Melbourne chill, lost the knack
for wet heat.
    And then they passed under the familiar tangle of mango, frangipani,
bougainvillia, and she cried, 'Hey! You can't see the house *at all*.'
'I told you. Pruning's not allowed, no cutting back, nothing. What we've
got here is five acres of new-growth jungle with room to walk sideways
round the house. Our own little Kakadu.'

Between the half acre of pineapple rows and the house, Maggie can see
flashes of yellow, bits and pieces of the bus. It is almost entirely covered
by passionfruit vine, though at the four points where its axles rest in the
earth, pawpaw trees rise in thick spiky clumps. He must dump the seeds
there, Maggie thinks; it's some new geometric ritual, the compass points
of whatever this latest obsession is. He could live on pawpaw and
passionfruit without leaving his rusty cocoon, she thinks. He could just
reach out through the windows and pick. The light inside must be green
now, like under water. He'd love that, Jug would, odd fish in his tank
(shark in angelfish clothing? dolphin in sharkskin?), jugging it down, *jug
jug*, tanking up in his tank, probably having a whale of a time, driving
them all round the bend. As usual.

She sees now what was impossible about Melbourne. It was having to explain this, him, Darwin, all of it, any of it; trying to explain it without having to endure *how quaint, how awful, how bizarre, how exotic, how horrible, how--*. She couldn't bear to expose her perfectly ordinary strangeness, her loony family's ordinary Darwin madness, to people who knew so very little. *Everyone's a bit troppo up there, aren't they?* they would laugh, nudge, nudge. *The Top End's a bit over the top, wouldn't you say?* I could scratch you, she would think, and you wouldn't be one sweat layer thick. But she'd learned to do it herself, play the clown, betray a memory here, the self there, one drink, two, it was easy, pile the accent on thick, get the laughs. Besides, only two years earlier, let's admit it, she'd been frantic to flee, *frantic*, indecently keen to put as much distance as possible between herself and her own little haywired Top End bubble.

I can't *breathe* here, she'd said.

She breathes the damp air, sluggish with pineapple musk, frangipani, white gingerflower. I'll drown here, she thinks. I'll never get away. I'm just part of this blissed-out vegetable world, slumping into the Arafura Sea. We're all drugged. We're all troppo.

*Hallelujah!* as Jug would have said.

She steps on another egg.

The whole bloody garden must be protein-enriched, she thinks. It seems to be doing wonders for the pineapples. Almost every plant has a plumed cone at some stage of ripening, and when she looks down the throats of not-yet-fruited clumps, she sees the telltale blush of things underway. How sexually blatant plants are, she marvels. She twists four ripe fruits from their serrated nests and cradles them in her arms. Squashing eggs as she goes, scratching her legs on the pineapple swords, she makes for the bus.

'Jug?' she calls tentatively from the door.

It was a school bus once, long ago put out to pasture, deregistered, bought at auction, on whim, for a song. Maggie thinks the most telling census question in Darwin might be this: how many deregistered, de-wheeled vehicles are slowly listing into your five-acre lot? The Darwin average, she suspects, would be three. Beyond the pineapples, beyond the bananas, the mangos, the vast overgrown lawn, the avocados, somewhere down among the compost heaps, there are, she surmises, four earlier family cars now all but invisible, bleeding rust into jasmine that has run amok.

In Jug's bus, all the seats have been removed. There's a galley kitchen in the driver's niche, a bunk where the back seat used to be, a chemical lav in one corner, a hinged lift-up table along the side, a couple of armchairs spilling stuffing. Everywhere there are cobwebs with watchful spiders as large as poached eggs at their hubs. Chickens, eggs, ants: the floor seems busy. A harmless carpet snake, thick as a forearm, has coiled itself neatly into a chair.

'Jug?' There's no answer so she climbs in. She sees him lying on his back on the bunk at the rear of the bus, arms folded behind his head, staring at the ceiling. He is wearing khaki boxer shorts and a singlet, nothing else, and the bus is ripe with the smell of unwashed male. Light comes through the passionfruit leaves, amber green. 'Four pineapples,' she says brightly. 'Real beauties.' She puts them into the miniature stainless steel sink. 'Mum says you've given up on roads and bridges and gone into vegies and fruit. The market man, the green-fingered genius, she says.'

*Speak, you stubborn old bastard,* she wills him. She can feel the usual dual pull of rage and protectiveness. For a big blustering man, he looks unexpectedly frail, and she is alarmed by the sight of his skinny legs and bare feet. His face and shoulders and arms are like old leather, but the legs and feet – trousered and shod throughout his respectable years as a civil engineer – are as pale as the skin of young children. She feels embarrassed to see her father this way. It's like seeing some soft creature with its shell peeled off. Improper. She lifts the lid off his icebox and takes out two cans of beer, watching him. She peels the tab off one can. It makes a slight hiss, and brackish foam bubbles out and spills over her hand. She sees his eyes swivel in her direction and she walks down the bus. 'Mum tell you I was coming home?'

'Nope. But I reckoned you would, sooner or later.' He accepts a beer and swings himself upright. 'Told you I was bonkers, did she?'

Maggie sits cross-legged on the floor in front of him. 'Didn't need Mum to tell me that,' she says, cuffing him on the leg. Tactful, she makes no comment about the beer, which he had so dramatically renounced ten years ago. Maggie had been fifteen at the time, her brother Ben, eighteen. 'The Lord has delivered me,' Jug told them. 'I've been born again, pure as the driven snow.'

'Not much call for snow round here,' Ben said, asking for it. But there had been no oath, no swipe at Ben, no bash across the side of his son's head, so that they had all marvelled and had known something eerie had occurred. Only the rigging in his neck, corded tight, told them the old Jug was still down there somewhere, inside the new one.

'It's funny,' Jug says meditatively now, looking around the bus. 'Well, not bloody funny at all. Something plays bad jokes on us, eh? I lived in the back of a truck when I first ran away to Darwin, fourteen years old. Jeez, jeez, jeez, I hate the way stuff comes back. Like bloody spiders crawling into your head.'

He never speaks of his childhood unless he's drunk, and it's a bad sign when he does. They know almost nothing about it. He began brand new on his wedding day, no baggage, no past, except for the bits that sometimes leaked out of beer-soaked cracks, or showed up, mangled, in rage. He was a famously hot-tempered boss on the road gangs, a short-fused husband and father, a weekend roisterer and larrikin of note.

And then the Lord spoke to him from a Gospel Hall pulpit. It was a steamy Sunday night, and Jug, guzzling from a large Darwin stubby of tarblack bitter, was weaving by the chapel's open door on the esplanade when the Lord shouted at the top of His almighty lungs: 'Jug Wilkins, it is required of you this night to be a juggernaut for God.' Jug broke his teeth on the neck of the bottle in shock, and cut his lip, a potent sign. Blood streaming from his mouth, unnerved but belligerent, he staggered into the chapel and walked down its central aisle. 'Who the fuck do you think you are?' he demanded, teetering on his feet. 'I am the Lord your God, Jug Wilkins.' God fixed him with His pulpit eye, and Jug just stood there, confused – like a kangaroo in truck lights, people said later, swaying at the lip of some steeply pitched gulley. 'Decide!' God roared. And Jug did. He jumped. He crossed over. He became an enforcer for the Lord, a role that not infrequently brought him into collision with his rebel daughter and resisting son. Bible in hand – his surveyor's chart – he would chapter and verse them, laying down markers, calling the shots, mapping everyone's road to Eternity.

'Watch out,' he tells Maggie now, fretfully. 'I'm infectious. I got these old dreams, bad dreams, coming back.' He bats vaguely at the air and she sees mosquito swarms of nightmares buzzing him, giving him no quarter. 'Western Queensland somewhere,' he says, ducking. 'Must've been. Between Charleville and the Territory border, I reckon. I'd just nicked off, me old man didn't believe I'd ever do it. I hid in the back of a roadtrain, see.' He is not so much talking to *her*, Maggie thinks, as talking in a waking sleep. His voice seems very far away, inside a bubble in his head. 'It was cold as the bloody South Pole, that's the way it is out there, nights, June, July, cold as the bloody South Pole. You wouldn't believe the difference between night and day, she's an oven by day (you could fry an egg on the road), and deep freeze after dark. If you tripped over your foot in the dark, it'd snap right off, you'd get ice in your eye. Blimey, it's cold, it's cold.' He huddles into himself and begins to shake. 'I'm shivering under this tarp, which, let me tell you, stinks of bloody cowshit, *stinks*, and me old man steps out of nowhere with his whip in his hand. Steps out of the air, *abra*-bloody-*ca-dabra*, and into the back of the truck and rips off the tarp. He's got horns on his head.' Jug drops the beer and puts his arms in front of his face, warding off blows. He is trembling violently.

'Jug!' Maggie says, alarmed. 'Jug, you're drinking too much.'

'"*Gotcha*," he says. "*Gotcha, gotcha, gotcha*. You'll never get away from me, you little bugger, you little twerp."'

'Jug, it's okay, it's all right.' Maggie takes hold of his hands, which are clammy. He's sweating like a pig, but feels dangerously cold to the touch.

'He *laughs* when he does it,' Jug says. 'And I never did, I never did, he was right about that, I never got away from him.' He's shivering, curled into himself, barricaded behind his arms. 'He's back again,' he says. 'He's back. He's showing up after dark.'

Maggie can't bear it. 'Dad,' she says, hugging him. 'Oh Dad, you've got the DTs again.'

But it's the wrong thing to say. Wrong word. A sort of spasm passes through his body, and lucidity, like a brilliant tropical bird, swoops down on him. He leans toward her and takes her chin in his hand. 'I do not have the DTs,' he says distinctly. He repeats himself intensely, enunciating each word as only challenged drunks can, exaggerating syllables to such a degree that Maggie, helplessly, thinks of stepping on eggshells, thinks of his chook-mad garden, thinks of the crusted goo on her feet.

'*Take my yolk upon you,*' she splutters, on the edge of something, anxiety, compassion, hilarity, fearful hysteria. But this does not help.

'That's cheap, Maggie, cheap. Is that what they taught you in Melbourne? Cheap blasphemy? Blasphemy is cheap. Making fun of the Bible is cheap, making fun of your father is cheap.' His grip on her jaw is tighter, tighter. 'Your father does not have the DTs. Can you get that into your fucking head? I do not have the DTs. I know what's fucking real and what's not.' Any second now, Maggie thinks, my jaw will crack. 'This world,' he says furiously, 'is full of fucking people who don't know what's real and what's not. DTs, they say. Visions, they say. Bonkers, they say.' For emphasis, he bears down on her face with rhythmic force as he makes each point. Because she cannot speak, quite literally *cannot* speak – she can feel her bones giving way – Maggie focuses her outrage in her eyes, and he glares right back. 'Don't you look at me like that, young lady, with the devil between your eyes, and between your legs too, I reckon. Honour thy father, young lady, and fucking remember this: I fucking well know what I've seen and what I haven't, don't you fucking forget it.'

'If I ever kill anyone,' Maggie tells Ben and Liz. She's still crying. 'If I ever kill anyone,' she sobs.

'Yeah,' Ben says. 'I know. Hey, it's okay, kid. It's okay. We won't. I've thought it a thousand times, but we won't. We love the old bastard, and we won't.'

'But I would've,' she says. 'If I'd had a gun or a knife in my hand, I would've aimed straight for his gut. I *wanted* to.'

'Yeah, well you didn't, and you won't.'

'Ben came close once, though,' Liz says. 'In high school, remember?' Ben frowns, a warning, but Liz barrels on. 'The night he kicked Ben out. I nearly killed him myself that night. '

'Yeah,' Maggie says. 'I remember.'

She remembers the two of them standing there, Ben and Liz, and Jug screaming at Ben: 'The beginning of the end, that's what it is. A man starts fucking *boongs*, that's it, he's into the sewer, mate, and it's all downhill, all fucking downhill from there.' This was before God had grabbed Jug by the scruff of the neck. Weeks before. 'No son of mine,' Jug had roared, 'is

going to screw around with some black fucking ginn. You wanna fuck *boongs*, go and live in their stinking camps.'
There had been fists and blood and mayhem.
'Get out,' Jug had yelled. 'Get out, and take your black slut with you, and don't ever come back.'
'Too bloody right,' Ben yelled. 'You can count on it, mate.'
Weeks of storm weather had prevailed, weeks of walking on eggshells. And then God had spoken.
And then Jug had pulled in his horns.
'She's all right,' he'd say gruffly of Liz. *For a boong*: you could hear him refuse to think the thought. 'Red and yellow, black and white, All are precious in His sight,' he'd say. In fact, Liz got on better with the born-again Jug than his son or his daughter did. It's my Mission School background, she'd say. I know that country.
'How long's he been like this again?' Maggie asks.
'Didn't Mum tell you?'
'No. She never said a word in letters till the chooks got her down. So how long has it been?'
'Since the new road from Jabiru,' Ben says.
'Mum says nobody knows what happened.'
Ben says nothing.
'Well?' she says, watching him closely. 'Is that true?'
'Yes and no,' he says. 'I don't want to comment. I can't comment.'
'I can,' Liz says. 'He's been sung.'
'What?' Maggie blinks at her. 'By who?'
'By my mob,' Liz says. 'By the elders of the tribe.'
'Why?'
'The road,' Ben says. 'The mining company. The new road through Kakadu. It runs through sacred sites.'
'He knew that,' Liz says. 'We made depositions. The press refused to cover it, per usual, but everyone knew. I faced him one day, with the demonstrators. Nose to nose.'
'So that's it,' Ben says. 'You never told me.'
'No.'
'What'd he do?'
'We just stood there staring at each other. And he said: 'What can I do, Liz? I'm a working man, I build roads, what else can I do?' And I said: "You can cross the line, Jug.' And he said: 'Easy to say, Liz. Easy for you." And I said: "Don't do this, Jug, please. It's our land, it's our Dreaming, it's our old people, you're tearing us up, it's our country." And we just kept standing there, looking at each other, eye to eye, people pushing and shoving, but it was just us two, him and me.'
She is staring at the backs of her hands.
'Yes?' Ben prompts.

'I don't know,' she says. 'I felt he was standing right on the line, I felt he was thinking about it, I thought maybe he just might step over and join me, he just wanted a nudge, so I said....'

Maggie pictures the scene: the graders, the steamrollers, the tiptrucks of crushed stone, the sharp smell of tar, the demonstrators, the workmen in their heavy boots and singlets, the heat. She watches Liz remembering it. She watches Ben watching Liz. *This is a taboo subject with them*, she hears her mother say.

'What happened?' Ben nudges.

'I said something....'

They wait. Liz studies her hands. '*What?*' Ben says. 'What did you say?'

Liz sighs heavily. 'I said the wrong thing, I reckon.'

'What was it?'

But she's back at that line, nose to nose with Jug, her mob and his mob, stalemate.

'What, dammit! What did you say?'

'I said: "You've got a granchild coming, Jug. It's his Dreaming you're messing up. It's his place, it's his country, your own *granchild's*. You're desecrating his birthright, Jug."'

Maggie watches Liz's breathing, she knows the way of it, how the ragged tempo takes you over, it's like a weather pattern that you enter when you get too close to Jug. 'What did he say?' she asks.

'He said: "You fucking manipulative *boong*."'

Ben puts a hand over his face.

'And I told him, I hissed it at him. I said, "You're being sung, Jug Wilkins. You'd better make arrangements, because you're gonna be sung."' She starts collecting dishes with extraordinary vehemence and banging them into the sink. 'Fucking boong-hater,' she keeps saying. 'Fucking boong-haters, all of you, deep down.'

When she passes by him, Ben lifts a hand to touch her, but drops it again. Maggie has a sudden lurch of panic: they'll fight, she thinks; they'll say things they can't take back; he'll turn into Dad. Maggie wants a lightning bolt, she wants to point the bone somewhere, she wants someone to unsing the country, she wants to stop all of this. She gets up and puts her arms around Liz, but Liz pushes her away, furious. 'Don't you bloody *touch* me!' Liz yells, but the words puncture her rage which leaves her in a sudden rush, half sob. She looks deflated and unutterably weary. 'Oh shit,' she says helplessly to Ben: 'I'm sorry, mate. I really thought, you know, he was going to cross the line. I was so fucking *disappointed*.'

She says to Maggie: 'Anyway, they did. Sing him, I mean. They did it. He's been sung, and he knows it.'

Maggie is standing at the very back edge of their lot. It's night, still stiflingly hot and humid, but there's a full moon and just the suggestion of a breeze beginning to snuffle in off the sea. Around her rise the burial mounds of old cars. What would an archaeologist make of this? she wonders, this humpy terrain of rusted frames and compost heaps, all smothered and choked with jasmine, allamander, bougainvillea, and the ever rapacious morning glory, all of it sliding back into bush. Who knows where the boundary lies? What mad surveyor ever tried to mark such a thing?

'So wha'dya reckon, Maggie?' His voice is slurred, rising from somewhere in the smothered heaps of junk.

'Oh God, Jug, don't *do* that, you nearly gave me a heart attack. Where are you?'

'Where you gonna place your bet, Maggie?' He knocks on a creeper-clothed mound, and it gives back a hollow note, faintly metallic. 'The Earth our Mum? Or the cars? Wha'd'ya reckon?'

She's still too angry with him for patience, she wants to hurt. 'I've been to Ben and Liz's,' she says. 'You shouldn't've worked on the road. I know why you've gone loco, you've been sung.'

'On the road to Ka-ka-du-uu,' he sings drunkenly, 'where the crocs and the jabiru play—'

She will make him bleed. She will. 'They've turned you into the fruit and vegie man,' she says.

But he's not listening to her. He's not paying attention. He comes crawling out of the undergrowth on all fours, his head cocked to one side. He's listening for something else. She thinks of the cats watching invisible birds in the bush, that fixed intensity, his concentration focused at the point where the car humps merge into impenetrable wetland scrub. She peers into the moon-washed darkness, curious. 'What are you looking for?'

He gives no reaction, no sign, she might as well have ceased to exist.

'Jug,' she says, irritable. She wades through ground cover, creepers, rotting matter, she crunches sticks and eggs as she goes. 'What are you looking at?' And when he ignores her, she pummels his shoulders with her fists. He yelps, and throws her a brief startled glance, but whirls back again as though he dare not waver in his attentiveness. She has the creepy sensation that they are both being watched.

'What are you looking at, for God's sake?'

'Them,' he says.

'Who?' She batters him with her fists, years of rage, anxiety, helpless compassion all shouting through her white tight knuckles. 'Whad'ya mean, *them*, you bloody loony?'

He catches hold of her wrists. She can see he's snapped out of it now. He's with her again. He's just Jug. 'You see, Maggie,' he says quietly, 'that's why I can't tell you. I can't tell anyone. You'll say drunk, loony, the DTs. It's too big for that. It's too—' He can't even find a word.

But she knows suddenly, intuitively, what he's talking about. She has a sharp vision of a Melbourne dinner party, the usual little terrace house, cast-iron lace balconies, North Carlton, candlelit table, a whole roomful of elegance, brittle wit, and glibness. Maggie's in mid-flight, and all eyes are upon her, waiting. They are waiting for the laugh. *And as for Jug...?* someone prompts, but Maggie has fallen silent. There's a line she won't cross. She has bumped into sacrilege and recognized it in time. I forget, she says politely. I forget what I was going to say.

'Except maybe Liz,' Jug says. 'I could tell Liz, but I won't give her the satisfaction, me pride won't let me. And I can't tell anyone else.'

'It's okay, Dad,' Maggie says. 'I know what you're talking about.'

He puts out a hand to steady himself. 'I got vertigo,' he says. 'Comes and goes. Ever stood over a crack into nothing?'

'Yeah,' she sighs.

He holds his two hands up against the moon and brings them slowly together. He matches them carefully, palm to palm, finger to finger, thumb to thumb. 'There's two worlds,' he says, trying to explain something to himself. 'They're both as real as can be. They match exactly, so you can only see one at a time.' They both study his hands against the moon, a single dark silhouette. He could be someone praying, Maggie thinks. He sighs heavily. 'They match exactly,' he says, 'but they don't fit.'

'Yeah,' she says. 'I know.'

He looks at her warily and she gestures with her hands, palms up. Who has answers? her shrug implies.

He is assessing something. He reads her gestures and her eyes. He makes a decision. 'I saw something,' he says.

She nods.

'But I can't tell you. It's too–'

'I know,' she says. 'It's okay.'

They watch each other for a long time in silence. Then she raises her hands, palms facing him, and he brings his up to meet hers. They sit there like two children, fingertip to fingertip, palm pushing lightly against palm, an imperfect fit.

'If I told you...,' he says gruffly.

'You don't have to tell me. It's okay.'

'If I tell you, you gotta promise–'

'Cross my heart.' She licks an index finger and gestures over her breast.

'It was before they sung me anyway,' he says. 'It was just after me and Liz – well, I blew me top.'

'Yeah, she told us.'

'Didn't mean to. And then afterwards, I just wanted to smash something. I climbed up on the steamroller. We had the first bed of gravel down, I wanted to crush it meself, I wanted to mash it in, flatten it. I saw Liz leave with her mob. Good riddance, I thought, and I moved 'er up to full throttle. You could hear the road crunching into dirt, it's a good sound that. I was up there behind the wheel, and I suddenly had this giddy feeling I was on the spine of a razorback. Each side of me there was nothing. *Nothing.* I mean, if I moved, I could've fallen right off the world. And then

I got this funny feeling on the back of me neck, this prickle, like when you know someone's watching you.'

He opens his eyes very wide, the pupils dilated. The moon, bright orange, sits behind his head like a plate. Maggie sees herself, twice over, in his eyes.

'I turned around,' he says, whispering now, 'and there were hundreds and hundreds of them, thousands maybe, just standing there with their spears in their hands, watching me. They didn't make a sound. They were naked except for those little things they wear, and white bodypaint.'

He clutches at his heart, a sharp pain grabbing him again. 'It spooked me,' he whispers. 'The way they just stood there watching. They never made a sound, but I knew what they were waiting for.'

He looks at Maggie intently. 'They are *with* us,' he says. 'I never realized before, but they're with us.'

Maggie swallows.

'I climbed down off the steamroller,' he says. 'And I walked away. I never went back.'

'Dad,' Maggie says gently. 'Let's go back to the house.'

But he doesn't want to. He stands there staring into the wetlands. 'Alpha and Omega,' he murmurs. He seems to be sifting through clutter in his mind. 'The first and the last,' he says. 'The First Ones. *The last shall be first.*'

Maggie tugs at his hand. 'Dad,' she says.

'*Seeing we also are compassed about with so great a cloud of witnesses,*' he says, pulling at a creeper from the scrub of his Gospel Hall decade. He thinks he's got hold of something. 'And in those days, the last shall be the First Ones, and they shall be with us in the land.'

'Dad, you're mixing things up.'

'Nothing fits,' he says, turning to offer his puzzled benediction. 'That's the problem, Maggie. Nothing fits. But I know what's real and what's not, and they are with us.'

# KATE GRENVILLE

Kate Grenville was born in Sydney, Australia, in 1950, and holds degrees from the University of Sydney and the University of Colorado (U.S.A.). Her fiction includes *Bearded Ladies*, *Lilian's Story* (winner of the Australian/Vogel Award), *Dreamhouse* (recently released as a film), *Joan Makes History* (awarded a Bicentennial Commission), and *Dark Places*. These have all been published in the UK and the US, and several have been translated into German and Swedish.

KATE GRENVILLE

# Why I Write

I write as a way of exploring issues I don't understand: writing about something is my way of thinking about it. Mainly, the issues I don't understand have to do with women. Why might a woman choose to become a bag-lady (*Lilian's Story*)? Why do women stay in miserable marriages (*Dreamhouse*)? Why aren't there more women in history books (*Joan Makes History*)? Where does misogyny come from and what does it feel like (*Dark Places*)?

I don't write out of a theory about these issues, but in order to find something out. I feel that fiction is perhaps the best way to get under the skin of an issue, approaching it in a shamelessly subjective way – the way of intuition and empathy rather than the way of analysis – a way that can produce its own powerful revelations. Writing for me is a way of listening to my unconcious, and through it to the unconcious or hidden parts of the culture of which I'm a product.

Writing is a permitted way of exploring taboo subjects, or taking seriously subjects that are usually trivialised: and writing is a way of making visible the invisible biases of our culture. These taboos or attitudes can't easily be tackled head-on, but they can be embedded in the rich and seductive texture of a novel.

I think that, especially for women, there are many subjects that haven't been dignified with substantial treatment in the arts. Where is the great novel about housework? Where are the great novels about being a parent? Where are the great novels about the world of offices?

The novel can speculate in a way not possible in other disciplines – what might history look like if it was all about women rather than all about men? What does it feel like to hate and fear women? Speculative histories and experimental identities such as these are the kind of thing the novel does best, I think.

I write, too, because writing is a way of making life bearable, giving it meaning. Not that my life is terrible – it's not. But when it seems futile, or failed, or bleak, writing gives me a way to use all those feelings in a positive way. I can invent a character who's a failure and feels futile – and in being permitted to fully explore the feeling through writing about that character, insights can happen that might not otherwise. Perhaps I might discover through my invented character that failure has its own glories. Perhaps, in the course of the writing, it will emerge that futility is the only road to purpose. These insights are not personal – writing is not therapy. With a starting-place in the personal experience, writing can extrapolate and reveal things we all share.

KATE GRENVILLE

# Albion in Love

This is Albion Gidley Singer at the pen, a man with a weakness for a good fact. The first fact is always the hardest: you must begin somewhere, and such is the nature of this intractable universe that you must start with a thing admitted but undemonstrable. Myself, for example. I am a thing admitted, I close a drawer on my hand or slice my chin with my razor and admit myself to be, but it is a source of grief to me that I am undemonstrable, in spite of hands scarred by drawers, and blood spurting from my chin.

I inspect the things I own, but they do not give me back myself. I grasp a poker, or the Dresden shepherd on the mantelpiece, and snap off the flute in his silly pink hand, but such things remain strangers to me. I am a hollow link in the endless chain of proof which stretches back to a time when Albion Gidley Singer could not be imagined, back to simians swinging through branches, back to the jellies eddying in the currents of brand-new seas.

Mirrors show me a stranger, and there are long dark nights of hissing emptiness, of the voids between the stars, when I am hot with panic. *God!* I cry silently then, into the quality down of my pillow, which has swallowed so many cries for help. *God!* In the morning, with yellow sun lying silkily over the end of my bed, the hissing voids retreat beneath the sound of sea and kookaburras. I don my wing-collar, that keeps my head on my shoulders, and remind myself that I am a philosopher and a gentleman.

Hollow man that I was, I found true love at last with Eadith: Eadith of the rust-coloured hair, simple Eadith who admired Albion Gidley Singer for his place in the world and his immaculate wing-collars.

Eadith! When I met her she was laughing and if she had not been, I might never have known love, because when she was not laughing her mouth was like a fish's, with a tendency to turn down at the corners. Laughing Eadith was chasing a feather that cavorted out of her grasp at each jump she made for it, in the park under the paper-barks, where feathers often floated down to the grass from the birds that perched and soiled overhead. I watched, because I did not wish Albion Gidley Singer to make any kind of fool of himself, rushing in and catching floating feathers like a madman if in fact this woman was brushing away a fly, or simply a lunatic who was trying to catch God, perhaps, as he sported with her.

I stood watching, then, with my cane planted at an observer's angle in the grass, and this rust-coloured woman in her dark-green costume laughed and leapt in an inefficient way at the feather buoying itself up on the currents of air she was producing. She laughed so that I saw her bad teeth, and the artlessness of her beginning to shine with effort and frustration and the consciousness of being watched by a gentleman with a cane. *Madam*, I said, and took a few steps closer, so that I could see that she was not in her first youth, *Madam, may I offer you my assistance?*

She was no coquette, this woman in her ugly green, and she smiled so that her face creased, but looked me guilelessly in the face as she said, *Oh sir, you are kind, it is that I collect them, you see, and make pictures from them, and this is a Sydney feather, and a very good one.* As she spoke the feather wafted down between us and with one decisive movement I had it caught in my hand. *Maps of Australia*, the rust-coloured woman was saying, *and of course religious motifs, my father was a clergyman of the Church of England.*

She smiled with her bad teeth, as if I would know all about maps of Australia and clergymen, and would care, and she smiled in a warm vague way that would have been an invitation in another woman, but she was too artless and plain to know how to make an invitation with a smile. She smiled and lingered, this woman with small unlovely eyes the colour of soil, and wished to go on talking, I could see, about her feathers and her father.

I saw her hands, like a child's, square, the nails cut short. They were not the clever hands of my wife Norah, soft and skilful with embroidered parrots, and deft among the combs of her complicated hair, and they were not the hands of Agnes and Una, with cheery painted nails and a thousand small secrets of skill with a gentleman's manhood. They were the hands of a lost soul who made maps of Australia out of feathers, and smiled at gentlemen in a way that said she knew nothing of the world. *Maps of Australia*, I said, and she nodded with eagerness. *I have been needing Cape York Peninsular, and now you have given me the very tip that I needed*, she exclaimed, and I thought of another tip I was beginning to feel I would be prepared to give her. *I should very much like to see such a work*, I said, *as a map of Australia in feathers*, and my voice was mild, Albion Gidley Singer at his mildest, for this was a woman no man had to labour with. She smiled and her face was pleased to be spoken to, and she was proud to take Albion Gidley Singer home to her tiny rented room by the sea, to show him her treasures, and her unfinished map of Australia.

Ah, Eadith! She was like a peach, in need of a shave. The down softened the contours of her features and gave her an expression of softness, a vagueness, that I liked: and, of course, I longed to reach out my hand and feel that fur under my fingers. Eadith was not beautiful, if she had been she would not have been spending her days making her widow's mite go a little further in this damp seaside place. She would not have remained a widow, growing slowly old under her fur without the flame of the touch

of a man to bring her to life. Nor was she a wit, my poor Eadith, or even
a person of brains like my ugly daughter. Eadith was a silly woman, given
to clucking at babies in the streets, embroidering small dainty pointless
bits of things, and gathering pictures from *The News Of The World* on the
subject of the Royal Family. *You can tell they are Royalty,* she said, showing
me the smudged photographs. *Do you agree, Albion, you can see the royalty
in their faces.*

It was her silliness, her earnest silliness, that I loved her for: she became
solemn and pink, persuading me that the Royal Family had royalty in
their very jaw-bones, and her mouth tightened in pride, smoothing the
idiot pieces of embroidery on her knee. *It makes the time pass,* she
explained, with her head on one side smoothing a rose-petal embroidered
in dark-green, and I wanted to seize her in her solemnity and turn her
simple spirit towards me. *My peach,* I wanted to say, and see her flush
with pride at being the peach of Albion Gidley Singer, and of course never
guessing why she was my peach rather than my angel or my rose.

But, now we sat, still, with my yellow gloves lying on my knee between
us as I hoped Eadith's hands would one day lie. *Let us take the air,* I said,
and Eadith brightened like a fanned fire and jumped to her feet in a way
Norah would never have done, with enthusiasm at an idea of mine.

There was a sea-wall with a promenade, and on one side the sea slapped
and pounced, and on the other we could see the narrow strip of the town,
and then the railway line keeping the houses hemmed in, and beyond the
railway line the mountains rose up steeply, lowering down on us in a way
I disliked. I turned my face away from those overhanging mountain slopes
and faced into the sea breeze as Eadith was doing, she was *taking the air*
as if it was medicine, in great gasping breaths. *Oh,* she laughed suddenly,
pink in her cheeks, more peach-like than ever, *Oh Mr Singer, I am come
over dizzy, it is all that air,* and she stood with her hands balancing on the
air in front of her breasts so that it was clear to me that Eadith was a minx
too, and was probably not dizzy, or only with passion. I took her hands,
then, and pressed her against me, saying *Mrs Heron, it is all right, you will
be well again shortly, just rest for a moment.* I spoke into her hair and against
my fine woollen chest I could feel the thrust of her breasts, heaving up
and down against me in an inflammatory way.

The drone of the sea was making me irritable now. *Eadith, it will rain, we
must return,* I said, and could not look at her eager artless face, that
showed up my perfidy and the depths of my animal lust. *Eadith, I would
hate you to get wet,* I said, speaking mindlessly, my mind on other things,
but Eadith's mind was on nothing but me, and I felt her looking up at me
watching the words fall out of my mouth, and I was comforted by such
embracing attention. *Eadith,* I said, *I would like, I cannot say, I am too full of
it, too much feeling, Eadith.* Poor innocent Eadith, listening to my riddles
and trying to read my face, I saw the power fill her face as water fills a
sponge, saw her think she understood, and I stood within my falsity and

felt her eyes smiling all over my face, and her loving innocent spirit come to meet me. I *adore*, I murmured, so I knew she could not be sure just what she had heard. *Adore*. Her eyes watched my mouth and I caused it to smile a non-committal sort of smile, that would keep her puzzled. *You are an intrigue to me*, I said, and her face was radiated with pleasure, hearing the words, and I mumbled some more, but knew she would not break the spell by saying *Pardon? Pardon, Albion?* I let her hear another teasing word then: *Besotted*, I said and then I bowed my head as if overcome, and Eadith could do nothing more than clasp her hands, poor fool, and wait for me to become clearer, or burst into a passion of tears on her shoulder.

I did neither of these things, but straightened at last and looked at that heavy sky lowering down on us. *Well*, I said, and took a small step away from the woman gazing at me, and from that small distance gazed back into her eyes for a moment, smiled another mysterious smile, and then bit it off under my teeth. *Well, Eadith, I would not have you get wet for the world*, I said in a voice as tender as milk. *And I know you wish to return now. I can see you do not like to say so, but you are eager to go back.* I smiled, and saw her frown a little, and I smiled more, because I knew there was nothing she wished more than to go on standing with me, but she did not know how to contradict me.

On the way back to her dank rooms we stood by the shallows watching the smooth grey surface of the water scattered by the flash of fish cavorting there, a shoal of silver backs churning the water. *Look*, Eadith said, and took advantage of the moment to lay her hand on my arm, as if I could not see those roistering fish. *Look, Albion, fish!* I stopped, and lifted my arm a little so she felt emboldened to leave her hand there and I could feel her tremulous through my tweed. I felt myself becoming a man in my trousers, feeling her quivering against me, and said: *It is some kind of courting ritual, Eadith, it is their mating dance, they are preparing to copulate.* Ah, what an unscrupulous rascal I was! I felt Eadith flinch, but not flinch so much that I did not know that she could be mine, whenever I wished, now: talking of those copulating fish had tested her waters for me, and she had not flung away in disgust, had not even removed her hand from my arm: I was an unscrupulous rascal, but she was a trollop of the first water, like all the women I had ever known: she just concealed it differently under her plain peachy cheeks. I smiled to myself then, a special and private smile which I saw her wonder at: but I had her bluffed, this foolish fond hairy woman, and she would not dare approach that secretive smile of mine and ask what lay behind it.

Gulls wheeled and rudely screamed, a small ungainly boy ran past and shot us a knowing glance, and the shadow of the land lay dark on the water. *Come then, Eadith*, I said with rather more volume than I had intended. *Come, Eadith*, I repeated more gently. *Come, let us return now, and discuss the nature of your void, and mine.*

# The Story-teller's Revenge: Kate Grenville Interviewed by Gerry Turcotte

*Could we start this interview generally, perhaps with your background as a writer. How you started and why.*

I never quite know how to begin with that question. I had a few false starts when I was at school. I wrote a short story and sent it to the Australian *Women's Weekly*, and when I was at university I wrote a novel and a few short stories which I didn't finish. But then I got going seriously when I went to England in 1976. I'd always had a yearning to see if I could write or not so I thought I'd take six months off and live on my savings in a garret in Paris. I thought if I was going to do the cliché I might as well go the whole hog! So I wrote two novels in the space of nine months which are both absolutely appalling. They're the ones you write to get a certain amount of junk out of your system before you can start really writing. The urge to write came out of the fact that I couldn't find anything to read that seemed to be about the kind of life that I lived, the kind of problems that I was dealing with. There was a lot of that rather uplifting feminist writing, like Erica Jong and Lisa Alther, and they made me feel discouraged because they were so cheery. In spite of their anguish and self doubts they had some kind of control over their lives. And they had gusto and they weren't afraid. I was terribly timid. And then at the other extreme there were those British women: Angela Carter, Emma Tennant, Micheline Wandor, the Women's Press sort of books. And they seemed to me like another extreme. They were writing a kind of highly analytical feminist fiction, and I wasn't one of those either. And I felt as a reader I was caught between two stools, and when I began to write I realized that I was still falling between two stools. I sent some of the early stories to the Women's Press and they were rejected, with a note saying they weren't feminist enough. I sent the same stories to conventional outlets too, and the men there also rejected them, saying they were too radically feminist and angry. So I started writing out of that sort of frustration of there being no reflection anywhere of the reality that I seemed to be dealing with.

*You're a favourite as a Creative Writing teacher. How much of the techniques you use are the result of your studies in the USA?*

Almost all of them. What I learned there was to free up. I had a teacher there who said, 'Look, they're quite good Kate but they're full of closure.' Well, that really seared me to the heart. What he meant by closure was what I thought a well-made story looked like. All the threads tied up. The gun on page one fired by the end of the story. I thought that was what good writing looked like.

What I learned studying with those American writers was that good writing could look like many different things. And open-ended, exploratory ways of writing can be more exciting, more risky too, than safe, traditional, highly controlled forms. As a writer I learned to trust instinct, and not to feel I had to know everything about the story before I started it. The notion of writing as discovery, rather than as just tale-telling, was revolutionary for me. The British-inspired literary education I'd had was very prim and straight-laced – the worst thing you could be was out of control. What I learned in the U.S. was that if you're never out of control, you never break out into discovery.

*Can you say a bit about the differences between the North American approach to Creative Writing and the Australian approach?*

There is no belief in Creative Writing here. Even the term is sneered at. Creative Writing is considered the kind of thing that you do at WEA[1] along with macramé and pottery. The image is of little old ladies writing about their lives. In this country when you're a Writer-in-Residence you still have to go through that dispiriting argument about whether you can teach writing. As part of our British baggage we have taken on board the Muse theory of writing, the theory that writers are an elect group, an elite touched by the finger of Art. Academics like to keep the study of literature firmly in the realm of the theoretical: the idea that you can learn things from Shakespeare as a writer that you can never learn as a critic, has not made much headway. And our British heritage also gives us a distrust of experimentation and innovation. We would rather go on perpetuating old forms of excellence than discover new ones.

*You have said elsewhere that you get very bored with anything which isn't structurally challenging.[2] More than this, that you felt inhibited by 'form' and felt you had to fracture it in order to speak as a woman. How did this surface in your earliest work,* Bearded Ladies?

Those stories...some of them are attempting to be traditional well-made stories, but some of them under the influence of Americans I met in Paris, are kind of pale imitations of John Hawkes, John Burroughs.

*All men?*

Yes, the mainstream, even in innovative writing, is still male. Who are some women? Oh, Kathy Acker, of course. So a story like 'Making Tracks', began as a traditional well-made story. Eventually I realized that what I really wanted to write about was a kind of nightmare state of mind. And I knew that that mood was going to be trivialized in any conventional way of telling that story. It would be reduced to either/or: either it's a dream or it's reality. What I had to do was to find a form in which what happens to that woman was simultaneously fantasy and reality. The woman does go back, and she doesn't go back. The power of her imagining the return makes it real. Something doesn't actually have to have happened in real life to be real. So I wanted to get in these simultaneous impossibilities. Or a story like 'Blast Off': what I wanted there was to find a model for pure rage. I had no model for a story as angry as I wanted that one to be. So it came out in those chipped little fragments of pure black hatred.

*In your mind, is the ending of* Dreamhouse *sufficiently open to be successful according to what you outlined earlier in your comments on closure? It's really ending in a beginning, but is that sufficiently open?*

No. I tried to do a bit of closure with that. I was still learning to let go of the safety-line of closure at the time, because I wrote that book during the two years I spent in America. The fact that Rennie has to have some kind of cathartic scene with the hat – which never seemed to me an adequate kind of object on which to hang that catharsis – the fact that he has to have a catharsis before she can leave, I think it is a bit too neat. Life isn't really like that and I don't think fiction has to be either. However it's very much better than an earlier version of the book in which I had a whole section, fifty pages, showing Louise and Viola living happily ever after. That was real closure, closing up and nailing it down and tying it up.

*I wonder if you could discuss the rather fascinating structural peculiarity of* Lilian's Story. *Its original form was quite different, and then you re-shuffle the chapters. Why was that necessary?*

It was the first book I wrote after I'd done the two years in America and I thought, 'All right, learn your lessons, just write whatever comes to you each day. Write where the energy is instead of following where the plot is.' In fact I never knew what the plot was going to be right up until I had almost finished the book. I didn't quite know what was going to happen in the end. And I thought, write a lot of fragments then rearrange them in neat chronological order in chapters, so I did that. I wrote about a hundred pages of fragments and then typed them all up and put them together in a very neat orderly way. I found to my surprise that they dovetailed beautifully. But when I strung them all together some indefinable thing happened to the structure. It just became flaccid and dull. It lost some tension. So I went back to the fragments: the fragment-instinct seemed to have been right. And the structural shape that suggested itself then was to gather them into big loose bags: a girl, a young lady and a woman. Those seemed to be convenient bags in which to put fragments of various kinds. I'm still traditional enough to think that you have to have some kind of thread of action – it doesn't have to be plot – but there does have to be some kind of growth, a sense of organic growth. So there's an overall steady shape, chronological structure, but within that, a very loose assemblage of scenes.

*What about the lack of quotation marks?*

I'd always been unhappy with the way quotation marks set off dialogue. It insulated it from the rest of the narrative. And for various reasons I thought that this was very false because in life it doesn't happen like that, dialogue is usually part of action, it's very seldom that someone sits down and gives a speech. So I wanted to convey that kind of simultaneity instead of cutting it off in time. I also wanted to convey the fact that things between quotation marks have no different status than things not in quotation marks. In other words, it's all made up by the writer. There's that illusion with quotation marks that you're quoting something that happened out there in the real world. And particularly in *Lilian's Story*, where it is a first person account by somebody who might in fact not be a very reliable narrator, I wanted to clue the reader in that the dialogue is also going through the filter of this woman's consciousness. That mightn't be what the people said at all, it's what she *heard* them say. Italics seemed to work because I didn't want much dialogue. It's not a technique that would have worked if I'd had a lot of dialogue. And it wouldn't have worked with realistic dialogue. Italics help to make the dialogue stylized and slightly unreal.

*Both your earlier novels have been published outside Australia. I know in* Lilian's Story *your New York editor asked you to add in a chapter, but that had more to do with character development than with explaining Australia and its language.*[3] *But there must be a lot of work to do in order to translate the Australian lexicon for a world market. How have goannas and damper fared overseas? And do you care?*

Well they haven't gone down very well. My American editor for *Joan* gave me a whole list of things that needed translating like damper, goanna, short back and sides and choko and all *kinds* of things that you take for granted. And I'm in a quandary here. I don't want the book to be so foreign that it's inaccessible. I *want* it to be accessible. But I also don't want to reduce its Australianness. So somehow I have to try and approach each of those problems and write around it so that it's self-explanatory, so that I could keep the word but elucidate the meaning. But for some things it was just impossible. I mean a goanna. Without making the prose ridiculous it's really hard to describe. 'A large lizard, which we call a goanna, rumbled across the stage.'

*Footnotes?*

Yes, footnotes would do it.

*A glossary?*

A glossary. Well, they thought of a glossary for *Lilian* but they decided they didn't need it. In the end I wrote back to the editor and said, 'Look! I've done what I can but you have to remember that we learned what coyotes were by reading cowboys and Indians comics, and American readers are probably smart enough to work out, in context, what a goanna is.' And if they read enough of Australian writing they soon will because the same words will keep popping up. But it's one of the not-so-subtle pressures on Australian writers to become much less Australian, to become transpacific and transatlantic writers. It's a terribly distorting thing which I suppose any small culture has to deal with; to what extent you're willing to distort what you have to say, to make it international. Which means of course that you tend to fall back on those universals, you know, like human psychology and human relationships. Unfortunately I'm now less interested in those things and more interested in things that have to do with the history of a particular place and the politics of a particular place. And the more I get interested in that the sharper the problem is becoming, because you have to sell your books overseas to make any money.

*You begin,* Joan Makes History, *with an obvious allusion to biblical history: 'In the beginning was the word.' But, of course, since* Joan *is a re-vision of history, particularly masculine history, you change the quote. 'In the beginning was nothing much.' How conscious were you of somehow rewriting patriarchal history; of wanting to substitute feminine history for it, even at this level?*

I began the book as a very conscious exercise in a feminist rewriting of Australian history. But as I got involved in the book I got interested in other aspects of the problem. The current dilemma for women is the age-old dilemma of how you combine the desire to have a family – the domestic dimension – with being out in the world, being an achiever. And simply rewriting the past in a new shape didn't seem adequate to confronting that problem. I came to see that it's not just a matter of rewriting history, it's a matter of rethinking our whole role.

*Much of what you offer for 'inclusion' into history is the rather large, though unacknowledged, contribution of women which has little place in the masculine spectrum: motherhood, companionship, and so forth. More than this, you focus on what Don Anderson has called 'the importance of the minutiae of everyday life in the writing of history.'[4] Can you comment on this?*

When I began *Joan* what I was going to do was pretend that a woman was actually there at the great achievements of Australian history: that a woman was really the one to discover Australia, that a woman was really the first one to step ashore. In other words, I had women simply stepping into the shoes of men, dressing up in drag if you like. It was a kind of drag version of history. And that's how the book begins. The first couple of scenes are like that with women playing out the male role.

*But later on, the contemporary Joan actually does do this, doesn't she? She actually does become a man.*

Yes. But she rejects this, just as I rejected it, as I was writing it. I realized that it was no solution to say, 'Look, women were there and they were making history in the male way.' That still goes along with the assumption that the only history worth talking about is the kind where someone discovers something, or leads an army, or rules a country. As I went along further with the book I realized that what I wanted to say was, those things matter, but what also matters are the humble things, and the people who do them. The person who 'just' brings up the kids and washes the socks is as necessary to the whole picture as the kings and explorers. She, or he, is also making history in the sense that they are creating the climate in which humanity lives. Beside, if no-one got the dinners there wouldn't be much exploring or ruling. That's why Joan turns her back on the great achievements and becomes a washerwoman and a mother. It's why, in the specific scene in which she becomes a man, and literally dresses in drag, she realizes that the achievement of being a man is a hollow one. There are more satisfying things to do than just ape men.

*One of the particularly interesting, and also confusing, occurrences in one of those 'drag' scenes is that as soon as Joan becomes a man she begins to use all the same pressure tactics against women that men do. Why is that?*

I've always enjoyed that feeling of what a lovely revenge it would be on the system.

*Except that it's a revenge on women.*

Yes. It's part of the patriarchal oppression of women that women are the real warders of other women. It's always been the case because women have internalized it all so thoroughly. You know, certain slaves have been given favoured treatment so that they can be placed above the other slaves.

*A type of* The Handmaid's Tale.

Yes! You can talk from a woman's point of view about what it's like to be pressured by men, and it sounds as if you're just whingeing about trivial things, or that you're just being paranoid. You know, men are not *really* whistling at you on the street, they're just passing the time of day. But to reverse the whole thing so that it's a woman acting the part of the oppressor – that makes it more convincing as the bullying it really is.

*You've said that initially, your short stories were rejected by feminist journals for not being radical enough, and by male journals for being too radical. Notwithstanding the response of the feminist journals, your first collection of stories was extremely well received by the women's community at large. Since then you've been under increasing fire for, as some might put it, not remaining faithful to a radical degree of feminist thought. This criticism has been particularly bad in terms of* Joan. *What do you see has changed in your writing, if anything, to cause such a feeling? Is it that your investigations, those levels you're playing with now, are just too subtle?*

I hope not. Because I think they're the level that most women are trying to come to terms with. I think that thoughtful feminists understand *Joan*. Dale Spender, for example, saw exactly what I was trying to do in *Joan*. But feminism can harden in the arteries like any other vigorous set of ideas. It begins, or began for me anyway, as a blinding flash – you grow up in patriarchy and you accept the patriarchy. Then you do some reading and some thinking and you have this epiphany and you see that it's all wrong. Then you rethink everything. And having rethought everything to a certain point it takes another leap, another epiphany, to think still further, to adapt to new streams or ideas or desires. Many feminists like myself are trying, somehow, to incorporate the fact that many of us want to lead this difficult life of motherhood and being a member of a family. Somehow our feminism has to change shape to absorb that fact. Feminism for me has always been about broadening options – it's been a response to the gap between the real and the ideal and trying to bridge that gap. It's not dogma. Now the choices that Joan makes might appear to be re-enforcing that terrible old idea of 'A woman's place is in the home'. But what I'm trying to say is that if a woman chooses that her place *is* in the home, then she should be given full honour for that. That should be *her* choice. What the book is about is giving glory to occupations type-cast as inglorious – women's occupations. Judy Chicago's 'Dinner Party' is an obvious analogy – glorifying female skills – glorifying tapestry rather than demanding bronze statues.

*There were also women enacting what masculine historians would consider 'larger' or more 'heroic' gestures. Caroline Chisholm for instance.*

And Daisy Bates.

*I can understand that you wouldn't have wanted to represent exclusively this type of achievement, but were you tempted to tell these stories at all?*

Yes. And in my first plan of the book that's what it was all going to be. Women of achievement. But I got interested in the other idea: to talk about the utterly ordinary women, not the remarkable ones. The reality for most women was that they have been wives and mothers...enormous numbers of women are still choosing that as their life. So you have to tackle those women, if you're going to say something useful to women today. You have to say, okay, our history was about being drudges and wives and mothers, a slave race, and *that* was glorious, that was history! We have been magnificent! Rather than to say, the only women worth remembering are Caroline Chisholm and Daisy Bates because they did those masculine things, were individual achievers.

*When we spoke earlier about* Joan Makes History *you said, 'I felt very strongly writing this history that I wanted to put in at least some of the groups that had been left out – mainly the women, but also the Aborigines.'[5] You also suggested that you felt 'uneasy' about doing this. Was writing the Aboriginal passages made all the more difficult knowing the book would be associated with the Bicentennial?*

Absolutely. At the time that I wrote them it was still a long time before the Bicentennial and the full horror of the way it left out those people wasn't apparent. I probably should have guessed, but I didn't then, how insulting the Bicentennial would be to the Aboriginal people. But as the day got closer, as the book was finished, it became obvious that the Bicentennial was going to be an exercise in dismissing whole areas of human experience.

*Did that cause re-writes?*

No, but I was in a bit of a dilemma. I didn't want to leave the Aborigines out of the book because one of the things I was doing was putting back into a history book some of the groups left out of other history books – among them women and the Aboriginal people. But I also didn't want to tell their story for them, or do any of that patronizing White-novelist-telling-the story-of-the-Blacks thing. So I was in a bit of a dilemma, and the only way that I could see out of it was to write a totally subjective account that was shamelessly myself imaginatively projecting. The other thing that I wanted strongly to do was to say, Aborigines, the women too, were not the passive creatures that we've always learned about in our history books. So I've made both the Aboriginal women fairly active, especially the second one. Of course, they weren't just decorative plaster statues standing around the landscape. They were actually – as we know now – fighting a fierce guerilla war. I wanted to make the gesture, and leave it at that – not go too far on someone else's territory.

*In* Joan *you set up very clearly a dichotomy between the 'Brits' on one side, and the non-Anglo-Celtic, the marginal and the female, on the other. This continues your investigation of themes of imperialism and colonization doesn't it?*

Yes. Again when I first conceived the book it was as a reaction to Ann Summer's *Damned Whores and God's Police*, where she draws a parallel between the colonizing of a country and the colonizing of women as a class. I thought, wouldn't it be interesting to write a story that was a parallel of exactly those two events, the literal colonizing of a country, namely Australia, and the metaphorical colonizing of a woman, Joan, to show those two stories and to intercut them side by side. And that thread, as often happens in a book, the thread that begins it, becomes buried after a while in the elaboration, in the other things you get interested in. And also simply in the human momentum of the human beings and the stories that you put into action. That parallel is very clear in the first couple of sections. I've got the conception of a nation – they're sitting on the Endeavour, saying 'What will this Great South Land be like?' – and the images I use are of a pregnant swelling womb the country swelling in its unknown home over the sea somewhere. And in a parallel chapter the foetus is swelling within the womb, and it's another great unknown being speculated over. I set the parallel up mechanistically and what happened was that I realized that such a mechanical schema was too rigid for the book that I wanted to write. I wanted to have much more elbow room than that, and I kind of faded that parallel away. I hoped that enough of it would echo at different points of the book, that the parallel would still be there. Federation is the point where it parallels again very obviously with the coming-of-age of a nation and the coming-of-age of a daughter. It was an important organizing structure for my first ideas about the book.

*There's an interesting parallel too between* Lilian's Story *and* Joan. Joan *begins with the discovery of Australia by Whites, and* Lilian's Story *with the consolidation of that discovery, Federation.*

I wanted them to dovetail. I was even going to put a date on Madge leaving home which happened to be my particular birthday. But I thought that would be too subtle. A bit of an in-joke.

*We spoke elsewhere about your propensity for the Gothic, at least in* Dreamhouse *and* Lilian's Story. *Is the Gothic voice something you're moving away from? Certainly* Joan *doesn't have that type of darkness.*

No it doesn't. You mean the darkness of sinister images? When I began to have all those thoughts about what I regard as the new wave of feminism, where you combine feminism with the old values that we have from our mothers – when I began to think about that it was a terribly freeing thing. For years it had really blocked me up in a quandary, how to combine being a mother, where you're totally the slave of another human being, with being completely your own person. So when I began to see in *Joan*, as in my own life, that it was in fact possible to find a way out of that quandary, it was like a huge opening of delight. It was a really positive thing. There didn't seem much impulse toward the darkness of the earlier books.

*You've described the Gothic as a playful convention.*

It's playful in the sense of being exaggerated and not like real life, so you can slip under people's guards. I suppose that now I think that there are other ways of slipping under people's guards; other interesting things to do. And I suppose the Gothic suits tearing down, it suits the destruction of the old icons, but perhaps it doesn't so much suit the exploration of new positive directions. So I hope *Joan* is playful as well, but with other conventions.

*As a final question, now that you've covered the history of the universe, what will you turn to for subject matter? What's in need of revision?*

It's a real problem. I thought of writing a utopian novel, rather than revising what's already been, to invent completely. But I actually prefer to deal with what there is rather than make something up. In the book I'm writing now I'm burrowing downwards, I'm writing Lilian's father's book.[6] And I'm burrowing downwards into that idea of patriarchal oppression from the man's point of view. But I'm getting in a way slightly less interested in that aspect and more interested in a notion that patriarchy is bound up with a kind of ruthless law-of-the-jungle set of political or philosophical beliefs: the thought-system that says the strongest deserves to win. Which is a very topical thing to be thinking about. At this place and moment in history, it's quite hard not to think about it at the moment.

*Although Darwin helped that idea along.*

Yes, he gave justification, the ultimate scientific justification. And the animal analogy is one which we still have to come to terms with when we transfer it to human things. So Father, as well as being an oppressive patriarchal figure, is representative of those beliefs: the market place as jungle, the weak must go under, the trickle down effect, there is no equality in nature so why should there be in the affairs of men. He represents that whole way of thinking about human affairs. What I'm trying to do is to show how wrong he is, that human affairs are more complicated than that, and that we have to acknowledge that there are, for want of a better word, *moral* imperatives as well as power imperatives. So I'm trying to explore patriarchy's deepest beliefs. As well as have a lot of fun at the expense of this particular man.

*I guess this also gets you back to Malthus.*

Yes, the *Doctrine of Necessary Catastrophe.*[7] Well, I'm fascinated by that. I deeply envy people who hold those beliefs, because for them it is so simple, their position is so logical you cannot attack it logically. There's nothing you can do with it except appeal to these terrible woolly half-baked notions of goodness and compassion and looking after the weak. All you can do is appeal to this mumbo-jumbo, so that the challenge is to find a kind of alternative logic with which to battle it. So it's always interested me. Like most people I've been exposed to a lot of that conservative philosophy and never been able to argue against it really effectively.

*Except to become a story-teller.*

Yes. It's such a good revenge. I mean, apart from people like you challenging me, I can say what I like. And get away with it. No reader is going to leap up off the page and say this is all wrong, this is nonsense. So yes, it's a great revenge for those of us who believe in the woolly values.

*Well that seems to be a good place to end. We have, after all, recorded this in the Woolley Building at the University of Sydney.*

## Notes

1. An organization providing adult education courses. The acronym stands for Workers' Educational Association.
2. Gerry Turcotte, 'Telling those Untold Stories: An Interview with Kate Grenville', *Southerly*, No. 3 (1987), pp. 284-99.
3. Kate Grenville, 'A Time of Hard', *Scripsi*, Vol. 4, No. 3 (1987), pp. 51-59. According to Grenville, this chapter was added to the American edition of *Lilian's Story* because her 'editor in New York suggested that Lil got too old and too mad too suddenly ... that a transition was missing'. *Southerly*, p 290.
4. Don Anderson, 'You've met Joan – Our Everywoman', *Sydney Morning Herald*, 30 April 1988, p. 70.
5. *Southerly*, p. 297.
6. Albion's Story is to be published in Australia and the UK by Macmillan in 1994 and by Harcourt Brace in the US, under the tittle *Albion's Story*.
7. Rennie, in *Dreamhouse*, is writing his doctoral dissertation on Malthus' infamous *Doctrine*.

# JENNIFER STRAUSS

Jennifer Strauss was born in Heywood, Victoria in 1933. She has published *Children and Other Strangers* (Nelson, 1975) and *Winter Driving* (Sisters Publishing, 1981). She is currently a lecturer at the Department of English, Monash University, Victoria.

JENNIFER STRAUSS

# Why I Write

I find it very difficult to talk about myself as a 'Poet'; everything seems to fall into the language of false pride or false modesty or else an evasive irony that escapes neither. Even in talking about simply writing poems, I'm abashed by the smallness of my output and my lack of an articulated 'poetics'. I've never been able to produce a finished poem by making up my mind to write a (=any) poem at any particular time, much less by making up my mind to write 'a sonnet', 'in tercets/hexameters/dialogue-/heroic handstands.' I can only write when the idea of a particular poem germinates in experience – usually the kind of experience in which there is some kind of intersection; of feeling and thought; of past, present and speculative time; of particular and type. The 'idea' of the poem isn't an idea at all in a philosophical or even discursive. It's a kind of dimly perceived shape, and the defining of that shape is a process of discovering as much as of 'making'.

All my poems are personal; very few are unequivocally autobiographical. Mostly, I write because things disturb (rather than distress). I want to make an order out of that disturbance, which isn't always caused by chaos, obvious dis-order; the wrong kind of order can disturb even more. And the poem doesn't exorcise the original feeling; poems aren't problem-solvers, not even dissolvers.

I write the only kind of poems I can. I admire a great many other kinds.

# Jenny Strauss

## DREAMING OF HELLFIRE AND DAMNATION

A T-junction ends the passage
'Choose!' her escort says
'To the left –
            eternal silence
perpetual discourse on the right.'


'Hell à la carte?' she quips
playing for time.
                    *Lesson One:*
*The Jokes are Only on You.*


'You can't decide? Have both.'
The trap-door trick:
                        feet-first,
she falls to a room
ablaze with conversation, tongues
of fire, darting flames
                        dancing
in disembodied mouths.


The crossfire rakes her nerves
as droplets
            cool with significance
tantalise
            sizzle
                evaporate...

She will never master the lingo.

In this black Pentecost
        the bread of language
        will turn on her tongue forever
            to bitter stone.

# THE MELANCHOLIC AT THE DINNER PARTY

Watching her love in animated talk
she's overcome to see
that glowing territory of otherness
ignite with all
its fiery first attraction;

averts her gaze, as if afraid
a speaking look might cry:
*Remember me!*
*Aquarius the waterbearer,*
*quencher of flames.*

Sadness drags at her spirit's gut,
a menstrual pain
that will not bleed away
but cramps and grinds.
'How long,' she asks impassively, 'can love

survive the dwindling of desire?'
The conversation hiccups,
rejects this tasteless morsel,
flows again. She knows
the answer must be sweated out in silence.

# VANISHING SPECIES

The child
(computer games abandoned)
comes tidily to breakfast
on coffee and croissants,

declares
'I didn't much care
for last night's sitter.
She talked too much.

She wouldn't
let me play my video,
she didn't read from a book,
she talked a story.

It was weird –
there was this naughty mother
sent her own little girl out,
all by herself, into the woods.'

Order's
foundations are shaken:
in the mock-adult face
a muscle quivers.

'Daddy
I don't understand:
What <u>are</u> woods? What's a wolf?
What's a riding hood?

What's a red?'

# ———YASMINE GOONERATNE———

Yasmine Gooneratne holds a Personal Chair in English at Macquarie University, New South Wales, and is also Foundation Director of the University's Postcolonial Literatures and Language Research Centre. Her books include *Jane Austen* (Cambridge UP, 1970), *Alexander Pope* (Cambridge UP, 1976), *Silence, Exile and Cunning: The Fiction of Ruth Prawer Jhabvala* (Orient Longman, 1983), *Relative Merits: A Personal Memoir of the Bandaranaike Family of Sri Lanka* (C. Hurst & Co., London and New York, 1986); and, most recently, a novel, *A Change of Skies* (Picador Australia, 1991), winner of the Marjorie Barnard Award for Fiction in 1992.

YASMINE GOONERATNE

# Why I Write

Primarily, I'd say that I write because I enjoy it. The sheer act of writing is a source of great pleasure for me. In the process of writing poetry or fiction I begin to discover what my deepest concerns and desires are, and I have found to my delight (like a secret gift built into the medium I use) that I have the technical ability to explore them. This is not to say that I write in order to 'express myself' because, frankly, my way of life gives me plenty of opportunity to do that. When I come across 'self-expression' in a book or an article – it's easy to recognize, it's the literary equivalent of posturing before a mirror – it's an instant turn-off as far as I am concerned. I become extremely suspicious of the author's pretensions and motives. The book becomes boring. I abandon it.

By reacting in this way, I've left a fair number of bestselling, even prize-winning books half-read and therefore unreviewed and undiscussed. My conscience, I should add, is perfectly clear on this matter. Life, as I see it, isn't long enough to allow one to read all the good books there are in the world, so why waste precious time reading bad ones?

A second reason for writing is, that I hope one day to create work that will do for its readers what my favourite books do for me: become life-companions, and be frequently re-read by them for the sheer pleasure of it. A third reason is, that as a teacher and lover of the English language, I want to explore its creative possibilities as fully as I can.

The writer who works in English, as I do, has what is potentially one of the largest audiences in the world. I am concerned to see my medium kept as healthy, clean and vigorous as possible. However, a language is shaped by the history of the people who use it, and over many centuries of colonial and patriarchal exploitation the English language has become stained by a vocabulary of denigration unmatched, probably, by any other in the world. Writers who oppose racism or sexism face the intellectual challenge of cleaning up a contaminated medium and, until it is cleaned up, of finding ways to let the spirit of literature breathe within that contamination.

In my homeland, Sri Lanka (as in India), the art of composition is still believed to be a gift of the goddess Sarasvati. In ancient Greece nine Muses were believed to preside over the arts. The old gods may be thought to have lost their power to influence contemporary life, but any one who has had the good fortune to compose an original poem must have some inkling of what it means to be touched, however fleetingly, by forces that are beyond explanation, a power that our ancestors would have called 'inspiration'.

We have different ways today of explaining the process of composition, we might say our writing springs from the memory or the imagination. I have heard some writers describe the moment when imagination takes over from logic and the words flow free as being 'on a roll', of being in 'free fall', or in 'full flight'. But in the end, I think, the experience is the same as it was in the ancient world. There comes a moment when thought and feeling fuse, when memory and the imagination work in harmony, when all five senses are alive and singing, and all of this comes together, flowing through our pens or our fingers on to paper or a computer screen.

There are few moments to match it, I imagine, outside religious or sexual ecstasy. Maybe some active individuals approach it when they are abseiling, hitting a six, winning Olympic gold or climbing Mount Everest. Writing, however, gives you more than a medal or a memory, it results in something permanent, words on the page. In that moment of 'free fall' writing, a writer can transcend what had been previously thought to be his/her capabilities or limitations, can 'snatch [as the poet Pope put it in his *Essay on Criticism*] a grace beyond the reach of art'. It is probably the desire, once we have experienced it, to recapture that moment of supreme achievement, that keeps authors such as myself chained to the pen or the computer screen endlessly working towards the moment when diligent labour turns into enchanted flight.

YASMINE GOONERATNE

# From a Novel in Progress

The island's single international airport was crowded. This, I soon discovered, was because His Excellency the President was expected to arrive any moment now, from a conference he had been attending in Rome. Half the population of the city, seized, it seemed, with a burning desire to welcome him home, had converged on the airport which was decorated as far as the eye could see with coloured banners and huge posters which carried pictures of His Excellency's smiling face. Flag-waving crowds and cheering school-children lined the approach to the airport. It was impossible to get a taxi – security police had cordoned off the taxi rank, and arriving passengers were ushered into an air-conditioned lounge where they were politely told they would have to wait until the President was safely on his way to the city, and the Customs and Immigration desks could re-open for business.

'Oh, *God*! isn't this a pain!'

The young woman who had spoken, half to herself, half to me in the way irritated travellers occasionally do at airports when their itineraries get fouled up, took a book from her carry-on bag and began to read. I couldn't have agreed more. But she was clearly not expecting a response from me, so I bought a copy of the *Daily News* to check out the weather up-country. During my time on the paper the weather forecast had always been on Page One, but the format had obviously changed since I'd left, for I had to work through the whole paper, Local News, International News, Tea Prices, Stocks and Shares, Women and Culture, and Auction Notices, before I discovered the forecast on the Sports page, above the football and cricket scores. And that was how I learned – from Auction Notices – that Mrs Edith Crocker's property was on view that weekend, and was to be auctioned on the following Tuesday.

I hadn't thought of Mrs Crocker in years. But the auctioneer's notice brought her back so vividly to my mind that it was as if she had never left it. 1957. The island's social world had moved up for the 'season' to the misty blue line of the hill country, escaping the heat of April in town. Its members had redistributed themselves among the hill-stations that the British had built in the last century, focusing their attention as the British had done before them on the tennis courts in one little township, on the golf links in another, on the racecourse set among lush green paddocks at the third. The centre of all this activity had been, of course, the Grand

Imperial Hotel, older than the Raffles in Singapore, grander than the Great Eastern in Calcutta. Its sweeping lawns and long reception rooms with their log fires and parquet floors, once venues for Fancy Fetes and Governors' Balls, had become, since Independence, ideal locations for the operation of the local marriage market. There new saris were paraded by young women, and marriages were planned by mothers and aunts, a feverish business from which the men sought refuge in billiards or beer in the Grand Imperial's famous teakpanelled bar.

Not that I'd been involved in any of that. I was a working girl then, as now, with no fond mamma to make matches for me, no papa to negotiate a dowry. As a free-lance journalist, writing occasionally for the Women and Culture page of the *Daily News*, I knew something of what lay behind the glamour: I knew, for instance, that the drinkers in the bar on whose behalf marriage settlements (their daughters' or their own) were being delicately negotiated in the reception rooms didn't give a damn about the fashion show going on upstairs, just as they didn't give a damn about the classes in *haute cuisine* and dress-making in which their daughters or future wives were hopefully enrolling as qualifications for marriage. How did I know this? As a working girl living on her own in a city flat, obviously unattached and far from unattractive, I'd been propositioned too often to remain naive about men, married or single, or to retain many illusions about marriage.

There was a stir and bustle in the airport, and a line of officials snapped smartly to attention. I looked up and I saw, through the thick plate glass that separated our lounge from the main lobby, an imposing figure in snow-white national dress and dark glasses, garlanded with flowers and surrounded by a cordon of security guards.

My fellow passengers pressed forward to have a look at an Asian President, and he, pleased by their respectful attention, folded his hands and smiled, bowing graciously in our direction. I scowled back at him. I recognized him all right, he'd been a Junior Minister in the cabinet that Peter, working in association with his friends in the group they code-named 'Camelot', had gallantly attempted to remove for their country's good by means of an army coup in the fifties.

Who had Peter thought he was? I asked myself, not for the first time. Sir Lancelot of the Lake? Simon Templar? James Bond? And as for 'Camelot' – David, Jeremy, Colin, Nigel and company - who had they thought *they* were? Knights of the Round Table? 'A League of Gentlemen'? Just what had they thought they were doing? Their miserable 'coup', undertaken in the joyous spirit of a *Boys' Own Paper* adventure, ill-conceived and hopelessly mismanaged, had stripped Peter and his friends of their rank and decorations. It had landed some members of 'Camelot' temporarily in jail (where they had had to wake up rather abruptly to living conditions which were certainly medieval), and had pitched others with their families (including Julian and me) abroad, into permanent exile. Yet it was obvious that the same coup which had altered our very lives had been but a tiny hiccup in the political career of the man who was now smiling blandly at me through the plate glass of the airport lobby.

I rummaged in my bag for my passport and immigration card. When I glanced up, the young woman beside me had disappeared. I looked about in vain for her that night in the lobby of my transit hotel. I needed someone to talk to, but could find not a single soul to whom I could relate in a place which was crammed with people, tourists on charter flights from Europe and journalists who, it seemed, were winging into the capital on every jet, intent on filing reports to their papers on what was expected to be the news sensation of the year. I gathered from the animated conversation around me what I had not learned from the Government-controlled *Daily News*, that a push by Government security forces was expected to take place at any moment, an offensive by air, land and sea that the Government hoped would end once and for all the problem posed for the country by the terrorists concentrated in its Northern Province.

Waiting for the news story to break, the journalists sat about in the bar and the lobby, jockeyed for places at official briefings, bribed their way on to helicopters bound for the north, and chatted up middlemen who swore they could fix up interviews for them with terrorist leaders. Everywhere in the hotel telephones were ringing. Barefooted bell-boys raced along corridors carrying telefaxed messages. It wasn't difficult to tell the tourists from the journalists: while the tourists herded like terrified cattle into the comforting waters of the hotel's three swimming pools, the bar rapidly became the headquarters of men equipped with pocket microphones, mini-computers and cameras, trading information and busily comparing notes on their experiences in Cambodia and Vietnam. (Some of them had memories that went as far back as Korea.)

A list had been posted in the lobby for tourists who wished to go on a guided tour of the old colonial city, another for visitors who wanted interviews with Government spokespersons. The old hands among the newspaper-men delightedly took the tour and pointedly scorned the interviews, preferring (where the 'war' was concerned, at any rate) to impress one another with the superiority of their inside information. One was able to tell his drinking companions that the city hotels were flying in bargirls from Bangkok for the benefit of the assembled *paparazzi*. These would be available for viewing from 7 pm that very evening, when the festivities would begin with a cabaret in the hotel's Pink Elephant night-club for which tables were being reserved *now*. Another touched his mates for a ten-rupee note in order to demonstrate from the devices printed on its surface, front and back, an obscene joke at the President's expense that was currently circulating in the city. The *Post* representative had been filling in his time making an in-depth study of island culture. He wanted, he said, to get the background right, and he regaled his comrades with snippets of island history.

'In a society like this,' he said, 'time stands still. What was true in the 5th century B.C. remains true today. Did you pick up yesterday's story about the military commander the Security Forces saved from being walled up and starved to death? Well, it happened in the 10th century, to a chieftain of the Inner Kingdom. His wife saved his life. Granted permission to visit her husband, she pounded rice into a paste and rubbed the paste into her body. When she met her husband, and they were left alone together in the privacy of the prison, he licked the paste off her. Sexy, eh?'

The man from *Time* was researching the colonial period, and had discovered that the area in which terrorists were currently concentrated was one in which Sir Samuel Baker had once dreamed of founding a British colony.

'This was before the old boy went off to explore the source of the Nile. Imported a bunch of English villagers, complete with ploughs and tools and aprons, imported a pack of foxhounds, too, so he could hunt sambhur in the uplands. Built a brewery, a court house and a church, in that order. Ran the place for six years as if it had been a private estate, before giving up the idea and moving on to Africa. I've fixed up an interview for Monday morning with a descendant of one of Baker's villagers, an ancient who's holed up in a nursing home in the city. Monday afternoon I've been promised Padma Devi, queen of the terrorists in that area. Thought it'd make a nice contrast – old colonial Brit, clinging to his life, young Asian revolutionary throwing away hers.'

All night long a typewriter tapped in the room next to mine. I buried my head in my pillow and tried to ignore the noise, but the guest on the other side of the wakeful typist didn't. 'Stop that bloody racket!' yelled a female voice. The protest was accompanied by a furious banging on the sturdy connecting door. The typing ceased immediately, but it was by then five o'clock in the morning. Unable to sleep, I got up, dressed, and went for a walk.

All along the beach front in the early light of dawn, beneath the tossing fronds of a long line of palms, plump, pale tourists were jogging along the promenade or standing in their minuscule beach gear, facing the ocean waves and taking deep breaths of invigorating ozone.

'*Un! deux! trois! quatre! cinq!*' puffed one of the joggers as he thudded past me in his boxer shorts and Reeboks, lifting his white-skinned knees high in the air.

# CHANDANI LOKUGÉ

Chandani Lokugé is Sri Lankan now living in Australia. She came to Australia on a Commonwealth scholarship to work at the Centre for Research in the New Literatures in English at Flinder's University, South Australia. She has recently completed her doctoral thesis.

Her first collection, *Moth and Other Stories* was published by Dangaroo Press in 1992.

CHANDANI LOKUGÉ

# Why I Write

One afternoon, a colleague said to me that one of my students had committed suicide the night before. Sadly, she told me why. I walked away dry-eyed. I felt her eyes bore holes in the back of my head. I sat down at my desk and stared at the wall. I had known this student so well and she enveloped me now with her presence, her innocence and her smile. I had seen her between classes just the other day. I'd thought she looked stressed. But I was rushing madly from one class to the next. And had not the time to speak to her. I turned to the type-writer. And within an hour and a half I had written 'The Falling Star'. I hardly revised it. All thirty pages of 'The Man Within' grew out of a news brief in the *Daily News*. 'The Intruder' happened to a friend. And so it goes.

CHANDANI LOKUGÉ

# Wild Blossom

Shanthi. Shanthi. Let shanthi soothe my mind. But it eludes. The anguished body still lives. And the sporadic screams that rent the silence. I clawed the earth and the foetus struggled to be free. Struggled to push out of the tightening cervix. Father? It cannot be. You do not know of this, yet. You sought from me such glory. And I have failed. I have failed. What have I given you but a useless grand daughter. A curse. Sumana. Sumana, take her away. I must give her away. The blood oozes and soaks the thighs. The body still quivers with remembered spasms. There was passion before. Yes. Rohana would say to me, Rukmali you are so full of passion – you attract chaos. But I have no passion left. I am emptied. Rohana, you and the country. Together, you have sucked it out of me. By the empty well, I thrust the endaru between my legs and through the vagina. Searingly, it penetrated. And it was eight months too late. I was insane. And the hurt struck like lightening. Streaks of lightening. I clutched the pain. I would force it back. But it streaked through the body like the death shriek of friends. Later some of their bodies were thrown into the river. The bodies floated in the water and the swollen river bore them away. All is black-red again and I am a spasm of pain. It tore my insides, the doctor said. The hospital walls are white and stark. The nurse bears a hard cold face. You didn't think of the pain when you conceived the brat? And where is the father? Her words echo like drum beats in a silent night. Or like gun shots. My father. I have shamed and humiliated you. Neighbours will throw stones and buckets of dirt at our front door. I had to do it. I had to get rid of it. I would hide it in the bottom of the shallow well. And it would dry up there wrapped in the scrap of cloth. A stray dog would find it in the morning. And leave no trace. Except the bloodied rag. In the dark hours before dawn, it struggled free of my body. And I held it. I could not drop it in the well. My daughter. Forgive me. I have wronged you. You must live. You have mind and body, feeling and perception. And I will call you Shanthi. And you will be peace.

    The two old people sit by the bedside. The old man stands up tiredly and moving up to the low parapet wall, spits red betel juice into the drain outside. The crow caws loudly, perched on the roof just above. The old man shoos it away, and looks hastily over his shoulder at Rukmali, stirring restlessly on the narrow hospital bed. White as the sheet she is, he mutters – my beautiful flower. But he does not desire her recovery. In all his actions there is love. But he cannot accept what she has become, possessed by Mara and defiled. He presses his fingers to his eyes. He remembers how she was crowned Avurudhu Kumari at the village New Year Festival, two years ago. He hears the cheering. He sees her lovely face and slender form as she walks up the stage. The long dark eyes like blue lotus-buds and the lips like tender na leaves. Long, long black hair. He sees her presented with fresh-hued flowers and crowned with a gold paper crown. As she walks away she turns and smiles with him. And he chokes with pride. She made up for a hundred sons. In every way. Just as her horoscope had predicted. There was no son to till the land, but there was Rukmali. She was destined for greater things than the land. She would bring the family fame and glory. His clever, beautiful daughter. He removes his fingers from his eyes. He gazes at them emptily. They are wet with tears. And calloused. The nails are broken and edged with dirt. What was he but a humble farmer. But he had walked proud and straight because of Rukmali. She had entered the university. *His* Rukmali. No one else in his hamlet had managed that. Not even the magistrate hamudoru's son from the neighbouring big town. He could barely meet the expense. And so he had mortgaged the land even against his wife's wish. What about the rest of the family, she had protested. What about the younger girls? Rukmali will look after them, he had silenced her confidently. When she graduates and gets a good government job, she will support the younger ones. I tilled the land for her, he said, for Rukmali. For no one else. His hands tremble and he lets them drop to his sides. And then suddenly she vanished. Out of his reach. They whispered in the village that she had joined the insurgents. That she lived in the jungles many miles away. They said she was a leader. He knew then that he had lost her. And he wept. When she was a little girl and fell into the mud in the paddy field he had picked her up. He had wiped her legs roughly with his palms and steadied her. When she ran ahead of him again, along the narrow bund, he had warned her, gently, of the mud on either side. He had coerced her swift passionate spirit to the temple where the monk had taught her the dhamma. He had watched her offer flowers at the sacred feet of the Buddha, in a long flowing white cloth. And thought her disciplined at last, and subdued. But she had yearned to fly. And he would not tether her like his buffalo to the threshing floor. When he boarded her in the Central School many miles away from the village, he had said to her – May you achieve your desires. You are a pride to me, daughter, all my hopes bear fruit in you. And he had bestowed on her the blessings of the Triple Gem. There had been sadness in his heart but overriding the sadness, pride and joy.

The crow caws again loudly. The old man walks vaguely out of the ward, picks up a stone and aims it at the crow. It must not disturb Rukmali with its noise. He turns to go back to the ward. The old woman has risen and is bending over Rukmali. He sees her tears fall drop by drop on the blanched face. Rukmali is dead. The light is extinguished. Darkness falls over darkness. What has he now, that his daughter is dead? She is borne away by the strong winds of Mara. His lovely wild blossom, full of vibrant colour; full of potent fragrance. And now she is faded; malodorous and unlovely. Where would her consciousness find refuge? He is spent with the griefs of attachment. Fleetingly, he remembers his two younger daughters. The police had dragged them out of the house, once they had heard about Rukmali's part in the revolution, and had shot them before his eyes. He begins to understand a dhammapada that he had chanted meaninglessly all his life: 'From affection arises sorrow; from affection arises fear; to him who is freed from affection there is no sorrow and there is no fear from anywhere'. Sumana lifts the infant out of its crib and carries it out of the ward. His wife, still bending over Rukmali gazes after Sumana and then turns round and looks at him. But he will not meet her eyes. He would be free. He seeks nothing to rest beneath the bo-tree in the village temple. He begins to walk away.

But father, the child is mine and I will hover over her. Conceived in tortured passion when the full moon sparked impossible dreams. We conceived freedom. Employment! Equality! We would be free of feudal bondage! But we miscarried. And died miscarrying. Later, we dragged out the bodies. Mostly dead. Mostly body parts. Those who still writhed were put to sleep like dogs who were in agony and of no further use. I saw Rohana shoot Asitha through the ear. Rohana who had lain in my arms a few nights before. Our passion was frenzied. There was no time. No time for anything but the guns, the bombs, the freedom we sought – for ourselves, for the country. For our children. We will create a child, Rohana said, yours and mine – for freedom. He will reap the harvest of our toil, Rohana said. We made love. We were not sane. Victory or death was just around the corner. We crouched in the jungle. We awaited the appointed day, the hour. The final night stretched endlessly. Suddenly, the hyena laughed and signalled in human voice. Soldiers swarmed around us. Bullets raped the night. The government did not fall into our hands. We fell into theirs. Those who died were fortunate. I was dragged through the village centre. Later, I was raped by the soldiers at the station. One after another they raped me. I bit my lips and held back the screams. It was cold and brutal. Then they took me away to the prison. My nails were split for information. Eight months later, heavy with child, I escaped. To the well. To the empty well that lay forgotten in the vacant lands behind the university. Whose child have I given life to?

Peace is maya. Happiness is maya. Freedom is maya. I am denied. The consciousness wanders between births. Deluded. But through the infinite distance of my childhood, I hear the temple bells. And the chant of monks. I run to my father. Together, we insert bo-leaves between the pages of my book of scriptures. Each week, out of the golden sand, we pick a fresh green leaf that the tree has just shed. At the end of the year, I flick the pages and the leaves flutter down to the table, in different shades of green-brown. Some are worn away to skeletons. I touch the slight veins on a dried leaf, so fragile and brown. You too will go to the temple, my little one. May you be drawn by its peace like my father was. My first and last wish for you is shanthi.

(Ext. from a novella in progress based on the 1971 youth insurrection in Sri Lanka.)

Ania Walwicz

ANNE BREWSTER

# Ania Walwicz's Vagrant Narration: Cosmopolitanism vs Nationalism in Australian 'Migrant Writing'

Australia is a nation formed by immigration. Nationalism's project is to recuperate or domesticate the centripetal forces immigrant constituencies engender within the culturally homogenous formation of the nation. It aims to construct a national ethno-history but in Australia ethnic constituencies' memory is plural and recent. One means by which compatriots can be turned into co-nationals is through their mobilisation into the vernacular language. Language plays an important role in the construction of any nationalism as it is the medium by which individuals are interpellated as subjects in culture. It has what Etienne Balibar describes as a specifically 'plastic' role in multi-ethnic communities,[1] in the sense that it naturalises new speakers quickly and assimilates them, but without providing the closure and exclusion that nationalism has traditionally needed to function efficiently. This closure has been supplied in the discourse of Australian nationalism by the rhetoric of multiculturalism and ethnicity.[2]

In this paper I examine the work of Polish-Australian writer Ania Walwicz. Her recent book *red roses*[3] exemplifies this 'plasticity' of language and discourse; its emphasis on the performative nature of ethnicity and gender, parody multiculturalism's project of institutionalising memory and museumising ethnicity. By foregrounding the performative body and the performative voice, the text focuses on the fictionality of representation and the instability of meaning and evokes the fluid, shifting and composite space of the traveller. My discussion of *red roses* will suggest that Australian literature is characterised as much by cosmopolitan as by national formations, by figurations of migrancy as much as by those of national situatedness.

*red roses* is clearly a book that hovers on the border between autobiography and fiction. Autobiography has traditionally explored the lives of representative individuals, where representativeness articulates dominant cultural discourses. *red roses* can be seen as similarly representative, but of the collective memory of a minority group, a constituency that has been silent. It is also representatively political in the sense that Deleuze and Guattari describe all minority texts as political.[4] The autobiographies and the memory of minority constituencies cannot be unscrambled from the representations of dominant cultural discourses.[5] However, these representations, I argue, are appropriated and fragmented by minority constituencies' memory in a way that foregrounds their relativity and fictionality. As the text of a minority group that has been silent, the role of memory is very important in that constituency's project of constructing a self. As one shall see from my analysis of red roses, this self is self-reflexive and performative, and interrogates the notion of representation rather than simply replicating dominant discourses. red roses is a fabrication of the self that names itself as such.

Remembering is an important aspect of fabricating a self: 'i believe that a person's life really begins with what they can remember for themselves' (p. 129), states the narrator. Her journey into the past takes as its starting point the image of the mother and makes forays into the past in order to 'return to a former time. I want to buy my time back. I am getting her time' (p. 52). This is a project that is fraught with mismatching and illusion however: 'i am returning to a former time in history books they are telling her stories and mine i'm never just here at the right time' (p. 93). The narrator rejects history, ultimately, in favour of a form of recollection that acknowledges the slippages, the gaps, the unreliability of memory and discourse: 'i wanted to invent myself' she says; 'i was overburdened with all that history' (p. 176). This form of recollection, which gives rise to the collage textuality of red roses, could be compared to Foucault's notions of archaeology and genealogy[6] rather than the conventional discourse of history and the linear narrative of the historian.

In the first few pages of the text the narrator explores fantasies of origin. She seeks out her 'certificate of birth' (pp. 3,15); this is followed by a number of scenarios in which she plays around with plots or scripts which invent different parents ('i was a daughter of barons they left me on her doorstep i was born an egyptian princess' (p. 16); 'my father was an admiral an owner of hotels she was a opera singer' (p. 18); 'my parents were french they were fashionable people farming' (p. 19); 'my parents were nobles in england i was sent to boarding school' (p. 37) etc). These fantasies serve to foreground the fictional and inventive nature of memory.

The journey into the past is one from silence into language: 'i am a beast underground i come up after thirty five years of being hid' (p. 11). The image of being hidden underground in a sub-human state is a metaphor for minority people's condition of being voiceless and invisible. The journey into language starts with making contact (metaphorically) with the mother. This is a dialogic process; the narrator speaks (to) the mother/the text and in turn the mother/the text 'speak' her. The text makes frequent use of the vocative voice as the narrator exhorts the mother to reply: 'will you send me aletter [sic] or a telegram will you tell me ... your address your telegram number' (p. 2); 'please return my letters' (p. 3). Inevitably, there is no response directly from the mother; the process of writing can be seen as the invocation of an addressee/muse who is always necessarily absent. In this way writing epitomises the paradox at the heart of signification or representation, namely that the referent is always absent. The journey in search of the mother/language is thus a journey which never finally realises its destination. The mother symbolises the absent referent which can never be fully realised in language: the narrator describes her and her 'talk' as a phantom and a ghost: 'she is saying me now the phantom talk of mum the ghost' (p. 11). Paradoxically, language, like memory, 'speaks' (from) absence. This paradox, by extension, foregrounds the phantasmatic nature of the metaphors of the mother-tongue and the mother-country so intrinsic to the originary discourse of nationalism.

Although the mother is positioned as the addressee or narratee of the text, there is slippage in the pronoun 'she' which is rarely attached to a proper name, and yet clearly refers to more than one particular woman. Throughout the course of the narrative the pronouns 'she' and 'you' apparently refer to several women, however the lack of differentiation between these women collapses them back into the mother: 'i am writing a letter to you i am writing a letter to mother' (p. 14). The narrator makes this point even more succinctly when she says: 'i substitute one woman for another woman' (p. 170). The narrator also adopts the persona of the mother ('i am writing a letter to my daughter but she won't answer' [p. 85]); in this way the mother is seen to 'speak' the daughter. Writing is thus seen as a dialogue with an absent woman. Ultimately this dialogue is a 'conversation' with or representation of oneself: 'she is writing letters to herself' (p. 14).

The conventions of the narrative strategies of letter-writing by which we invoke and construct both addresser and addressee are parodied in a long sequence which begins as a letter to the narrator's mother and which turns into a love letter, then a letter breaking an engagement, a legal letter, a sympathy letter, a thank-you letter, a letter of introduction etc. (pp. 145-147). This collage of phrases foregrounds the conventionality of written communication; it also announces which rules Walwicz is breaking in this text: she opens the sequence with the statement, 'the sentence can be the beginner' (p. 145), drawing attention to her own delegitimisation of the sentence as the basic unit of written communication. The sequence finishes with the statement that 'excessive punctuation tends to destroy the flow of a piece of writing' (p. 147); this reads like a rule of grammar but it is a rule which Walwicz parodically pushes to its limit.

Through the use of the vocative case in the constant address to the mother, we have a strong sense of the oral transaction of language: the narrator tells us that 'i'm eavesdrop and listening and hearing' (p. 122), that she's garnering her voices from the world around her. This orality in turn evokes the body. There are many references to the mouth and the notion of language as exchange, as something we borrow or steal from other people – a process which the art of the collage-maker and the bricoleuse exemplify – and which never comes to us except by way of someone else ('you have a way with words they get into my mouth' (p. 88). The act of exchanging words is a focal one in the text: the mother often exchanges words by singing (pp. 1, 3) and they are also likened to blood (p. 108) or milk (p. 144) in the mouth. The metaphor of language as food is explored on more than one occasion e.g. pp. 30-31. The pre-Oedipal relationship with the maternal body is evoked here, and language is seen not as an aspect of paternal law (as in Lacan) but as having a somatic function, a continuation of the infant's physical bond with the mother's body. Other women in the text are seen to evoke this bond with the maternal body and to facilitate language in the same way that the mother does: 'you talk her through my trance mouth' (p. 5).

The orality of language is further emphasised in the use of voice as theatre. At one stage the narrator says: 'i am getting ready the scenario the inevitable play script the necessary language i am monsieur and she is countess' (p. 58); 'i speak behind a mask' (p. 88) she adds. These small theatrical 'scenarios' are scattered throughout the text which comprises a collage of 'character' voices ranging from Disney cartoon characters and childhood personae to an array of other voices. The collage represents the range of available discourses and representations from which identity is constituted, discourses and representations which are mobilised playfully in the service of desire: 'i was tired ... of having to be just myself i wanted to be other people too' (p. 175). What Balibar calls the 'plasticity' of language is demonstrated by Walwicz's virtuoso appropriation of different voices in the collage of red roses. Clearly the vernacular language naturalises the writer and assimilates her to a degree but, by the same token, the narrative voice splits into multiple voices, and thus resists the closure that discourses such as nationalism require.

The sense of the voice as theatre foregrounds the performative aspect of language; 'all statements are performative' (p. 119), the narrator tells us and, 'it's not what is said it's in the way of telling' (p. 130). The notion of the self as performative through language is explored principally in the notion of gender, gender 'roles' being epitomised by the various film stars whose voice and image the narrator appropriates at will to fabricate the absent mother and through that metaphor, the self. Ethnicity, like gender, is seen as an assemblage of utterances which can be mobilised in many different ways. In its strategies of pastiche and mimicry, collage promotes thus the play of difference without privileging any discourse over another and avoids the establishment of a hierarchy of discourses. Strategies of pastiche and mimicry are characteristic both of women, for whom femininity is essentially a masquerade,[7] and of minority people whose experience of the dominant discourse is mediated and relativised.

By focusing on language as performance, that is, on its oral and theatrical aspects, the narrative of red roses foregrounds the power of language to fascinate and seduce. Storytelling and the fairy tale have pride of place in this narrative as they epitomise the experience of fantasy. The magician (p. 131) becomes a metaphor for the writer, whose work is likened to invention (p. 128) and make believe (p. 105). Language, like memory, is unreliable and illusory; the writer is a liar (pp. 9, 26, 68) and a stealer of other people words (p. 74). Also, because it lacks linearity and plot, the collage narrative of *red roses* is inconclusive, unfinished and open-ended; like the folk story on page 85, it is made up of repetitions with variations and 'never ends'; with collage, as with memory. 'there's always everything unfinished' (p. 140). Collage, because of its 'vagrant' and random nature, militates against the closure of discourses such as nationalism and multiculturalism which produce reified stereotypes. Ethnicity, like gender, is an assemblage of performative acts and choices; it is open-ended and unfinished.

The emphasis on language as performance and on the self as an assemblage of voices, points to the fact that performance is always in excess of knowledge for, as Spivak would have it, 'knowledge is never adequate to its subject'.[8] The activation of voices in an open-ended collage produces 'a whole composed of parts and bigger than the parts' (p. 58); in the telling of the story meaning proliferates: 'i'm all telling by not telling in that way i tell more and more than i even know' (p. 147). This type of text clearly involves the reader in a highly participative role as the narrator points out:

> i just outline a sketch you never reveal her completely or yourself why do should i you have to make her up i'm just giving suggestions i don't want to say completely and fully i'm just hinting at a story then you just read me carefully the reader participates the reader reads the reader makes me. (pp. 115-6)

So, although the narrator in her playfulness, which lends a high degree of uncertainty and risk to the process of making sense of the text, is essentially seductive, this is not a passive process for the reader. The reading of collage is highly performative because the syntactic breaks and edits signify in a way that is ambiguous and polysemous. The reader actively makes sense of the text in the same way that we actively construct memory.

Language and memory, as I have suggested, are personified by the mother who is a metaphor for the crisis of representation and identity. Originary notions of identity are replaced in *red roses* with ideas of fabrication and constructedness: 'i didn't have a mother i am making one up here to ... fill a gap a void i am making up i am making mum talk' (p. 32). The narrator says 'i'm just making myself from her and many other things' (p. 206) signalling the arbitrary nature of the way we construct our origins in memory. The text's fabrication of the mother draws, as I've mentioned, on the techniques of collage: 'i am sticking toget her [sic] i am attaching with glue out of bits i am making a mother' (p. 12). Memory's *modus operandi* could be said to be that of collage; the narrator constructs the mother from fragments of language: 'i am making up a mother a biography out of what's said' (p. 79). The collage nature of *red roses* is most obvious in the fractured syntax and Walwicz's abandonment of the sentence and of punctuation as the structuring principles of writing. The incongruity of syntactic 'edits' imitates the figurative condensation of metaphor or dreaming.

Another level of collage is demonstrated by the many different discourses whose languages erupt into the text. Many of these are discourses from childhood such as fairy stories, folktales, tv cartoons, comics and nursery rhymes. Others are from the media such as advertising, journalese and popular science; also literary genres such as the detective novel, the romance novel, biographies of film stars, literature and literary theory; and still other genres such as pornography, tour guides, grammar books, women's magazines, travel diaries and the discourse of gardening. On a linguistic level, there is a collage of snippets of French, German and Polish in the text, a multilingualism which creates what the narrator calls 'wordy salads' (p. 77).

As the image of 'wordy salads' suggests, the purpose of collage is not to unify fragments in order to create a coherent, seamless whole but to allow the fragments to maintain their alterity within the whole. The effect is one of randomness and dislocation. Collage encourages a double reading: the fragment is read in both its original context (that is, in relation to its text of origin) and in its new context.[9] In collage intertextuality reigns: 'everything refers a reference' (p. 181). We are reminded of the instability, temporariness and relational and provisional nature of meaning and representation. Discontinuity – between cultures, between childhood and adulthood, and between received representations and the performative aspect of gender and ethnicity – is foregrounded in the collage text of *red roses*.

The formative trope of collage could be described as metonymic rather than metaphoric. Words are found objects rather than moments of originary consciousness. The modes of detachment, readherence, graft and citation evoke the notion of the world as representation and the notion of the constructedness and intertextuality of language; collage thus exemplifies the condition of the diasporic, the migrant, the exile, the tourist, the refugee, the cosmopolitan and the traveller. *red roses* can, in this light, be read as a travel diary, a journal or a map. In this last instance Steven Connor's use of the image of the periplus,[10] which maps out a journey one step at a time rather than providing an overview, is relevant, as the narrative of *red roses* avoids any easy chronological interpretation.

These three genres – the travel diary, journal and map – (and also the genres of tourist guide and phrase books) – are each invoked in the narrative, which moves from place to place (Perth, Sydney, Melbourne, Singapore, Paris, Germany, England, Italy, Poland etc). The journey motif is a dominant one; the narrator announces that 'i am preparing journeys and maps' (p. 98), that 'i have reisen [sic] fieber the fever of travel i am going away soon' (p. 94) and that she is writing 'in my travel diary in my diary of travels' (p. 186). The collage mélange of the narrative, which rarely provides any preamble to a change of setting, invokes both the shifting, fluid world of the traveller and of memory. The narrator's 'lack of a solid world' (p. 206) suggests not only the traveller's sense of space but also the fluid, shifting, 'vagrant' and intertextual nature of representation and signification.

The motif of the journey is also used in the context of the process or passage of reading. The image of the (un)winding thread appears several times and becomes a metaphor for the seduction of the reader. There is an extended passage which starts with the images of first, ravioli, and then a jumper unravelling, and precedes, in a style reminiscent of magic realism, to follow the thread around table and chairs, through a room and a dance etc. In this passage the thread clearly symbolises the narrative thread, and the narrator demands cheekily 'where's the story now answer a comprehension test' (p. 66). She adds to this a confession and a prescription: 'i'm just a fascinator read me slow' (p. 65).

The most frequent use of the journey motif is, of course, that of the pilgrimage to the mother. This journey is a journey into the past and into memory as I have suggested; its map is the map of collage, a map that is not linear but rhizomatic, fragmented and episodic, like language and memory:

> i am trying to solve a riddle or unwind a thread the signs are not systematic they are all intermittent they are flashing on and off i am using an absence in my code a langue i am a signwriter of a sign i am not the i the writer i am just my mum and mums i'm a memory now a flashback. (p. 120)

The pilgrimage to the mother, which concludes in one sense at the Eiffel Tower, is also a 'reverse jurney' [sic] from the past and memory into the present and language (symbolised respectively by the umbilical cord attaching to the mother and by the typewriter): 'a reverse jurney [sic] now i've by now unwound a knot in my stomach a typewriter ribbon' (p. 207).

If textually the collage of *red roses* can be said to invoke representational relativity and 'wandering', and I have titled this paper the 'vagrant narration of Ania Walwicz' to emphasise this idea, collage can be further seen to articulate a political strategy, namely the strategy of migrants and minority constituencies reinscribing themselves not in terms of fixed identities, of an originary, nativist or ethnicist discourse such as multiculturalism, but through mimicry and pastiche of dominant representations. Memory constructs and fabricates a collage from these fragments of discourse and inhabits not the fixed and definitive borders of the multicultural nation but a floating and unstable world, moving along the trajectories of the traveller and the vagrant.

NOTES

1. Etienne Balibar and Immanuel Wallerstein, (*Race, Nation, Class*, London: Verso, 1991), p. 98.
2. Throughout this discussion I use the term 'ethnicity' to invoke the notion of a cultural construct rather than an inherent, instinctual or natural essence. 'Ethnic' markers are always mobilised within specific economic, political and cultural contexts. When mobilised by non Anglo-Saxon minorities in the UK, the USA and Australia, for example, ethnic behaviour and assertion of difference is an expression of resistance to Anglo-Saxon hegemony. When institutionalised, as in the rhetoric of nationalist multiculturalism, the promotion of ethnicity and multiculturalism masks many kinds of difference and conflict, for example, of class relations. See Marie de Lepervanche, 'From Race to Ethnicity', *ANZIS*. 16 (1), 1980, pp. 24-37.
3. Ania Walwicz, *red roses* (St. Lucia, Queensland: University of Queensland Press, 1992). All references to *red roses* are to this edition and are included in the text.
4. Gilles Deleuze and Felix Guattari, 'What is a Minor Literature?' in *Mississippi Review*. 22 (3) pp. 13-33, p. 16.
5. See the work of the Popular Memory Group on this issue. Popular Memory Group, 'Popular memory: theory, politics, method', in *Making Histories*, eds. Richard Johnson et. al. (London: Hutchinson in association with the Centre for Contemporary Cultural Studies, University of Birmingham, 1982), p. 211.
6. Michel Foucault, *The Order of Things: An Archeology of the Human Sciences* (London: Tavistock, 1970); *The Archeology of Knowledge and the Discourse on Language*, trans. A.M. Sheridan Smith (New York: Pantheon Books, 1972).
7. Joan Riviere, 'Womanliness as Masquerade', in *Formations of Fantasy*, eds. Donald and Cora Kaplan (London:Methuen, 1986).
8. Gayatri Chakravorty Spivak, *In Other Worlds*. (New York: Methuen, 1987), p. 254.
9. Marjorie Perloff, *The Futurist Moment: Avant-Garde, Avant-Guerre and the Language of Rupture* (Chicago: University of Chicago Press, 1986), p. 47.
10. Steven Connor, *Postmodernist Culture* (London: Basil Blackwell, 1989), pp. 227-228.

# NEW ZEALAND

# PATRICIA GRACE

Patricia Grace was born in Wellington in 1937. She is of Ngati Raukawa, Ngati Toa and Te Ati Awa descent. Patricia lives on ancestral land in the coastal suburb of Plimmerton, near Wellington. She is married with seven children. Her first novel, *Mutuwhenua: The Moon Sleeps* (1975) was short-listed for the New Zealand Book Awards and was followed by a collection of short stories, *The Dream Sleepers* (1980). *Potiki* (1986) her second novel won the New Zealand Fiction Award in 1987. Since then she has published two more collections of stories and a novel. Her new collection of short stories, *The Sky People*, Penguin, from which 'Flower Girls' is taken, was published in 1994. Patricia has written three books for young children – *The Kuia and the Spider* (1981), which in 1982 was awarded Picture Book of the Year, *Watercress Tuna and the Children of Champion Street* (1988) and *The Trolley* (1993). These three books are accompanied by Maori language editions. *Wahine Toa* (1984) is a book of paintings by Robyn Kahukiwa, depicting women in Maori mythology, for which Patricia wrote the text. In 1989 Patricia Grace received an Honorary Doctorate in Literature from Victoria University, Wellington, New Zealand.

PATRICIA GRACE

# Why I Write

Sometimes when I am asked why I write I say it was because my father was a stationery manufacturer and I always had plenty of paper to write on. However, reading and writing was always something that interested me. As a child I was not an extrovert so that writing was one means of self-expression.

PATRICIA GRACE

# Flower Girls

When the big man died people began arriving at the gates at five in the morning, waiting to be called at daylight, shifting in their coats and rugs and passing the envelope. Cigarette tips spotted the dark.

While one group was being called, more cars and buses would arrive and another group would prepare itself. This kept up throughout two days from early morning to nightfall.

The women doing the calling and the men making the speeches had to have a rotating system so they could have time to eat and sleep. The cooks never got off their feet, nor did those who were cleaning and setting up tables every hour, and nor did the ones who were bringing in supplies.

Once it became obvious that the usual facilities wouldn't cope with the numbers of people arriving, a marquee was put up as an extra dining room and truckloads of mattresses were borrowed from another marae and put down in the assembly hall of the local college.

Both out on the marae and in the house many words were spoken about the man and his work. The family itself, as well as the managers of catering, accommodation and protocol, made sure that nothing that could be done was left undone in order to honour the man at the time of his attaining his ultimate chieftainship. Visitors came with full envelopes to put down.

The big man wasn't big. He was small in build and stature, and the brothers and nephews who carried him into the meeting house held a light load.

When the lid was removed, and beneath the flow of words from the minister and as the cloaks, ornaments, photographs and flowers were placed, there was satisfaction expressed that a good job had been done by the undertakers. This husband, father, brother, cousin, friend, who had become a bone of his usual self during his illness, now appeared as if in reasonable health. In fact he was young and smooth again, round-cheeked almost. His jaw had been frightened into a suggestion of a smile to show that he had died peacefully.

His sister and sister-in-law were the ones who had seen to it that he was dressed in his best for his final journey and that his badges, service medals and ribbons were displayed in a suitable way amongst the more ancient treasures on the casket.

So everything was all right. Everything was as it should have been for such a man – that is, except for the blight of his daughters all named after flowers. They were Hyacinth, Violet, Lilac, Verbena and Marigold.

Hyacinth was the most un-flowerlike. Summer and winter, over her great pod of a body, she wore sleeveless tent dresses splitting beneath pouchy underarms. Curved under her bluish rolls of feet she wore sandals no matter what the weather. Her face was a great round cake. In fact she had two faces, the large cake-face being centred by the little face that had been hers when she was a girl. She was butter-coloured, untouchable, and she wheezed in late on that first day smelling of mutton and cabbage, crying hideously for Daddy.

No one would have thought it inappropriate for Hyacinth to cry and call out for her father if she's been anywhere in sight during the time of his illness. But he'd been in hospital, dying, for some weeks before being brought home to spend the final week of his life. In all that time she'd visited him just once. That one time she'd been up and down, in and out like a fretting animal. So calling for Daddy now, splashing tears, keeping the minister waiting, didn't go down very well with those who knew.

And afterwards, instead of staying there by the man, Hyacinth left the meeting house and went to the dining room, where she bungled about getting in the way of workers who were trying their best to respect her as a bereaved daughter. Two aunts came out and cornered her at last, spoke hard in her ears and took her out to the house, where they put a rug round her shoulders and sat her by her mother. The sister and sister-in-law managed to keep her there, shut up, for the rest of the day.

Violet came in at dusk on the first day wearing a full-length leather coat with fur collar and lapels, dosed to the eyeballs and unable to manage her own two feet. She had left home at fifteen to tote herself up and down the waterfront. It was an easy way to make money, though it wasn't money she wanted then. If she had been asked what it was she wanted, she may not have been able to bring to articulation the word 'forgetting'. But it was 'forgetting' that being laid, paid, robbed and jabbed with cigarette ends could help her do.

At nineteen she married a man of moderate means, and in the five years after that had three children.

But she had a habit as well. In the end she left the children with their father and went back to business. In spite of all this, deep inside herself she knew she was half sensible. She could feel it sometimes. One day she'd beat the habit, find Roxy, Maadi and Palace, who would love and adore her, and there'd be a new life for all of them.

When this Violet came in, strung between two friends, it was some younger cousins who managed to put the coat and her belongings into the boot of a car for safekeeping, roll her in a blanket and put her into a corner amongst the pillows, out of the way, faintly snoring.

Lilac was the one who had been saved by the Lord, but it was only her soul that had been saved. Sickness was eating away at all the guilty places of her, and the women had made a bed up for her by the man and helped her to get comfortable there. Medication allowed her to sleep, and each time she woke, the aunts washed her face and hands, tidied her hair and propped her up on pillows.

The one called Verbena had become unhinged years before, and during the time of her father's illness had had to be readmitted to hospital while the family coped. No one could stop her from laughing. She wasn't brought in until the evening of the second day, tranquillised but still giggling. However, people knew they should tolerate this. Verbena was a loved one, a special one, as was Lilac too. This was mentioned several times in speeches so that everyone would understand.

Marigold, who was the youngest, had run away to save herself when she was ten. She'd been encouraged to do this by Lilac, the good one, and had spent two years living on the streets, sleeping under bridges and in old buildings. She'd learned to steal and sniff glue, but somehow she felt this wasn't really her style. One day she went looking for Violet, of leather and fur, who took her in, gave her clothes and thirty dollars and told her to go and get a room, a job as a waitress and to work herself on from there, which she did.

Her first job was in an all-night café, midnight until eight in the morning, and what she liked most about it was being warm in the night and eating. At the time of her father's death she was working as a receptionist-cashier in a restaurant specialising in deep-fried family meals. Sometimes for this job she was required to wear clown clothes, pirate outfits or animal suits, and to paint her face in different ways. This was something she enjoyed. She was beige-coloured and had eyes like sea anemones. She had a boyfriend too, and a taste for top shelf.

Now she was twenty and, though she came home fortified with bourbon, she was, at least, on her own two feet, which were in their own diamante stockings and in their own spike-heeled shoes. She was the last of the sisters to arrive. Because she had left home at such an early age, she knew nothing of protocol and strode onto the marae in her skimp of a skirt and sat at the end of the paepae, chewing. But she was put into place after a while, with only the next day to go.

All of the flower-named ones had been beautiful and sister-looking when they were little girls, was what everyone said. The aunts were nearly exhausted as they went about doing what they could to make the behaviour of the sisters less conspicuous.

It was the mother, wife of the man, that everyone felt sorry for. She deserved better in the way of daughters, especially at a time like this. She'd been a true support to the man in all that he did. She'd been a loving mother. It was said over and over again.

Actually the aunts could've wished for a little more responsiveness from their sister at this time. The occasional trickle from their sister's eyes they thought insufficient, really, though when they thought about it they realised she'd always been pasty. And they didn't think the smock and cardigan appropriate either for such a big occasion, but they were kind and didn't say so. After all, their sister was exhausted after their brother's long illness and there was not one daughter with sense enough to be of use to her.

However, on the day of the burial they insisted on lending her some clothes. They couldn't let the newly widowed sister send their brother off dressed the way she was, not when he'd always been so particular. It was bad enough the daughters being circuses.

They helped her while she dressed, and locked themselves either side of her when the time came to follow the casket to the cemetery ahead of the large crowd.

At the graveside the mother just waited the time through, letting go a thin sigh as the shovels mounded the last of the earth over the big man. After that she allowed herself to be taken back to the wharenui, and allowed herself to be cheerful when it was the right time.

She was the only one who knew what good girls her daughters really were. They were good girls, deserving of the names of flowers, who had kept the secret of themselves and the big man – kept the secret, kept the secret, kept the secret.

# LAURIS EDMOND

Lauris Edmond grew up in Greenmeadows, a small country town in New Zealand. She trained as a teacher and speech therapist and then went back to living in small towns as the wife of a school teacher and, eventually, the mother of six children. She has written poetry in private since childhood, but did not publish her first collection until 1975. *In Middle Air* won the PEN Best First Book Award. She went on to publish nine other volumes of poetry, including the *Selected Poems* which won the Commonwealth Poetry Prize in 1985, and, more recently, *New and Selected Poems* from which she has been reading on a tour of Germany and England. In 1986 she was awarded an OBE for services to literature and in 1988 an Honorary Doctorate of Literature by Massey University, Palmerston, North New Zealand. She has published a novel, a number of plays, and a three-volume autobiography. She lives in Wellington, New Zealand.

LAURIS EDMOND

# Why I Write

My primary impulse is a private, individual one – a powerful urge to say the unsayable; this is one of the ways in which I think of poetry, its purpose and function. The desire to make sense of the amorphous and chaotic experience of living is part of this; I can't do better than quote Picasso: 'Art stabilises us on the edge of chaos'. From as far back as I can remember in my growing up, the way to 'make sense' was through words, so I have a lifelong passion for the power and intricacies of language. I write to discover, not to tell what I know. The flash of something new (even if in one sense familiar) is where a poem begins; the writing of the poem elucidates for me what that first glimpse meant.

But because I live in a young, small, remote country there has always been another less defined reason for being a writer. This is that the collective urge to define ourselves as a new and cohesive society, a nation, is still very strong here. Before I had published a single poem (I wrote for many years before I tried to publish my work), I knew that there had been few writers who had tried to re-create the authentic experience of life in these islands, and fewer still who were women. I did not know then, though I do now, that there was a significant prejudice operating against women who presumed to enter what was seen as a male field.

I published my first volume of poems in 1975, at a time when this climate was changing. That was International Women's Year, and this new consciousness came, here as elsewhere, after some years of vigorous re-examination of women's own attitudes and habits. The late 60s and early 70s was the time of 'consciousness raising', and among other effects was a great burgeoning of women's writing. The whole movement had great significance for me. In simple terms, it gave me the courage to express a view of the world I had always till then kept secret.

I have now published a three-volume autobiography, which I set out to do in order to define and document the changes and the upheavals brought about by this revolution in my life and work. As it has turned out, these volumes have been read by many women as their own story, despite obvious differences in detail.

But first, for ten years I wrote poems constantly, and published, on average, a book a year - a state of hyperactivity which was, no doubt, one effect of finally breaking the unnatural silence of my first 50 years. I also began to travel. This is the habit of islanders like ourselves, but for me it had, like much else, been delayed till middle age. This widened my view of my place in a broader scheme of things, and gave me, by one of the paradoxes of travel, a stronger sense of my identity as a woman, a writer, a New Zealander. I met women from other countries and cultures whose experience held parallels with my own; I felt both more local, and more universally a woman writing of my time and my generation.

I should add that my long 'apprenticeship of silence' was not spent in some kind of waiting inactivity. Conforming to the dictates of my conditioning – as we now know to call it - I married and brought up a family, as it happened a large one. I do not, of course, regret my maternal function, but even in a literary sense I now believe that beginning to write in one's middle years has certain advantages. You have a kind of inner assurance (however unsure you may be on the surface) that expresses itself as the voice in your writing.

The Nineties are for me the post-autobiography period. I have as it were recovered from that five-year labour, and am writing poetry again, with a freedom I appeared to have lost during that time. I also plan to write my second novel. But the interesting discovery for me is that the inclination towards poetry rather than prose is still there, though it may have been in abeyance for a time. I surmise that it is to do with typical – and preferred – kinds of intellectual and emotional response. I don't, characteristically, want to make up stories about what I see and know, as I think novelists do. I see quick flashes, encapsulated stories if you like, without the development of plot or theme; I like to try and grasp the experience all in one. I don't know why this is so, and neither perhaps do other writers, poets nor fiction writers. An intriguing question.

# Lauris Edmond

## A FINE NIGHT IN THE CITY

At midnight in the breathing dark
I walk through my house: it is
lit from beyond itself by the light

of the city, translucence of
moonlight, white stars asleep on
the harbour water. This is home,

I whisper, amazed; this is where
I live. If anything is mine it is this
vision, this luminous gift held out

to the unknowing dark. Last week
I was busy about the world's airports
pursuing the traveller's ridiculous

industry of survival, each moment
bursting with trifles like over-stuffed
luggage. In this stillness I neither

lift nor handle, I stand at the window,
weighing nothing, carrying nothing.
I breathe, and the light grows

within me. Home is where your life
holds you in its hand and, when
it is ready, puts you quietly down.

## TAKING DOWN CHRISTMAS DECORATIONS

I was first in this room twenty years ago,
alone - I crouched over there on a bare floor
and leaned on the low window sill;

without knowing it, I was looking for signs –

the future. Any future, I wanted.
Time that would know how to pass, how to take on
one by one the difficult days
at the end put each one
carefully, steadfastly to rest.

A place too. A new place, where the death which had made
vagrants of us in our own house, and now followed us
everywhere, might sit down and speak at last
with a low-toned, trusting sorrow:

I looked out on this lumpy hillside garden,
the shifting sea, felt the October sun
strike coolly across the empty floor
and I made some kind of wordless affirmation
to weather and water, the harsh and tangled growth
of hillside plants. A small wind came up, I remember.

This Christmas children were here, perched on
the furniture, tacking up cardboard stars and trees,
reaching up to tie shiny things
to the tree's bristled branches, its piney smell
fresh and sharp. This morning as I drag it over the floor
the smell still hangs within its spikey niches.

Always after celebration there are small griefs,
a coming down, the old apprehensions still waiting about
unchanged. Yet I am glad to be here. We have
neither solved nor relieved our loss; rather
it has come with us,
we live in its constant knowledge. Each Christmas is now,
or the last one she spent with us,
or perhaps next year –

and hills are instructive: whatever grows here,
each green cell, each pinprick of sap,
knows in its very fibre that to live and breathe at all
is to act provisionally.

At the door I look out to pohutukawas
burgeoning all over the hillside,
their lavish blooms so lightly held
that even by tomorrow
those imperial crimson threads
will already have begun to blow away.

# POSITIONING

In a rainy spring my house is often dark;
I stand at a window watching it drift past,
the grey and silver weather; closer in,
there's a box of curled impatiens flowers
holding up minute green saucers to the rain
on my bedraggled but luxuriant balcony.

Here is the action, of course I stand and stare.
It's beautiful, this expanse of growth and
seasons, nights and rainy days – and it is mine,
which is to say I am enclosed within it.
An imprisonment benign, magnificent, and no less
ruthless for being what I exactly chose.

Downhill, in the bus shelter at Courtenay Place,
the old man will be staring outwards too, his
ancient tweed unkempt, his yellow beard
tattered at the edges. He'll watch the rain,
its gentle remorseless wetting of his entrances
and exits – he who has so many, and so few.

His eyes are watery, blue-white, alight with
calculation, his wits continually at work
pursuing restless appetites – a roof, a drink,
a word. I shiver at his journeys in the rain
and frost, the thirst that drives him over gritty
asphalt, his only gardens City Council plots –

and turn back to my dim interior: it seems
that I, directing my wayward years towards
this privacy - and dryness in the rain - now have
what he must struggle for. Yet each of us
has chosen our servitude. Like rain, our
inward seasons drive, confine us, equally.

## THE SEVENTH DECADE

I am not a battery hen
I am free range.
Distance opens around me
filled with the cloudy weather
of other peoples' lives.

Their sharp rain chills me too
of course, but they
do not know
of my nesting.
It is in the deep hillside

it changes
and draws me further and further
away. It is not
one place. It is unknown
even to me.

## SHE

It's late, she's got time at last to sit still
with a cup of tea – or rosehip syrup perhaps,
or flower water, or a mud-and-parsnip-leaf

concoction left out by children now mercifully
asleep; her feet stir a coloured mosaic of
Lego pieces to find a place, and her eyes fall

on a blue hem still to be stitched, as she
fingers her way through more mystifying
fragments the day has left lying about,

unseen now but alive as a nest of spiders
(those fierce tears, the kicking, a fainting  ...)
She's tired, and beautiful in her tiredness,

not in the allowed way (a mother's such a servant
for decency's sake you say she's pretty), but
because pieces of the life she cares for remain

in her, on her, a crystalline magnetic collage,

reflecting not only children picking their noses
and discovering God peering out of their belly-

buttons, but the presence of the oldest goddess,
her peasant spirit waiting still in this warm
crumpled kitchen, with a capacious wisdom that daily

connects danger and dirt with the songs of the stars
– waiting, I say, for the homage long, long due
from her race, and never sufficiently given.

## AUTUMN IN CANADA

Naturally, it's the fall – what else could it be,
this loosening, letting go, these faint purposeful
dry showers, the crushed mosaic under my feet?
The fall. It passes through me with an airy rustle,

as though I too relinquish a burden – all that earlier
bursting out and youthful fullness, the imperceptible
change to a more attenuated quality, a leaning or
slackening, the occasional quick-smothered yawn

that tells you (or would if you listened) that a seasonal
wind will one day take from you what you have already
long been losing. Beside me on the grass are hundreds
of big dark birds: 'Canada geese' says an old woman

on a bench, 'they come every year.' I stand close but
they don't care, sea birds awkward on land, yet not wild,
carrying within their oddly asymmetrical bodies a map
of the seasons they too know by watching for signs.

# SINGAPORE
and
MALAYSIA

# CATHERINE LIM

Catherine Lim is a writer in Singapore. She has published seven collections of stories, three novels, and
a book of poems. Two of her short story collections
were used as literature texts in the G.C.E. O Level
Examinations conducted by Cambridge University,
College, Australia. Some of the books have been
translated into Chinese, Japanese and Tagalog. Before
she became a full-time writer, Catherine Lim, who
holds a Ph.D. in Applied Linguistics, was a lecturer
in RELC (Regional Language Centre), Singapore,
training teachers from Southeast Asian countries in
the subjects of Sociolinguistics and Literature. To
maintain her  links with the academic and
professional worlds, she continues to give lectures at
seminars and conferences both at home and abroad.
She is divorced and has two grown-up children.

CATHERINE LIM

# *Cheongsam* Misadventures

I was therefore all ready for the grand conquest, envisaged as comprising a series of individual conquests, as my *cheongsam* and I cut a victorious swathe through the decks, corridors and glittering function rooms of the QE2 denizens.

Alas once more for the gap between proposal and disposal! *Cheongsam* misadventures they turned out to be, not the glories I had imagined.

The first was on the very evening after the story-telling debacle. The dress code was formal. I chose a bright red *cheongsam* with small green bamboo patterns, and delicate piping of exactly the same shade of green at the collar, sleeves and hem. A row of three green frogs sat demurely on my right shoulder. Bright red being a lucky Chinese colour that brings happiness and prosperity, I was hopeful of quickly securing the first through the second. As if in answer to my wish, a very prosperous-looking gentleman suddenly materialised in front of me. I had not seen him before; it was possible that he had newly arrived on the ship. I was sitting in one of the plush green velvet chairs lined along the side of the ship, looking out at the ocean, in the half hour before dinner. The gentlemen was prosperous-looking by the one unfailing Chinese criterion: he had an enormous paunch. (This could be explained by the Chinese instinct to equate prosperity with eating. A large male belly meant food in excess and running over, to benefit others, including wives and concubines. It became a general symbol of happiness, peace and well-being, hence the representations of Buddha and monks as pot-bellied in well-known Chinese paintings and sculptures in no way contradicted their asceticism.)

Other criteria were fulfilled by the gleaming expanse of the gentleman's forehead, the largeness of his nose, the length and fullness of his ear-lobes and the fleshy substance of his hands, all of which I registered within the first few seconds of his appearance. His large hands laid comfortably on his enormous tuxedoed girth, he surveyed me with intense interest, as if I were an alien on the ship. When he saw me look up at him, his large florid face broke into a smile.

'May I sit here?' he asked, indicating a seat next to mine. Then, as if suddenly realising he was unfairly imposing his own language upon an alien, he said, slowly and painstakingly, 'You Chinese, Japanese? You speak some English, yes?' I nodded. He looked at me with increasing

patronage. He pointed to the *cheongsam* and said 'Nice dress, this. Yes?'
Then he pointed to himself and said, 'I Charlie. From the United States of
America. You know Ama-ri-ka? Yes? Where you from?'

I said, 'Singapore, which, by the way, is NOT a part of China as some
Americans still think. Yes, I speak some English. It is not my native
language but an imposed colonial language which I suppose I speak well
enough to communicate with any well-meaning gentleman on the QE2.
And yes, I know the United States of America, but I fear my knowledge
has been influenced by those TV programmes which you have been
exporting to the world and which show the least commendable aspects of
your culture.'

The gentleman stared at me. Then he looked away and exclaimed,
'Jesus!' pressing a finger to his forehead. Then he turned back to face me,
exploding in a series of sharp barks of pure astonishment: 'Hey, this is
wonderful! You speak English real good, without an accent! Isn't that
something? Hey, I'm sorry. I was an idiot. A blundering fool. Please
forgive me. I couldn't place you, was why. In that dress. Marvellous dress
that. Hey, I'm real sorry.' He was genuinely contrite.

I could not resist, though, telling him the well-known anecdote about an
American socialite who was seated next to a very silent Chinese gentleman at dinner, trying to make conversation with him by saying, 'Likee
fishee? Likee soupee?' When it was time for the speeches, she was
astonished to see the Chinese gentleman get up and address the gathering
in flawless English. Sitting down again, the gentleman smiled at her and
said, 'Likee speechee?'

'Likee Speechee! Likee speechee!' echoed Charlie in booming enjoyment,
almost choking in his laughter.

'Isn't that something?' he said finally, wiping his eyes. 'Hey, wait I tell
my folks back home.'

As if to make up for his presumptuousness in doubting that I could
speak his language, he now insisted on learning some words of mine.

'What do you call this marvellous dress?' he asked.

'*Cheongsam*,' I replied.

The word sounded strange to his ears. He tested it on his tongue
gingerly, like some strange spice. Then he got ready to mobilise the full
range of his vocal equipment for the task of properly articulating this most
exotic word. It kept eluding him, tying up the poor vocal organs in a
hopeless jumble of sounds that belonged to no human language. But
Charlie would not give up, and at last came up with some semblance of
the word.

'Shawn-sam,' he said, looking at me hopefully.

'That's close enough,' I said quickly, not wanting to witness more of that
fearful oral struggle.

'Shawn-sam,' he boomed, beaming.

He had on his face the pure delight of a small child who has at last mastered some intricate operation in a toy. Like a small child, he needed confirmation of his triumph, so he kept repeating 'shawn-sam'. Gaining confidence, he wanted the word expanded into a sentence and asked me to teach him a full Chinese translation for 'I like the *cheongsam* very much.' With growing weariness, I did, leading him through a tedious practice session from which he emerged even more enthusiastic, repeating the sentence endlessly until I thought I would grow quite mad from it. By the time we went to dinner, he was still murmuring 'shawn-sam', like a mantra. His interest, so promising at the beginning, had become purely academic.

Then I realised I was witnessing a rare but very real phenomenon of form overtaking substance, of abstraction superseding reality. The good gentleman, caressing the name of the *cheongsam*, had become oblivious of its reality. Silky sinuousness and high slits had been left behind for a mere linguistic abstraction. I had never thought the *cheongsam* could be subverted by its own name.

The subversion was complete when the gentleman said happily to himself, 'I'm going to write it down, so that I won't ever forget it. Isn't that something?' And he pulled out a little notebook, opened it at a pristine page, took out his glasses, put them on and carefully wrote the word down with the full absorption of the research-scholar.

My next *cheongsam* adventure involved a very old gentleman, possibly one of the oldest on the ship. He was English, aged eighty-six, either divorced or widowered and clearly enjoying his freedom. He was one of those octogenarians who are interesting for the harbouring of a robust libido in a very frail body. Indeed, the vigour of this particular aspect of the gentleman's constitution could only be guessed at by his exclusive choice of female company. Wherever he was – in the boat decks, the games decks, the shopping arcade, the restaurants, the lido, the function rooms – he sought to be close to the young waitresses, stewardesses, shopgirls, croupiers and the not-so-old female passengers. However, so much libidinal buoyancy in a general wreckage of sagging skin, spotted hands, knotty legs, rheumy eyes, wispy hair and quavering voice meant that a great deal of his life must be lived in the imagination only. In the imagination, he must have divested a long line of sun-bathing and sauna-frolicking ladies of their swimsuits and bikinis, and dancing or gambling ladies of their sequined gowns. By the way he studied the straps of swimsuits, the zips of shorts and sundresses, the buttons of shirt-fronts, one could tell that he was already happily engaged in the different stages of divestment.

Paralleling the intense life of the imagination was an equally obsessive concern about his health. I had never seen anyone who carried around so many bottles of pills which would appear from inside his jacket, shirt, coat, trousers at various times, the pills shaken out gently into a cupped hand and popped into the mouth. I suspected that these were a desperate means to narrow the wide gap between the health of his body and that of his libido. I also suspected that in the event of a decision involving a conflict between the two, the health of his body would be the more important consideration. Having almost reached the Biblical ideal of four score years and ten, he was not about to squander it all away by some foolish adventure that would cause the old heart to fail. Meanwhile, with the help of the pills and frequent checks in the ship's hospital, this English gentleman whose name was Robert, was able to pursue a thoroughly enjoyable and unique life of double-barrelled pleasure: innocent open flirtation and not-so-innocent secret disrobement.

It would only be a matter of time before the *cheongsam* came within his amatory orbit. Which it did, three days after the disappointment of Charlie's misdirected zeal. He saw me in the QE2 Grand Lounge, after the cabaret was over and people were getting ready for the late-night dancing. He told me, with the bold confidence that only very old gentlemen could have towards much younger women they are accosting, that he had been observing me for some time, and that the pants and shirts I wore during the day were far less flattering to the figure than the *cheongsams* I wore in the evenings. He learnt the name easily but preferred to refer to it as 'your Chinese dress'. Over drinks, he talked freely, his eyes keenly taking in every detail of the *cheongsam* which on this occasion was pale pink with the three frog buttons of the same material. Now with the light colours, the contours of the *cheongsam* are made even more conspicuous, and no true *cheongsam*-wearer is unaware of this fact.

The free flow of talk was interrupted only by his twice reaching inside his jacket to pull out a bottle of pills. The first time he shook out a brown capsule, the second time, two little green pellets.

I ventured to ask what they were for.

'My heart,' he said. 'I must take good care of my heart.'

The heart being thus taken care of, he now proceeded to feed his eyes, which ran the whole length and breadth of the *cheongsam* with the connoisseur's expert scrutiny. Soon I became aware of a look of growing puzzlement on his face. I was myself puzzled until, by observing that he was craning his neck a little here and twisting it a little sideways there, I realised that he was trying to establish the various points by which the fortress of the *cheongsam*'s virtue might be stormed. There being no visible sign of hook, button or zip, the gentleman became exceedingly perplexed. Then his eyes rested on the frog buttons which he began to study intently. An expression gradually appeared on his face, accompanied by certain slight movements of his fingers that unmistakably told his imaginary assault on them had already begun. His excitement on making the Great Uncovery was itself exciting to behold.

Now, as I had earlier mentioned, uncompromising tightness is the very essence of frog buttons which comprise small, firm, round heads of cloth forced through the narrowest loops. No self-respecting *cheongsam* tailor would have them otherwise. The buttons, once done, defy even the deftest male fingers. If Alexander the Great had been Chinese, he would have had to cut through not one but three Gordian knots. The arthritic fingers of octogenarians therefore stand not a chance. By the time they struggle through to the third and final button, a combination of the physical exertion and the mental anticipation will have rendered the undoer unfit for anything else. Worse, the strain may prove too much for an old heart. Of course, all this can be avoided by the simple expedient of securing, from the start, the lady's cooperative efforts. But for intrepid, committed disrobers like Robert, that would rob the exercise entirely of its pleasure.

All this must have going through the gentleman's mind, for a thin film of sweat appeared on his brow. He wiped it with a silk handkerchief and took out another pill. I thought it was to fortify himself for the next round of assault but clearly it signalled defeat. He said he was feeling tired and would like to retire for the evening. The *cheongsam* beginning as libido-challenging, had ended as life-threatening. While alarmed by the fact that it seemed to be having a life of its own and was taking me along the most unexpected paths, I nevertheless accorded it the increased respect it deserved.

'The cruise is not even half way through,' I consoled myself, 'and there may be happier outcomes yet.'

We were approaching Bombay. How could I have guessed that at this stage in the cruise, the *cheongsam* was to suffer its great humiliation?

Two days before reaching Bombay, the *cheongsam* caught the attention of a gentleman who, to my secret delight, was more elegant and younger-looking that either Charlie and Robert. Indeed, he came quite close to the image of the ideal gentleman whom middle-aged women on a pleasure boat dream of meeting – tall, slim, tanned, exuding confidence, with elegantly greying hair and equally elegantly greying sideburns. I was having a pre-dinner drink with someone I had earlier met, an Australian lady named Laura who, during the day, wore amazing T-shirts with slogans such as 'Downunder, not Downandout' blazing across the enormous expanse of the chest and in the evenings, dense black outfits with strange mythical animals in rhinestone. She wore only silver ornaments and her favourite ear-rings were a pair of long scimitars that flashed and slashed dangerously each time she threw back her head and laughed, which was very often. I noticed that the bartender, a reserved hollow-cheecked young Turk, twitched nervously each time the scimitars swung in his direction, probably conjuring some painful ancestral memory.

Laura had been to Singapore and Hongkong many times, she told me, enticed back again and again by the famous steamed chicken and roast duck, suckling pig and Emperor's goose. Her greatest complaint was: how did Chinese women in the midst of the world's greatest gastronomical delights, manage to stay slim while their Australian sisters ballooned within a week?

'Won't I need at least six of these to get into?' she shrilled, pointing to my *cheongsam*, and laughed seismically, spilling her drink.

The gorgeous-looking gentleman came in, looked around, walked straight to our table and asked if he could join us. Now in the presence of a promising gentleman, there was a distinct advantage in having someone like Laura around. This advantage, which I confess I was quick to exploit, was the effectiveness with which a very large figure, side by side with a slim, *cheongsam*-clad one, could become its best advertisement. Advertise me Laura did, not just by being there, solid and immovable, but by loud declamations to the gentleman, as soon as he was seated, of the unfair slenderness of Singapore and Hongkong women.

'Don't I envy them their slender bird-waists, their tiny ankles?' she decried rhetorically and added plaintively, 'and just look at me! Is it fair, I ask you?'

The gentleman gallantly complimented her on the vibrant red hair, then turned his full attention on to the *cheongsam*. It was a green one this time with sprays of purple orchids, and double piping of purple and green. The frogs were also in purple and green, twisted around in an ingenious blend. I had on a pair of jade ear-rings that were exactly the same green shade of green and carried a gently scented fan of pale green silk (non-functional, purely ornamental, as the ship was fully air-conditioned), presenting myself as the very essence of Oriental-tropical exoticism. The gentleman was clearly charmed.

He escorted me into the dining restaurant and after dinner, waited to escort me to the lounge, to get ready for the evening's show. During the show, he leaned over to whisper the warning that he was going to monopolise me for the after-show dancing, and maybe after that, for the after-dancing midnight buffet supper. His soulful eyes hinted at a monopoly well after the cruise itself. This gentleman who was called Herman and who came from South Africa, said he looked forward so very much to seeing the next evening's *cheongsam*. The next evening I tried not to disappoint him by choosing one that was the closest to peacock blue, having recollected a small snatch of conversation in which he had extolled that colour. It had daintily rose-like patterns and black piping. The frogs were in severe black which gave them a dramatic appearance. The effect was completed by a pair of long black bead ear-rings. Herman was enthralled.

And just when I thought the *cheongsam* could claim unqualified success, we reached Bombay. On board came a troupe of sari-clad women, like a flock of brilliantly-feathered tropical birds. One stood out among them, a statuesque dusky goddess who stunned everyone into attention when she swept into the dining restaurant in a flame-red and green sari with a gleaming gold border. The lady's kohled eyes flashed challengingly, and from that moment Herman was smitten.

From *cheongsam* to sari was an easy step which Herman effected in exactly the time I turned my back to have my glass refilled, and the Indian Venus made her entrance into the bar. There she stood at the doorway, a tall imposing queen, this time in a deep purple sari, rich ornaments of gold adorning her ear-lobes, throat and wrists, one bare arm regally flung across her waist, surveying her new queendom with hauteur. I had hoped that she was travelling with a strict and conservative parent or better, a surly, possessive husband, but her bold entrance by herself in the bar announced that she was being shackled by neither and that like me, she was a solo traveller.

The *cheongsam* thus defeated, I tried to analyse the causes, that is, its deficiencies in relation to the sari. I found many, alas, so that I was forced to revise my earlier assessment of its power. For I had to sadly admit that worn by someone like this proud beauty from Bombay, the sari was alarmingly ahead of the *cheongsam*.

Firstly, its fluidity and flow, allowing the wearer the sway, turn, glide, slide, duck, pirouette, showed up all the formal stiffness of the *cheongsam*. Secondly, its baring of the midriff, a middle pleasure zone suggesting a greater pleasure on either side, immediately reduced the *cheongsam* side slits to a paltry promise. Thirdly, on a windy boat deck, its end could be drawn over the head and partially across the face, while the rest of the filmy stuff floated around the body. Now an Indian woman, face lowered, her large dark eyes peeping from behind this sari-veil which her fingers clutch tightly against the wind, is a definite male fantasy. By contrast, the *cheongsam* remains unaffected by oceanic breezes, except the lower part which flaps untidily about the legs, like some foolish trapped bird.

Lastly – and this must be the ultimate advantage – the sari claims an ease of disrobement the *cheongsam* never can. Unhindered by buttons, hooks and zips, the sari can be removed by the simple procedure of unspinning the lady out of it. Its great length of many meters allows for the pleasure of a full and vigorous unspinning with the added advantage of dizzying the lady so that she totters romantically into the unspinner's arms. By contrast, the unhooking of the *cheongsam* collar, the demolition of the three sentinel frogs and the laborious unzipping at the side, add up to a mundane operation. Just as the presence of Laura's large T-shirts had enhanced the appeal of the *cheongsam*, so now, by same Principle of Contrast, the dazzling sari had cast it into the shade.

I conceded defeat.

In my more spiteful moments, I imagined the gentleman in his ardour being frightfully entangled in the treacherous lengths and folds of the costume, choking and suffocating and myself whispering in malicious glee, 'Who's sari now?'

Months later I received a postcard from Laura, that exclaimed: 'Wasn't that a splendid cruise? Didn't your *cheongsam* just floor that gorgeous guy from South Africa?' and I wrote back, casting my sentences in the same breathless mode of the rhetorical question: 'Hadn't we, alas, over-estimated the power of the *cheongsam*? Shouldn't I now try my luck with the sarong?'

So the second strategy was an equally dismal failure. I was in a wretched state indeed.

# ——— SHIRLEY GEOK-LIN LIM ———

Shirley Geok-lin Lim was born in Malacca, Malaysia, to a Nonya (Malaysian assimilated) family. She received a Ph.D. in English and American Literature from Brandeis University in 1973. Her first book of poems, *Crossing the Peninsula*, won the 1980 Commonwealth Poetry Prize. She has published two other poetry collections and a book of short stories, *Another Country*. Her critical volume, *Nationalism and Literature: English-Language Writing from the Philippines and Singapore* is forthcoming. She is co-editor of *The Forbidden Stitch: An Asian American Women's Anthology*, which received the Before Columbus American Book Award in 1990; co-editor of *Reading the Literatures of Asian America* and *One World of Literature*, and editor of *Asian America: Journal of Culture and the Arts*. She has published in numerous critical volumes and journals, including *The Journal of Commonwealth Literature*, *New Literary History*, *Feminist Studies*, and *Poetry Review*. She is currently Professor of Asian American Studies and English at the University of California, Santa Barbara.

SHIRLEY GEOK-LIN LIM

# Why I Write

'Work' is a word freighted with sacrifice and honour. My 'work' includes poetry, fiction, criticism, pedagogy, and more recently, a kind of non-specific-genre that begins with the autobiographical subject to span all these. My early readings were formed by a colonialist education; I love(d) the English of English geniuses, including Shakespeare, Keats, Wordsworth, Austen, Dickens, and Yeats. Exposed to a United States Ph.D. requirement, I learned to counterweight these with American voices: Creeley, Roethke, Adrienne Rich. Returning to Southeast Asia, I found all of the above weightlessness, learned instead to read against the Western grain, within the particular locus of the post-colonial Anglophonic Asian, prey to multiple misplacements and dislocations, but also a predator of sorts of cultures set free-floating on the currents of global capital, media, war, and human exchanges. I would like time for the work of concentration – the poems and short stories. In the meantime, I teach and write criticism.

# Shirley Geok-lin Lim

## LOST NAME WOMAN

Mississippi China woman,
why do you wear jeans in the city?
Are you looking for the rich ghost?
to buy you a ticket to the West?

San Francisco China woman,
you will drink only Coca-cola.
You stir it with a long straw,
sip ss-ss like it's a rare elixir.

Massachusetts China woman,
you've cut your hair and frizzed it.
Bangs to hide your stubborn brow, eyes
shine, hurricane lamps in a storm.

Arizona China woman,
now you are in Gold Mountain Country,
you speak English like the radio,
but will it let you forget your father?

Woman with the lost name,
who will feed you when you die?

## THE REBEL

Tonight I will think of my uncles.
For once I will walk in their spirit.
Pile mahjongg tiles in great walls
and crash them down with two big fists.
I will be reckless and roast opium
balls over spirit lamps. I will close
my eyes in fox women harems
and wake to male children, this one
with my bulbous nose, these
with staggered pointed teeth

like handsome crocodile,
a dozen black-headed sons
to curse and gamble like me.
What fun my uncles had, springing
knives, fighting, using their
full confident voice.
This morning I sang with the car windows up,
letting my voice go its natural length.
What a revelation to hear my voice
as it is, booming in natural rhythm.
Did my uncles always speak in their voice?
Did no one tell them to be quiet,
be gentle, be soft, to whisper,
to hush? I with seven uncles
am forbidden to walk their path.
Tonight I'll speak like my uncles,
I'll tell those who taught me to be
a girl, I'm not, not, not, not, not.


## AH MAH

Grandmother Lim was smaller
than me at eight. Had she
been child, forever?
Helpless, hopeless, chin sharp
as a knuckle, fan face
hardly half-opened, not a scrap
of fat anywhere: she tottered
in black silk, leaning on
handmaids, on two tortured
fins. At sixty, his sons all
married, grandfather bought her,
Soochow flower song girl.
Every bone in her feet
had been broken, bound tighter
than any neighbour's sweet
daughter's. Ten toes and instep
curled inwards, yellow petals
of chrysanthemum, wrapped
in gold cloth. He bought the young
face, small knobby breasts
he swore he'd not dress in sarong
of maternity. Each night

he held her feet in his palms,
like lotus in the tight
hollows of celestial lakes.
In his calloused flesh, her
weightless soles, cool and slack,
clenched in his stranger's fever.


## MANGO

Mango at the New York A & P.
at eighty-nine American cents each:
stone-red, fore-shortened, puffy

hybrid all the way from Acapulco,
from corporate farms and rich Yankee
enterprises. Two days later,

my brother slowly drives me, Straits-born,
home through narrow, rewritten, Melaka.
Before despairing houses whose sons

and grandsons have left for Australia,
umbrella trees drop welcome shade.
Crescent mangoes thrusting as smooth-thighed trailer

girls from Siam gleam among sickle-drawn
leaves. I eat a green mango. Solid,
sour, it cuts the back of the throat, torn

taste, like love grown difficult or separate.
More chillies, more salt, more sugar,
more black soy – memory of tart

unripeness sweetened by necessities.
Where do we go from here, carrying
those sad eyes under the mango trees,
with our sauces, our petty hauntings?

# SRI LANKA

# JEAN ARASANAYAGAM

Jean Arasanayagam is a Sri Lanka writer of Dutch
Burgher origin married to a Tamil. She writes fiction,
poetry and drama and her work has received increasing critical acclaim. She has, as Neloufer de Mel
pointed out always been concerned with what it is to
be a woman, adult, wife and mother, but of recent
years she has added to that agenda the problems of
country torn apart by conflict and political strife. Her
most recent publications are *Reddened Water Flows
Clear* (Forest Books) and *Shooting the Floricans*
(Samina). Dangaroo Press are planning to publish a
collection of her short stories and poems plus a book
about her Burgher background in the near future.

JEAN ARASANAYAGAM

# Why I Write

I want to stretch the world as wide as possible to accommodate my ideas.
I want to sling those words like jewels across space, to let them fall and
scatter everywhere. When I look out of my window, nature is a map of
greens, blues, yellows. There are innumerable mutations of colour and I
set up my own landmarks on the pages of this seasonal atlas. I shift
frontiers and boundaries to give me the freedom of a limitless territory but
I do this without causing death and violence or displacement to other
inhabitants or living creatures of the universe. I can people that world
with all the characters that I encounter from day to day, not only the real
with the nuances of individual human speech but with those fictional
characters sometimes much larger than life who I create. The journeys I
take are never straight journeys. They are often allegorical. I speak in
parables and fables. Reality alone is insufficient. I want to enter into every
nook and cranny of experience to search out the significant. I do not want
to leave this world without making some impact/shedding some
light/discovering the revelatory experience. I want to show how my life
has suffered a sea change through all the experiences it has been subjected
to from childhood to adulthood and to use language with all its new
discoverable and exploratory strengths, metaphor, imagery with visual
and palpable force, parallels, relevances. I want to discover and explore
the resonances not of the single voice, but the innumerable voices around
me.

I want the world to hear my voice. I want my country to hear my voice
and not turn aside or ignore its echoes and reverberations. My voice as I
hear it should be/is/will be an influential voice but that would entail that
my utterances be responsible or even prophetic ones. Changing ideologies,
political and social awareness, war and violence, identity, women and
their needs and concerns, victims/victimiser, the colonized and the
colonizer all play a role in the limitless universe of my psyche and
consciousness. I explore hierarchies through marriage into a different
culture, rejection and alienation within closely structured societies which
refuse to accept me. I am deeply, indeed, profoundly aware of my own
colonial inheritance. The hybridity adds multifarious dimensions to my
view of life - say rather, my vision of life. Being Sri Lankan is an
important part of my identity, belonging to the Dutch Burgher lineage is
very important to me. I can weave strands of that blood lineage in vivid

or sombre threads to create fantastic tapestries out of those voyages that my ancestors took, their arrivals, their departures. Colonialism is a fact of history. Its vast saga, its legacies, its oppressions, its statements in terms of inheritance, descendants, is something I feel is important to analyse on more intimate terms than historical documentation alone.

I explore the revelations of visions and prophesies, folk-lore, mythologies, all levels of fantasy and realism. I create/visualise, entire poems, fictions, plays, whole areas of life and history. I create evidence where there is no archival documentation and I go very deep into memory and the past to relate it to the present and the future.

Writing is breathing. It is living to me. What a struggle life is, often so agonising. What else can I do but use it, contend with it in my work? It's a very physical thing too. I feel complete after the act of writing, if I feel it has worked. It has very often been a cathartic experience to me. Sometimes, of course, the process takes time and for the entire experience to be realised I move from form to form, shift from one genre to another, change register so that realization could emerge first through a poem, next moving onto a play and eventually becoming a short story. Likewise, the short story could extend itself into a novella or novel. The potential is infinite. I need experience to write. Travel. The refugee camp in which I spent week after week, month after month, with my family (and which I still inhabit in my mind), my identity, search, love and personal relationships, pain and suffering of my own and that of others.

I have a rich store of stories to relate. My mind is full of them and they relate to the universal human condition. I have poems that fall like meteorites from the sky and people interacting in my plays ... autobiographies too. I have all the feelings and emotions I want to express at hand. They are all part of my writing. To write of them, to explore those endless metaphors of life and death, that's my exploration. I search for that significant moment, the moment of truth... Writing helps to contend and deal with those agonising experiences of life and death, love, pain, sorrow, not only of my own but those others too.

JEAN ARASANAYAGAM

# The Mother-in-Law

My mother-in-law, a stranger to me had been brought to her son's home. The years between us had been barren years, sterile with the desert of silence. I had tried many times to traverse this desert, in search of that illusory oasis, but it was only the mirage that led me on and on. I ended up gaunt and starved, parched with craving for that which would never be. Here, finally I had stopped, with the barriers of dunes before me and the sand prickling against my skin. Those conduits, those springs, those lost oceans were dried up. We were strangers to each other. Yet we were both women to whom this man, her son, my husband, belonged. She, my mother-in-law, who was once a matriarch, who was proud in a sense of her hierarchy, with the pride of possession, a caste, a name, six children was now gradually losing everything. A tree that was being denuded of fruit, leaf, flower. I was the daughter-in-law who had desired more than anything else to know who they were, this family, whose lineage made them a people apart in their village. In their village in the North they possessed all the prerogatives of caste, the Vellala caste, both at the temple festivals and in their daily life. This family of Saravanamuttu of Mailvaganam of Supramaniam. My father-in-law Saravanamuttu had always worn the sacrificial tetpai grass when he partook of the temple rituals. The temple was built on their property and my husband as a child had often felt their permeation, emanations from those holy sanctums within the groves of palmyrah. My mother-in-law had lived as a child in Colombo for many years. My father-in-law and she had been cousins: he had left the village to come to the city to do business. He lived his early days in a chummery with other young men from the North, the austere life style which he followed from the beginning, persisting to the end of his days. My mother-in-law had married him when she was sixteen years old. She too had left the village when she was very young and had been brought to live in Colombo with her guardian, an uncle, gradually being uprooted from the village. Whenever she went back, she returned to the old way of life, to the ease and comfort of being waited upon and served by the traditional caste groups; the compound being swept of every leaf by Sinammah, the water fetched from the well and stored in large earthenware pots, or drawn by Sinnian for baths. The women came to help in the kitchen, to pound the rice, to boil the paddy from the fields, to pick up the hundreds of mangoes that fell from the laden trees, to spread the pinatu to dry on the woven mats... a hundred thousand tasks which were performed for this family. In the city it was different; they had servants whom they paid with money who did not serve them through the hierarchy of caste – they had Kochchi cooks, men from Kerala, gardeners, chauffeurs of their cars, ayahs from the Southern villages to look after the children. My mother-in-law led a life that was cosseted and pampered because she belonged to a family that had wealth, property, land, houses, money. Right from the start she was made to feel that others were lesser beings if they did not belong to the same caste and lineage that she did. I was one of those lesser beings. I did not belong. I had made an opening in the wall to enter into her territory. What was this territory? A dichotomy existed within it. In the village it was the vast house with its pillars, its carved doors, its inner courtyard, the tinnai, its palmyrah grove and paddy fields and its temple. In the city it was the house that my father-in-law had built on land that had been purchased for a price, the deeds going back to Colonial times in the Dutch period. These were not hereditary lands but land bought with money earned by my mother-in-law's ancestors.

Still, part of her life had been entrenched in this house, in this village in the North for she went back to where the earth, the soil, the water were familiar, were part of her. And here, in this house, the family guru Yogaswamy would visit them and she would wash out the home with turmeric, spread a kambalam for him to sit on, prepare vegetarian food for him in the shining utensils and listen to his discourse. How then, could I, a different being altogether, be accepted. There was room for extreme cruelty on the part of the one who wielded power. Her world was not my world. Her mythology was not my mythology. Our language was different. I was too young and naive to stop at those closed gates.

I wanted to go inside and feel myself part of my husband's life. It was never to be. The silence grew between us. But I saw what they, that family, refused to see, the breaches made in that hierarchical wall where invaders and intruders, other than myself, insinuated themselves and began to enter as an enemy would.

Their subtle conquest laid that empire low and she, my mother-in-law, laid down the last symbol of her matriarchy with the removal of the thali from round her neck; gradually her jewel boxes were rifled, the knots in her bundles of brilliants, diamonds and gold sovereigns were undone and vanished. Where? Who knows? Those who were themselves of her own flesh and blood, her kith and kin, laid hands on the booty. And finally after Pata's death, my father-in-law's death, the erosion had begun with a vengeance and she began to find that loss of power eating into her very being, leading to her derangement, her delusion and displacement, far away from the village where she had gone for each new birth. Even her city home was no longer her own. It had to be relinquished to her younger daughter. Her nature had gained strength from the sacred hierarchy, from the hundred thousand poojas she had made. She was confident that by handing over the apportioned out property to those who obeyed her traditions the gods would bestow blessing on her forever.

The courtyard in the Navaly house with its pomegranate tree which always bore fruit, now spread only thorny branches, and there was no more grain left to dry on the spread mats. Who would carry on the temple rituals? Who would care to come and serve her with respect for her lineage? Her nature grew as bitter and corroded as the stagnant water in the well in the grove. Her strength had to assert itself against the usurpation and loss of power. It was this assertion that split her mind in fragments and made her spew out curses and pronounce blessings. She was blind, so blind that she could not see who had stolen her power and emptied her coffers. She still clung to an identity that she fought with every weapon to preserve, but how could she, in this house, the house of that outsider whom she had never fed, never given drink to, whose life had been less than dust to her, my life, mine, her daughter-in-law's?

She stepped into my home, brought by her grandson and his wife. She had just one suitcase with all she possessed. No longer did she have bracelets and rugs and chains of gold. Sold. Given away. Stolen. Right from the beginning the note of discord sounded.

'Do you like to live in Kandy?' I asked her politely.

'What difference does it make,' she snapped, 'Colombo, Kandy, Jaffna, what difference. It is all the same.'

'Don't talk to her,' my husband whispered, 'she will only be rude to you. Akka has told us not to talk to her. To leave her alone. There has been enough trouble in the house of my sister and brother-in-law. They cannot live with her. She interferes in their lives. She does not know how not to step into another's territory.'

How could she? Her privilege was that others should not step or impinge on her territory.

I could not help looking back on the past. The day she came on that formal visit to see her grandchildren.

'I have come to see whether my son is happy,' she had said defiantly at me. My mother too had come to see me. My mother and she, my mother-in-law. My mother with her soft amber eyes resting on me, her daughter, with so much love. Who had sung to me, kept me close to her, spelled out her fictions to me, both of us caught up in that magic mythology that no one could destroy. She had not wanted me to marry into this unknown family, into a culture which was not prepared to admit any intrusion and yet once I had married she had accepted my husband and welcomed him by offering him all the largesse of a generous, open-hearted spirit. Although she did not know it, my mother-in-law had already lost her son. She could not distinguish between what lay within her coffers and the wealth that she had in that life of his. To her the brilliants glittered with

a more piercing and more scintillating light than the love which could
have illuminated her present dark.

She had come prepared to be rejected as one who had shown no love,
who could not expect love. Yet even her traditional, chosen daughters-in-
law disliked her. Her own daughter could not live with her. 'They will
chase you away in six weeks' was what one family friend had said; what
her own son-in-law had said. They had taken no pains to bring us two
strangers together either. So she stood her ground and lashed out, flailed
at me with her own bitter words.

'I am a beggar. Begging bowl.' Begging bowl! 'A beggar. A pauper.'
'Whose fault is it?' I ask.

'I don't know,' she shrugs. 'It is the son's duty to look after the mother.
For many years my son-in-law Supramaniam looked after me. For big
operation he sent me to India. Now they say it is the Mahen's turn, my
son, Rasa.'

'But for twenty years Rasa did not exist for you, you had forgotten your
son, you never turned and looked at him after his marriage. Because he
had not married according to your wishes. You visited us only once in
those twenty years.'

For Achchi, her son-in-law Supramanian, the man of wealth and
property, who had married her elder daughter Lakshmi, was the man she
had admired and looked up to. This was the man whom she and Pata had
chosen with the advice of their guru Yogaswamy. Her daughter would
always have the security of a great house, many houses, estates, holiday
houses, money to indulge herself, to eat, to drink, to entertain, to travel all
round the world. It was one of those traditional marriages ordained by the
hierarchies of their kind. But now that Achchi was old, interfering, difficult, even this son-in-law did not want her in his house. I had invited her
to come and stay with us but I did not know that her mind was giving
way through her displacement, through the violent quarrels which had
been hidden from us, with her son Rajan and his wife Mohini.

'You never visited us,' I repeated. 'Never to see your son, never to see
your granddaughters, never even when they were ill. We were never invited to your house for festivals or almsgivings. You kept us out. Your
children kept us out. Lakshmi with all her wealth never wanted us to
come into her mansion. "If you come," she said once, "you must do everything for yourself. I cannot put myself out for you or your family." The
wealth had to be conserved for herself and her children. A mansion with
many rooms but no room for you any longer Achchi,' I said.

'Pata did not like me to go anywhere.'

'You went only where you wanted to. Places which were important to
you. To the temple. On family visits. To the cinema. Not to the house of
the outsider. When you came to see your grandchildren you brought your
own food, but only for yourself. You sat and ate it alone. Did you think

our cooking vessels were defiled? You did not bring food for us. Just enough for yourself. If anything were to remain that was for us.'

'Begging bowl!'

I felt the weight of the oppressor. Not just that of an individual alone, but that of the whole society which had denied me recognition or acceptance. It was the arrogance of the invader who had grown proud with conquest. From where had Achchi's people come. And Pata's? As long as their wealth and property endured the mythology of birth could be sustained. Ganesh was the god of wisdom. Lakshmi the goddess of wealth. Saraswathi for the Arts. Worshipped by the family. The images and myths, the epics, the legends, the thevaram, the Sivapuranam, the Vibukhti that she put on her forehead made Achchi declare, 'I am different to you. I am higher than you. What is your God? I eat only vegetarian food. I pray. I bathe. I put holy ash, Tirunuru, every day. How can I ever do wrong?'

In their grove were the rusted links of the elephant chains that tethered their elephants to the palmyrah trees. Their ancestors had been carried on the elephants to the temple of Nallur to annoint the kings. Was this to bestow virtue on them, this and this alone? My people too had their histories, but we were not going to delve into our individual archives to discover whose history was greater. I felt the weight of this oppression, the being made to feel the outsider. I had gone to that village to discover for myself the mythology of that family. It was a different world. The grove closed in upon me yet I followed the pathway to the house where my husband had spent his childhood. I walked through room after room and found them empty of all but ghosts. No one would return here.

She could not be forced to love me. There was no obligation on her part. But had I not wanted to be accepted by her? Yes. At the beginning I had wanted it. Because I could not think that her pride of lineage should be a barrier. Later I was to know that what had been done was to wound her sense of pride in the inviolability of not wanting to sacrifice, in any way, her sacred hierarchy. The ring of tetpai grass would never unite us because her gods were not mine.

'Perhaps you did not like me because I was not your kind?' I asked.

'Maybe,' she said ambiguously.

I brought the portrait of her parents to her room. She cringed away from it. She did not want to look upon those images. I gazed forever at them, trying to see my mother-in-law in those faces. Her mother in a gold bordered saree, many yards in length. Decked out in gold and jewels. Attiyal round the neck and double chains, pahato malee. Mukutti for the nose, of brilliants. Padakkams studded with emeralds, rubies, diamonds. The chains reach to the waist. She appears to be some kind of deity. Fit her into a temple. The goddess of prosperity. Lakshmi. Her body is firm and fully fleshed for she must fulfil her role in life and produce children. Three daughters and one son she had and died before her prime. She could not breast feed Achchi who was given over to a wet nurse and drank milk from a woman who was not of her own kinship, a Sinhala wet nurse from whom Achchi suckled. Fire consumed that life. Fire was worship too. Walk around the sacred yaham at the marriage ceremony while the Brahmin priests drop seeds which crackle in the hot ghee in the sacred fires of Agni. Mount the flower bedecked Manaverai. Lie in the marriage bed. Bring forth heirs to preserve the traditions. The kum-kumum is bright red on the scar of the parting in the oiled hair. Yet in the pyre the flesh shrivelled the skin crackled in that same sacred fire of Agni. No, Achchi could not bear to look upon that portrait any longer because she had lost all that had given value to that hierarchy. Victim. She now clung to life fiercely trying to preserve, clutching on to it, holding its vessel to her lips to quench her inordinate thirst. And she had to sit beside Pata's bier. He had been her only protection. After his death she could be taken from place to place to live until her own death.

Pata's ashes were strewn in the ocean; they spilt out of the cracked urn and lay like a skin on the water, salt and ash sucked in by fish. Bounty and riches, caste, hierarchy, homage. That was how the family had survived. The koviyars carry the bier in the village to the burial ground but here in the city it is taken away in a hearse. Now the compound is unswept, the leaves pile up on the threshold. The pillars are cracking. The pettagams are like empty coffins. The grove is a wilderness for the birds. The parakeets pillage the fruit and there are strangers who walk in and out of the house. The alari-poo fallen from the branches in a lavish carpet curl up their yellow petals. The toddy pots swing on the palmyrah branches. It is all changed now. The sound of bursting mortar shells reach the village. The militants wear cyanide lockets round their necks. Bridegrooms of death. New invaders march in and out; one supplants the other. Where jewels were once locked away, arms caches are now found. Strangers have taken over everything. The children no longer go to the temple to carry on their rituals. The Brahmin priest carries on the Kodiyettham ceremony on behalf of the family. No one can ever return.

# ——PUNYAKANTE WIJENAIKE——

Punyakante Wijenaike is Sri Lanka's most distinguished novelist writing in English. She has published
four novels and four collections of short stories and
one of her novels, *Giraya*, has recently been made
into a very successful television series. Though she
was born, bred and educated in the city of Colombo
the roots of her writing very often go deeper into the
rural areas. In 1985 she was awarded the Woman of
Achievement Award and in 1988 the Rank of Kala
Suri Class 1 was conferred on her by the President of
Sri Lanka. She also served on the panel of judges for
the Eurasian region of the Commonwealth Writers
Prize and was chairperson of the panel of judges for
the Michael Ondaatje Prize. In connection with the
State Printing Cooperation of Sri Lanka Dangaroo
Press is going to publish her most recent novel,
*Amulet*, in 1994.

PUNYAKANTE WIJENAIKE

# Why I Write

I do not know, to date, what led me to write. All I realize is that, as a lonely, introverted child, there was this enormous need to create and express myself because I dreaded to communicate through speech. I needed to express my thoughts, feelings and emotions in an indirect way rather than talk face to face. Long before I began to write, however, I was living in a fantasy world of my own creation, where I created people and situations the way I wanted them to be. I spent many happy hours creating live characters out of inanimate dolls, giving each a name and personality. I made them walk and talk and live through experiences which entertained and amused my younger sister and brother. Next I turned to play-acting with real live people, namely my cousins. We used to don costumes and put out plays for an appreciative audience, our parents, grandparents, aunts and uncles.

As a child I was happiest in a world I created around me. A tree was not just a tree. My imagination turned it into a ship or a trapeze where I experienced adventure. A pathway turned into a stream where I paddled a canoe.

Then I learned to read. A whole new world opened its doors to me. I began to devour books by the dozen, often to the dismay of my grandmother who saw nothing worthwhile in my lying about and reading. I would read while eating, while lying down or even in the toilet. My first love was Enid Blyton's 'The Magic Faraway Tree'.

Slowly I began to write. I kept diaries of my thoughts, feelings, impressions, fears and happy moments. I found, when writing, that I was uninhibited, unselfconscious, not ill at ease, like when I attempted to speak to anyone. If I wanted to communicate with my parents on a matter that was serious to me, I would note it down on paper and present it to them. Once my father was amused. 'Why don't you turn to creating stories?' he asked me.

Yet it was only after I was married that I began writing stories. At first it was just a break from the routine of housework and child-rearing. Once more I had found a way to break the dreariness of day to day reality. As I progressed as a writer I found I was developing as a person as well. I met new people, learnt to observe, listen, understand. I came out of a narrow house-bound world. I also came out of fantasy into reality or rather made a blend of both. I could cope with reality as it formed a base for my writing. I wrote of everyday lives, of people living in the village as well as in the city. I would take a character or a situation and create my own interpretation of the person or situation.

My approach to creative writing is simple. I don't write to change people or society. I don't attempt to separate black from white. Each human is equipped with good as well as bad. I know when I am writing well. I am happy and absorbed and the type-writer or pen cannot keep pace with the flow of thought. On the other hand, there are days when I tend to pause, day-dream and do not get enough satisfaction out of what I am writing. I know then there is something wrong, something missing in that piece of creative work.

In the beginning I wrote for the mere pleasure of writing. But now, with demands for more stories for television and books, it has taken a positive role in my life. It has got deep into my blood and has become 'a way of life'. It has become part of me.

To date I have seven published books, a hundred stories in newspapers, journals, anthologies here and abroad. The B.B.C. broadcast four of my stories and the local Radio has broadcast many. I have won an honour from the Sri Lankan government, a title called 'Kala Suri' which means 'class one' in the field of creative arts.

The financial rewards are small and limited. The real reward comes with the acceptance of my work and the personal enrichment I derive from writing about people and situations I feel deeply about.

PUNYAKANTE WIJENAIKE

# *Amulet*
(an extract)

As a child I grew up in the care of Punchi Menike, not my mother. She is the one who influenced my thinking and feeling. She was a round faced woman, a moon face with dark hair oiled back into a tight knot, low at the nape of her neck. I was fed, bathed, dressed primly and properly, rocked to sleep on her out-stretched legs. She used to pick lice out of my hair and kill them pressed between the nails of her two thumbs. Punchi Menike had one other task apart from following behind me all the time. She was given the important task of preparing mother's daily chew of betel. I would watch, fascinated, her washing of the dark green, freshly plucked leaf, breaking the arecanut into pieces with the giraya, squeezing the chunam and other ingredients onto the leaf. While performing this daily task she would tell me stories of the good and the bad – the bad always ending up in hell worlds, the greedy as hungry peretayas always in search of food to fill their bellies. Despite this constant eating and satisfying of their hunger, they remained thin, skeletons always hungry, always greedy, wandering the earth lost and lonely. Often when I was frightened by these tales I would long to run to my mother but she remained a distant busy person, with a bunch of household keys dangling from her waist, tending to the drying of paddy, the cooking of meals or the garden. We drank milk freshly drawn from mother's cows and then, of course, mother had brother to look after. She devoted her life to him, personally bathing, feeding. She entrusted him to the care of no hired woman, like she did me. I remember mealtimes clearly. While Punchi Menike rolled my rice into balls and forcefully overfed me by frightening me with stories of peretayas who would eat me if I did not eat, mother would distract brother's attention by a story of a handsome prince who would become rich over-night and feed him unawares.

Every poya day Punchi Menike observed sil. Dressed in immaculate white cloth and white long-sleeved blouse and with a white shawl across her shoulder, she would retreat into the temple. On such days only, mother took care of me. Punchi Menike drilled me early into a superstitious belief in religion. Today I know Buddhism is a philosophy, not a superstition. But I cannot shake off early inhibitions. It was a sin to eat beef. It was a sin to even think of sex. Punchi Menike herself had four children in the village looked after and brought up by her mother-in-law, but to Punchi Menike children were something apart from sex. I wonder now how she conceived. She never permitted me to read or think or meet people. She was always following me with advice, especially how important it was not to go against the wishes of parents. If I did I would go down into hell forever.

On such ground was the foundation of my life laid. Yet when I grew afraid, when I suffered from nightmares, it was Punchi Menike who cuddled and soothed me. When I attained puberty, it was Punchi Menike who protected me from 'kila', from demons. Punchi Menike had a favourite story about the last King of Kandy. I now wonder why she kept drilling this into my mind? Was it a kind of unconscious forewarning?

'Bahirawa deviya was a brother of God Kataragama,' said Punchi Menike. 'He loved beautiful young women, especially fair Kandyan women. Once there was a severe drought. The water tanks ran dry, the rice fields lay with parched, cracked lips aching from water. But no rain fell. The river shrivelled up into a stream and even the waterfalls ceased to fall. It was a curse from God. The annual Esala Perehera was held by the King, Kapuralas were set praying daily, yet no sign of clouds. A merciless sun kept appearing in the sky every morning, sucking up whatever moisture was left anywhere. This was making the King very unpopular. People were whispering that he must have done something very bad to have made the God so angry. That he should do something to appease the angry God. The King had another problem. The British were occupying the lowlands and if there was a crop failure they could march into his kingdom saying he was a failure as a King. To save himself the King was compelled to sanction a 'dola', a sacrifice to the God to appease him and bring on the rain. A beautiful girl was to be sacrificed to Bahirawa. A virgin.

The girl was chosen. She was already in love, this seventeen year old girl, with a handsome young man of her own kin. Yet she was selected for sacrifice.

She had been selected to save the land from drought. It was an honour to be selected by the King but the girl did not think so. She wept and wept, yet if she refused the King it would bring dishonour to her father,

On an auspicious day, the beautiful young woman came walking on white pavada to the porch near the King's palace converted, for the occasion, into a magul, bridal platform. Bands of red and white calico spiralled the columns, arched like rainbows, composed of a thousand frills of red and white cloth. On either side of the pavada the floor was festooned with young coconut palms twisted and turned into decorative art. The bride was the only thing that looked wilted, like a freshly plucked lotus dying without water. She hung her head and stepped listlessly although she was decked as a bride with pendants on seven chains, gold bangles, emerald and ruby rings on her delicate fingers and tinkling silver anklets. Despite all this finery, tears coursed down her cheeks for she knew she was being led to the slaughter –.

'Why couldn't she have run away?' I remember asking.

Punchi Menike looked stern. 'A King's word is law and by running away she would only have bought shame and dishonour on her family. And, besides, where, to whom was she to run to?

'But it was her life they were sacrificing,' I had protested. 'Surely she has the right to her own life?'

'Her life belonged to her parents who had brought her into this world and they could not displease the King!'

'Why couldn't she kill herself rather than be shamed or tormented by an unknown demon God in the jungle? It would have been easier to die in dignity.'

'It is a sin to take even your own life,' said Punchi Menike who observed the religious rites every full moon day clad in white. 'If you take your own life you have to pay for that sin in the next life!'

'If you are born a King have you the right then to sacrifice other peoples lives and yet not pay for it in the next life? Do you have that privilege over life and death?'

Punchi Menike's simple mind had no answer to my question. She looked frightened that I should hold such thoughts, put such questions. Religion was to be accepted, not questioned. Then triumphantly she found the reply to silence me. 'The King ordered the sacrifice to save the country from drought. It was his duty to see that the crops were not ruined.'

The answer did not satisfy me but I kept silent because I did not want to harass my beloved old ayah. Besides she might refuse to repeat the tale if I requested it again.

As I grew from puberty into young womanhood, in my imagination I formed a love relationship with the only young man I came into contact with apart from my brother, Niranjan. I began to see him in my dreams, blush whenever our eyes met in brief encounters. He began to visit our house frequently on some pretext or other. Often it is was a message from my Loku Amma, mother's elder sister. I once saw mother glance from him to me. I turned away and went inside my room. Even so his visits to our house ceased over-night. I remember nights of weeping and a bewildered Punchi Menike sitting up on her reed mat beside my bed, stroking my hair. She had not guessed how far my imagination had taken me. I felt, in some way, like the cheated girl in history. Niranjan was my cousin, my mother's elder sister's son. We had not even talked to each other, only exchanged looks. I realised then the prison I was in. I used to wake up in terror from sleep, screaming. Punchi Menike would wake up and rock to and fro in grief. 'My poor child, my poor baby, possessed by some demon ...'

I remember they held an exorcism ceremony for me. And then my parents hastily arranged this marriage for me with a man I had not met...

I wore traditional white and gold. Seven gold necklaces hung like seven heavy chains around my neck. The nalal patiya, the headband of the bride seemed to grip my head in a tight hold. Three gold bangles on each hand, anklets round my feet. A bouquet of white roses and gold high-heeled shoes was the only difference between me and the girl of Punchi Menike's tale. Western influence had not yet touched the King's kingdom when the sacrifice took place. I consoled myself with the thought that I was not going to spend a night tied to a stake in the middle of the jungle.

I stood by Senani's side on the poruwa. I was with the man who would become my husband. I knew nothing of him yet the Mangala Ashtaka was chanted invoking the blessings of Gods and devas over us. Each of our two small fingers were tied together with gold thread binding us to each other for life. Betel leaves were dropped on the poruwa calling on mother earth to be witness to our marriage. The earth that bears up anything must be the woman. Out of the corner of my eye I saw my cousin, my first love, looking as dejected as I felt. What chance had we to be together? We had been like unopened buds plucked from a tree before we had a chance to open our petals to the sun. We had been plucked and laid on an altar of sacrifice by our parents. A sacrifice of our feelings, our love, nipped in the bud. Senani tied yet another gold chain around my neck claiming me as his wife. I fed him milk rice symbolising our relationship. My mother was gifted with a roll of white cloth, as was the custom, to repay her for looking after his wife to be and compensate her for my loss. I looked sadly at Punchi Menike. It should have been given to her. What would happen to her now? Most probably she would put on white and retire as a Sil Matha into a nunnery.

Young virgins clad in pure white sang the 'Jaya mangala gathas' wishing us well in our new life. I dared not even look sideways at my bridegroom, for fear he would think me forward. But I was aware of him with every beat of my palpitating heart. What would our life together be? Would he understand my fears like Punchi Menike had? What would it be like, this wedding night ahead of me? Would it be a sacrifice of my body as well as myself? Or would it be the beginning of a new life of happiness and friendship? Above all I wanted my husband to be my friend, even before he became my lover. He should understand that he must handle me with care and gentleness knowing the kind of inhibited life I had led. I saw Punchi Menike weeping openly.

\* \* \*

The view from the attic room remains unchanged. My instinct as a young, ignorant bride had nevertheless been correct. Even today hours pass without his wondering where I am, without his coming to look for me. As a young virgin bride I had feared the wedding night. Now I know it had not just been 'wedding nerves.' It had been a fore-warning. I had over-estimated his capacity for feeling, for tenderness. Today I sit motionless before the statue of the Buddha in this secret room where I can at last be myself. I sit motionless, like the Buddha, knowing that he, Senani, will not come looking for me here. But unlike the Buddha, I am not beyond feeling. I suffer pain, knowing that he never wanted me for myself.

* * *

The wedding night will remain with me until I die. I hope I do not carry a repetition of it into my next life. While he was in the toilet brushing his teeth and changing into black silk pyjamas, I was sitting on the large hotel double bed in my white silk nightgown with the rosebuds embroidered on it with loving care by Punchi Menike. I was shivering and shaking as if with a fever, my teeth chattering. Earlier Senani had helped me undress. It was always Punchi Menike who had undressed me and prepared me for bed. Silently, like a child, I wept for her. My brand new husband had taken off my chains, bangles and engagement ring and earrings and locked them in the hotel wardrobe. The key he put inside his wallet. I thought he was protecting my jewellery for me to use later. But he never gave them back to me. I went with only my ear studs on for the home-coming. Later he locked my jewellery in his home iron safe, the combination to open it being a secret to him. I was terrified of the white cloth spread over the hotel bed sheets. My moment of surrender was approaching. I recalled the maid tied to a stake at the top of the hill Bahirawakande and thought: 'Was she more frightened of the demon than I am of my brand new husband?' Then he unlocked the toilet door and came into the bedroom. On the pocket of his black silk pyjamas was embroidered his initials Senani Seneviratne- S S. He got into bed and waited for me to follow suit. There were no kisses, no fondling, no endearing words to coax a frightened virgin into sex. He acted as if I was another possession, like the jewellery he had taken over and locked up.

He was quick and brutal with me. He ignored my cry of pain and performed his act of penetration as if it was something he had to accomplish that night and when it was all over he left me crying, turned his back on me and went to sleep. Soon I heard him snore. I lay silent, looking up, tracing the patterns on a strange new ceiling.'

* * *

The morning after the wedding night I rolled up the cloth that bore proud proof of my virginity and hid it in a paper bag inside the suitcase. No one came from my husband's side to inspect it. But I kept it in case at the home-coming I was asked to produce the evidence.

From then on it was just the two of us in strange places and situations. He took me to places I had never seen before and was afraid of. We went into the heart of the jungle, into Yala game sanctuary. Often he left me alone in the bungalow with an old cook, who was often drunk, while he went shooting wildlife with his camera. I begged him not to leave me alone. He smiled an unreadable smile and took me with him. When the jeep went over ruts or when he came across a wild elephant or bear, I would cling to him, and although he smiled with amusement, he held me close. Once I became hysterical when we came very close to a lone elephant, who, startled by the jeep, raised his trunk and made as if to charge us. Even the tracker became excited and said urgently: 'Go faster, master, go fast.' But Senani took his time, watching me weep and cower down in the seat. When we passed the danger he said: 'See Shyamali, you must have more faith in my control over events. I would not have let that elephant harm you.'

Suddenly we came to a clearing. A cobra was moving slowly, heavily, on its belly towards a prey we could not see. A Gurulla bird circled the air, watching, ever watching the movements of the cobra. Suddenly it decided to swoop down and peck at the snake. The cobra began to go round and round in confusion forgetting its prey, a small jungle fowl who bounded away in relief. The bird kept on circling and swooping and pecking the snake, wounding it until it could take no more. It raised its hood to strike. But the cautious and cunning bird flew into the air and hovered about until the cobra writhed in agony and finally succumbed to its injuries. Then the bird returned to eat the flesh. Senani waited, watched and filmed the whole episode before going into the forest again. I had been crying through the whole unfair fight and now I felt sick.

'That is life, that is reality, Shyamali,' he told me. 'The strong always overpowers the weak. The cobra was going to eat a helpless, small jungle fowl anyway. It deserved the fate that awaited it.'

I felt a strange excitement in his voice, a savouring of the episode. Suddenly I felt cold, lonely.

From there we went to the cultural sites of Anuradhapura, Polonnaruwa and Sigiriya. But Senani never halted at the places of worship. He only stopped the jeep he had borrowed from a friend, to take a snap of the Sri Maha Bodhi and Ruwanveli-seya like any foreign tourist. But he made me climb right up Sigiriya rock despite my feeling giddy. He made me look down the steep precipice, holding me firmly by the hands. One moment I thought he was letting me go, letting me plunge to my death, but the next moment he had me pressed firmly against his warm body. I began to cry. 'Why do you weep so easily Shyamali?' he asked.

I changed the subject, ashamed of my fear of heights. 'Didn't Kasyapa murder his own father?'

'He walled him in,' said Senani abruptly. Then he turned his attention to the filming of the moat, the rock, the lion's paws, the water lilies and white storks. I wished then I had canvas and paints with me. Mother had discouraged my interest in painting but maybe Senani could be persuaded to let me follow my interests. New hope arose. I began to look upon my husband with tolerance.

We returned to Colombo for the home-coming. The honeymoon was over and although I had formed a kind of hero-worship of my new husband, proud of his dark, haughty good looks, still I was not completely happy. A certain unease had crept into my being which had been hitherto innocent as a child.

We drove straight into the house along a short driveway lined with palm bushes, past a smooth green lawn dotted with flowering trees and parked under the porch. I remember that porch very well for today's houses have no space for porches. The cars drive straight into garages. Inside the house there was no one to greet us, no lighting of crackers, no nekath time nor kith and kin. No lighting of the oil lamp although I saw that the lamp had been polished to a high shine. There was only Ramon, his male servant, who carried in our bags and Pinchamma the kitchen woman. She was a strange looking creature, squat, shapeless, with a square face as if someone had pushed it into place. Senani had not even informed my parents of our return. Quietly I went into the back of the house and threw the soiled wedding night cloth into the dust-bin. I saw Pinchamma watching and grinning. I felt the first chill run up my spine.

I became the mistress of a new household. I was like mother. Yet it was not the same. I felt the house did not belong to me. I was the mistress but was I really in command? In my uncertainty I began to constantly finger the amulet that my mother had hung for my protection prior to my leaving home. She had hung it on a thin gold chain with the barrel, the amulet itself hidden under my clothes, nestling between my breasts.

* * *

She had had this amulet made a month prior to my marriage. Why? I had heard Punchi Menike pleading that I was constantly in tears. Perhaps it was on account of this or was it because our horoscopes had not matched completely? I knew mother was a practical woman. Because of my involvement with my cousin and because she may not have been able to find a Kandyan who was willing not to have a share in the property, she may have fallen on the resources of the Kapurala to protect her child. Certainly mother spared no pains nor money to prepare the amulet. A special room was set apart in the house for the Kapurala to 'charm to life' the jeevan kireema, of the talisman. It took seven days and seven nights to endow it with the power of protection. Within the gold barrel was hidden the charm, a strip of copper engraved with protective symbols. Symbols strong enough also to bind a man to a woman for life.

NELOUFER de MEL

# Woman as Gendered Subject and other Discourses in Contemporary Sri Lankan Fiction in English

Sri Lankan literature in English is not a major player in the country's mass media scenario.[1] Those who choose to write in English are people who, through education and family background, have their roots in the history of English as the language of colonialism and socio-economic privilege in Sri Lanka, and, consequently, belong to a very small group. Failure to teach English as a vital second or third language, along with continuing institutional marginalization of Sri Lankan English, have meant that only a handful of writers are confident and fluent enough to write in English.[2] The lack of a large reading public for books in English results in commercial reluctance by major publishers to publish more than one, or at the most, two books per year. Those writing in English are forced therefore to publish privately, or collectively through The English Writer's Cooperative. They may also look to an interested NGO, or put their faith in the Arts Council of Sri Lanka which, after competition, awards Rs.10,000/- to different categories of writing, or the National Library Services Board which at most agrees to buy Rs.25,000/- worth of books but only after they have been printed by their authors in the first place. The fact remains then that most books published in English are self-financed.

An examination of Sri Lankan fiction in English produced in 1992 and 1993 (including works published abroad by expatriate Sri Lankan writers which engage with the dynamics of the Sri Lankan socio-political fabric) points to the missed opportunities caused by this unhelpful publishing environment. For apart from the very limited exposure to a wider reading public achieved at present only by the few authors rich enough to publish their own work, the paucity of translations from Sri Lankan English into Sinhala and Tamil and vice versa preclude the vital dialogue required within the country, at multiple levels, for the creation of a truly dynamic body of literature.[3]

This lack of dialogue is particularly unfortunate with regard to works which show a relatively sensitive awareness of how gender operates and is articulated in contemporary society. Such representations could make a vital contribution to a wider discussion amongst the reading public on issues such as the construction and appropriation of gender, the commonalities and differences that bind the experience of women, the grip of patriarchy and the contradictions and diversity that abound within a marginalized group itself such as women under the rule of patriarchy.

I stress gender for many reasons. Our gender is produced both by biological factors and by processes socializing us into playing the roles of male or female. Because these roles are constructed in relation to each other, an unpacking of the discursive underpinnings which inform constructs of both male and female identity, and an insightful listening to the dialogue – most often on unequal terms – between male and female cannot be achieved through a focus on the feminine solely in terms of biology, divorced from the patriarchal socio-cultural practices which construct and police it, often with its own complicity. For even in a work of fiction which has no male characters, the reader is constantly called upon to evaluate, condemn or praise female thoughts and actions on the basis of a cultural conditioning which privileges patriarchal norms. These enter a Foucauldian archive, a network of all which conditions us and governs our behaviour and is all the more complex because we are not always conscious of all the ideological strands contained in it and which produce us. In fact the Foucauldian archive derives its potency from those elements of our own conditioning which we are unconscious of and which are therefore difficult to locate, more so as they are ever shifting. In a patriarchal structure therefore, much of what we take for granted in terms of dress codes or model behaviour for women has its roots in a patriarchy which dictates an identity for a woman which is then disseminated through popular culture, education, family upbringing and literature. It is against such an identity, within which many women have felt imprisoned, that many of the characters in the stories I will be looking at rebel.

A related debate that raged elsewhere in Aijaz Ahmad's critique of Edward Said's *Orientalism*[4] is useful however in guarding against an exclusive focus on gender as the only form of Otherness against and from which identity is derived, and showing that this Otherness is not always constituted in Manichean terms. What Said called Orientalism was the manner and stereotyping by which the West constructed an identity for the Orient which then allowed it to manage and colonize the latter, because the stereotypes justified the West's need for the Orient as something it developed, civilized and acted upon. A central insight of Said's, (influenced by Fanon), was that the West in fact was constructing its own identity at the time of its imperial ventures, in relation to this Orient. It evaluated its own civilization and histories on the basis of their difference from the Orient which was coded as underdeveloped, pagan, irrational and effeminate.

Ahmad takes Said to task for implying that 'as Europe establishes its own Identity by establishing the *difference* of the Orient...all European knowledges of non-Europe are bad knowledges because they are already contaminated with this aggressive Identity-formation.' According to Ahmad, the implication of Said's argument is that 'Europeans were ontologically not capable of producing any true knowledge about non-Europe.'[5] Although this critique in turn implies that identity formation is a conscious and deliberative act – when in fact Said's discussion of the nature of the discursive terrain on which such identity is mapped problematizes such positivism – Ahmad's argument is useful when appropriated into the terms of the gender debate. For it warns against looking at patriarchal constructs of female identity as always made in bad faith; that male and female identities should not be seen purely in manichean terms as polarities which contaminate but never enablingly inform each other. It should also remind us that patriarchy constructs itself in relation not just to the female gender but to other paradigms such as the State, nationalism, patriotism, race and class as well.

Just as the West imposed an identity on the Orient, patriarchy constructs woman as a gendered subject, and through the hegemony of a patriarchal literary establishment and tradition, women writers have been given a particular space – that of autobiography and domestic life. The long involvement of women authors in the genres of letters and journals (which record that most private space) has its roots in this history. Traditionally too, the autobiographical nature of women's writing resulted in its marginalization by a male-dominated literary critical establishment, dismissed as inconsequential in terms of public/'world' affairs and unable to contribute to great debates on culture and morality. But women readers of women writers have always known that the strength of these works lies in the personal as political, and see their collective concerns mirrored in these autobiographical/ domestic settings. Women authors, then, have made creative use of this space conceded to them to challenge and problematize patriarchy and explore questions of womanhood.

Sita Kulatunga relies on the autobiographical intimacy of letters in her novel *Dari the Third Wife*[6] to explore the ramifications of polygamy from the point of view of a young Nigerian girl married off to a rich man as his third wife. The novel is structured as a series of letters written by Dari to a Sri Lankan school friend[7] and this fictitious creation of 'authentic' correspondence – fictitious because it is both figment of an author's imagination and a representation by Dari of herself as a cohesive entity which, discursively, she can never be – invites the reader into a privileged intimacy, for letters are confessional by nature. They skilfully evoke a young girl caught in an ambivalence that problematizes stereotypical notions of the harshness of polygamy and adolescent marriage while also conveying the frustrations and injustices they cause.

The success of the book lies in this ambivalence which is represented through an exploration of Dari's predicament. Dari is naturally shocked and frightened at having to marry an unknown man and regretful at a missed opportunity for higher education. But the author also charts a young girl's sexual awakening which makes Bello's attention exciting to her. That Dari can and does fall in love with her husband and that her love is reciprocated is what forces us to acknowledge creative possibilities in a cultural system – particularly one that is unfamiliar to us – and this problematizes our own relativist assumptions which prompt an easy dismissal of polygamy as completely abhorrent and always discriminatory towards women.

Yet it is the contradictory duality underlying the experiences Dari writes about which makes her story really meaningful. Because of the couple's love, Bello's death in a car accident at the end is a harsh tragedy for Dari to bear, but ironically, it frees her to pursue her higher studies. Dari is the favoured wife – the one Bello chooses for companionship and the only one to move with him to the town house, but she is imprisoned nevertheless in her identity as the third wife. She is dependent on Bello for everything and totally isolated. Ameena the second wife, predictably scorns her, while Fatima the traditional, 'accepting' first wife talks to and advises Dari but is shown to be destructive in unwittingly frightening her about Ameena's evil charms. Dari in fact ends up believing that the still-birth of her first child is the culmination of those charms. This sense of isolation – she can only express her fears to her two friends through her letters – is skilfully underscored by the prison-like compound she lives in. The only window in her room is a 'pitifully small square' at the back, so high Dari has to climb on a stool to reach it.(p. 50)   Acknowledgement of her ability by her school teachers is a source of encouragement for Dari, but she has no real chance to use it. Her greatest encouragement lies in her own restless feminist sensibility which makes her relentlessly aware of her situation, guilty about her complicity as an all too consenting third wife and frustrated at not being able to further her education or have money of her own. But here again, 'Only God knows best what the future holds and sometimes I wonder', a refrain recurring throughout the letters, forces our acknowledgement of the complexity of a cultural system that prevents the heroine from developing that restlessness into an active bid to set different parameters for herself. The refrain echoes Dari's doubting of her religion (there is however a slippage here in that the author shows this religious uncertainty to emanate wholly from exposure to Western books and knowledge), but its soothing chants and prayers are what she misses when she moves into town.

The novel's ambiguity also throws light on other discursive pressures reflected in the text. On the one hand it gives voice to the ambivalent position of Dari as a woman at the fluid intersections of burgeoning awareness of herself as an economic pawn, sensual woman, wife and mother. In its concentration on the intensely personal it travels well to other cultural contexts where the father figure of Bello represents a patriarchy that is familiar, and in doing so, reinscribes the validity of the personal as political which energizes so much of women's writing. On the other hand, the creative possibilities within polygamy stressed in the novel, mainly depicted through the couple's love, are discursively constructed by the author at the expense of Bello's other wives, who are not only denied a meaningful agency throughout the work, but are presented much less sympathetically than Dari as she competes with them for Bello's attention and buys into the system. Moreover, Dari's reliance, as a widow, on the charity of Bello's son by his first wife is shown as a fate she is resigned to, and a positive respite from the rapaciousness of Bello's brothers, rather than an oppressive disempowering she needs to fight against – all of which precludes a keener and more overtly feminist critique of polygamy as it impinges on the lives of these women, and as a patriarchal structure which *controls* their sexuality. It is possible to recognize the operative discursive pressure which makes the author, an outsider from another cultural context, tentative in critiquing polygamy from a relativist stance. And this, while it signals an admirable refusal on the part of Kulatunga to be judgmental from the outside, means that her novel does not explore as creatively as it might the issues confronting women in polygamous cultures.

In Chandani Lokugé's title story in the collection *Moth and Other Stories*[8] it is the Janus-faced portrayals of the women that disappoint. But we must remember that the narrative voice is Lalith's, the village boy, who though in love with a rich young girl Mala, is seduced by her mother. The story, drawn in bold strokes, merits analysis of the way it articulates gender and sexuality and particularly for how the protagonist's psychological resistances throw light on common cultural codes operating in Sri Lankan society.

It is important that the story criticises Lalith for his opportunism in seeking instant socio-economic advantage by marrying into a rich family. Marrying Mala was for him, 'the chance of a life-time', 'a lottery ticket to a new life.'(p. 3) As a result, we distance ourselves from Lalith and learn to recognize that the virgin/whore dichotomy he slots women into reflects the cultural and individual codes that produce him rather than authorial endorsement of its reality. Lalith's mother, in this stereotypical framework, is the steadfast, simple, devout village woman who acts as the voice of conscience within Lalith. Guilt ridden at being seduced by his future mother-in-law, he thinks of his mother after the climactic moment of sexual intercourse. 'She (mother-in-law) came towards me...She held out her hand and body. I jerked forward. When I slept I dreamt of the full moon riding the sky in the village. Mother and I were in the temple.' (pp. 7-8)

Identifying this moral conscience with a 'pure' mother figure, rural existence, and Buddhism, by linking the mother with the village temple Lalith *always* sees her at, taps into widely held constructs of gender and culture that circulate amongst the Sinhala urban and rural middle-class.

It reiterates the forceful impact of a Buddhist ethic which subsumes the erotic and, within a particularly current nationalist framework, codes sexuality, often blurred with the urban and the West, as corrupt and sinful. There is enough evidence outside the texts I discuss here to suggest this is a construct which circulates widely in the media. The most cursory glance at contemporary Sinhala theatre and cinema shows how familiar are the stereotypes of women impressed in Lalith's mind. They exist as a polarity: the steadfast, poor, devout rural mother at one end and the sophisticated, Westernized, urban seductress at the other. They also constitute a norm where a further association between sexuality and a capitalist/business ethic is a further black mark against urban Westernized values. (And here Lokugé is guilty of having internalized these values, for the bewitching intended mother-in-law in the story is a successful hotelier – the tourist hotel again a signifier of a corrupting commodification of local culture weakened by the intrusion of alien (usually Western) tourists.) The Sinhala film *Kulageya* (1992) also marks this set of associations by having the dialogue between Mervyn and the business friends (one a drunkard, the other a seductress) who drag him into a world that alienates him from his family *entirely* in English. The character of Ramya in the film is a familiar figure – an English speaking, urban and Westernized seductress. Acceptance of this relatively widespread stereotype allows Lalith in Lokugé's story to present himself and Mala (her youthfulness an indicator of innocence and helplessness) as victims of the sexually rapacious mother, the moths who burn to her flame.

Other representations of women in Lokugé's short stories militate against Lalith's essentialist views of women, except in the disappointing 'In the Name of Charity' where the rich woman remains, without any subtle nuances, stereotypically haughty and insensitive. But generally the stories reveal sensitivity to the burden of women, often helpless and victimized by their families. 'Non-Incident' represents this very clearly, portraying a mother who carries the triple burden of being a woman, Tamil and underclass/uneducated. A tea plucker married to a Sinhala planter (most improbable given the social hierarchy that operates, but more of this later), she is the butt of her husband's racism and victim of brutal rejection by both husband and a son reared by his paternal grandmother never to know the embarrassment that is his mother. Their refusal to claim her body from the lunatic asylum continues their denial of her basic rights and their cruelty to her while alive. But if this story depicts the plight of women in its darkest aspect, there are others in which women playing the usual socio-domestic roles, are all shown to be victims of domestic violence, or at least of economic pressure and loneliness. Manel in 'A Man Within' copes with her husband, two children and growing debts, but just barely, leading a strenuous, routine life with no future. This is a masterful story describing how Sunil the protagonist, caught in a web of debt, becomes a target for terrorist blackmail, picked to carry a bomb into the Central Telegraph Office where he works in return for a large sum of money.[9] Lokugé's emphasis, however, on recording experience wholly from Sunil's perspective, necessary in her portrayal of a man under enormous pressure, means that Mala the wife is denied a voice of her own. We are aware of her through Sunil and while this denial of her own agency prevails it is impossible to show her as capable of overcoming the situation she and her family are in on her own terms.

The one woman who does try to make something of her life is Roshini in 'Point of Contact'. There is an astute construction here of one of the most difficult domestic scenarios with Roshini, a beautiful and capable young woman, trapped in a marriage where she has to make do with being a housewife. The complexity of the story and its setting arises from Roshini's guilt over her frustration, for her husband is kind, gentle and patient. But, without sensitivity to Roshini's needs for herself as a capable woman both within the home and outside it, as well as her sexuality, her husband's good qualities are shown as inadequate for a fulfilling marriage. When Roshini tells Nihal she would like to go out to work because she is bored and would like to earn her own money, his response is:

> Roshini, listen to me. I love you – I love to come
> home to you in the evening and find you waiting for
> me, looking so fresh and beautiful. I love to have my
> meals cooked by you, served by you. Who will see to
> these things if you go for a job?...Anyway, the women
> in my family don't work. (p. 87)

This is patriarchy, buttressed by tradition, at its most insidious, for although there is no overt cruelty a powerful hegemony is still asserted. It sets out parameters most limiting to the woman, as she contends with her guilt at being frustrated.

Roshini is vulnerable now to other men looking for sexual escapades, yet mature enough in this case to see the man she meets on the beach as 'all froth and bubble'. But from this point, the imagery in the story turns violent. 'Waves curled in whirls of blue, swell, loomed pregnant, laboured...shockingly smashed' and 'The sky seemed on fire, like a burning funeral pyre.'(pp. 90-1) The longing for motherhood – maternal imaginings – as an escape from boredom is here infused with a sub-conscious violence that carries Roshini's disturbed psychological state well. Finally she is shown to crack under the pressure and maniacally cut off her long tresses of hair – that symbolic marker of South Asian femininity – which coil around her feet. We know this will incur her husband's wrath. As for liberation, cutting off her hair is likely to be only a momentary act of rebellion as she slides into a psychotic state, for there is nothing within the story to signal a consciously mature awareness of how she can help herself.

All Lokugé's stories then end in displacement, rupture and violence both at domestic and public levels. But if Lokugé's women characters end weakly and tragically, we also need to be aware that these endings are influenced by other discursive pressures that determine a writer's particular stance. It is possible in this case, to see the discursive pressures on an emigrant writer such as Lokugé now living in Australia, which may cause the abandoned homeland to appear as a place of fracture where resolution is endlessly deferred. The whole collection is in fact an interesting site of how the pressures on an emigrant writer both buttress and overdetermine the exploration of gender issues. In *Moth and Other Stories* the land of birth is continually represented as violent. This is made possible by a general effacing of the *agency* of that violence. Apart from the story 'A Pair of Birds', which represents with subtlety and skill the rupture of a friendship after the 1983 Sinhala-Tamil riots, terrorists, whether LTTE or JVP, are shown to be shadowy figures, penetrating private and public space but faceless, with only 'unblinking, pitiless eyes ferreting into him, exploring, exposing his soul' as in the story 'The Man Within' (p. 62), known only by a serial number. The impact terrorists have on people and landscape is mapped through the perception of different voices that structure these stories, none however from the terrorist's point of view. Without any dialogic relationship between protagonist and terrorist, except in terms of the latter's impact upon the former, the landscape filled with bombs and terror, which make even its flowers violent, the crimson of the Nelum turning into a 'Red-shot smudge on white-gold temple sand'(p. 63), legitimizes the nihilism in the whole collection that Sunil expresses in 'The Man Within': 'Wasn't the country as helpless as he was? A country stripped and exposed starkly, just as he was unprepared and incapable of self-defence or self-control'.(pp. 62-3) It is significant that in contrast, the one story set in Australia has a landscape that is welcoming, a place of refuge, although of course for the immigrant character in the story there is no real sense of belonging. She and the landscape will always be alien to each other. Nevertheless lives can be lived here in contrast to a native land which 'cring(es) in terror.'(p. 95)

This same possibility of change in a different cultural setting is central to the theme of *A Change of Skies* by Yasmine Gooneratne[10] who emigrated to Australia in 1972. Gooneratne depicts the migrant experience as a series of trade-offs. What one gains is always offset against what one loses. The protagonists in this novel undergo a symbolic name change. Bharata and Navaranjini Mangala-Davasinghe, with all the attendant cultural baggage these names imply – associations of India, the scholarship in Indian languages of Bharata's father, and the rich heritage behind the name of the woman – are changed to Barry and Jean Mundy. In changing their names these two conform to Australian habits of shortening names. It is a gesture

towards integration which has however its satiric repercussions. The
sound Barry translates into Sinhala as 'beri' meaning 'cannot' and so, in
the context of the male, impotence.

In terms of gender hierarchy which this novel is always conscious of in
nuancing Barry's pomposity and condescension towards his wife, the
name change allows Jean access to an equality, a partnership with her
husband that the Asian name Navaranjini would have foreclosed. But is
it all in a name? Gooneratne's satire exposing the absurdities of the
pompous husband, the national stereotyping of one another by Asians and
Australians, the emigrant nationalist, academia and the trendy
feminist/ethnic activist, mocks gender, racial and pedagogic hierarchy
anywhere. In cocking a snook at a brand of militant feminism through her
heroine Jean who becomes a successful businesswoman in Australia by
making a profession out of oriental cookery – that drudgery of most
housewives – Gooneratne asserts a woman's right to choice that jabs at
'politically correct' stances which downplay and deny a vision and
capability such as Navaranjini's.

It is when one examines Barry and Jean's 'development' in Australia in
the larger context of patterns that inflect emigrant experience and writing,
that Gooneratne's work testifies to the tensions abounding in such
constructs. For there are contradictions – what Stephen Greenblatt calls
'small textual resistances'[11] – in the work which can be read as
symptomatic of the emigrant writer coming to terms with that migration.
Uncovering them leads us to understand the ambivalences that frame an
emigrant writer such as Gooneratne who, while laughing at her immigrant
characters, exposes her own tense stance towards both her native and
adopted lands. Take for instance the astounding arranged marriage in this
novel between the Sinhalese Bharata and Tamil Navaranjini, which even
the friendship of the families doesn't make credible, given the social
customs that prevail in Sri Lanka which insist on arranging marriages
according to caste, class and ethnicity. (The marriage between Tamil tea
plucker and Sinhala planter in Chandani Lokugé's story 'Non-Incident'
resonates here as it can be read as a similar textual resistance.) In the
scheme of Gooneratne's novel this is a small point and not particularly
important to the story, except that it throws light on her attempt to bring
together in the Sinhala Barry and Tamil Jean a composite Sri Lanka even
as she satirizes her characters for seeing others in such generalized terms.

My emphasis on placing both Lokugé and Gooneratne within the context
of emigrant writing is deliberate, for we have to remember that although
women's issues figure prominently in the works of these women writers,
they do not comprise the only issue. Nor are feminist discursive pressures
the only set of parameters that produce these texts. For we see in the
works of both Lokugé and Gooneratne particular pressures on the
emigrant writer which construct the native land as a ruptured, terror-filled
entity with cultural practices restrictive as manacles, overdetermining and

underpinning the way feminist issues are presented. Gooneratne's statement in an interview with Anne Susskind is interesting in this respect. She said, 'Many migrants concentrate on what they lose – their homeland, language, culture and bringing their children up in alien environments. I think I'm writing about people's capacity to change, a country's capacity to change, that no one needs to get stuck at a stereotype. Jean has no concept that she will develop a career when she comes but she does.'[12] What is crucial here is that it is the new land which affords the possibility of self-awareness and change. In fact the difference in emphases between the texts of Lokugé and Gooneratne who have migrated to Australia, and Sita Kulatunge whose sojourn in Nigeria was temporary, points forcefully to the presence of these discursive pressures. In Kulatunga's work, Dari's letters to her Sri Lankan friend imply that the latter has access to opportunities Dari is cut off from. In Gooneratne, it is not that everything about the native land is abhorrent. But it is symptomatic of her position as a writer that what she values in the homeland is the past, the ancestral walauwa, which is treated with a far gentler irony than the harsh satire aimed at contemporary Sri Lanka which is hollow, violent and chaotic – everything the airline magazine Barry and Jean's daughter, Edwina, reads on her trip to Sri Lanka clumsily tries to erase. The differences then indicate that textual variations are not wholly the result of individual differences and choices on the part of their authors, but are also produced by various overdetermining discourses which vary through locale and time.

Similarly, when one looks at Jean Arasanayagam's *Fragments of a Journey*,[13] we see yet another set of parameters – textual requirements of travel writing – impinging on how gender is represented in the short stories. Women's travel writing as a popular genre came into its own during the late 19th and early 20th Centuries when women started writing about their adventures in and impressions of the colonies where their husbands, sons or relatives were posted.[14] As in letters and diaries (often included as textual strategies in women's travel writing), it is the subject position that is central as the author recounts experiences through a personal involvement and vision. Often authors embark on journeys of self-discovery, whether consciously or not, and the characters depicted are shown, together with the author, to be taking part in one dramatic narrative.

Arasanayagam's title story 'Fragments of a Journey' makes clear that the woman traveller Dewa, journeying in India with her husband and daughter is on such a voyage of self-discovery.

All her life she had begun these journeys, some
of which were completed, the experience gathered
from them, stored in her memory-house to be relived
and rethought of...'Journeys are then in a sense,

never complete. They must begin all over again. They
become pilgrimages of discovery...These then are the
diaries that I write in my mind, that I carry back
with me...' Dewa thought to herself. (p. 66)

We enter into the intimately personal here, and the closeness of the
author's voice to that of her protagonist is obvious to readers of
Arasanayagam's poetry where the images and metaphors that Dewa
thinks in echo and resonate. For instance Dewa pondering over her
journeys – 'as if, taking up a book of paintings of ancient temples and
murals she slipped into those pages and walked in that re-incanatory
passage along the shores of Mahaballipuram where the rathas lay
drowned in the sea bed watching the sunken chariots whose stone wheels
had ceased to churn the path of war in some warrior's destination' (p. 66),
is completely in keeping with Arasanayagam's own emphasis on, and
admiration of Hindu myth and religio-cultural ritual which feature
prominently in her poetry.

Traces of a colonial discourse that required the travel writer to present
him/herself as an explorer/adventurer who conquers the arduous and
strenuous obstacles the new land presents can be seen in this story. The
reader is taken through a journey in which Dewa moves from hotel to
hotel, sleeps on soiled mattresses, journeys eight hours in a bus, travels
throughout the night, sprains an ankle, attends to a sick daughter and is
cheated by locals. 'Repetition becomes wearying' Dewa realizes, and the
exploration is strenuous. (p. 68) Here is a woman taking on the mantle of
a male adventurer, coping with the obstacles with stiff upper lip and a
sense of resignation. It is significant that when Dewa does feel completely
integral to the new landscape and culture it is at a moment in which she
is 'detached, momentarily from her family' (p. 79), and so, divorced from
wifehood and motherhood. Yet, in the detail that catches Dewa's eye is an
emphasis on the domestic that points to feminine interests. She often
describes various foods, cooking utensils, men ironing clothes, flowers,
gardens, women's clothing. Is this a significant contradiction? Sara Mills
argues in Discourses of Difference that this is a common discursive practice
in women's travel writing. The stereotype of the adventurer who
overcomes numerous obstacles is so obviously masculine, women writers
have difficulty in completely adopting this role with ease.[15] Thus there are
constant disclaimers in the texts by the women authors of their masculine
ability through humorous interventions and self-negations. It is possible
to see Dewa's attention to domestic detail in Arasanayagam's story, as a
discursive negotiation with which she dilutes somewhat the identity of a
resourceful and stoic masculine explorer that this genre of writing requires
her to take on for herself.

The multiplicity of discursive pressures on a text and its author include
the pressures brought to bear by reader responses. While women's writing

was never taken seriously in the public domain until the feminist debate forced both the publishing and critical establishments to take note, contemporary readers – particularly women – expect of female writers a greater understanding of the issues surrounding women's lives and a dedication to exploring, analyzing and even offering solutions to women's problems in their work. My reading so far, in focusing exclusively on women authors and how they articulate gender is a case in point. It is precisely this pressure we bring to bear when reading a text, looking for representation of multiple and overdetermining factors that interest us which makes us disappointed when a text, authored by a woman in particular, fails to take issue with women as gendered subjects in all its ramifications. An exclusive focus on women's writing is however an act of bad faith, and does not suffice for an understanding of how reader expectations produce differences in the work of female and male authors in the way gender is articulated.

There can be seen on the whole, a more honest confrontation with patriarchy in the work of the women authors I have looked at which is lacking in the work of contemporary male writers. In James Goonewardene's *One Mad Bid for Freedom*[16] women figure briefly just twice in the whole work. In an otherwise interesting novel which depicts facets of contemporary Sri Lanka in absurd exaggeration – a form which comments with irony on its subject matter – women are mere sex objects, giggly sexual partners of Korale and the members of his club. In Rajiva Wijesinha's *Lady Hippopotamus and Other Stories*,[17] when women characters function centrally in the narrative, or are drawn in bold cameo roles, it is their subliminal sexual desires that provide the twist in the tale. This in itself – returning the sexual to women whose spinsterhood and widowhood has meant a denial of their sexuality by society (this group includes the male Christian priest who is subject to similar moral censure) – would have been refreshing if not for the fact that, except in the story 'Exposure' which deals starkly with the economic necessities of prostitution, the subject is not given full treatment throughout the whole collection. When, as in 'Lady Hippopotamus' the sexuality of the boarding-school mistress becomes a subject of scandal, the tone of insensitive adolescent schoolboys the narrative voice takes on, precludes anything more than a gossipy, shocked moral judgement. There is a daring and refreshing presentation of both male and female sexuality in Carl Muller's *Jamfruit Tree*,[18] but the Burgher girls, unlike their resourceful, stoic mothers who are shown to soldier on with drunken husbands, economic deprivation and the struggle to maintain respectability, are depicted as being just sex mad, reinforcing a familiar cultural stereotype of the young Burgher woman as sexually free and therefore tainted.

This leads us to the question of biological determinism. Are men incapable of portraying women characters and their concerns in any realistic and complex way? The history of literature, drama, poetry and fiction have shown us that this is not the case for there are many portrayals of women by men which convince. In contemporary Sri Lankan Fiction in English, it is Romesh Gunasekera who delineates the inner compulsions of women characters most skillfully in his collection of short stories *Monkfish Moon*.[19] In three of the stories Gunasekera concentrates on women, deftly sketching in 'Carapace' the flitting nervous ambivalence of a young girl as she awaits a visit from an intended marriage partner from Australia who offers her an opportunity for a life of glamour she dreams of, while her love, although unarticulated, lies with an older but less acceptable beach-hut chef; or probing a daughter's reflection on her father's politics in 'Ranvali'. But it is 'Batik' which contains the most skilful portrayal of how a woman is affected when politics encroaches upon the domestic space. In England, Tiru and Nalini (he a Tamil, she a Sinhalese) are shown to invest equally in their home; their best moments together come when they redecorate their house, sharing ideas, compromising on differences. Nalini's entire world is this home and her husband, and so it is in order that the fissures which arise from Tiru's preoccupation with Tamil Eelam politics and his subsequent neglect of her, erupt most keenly in this domestic space. Gunasekera's depiction of the tension between husband and wife is deft and at the end, contrasting with the tender sexuality the couple shared before this intrusion of politics into the personal, is Nalini's controlled but slightly hysterical stabbing of a chilled chicken she prepares to cook which grows into an act of violence as she smashes a cup when even her pregnancy fails to evoke interest in her husband.

In contrast, an example from the popular press illustrates an almost total neglect of woman as a gendered subject in the work of authors writing in Sinhala. An article by Ranjit Dharmakeerthi citing eight short stories that appeared in the *Ravaya* – a popular weekly newspaper in Sinhala – representing popular cultural attitudes which speak to and are reinforced by a larger Sinhala speaking public, throws light on the different preoccupations of writers within this milieu.[20] Seven of the stories by male writers emphasize variously the pitfalls of the open-economy framework within the country, human rights abuses by the government and the psychological pressures on men imposed by the socio-political and economic crises in the nation. It is only the one female author, Kumuduni Manel de Silva whose protagonist is a woman, who charts in the story 'Agadhaya', a widow's struggle against economic problems and isolation which drive her into the arms of Perera a boutique keeper.

What this points to is a continuing discursive pressure on male authors to intervene in matters of 'public' importance such as political crises or public morality where giving voice to women's concerns is not a priority, while the female author continues to examine what is seen as the private space. To a large extent this is induced by artificial divisions at the level of reader expectations, and by extension a larger public and culture, which demand from male authors radically different interventions to those expected from female authors. These expectations in turn dictate the texts that foreclose male authorial acknowledgement of gender issues. If the publishing and literary critical establishments in Sri Lanka take a more activist stance in facilitating publications, translations and debate on these issues, we will see in the near future a more complex engagement on the part of both male and female authors and their readers with gender and other discourses that frame us.

## Notes

1. This paper was first presented at a seminar on 'The Media and Women' sponsored by the Women's Education Research Centre, Colombo, Sri Lanka, August 1993.
2. The medium of instruction in Sri Lankan schools is in one of the indigenous languages – Sinhala or Tamil.
3. In 1993 there were just three translations and one adaptation of works from English to Sinhala.
4. Edward Said, *Orientalism* (Harmondsworth: Penguin, 1978).
5. Aijaz Ahmad, *In Theory: Classes, Nations, Literatures* (London: Verso, 1992), p. 178.
6. Sita Kulatunga, *Dari the Third Wife* (Colombo: Kulatunga, 1993). Pagination will be from this edition.
7. Sita Kulatunge taught English in Nigeria for two years (1984-1985) and draws from her observations there.
8. Chandani Lokugé, *Moth and Other Stories* (London: Dangaroo, 1993). Pagination will be from this edition.
9. In 1986 a bomb did go off at the CTO killing over a 100 people. Lokugé roots her stories in a Sri Lankan reality by continuously referring in them to real incidents such as this.
10. Yasmine Gooneratne, *A Change of Skies* (New Delhi: Penguin, 1992). Pagination will be from this edition.
11. Stephen Greenblatt, *Marvelous Possessions* (Oxford: Clarendon, 1992), p. 65.
12. Yasmine Gooneratne quoted in Anne Susskind, *Sydney Morning Herald*, 27th July 1991. p. 17.
13. Jean Arasanayagam, *Fragments of a Journey* (Colombo: WERC, 1992).
14. See Sara Mills, *Discourses of Difference: An Analysis of Women's Travel Writing and Colonialism* (London: Routledge, 1991).
15. *Ibid.*, p. 78.
16. James Goonewardene, *One Mad Bid for Freedom* (New Delhi: Penguin, 1990). As there are few Sri Lankan male authors writing in English, I have had to look beyond the '92-93 time frame to illustrate my point.
17. Rajiva Wijesinha, *Lady Hippopotamus and Other Stores* (Colombo: English Writers' Co-operative, 1991).
18. Carl Muller, *The Jam Fruit Tree* (New Delhi: Penguin, 1993).
19. Romesh Gunasekera, *Monkfish Moon* (London: Granta, 1992).
20. Ranjit Dharmakeerthi, 'An Examination of Short Stories published in the Ravaya from January to March 1993,' *Ravaya* 4.7.1993. p. 6.

# PAKISTAN
and
INDIA

# BAPSI SIDHWA

Bapsi Sidhwa was born in Karachi, Pakistan. She graduated from Kinnaird College for Women, Lahore. Married and with three children, she resides in the United States but travels frequently to Pakistan. An active social worker among Asian women, in 1975 she represented Pakistan at the Asian Women's Congress.

Bapsi Sidhwa has published four novels: *An American Brat*, *Cracking India* (published as *Ice-Candy-Man* in England), *The Bride*, *The Crow Eaters*, and short stories. She has been translated into German, French and Russian. She is currently working on a collection of short stories and compiling a book of essays and reviews.

Sidhwa has been nominated for the Lila Wallace-Reader's Fellow at Radcliffe/Harvard in 1986-87 and was a Visiting Scholar at Rockefeller Foundation Study Center, in Bellagio, Italy. She was awarded a National Endowment for the Arts grant for Creative Writing in 1987. She received the *Sitara-i-Imtiaz*, a Pakistan national honour in 1991 and the *Litteraturepreis* in Germany for *Ice-Candy-Man (Cracking India)* also in 1991.

BAPSI SIDHWA

# Why I Write

I began writing because the itch to write was compulsive. I analyse it now as an obsession with self-expression – something I was denied as a child. For me writing is a natural condition of existence, and very often an act of joy. Of course it can be painful, slow, and difficult at times, but it is always a labour of love.

The moment it ceases to be so, I'll give it up; although by now it has become a habit.

When I'm not writing my life seems to fly apart, and I get embroiled in needless complexities. So, why complicate life? It's easier to write.

BAPSI SIDHWA

# The Trouble-Easers

It is Friday: the day to remember the Trouble-Easer and Behram Yazad.
Mother mops the brick floor in the bedroom and closes all doors. I
dawdle on the bed, my prayer cap on my head. I am impatient. I wish my
mother would get along with the ceremonial story, and not take so long
with her prayers. I hear the Swish-swish of the *Kusti* as she whips the
sacred-thread behind her to banish evil. She will tie the thread thrice
round her waist, knotting it in the front and in the back, and, so, gird her
loins in the service of the Lord.

When Mother emerges from the bathroom, the gauzy scarf covering her
head tied in a soft loop beneath her chin, her face devout, the bedroom air
smells holy. And she has not even lit the joss-sticks or the fire yet.

I help her spread the *durrie* on the floor, and, on it, a spotless sheet. It
is immaculate except for a few holes burnt by errant sparks from previous
prayer-fires. Mother places the fire-altar tray, with its portion of
sandalwood shavings and frankincense, in the centre of the sheet. Around
it she arranges a portrait of our Prophet Zarathushtra – one finger raised
to remind us of the one and only God – and of the ragged-looking saint
Mushkail-Asaan. A silver bowl containing water, a mirror, chickpeas and
jagged lumps of crystallized sugar, complete the arrangements.

I take my place across Mother. Shaded by the scarf, her features acquire
sharper definition. The chin, tipped to a dainty point, curves deep. The
lips, full, firm, taper from a lavish 'M' in wide wings, their outline etched
with the clarity of cut crystal. The soft her cheeks is framed by a jaw as
delicately oval as an egg. The hint of remoteness, common to such
classically sculpted beauty, is overwhelmed by the exuberance and
innocence that marks her personality. Mother is beautiful beyond bearing.
My heart beats fast. She does not look at me. I am observing an aspect of
her that is too private. A shy and guilty voyeur, I remove my eyes from
her face.

We sit cross-legged. Praying under her breath in sibilant whispers,
Mother lights the joss-sticks, and arranging the sandalwood in a crisscross
atop a thin bed of ashes in the fire-altar, sets it alight with a match-stick.
Turning her face slightly to avoid the smoke, she gently fans the
sandalwood to start a crackling little fire the size of a fist. She adds a
pinch of frankincense and the room is so filled with smoke and fragrance
that I can feel the presence of the angels. My eyes and my nose water.

At last Mother utters the words that will start the story of Pir Khurkain and Mushkail-Asaan.

'Once upon a time there was a wood-cutter named Pir Khurkain.'

'*Jee ray jee* (Yes jee yes),' I respond reverently.

I too have a part to play. Each time Mother comes to the end of a sentence I must say, '*Jee ray jee.*' If I fail to respond promptly, Mother peeks into the mirror and quickly says: 'Yes jee yes,' to herself, becoming both the teller and the listener, and I am done out of my part.

Right through the ceremony we shell the chickpeas and collect them in a dish. The discarded dark brown husk floats in the silver bowl. The bowl's contents will be reverently tipped into a fern-pot or a gardenia hedge later.

As the story progresses my mother's pure, rich voice picks up the spellbinding rhythm of all great tellers of tales:

Once upon a time there was a woodcutter,

'Yes jee yes.'

Everyday he chopped wood and provided for his wife and daughter.

'Yes jee yes.'

One day his neighbours cooked liver. The fumes from the frying liver drifted to his house and made his daughter's mouth water.

'Yes jee yes.'

The girl wondered, 'What excuse can I make to visit their house?' She decided she would pretend she needed some fire.

*I don't recall anyone telling me, but I know that everything in the story happened a long time ago, before matches were invented. People lit their fires from a central hut – or a temple – where a fire was kept alive all the time, or they took it from each other's hearths.*

When the girl went to her neighbours house to ask them for fire, they told her to get it herself, and no one offered her any liver.

Then she went to the neighbours again. This time they brought her the fire, but no one gave her any liver.

The woodcutter's daughter felt brokenhearted.

In the evening when the woodcutter returned, he asked his daughter: 'What is the matter, why are you so sad?'

Then the girl told her father, 'The neighbours were cooking liver..I went to their house to ask for fire. They did not bring me the fire, but asked me to get it myself. Thrice I went to them, the third time I went they had sat down to dinner. This time they fetched me the fire, but no one asked me to stay to dinner. My heart and soul were in the liver, but they did not give me any: that's why I'm sad.'

The woodcutter said, 'Don't worry, child. Tomorrow I will cut a huge stack of wood and buy you all the liver you desire.'

Pir Khurkain went to the forest to cut wood early the next morning. He chopped the trees until he had gathered a large stack of wood, but when he went to collect it in the evening, there was nothing there. The stack of wood had burnt to ashes.

Pir Khurkain was too ashamed to face his wife and daughter empty handed, and he decided to spend the night in the forest.

The next day he cut another stack of wood, but when he went to fetch it, the wood had again burnt to ashes.

The woodcutter could not bear to face his family empty handed, and again he spent the night in the forest.

Pir Khurkain spent the third day cutting and chopping an even larger stack of wood, but when he came to take it to the market, he found only ashes. Pir Khurkain thought: It is three days since I've eaten, but I cannot bear to show my face to my wife and daughter empty handed. He became very dejected.

'Yes jee yes.'

The woodcutter waited in the forest till the evening became dusky. He thought he would sneak into his house late at night and spend the night quietly in some corner.

When he arrived at his street he concealed himself in a shaded spot, waiting for the night to advance.

Now it so happened that the angels who ease troubles, Behram Yazad and Mushkail-Asaan, were out for a stroll in the city, and while wandering through the streets, they came upon Pir Khurkain. They asked him, 'Why are you standing out here in the dark? Is anything the matter?'

The woodcutter was too embarrassed to give them a reply and he kept quiet. On their way back they saw him again. 'Why are you still standing out on the street?' they asked. 'Tell us what is worrying you and we will ease your troubles.'

*At this point mother adds a pinch of frankincense to the fire, and holding her palms together and bowing her head, asks the angels to ease her troubles. She makes a motion with her hands, as if drawing the smoke towards herself, and continues.*

The woodcutter told them the tale of his misfortunes and suffering. (*Mother repeats the story almost from scratch, starting with:* One day the neighbours were cooking liver – I can *listen to the sad litany of the poor woodcutter's woes a million times and not get fed up.*)

Then Mushkail-Asaan and Behram Yazad were moved to pity by the woodcutter's misfortune, and scooping three fistfuls of sand from the ground, they poured it into his lap. 'Cherish what we have given you,' they said, 'and keep it safe. Distribute some chickpeas and sugar or sugared-cardamons on any auspicious day you like, and think of us.'

The woodcutter thought: 'What good will this sand do me? I will throw it away as soon as they leave.'

But Behram Yazad and Mushkail-Asaan could read what was going on in his mind, and they said: 'O Pir Khurkain, don't throw away what we have given you. Cherish it and guard it with your life. Each grain of sand will be useful to you. Sell it at a high price, don't sell it cheap; and remember to remember us.'

'Yes jee yes.'

*Mother must again place frankincense on the fire. She does so, saying, 'I will never forget you O Behram Yazad and Mushkail-Asaan.' I also add a pinch of frankincense and parrot her words.*

When the woodcutter returned home, his wife and daughter were asleep. He poured the sand into a corner, and lay down.

Shortly before dawn, when his neighbours set out for work, they called to his daughter: 'Wake up, girl, wake up. Your house is on fire.'

When the girl woke up it seemed to her as if their house was lit with lamps. She awakened her father and told him that their house was on fire. The woodcutter said: 'Go back to sleep, child, it must be one of our neighbours' houses that is on fire. What do we have in our house that it could burn? We own nothing.'

The girl went back to sleep. Now Pir Khurkain got up and saw that the whole house was filled with light and dazzling bright. He looked around, and saw that the sand that he had thrown into a corner had turned into an incandescent heap of diamonds, emeralds, rubies and pearls.

'Yes jee yes.'

The woodcutter gathered the gems in a rag and went back to sleep.

'Yes jee yes.'

The next morning the woodcutter selected one gem from the heap and took it to a jeweller's to sell. The jeweller asked him: 'What should I give you for this, one billion rupees or two billion?'

'You are mocking me,' cried the woodcutter and went to another jeweller.

The other jeweller said: 'I don't have enough money to make you an offer for a gem like this.'

Then the woodcutter went to the biggest jeweller in town. The jeweller said: 'I cannot fathom the value of such a magnificent jewel. But here's what I can do: I'll make three mounds of gold sovereigns of different sizes. Throw the jewel into the sky and which ever mound it falls on, will be yours.'

The woodcutter threw the gem up into the sky and it settled on the largest mound of gold.

The woodcutter collected the gold coins and went to the market. He bought meat, liver, bread, sugar, butter, flower etc. and all the other groceries he could think of for his house. Next he hired some labourers, and after helping them to raise the loaded baskets to their heads, directed them to his house. When he had finished buying everything he needed, Pir Khurkain bought some roasted chickpeas, and repeating to himself the story of his meeting with the Trouble-Easers, and giving three chickpeas to whoever happened to cross his path, he took the road home.

In the meantime the first lot of hired men had arrived at his house. Pir Khurkain's wife and daughter were standing outside, and the men asked them if this was the woodcutter's house.

'This is the woodcutter's house,' they said, 'But the poor woodcutter could never afford such fancy purchases.'

They told the hired men that they must have made a mistake, and sent them away.

The labourers met the woodcutter on the road. He turned them back and walked behind them repeating the names of Mushkail-Asaan and Behram Yazad and giving three chickpeas to whoever crossed his path.

But when the woodcutter returned with the merchandise, his wife cried, 'We're poor folk. How can we suddenly afford to buy all this? You must have committed a theft.'

Then the woodcutter told his wife and daughter the story of his meeting with the angels. They put everything away in its proper place, and then washed and cooked the liver. They ate and drank their fill and had a marvellous time.

'Yes jee yes.'

The woodcutter heard that some of their neighbours were going to Mecca on a pilgrimage, and he told his neighbours that he would go with them.

But before he left he made a necklace out of those diamonds, emeralds, rubies, and pearls. He put the necklace round his daughter's neck and told her: 'Daughter, you can build an even larger and more resplendent house than the King's palace with this money. But don't forget, we owe all our happiness to the Trouble-Easers Behram Yazad and Mushkail-Asaan. Remember to think of them every Friday, and distribute three pice worth of roasted chickpeas after you pray.'

Then the woodcutter went away to Mecca to perform Haj.

'Yes jee yes.'

The woodcutter's daughter built a house like a palace. They entertained lavishly and the house resounded to the sound of laughter and the chatter of new friends.

One day it so happened that when the woodcutter's daughter went to the bath-house she found that someone was already inside and the doors were closed to her. She asked the maid who was waiting outside, 'Who's in there that you won't allow me to enter the bath-house?'

The maid told her that the Princess was having her bath.

When the Princess heard them talking, she called to the woodcutter's daughter and said, 'Let us bathe together, after all, you are a woman, and I am a woman.'

When they came out of their baths, the Princess sent for round silver platters of pillaf and sweets and invited the woodcutter's daughter to eat with her.

Pir Khurkail's daughter wondered how she might repay such royal hospitality. She removed a diamond from her necklace and gave it to the Princess.

'Yes jee yes.'

When the Princess returned to the palace she showed the diamond to the King and complained, 'Father, you are a King, and yet you don't have a single gem to compare with this diamond given to me by a woodcutter's daughter.'

The King said, 'Daughter, God has not made all men equal. Some wear crowns and sit on thrones, some toil and reap poverty, some live by honour and some by pride, and some have strength and some ill health. One man's fate is not the same as another's.'

The Princess and the woodcutter's daughter became devoted friends.

'Yes jee yes.'

*At this point mother interrupts the narrative to say, in an almost childishly self-righteous way, 'The woodcutter's daughter forgot you, O Trouble-Easer, but I will never, ever, forget to remember you.' Mother puts more sandalwood on the fire, which has almost become ashes. Then she joins her hands, and bows her head, and asks for blessings on her house. When she passes her hands over her face, I sit up. The interval is over, the story will continue.*

One afternoon the woodcutter's daughter and the Princess came upon a lake in the forest. The Princess said, 'How inviting the water looks. Let's swim.'

'I can't swim,' her friend said. 'But I'll sit by the lake while you have a swim.'

The Princess removed her clothes, and, last of all, the diamond necklace round her neck, and hung them from the branches of a tree. She told her friend to mind her belongings, and slipped into the water.

Then Mushkail-Asaan came in the guise of crow and took away the diamond necklace.

When the Princess came out of the water she discovered that her necklace was missing.

'Yes jee yes.'

They shook the branches of the tree and searched the underbrush but they could not find the necklace.

Then the Princess cried: 'There is no one here but us. I told you to mind the necklace and now you say you don't have it. You have taken it.'

The Princess took her complaint to the King. The King questioned the woodcutter's daughter, but she told him, 'I have not taken anything.'

The King cast the woodcutter's daughter into prison.

'Yes jee yes.'

When she heard that her daughter was in prison, Pir Khurkain's wife ran to the palace gates crying, 'O King! How can I leave my unmarried and chaste daughter all alone in prison? Put me in with her!'

The King now cast both mother and daughter into prison. He confiscated their property and all their possessions in lieu of the necklace.

'Yes jee yes.'

On his way back from the pilgrimage to Mecca the woodcutter was robbed by bandits.

When he arrived at his house he found it dark and gloomy and frighteningly desolate.

The woodcutter knocked on his neighbours' doors. His neighbours told him that his daughter had stolen the Princess' necklace and the King had cast both his wife and daughter into prison.

Pir Khurkain ran to the palace and standing before it cried: 'O, King! What manner of justice is this that I, a man, sit at home free, and my wife and daughter are in prison?'

The King told him, 'Your daughter has committed a theft, that is why I have put them both into prison.'

The woodcutter pleaded, 'O King, release them, and lock me up in their stead.'

The King freed both women and cast Pir. Khurkain into prison.

That night Mushkail-Asaan appeared before the woodcutter in a dream; 'I gave you every happiness that your heart desired,' he said. 'Yet you could not remember to pray over a few chickpeas for me?.'

In his dream the woodcutter wept and cried, 'O Trouble-Easer, forgive me. My daughter is young and heedless. She has made a mistake.'

And because Pir Khurkain was a truly good man, Mushkail-Asaan said, 'When you awaken you will be free of your chains. You will also find three coins to the right side of your head. Send for the chickpeas and sugar with the money and remember us; we will ease your troubles.'

*Another break in the story. Another pinch of incense added to the fire, a folding of hands and bowing of heads. Mother says: 'When you ease other people's troubles, O Mushkail-Asaan, ease ours as well.'*

Next morning when Pir Khurkain woke up, the chains that bound his hands and legs fell away from him. He looked to the right of where he had laid his head and found the three coins. He sat by the barred prison window thinking of the Trouble-Easer.

Presently he saw a Passerby who was on his way to buy clothes for a wedding. The woodcutter begged him to bring him three pice worth of roasted chickpeas.

The Passerby was brusque and rude. 'I have no time to waste,' he said, 'My daughter is getting married, and I am too busy in the bustle of wedding preparations to get you chickpeas,' and he went his way.

The woodcutter angrily muttered. 'May you hear news of a death instead of a wedding, and may you need a shroud instead of wedding garments.'

The Passerby was on his way back to his house when some men rushed up to tell him, 'Your son-in-law has suddenly taken very ill. He's unconscious and on the verge of death. You must buy clothes for the funeral.'

The Passerby turned back sorrowfully to buy clothes for his son-in-law's funeral. The woodcutter saw him, and again begged him to buy three pice worth of roasted chickpeas.

The grieving Passerby went up to the barred window and said, 'Give me the money brother, and I will get you the chickpeas. Earlier I was on my way to buy wedding clothes; now I have news that my son-in-law is deathly ill, and I'm in no hurry to get burial clothes.'

The Passerby brought the woodcutter the roasted chickpeas.

Then the woodcutter blessed him and said, 'May your sorrowing house be filled with joy again.'

Once more the men rushed to catch up with the Passerby. 'Your son-in-law has recovered,' they said. 'Go quickly and make arrangements for the wedding.'

The woodcutter repeated to himself the story of his meeting with the Trouble-Easers and the help they had given him, and handed three peeled chickpeas to whoever went past his window.

'Yes jee yes.'

The next day the King and the Princess went for an outing in the forest. They got tired and sat beneath a tree when lo! The diamond necklace fell into the princesses lap!

'Yes jee yes.'

They looked up and beheld a peacock. Mushkail-Asaan, in the guise of the bird, had returned the necklace.

The King thumped his daughter on the back and scolded her. 'You have accused an innocent girl of theft! You have committed a very grave wrong.' The King and Princess became very sad and were sorry.

The next day Pir Khurkain was released from jail with great pomp and celebration. The King took the woodcutter to the palace and said, 'Can you forgive us, O Pir Khurkain? My daughter has made a terrible mistake!'

The woodcutter wept and cried: 'You have dishonoured my family and disgraced my daughter! Who will marry her now?'

Then the King said: 'Would it please you if I marry her to my son?'
And so it came about that the daughter of a humble woodcutter was married to a prince.
The King removed his crown and placed it on the woodcutter's head.
'Yes jee, yes'
The story ends. Mother asks blessings for our family: 'As Pir Khurkain's troubles eased: as a woodcutter's daughter married a Prince: as the Passerby gained his son: so help us great Trouble-Easer and Behram Yazad and make our wishes come true. Amen!'
The room is scented with incense and foggy with smoke. Almost all the golden chickpeas are peeled, their dark husks floating in the silver bowl. Mother gives me three chickpeas and pops some into her mouth. She will now distribute them, giving more than the prescribed three to visitors and members of our household.
My bottom hurts with sitting so long on the hard floor. It is worth it; I feel ennobled – God blessed.
It didn't occur to me until many years later to wonder how a Muslim woodcutter, who went for Haj to Mecca, got tangled up with Zoroastrian angels and Zoroastrian prayers. But that is what happens when one lives cheek by jowl with people of other faiths – saints jump boundaries and the barriers fall.

# SHASHI DESHPANDE

Shashi Deshpande was born in Dharwad, India, daughter of the renowned dramatist and Sanskrit scholar, Shriranga. At the age of fifteen she went to Bombay, graduated in Economics, then moved to Bangalore, where she gained a degree in Law. The early years of her marriage were largely given over to the care of her two young sons, but she took a course in journalism and for a time worked on a magazine. Her writing career only began in earnest in 1970, initially with short stories, of which several volumes have been published. She is also the author of four children's books and five previous novels – *The Dark Holds No Terrors, If I Die Today, Come Up and Be Dead, Roots and Shadows* and *That Long Silence* (Virago, 1988), which won the Sahilya Akademi award and has been widely translated. Shashi Deshpande lives in Bangalore with her pathologist husband. Her most recent book is *The Binding Vine* (Virago).

SHASHI DESHPANDE

# Why I Write

I started writing rather late in life; I was nearly thirty when I began. Until then, though I had read voraciously since childhood, and had been obsessed by – no, let me not be pompous and say literature – the written word, I had written nothing, nothing at all. One day I began. And then, as if the floodgates had been opened, I wrote and wrote and wrote. It was a deluge, as if what had been pent up in me for years was flooding out. I wrote short stories initially. All about women, as my very few readers as well as family and friends never failed to inform me. I had a serious sense of doing something not exactly wrong, but something rather shaming. Surely writing about women was not serious writing? Serious literature was written by men, about men. But there was nothing I could do about it. Sometimes I cheated. I wrote in the persona of a man. A male narrator. But the stories turned out to be about women after all.

They kept coming out of the dim corridors of my mind, places I hadn't even known they inhabited. Girls and women I had seen since childhood. Girls being 'shown' around to eligible 'boys', waiting patiently, humbly to be approved by them, by their parents, their sisters/brothers /aunts/uncles/grandparents so that they could get married and fulfil their destinies. Girls who had been lively and sparkling, looking after marriage placid perhaps, but dimmed, as if a spark had been extinguished. A great aunt who had been widowed at 10 and lived the life of a shaven widow ever since and another who was, they all said, 'so clever she should have been a lawyer' but became a widow instead. And we took it for granted that their roles were to serve anyone, everyone in the family for all their lives, with never a respite.

I wrote a story about a young woman's feelings on the first night after her (arranged) marriage. Of her fears of having sex with the man who was to her 'not even a friend, but only a husband'. A novel about a woman who thinks of herself as the 'skeleton in her own cupboard'. Another about a marriage which a woman suddenly discovers is nothing more than a yoking together of two animals: 'it's more comfortable to move in the same direction. To go in different directions would be painful; and what animal would voluntarily choose pain?' I wrote about a woman who – but why go on? Yes, I write about women.

Sometimes, in my more expansive moments, I say 'I speak for women.' In more sensible moods, I know that is claiming too much. Social responsibility, social commitment – these are words that occur with monotonous regularity in India when writers speak/are spoken of. Yes, in a country like ours, these can never be ignored. Yet I know I do not write to change the world. I would like to; who wouldn't? But I know I cannot. I can only tell it as it is. Rejecting all that has been said, written and told to me about people, specially about women who have always been spoken for, discarding images, stereotypes, re-questioning myths and starting afresh, crawling into the minds of women, painting their inner landscapes – I tell it as it is. Rather, as I think it is. And taking pains about how I tell it, shaping my work with care and love, because the form of my creation is very important to me. This is what I have done and, hopefully, will go on doing.

SHASHI DESHPANDE

# The Homecoming

Pushing the bucket of dirty water away with her foot in an unconscious imitation of her mother, she swiped the floor in a final wide arc and thought of her mother's words – after you've mopped the floor, you should be able to see your face in it. Can I, she wondered? No, there was nothing. That's just Ai's way of talking, she thought scornfully. And she didn't want to see her face, anyway. She remembered the day she had looked at herself in Anju's mirror - it was new then, Anju had just bought it with her first pay – and how startled she had been to see her face so clear in it. This square face with the thick eyebrows and frizzy hair – is this me? She much preferred the grey ghost the old mirror showed her. Anju never had enough of looking at herself in the new mirror, though. She would turn it this way and that to get the maximum light from the one small window set high in the wall. But then, Anju was pretty – her fair complexion, her straight nose...

'Finished, Suman?'

She turned round startled. Her face changed, it took on a look of utter devotion. How silvery Tai looked standing there in the morning sunshine that poured in through the window. Even her voice was silvery.

'Yes, Tai.'

'Had your tea?'

'No, Tai.'

'Go in and have it, then. Have a good breakfast, mind.'

'Yes, Tai.'

'You'll get a good breakfast,' Ai had said when she was trying to persuade Suman to work in Tai's house the two mornings a week she went to the temple.

'Yes, yes, teach her to become like you - to work like a dog and then be grateful for the scraps they give you, this pigsty they allow you to live in.'

'You be quiet. You don't want to work yourself, and you don't want this girl to do it, either. What's wrong with her doing a little work and having something filling in her stomach before she goes to school? What can I give her, anyway?'

But for Suman it was not the breakfast. It was Tai – the way she looked, so light and airy in her saris that seemed to float around her, her soft voice, her smile, the way she spoke to her, called her Suman...

'Baby?' she had smiled when Ai said, 'Baby will do your work Mondays and Saturdays.' 'If she's big enough to work, she's too big to be called Baby. I will call her Suman.'

That was the beginning of a happiness she could not speak of to anyone. She had kept it locked within herself, guarding it jealously. At night she had lain awake, her eyes fixed on the light that came in through the small, high window from the veranda of Tai's bedroom. Looking at it, she could imagine Tai reading, or listening to music, maybe. Sometimes, rarely, both of them sat outside on the veranda and then she could hear their voices. One still night she had heard Tai's laughter and suddenly a kind of sob had welled up in her, taking her unawares so that she had not been able to stifle it.

'Baby?' Ai's voice had come immediately out of the darkness. She had lain rigidly silent. 'Anju? Anju?'

'What is it?'

'I thought I heard someone crying.'

'I wasn't crying. But I feel like it all right. God, one can't even get a bit of sleep in this place.'

With the four of them sleeping in the little room, it was a tight fit. Suman had the worst of it, actually, sandwiched between Anju, who got furious if she as much as moved a finger and the little fellow who wet himself every night.

'Why don't you send him out with Suresh?' Anju had complained. 'He's big enough, nearly six now.'

Ai had tried. But it was no use. He invariably came back, clambering over their bodies until he found the soft mound that was his mother. And, in a while, he would wet himself. That night, he had done it again. Suman, feeling the wetness, had woken up to Anju's angry outburst, more vicious than usual.

'I'm going to get out of here, I've had enough.'

'Not if I can stop you.'

It was then that Suman had come out of her dream world to realise the conflict raging between Ai and Anju. She had cowered in her blanket at the cruel hurting things they said to each other.

'Marriage? You think it's a child's game? A doll's marriage? You meet a boy you know nothing of – neither his caste, his home nor his family and you want to go and put a garland round his neck?'

'I know why you're trying to stop me. You don't want to lose my pay.'

There had been silence after that and the next morning Ai's face had the same defeated look it had once had when Anju had said, 'I don't want to become like you – cleaning dirt out of other people's homes all my life.'

Ai stopped speaking to Anju after that and one day Anju just went away and got married. Ai wouldn't let them even mention her name. But when Anju had come back, in all her newly married glory - green bangles, silver toe-rings, black beads and a beautiful blue China silk sari - Ai had done all the things that were done to a newly married daughter, her face stern and unsmiling. And when Anju had left she had stayed inside. It was Suman who had stood in the doorway, watching Anju walk daintily down the mud path in her high heeled slippers, as if she had never walked there before, her sari-end tucked round her waist, accentuating its slimness, her hair clips glinting in her sleek dark hair. She had turned back when she reached the gate, waved casually to Suman and was gone. Suman, giving a faint sigh, had come in to find Ai sobbing, a terrible, rending kind of sobbing.

'Ai, what is it? What's happened?'

She had straightened up. 'Nothing' she had said and gone on with her work. She had said the same thing when Suman had come home and found Anju lying in a corner a few days back. 'What has happened? Anju? Ai, what's wrong with her?'

'Nothing,' Ai had said once again.

Nothing! How can Ai...? I will tell Tai...

'Finished, Suman?' Tai was asking her.'

'Yes, Tai.'

'All right, you can go. Tell your mother to come a little early today. I have to go out.' As the girl hesitated, not making any move to go, the woman asked, 'No school today?'

'I can't go, Anju is...' She bit off her words.

'Anju? Has she come? Why hasn't she come to see me this time?'

She had visited Tai last time. Suman had followed Anju and she could remember Anju trying to look as if it was a casual thing for her to be talking to Tai so easily. And how Anju, who had seemed so beautifully dressed until then, had looked gaudy and loud. Her voice too – why was it so shrill, so loud? Suman had been suddenly angry – with Tai? with Anju? or with herself? She had not known.

'Tell her to come and see me before she goes back.' Seeing the girl's face, Tai asked, 'What is it, Suman?'

'Tai, Anju says she is not going back.'

'Why? Started fighting with her husband already?' Tai's smile faded. 'Is anything wrong?'

'She doesn't say anything.'

Since her return, three days back, she had said nothing, except, once, 'I'm not going back.' It was Suman who had seen the marks on her back. Anju had been sleeping on her side, leaving her back uncovered. Seeing it, Suman had called out in a strangled voice, 'Ai... Ai...'

'What is it?'

The girl had just pointed to Anju's back. Ai saw the scars - some of them still raw, oozing blood – and cried out so loudly that Anju had woken up with a start. She sat up, her hands held out before her, her eyes those of a frightened animal.

'What did he do to you, Anju? What did he do? Tell me.'

Awareness had come slowly into Anju's face. Eyes fixed on them, she had moved backwards on her haunches – like an animal, Suman had thought, staring at her with fright, yes, she had even grunted like an animal - until her back had touched the wall. She had not moved from that spot since then.

'Tai, help us. Ai says Anju must go back, she says she's married and Anju...how can she? I saw her back. She's hurt.'

'Oh my God.'

'Tai, please come and talk to Ai.'

'All right,' Tai said finally. 'I'll come in the evening. I have a meeting. After it's over...'

'Tai, please don't tell Ai I told you,' she wanted to say, but lacking the courage walked away.

'No, I'm not going to tell her,' Ai had said angrily when Suman had suggested it.

'But why, Ai?'

Ai had been squatting as she cleaned the vessels, her large feet firmly gripping the squelchy mud under her feet. The fetid smell of left-over food came from the vessels.

'This is our business, we don't want anyone to interfere.'

'But Ai, Tai can do something, she can talk to Anju's husband...or...or she can do something.'

Ai had laughed at that. 'Something! No, no one can do anything. Move aside, don't just stand there. You can pour out the water for me while I wash. No,' she had gone on, throwing the clean vessels into the wicker basket with bad-tempered clangs, 'this is our business. Keep your mouth shut, I'm warning you.'

If she knows now what I've done, the girl thought fearfully, imagining the weight of her mother's hard hand. But I know Tai will do something and then Ai won't be angry any more.

As soon as Ai went out in the afternoon, Suman frantically cleaned the house. She pushed everything that was lying about into the large steel trunk and then looked at Anju, sitting in her unwashed clothes, her uncombed hair. There was a dark spot on the wall behind her where she had been resting her head. The room reeked of sweat – and something else. What was it?

'Anju,' she said gently, 'Tai is coming. She'll help you.'

There was no reply. Anju's face was blank as if she hadn't heard Suman, no, worse, as if Suman hadn't spoken. 'Anju,' she repeated. 'Tai is coming. Shall I comb your hair?'

Anju was still silent. Nevertheless, Suman got out the comb and mirror, the old one Anju had despised so much, and gently removed one of the clips from the ugly tangle of Anju's hair. Immediately, like a puppet whose strings had been pulled, Anju began to twist about, moaning, 'No' over and over again. Suman watched her helplessly. The cries went on and on. Finally she got up, put the clip and comb away and went out. She plucked all the washed clothes off the bushes, folded them, put them away and sat down from where she could see Tai's house. *Hasn't she come as yet? She must have come.* In a while it became dark. *She did say she had a meeting and she would be coming late. Has she forgotten? No, she told me she would come. I'll count to a hundred.* She counted hundred, two hundred, three hundred, and gave up. She sat trailing a stick on the ground, drawing meaningless patterns in the dust, feeling a kind of pain inside her. Ai came in through the small gate, Barkya clinging to her as usual. She went straight in, without looking at Suman. Soon Suman heard the Primus hissing. Suresh vaulted over the wall and went in calling out, 'I'm hungry.'

'Baby, Baby ...' she could hear Ai calling.

She felt the pain grow inside her; she crouched, trying to find a position which would give her some relief. She said she would come, she told me...

Ai came out. 'Baby, didn't you hear me? What's wrong with you?'

'I have a pain.'

'Where?' Ai's face was suddenly suspicious.

'Here.' Suman pointed to her stomach.

'Is it...? Get up, let me see...God knows I have enough without having you too... Thank God. Come inside, anyway and get the plates. And stop crying. A big girl like you crying like a baby! After you've had your food, we'll see about your pain.'

She went in and got out the plates. She picked up Anju's and was about to take it to her, when Ai said, 'No, leave it here. Let her come and eat with us.' Suman, plate still in hand, looked hesitantly at Ai.

'Put it down, didn't you hear me Anju, come and have your food here. Anju, did you hear me? Anju...Anju, look at me!'

The cry was so compelling that Anju looked straight into her mother's face. The mother and daughter stared at each other for what seemed to Suman a long time. Then Anju's eyes went blank again. Ai began to cry, hitting herself on the forehead with the back of her palm, the serving ladle still in her hand.

It seemed strange to Suman, when they went to bed, that it could be a night like any other, that the same night sounds could be going on outside. They were all as usual - the croaking of frogs in the garden pond, the howling of a dog and a snapping, barking reply from far away, footsteps and voices on the road, someone coughing. She lay still watching the window. It was still dark. *She has not come back. That's why she didn't come.* Once she moved and felt a quick convulsive movement of Anju's body. 'Anju, it's me, Baby,' she said and Anju's body became still.

She woke up suddenly to a jumble of sounds - shouts, cries, thuds, a clatter of things falling. She felt a blow – there was something, someone on her. She felt a small, trembling arm. It was Barkya – what was he doing? And then it penetrated, a sound that chilled her, a thin scream that seemed scarcely human. It was Anju, Anju screaming as if she had been saving up her voice all these days just for this. Suman got up, wrenching the little fellow off her. Now she could see the man who was holding Anju with one hand and with dull rhythmic thuds hitting her with the other, anywhere, everywhere, banging her head against the wall at the same time. Each time he moved her head, she could see Anju's face in the squares of light on the wall, her eyes blank, mouth open. Suresh – yes, that was Suresh throwing himself at the man, trying to drag him off Anju. And Ai too. She joined them. She could feel blows on her body, but she ignored them until a hand – or was it someone's leg? - smashed into her chest. She gasped with the pain, stood back trying to recover her breath and suddenly realised what the light on the wall meant. Tai was back. She ran out of the door, down the mud path. For the first time she went to the front door and threw herself against it, hammering at it, her body heaving. She could still hear the tumult she had left behind her, as if she had brought it with herself. She realised with surprise that part of the noise was her own loud sobbing. She hammered again. The door opened. It was him, not Tai.

'Tai,' she gasped, 'I want Tai.'

'What is it?' he asked and it was echoed from within by Tai.

'Tai, please come, he's here, he's killing Anju, he'll kill her, Tai, please come...'

The sounds were louder now. She looked back and saw that he had brought Anju out and was dragging her along the path she had walked so proudly on, while Ai and Suresh tried to stop him.

'Oh my God!' the woman gasped, shrinking back into the house. Suman didn't hear her, she didn't see her terrified face as she took in the scene of utter violence. She ran back, stumbling, frantic; perhaps she heard a cry, a voice calling out 'Suman, Suman...' but she didn't stop. As she got to them, the man pushed Anju through the small gate, giving Suresh a final blow that flung him against the wall. The boy fell down, lay still. Ai ran to him crying out his name. He got up, looking dazed, his face bleeding.

'Suresh, are you all right?'

'Leave me alone.'

They helped him back into the house, Barkya clinging so tightly to Ai's legs that she could scarcely walk. It was Suman who cleaned Suresh's face, though he kept brushing her hand away, pushing her of saying, 'Leave me alone.' When it was done, he turned his back on them and lay still, but occasionally his body shuddered as if he was crying. She went in to Ai. The little fellow, head pillowed on her lap, was crying in hiccups. Ai's tattooed hand mechanically stroked his head. Suman stood and stared. The room looked like the scene of a battle.

'Ai, shall I clean the room?'

She waited a moment for a reply, then began cleaning the room methodically while her mother watched her with lack-lustre eyes. As she shook the sheets, something fell down with a dull clink. She picked it up and stared at it.

'What is it?'

Instinctively her fingers closed on it Then she opened her hand and showed it to Ai. It was Anju's clip, a hank of her hair entangled in it. Ai's face worked. The tears came.

'Ai, don't...'

'Throw it away,' Ai said suddenly, fiercely. As the girl hesitated, she repeated, 'Throw it out. She's gone, she won't come back, she'll never come back here.'

Suman stood staring at the pin in her hand.

'What is the matter? Are you hurt?'

Yes, she felt bruised all over, but it was not that. It was the picture she saw as she looked at the clip - Anju walking, her head held high, the clips gleaming in her dark hair. Suddenly she made up her mind. Carefully she removed the screw of hair from the clip.

'What are you doing?'

'I'm keeping it.' She put it carefully in the box with the other clip she'd removed in the afternoon. Then she turned back to Ai.

'She'll come back. We'll bring her back, Ai.'

'Bring her back? How? You're talking big. Big girl, huh?'

Suman said nothing but looked back, unflinching, at her mother. It was the woman who spoke finally. 'All right, keep it,' she said, her body slumping. Her hands went back to their soothing patting. Suman tidied up the room and lay down in her place. For the first time in months she did not notice the light streaming in through the window.

\* \* \*

A brief note about the title: A daughter coming to her parent's home after her marriage is an event of importance and a number of rituals are associated with it.

'Ai' is 'mother' in Marathi. 'Tai' is literally 'elder sister', but is also used as a respectful form of address.

# ─────GITHA HARIHARAN─────

Githa Hariharan was educated in Bombay, Manila, and in the United States. She has published several short stories in magazines and journals, and edited *A Southern Harvest*, a collection of stories translated into English from four south Indian languages.

Githa Hariharan's first novel, *The Thousand Faces of Night,* was published by Penguin India in 1992, and won the Commonwealth Writer's Prize in 1993 as the best first novel. She has since published a collection of short stories, *The Art of Dying* (Penguin, India). 'The Remains of the Feast' is from that collection. Githa Hariharan lives in New Delhi with her husband and two sons, Rishab and Nishad.

GITHA HARIHARAN

# Why I Write

The question 'why do I write?' bewilders me somewhat. I know (or can make a reasonably good guess) why I do not do certain things: drive a car, for example, or cook wonderful meals every day. Perhaps disabilities lend themselves more easily to explanation. You have to constantly justify, to yourself and others, why you cannot do these things which make life so much more pleasant.

The point I am making, in rather circuitous fashion, is that I can talk about motives for writing (mine or anyone else's) with far less confidence than I can about an assortment of skills that are recognised as survival-helpers.

To avoid escaping the question altogether, I can offer a combination of possibilities. First I cannot imagine my life without either talking or reading; without the constant intrusion of, and involvement with, words. Some words, some combination of words seem to demand that they are put down on paper. Then, I have opinions, ideas and theories – a good deal of which may never get the chance to be aired if I do not write. And finally, like the woman in the Indian folk tale who gets fatter and fatter because she does not tell the stories swelling up her insides, I need to communicate the designs and patterns I constantly see – stories – if I am to move further, carry on with the business of living. The woman in the folk story finally learns to tell her story to the walls. I feel some kinship with her; perhaps I too write to remain, at least metaphorically, slim and healthy.

GITHA HARIHARAN

# The Remains of The Feast

The room still smells of her. Not as she did when she was dying, an overripe smell that clung to everything that had touched her, sheets, saris, hands. She had been in the nursing home for only ten days but a bedsore grew like an angry red welt on her back. Her neck was a big hump, and she lay in bed like a moody camel that would snap or bite at unpredictable intervals. The goitred lump, the familiar swelling I had seen on her neck all my life, that I had stroked and teasingly pinched as a child, was now a cancer that spread like a fire down the old body, licking clean everything in its way.

The room now smells like a pressed, faded rose. A dry, elusive smell. Burnt, a candle put out.

We were not exactly room-mates, but we shared two rooms, one corner of the old ancestral house, all my twenty-year-old life.

She was Rukmini, my great-grandmother. She was ninety when she died last month, outliving by ten years her only son and daughter-in-law. I don't know how she felt when they died, but later she seemed to find something slightly hilarious about it all. That she, an ignorant village-bred woman, who signed the papers my father brought her with a thumb-print, should survive; while they, city-bred, ambitious, should collapse of weak hearts and arthritic knees at the first sign of old age.

Her sense of humour was always quaint. It could also be embarrassing. She would sit in her corner, her round, plump face reddening, giggling like a little girl. I knew better than ask her why, I was a teenager by then. But some uninitiated friend would be unable to resist, and would go up to my great-grandmother and ask her why she was laughing. This, I knew, would send her into uncontrollable peals. The tears would flow down her cheeks, and finally, catching her breath still weak with laughter, she would confess. She could fart exactly like a train whistling its way out of the station, and this achievement gave her as much joy as a child might get when she saw or heard a train.

So perhaps it is not all that surprising that she could be so flippant about her only child's death, especially since ten years had passed.

'Yes, Ratna, you study hard and become a big doctor madam,' she would chuckle, when I kept the lights on all night and paced up and down the room, reading to myself.

'The last time I saw a doctor, I was thirty years old.'

'Your grandfather was in the hospital for three months. He would faint every time he saw his own blood.'

And as if that summed up the progress made between two generations, she would pull her blanket over her head and begin snoring almost immediately.

I have two rooms, the entire downstairs to myself now since my great-grandmother died. I begin my course at medical college next month, and I am afraid to be here alone at night.

I have to live up to the gold medal I won last year. I keep late hours, reading my anatomy textbook before the course begins. The body is a solid, reliable thing. It is a wonderful, resilient machine. I hold on to the thick, hard-bound book and flip through the new-smelling pages greedily. I stop every time I find an illustration, and look at it closely. It reduces us to pink, blue and white, colour-coded, labelled parts. Muscles, veins, tendons. Everything has a name. Everything is linked, one with the other, all parts of a functioning whole.

It is poor consolation for the nights I have spent in her warm bed, surrounded by that safe, familiar, musty smell.

She was cheerful and never sick. But she was also undeniably old, and so it was no great surprise to us when she took to lying in bed all day a few weeks before her ninetieth birthday.

She had been lying in bed for close to two months, ignoring concern, advice, scolding, and then she suddenly gave up. She agreed to see a doctor.

The young doctor came out of her room, his face puzzled and angry. My father begged him to sit down and drink a tumbler of hot coffee.

'She will need all kinds of tests,' the doctor said. 'How long has she had that lump on her neck? Have you had it checked?'

My father shifted uneasily in his cane chair. He is a cadaverous looking man, prone to nervousness and sweating. He keeps a big jar of antacids on his office desk. He has a nine to five accountant's job in a government-owned company, the kind that never fires its employees.

My father pulled out the small towel he uses in place of a handkerchief. Wiping his forehead, he mumbled, 'You know how these old women are. Impossible to argue with them.'

'The neck,' the doctor said more gently. I could see he pitied my father. 'I think it was examined once, long ago. My father was alive then. There was supposed to have been an operation, I think. But you know what they thought in those days. An operation meant an unnatural death. All the relatives came over to scare her, advise her with horror stories. So she said, no. You know how it is. And she was already a widow then, my father was the head of the household. How could he, a fourteen-year-old, take the responsibility?'

'Hm,' said the doctor. He shrugged his shoulders. 'Let me know when you want to admit her in my nursing home. But I suppose it's best to let her die at home.'

When the doctor left, we looked at each other, the three of us, like shifty accomplices. My mother, practical as always, broke the silence and said, 'Let's not tell her anything. Why worry her? And then we'll have all kinds of difficult old aunts and cousins visiting, it will be such a nuisance. How will Ratna study in the middle of all that chaos?'

But when I went to our room that night, my great-grandmother had a sly look on her face. 'Come here, Ratna', she said. 'Come here, my darling little gem.'

I went, my heart quaking at the thought of telling her. She held my hand and kissed each finger, her half-closed eyes almost flirtatious.

'Tell me something, Ratna,' she began in a wheedling voice.

'I don't know, I don't know anything about it,' I said quickly.

'Of course you do!' She was surprised, a little annoyed. 'Those small cakes you got from the Christian shop that day. Do they have eggs in them?'

I was speechless with relief.

'Do they?' she persisted. 'Will you,' and her eyes narrowed with cunning, 'will you get one for me?'

So we began a strange partnership, my great-grandmother and I. I smuggled cakes and ice cream, biscuits and samosas, made by non-Brahmin hands, into a vegetarian invalid's room. To the deathbed of a Brahmin widow who had never eaten anything but pure, home-cooked food for almost a century.

She would grab it from my hand, late at night after my parents had gone to sleep. She would hold the pastry in her fingers, turn it round and round, as if on the verge of an earthshaking discovery.

'And does it really have egg in it?' she would ask again, as if she needed the password for her to bite into it with her gums.

'Yes, yes,' I would say, a little tired of midnight feasts by then. The pastries were a cheap yellow colour, topped by white frosting with hard, grey pearls.

'Lots and lots of eggs,' I would say, wanting her to hurry up and put it in her mouth. 'And the bakery is owned by a Christian. I think he hires Muslim cooks too.'

'Ooooh,' she would sigh. Her little pink tongue darted out and licked the frosting. Her toothless mouth worked its way steadily, munching, making happy sucking noises.

Our secret was safe for about a week. Then she became bold. She was bored with the cakes, she said. They gave her heartburn.

She became a little more adventurous every day. Her cravings were varied and unpredictable. Laughable and always urgent.

'I'm thirsty,' she moaned, when my mother asked her if she wanted anything. 'No, no, I don't want water, I don't want juice.' She stopped the moaning and looked at my mother's patient, exasperated face. 'I'll tell you what I want,' she whined. 'Get me a glass of that brown drink Ratna bought in the bottle. The kind that bubbles and makes a popping sound when you open the bottle. The one with the fizzy noise when you pour it out.'

'A Coca-Cola?' said my mother, shocked. 'Don't be silly, it will make you sick.'

'I don't care what it is called,' my great-grandmother said and started moaning again. 'I want it.'

So she got it and my mother poured out a small glassful, tight-lipped, and gave it to her without a word. She was always a dutiful grand-daughter-in-law.

'Ah,' sighed my great-grandmother, propped up against her pillows, the steel tumbler lifted high over her lips. The lump on her neck moved in little gurgles as she drank. Then she burped a loud, contented burp, and asked, as if she had just thought of it, 'Do you think there is something in it? You know, alcohol?'

A month later, we had got used to her unexpected, inappropriate demands. She had tasted, by now, lemon tarts, garlic, three types of aerated drinks, fruit cake laced with brandy, bhel-puri from the fly-infested bazaar nearby.

'There's going to be trouble,' my mother kept muttering under her breath. 'She's losing her mind, she is going to be a lot of trouble.'

And she was right, of course. My great-grandmother could no longer swallow very well. She would pour the coke into her mouth and half of it would trickle out of her nostrils, thick, brown, nauseating.

'It burns, it burns,' she would yell then, but she pursed her lips tightly together when my mother spooned a thin gruel into her mouth. 'No, no,' she screamed deliriously. 'Get me something from the bazaar. Raw onions. Fried bread. Chickens and goats.'

Then we knew she was lost to us. She was dying.

She was in the nursing home for ten whole days. My mother and I took turns sitting by her, sleeping on the floor by the hospital cot.

She lay there quietly, the pendulous neck almost as big as her face. But she would not let the nurses near her bed. She would squirm and wriggle like a big fish that refused to be caught. The sheets smelled, and the young doctor shook his head. 'Not much to be done now,' he said. 'The cancer has left nothing intact.'

The day she died, she kept searching the room with her eyes. Her arms were held down by the tubes and needles criss-cross, in, out. The glucose dripped into her veins but her nose still ran, the clear, thin liquid trickling down like dribble on to her chin. Her hands clenched and unclenched with the effort and she whispered, like a miracle, 'Ratna.'

My mother and I rushed to her bedside. Tears streaming down her face, my mother bent her head before her and pleaded, 'Give me your blessings, Paati. Bless me before you go.'

My great-grandmother looked at her for a minute, her lips working furiously, noiselessly. For the first time in my life I saw a fine veil of perspiration on her face. The muscles on her face twitched in mad, frenzied jerks. Then she pulled one arm free of the tubes, in a sudden, crazy spurt of strength, and the I.V. pole crashed to the floor.

'Bring me a red sari,' she screamed. 'A red one with a big wide border of gold. And,' her voice cracked, 'bring me peanuts with chilli powder from the corner shop. Onion and green chilli bondas deep-fried in oil.'

Then the voice gurgled and gurgled, her face and neck swayed, rocked like a boat lost in a stormy sea. She retched, and as the vomit flew out of her mouth and her nose, thick like the milkshakes she had drunk, brown like the alcoholic coke, her head slumped forward, her rounded chin buried in the cancerous neck.

When we brought the body home – I am not yet a doctor and already I can call her that – I helped my mother to wipe her clean with a wet, soft cloth. We wiped away the smells, the smell of the hospital bed, the smell of an old woman's juices drying. Her skin was dry and papery. The stubble on her head – she had refused to shave her head once she got sick – had grown, like the soft, white bristles of a hairbrush.

She had had only one child though she had lived so long. But the skin on her stomach was like crumpled, frayed velvet, the creases running to and fro in fine, silvery rivulets.

'Bring her sari,' my mother whispered, as if my great-grandmother could still hear her.

I looked at the stiff, cold body that I was seeing naked for the first time. She was asleep at last, quiet at last. I had learnt, in the last month or two, to expect the unexpected from her. I waited, in case she changed her mind and sat up, remembering one more taboo to be tasted.

'Bring me your eyebrow tweezers,' I heard her say. 'Bring me that hair-removing cream. I have a moustache and I don't want to be an ugly old woman.'

But she lay still, the wads of cotton in her nostrils and ears shutting us out. Shutting out her belated ardour.

I ran to my cupboard and brought her the brightest, reddest sari I could find: last year's Diwali sari, my first silk.

I unfolded it, ignoring my mothers eyes which were turning aghast. I covered her naked body lovingly. The red silk glittered like her childish laughter.

'Have you gone mad,' my mother whispered furiously. 'She was a sick old woman, she didn't know what she was saying.'

She rolled up the sari and flung it aside, as if it had been polluted. She wiped the body again to free it from foolish, trivial desires.

They burnt her in a pale brown sari, her widow's weeds. The prayer beads I had never seen her touch encircled the bulging, obscene neck.

I am still a novice at anatomy. I hover just over the body, I am just beneath the skin. I have yet to look at the insides, the entrails of memories she told me nothing about, the pain concealing into a cancer.

She has left me behind with nothing but a smell, a legacy that grows fainter every day. For a while I haunt the dirtiest bakeries and tea-stalls I can find. I search for her, my sweet great-grandmother in plate after plate of stale confections, in needle-sharp green chillies, deep-fried in rancid oil. I plot her revenge for her, I give myself diarrhoea for a week.

Then I open all the windows and her cupboard and air the rooms. I tear her dirty, grey saris to shreds. I line the shelves of her empty cupboard with my thick, newly-bought, glossy-jacketed texts, one next to the other. They stand straight and solid, row after row of armed soldiers. They fill up the small cupboard quickly.

# SUNETRA GUPTA

Sunetra Gupta was born on March the 15th, 1965, in Calcutta. She spent her early childhood in Africa, but most of her schooling was in Calcutta. She graduated in 1987 from Princeton University in Biology and completed her Ph. D. in Mathematical Biology at Imperial College, London, 1992. She is currently Research Fellow at Oxford University (Merton College & Dept. of Zoology), studying infectious diseases.

She has published two novels, *Memories of Rain* (Grove Press, USA, and Orion Books, UK) in 1992 and *The Glassblower's Breath* in 1993 (same publishers). She is now working on her third novel.

SUNETRA GUPTA

# Why I Write

For me, writing is an adventure, an excursion into the depths of my self. In this sense, writing is for me a kind of structured dreaming, where I am able to tap into my (sub)conscious in a more controlled manner than while I dream. This control is, of course, afforded by narrative, and while my dreams quite often have sequence, they are rarely harnessed by narrative. The act of writing therefore embodies for me a very tender junction between the chaos of my dreams and the stern order of the universe. It is this exhilarating coalition that I seek to celebrate when I write.

'Je n'ai jamais éprouvé que le sommeil fut un repos', said Gerard de Nerval. Dreaming is hard work, and writing is no repose either. The strenuous task of pouring my own dreams and memories into the mould of other invented lives brings me closer I feel to the truth of these experiences. Writing is therefore a constant act of reinterpretation, reinscription and regeneration. In this way it serves as an alternative mode of analysis than that which I employ in my scientific research. The language of scientific rationalism can fail miserably when one is trying to make sense of emotion. Creative writing allows me to develop a language with which to probe the deeper recesses of my being. Writing is, in this sense, as much about discovering a new language as using the language to look further into yourself and those around you. I feel the need therefore to experiment with language, not in some directed way, but when the need arises. I feel it is important to communicate to the reader that language is pliable, and that creating your own language is the primary act of personal and political independence.

Finally, I write because I must. I only say this because I believe that passion plays a very important role in creativity. If this personal odyssey were not driven by such irrational visceral concerns such as the simple engulfing desire to write, I think I should be in grave danger of dishonesty. I say this to an increasingly graphomatic society, where writing has come to be viewed as a social responsibility rather than a maddening imprecise urge to which one is forced occasionally to submit. In this sense, the moment I can articulate very precisely 'why I write', may be the moment when I cease to do so. Happily, for now, it is a question that I can only respond to in this very unstructured manner.

SUNETRA GUPTA

# Strangers and Other Ghosts

Mother, it is the smoke in your kitchen that teases these tears from my eyes, this thin smoke, ruinously tinged with old mustard, that you have inhaled daily for so many years, it is the smoke, mother, not the fallow weight of my fattened prose that brings tears, today, to my eyes, as I sit to compose another episode of the unending saga that brings us our daily bread, to drag my characters through another week in their lives, brushed always by deadly fronds of their histories. This week we will have a chance encounter with a young woman, a rainy Wednesday afternoon, perhaps, much like this one, on the long verandah of the Marble Palace, the Mullick family mansion, mother, that you have never visited, one of this city's few attractions, I must take you there, mother, perhaps next year, after you retire, you will have time then mother, darkthroated afternoons of endless silence, afternoons that once would have been measured out for you by the chime of the school bell, but I digress, as always, I digress, and how my audience feasts upon my digressions, mother, it is a habit that I get from you, I believe, a childhood of opened parentheses, the glorious insulation of nested anecdotes, that is the essence of a child's security, is it not, mother? And now it is I that am charged with the duty of building a labyrinth of tales for my readers to hide within, where one story dives into another and resurfaces without its fins, we will have a chance encounter this week in Marble Palace, a young woman, newly graduated, born and bred in North London, shall we say, come for the first time to this city, to excavate her roots, no, not for the first time, for she will have been brought before as a child to be exhibited to the grandparents, the aunts and cousins. With one favourite cousin, her age, she will have maintained a correspondence, will have sent her precious posters of Madonna, slipped chewing gum slices into the crevices of excruciatingly coded letters, this cousin will have been married now for a few years, our young woman may even have attended her wedding, a brief two weeks in the tropics between college terms, but much has changed within her since then, her horizons have broadened, but with nothing much to fill them, the undergraduate romance with the fiery Welshman has ended, all too trivially, her dog has been run over by an ice-cream van earlier in the year, her best friend has left for graduate school in Canada, all she has left to her are her secrets, old now, and rusty at the edges, and all she wants to do is to sit in a corner somewhere and write poetry, and for someone to read it, endlessly read it, drink deeply of her mindbroth, and smack his lips in limitless delight. Such are her thoughts as she stares into the dull August rain, falling breathlessly into the old courtyard of the Marble Palace, falling without adjectives into the curled phrases she longs to use to describe a tropical downpour, if only someone would give her the run of a place like this for a year, she muses, or better a ruined mansion in the tangled heart of a forest, hung with diseased mirrors, and peopled only with the shadows of strange and useless furniture, would she not then be able to wring music from words, words within her that have never been given space to breathe, jostled by traffic and smoke, trivial social intercourse, and the felted shoulders of other words, packed too closely together. Such are her thoughts, mother, when he comes upon her, not our regular protagonist, but his rarely mentioned older brother, the introverted business executive, Arunavo, he has taken the afternoon off, feeling a cold coming on, and then on sudden impulse (what other can be the nature of impulse, mother?) he has directed his driver to the Marble Palace, and not home, where his daughters will be returning around this time from school, and though he does not directly make this connection, we will make it for him, that he has chosen to spend a few quiet hours in the antique insulation of the Marble Palace, to rest awhile amid sweet Victorian decay, before returning to his luxurious but busy Alipore flat, for he has three daughters, our Arunavo, all popular with their schoolmates, whom they drag back in hordes to fill the afternoons with wide giggling and sandy whispers, that he cannot bear to return to this he does not know, but my audience will suspect it, for they know that Arunavo is a man with a passion for silence, that years ago he lost the woman he loved because of his addiction to silence, for he had not dared speak his love, silently he had worshipped her, and with ardent silence she had responded to his adoration, but he had never declared his love, not even when the threat of an arranged marriage loomed large, he had not intervened, and she had married a young doctor, and left with him, a year later, two months pregnant, to find a new life in the United Kingdom. You can see the beginnings of the intertwinement, can you not, mother, of these two separate threads, my young woman, thirsting for poetry, staring into the rain, and my middle-aged executive with a sore throat, come to seek silence in the clammy ruins of the Mullick family mansion, you can see now, can you not mother, the clumsy node, the fat and crude knot I am about to tie?

Intellect without emotion, arrogance without passion, violence without pain, these are the worst of evils, she decides, staring into the numb rain, and my readers will excuse her, for it is the fragrance of these musings that arrests Arunavo, as he passes by her in pursuit of a mustier silence than the empty courtyard can offer, but it is only the train of his thoughts that is interrupted, polite momentum propels him into the dark picture gallery, where he finds himself deliciously alone.

But he will not wallow for long in this half-light, thick with the floating scabs of old dreams, her thoughts curve like elbows around his head, she follows him in, treads softly, slipperless, into the picture gallery, as the rain suddenly rears and bucks and comes pelting onto the verandah.

He turns to her and smiles, he is not shocked to find hovering beneath her ghostly features, a pentimento of his long lost beloved, I loved your mother, he longs to tell her, I am almost certain I loved your mother, think, but for my silence you would not have been. But he is a man of few words, Arunavo, and my audience would not tolerate such an indiscreet outpour on his part, and least of all you, mother, you would never countenance such appalling behaviour on his part, he is frightening the child, you would protest, thinking of your own granddaughter, my dear niece Urmila, whom we saw off last night, put her on the plane to Heathrow, she did not look well, mother, did she, last night, three months in the tropics had eaten deep into her unaccustomed flesh, so terribly pale and thin she looked, last night, mother, drained of all the youthful enthusiasm she had come with to our household, three months ago, she had great hopes of these three months, mother, three months with you and I, her literary maiden aunt, the madwoman in the kitchen, scratching away among the mustard frowst and the fennel fumes, she had great hopes of me, mother. And instead I simply milked her for details of her North London life, borrowed shamelessly from her breathless confidences to spice the lives of my characters, hunted for authenticity in the labels of creams and potions, the tags upon her T-shirts, these scraps that my audience savours above the convolutions of my narrative, but it is a common affliction, they tell me, the disease of brand-names, the martyrdom of Marks and Spencer, the detached benevolence of Boots, the asthmatic solicitude of Harvey Nichols, all are palpable to me now, I who have never crossed the seas.

But my young woman in the Marble Palace is not Urmila, mother, you will see so, soon, for Arunavo will describe her as delicate, her nose shaped like a reedpipe, her eyes large and quiet, her lips full but always in grim compression, she is certainly not our Urmila, mother, with her rooster hair, and collandered earlobes, no, mother, my young woman has hair that hangs like autumn clouds about her neck, and her ears have holes enough only for a pair of diamond studs that serenade the rainlight in hasty, abrupt flashes.

Arunova sneezes. Excuse me, he says to the girl.

Horrible rain, she says, a soaking in this is worse I am sure for the health than a miserable cold English drizzle. And a cold in hot weather is so much less tolerable than a cold in cold weather, where it can be nursed with fires and brandy, and mugs of hot chocolate.

Colds are good for you, says Arunavo, perversely. There was a belief in North Bengal, he remembers, that colds protect from insanity, a stuffy nose flattens unwary convolutions of thought, popping ears distract from the obsessions of moonless wind, dense tropical silence will sear a wakeful mind unless it is cloaked in the midst of rheum, he tells her so.

Colds, says the girl, and all manner of respiratory infections have been elevated to the level of ideal to curb the creative impulse within man, as with the image of the ailing domestic angel that enfrailed so many generations of women. Yes, colds can protect against madness to be sure, for colds will divert from the energy of authority, that first clause of madness: the total recognition of the self.

You remind me, says Arunavo, of a schoolgirl to whom I gave private tuition, many years ago, when I was in college. She had strange ideas about everything, and was just as eager as you to communicate her fancies to strangers.

I was in love with her sister, he longs to tell her, I loved her sister, loved her with the deep boundless energy of silence, her every action encrusted in silence would repeat endlessly within me, a glimpse of a hand pulling in the shutters in the outside corridor would chorus inside me all evening as I discoursed with my precocious student, tried to straitjacket her wild thoughts into sentences, it was I that gave her the curse of coherence, thinks Arunavo, and now she writes cheap serials for women's magazines.

It is only to strangers that I would communicate such fancies, says the girl, to strangers and ghosts.

I may be a ghost, for all you know, says Arunavo.

This is uncharacteristic of him, my readers will frown, we know Arunavo, he is not schooled in such verbal indulgence, we have known him now for many years, my readers will protest, and never has he been so inclined, Arunavo, we know, is a man perpetually sucking in the sprouts of his thoughts.

But I have known him longer than they, and I know what lies buried behind those walls of stone, I know what labyrinths are still packed with the translucent folds of unspent passion, I know what sighs still remain unburnt between tall corridors of dream, I know the window from where she would watch him waiting for his tram, I know the strange disquiet stirred within her by his utter lack of agitation, as tram after tram would pass, and not one of them going his way, I know the restless brush of his frayed shirtcuff against the tea saucer, as he fought with his student's plaintive oxymorons, and thought incessantly of her sister.

I might easily be a ghost, he pleads to the young woman, in a roomful of scrofulous oil paintings, he has been a ghost, all his life, to his family, to his friends, a mere outline of a man, even to her, who had loved him with passion, how quickly he must have lost substance, become a faint shadow in her past, she who had been driven to distraction once by the proximity of their fingers as she handed him the discreet brown envelope, his monthly wage, mother you sent it often by her, did you not, did you hope, between all hopes, of encouraging their tenderness, did you hope that he might declare his love to her, save her from impending sacrifice, the marriage that her uncles were already arranging, for we have had no father for many years, lived on the charity of our uncles, supplemented by your meagre teacher's salary, mother, and now by my inadequate earnings. Did you hope he would rescue her, mother, from a lifetime of submission, or rescue you, rather, from a lifetime of gratitude, my uncles did not spare any expense at her wedding, oh rivers of curry flowed between rice dunes at that wedding, and I stood behind the mountains of cutlets and wept, and resolved never to marry. Was she to be a vehicle of your protest, then, mother was that why you sent her so often with the tea and the sweetmeats, and his pay, always in a used envelope, the address scratched out, did you hope that he would give you the courage to refuse my uncles' charity, that in this one matter, the marriage of your daughter, you might have a say, that you might proudly declare that the nice young tutor was in love with her, had begged her hand in marriage, of course they would have to wait, for he had barely finished his Master's degree, but his prospects were brilliant, that much was clear, he was a prize catch, but he slipped your nets, mother, never dignified their solemn ardour with vows, perhaps you knew he never would, mother, perhaps this was your cruel way of acquainting us with the monstrous proportions of our misfortune, perhaps you wanted her to love him, only so that the keenness of her loss would echo your anguish, mother, as you handed her destiny over to my uncles, for their eager hands to knead into shapes far beyond your control.

And so you watched helplessly as they gave her away to a squat engineer, how we grieved at his appearance, for he a good halfhead shorter than her, and his nose squashed like a warthog, and how old he seemed, thirty-four, we were so young then, mother, you will forgive our youthful distress, will you not, for we all came to appreciate him in due course for the gentle and loving husband that he was to her, and our dear Urmila was born of their union, his dark eyebrows arching over her claysmooth features, the fatness of his nostrils pulling down upon her fine nose, our Urmila is no beauty like my sister, but she has a pleasant face and a cheerful disposition, has she not, mother, but three months were too long in these humid climes for her, she returned sobered and spent, grateful to climb into the stolid pegasus that would bear her back to the land of her birth, you dabbed your eyes as the plane took off, mother, who knows when you will see her again.

But my young woman in the Marble Palace is not Urmila, mother, I promise you, she is a true figment of my imagination, she has come to this city in search of something quite different, and now in the sumptuous decay of the Marble Palace she finds sudden reason for hope, for the man before her has declared himself a phantom, and now she knows, that wherever she goes she must take her own ghosts with her, and those of her fathers, and their fathers before them, and that wherever she goes, there will always be within her a feast of phantoms, that their laughter and their tears will forever softly percolate into her consciousness, and she will be content.

We will leave them there, I think, the sore-throated executive, and the dreamy young student, we will leave them before the knot that ties their fates together becomes a noose, we will leave them with their deliciously unfinished conversation, that had begun with such promise of unrestraint, we will leave them to their own devices, for the moment. Perhaps I may bring them together again, if, as I have often schemed, I send Arunavo on a business trip to London, where he is sure to bump into his lost love through the North London Bengali network, and your daughter, he will ask, after the first trivial disillusionments are cleared from his palate, your daughter, whatever became of her?

My daughter? his lost love will echo, why she is well, though still seeking suitable employment, why not have her show you around London tomorrow, she has little better to do, and knows the city much better than any of us.

And so they find themselves again among the debris of a past that is not their own, within the holy coffers of Sir John Soane museum perhaps, exchanging absurdities in the alabaster stillness, until the meaning of his life will have been unravelled to a point of excruciation, and knowing that the time has come when finally he must abandon silence in favour of the firmer insulation of the ridiculous, he will wave the girl goodbye, return to a solitary park bench, and there he, who robbed me of my imagination, denied my sister the dignity of choice, and denied you, mother, the defiance of fate, he will bury his eyes upon the rancid sleeve of his borrowed overcoat and weep.

# MEIRA CHAND

Meira Chand was born and educated in London. Her mother is Swiss and her father is Indian. She is married to an Indian businessman and they have lived in Japan since 1962, as well as in India. Meira Chand is the author of *The Gossamer Fly, Last Quadrant, The Bonsai Tree, The Painted Cage* and *House of the Sun*. *House of the Sun* was adapted for the stage and presented in London by Tamasha at Theatre Royal Stratford East in 1990. It was the first Asian play with an all-Asian cast and production team to be staged in London. It was voted Critic's Choice by *Time Out*, London's main entertainment guide. *The Gossamer Fly* is to be made into a major film.

MEIRA CHAND

# Why I Write

In the year E.M. Forster published *A Passage to India*, my father was enduring an opposite voyage. The wind blew colder by degrees on his face, the sea tossed irritably beneath the ship in the Bay of Biscay. Although the sun paled visibly my father, looking up and ahead, discerned a glow behind clouds that seemed brighter than any in India. He was on his way to England to study medicine.

When he arrived in England in 1919 he had to travel ten miles across town to seek out the only other Indian he knew. The London of that far away time was not the multiracial place of today. He met prejudice in that monocultural society, although he spoke more of the kindness received. He met and married my mother who, although of Swiss parentage, had grown up in England. He stayed for a lifetime and did well for himself, and gave back to his foster society as much as he took. It was not a bad cultural relationship. Yet, as much as he wished it not to be so, its undercurrents and duality came down to me.

Each year our family went for summer holidays to Devon, in the south west of England. I was four, maybe five that summer. I remember standing on the beach near the sea, alone. I remember a strange Englishman coming to talk to me. He pressed a half crown coin into my hand and asked me where I was from. I remember nothing of what he looked like, except that he was tall. But I at four was near the ground and everyone was tall. Nothing of a dubious nature took place because my father, some distance away in a deck chair, had seen the encounter and came rushing up.

The next fragment of memory I have is of my father towering above me, angry and muscular in a red woollen swimming suit. He shouted at me when the man was gone, demanding to know all that was said. The conversation with the man had not progressed far. I was pleased with the silver coin and had only been asked where I was from.

'And what did you reply?' yelled my father.

'I said I came from India,' I answered.

To give this answer I must, in my childish identity, have felt a natural affinity with my father and his country, although I had no conscious association with the place. I had never been to India. I knew only my home in London, the beach in Devon and few Indians other than my father. My father seemed then to draw himself up to full height, which was well over six foot.

'Never tell anyone you are Indian. Say you are English,' he ordered.

We both then turned to look back on the beach to where my mother slept in a deck chair, pale eyes closed, pale hair stirred by the breeze, unaware. Although nothing was said I knew immediately, this was to be a secret between us.

My father took the coin the man had given me and threw it far out to sea. He seemed so large and powerful. I remember the great shadow of him still in his red woollen swimsuit, straps crossed upon his dark back. I remember the sky as grey and the wind as cold and sharp. I remember the bright coin in the palm of my hand before it was taken from me. The moment never left me.

To my father, as an immigrant in an alien land, the word survival had a special meaning. He applied it to me on the beach that day. As a parent now I understand only too well my father's fears when he saw me approached by a strange man. I understand too, knowing his battle for acceptance in a discriminating world, his deeper anxiety as I stood on that beach, dark-eyed, dark-haired, dark-skinned like himself, vulnerable before a world he knew too well and without the tools for survival. In his panic he gave me the first that came into his head. He told me quite literally to turn brown into white. He ordered me to deny him and so to deny a whole half of myself. The very identity he had given me and that only moments before I had voiced so easily on that beach, he told me to reject. The confusion grew in me and filled me for life. If already my cultural fragmentation was not enough, I had now been spliced through the root.

Many, many years later, living then in Japan, a sentence came into my head. It appeared to come from nowhere. It would not leave until I wrote it down. The sentence became a paragraph and the paragraph a page about a child I did not know. Eventually the page became a book. I wrote until I felt I had got to the end. And I seemed to know instinctively where that end was. The tale the book told was pure fantasy, in no way autobiographical. Yet, the child I wrote about seemed to carry a pain similar to the pain I had carried as a child. Cultural duality and spiritual isolation afflicted her. Stranger still the child had crossed cultures and seas and had become Japanese. The transformation was empowering, and placed objectivity upon experience. For the first time since that long ago day on the beach, I was free of an inhibiting, obsolete skin. Through writing a process of healing was begun. Almost unconsciously, I had written my first book.

MEIRA CHAND

# House of the Sun
(Chapter One)

Bhai Sahib examined Mrs Hathiramani's horoscope. He sat cross-legged on the stone floor in a once-white vest and *dhoti*. The vest had a hole, and a remnant of his lunch, eaten hurriedly at the sound of Mrs Hathiramani's arrival in his temple, had left a deep yellow stain upon it.

Mrs Hathiramani had arrived out of breath after the climb downstairs from her home on the fourth floor, two stories above Bhai Sahib in the building they called Sadhbela, and shouted, 'O, Bhai Sahib. Anybody there?' She carried a plate of cashew nut sweets, covered by a yellow checked cloth.

Behind the faded curtain dividing his living quarters from the front room of his home, set aside for use as a temple, Bhai Sahib stopped eating. His wife frowned and rested a spoon in a pan of *dal* before continuing to serve her husband. She gave him a meaningful look. Neither replied to Mrs Hathiramani's loud summons.

'Do as you wish, then. I know you are there. I am waiting,' Mrs Hathiramani threatened. Her voice was gruff and masculine. She removed the cloth from the plate of sweets and put it on the altar under a picture of Guru Nanak, beatific and serene. Then she lowered herself awkwardly on to the floor, placed the red, cotton-bound horoscope before her and stared grimly at the curtained doorway, beneath which she could see Bhai Sahib's bare, sandalled feet, and the legs of a table and chair.

Bhai Sahib returned with a sigh to his lunch. Soon Mrs Hathiramani heard him hawk and rinse out his mouth. He appeared from behind the curtain, wiping his nose on a small blue towel. He was a corpulent man with protruding eyes, cheeks of grey stubble, and a coarse moustache.

'I was eating,' he announced, folding the towel over a shoulder. Mrs Hathiramani gave him a well-rounded look.

'Only *dal* and rice every day,' Bhai Sahib informed her and sucked his teeth.

'I too can eat only *dal* and rice and not complain,' said Mrs Hathiramani in reference to past bad times and her fortitude through them.

'Nowadays, even for God, people will not pay,' Bhai Sahib grumbled. Mrs Hathiramani ignored the remark.

Bhai Sahib squatted down before her, picked up the horoscope and sighed. In the open window a crow alighted, folded its wings and strutted about the window sill. Bhai Sahib belched and settled to his work. Outside the sun was high, white and hot upon Bombay, carrying the stench of drying sardines from the beach into the room.

Very little of the room was left to the temple, Mrs Hathiramani noticed with disapproval. When Bhai Sahib had been younger, his family smaller and his faith less easily compromised, the room had been unadulterated by worldly objects. Now, a grown family of married sons, a widowed mother and the constant arrival of new grandchildren pressed hard behind the curtain, and had finally spilt beyond it. The altar, upon which rested the sacred book, was bulky as a fourposter bed, draped and cushioned and garlanded, but the space where Mrs Hathiramani and Bhai Sahib sat, once bare and serene, was now hemmed in by walls of tall metal cupboards in a depressing faecal colour. Upon them were stacked boxes and suitcases and plump bedding rolls, jars of pickles and tins of oil. Some shelves of medicines and a water jar occupied a corner beside a long bench. Space had recently been made before the altar for a large, imported television upon a black metal stand.

Once, coming down a few weeks ago in the evening to see Bhai Sahib, Mrs Hathiramani had been unable to enter the temple for the crush of Bhai Sahib's family before the lighted screen. And Bhai Sahib himself suggested she return later, his eyes riveted upon the box. Mrs Hathiramani had vowed she would never return at all.

Bhai Sahib examined the close lines of faded blue script, written down long before at the time of Mrs Hathiramani's birth, and the symmetrical designs in the worn booklet. At a page with a drawing of a sun surrounded by lotus petals, he paused. The sun, besides long rays emanating from it, had a human face with large sober eyes and a heavy moustache. Within each of the lotus petals was more blue script which Bhai Sahib read with a serious expression.

'What is it?' Mrs Hathiramani asked, leaning forward. She was alarmed, not so much at what might be written in the horoscope, but at the change in Bhai Sahib's expression. She sensed already it would be difficult to dilute the course of whatever destiny was in store for her.

Bhai Sahib shook his head, squinting at the booklet. 'The Sun is now Lord of the Tenth House and occupies the Ninth. In March Saturn is coming into the House of the Sun. Saturn is strong and will bring trouble. Be careful, otherwise he will do you harm.' Bhai Sahib looked sternly at Mrs Hathiramani over ancient spectacles, as if she had deliberately arranged this beleaguered state in her affairs.

'Aiee,' Mrs Hathiramani moaned softly. 'How long will he stay in the House of the Sun?' She pulled the end of her sari tighter about her ample breasts. She was a soft-fleshed, mountainous woman with a small, beaked nose, and small, hooded eyes.

'He will not move out until June. Three months he will be in the House of the Sun,' Bhai Sahib announced. He stood up to spit out of the window. The crow rose with a squawk, Bhai Sahib sat down again. The bird settled back, a mean look in its eye, its gaze upon the cashew nut sweets.

'What shall I do?' Mrs Hathiramani implored, hands to her cheeks. The upper half of her face was narrow, as if all the flesh had suddenly slipped to her jaw.

'The only thing Saturn fears is a sapphire. Wear a sapphire; then nothing can harm you,' Bhai Sahib replied and suppressed a yawn. The air in the room was unmoving, he stood up to turn on the ceiling fan. From the window the crow croaked in an insolent manner.

Mrs Hathiramani nodded at Bhai Sahib's advice, and held down her sari against the sudden gale sweeping the room. She looked up at the creaking, speeding fan apprehensively.

'I will buy a sapphire,' Mrs Hathiramani decided hurriedly. 'I will buy one right now from Mr Bhagwandas. He will be home for lunch.' She paused, then asked, 'A cheap one will do?'

'The quality is not mattering, only the stone is mattering. It must be a sapphire,' Bhai Sahib replied. 'I will also perform some rites, so that no real harm can come to you,' he added, averting his eyes.

'How much will that cost?' Mrs Hathiramani asked. 'You have only just finished those prayers for Mr Hathiramani's health, and that was costing too much. Mr Hathiramani has no belief in these things; he was angry. He is an educated man and you know the harm education does a man in these matters. How much?' Mrs Hathiramani's small eyes grew bright. There was the sudden shrill sound of children in the corridor outside as she spoke.

Mrs Hathiramani rose, levering her bulk up in stages. As she approached the door Bhai Sahib's three grandchildren burst noisily through, dancing about upon bare feet. One collided with Mrs Hathiramani, knocking the horoscope from her hand.

'Even your grandchildren you cannot control. You are only charging money and doing nothing,' Mrs Hathiramani shouted in sudden angry frustration at Saturn. As she bent with difficulty to retrieve the horoscope, her sari slipped from her shoulder, and her flesh spilt forward.

Bhai Sahib yelled at his grandchildren and flicked out at them viciously with the blue towel. They jumped about, laughing louder before finally retreating. As Bhai Sahib slammed the door upon them the crow dived in, snatched up a sweet and flew off to a mango tree. Mrs Hathiramani, out of breath from levering herself up and down, gave Bhai Sahib a look of disgust. She rearranged her sari, opened, then banged the door behind her.

The corridor, like all the passages in Sadhbela, was narrow and dark; Mrs Hathiramani's hips almost filled the space. Some light filtered through from the lift shaft and Mrs Hathiramani lumbered towards it. She shook the ancient bars of the grille vigorously; the bell would not work. The metal clattered and Mrs Hathiramani called loudly down the shaft, 'O, Liftman. Lift.'

But no lift appeared. The liftman was chatting with a sweeper and refused to hear. By pushing her face up to the bars and squinting down the long dark shaft, she could just discern, far below in a pool of sun, a hairy leg and a portion of his khaki shorts as he lounged against the open door. She would see to him later, he would not get away with such insolence. She had already been forced to walk downstairs to Bhai Sahib, he had been unavailable then.

Mrs Hathiramani gathered her sari clear of her ankles, and began to climb the stairs to Bhagwandas the jeweller, who lived on the floor above Bhai Sahib. An odour of garlic sank into the sour stairway, stained with the red spittle of betel nuts and the filthy discharges of lazy servants, who used it sometimes as a urinal. Mrs Hathiramani reached a landing and there met the mad beggarwoman who inhabited the corridors of Sadhbela. She was haggling with a vegetable vendor for a cabbage leaf to cook, jumping dementedly at the wide basket of produce he balanced on his head.

When the beggarwoman saw Mrs Hathiramani she turned upon her and began to pull at her sari. Mrs Hathiramani, who would normally have flung her away, thought now of Saturn before the House of the Sun. She dug down the front of her sari blouse and produced a warm one-rupee note that she thrust at the beggarwoman. A donation of such proportion had not been known before from Mrs Hathiramani - the beggarwoman drew back in. amazement and forgot to appear quite mad. Mrs Hathiramani pushed past her and climbed heavily on her way, arriving at last upon the third floor.

As she pressed the Bhagwandas' doorbell she heard the faint sound of Mrs Murjani's cuckoo clock float down from the seventh floor. It cuckooed twice to mark the hour. Mrs Bhagwandas opened her door, and waited to listen with Mrs Hathiramani before inviting her in. As they looked up at the flaking ceiling, wishing their gaze could penetrate Mrs Murjani's elegant lounge, a dull grating sound swelled up from below and the lighted cage of the lift came into view, rising slowly. Mrs Hathiramani turned to see through the bars the smug grin of the liftman, Gopal.

'Rascal,' she shouted. 'You are not paid to gossip with sweepers. I'll see to you; you wait.' She raised a fist, then caught sight of Mr Murjani in the rear of the lift, on his way home for lunch. 'He is only wasting the building co-operative's money,' she informed Mr Murjani as he rose up before her.

Mr Murjani cleared his throat, touched his moustache and said a word of greeting. His face came level with Mrs Hathiramani and travelled on. His polished shoes and Gopal's bare, hairy legs, sturdy as mahogany, were suddenly before her. Then there was the empty, silent darkness of the shaft again, all illumination gone.

'When we fled Sind, Murli Murjani was still a child,' Mrs Hathiramani remembered, marching angrily into Mrs Bhagwandas' living room. 'On a refugee train from Karachi after Partition, he sat upon Mr Hathiramani's lap and wet himself as he slept. Mr Hathiramani had only the trousers he wore when we ran from our home before the knives of those Muslims. Not until we reached Delhi did Mr Hathiramani get more trousers at a charity camp. Two months he carried upon him the stain of Murli's pee. And now, just see, he is such a big man he cannot speak with us. See how money changes people.'

'But in Sind the Murjanis had money. They were great landowners,' Mrs Bhagwandas reminded her, apprehensive as always of contradicting Mrs Hathiramani.

'I'm not talking about our Sind,' Mrs Hathiramani frowned. 'Rich or poor, we left everything there at the time of Partition. I'm talking about money Murli has made in Bombay. This money is new money, the other was old. Both have a different effect.'

'In Sind we were happy,' Mrs Bhagwandas sighed.

'There we lived a pure life.' Mrs Hathiramani pursed her lips, looking out of the window at Bombay. For a moment they sat, side by side upon a black rexine couch, silenced by thoughts of the past.

In Sind, Mrs Hathiramani had not known Mrs Bhagwandas, who came from Sukkur, a short distance from her own home in Rohri; but she had heard of the family by the same flow of gossip that had made her own people known to many. Almost all the residents of Sadhbela were from Rohri or Sukkur, towns either side of a bridge across the Indus river. All had been Hindu refugees at the time of Partition, all had fled from Sind. Their land lay to the north-west of what was once India, and is now Pakistan. The people of Sukkur had been known to show their superior wealth extravagantly, riding about in ostentatious horsedrawn carriages. The people of Rohri had made do with rickshaws and thrift, and swore to their purer hearts and resident saints their hospitality and their food. In those far-off days before they all became refugees, fleeing from a Muslim Sind, each town disdained the other. History, chaos, poverty and death soon changed such parochial ways.

Mrs Hathiramani sat silently in Mrs Bhagwandas' bare, spacious room, with its stone floors, and hardbacked chairs pushed up against the walls in the manner of a waiting room. In spite of a substantial accumulation of money, Mr and Mrs Bhagwandas were not ambitious. The diamond solitaires that pierced his wife's nose and ears were of such superior quality that Mr Bhagwandas' status in Sadhbela was never threatened; only Mrs Murjani owned diamonds to equal them. Mr and Mrs Bhagwandas had never got used to all the unnecessary things the owning of money seemed to require. It was too much of a bother to keep up with their wealth, and the life it demanded was too far from the cool, cracked floors and string beds, the whitewashed walls and the bushes of jasmine they had known in Sind. 'I'm a poor man,' Mr Bhagwandas insisted with a giggle. The men about him laughed and poked him in the ribs.

Early on, Mr Bhagwandas had secured a sea-facing flat on a corner of the third floor. His knowledge of gems had served him well in both Sukkur and Bombay. Throughout the business of fleeing and refugeeing, there had been no dearth of clients in camps or upon trains, anxious to part with their jewels to restart life, or continue its meagre flow. It seemed as if all the women of Sind had fled their homes with their jewellery knotted into handkerchiefs, and hidden beneath their saris. Many such bundles had been unknotted in desperation before Mr Bhagwandas, on his journey southwards from Sind. In Bombay he had established himself in the jewellery market, Zaveri Bazaar. He had prospered through the years.

Mrs Bhagwandas vanished into her kitchen and soon reappeared with a servant, who offered a drink of lemonade and some cashew nuts upon a greasy plate. 'He is still sleeping after his lunch,' Mrs Bhagwandas said of her husband. 'But soon he will come.' She sat down beside Mrs Hathiramani, who began to speak about Saturn in the House of the Sun. Mrs Bhagwandas listened, her head to one side, nodding in concern. She was a loose-fleshed woman, with flowing, grey hair tied back in a rubber band. Her teeth protruded in a goodnatured smile to rest upon her lower lip. She offered some cashew nuts to Mrs Hathiramani, and then a plate of cheese crackers she had ordered the servant to bring in. Mrs Hathiramani surveyed the two plates. In her own home she offered at least three or four plates of edibles to guests, and always something sweet, not just salty things – it did not show enough respect. Mrs Bhagwandas played up too much the matter of simple living. The sun refracted on her diamond ear studs, smaller in size than Mrs Bhagwandas' gems. The flash of light sparked off both women.

Mr Bhagwandas appeared suddenly in the room, smiling and rubbing his hands together. 'What can I do for you, sister?' he asked. He was a stout, smooth-faced man with narrow, liquid eyes creased in a permanent smile. His hair was dyed an immaculate ebony.

'Bhai Sahib is indeed correct. A sapphire can overcome the evil of Saturn,' Mr Bhagwandas confirmed when Mrs Hathiramani had finished explaining. 'Leave it to me. I will find the right one.'

Unlocking a metal cupboard, he threw open the doors to reveal shelves of boxes and leather pouches. Sitting down at a table with a small suede bag, he fitted his jeweller's glass to his eye, spilled out a pile of translucent stones, and poked about amongst them with a pair of tweezers.

'Any cheap quality will do,' Mrs Hathiramani assured him as casually as she could.

Mr Bhagwandas chuckled. The glass protruded like a growth from his eye. He sat back and picked up a small stone with the tweezers.

'This will be the correct one for its job,' he decided.

Mrs Hathiramani heaved a sigh of relief as Mr Bhagwandas wrapped it up in crisp, magenta tissue paper. She pushed it down the front of her sari blouse into her cleavage, on top of some one-rupee notes.

She had to ring her own door bell on the fourth floor several times before the servant boy Raju appeared, rubbing sleep from his eyes. Usually the door stood wide open.

'Donkey,' she shouted. 'How long must I ring? Why was the door shut? What were you doing?' She knew he had been sleeping, as was permitted, after his lunch.

'Memsahib, I was sleeping.' He yawned and scratched an armpit. He wore dirty drawstring shorts and a ragged vest of indeterminate colour.

'Sleeping?' Mrs Hathiramani lumbered up the hallway to her living room. 'Where is Sahib?'

'Sleeping, Memsahib,' Raju replied.

'Sleeping, sleeping?' Mrs Hathiramani exploded. 'Why are people only sleeping in this house?'

'Memsahib, at this time of afternoon, we are always sleeping,' Raju reasoned and slipped quickly behind Mrs Hathiramani as she raised an arm in a menacing manner. Mrs Hathiramani began to feel suddenly weak before the tribulations of audacious planets, servants and liftmen.

'Tea, get me tea,' she demanded.

'I have not slept yet,' Raju reminded her, standing back a safe distance. He was twelve years old and had no fear of Mrs Hathiramani. He was quicker in mind and body than she, and there were other jobs to be had in the building.

'Donkey,' Mrs Hathiramani roared. 'Tomorrow I will throw you out. Like a rotten onion from the window, I will throw you out. Tea.' She turned towards the bedroom where she knew she would find her husband.

She stood by the bed looking down at Mr Hathiramani's slumbering form. His grey hair was greasily askew, and the bridge of his large nose carried a permanent groove from the weight of his spectacles. These were now folded upon a side table on top of a magazine. Mrs Hathiramani sat down heavily at the end of the bed, unwinding part of her sari. She stretched and yawned; she too was used to a sleep after her lunch. She spread herself across the width of the bed at right angles to her husband's feet, and closed her eyes.

'Memsahib, tea.' Raju rattled the china on the tray.

'Tea? Who is asking for tea?' Mrs Hathiramani sat up. 'It is only three o'clock. This is the time for sleep. Get away.' She closed her eyes again.

As soon as he saw his wife was asleep, Mr Hathiramani opened his eyes, and reached for his spectacles and the *Illustrated Weekly of India*. The arrival of his wife had interrupted his reading of an article about a scandal of high-class prostitution in Bombay. He had put down the magazine not for fear she would disapprove of his reading matter, for Mrs Hathiramani could neither read nor write and so had no way of checking on him. He had feigned sleep so that he need have nothing to do with his wife for a further hour of the day; there would be more than enough of her after tea. He had already heard from Raju about Saturn in the House of the Sun. Raju had heard it from the liftman, who had heard it from Bhai Sahib's servant, who had heard it first hand, as he washed up after Bhai Sahib's lunch behind the curtain in the temple.

His wife was a disappointment to Mr Hathiramani, both for her lack of education and her inability to bear children. He had known about the education before he married her. He had protested his need for a literate wife, but because of the dowry promised, his pleas went unheard by elders during arrangements for the marriage. At that time an undeniable ripeness had enfolded his wife, in anticipation of which Mr Hathiramani, on the one occasion he had been allowed a glimpse of her, had finally agreed to the wedding. But both his anticipation and Mrs Hathiramani's voluptuousness bloomed and faded quickly, like a delicate flower, but without the expected fruit. They waited, but there were no children.

Mr Hathiramani sent his wife to all manner of doctors, without success. In the end he considered sending her back to her mother in revenge. Soon the old lady arrived on their doorstep, bringing things to a head. Mrs Hathiramani had sat on a tin truck, which was covered by a pink and white checked cloth and contained most of their belongings, and sobbed. Mr Hathiramani strode up and down, yelling about the mistake of educated men marrying uneducated women, and the fate of the Hathiramani family line without an heir. During this outburst his mother-in-law did an unusual thing; she kept quiet. Mr Hathiramani wondered about this even as he strode about. When he stopped yelling and his wife ceased sobbing, and all three sat in silence, the mother-in-law spoke at last, a crafty light in her eye.

'If that is what you want, we will take her back. But what shall we tell everyone? How will we face them when they know her husband was impotent? What will everyone say?' Mr Hathiramani had opened and shut his mouth, his wife looked at her mother in admiration, and the old lady stared demurely at her feet.

Soon after this event, they had been forced by Partition to flee their home in Rohri. In Bombay Mr Hathiramani had no choice but to abandon the intellectual life he had led until then as a journalist, and to establish Hathiramani Electricals, a dark, greasy but successful repair shop on Grant Road. They moved into Sadhbela and settled themselves into its few rooms with several tin trunks, and an armada of jars in which Mrs

Hathiramani stored everything from chutney to biscuits, mothballs, buttons and thread. Mr Hathiramani had made his presence in the building felt and he was soon the co-operative committee's secretary.

Mr Hathiramani considered himself above the superstitions of his uneducated wife. The three mechanics he employed in Hathiramani Electricals worked with such unusual diligence that Mr Hathiramani was able to spend much of his day at home. He lay upon his bed in his vest and wide-legged pyjamas, reading newspapers, magazines and a worn copy of *The Oxford Dictionary of Quotations*, of which he had memorized much. A recently acquired *Encyclopedia Britannica* of the year 1948 was piled beside his bed. Mr Hathiramani had taken several days off from work to read to the end of CER. But many pages were missing, or obliterated by graffiti, and his faith in the project was shaken. He returned to the newspapers stacked about the room, filling the air with their musty smell. He enjoyed diving into piles to extract news of forgotten years, contemplating the progress of things. Mr Hathiramani also put aside a part of each day for the writing of his diary.

Mr Hathiramani did not choose to spend his day stretched upon his bed for comfort, but because it was the most strategic spot in his home. The bedroom faced a short corridor to the front door, which was usually left open to reveal the lift shaft and the stairs beyond. In this way it was possible for Mr Hathiramani, from his bed, to keep an eye on all the comings and goings in the tenement. Those ascending or descending in the lift were viewed and timed by Mr Hathiramani, and anything of importance was noted in his diary. What he could not see below the fourth floor or during his absences was reported to him by the liftman, Gopal. For this service he paid Gopal a monthly wage. Mr Hathiramani's diligence was appreciated in the building. It had prevented some thefts or determined the culprits, and had once decided Mr Bhagwandas not to give his daughter in marriage to Bhai Sahib's son. By tracing the boy's movements through the pages of the diary, it was clear to Mr Hathiramani and Mr Bhagwandas that he was not of reliable character.

It was as if he had two businesses: Hathiramani Electricals, a lowbrow, bread and butter affair, and his diary, a true vocation. In Sind he had run for a time his own literary publication with a group of friends, but after Partition, in Bombay, his opinions seemed unwanted and a frost settled upon his life. Necessity had dictated the establishing of Hathiramani Electricals, but Mr Hathiramani considered he had betrayed himself and had suffered from depression and outbursts of temper until, moving into Sadhbela, he had begun his diary.

Mr Hathiramani used a large, blue ledger for his diary. Each double page was divided; the left-hand page had three columns, two narrow ones headed *Arrivals* and *Departures*, and a wider one for *Comments*. The right-hand page was divided into *Miscellaneous Past*, and *Miscellaneous Present*. Its writings had little to do with the life of Sadhbela but consisted, in *Miscellaneous Present*, of Mr Hathiramani's thoughts upon life and copied fragments from the newspapers he read upon his bed for a large part of each day. In *Miscellaneous Past*, he compiled from mildewing books of Sindhi script his own English translations of the history and culture of his homeland, which had flowered in the Indus valley two thousand years before the Aryans invaded India with their primitive ways. In 300 B.C., the great city of Mohenjo Daro already stood on the banks of the Indus, or Sindu, river. There were references to Sind in the Greek histories of Herodotus, Hecateaus, and Arrian. Sindhu soldiers fought in the army of Xerxes in Greece, and again against Alexander the Great, providing men and elephants to the Persians, and fierce resistance again when Alexander invaded Sind. It was a Sindhu soldier who eventually wounded Alexander the Great, and caused his retreat from the land. The Vedas emerged from Sind composed on the banks of Sind's mighty river. Even the esteemed Emperor Akbar was born in Sind of a Sindhi mother. Sind was the cradle of all ancient civilization.

When he pondered these facts, Mr Hathiramani was saddened further by exile. Pride in this heritage was lacking in Sadhbela, resettlement had eroded identity. There were young people now who knew nothing of Sind, and who found their only heritage in a language spoken but never written, a few regional foods, and their distinctive names. Mr Hathiramani considered himself alone in Sadhbela in intellectual prowess, and weighed down by the responsibility this placed upon him. Sometimes, waking at night with the moon on his face and the roll of waves in his ears, it seemed he had been chosen to lead his people back to a knowledge of themselves. It was for this reason he had recently begun, in *Miscellaneous Past*, a translation of the work of Shah Abdul Latif, medieval Sufi poet of Sind, mystic bard of their heritage. A knowledge of this heritage, thought Mr Hathiramani, implanted into every exiled Sindhi, was the only homeland they could now ever know. He alone, Mr Hathiramani was sure, was the sole instrument by which there could be an expatriate Sindhi renaissance.

Mr Hathiramani finished the article on prostitution; his wife still slept at his feet. It was as he had thought; all high-class prostitutes nowadays were college-educated girls. It did no good to educate a woman. In middle age he had come to agree with the views of his parents. He dreaded now to think of his position without the lever of education to hold over his wife. Mr Hathiramani leaned back and stared at the ceiling; at his feet his wife snored.

He reached for his diary and, opening it, retraced the recent movements of everyone in the building. It had become clear there was a need for extra vigilance. Two days ago Sham Pumnani had returned home after losing his job in Japan. He had been accused in that faraway place of embezzling office funds. A man of so few scruples must be watched, Mr Hathiramani noted. No one in Sadhbela, in the trauma of Partition and the flight to Bombay, had fallen so far into misery or failed so utterly to recover themselves, as the wretched Pumnani family. Mr Hathiramani underlined again the note to watch Sham Pumnani.

Apart from Sham there was the problem of Mohan Watumal, who must also now be watched. Only the night before Mr Hathiramani had described Mohan Watumal as a waster, who did nothing to help his ageing father, but sat about in coffee shops, discussing impossible schemes. Distant cousins of Mrs Hathiramani had unwittingly offered their daughter in marriage to Mohan, not knowing he lived in Sadhbela. At this revelation they had promptly appeared to seek Mr Hathiramani's opinion. Mr Hathiramani had not minced his words, and opened his diary to reveal Mohan's layabout traits, clearly shown by his irregular comings and goings. Mrs Hathiramani's cousins expressed gratitude for such frankness and left to call off the engagement. Mr Hathiramani had closed his diary with a satisfied smile, but Mrs Hathiramani was worried. She spoke of the vengeance his mischief would arouse in the Watumals. Mr Hathiramani remained unperturbed, but made a note now, under the one about Sham Pumnani, to observe Mohan Watumal as a precaution .

A thief and a waster. Mr Hathiramani sighed. Such now was the calibre of young Sindhi men. Impossible to think of a Sham Pumnani or a Mohan Watumal ever finding the courage to wound Alexander the Great. Mr Hathiramani turned once more to *Miscellaneous Past* in his diary, and the immortal Shah Adbul Latif. At his feet his wife snored lightly.

# BHARATI MUKHERJEE

Bharati Mukherjee was born in Calcutta. She attended the Universities of Calcutta and Baroda, where she received a Master's Degree in English and Ancient Indian Culture. She came to America in 1961 to attend the Writer's Workshop, and received a Master of Fine Arts and a Ph.D. in English from the University of Iowa. She became an American citizen in 1988. She is a professor of English at the University of California at Berkeley, and is married to the writer Clark Blaise.

Mukherjee is the author of six books of fiction: *The Tiger's Daughter, Wife, Darkness, The Middleman and Other Stories* (which won the National Book Critics' Circle Award in 1989), *Jasmine* and *The Holder of the World*; two books of nonfiction, written with her husband: *Days and Nights in Calcutta* and *The Sorrow and the Terror.*

BHARATI MUKHERJEE

# *The Holder of the World*
(an extract)

I LIVE in three time zones simultaneously, and I don't mean Eastern, Central and Pacific. I mean the past, the present and the future.

The television news is on, Venn's at his lab, and I'm reading *Auctions & Acquisitions*, one of the trade mags in my field. People and their property often get separated. Or people want to keep their assets hidden. Nothing is ever lost, but continents and centuries sometimes get in the way. Uniting people and possessions; it's like matching orphaned socks, through time.

According to *A & A*, a small museum between Salem and Marblehead has acquired a large gem. It isn't the gem that interests me. It's the inscription and the provenance. Anything having to do with Moghul India gets my attention. Anything about the Salem Bibi, Precious-as-Pearl, feeds me.

Eventually, Venn says, he'll be able to write a program to help me, but the technology is still a little crude. We've been together nearly three years, which shrinks to about three weeks if you deduct his lab time. He animates information. He's out there beyond virtual reality, re-creating the universe, one nanosecond, one minute at a time. He comes from India.

Right now, somewhere off Kendall Square in an old MIT office building, he's establishing a grid, a data base. The program is called X-2989, which translates to October 29, 1989, the day his team decided, arbitrarily, to research. By 'research' they mean the mass ingestion of all the world's newspapers, weather patterns, telephone directories, satellite passes, every arrest, every television show, political debate, airline schedule ... do you know how many checks were written that day, how many credit card purchases were made? Venn does. When the grid, the base, is complete, they will work on the interaction with a personality. Anyone. In five years, they'll be able to interpose me, or you, over the grid for upward of ten seconds. In the long run, the technology will enable any of us to insert ourselves anywhere and anytime on the time-space continuum for as long as the grid can hold.

It will look like a cheap set, he fears. He watches 'Star Trek,' both the old and new series, and remarks on the nakedness of the old sets, like studio sets of New York in 1940s movies. The past presents itself to us, always, somehow simplified. He wants to avoid that fatal unclutteredness, but knows he can't.

Finally, a use for sensory and informational overload.

Every time-traveler will create a different reality – just as we all do now. No two travelers will be able to retrieve the same reality, or even a fraction of the available realities. History's a big savings bank, says Venn, we can all make infinite reality withdrawals. But we'll be able to compare our disparate experience in the same reality, and won't that be fun? Jack and Jill's twenty-second visit to 3:00 p.m. on the twenty-ninth of October 1989.

Every time-traveler will punch in the answers to a thousand personal questions – the team is working on the thousand most relevant facts, the thousand things that make me me, you you – to construct a kind of personality genome. Each of us has her own fingerprint, her DNA, but she has a thousand other unique identifiers as well. From that profile X-2989 will construct a version of you. By changing even one of the thousand answers, you can create a different personality and therefore elicit a different experience. Saying you're brown-eyed instead of blue will alter the withdrawal. Do blonds really have more fun? Stay tuned. Because of information overload, a five-minute American reality will be denser, more 'life like,' than five minutes in Africa. But the African reality may be more elemental, dreamlike, mythic.

With a thousand possible answers we can each create an infinity of possible characters. And so we contain a thousand variables, and history is a billion separate information bytes. Mathematically, the permutations do begin to resemble the randomness of life. Time will become as famous as place. There will be time-tourists sitting around saying, 'Yeah, but have you ever been to April fourth? Man!'

My life has gotten just a little more complicated than my ability to describe it. That used to be the definition of madness, now it's just discontinuous overload.

My project is a little more complicated.

## 2.

THE RUBY RESTS on a square of sun-faded green velvet under a dusty case in a maritime museum in an old fishing village many branches off a spur of the interstate between Peabody and Salem. Flies have perished inside the case. On a note card affixed to the glass by yellowed tape, in a slanted, spidery hand over the faded blue lines, an amateur curator has ballpointed the stone's length (4 cms) and weight (137 carats), its date and provenance (late 17c., Moghul). The pendant is of spinel ruby, unpolished and uncut, etched with names in an arabized script. A fanciful translation of the names is squeezed underneath:

Jehangir, The World Seizer
Shah Jahan, The World Ruler
Aurangzeb, The World Taker
Pearl-of-My-Crown, World Healer

In adjoining cases are cups of translucent jade fitted with handles of silver and gold; bowls studded with garnets and sapphires, pearls and emeralds; jewel-encrusted thumb rings; jewel-studded headbands for harem women; armlets and anklets, necklaces and bangles for self-indulgent Moghulmen; scimitars rust dappled with ancient blood, push-daggers with double blades and slip-on tiger claws of hollow-ground animal horns.

How they yearned for beauty, these nomads of central Asia perched on Delhi's throne, how endless the bounty must have seemed, a gravel of jewels to encrust every surface, gems to pave their clothes, their plates, their swords. Peacocks of display, helpless sybarites, consumed not with greed but its opposite: exhibition. And how bizarre to encounter it here, the spontaneous frenzy to display, not hoard, in this traditional capital of Puritan restraint. Spoils of the Fabled East hauled Salemward by pock marked fortune builders. Trophies of garrisoned souls and bunkered hearts.

The Emperor and his courtiers pace the parapets above the harem, caged birds sing, and the soft-footed serving girl follows them at a measured distance, silently fanning with peacock feathers at the end of a long bamboo shaft. Below, a hundred silk saris dry on the adobe walls. Lustrous-skinned eunuchs set brass pitchers of scented water at the openings in the zenana wall. Old women snatch them up, then bar the venereal interior to the dust and heat. Above it all, the Emperor – a stern old man, sharp featured in profile with a long white beard – contemporary of the Sun King, of Peter the Great and of Oliver Cromwell, splices the sunlight with uncut gems. The world turns slowly now in a haze of blood, then glitters in a sea of gold, then drowns in the lush green that chokes his palace walks. He is the monarch of rains and absurd fertility, bred with dust and barrenness in his veins, this fervent child of a desert faith, believer in submission now given infidel souls to enslave, unclean temples to scourge, and a garden of evil fecundity to rule. How useless it must have seemed to those ambassadors of trade, those factors of the East India Company, to lecture an exiled Uzbek on monochromatic utility and the virtues of reticence.

The gaudiness of Allah, the porridge of Jehovah.

'CLOSING IN FIFTEEN MINUTES,' barks the curator, a pink-domed curiosity of a man with bushy white brows, a pink scalp and billowy earmuffs of white hair. His name is Satterfield, the captions are in his hand.

'Comes from the Old English. Slaughter Field,' he offers, uninvited. Perhaps he sees me as a searcher-after-origins, though nothing in my manner or dress should reveal it. High Yuppie, Venn would say: toned body, sensible clothes, cordovan briefcase, all the outward manifestations of stability, confidence and breeding.

'Masters,' I say. 'Beigh Masters.' I give him my card – estates planning, assets research. No one ever asks what it means: they assume I'm a lawyer or with the IRS. Back on the scepter'd isle, three hundred years ago, we were Musters, or musterers. A clever vowel change, in any event. 'Looks like 'Bee,' sounds like 'Bay-a,'' I say.

According to a brass plate in the foyer of this old clapboard house, now museum, on an outcropping of cod-, lobster- and scallop-rich granite where a feeble estuary meets the sea, from this house a certain William Maverick once guided sloops of plundering privateers. Each conquerer museums his victim, terms him decadent, celebrates his own austere fortitude and claims it, and his God, as the keys to victory. William Maverick credited his own hard-knuckled tolerance of cold and pain and hunger to a Protestant God, and credited Him for guiding his hand over the sun-softened Catholics. It pleased him to know that 'shark-supp'd Spaniards would have an eternity to offer their novenas.'

It is perhaps not too great an adjustment to imagine pirates sailing from comfortable homes like this after laying in a supply of winter firewood for the wife and family, and chopping it, then some fish and salt pork, molasses and tea, before raising a crew and setting out to plunder the Spanish Main. We're like à reverse of Australia: Puritans to pirates in two generations. Our criminal class grew out of good religious native soil.

The first Masters to scorn the straitened stability of his lot was one Charles Jonathan Samuel Muster, born in Morpeth, Northumberland. In 1632, a youth of seventeen, C.J.S. Muster stowed away to Salem in a ship heavy with cows, horses, goats, glass and iron. What extraordinary vision he must have had, to know so young that his future lay beyond the waters, outside the protections of all but the rudest constabulary, at the mercy of heathen Indians and the popish French. By 1640 he was himself the proprietor of a three-hundred acre tract that he then leased to an in-law recently arrived, and then he returned to Salem and the life of sea trade, Jamaica to Halifax. Curiosity or romance has compelled us to slash, burn, move on, ever since.

Ten years ago I did a research project which led to an undergraduate thesis on the Musters/Masters of Massachusetts for Asa Brownledge's American Puritans seminar at Yale; everything I know of my family comes from that time when I steeped myself in land transfers, sea logs and records of hogsheads of molasses and rum. And that seminar set in motion a hunger for connectedness, a belief that with sufficient passion and intelligence we can deconstruct the barriers of time and geography. Maybe that led, circuitously, to Venn. And to the Salem Bibi and the tangled lines of India and New England.

THE YEAR that young Charles Muster secreted himself among the livestock aboard the *Gabriel*, a noblewoman in India died in childbirth. It was her fourteenth confinement, and she was the Emperor's favorite wife. He went into whitegowned mourning for two years while supervising the erection of a suitable monument. So while the Taj Mahal slowly rose in a cleared forest on the banks of the Yamuna, young Muster was clearing the forest on the banks of the Quaboag and erecting a split-log cabin adjacent to a hog pen and tethered milch cow. Three years later, barely twenty, he abandoned the country and built the first of many houses on an overlook commanding a view of the sea and the spreading rooftops of Salem. For the rest of his life he scuttled between civilized Salem and the buckskinned fringes of the known world, out beyond Worcester, then Springfield, then Barrington, gathering his tenants' tithes of corn and beans, salted meat and barrels of ale, selling what he couldn't consume and buying more tracts of uncleared forest with the profit, settling them with frugal, land-hungry arrivals from Northumberland, while running his own sea trade in rum and molasses, dabbling in slaves, sugar and tobacco, in cotton and spices, construction and pike building. He was a New World emperor. Even today, five townships carry his name.

In this Museum of Maritime Trade, the curator's note cards celebrate only Puritan pragmatism. There is no order, no hierarchy of intrinsic value or aesthetic worth; it's a fly's-eye view of Puritan history. More display cases are devoted to nails, flintlock muskets, bullet molds, kettles, skillets, kitchen pots and pothooks, bellows and tongs than to carved ivory powder primer flasks and nephrite jade winecups. The crude and blackened objects glower as reproaches to Moghul opulence, glow as tributes to Puritan practicality. As in the kingdom of tropical birds, the Moghul men were flashy with decoration, slow moving in their cosmetic masculinity. What must these worlds have thought, colliding with each other? How mutually staggered they must have been; one wonders which side first thought the other one mad.

About children reared in our latch key culture, I have little doubt. I've heard their teachers on guided tours, listened to the whispered titters of Cub Scouts and Brownies: *We beat those Asians because our pots are heavy and black and our pothooks contain no jewels. No paintings, no inlays of rubies and pearls. Our men wore animal skins or jerkins of crude muslin and our women's virtue was guarded by bonnets and capes and full skirts. Those Indian guys wore earrings and dresses and necklaces. When they ran out of space on their bodies they punched holes in their wives' noses to hang more gold and pearl chains. Then they bored holes in their wives' ears to show off more junk, they crammed gold bracelets all the way up to their elbows so their arms were too heavy to lift, and they slipped new rings on their toes and thumbs they could barely walk or make a fist*

No wonder!

I move from unfurbished room to room, slaloming between *us* and *them*, imagining *our* wonder and *their* dread, now as a freebooter from colonial Rehoboth or Marblehead, and now as a Hindu king or Moghul emperor watching the dawn of a dreadful future through the bloody prism of a single perfect ruby, through an earring or a jewel from the heavy necklace.

The curator returns to an empty darkened room where he can watch me, while lifting the covers off two large, wooden crates. The tea-chest wood is nearly antique in itself, except for the crude, Magic Markered notation: 'Salem Bibi's Stuffs.' The Salem Bibi – meaning 'the white wife from Salem' – Precious-as-Pearl! I have come to this obscure, user-hostile museum to track her down.

The opened crates overflow with clothing, none of it from the Bibi's time. It's like a Goodwill pick up. Satterfield paws through the upper layers, lets them spill around the crates, unsorted, still in tangles. Only the moths will know this history.

More layers; the crates are like archaeology pits. I want to stop and examine, but the decades are peeling by too quickly. Not all that survives has value or meaning; believing that it does screens out real value, real meaning. Now we're getting down to better 'stuffs,' fragments of cotton carpets and silk hangings, brocade sashes and exotic leggings.

I think we're about to hit pay dirt. An old rug. Satterfield looks up. 'Closing time,' he says. Museum hours: Closed weekends, Monday and Friday and Wednesday afternoon. Open Tuesday afternoon and Thursday morning.

'I've come a long way to see this,' I say. 'Won't you let me stay?'

My eyes are more often called steely or forthright than pleading, but to Satterfield they convey, this day at least, the proper respect and sincerity. I get down on my knees, and help lift.

'Wherever did you get this?'

'A donation,' he says. 'People in these parts, they have a lot of heirlooms. A lot of sea faring families, grandfathers' chests and things.'

'You mean someone had all this in his attic?'

'Friends of the museum.'

'Looks Indian,' I say. 'Indian-Indian, not wah-wah Indian.' I hate to play stupid for anyone, but I don't want him to suspect me. Traces of the Salem Bibi pop up from time to time in inaccessible and improbable little museums just like this one. They get auctioned and sold to anonymous buyers. I believe I know her identity, and the anonymous donor.

Mr. Satterfield settles on one knee and lifts out the frayed wool rug with a hunting motif – old, very old – and carefully unfolds it. Inside, there is a stack of small paintings; he lifts one, then two, and finally five crudely framed miniatures from the folds of the carpet. Then he smooths the carpet out.

'Pretty good shape for the age it's in.'

I get down on my knees, smoothing the carpet in the manner of a guest who, with indifference but a show of interest, might pat a host's expansive hunting dog. 'Well, aren't those very interesting paintings,' I say. 'Don't you think?' My voice has caught a high note, I want to cough or clear my throat, but it would seem almost disrespectful.

'We don't keep pictures here. This is a museum of maritime trade.'

There is surely one moment in every life when hope surprises us like grace, and when love, or at least its promise, landscapes the jungle into Eden. The paintings, five in all, are small, the largest the size of a man's face, the smallest no larger than a fist. They make me, who grew up in an atomized decade, feel connected to still-to-be-detected galaxies.

The corners are browned by sea water or monsoon stains. White ants have eaten through the courtiers' sycophantic faces and lovers' tangled legs, through muezzin-sounding minarets and lotus blooms clutched by eager visitors from pale-skinned continents oceans away. But the Moghul painters still startle with the brightness of their colors and the forcefulness of their feelings. Their world is confident; its paints are jewels; it too displays all it knows.

Here, the Salem Bibi, a yellow-haired woman in diaphanous skirt and veil, posed on a stone parapet instructing a parrot to sing, fulfills her visions in the lost, potent language of miniature painting. She is always recognizable for the necklace of bone. Later, when the Indian imagination took her over, the bone became skulls.

'I need to pack these up,' says Mr. Satterfield.

Here Precious-as-Pearl zigzags on elephantback, by masoola boat, in palanquins – the vast and vibrant empire held in place by an austere Muslim as Europeans and Hindus eat away the edges.

In the first of the series, she stands ankle-deep in a cove, a gold-haired, pale bodied child-woman against a backdrop of New England evoked with wild, sensual color. The cove is overhung with cold-weather, color-changing maples and oaks, whose leaves shimmer in a monsoon's juicy green luxuriance. At the water's edge, a circle of Indians in bright feathered headdresses roasts fish on an open fire. More braves stand in shallow water, spears aloft, as grotesque red salmon climb the underside of giant breakers. Their wolf-dogs howl, neck hairs rising, as children toss stones in play from the shingled beach. Around her submerged high-arched instep, jellyfish, dark as desire, swirl and smudge the cove's glassy waves. Crouched behind her, in the tiny triangle of gravelly shore visible between her muscled legs, black-robed women with haggard faces tug loose edible tufts of samphire and sea-grasses. I was right – they were fascinated by us. The artist cannot contain the wonders, fish and bird life bursts over the border.

'Really. It's getting very late.' He begins to turn the miniatures over and folds the ancient carpet over them.

'Where will you be selling them?' I ask, but he shrugs.

'That's up to the owner, isn't it?'

In a maritime trade museum in Massachusetts, I am witnessing the Old World's first vision of the New, of its natives, of its ferocious, improbable shapes, of its monstrous women, that only the Salem Bibi could have described or posed for. Her hips are thrust forward, muscles readied to wade into deeper, indigo water. But her arms are clasped high above her head, her chest is taut with audacious yearnings. Her neck, sinewy as a crane's, strains skyward. And across that sky, which is marigold yellow with a summer afternoon's light, her restlessness shapes itself into a rose-legged, scarlet-crested crane and takes flight.

The bird woos with hoarse-throated screeches, then passes out of sight. The painting could be covered by the palm of my hand.

I lift the final one. I want to memorize every stroke.

In the largest of the series – its catalog name is *The Apocalypse*, but I call it *The Unravish'd Bride* – beautiful Salem Bibi stands on the canon-breached rampart of a Hindu fort. Under a sky on fire, villages smolder on purple hillocks. Banners of green crescent moons flutter from a thousand tents beyond the forest, where tethered horses graze among the bloated carcasses of fallen mounts. Leopards and tigers prowl the outer ring of high grass, the scene is rich in crow-and-buzzard, hyena-and-jackal, in every way the opposite of fertile Marblehead. In a forest of blackened tree stumps just inside the fort's broken walls, hyenas lope off with severed human limbs, jackals chew through caparisoned carcasses of horses, a buzzard hops on a child's headless corpse.

Salem Bibi's lover, once a sprightly guerrilla warrior, now slumps against a charred tree trunk. He grasps a nephrite jade dagger hilt carved in the shape of a ram's head and, with his last blood-clotted breath, pledges revenge. His tiny, tensed knuckles glint and wink, like fireflies, against the darkness of his singed flesh. The poisoned tip of an arrow protrudes through the quilted thinness of his battle vest. An eye, gouged loose by an enemy dagger, pendulums against his famine-hollowed cheek, a glistening pink brushstroke of a sinew still connecting it to the socket through which the smoky orange sky shows itself. The lover's one stationary eye fixes its opaque, worshipful gaze on the likeness of the Salem Bibi painted on the lover's right thumbnail.

Near Salem Bibi's dying lover, under a multirooted banyan tree smeared with oils and ashes holy to Hindus, the upper body of a lotus-seated yogi slain in midmeditation holds itself serenely erect. An infant, chubby and naked, crawls from blood-splattered shield to shield inventing happy games. A thief crouches behind a pretty purple boulder and eyes the necklets of pearls, rubies, diamonds, on courtier-warriors' stilled chests. Broods of long-haired monkeys with black, judgmental faces ring the heaps of dead and dying.

In the clean, green distance beyond the conflagration's range, on a wide road that twists away from ruined forts and smoking villages, a gloomy, insomniac conqueror on a sober eyed elephant leads his procession of triumph-aroused horsemen, foot soldiers, archers, gunners, lance bearers, spies, scouts, mullahs, clowns, poets, painters, bookkeepers, booty haulers, eunuchs, courtesans, singers, dancers, jugglers, wrestlers, cooks, palanquin bearers, tent pitchers, storytellers, to the next gory and glorious field of slaughter. Their eyes form a perfect, glitter-pointed triangle: Salem Bibi's, her Hindu lover's, the Moghul conqueror's.

On the low-parapeted roof of the fort, Salem Bibi chants stubborn and curative myths to survive by. Her braceleted hands hold aloft a huge, heavy orb of unalloyed gold and a clear, multifaceted diamond through which a refracted lion and a lamb frolic in a grove of gold grass as supple as silk. At her henna-decorated, high-arched feet, a bird cage lies on its side, its microscopic door recently ripped off its hinges. The newly exposed hinge glows against the cage's duller metal, a speck of gold-leaf paint.

'Thank you, Mr. Satterfield.'

It is a feast of the eyes, and I must steady myself, take a breath, palms outstretched on the museum's floor. You can study it for a lifetime and find something new each time you look. It's like an Indian dessert, things fried that shouldn't be, hot that should be cold, sweet that should be tart. And an art that knows no limit, no perspective and vanishing point, no limit to extravagance, or to detail, that temperamentally cannot exclude, a miniature art forever expanding.

Go, Salem Bibi whispers, her kohl-lined sapphire eyes cleaving a low-hanging sky. *Fly as long and as hard as you can, my co-dreamer! Scout a fresh site on another hill. Found with me a city where lions lie with lambs, where pity quickens knowledge, where desire dissipates despair!*

THERE ARE no accidents. My Yale thesis on the Puritans didn't lead to graduate school and a teaching career, but it took me here, no accident. My life with Venn Iyer, father of fractals and designer of inner space, is no accident.

I drove out to this museum to track down for a client what he claims is the most perfect diamond in the world. The diamond has a name: The Emperor's Tear. For five years, I have been tracking the Salem Bibi, a woman from Salem who ended up in the Emperor's court. I know her as well as any scholar has known her subject; I know her like a doctor and a lawyer, like a mother and a daughter. With every new thing I've learned, I've come imperceptibly closer to the Emperor's Tear. In that final

Gotterdammerung painting, she is holding it: I have seen the Emperor's Tear atop its golden orb. Three hundred years ago, it existed in her hands; I know where she came from and where she went. I couldn't care less about the Emperor's Tear, by now. I care only about the Salem Bibi.

I should have let the keyboard do the tracking, but, like shamans and psychics, I've learned to go with hunches as well as data bases. The easiest way for a white-collar felon to make a stone vanish for a while is to loan it to a small, grateful museum under a plausible alias. And if the museum, finding itself too cluttered already, and out of its curatorial depths, were to sell it in some obscure auction in Europe or Canada, and the owner just happened to show up and buy it, he'd have title, free and clear, wouldn't he?

What I hadn't figured on was the secret life of a Puritan woman whom an emperor honored as Precious-as-Pearl, the Healer of the World.

# 3.

SHE WAS Hannah Easton, only surviving child of Edward and Rebecca Easton, nee Rebecca Walker of Brookfield, in the Massachusetts Bay Colony. Brookfield, today, lies about midway between Worcester and Springfield in the foothills of central Massachusetts, east of the gentle floodplain of the Connecticut River. In Hannah's time it was Indian country: smack in the middle of Nipmuc land with Mohicans and Narragansetts to the south, Pennacook and Abnaki on the north all the way to New France.

The dates are not important. I'll summarize them later.

All of Massachusetts must have been an extended family. A cousin shipped out, an in-law followed, an uncle got news of free land, a chance for rebeginning ... like villages in Poland and Italy and Ireland emptying for America two centuries later.

Case in point: my family.

Rebecca Easton's nee Walker's grandmother was a cousin of Charles Jonathan Samuel Muster's father; her family, had been legitimate passengers on the *Gabriel* (two years later to sink off Pemaquid, Maine) that Charles had stowed away on. Vaguely, then, I'm part of this story, the Salem Bibi is part of the tissue of my life. Walkers appear on the ship's records, but Charles Muster never did. They'd probably settled in Boston, or even Rhode Island. Perhaps primogeniture did him out of land or inheritance, but by 1653 Elias Walker, his wife and infant daughter, Rebecca, arrived in Brookfield and leased, from their distant relatives the Masters (the three sons of Charles Jonathan Samuel Muster), three hundred acres of prime Quaboag River bluff and bottomland. By all accounts, Elias Walker was a frugal farmer and stockman; by 1665, he had purchased his land outright. My direct Masters ancestors pocketed the cash and further dissipated their father's wealth.

At that time, Brookfield was a hesitant hilltop Puritan outpost deep inside Nipmuc country. Elias Walker held the usual attitudes of his times, and ours, toward the Indians: they are children, they are trusting, they are proud and generous. Even capable of nobility. But at heart they are savages: bestial, unspeakably cruel. He counseled, and cultivated, the path of mutual avoidance. Eight years later, the Walkers gained a neighbor, a sickly looking but resourceful recent arrival by the name of Edward Easton, who purchased with his English savings a brown ribbon of a field, a rickety shed, a cabin with privy and two barns.

The stage was set: older bachelor farmer with education and some money. The robust farmer's daughter next door was only eight years old when first glimpsed, but no one was going anywhere. By the time she was sixteen, in 1668, Rebecca Walker was married to Edward Easton.

By eighteen, she'd had two pregnancies. The second, a daughter named Hannah, survived. In the remotest of ways, Hannah Easton is a relative of mine. Hannah Easton would walk the parapets of a Moghul fort, would hold the world's most perfect diamond in her hands.

This was country for those raw and strong enough to hack prosperity out of wild, volatile land. And this was country for the middle-aged and bitter, discontented city dwellers and immigrants to start over in the wilderness, where the Prince of the Air was said to reign. Edward Easton was forty-three (already living on borrowed time, statistically speaking) the year that Hannah was born.

| | |
|---|---|
| 1632 | Charles Jonathan Samuel Muster arrives in Massachusetts. |
| 1653 | Elias Walker and family arrive in Brookfield. Birth of Rebecca Walker. |
| 1661 | Arrival of Edward Easton. |
| 1668 | Marriage of Rebecca and Edward. |
| 1670 | Birth of Hannah Easton. |

Of Edward Easton's life before the winter of 1661, when he showed up in Boston, little is known. He sailed out of the Downs soon after Charles II, the Stuart restored to the English throne, had Oliver Cromwell's embalmed body dug out of its secret grave and decapitated, and the head stuck on a pole in Westminster Hall. They sent potent messages in those days; Edward, a Roundhead sympathizer, must have caught the first packet boat to the colonies.

In the Old World, Edward Easton had been an East India Company man with a sedentary occupation, a doughyskinned, soft-bellied, fact-fevered scribe hunched over ledger books, letters and memoranda in the Company's Leadenhall Street offices in London. Back in my junior year abroad, in London, I checked the Company's books and papers stored in the India Office in Whitehall. Edward Easton's entries stand out because of the singular primness and angularity of his handwriting.

I knew my own family's names and fragments of rumored history, of course. When I got to England, I went straight to the shipping records, the baptismal records, the recordings of deeds. Seeing the names of relatives, reading of their deaths and births and marriages all placed me within a context that I found somehow thrilling, as though nothing in the universe is ever lost, no gesture is futile. I've since then doubted the significance of many of those innocent discoveries, but seeing those 'Salem Bibi's Stuffs' boxes on the floor of the maritime museum, those Moghul paintings, brought the importance of those feelings back.

A twenty-year-old girl, really, contemplating her place in the universe and the ways of the world had discovered an ancestor, a man of her genes who had gone before her, and though he was writing of strangers, she read all his notes like an intimate letter from home:

*A petty ruler on the Coromandel coast of India is given the gifts of armour, a wool coat and a spying glass.*

*A ship on its way to Masulipatnam is stocked with 1420 hogs and 250 oxen.*

*The mother of a factor who died on board a Company vessel sailing home from Fort St. George is denied the diamonds she claims he was bringing back for her.*

*A cabin-boy is whipped and his lacerations brined for having stolen a vial of musk.*

Did the cabin boy live to be a sea captain? Did the petty ruler wear his bribe to his next battle and did the armor save his skin? Was Edward Easton's mind so demented with details that he fled to the wilderness? Or did he merely look up and out the grimy window, see the forest of mastheads and yardarms on the river and the white Crosses of St. George fluttering like birds on the Company's pennants and finally walk away from his old self? As his wife and his daughter would do, again and again.

Edward Easton arrived in Boston with sufficient skills and savings to make him desirable as a son-in-law to any Boston patriarch with too many daughters, but within weeks he bought himself a horse and cantered westward. Was it disgust with the old life, or was he enticed by a new, wholly imagined one that drove him away from safe and stable port towns like Boston and Salem? Did the Puritans, with their gloomy quest for godliness, hold for him more terror – as, later, they would for Hannah – than the presumed Satan who reigned over Pennacook, Abnaki and Nipmuc?

What is known is that he headed for the outer rings of settlements, stopping over first in Billerica, then in Chelmsford, then in Lancaster – where he was invited to sup at the home of John White, the wealthy landholder, and offered a modest bookkeeping job by White's son-in-law, Reverend Joseph Rowlandson, Lancaster's first minister – then in Worcester, and finally either running out of energy or finding in Brookfield the dreamscape for starting over.

For this accidental frontiersman, the 1660s was a decade of self-transformation. Like an alchemist who turns dross into gold, he hardened his slack and bookish body into the wiriness of a tiller, transformed the forest into farmland, and disenchantment into desire. And when desire grew carnal and kept him awake all the summer nights of 1668, he married, after perfunctory courtship, the Walker's bonny lass, strong and handsome, even comely, he wrote in that angular hand, with domestic skills and teachable aptitudes worthy of a free-born woman of this new land.

He felt he might give her twenty years of husbandly service, begetting upon her a brood of worthy offspring. Already, he was cultivating a second career as village selectman.

I gasped the moment I opened Brookfield town registries and saw the same angular hand I'd known from Leadenhall. I thought then, with all the melodrama of undergraduate training, of Keats' odes, or of his 'On First Looking into Chapman's Homer,' for here I was, perhaps the only scholar in the world who had traced the work of an obscure clerk from London to Massachusetts. I could sense all the movements in his life, his determination to remake his life before it was too late, to go west to the colony instead of east, where surely his East India clerkship could have led him. I felt the same psychic bond with Edward Easton that Keats did with the revelers on the Grecian urn. He became a footnote in my thesis, but an assurance to me that my research in that era was somehow blessed. Of all the billions of births, the fires and floodings that separate me and my time from Easton and his, that the mundane work of this lone man should be preserved struck me as nothing less than miraculous and conferred on me a kind of wonderstruck confidence.

For most English colonists and certainly for Indian sachems, however, the 1660s was a win-or-die decade. So while Edward Easton was cutting trees down to stumps, raking his field, sowing his wife's fertile womb, prizing rocks from the ground and hauling them to build a wall, burying his firstborn, trading wool stockings and blankets for herbs with the Nipmuc, the Wampanoag chief, Metacom (whom the colonists renamed Philip), was suing and skirmishing to oust alien usurpers, and the French *habitants* were selling flintlocks to Ninigret, sachem of the Narraganset, in hopes of stirring up anti-English riots.

In 1671, on September 29, the day that Hannah turned a year old and first toddled far enough away by herself to have to be brought back by a solicitous Nipmuc, and the day that, in a cold drafty hall in distant Plymouth, the colonial government curtailed the sovereign powers of the Wampanoag and humiliated the proud King Philip by imposing a fine of one hundred pounds for violating their laws, Edward Easton, while in his outdoor privy savoring the poetic paradox in an imported, treasured copy of *Paradise Lost* and the physical paradox of constipation's painful pleasures, died of a bee sting.

OF HER MOTHER, the twenty-two-year old widow whom Hannah lost when the Nipmuc laid siege to Brookfield in the scorched and septic month of August 1675, she had one long, disturbing memory.

Rebecca Easton loved to sing. She sang psalms by the light of a fish oil lamp, always to the same five or six tunes. And though she could neither read the words to the psalms nor the notes to the tunes that Edward, perhaps in a rare desperately nostalgic moment, had scribbled on the back cover of the Psalter, she taught the child to sing antiphonally with her. Hannah's memory is of one such psalm-singing night, their last one. Rebecca by the window, her neck long and arched, her throat throbbing with song. A voice so strong and sweet that it softens the sternest spiritual phrases into voluptuous pleas. The greasy, pale light of the lamp; the acute smell of the lamp oil. Rebecca singing each line by herself first, then nodding to encourage Hannah; Hannah repeating the line in a quavery, unformed voice. But, Hannah remembers, and this can never be separated from the angelic choir pouring from her mother's breast, there are faces at the window.

Of course, the memory coalesces several frames into a single emblematic moment. The child sees; the mother does not. The faces are listening, tomahawks held high, about to smash the window and door, but they are stilled in midflight. The Indians know these songs, especially the women who sit in the rear of the church, walking in and out during the sermons but rising with the congregation to sing. Her memory is a window, letting in the fecundity of an unfenced world.

She has also what she calls sightings rather than memories of that early childhood on the farm. Rebecca and some Indian helpers must farm alone; Rebecca is a widow. A Nipmuc woman teaching her to clean and dress deerskin. A boy-child promising to grow for her the plumpest squashes and pumpkins, the crispest beans, the brightest corn. A Nipmuc man hunting wild turkeys and pigeons, and she bouncing along behind in Rebecca's papoose. A season of drought. The same Nipmuc man, Rebecca and Hannah – a frontier family – scraping the last ladlefuls of stewed-together berries and bird eggs and ground nuts from a huge, carbon-encrusted pot. Her mother smiling as the Nipmuc presses a steaming gourd of coarse, spicy potage to Hannah's lips. She remembers her face against the soft deerskin of his jerkin.

King Philip changed Hannah's life as completely and as forcefully as King Charles II of England had changed her father's.

All through June and July of 1675, paranoia traveled up and down the Bay Path. Philip was arming his warriors for an all-out war! Wampanoag were breaking into and entering colonists' houses in Swansea and raiding farms abandoned on the thin, frayed neck of peninsular land. Isolated farmers were gathered up and garrisoned, losing their crops and cattle to the marauders. Messengers from Governor Winslow of Plymouth fanned their frenzy. Philip's men were looting and burning Middleborough, Dartmouth, Plymouth. The heathens were axing, scalping, abducting the decent Christian men and women and children of Mendon.

Hannah dreamed of Philip pressing his war-roused face at the window. Why not? Stray troopers coming through spoke of Philip as though he were an omnipresent phantom. One moment he was staking out pease fields, next moment he was fortifying snake-crowded swamps. And the next, he was impaling scalped heads and slashing the bulging sacs of milch cows.

Then, on the night of the second of August, Philip's War came to the Easton hearth in the person of Rebecca's Nipmuc lover. If he had intended the marking as disguise, it didn't work. Hannah knew him as her inadmissible father, the only man she'd ever seen her mother with. The child raised her hand. The mother stopped singing, and slowly turned around.

This is the night Hannah has willed herself not to remember. What happened survives only as Rebecca's neighbors' gossip, embellished with the speculations of scholars. The lover, now painted and feathered as befits a warrior, comes to woo her one last time. And Rebecca surprises him. Reading Hannah's eyes, she stands and slowly turns, facing the window without surprise or terror. She stands on a reed rug by the window, the very window where Hannah remembers her having led women and children through psalms, and peels her white, radiant body out of the Puritan widow's thick, somber bodice and skirt as a viper sheds skin before wriggling into the brush. Her body is thick, strong, the flesh streaked and bruised, trussed with undergarments.

The Nipmuc enters the cabin, suddenly immense in his full battle regalia. He cradles the whimpering Easton hound under one arm.

Rebecca scoops Hannah out of her bed, cradles her and weeps as though the child were dead. The Nipmuc jerks his arm, the hound lurches, and a spume of blood leaps from his arms across the table. He swabs Rebecca's old garments in the blood, smears them with his feet over the floor, stabs holes in the cloth as they darken with blood, then hands her something new and Indian and clean to wear.

Outside, a Nipmuc woman who had taught her to sew deerskin into breeches, takes the child. She watches the cabin grow small, and a fireball erupt from the spilled fish oil lamp, as Rebecca and the Nipmuc take off for the river, and the woman, running hard and low to the ground, cuts into the woods, along the path to the Fitch farm half a mile away. She does not cry, and the vow she makes, bobbing in the arms of the nameless woman she has known all her life, to remain silent about this night, to sustain her mother in the ultimate lie, the ultimate unnatural crime of Puritan life, she will keep for sixty years.

Hannah's subsequent years can be read as a sermon on any topic, as proof of any interpretation. But she wills the memory of this night away; she will orphan herself to that memory, deny its existence, for that is the way her mother has planned it. She alone knows the nature of her mother's disappearance; she must carry the denial of this memory – a lump tenfold heavier than the memory itself – the rest of her life, chastising the lump inside her that is Rebecca with self-doubt and self-hate. Had she been perceived the daughter of a fornicator, not the offspring of an upright widow, no family would have taken her in. It is necessary not only to retain the memory of her beloved, absent mother, but to deny its final blinding, lustful image. To preserve above all the orphan's tragic tale above the wicked woman's demonic possession.

Has any child been so burdened? She has witnessed the Fall, not Adam's Fall, Rebecca's Fall. Her mother's Fall, infinitely more sinful than the Fall of a man. She is the witness not merely of the occasion of sin, but of the birth of sin itself.

And I who have studied Hannah's life nearly as closely as I have studied my own would say that Hannah Easton, whatever the name she carried in Massachusetts, in England, in India or even into history to this very day, loved her mother more profoundly than any daughter has ever loved a mother.

I feel for Hannah as the Nipmuc woman carries her off and drops her noiselessly on a pioneer family's doorstep, deflecting forever the natural course and location of her girlhood. And I envy Rebecca as she, impulsively, carelessly, leaps behind her lover, who is already on his horse, and vanishes into the wilderness. She has escaped her prison, against prevailing odds that would have branded her. Her lover might have come to the window that night to kill them both. Instead, he became the first man to read the scene between them as something sacred, in the fish oil glow, to hear the music.

# KANCHANA UGBABE

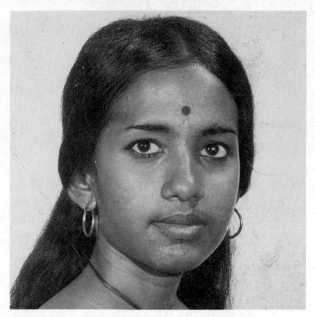

Kanchana Ugbabe was born and raised in India, is Nigerian by marriage and has a daughter and two sons. She has written widely on cross-cultural and women's issues. She is a graduate B.A. and M.A. (First Class), of Madras University and was awarded a gold medal for being the best female student of the University in her year. Her dissertation on *The Theme of Infancy and Childhood in Literature and Thought 1640-1750* gained her the degree of Ph.D. at Flinders University of South Australia in Adelaide. Dr Ugbabe has taught at Madras, Queensland, and Flinders Universities, and is now a Senior Lecturer in English at the University of Jos, Nigeria. In 1993 she was awarded a USIA grant to participate in the International Writing programme at the University of Iowa, U.S.A. Several of her stories have been broadcast by the BBC on its Overseas Service.

KANCHANA UGBABE

# Why I Write

I was born at Tamilnadu in India, gained my Master's degree at Madras University and my Ph.D. at Flinders University of South Australia. I married a Nigerian and now teach English at the University of Jos in Nigeria.

It is this cross-cultural perspective that gives me the impetus to write short stories. I feel I have a unique angle of vision: Indian from the outside and Nigerian from the inside. Each of my stories is born of some little incident or observation that sparks a range of associated ideas which have been brewing in my mind, and the story takes shape and form. Four elements contribute to this process: the impulse, the subject matter, the attitude, and the language.

Among the subjects which particularly interest me are the entire chaos of city life, the way people cohabit with the bizarre and the mundane in their everyday lives, and above all the responses of women to these and other situations in a society in transition. I write women's stories because I believe women have a voice and a vision that is peculiarly their own. I feel an urge about writing as a woman, a need to catch up and put across women's stories.

Living in an African country has made me strongly aware of the need to understand different cultures. My academic work is concerned with the concepts of childhood and the family in African as well as western literatures. In African literature, as in African society, the family is far from being a neatly defined and illustrated unit. It is, on the contrary, made up of a loose and amorphous group of people with a matriarch or patriarch at the centre, branching out into ever-widening circles of kinships and relations. It is a complex network of support-systems and value-building mechanisms.

Marriage in African society is not the union of two individuals but of two groups, two families, and African women writers in particular have gone to great lengths to explore the issues raised by such social structures. In my own way as a wife and mother in Nigeria, who is also familiar with Indian and Western attitudes to women, children, and marriage, I try similarly to explore these issues in my academic work as well as in my own stories.

Moreover, my years as postgraduate student and as teacher in Australia, and my recent extended visit to the United States of America have also in important ways contributed to my personal vision as a writer and to the craft of writing.

KANCHANA UGBABE

# Golden Opportunities

The caption under the wedding photograph in the local newspaper read, 'Claude hooks Hope,' as a matronly and obviously pregnant Hope, in white wedding dress and veil, stuffed a much-too-large piece of cake into the mouth of a bewildered and be-gloved Claude. Hope looked triumphant as the one who had 'hooked' Claude!

*Our* wedding picture was not quite so conventional. The photographer had me sitting on one of those wooden playground swings (a studio creation, of course), while my husband clutched at the chains. Very romantic, like a scene from the Indian movies. That was how I took my plunge into matrimony. It has been not just a turn on the swing but a regular roller-coaster ride ever since. My friend Daphne says that the sharp bit goes out of the situation if you stick it out long enough and that you arrive at a sort of benign indifference where the boat doesn't rock too badly, even if you keep wishing in the back of your mind that you were in a different boat ... My husband tends to be philosophical about these things. He maintains that women get the men they deserve and vice versa. I don't know if Kemi deserved the man she got, but she wasn't going to wait to find out.

When my husband told me his friend Debo's wife was coming from Lagos to stay the weekend with us, I felt the usual tingle of resentment. I disliked strange city women even before I met them. Kemi was coming to see her son, who was at a boarding school in our town. It was his free weekend. Debo and my husband had been at school together, but it was twenty years later, with both engaged in different occupations, when their paths crossed again in Lagos. They were both following up payments for completed army contracts. I had written Debo off from the start when I heard that he had two wives. Two wives and six children at forty! He must be one of those unreliable men, a womanizer, a spendthrift – a man who squandered his money on cars and clubs, I concluded. The two wives lived apart in separate houses, with Debo doing the rounds between them. For all practical purposes, he lived with Kemi, his first wife. But it was Biola my husband talked about, Biola who was shy, Biola who was mild-mannered and soft-spoken, Biola who baked cakes. Biola was Debo's showpiece. Kemi was an unknown quantity, and I didn't look forward to entertaining this Lagos woman, an employee of the National Shipping Company, at my home.

I stayed longer at work than usual, knowing my husband was at the airport to meet Kemi. On her arrival, Kemi bounced her way up the stairs and took me completely by surprise. After the initial welcome and introductions, we settled ourselves in the living room. Kemi sat across from my husband, her miniskirt tight about her thighs. He stared at her legs all evening, from the ebony calves up the smooth shaven legs to where the patchwork leather skirt ended. Her puffy childlike hands had rings on every finger. The painted fingernails danced wildly as she gesticulated. She had an endless repertoire of stories, from corruption in high places to armed robbery and drug dealing. She spun them out with confidence, shaking the silky brown hairpiece that was unobtrusively attached to her hair by a silver clasp. She was thirty-eight but looked and acted about twenty-five.

She punctuated her conversation with 'Darling, you have no idea...!' She rolled her big brown eyes and said, 'I'm going to leave him. You wait and see. I'm just praying that God will give me a good man. That's it.' With the appropriate gestures, she washed her hands of Debo. I rushed around to make her bed and carried a bucket of hot water to her bathroom. She sat like a princess, and, when everything was set, took herself to the bedroom on her spiky-heeled patent leather shoes.

Over the next two days, it was a total surprise every time Kemi emerged from the bedroom. You could never predict what the outfit might be. On Saturday morning, it was a burgundy wrapper and a flamboyant head-tie, with red lipstick that generously covered her lips. The pale edge of the wrapper read, 'Guaranteed Dutch Wax.' In the evening, it was striped culottes in black and white, the style accentuating her well-endowed bosom, and gold-studded sandals. On Sunday, it was a boubou[1] in gold that trailed after her, sweeping the harmattan[2] dust off my floor.

I didn't expect her to come into my kitchen, but there she was, blending the pepper and tomatoes, and browning the oxtail with Maggi cubes, early on Saturday morning. 'Darling, we have to be at the boarding school by ten o'clock,' she said, pouring a gallon of oil into the stew. So we cooked and we talked.

As she diced the carrots for the *jollof* rice, I noticed her smooth, well-rounded wrists and the pearl-studded gold bangle that fitted tightly around her wrist. 'Can we buy Kemi a gift? It's her first visit with us,' my husband had inquired, opening his wallet. 'Buy her something personal, like a bangle,' he had added. I had thought of something neutral, like an enamel saucepan or a Melaware tray.

'It's good to be independent,' Kemi said, 'then you can tell these men to go to hell!'

'How do you cope with your...with Biola, I mean?' I hesitated.

'Darling, I'm Debo's *only* wife!' she responded. 'If he chooses to keep a prostitute somewhere, that's his problem.' She volunteered more information, letting me in on a secret. 'Biola used medicine. She goes to witch doctors, and that's how she trapped Debo. I can't forgive Debo. I have had two children and four miscarriages. Every time I miscarried, Biola got pregnant. It's the medicine.' I warmed up to Kemi. 'Taste the stew,' she said, offering me a spoonful. The pepper singed my tongue and set my intestines aflame. 'It's too cold in this town,' she reasoned, 'you have to eat plenty of pepper.'

Her job with the National Shipping Company kept her comfortable; her contacts in Lagos gave her access to all sorts of loans. She was building a block of apartments. And she was into the supply business, buying garri[3] in bulk from the factory in Ibadan and supplying colleagues and friends every two weeks. She had her social clubs: the Inner Wheel, the Esteem Sisters, Ajegunle Women's Club, and the Fellowship of Business Women International. They met in each other's homes, drank beer and other local brew, and consumed huge quantities of fried meat and fish.

'You should come to Lagos,' she invited me, squeezing my hand. 'I have grand things planned for you.'

Biola was the bane of her existence. 'Do you know Biola has two children by an Alhaji, and she's now pregnant by an Igbo man?'

'What does Debo see in her?' I prompted.

'Darling, she is *ugly*. Crooked front teeth. Skinny, in buba[4] and wrapper. Oily, pimply face – that's the type Debo goes for...I'm just waiting for a nice man to come my way,' she concluded.

We got in the car. As we drove past the market, Kemi beckoned to me to stop at one of the shops. It was pretty much a shack, with wooden boards hastily nailed together, the nails still sticking out. 'Come to Blessed Spot and Enjoy Yourself,' urged a piece of paper nailed to the board. In this haven of bliss, this oasis, there stood a Coke machine in one corner and a photocopying machine in another. A cupboard with a glass front, roughly put together, housed lotions, creams, and other cosmetics in jars with orange, pink, and purple tops.

'How much is that facial mask?' Kemi asked the girl, who was squeezed between the various gadgets.

'Forty naira.'[5]

'What about the nail hardener?'

'Thirty-five naira.'

I shifted and discreetly eyed Kemi. What was she going to ask for next? After much haggling, Kemi declared that these things were cheaper in Lagos anyway, and promptly left.

We brought her eleven-year-old son home from the boarding school to spend Saturday with us – a scrawny lad with unkempt, dry scaly skin, and a shell-shocked look. Kemi gave twenty naira to the master in charge of the dormitory for his newborn child. 'Boy or girl?' she inquired, intending to send a gift on her return to Lagos. The chief prefect and the hall messenger got twenty naira each, to 'keep an eye' on the eleven-year-old Dele. 'He has to pass his exams. I'll hold you responsible,' she teased the chief prefect as she tucked the twenty-naira note into his palm. Once home, Dele was scrubbed from head to toe, washed, bleached, and disinfected, and fed a generous helping of jollof rice and the pepper stew loaded with oxtail, liver, and other choice cuts of meat. There was a brisk and practical air about it all – she had come from Lagos to do a job, and she had to do it well. Dele's appearance, lectures on studying hard, compliance with authority, taking care of personal belongings – she seemed to tick things off one by one on her mental agenda. Later in the day, we took Dele back to suffer the rigours of boarding-school life.

Kemi and I sat down to a cup of coffee. 'My life has been wasted on Debo,' she moaned, 'when I think about it, I get palpitations.' She talked of injustice, and it seemed as if all men were ogres exploiting and deceiving their wives, and lavishing love and money on mistresses. We exchanged stories of betrayal, of husbands who drove us to the outer limits of despair. It was our inner strength that had saved us from high blood pressure and heart attacks. We had acquired wisdom through experience.

Kemi couldn't sustain this sombre mood for long. As I brought the second cup of coffee, she launched into stories of erring husbands who got involved with several women and then dropped dead, leaving a labyrinth of woes for their wives. Lorraine, her friend, stood in her black scarf and black wrapper, she said, the picture of wifely grief, flanked by the boys on one side and the girls on the other. Kehinde, the 'other woman', burst in on them at the funeral, also clad in black, holding two children by the hand and a baby on her back. Lorraine was hysterical, Kemi said. 'You won't have peace where you are going,' she screamed to the man in the box, rigid in embalmed security. 'It's not the kingdom of God you are heading for. You'd better get up and sort out this mess!' I laughed till my sides hurt.

'How much do you have in the bank?' Kemi inquired casually. 'You know, I could send you wrappers and shoes from Lagos. Just add your profit and sell them quietly. Before you know it, you can buy a piece of land and put a few bricks on it. Then, like Debo, your husband will come to you when he needs a mere fifty naira.' I had meagre savings, put together erratically over a period of ten years. In a household such as ours, it wasn't easy to operate a bank account without my husband finding out about it. I hid the savings book and switched its place periodically – and panicked at being found out. My husband and I operated a joint account that was perpetually in the red.

My husband was not a notoriously difficult man, but Kemi's presence made the differences in our outlook more pronounced. He was the kind that filled his tank every time he passed the petrol station, while I flogged the old Toyota on reserve and then grudgingly drove in for maybe a quarter-tank of gas. He coaxed his car, keeping it in top form, changing its tyres periodically, checking its brakes. I left the windows down in the rain; I cursed the old car when it jerked and threatened to give up on me. All the trash over the past six months accumulated on the floor of my car – drugstore receipts, church programs, candy wrappers – you would even find an odd potato or onion nestling under the seat. The children treated my car with scant respect. His car radio played blues and jazz and he cruised along. He talked about joining the Road Safety Campaign.

I mulled over Kemi's proposal through the night. Lying in bed, I looked around the room. There were landmarks everywhere, milestones, souvenirs of my quarrels with my husband over other women, real and imagined, and my attempts to get even with him. The Sony Cassette player marked a major quarrel, when I rushed out and bought it as something belonging to me. I was going to put my feet up and listen to music. Another heated argument resulted in expensive lace curtains. The shrouded figures emerged one by one from the closet, women who inhabited my bedroom in silhouetted shapes, lurking in corners, insinuating themselves between the sheets. The names spilt out, echoing around my bed. I had never had an instinct for business or the initiative, but Kemi was going to launch me into the world of garri and palm-oil entrepreneurs. My life was at a crossroads, and the horizon held innumerable pots of gold.

Kemi and I entered the bank. 'Do not abuse the naira. Handle it with care,' said the Central Bank poster, with pictures of grubby and bacteria-ridden currency notes changing hands, tucked into sweaty blouses, in traders' pouches attached to petticoats, and crumpled into unrecognizable shapes by newspaper vendors. The shiny coins were so much better, though coins made you feel poorer than you were and made your purse heavier. I stretched out my hand to present the withdrawal slip to the cashier. A whiff of sardines emanated from the lady standing next to me; she continued with her crocheting, oblivious to everything around her. Kemi and I sat down on the bench. The women looked colourful, the men drab. Tight clothes reduced the sperm count, Kemi said. Sitting back, I watched backsides, big and small, in trousers, skirts, and wrappers, all provocatively tight. A woman with a baby sat near us. The baby bounced about and played with her fingers. Then, without warning, it pissed all over the man sitting next to the mother. 'Baby don piss O!' cried the man, jumping from his seat. 'Sorry O,' said the mother, mopping up with a tissue from her handbag. The baby said, 'Come, come.'

'No way,' said the man good-humouredly, gathering his naira notes and hurrying out of the bank. I handled my savings – with trepidation – as Kemi and I walked out of the bank. I felt hollow inside, having emptied out my savings account. I quickly put the money in an envelope and gave it to Kemi.

'Darling, just give me one week – seven days – and I'll be in touch.'

It is almost two years since Kemi's visit. I wait for letters and parcels and the passport to entrepreneurship and that peculiar independence that only Kemi could envisage. Maybe she has completed her block of flats at Ajegunle and moved in; maybe her prayers have been answered and God has given her that 'nice man'. She left behind a souvenir though – her gold-studded slippers and lipstick on the edges of my coffee mug.

## Notes

1. *boubou:* a long flowing garment worn in parts of Africa.
2. *harmattan:* a seasonal dust-laden wind on the Atlantic coast of Africa.
3. *garri:* ground cassava.
4. *buba:* a plain blouse, worn with a wrapper.
5. The amount is equivalent to about one U.S. dollar.

# AFRICA

# AMA ATA AIDOO

Ama Ata Aidoo was born in Ghana and is a pioneer in depicting the role of African women. Whilst she was still an undergraduate at the University of Ghana in Lagos she was awarded a prize in a competition sponsored by the Mbari Club in Ibadan. She has travelled widely in Africa, Europe and the USA, and apart from a distinguished academic career she was also Minister for Education in the Ghanian government in the 1980s. Her writing includes two plays, *Dilemma of a Ghost* and *Anowa* (the latter had a very successful season in London in 1991), two volumes of poetry, *Someone Talking is Sometime* and *An Angry Letter in January* (published by Dangaroo Press in 1992), a collection of short stories, *No Sweetness Here*, and two novels, *Our Sister Kiljoy* and *Changes* (1991). The latter won first prize for the African region in the 1992 Commonwealth Writers Prize. Her writing is sometimes experimental, and combines both African and Western traditions.

# Ama Ata Aidoo

SPICES
– for Pandi (Mutuma)


Actually,
I could handle the matter of
peppercorns
really well since
I can still see Mother
leaving them to ripen
on the *odupon*.

A proper parasite if ever there was one
who vinely and shamelessly
sprouted by giant roots
secured itself to massive ancestral trunks and
wove thin firm tendrils
singing a long and difficult solo
through the dappled undergrowths
                    then
lay queenly and luxuriantly on the branches and
on each wider, greener, thicker leaf,
until up and up and up
it reached its highest crescendo and kissed
the glorious sun
gloriously.


                    II

My Sister,
we shall not even discuss
ginger,
wild mint or
its more delicate kin
which acquired
the anti-chicken name *akoko-besa*
meaning *fowls-end*;
when grown in

old chamber- and water-poets, and
other closed-in spaces
behind the bedroom wall.

Can you believe that?

III

On the other hand,
The Pepper-master's and
The Pepper-mistress's
pepper
is another story.

There was a time when it was known only to
priests, priestesses, prophets and
sundry holy ones
who ate the sacred stuff to sharpen
their tongues

IV

When you first dropped your
artful reproof,
startling me with
its delicious wit and sweet censure,

I first and
guiltily
saw clear evidence of
my westernization,
or rather
the ease with which
the food-lover in me had taken to
'foreign cuts' of meat:
the steaks, the chops and

the briskets
duly cased in
condiments of exotic names and flavours;
– never mind their origins –

cardamom
origanum

rosemary and thyme . . .

But then, because
we try never to quite give in without a fight
I quickly recall that from
sweeping airports,
driving taxis and
cleaning rich old folks' bodies,

Cousin Kwaku, Bro Kofi, Sissie Yaa
and the rest of the extended family
go home to

New York's Flat and London's Shepherd Bushes
Amsterdam and Hamburg to
eat
more authentically and richly
than the kings and queens
we left at home.

So whose bourgeois palate
are we talking of
taking care of?

Eh, My Sister,
whose
bourgeois palate?

their visions of the future and
the immediate and urgent matter of
their sexual prowess.

Which name do you know it by, My Sister?

Shito
Piripiri
Miripiri
chili
cayenne
agoi
???

We speak of
the beginning and end of all heat . . .

Where I come from
we called it *muoko*
its etymology
completely lost in
millennias into which
harried wives
ground and ground and ground
the precious stuff . . .

If we insisted on counting,
we could end up with one hundred species, and
still not be done.

My Sister,
when The Pepper-person's pepper moved out of
the shrines and the temples,
it stayed for a thousand more years
in near-by habitations known only to locals in
Africa and Asia . . .

– another ancient and spicy secret,
valued in equal parts with gold dust
then, but soon to be

just one more Third World exotica
variously liked and apologised for.

These days,
between the mildest and the most abrasive,
green, red, yellow, thin, squat, full or hollow,
peppers
grace supermarket stalls from
Atlanta through London to Zurich . . .

from which places
we zero in
on the issue of how
we take care of our bourgeois palates.

# ── TSITSI DANGAREMBGA ──

Tsitsi Dangarembga was born in former Rhodesia, now Zimbabwe, in 1959. She spent her early childhood and received her first schooling in Britain but returned with her family to Rhodesia where she finished her schooling at a missionary school. In 1997, she went to Cambridge to study medicine but returned again to Rhodesia in 1980 just prior to black-majority rule and the emergence of Zimbabwe.

She worked for a marketing agency while studying psychology at the University of Harare. She took active part in the university's drama group and it was by writing plays for this group that her writing career started. She received second prize in a short-story competition sponsored by the Swedish aid-organization, SIDA, but the novel *Nervous Conditions* was to be her real breakthrough as it won the African section of the Commonwealth Writers Prize in 1989.

The book was published in Denmark and in July, 1991, Tsitsi Dangarembga visited Denmark in connection with the Images-of-Africa festival.

With her pungent points of view, Tsitsi Dangarembga takes a keen part in the debate concerning the position of women in modern Africa.

# Between Gender, Race and History: Kirsten Holst Petersen Interviews Tsitsi Dangarembga

*You start your novel* Nervous Conditions *with a very provocative sentence ' I was not sorry when my brother died.' and you continue rubbing salt into the wound 'Nor am I apologising for my callousness.' Do you find that your main character is justified in harbouring such an unnatural sentiment?*

When you write a novel you want people to read it. I thought I should say something stunning in the opening sentence that would focus very much on the issues I was dealing with. That sentence was really to open up people's minds. It has such an impact that nobody could ignore it. I didn't write that as a value statement, I really wrote it as a literary statement. What runs throughout the whole novel (*Nervous Conditions*) is a black, eight year old girl's quest for education; the novel is set in rural Zimbabwe in the sixties before Independence. The girl was actually more intelligent than her brother, but he was sent to school, he was groomed for stardom.She had to leave school because there wasn't enough money in the family to pay school fees for both children, so when he died she got the chance to be educated, which really meant that she got the chance of a better life. The brother's character was such that we can see that she would never be able to rely on him anyway, although she was making sacrifices for him by not going to school.

*What is the reason for this unequal treatment?*

The easy answer in the West is the Patriarchal system. I have become increasingly more reluctant to use this model of analysis as it is put forward by Western feminism, because the situation in my part of the world has one variable, which makes it absolutely different: the men are also in a position of powerlessness. So I would offer perhaps also economic reasons, for the family knew that she would not be in a position to help them afterwards; that is not purely a patriarchal problem, it is also a result of the state of colonisation at the time. And so it was a mixed problem, so one cannot say that it was purely a problem of gender.

*Nyasha's condition is not just nervous, she has a mental breakdown which takes the form of anorexia. Is it not – again – a provocation to transport, imaginatively, of course, this disease, which is a symptom of the affluent West, to a continent where people still starve to death? Do you think that it could in fact occur in Africa?*

It has happened! Cases of anorexia have been reported in Zimbabwe. The diagnosis of anorexia is something difficult. If a woman in Zimbabwe, rural or urban is depressed, loses weight etc. who is to say whether that is anorexia or not? Of course the extreme form is associated with these images of beauty, which developed in the West during the sixties. That is something else. I find this difficult to answer! When does a depression become so severe that it becomes a disease? And of course, we also have these images of beauty, we have Hollywood films in Zimbabwe, so women are becoming conscious of their weight. This happens particularly in the middle classes where the women have the leisure to read the magazines and decide that they want to look like these people. I would just like to make a point about the relationship between anorexia, beauty and studying: in the families where anorexia is common, even studying has a positive value, just like beauty, and I sometimes think that one of the reasons why the girls are so prone to this disease is that if you live a very intellectual life you do become more divorced from the physical aspects of yourself, and it may not be easy to determine what is affecting what. This may be the reason why these girls project themselves in that way.

*Education is always considered a possible way out for women, and yet in your novel you have a highly educated woman who seems to be every bit as oppressed as her village sisters. Why is that?*

This shows another classic myth of industrialised society. It was imperative to educate people to a certain standard so that they would be able to work; Africans were to be educated to a certain level, so that they could become hewers of wood and carriers of water. But the woman in this book has gone beyond that level; she has outlived her usefulness in terms of education as a way out. She has gone on to something that is beyond that, and there is no place for her in that system. She lives in a society that is still very narrow in two ways: on the one hand there is the traditional aspect and the role of the woman in the family, which she has broken out of, and on the other there is the colonial system and its attitude to black people. Her education enables her to see, to become conscious of it, but it really doesn't enable her to do anything about it. The question one could ask is should people really become conscious of the situation or should they not. I think that what is shown here is that consciousness always has a very great individual cost. But where one hopes that the benefit will derive is that as more and more people become conscious there is a basis for action, and action, at whatever level is always very therapeutic. One of the woman's problems was that this was very early, in the 1960s when there were not very many educated women around. The narrator actually observes this point: This family is very isolated, and the reason why I chose such an isolated family is that it pushes all the conflicts I am talking about to an extreme situation which I could build on.

*So you are actually more optimistic today. Do you think that woman would be able to act on her insight today and change her role in the marriage?*

Not really; she wouldn't be able to change her role in the marriage, but I think she would be able to seek more solidarity from other people, and maybe this is how a change within the marriage might come about: if she had solidarity outside her marriage, friends who encouraged her to use her potential, and if with encouragement from these friends she did act, then she would start feeling better about herself and would probably be a more competent marriage partner, anyway.

And yet, reality in Zimbabwe is not so simple. I am beginning to revise my thinking, actually. I used to adhere to a Western model of feminism, but even this problem between men and women in my part of the world, and in America as well, seems to me more and more to be a policy of divide and rule. If you think back to the time of colonisation when the families were split up, the men had to work in the towns, and the children would not see their father for half a year. I think it would be very difficult not to become bitter.

When people are talking about relationships between the genders they are always talking about going back to their roots, but that again is silly, because the tradition we are talking about is actually the tradition which came into being during the time of colonisation: women were bussed into the towns every weekend and beer-halls were put up, but no schools were built.. So many of the negative habits which are a problem between the genders in my part of the world actually started then, and it was done on purpose. Now we are forced to live with the results of that. And of course, the gender problem is always second to the national question. Therefore, I think, it hasn't received proper attention nor the right kind of analysis. One reason for this is that women in Zimbabwe are very wary of being called feminists. It is really a dirty word.

*Why?*

Well, Western feminists have a very bad name, let me tell you. People think about lesbianism, about breaking up families and... I actually don't understand it, quite frankly. I have tried to say to people that feminists want to make the world a better place, but I think men feel threatened, and then women don't want to lose the social security which they gain from having a relationship with a man. The feminist, who in Zimbabwe is usually a single woman , is a threat to the other women, and this means that actually there can not be any solidarity between the women either.

*What is your attitude to the vexed question of aid to the Third World?*

I think this attitude of wanting to help is problematic. The word 'good will' is something very interesting. When you speak of 'good will' you are talking about something willed, something intentional, something rational, and in this question of black and white we are going way back beyond rationality, so you never know what is actually going on inside. I may come to Denmark with the best will in the world, but the fact is that I have a history behind me, I have a personal history, a national history, not to mention a racial history, and this has built up a load of suspicion in me. I think that the only solution to this is for a bit more humility - on both sides. Whether this is possible when we have the whole history of these attitudes and these stereotypes of inferiority and superiority instilled into us is something I am not sure. It is not going to happen in a day. What we are doing now is something which hopefully our grandchildren will be able to benefit from.

*A final question: You obviously live between cultures. Who celebrates your victories or on whose shoulder do you cry when you get depressed. Who is your support group?*

I don't have one.

(This interview took place in Aarhus, Denmark on July 6th, 1991.)

HEIDI CREAMER

# An Apple for the Teacher?
# Femininity, Coloniality, and Food in
# *Nervous Conditions*

While preparing for an intertextual reading of women's oppression and resistance[1] in Tsitsi Dangarembga's novel *Nervous Conditions*, I found a video documentary which offered to simplify the task. This video, *With These Hands: How Women Feed Africa* is unsurprisingly neo-colonial and one dimensional, but it offers an interesting place to begin the complicated process of reading and writing about Dangarembga's more complex and progressive constructions of African feminist resistance. Both *With These Hands* and *Nervous Conditions* investigate connections between African women, food production, and symbolic uses of food. Also, the dangerous assumptions employed by the video reappear within the text of the novel as some of the many forces which the female characters must understand and negotiate.

*With these Hands: How Women Feed Africa* is divided into three segments, each a woman's first person story from a different post-colonial African nation. The women talk in what seems like their first language which the viewer hears for a short time before the translator's voice, that of a woman with an accent, is dubbed over it. They talk about cultivating poor soil, of growing cash crops whose profits benefit their husbands, and of not having adequate amounts of the family's land or of their own time to grow enough food. The end of each section is signalled by a quote from the UN Food and Agricultural Organization or the UN Economic Commission for Africa. The three quotes emphasize the amount of food production and preparation that women are responsible for and lament that in addition to this 'traditional' inequality of African women, 'agricultural modernization efforts have excluded them.' Each statement is used to cap off what each woman's 'authentic voice' is supposed to be saying. Gayatri Spivak in 'Poststructuralism, Marginality, Postcoloniality and Value' explains this search for a voice as part of an understanding which names the 'Third World' to 'cover over much unease ... [by giving] a proper name to a generalized margin.'[2] The proper name 'Third World' allows the 'anti-colonialist neo-colonialist' to make an unabashed request to hear 'a voice from the margin.' (p. 220) Trying to 'cover over [the] unease' about this film's relationship to its subjects, each statement emphasizes sexism from both the women's African cultures and from the UN and other 'modernization efforts' while failing to question colonialism and its own neo-colonialism.

By generalizing the experiences of 'women of Africa' from the blurbs of 'authentic voices' the film limits the kinds of resistance the women might have. In 'Under Western Eyes: Feminist Scholarship and Colonial Discourses,' Chandra Mohanty argues that 'using 'women of Africa' as an already constituted group of oppressed people as a category of analysis ... denies any historical specificities to the location of women as subordinate, powerful, marginal, central, or otherwise vis-a-vis particular social and power networks.'[3] In the section 'Zimbabwe: Cecilia's story,' Cecilia is shown talking about the difficulties getting land from resettlement policies as if the only problem is that the land is not reapportioned equally to women. There is no mention of the 15 years of war that led to Zimbabwe's independence in 1980, and that much of this struggle was to reclaim the disproportionate amount of fertile land settled by the English. Under the guise of a progressive concern, the film tries to align itself with women while it erases their lives and struggles. Therefore, as Mohanty puts it, through 'the debilitating generality of their object status' it also 'robs them of ... agency.' (p. 79)

The movie's strategy of 'concern' for women is not brand new. Franz Fanon in 'Algeria Unveiled' aptly, although through the use of rigid categories of colonizer and native, explains France's policy of concern towards Algerian women as a colonizing technique. Fanon describes how 'the dominant administration solemnly undertook to defend this [Algerian] woman, pictured as humiliated, sequestered, cloistered ... ,transformed by the Algerian man into an inert, demonized, indeed dehumanized object.'[4] Fanon sees this manoeuvre as an attempt to both destroy the 'Algerian culture' and to torture the Algerian man 'on the psychological level.' (p. 39) He argues that the French tried to 'defend' the Algerian woman and destroy Algerian culture by concentrating on 'a symbol of the status of the Algerian woman,' (p. 37) the wearing of the veil. The way in which With These Hands treats food production is similarly symbolic. From the beat of a pounding pestle which opens the film to the shots of women farming, women's large share of the responsibilities of food production is treated as the sign of their oppression within African cultures throughout the continent.

Criticizing With These Hands only by using the tools which Fanon provides does not thoroughly address the one dimensionality of the women in the film. Despite interpreting France's use of women as symbols of oppression, Fanon himself does not often treat women as more than symbols of national resistance. Where he addresses the psychological complications of Algerian men, he fails to address them for Algerian women. Tsitsi Dangarembga's direct reference to Fanon in the title Nervous

*Conditions* esteems Fanon's analysis of psychological implications of colonialism and simultaneously criticizes his reduction of women to symbols. Dangarembga's novel addresses the same symbol, food, that *With These Hands* uses to symbolize women's oppression. However, she does not reduce oppression to gender oppression or colonial oppression. Instead she creates a story of five women who have different ways of living within the systems of gender and coloniality that make up their lives. I will show in *Nervous Conditions*[5] that the narrator, Tambu, must understand how these systems and meanings of food intertwine with her ideas about liberation so that she can understand and tell the story of her 'escape.'

Dangarembga's narrative technique offers the structure for showing Tambu's escape. She employs the narrative technique of having an informed narrator telling the story of herself growing up. This narrator is telling a story of 'escape,' of a way to live with the contradictions in her life without being trapped by them. 'Coming of age' narratives are frequently used for many means in modern African and Caribbean literature. The narration can heighten or complicate oppositions between understandings of 'traditional culture' and its 'modern adaptations' to colonialism and postcolonialism.[6] In *Nervous Conditions* the multiplicity of voices of the narrator precludes a single 'authentic' voice, which could be appropriated in the way that what Spivak describes as a 'voice from the margin' is appropriated by *With These Hands*. The development of these narrative voices also helps create a framework for representing political complexity, psychological depth, and inner struggle. Dangarembga's informed narrator is not contrasted with a totally naive young Tambu. The informed narrator shows how Tambu's previous understandings of her actions might have been naive, but that not all her actions were naive. Dangarembga's narrative technique allows the young narrator to explain her education as a clear-cut escape from poverty and subsistence farming. Later the understanding is not that she was misled in getting an education but that she misunderstood what education and escape would mean. First, she sees her aunt Maiguru as having escaped through getting an education. She says:

> My mother said being black was a burden because it made you poor, but Babamukuru was not poor. My mother said being a woman was a burden because you had to bear children and look after them and the husband. But I did not think this was true. Maiguru was well looked after by Babamukuru, in a big house ... .Maiguru was driven about in a car ... .She was altogether a different kind of woman from my mother. I decided it was better to be like Maiguru, who was not poor and had not been crushed by the weight of womanhood. (p. 16)

Either Maiguru is neither black nor female or the definitions that her mother gave her don't work, or both. Maiguru's education has transformed many of the conditions from which Tambu wants to escape.

Tambu tries to escape from a life of cultivation by growing extra crops to sell for school fees. Her mother employs the same method to pay for Nhamo's education. But her mother translates food cultivation into education because she understands a son's education not as 'escape' from poverty, but as an investment that will return to the family, in the same way that Babamukuru's education returns to the family in the food and meat he brings them. Mainini sells hard boiled eggs and vegetables at the bus stop in order to have extra cash to pay for school fees. Similarly, Tambu not only works on her family's fields, but starts growing her own crop on a small unused portion of land. She decides to continue growing crops, a traditional aspect of womanhood which she has learned from her mother and her grandmother, so that she can both get a colonial education and attain her brother's position in the family. She grows food so that she will not have to continue growing crops for herself or for a family of her own.

The education of a son fills familial expectations, but the education of a daughter does not. Whatever wealth she gains would go to her husband's family. Thus Tambu's family, especially her threatened brother, try to thwart her attempts at escape. When her crop grows well and her maize is ripe, it starts disappearing because her brother is stealing it. Returning to her mother's definition, suddenly it is not her blackness but femaleness that is more involved in making her poor. It is more complicated than saying colonialism burdened her, because her brother was the one who stole the mealies. Finally someone outside the family, her teacher Mr. Matimba, helps her to sell her crop and makes sure the money goes towards her education. He takes her to the white town where she can sell her mealies for more money. Ironically she gets the funds for her education, her idea of escape, from a colonialist's pity and power.

Tambu's fees are paid by a white woman in the town, Doris, who self-righteously entertains the contradictory thoughts that Tambu is too lazy to be in school and that Mr. Matimba is using her for slave labour. She gives Tambu money when she finds out a story closer to the truth from Mr. Matimba. However, Mr. Matimba exaggerates in a way that helps her get the money. He tells a story that appeals to Doris' sense of pity and charity. He says that Tambu is an orphan who is trying to earn money for school fees that he can't afford to pay because he has 13 other children. Doris' money helps Tambu get the education that she wants. It also undermines her father's authority over her. Jeremiah argues that his daughter is his so her money is his as well. Because the money is from a white person and has a receipt, Jeremiah can't have it, and Tambu alone benefits.

When after her brother's death, Tambu is chosen to go to the mission school with her uncle, she rejoices over what she considers to be further separation from the subsistence culture of her family. The young narrator creates an opposition between the homestead and the mission that the informed narrator shows is not completely accurate. The young Tambu thinks that 'at Babamukuru's I would have the leisure, be encouraged to consider questions that had to do with survival of the spirit, the creation of consciousness, rather than mere sustenance of the body.' (p. 59) When she arrives at Babamukuru's house, she sees the plants like the ones that belonged to 'the pages of my language reader, to the yards of Ben and Betty's uncle in town.' (p. 64) She describes seeing these plants as 'a liberation, the first of many that followed from my transition to the mission,' and rejoices at the thought 'of planting things for merrier reasons than the chore of keeping breath in the body.' (p. 64) However, the informed narrator has shown that young Tambu had already planted things not just for keeping breath in her body but so that she could go to school. Tambu did spend much time at the homestead growing food to survive, but she also cultivated a crop to fund her education. She had not yet planted just for beauty, especially 'Ben and Betty' beauty, which is beauty as defined by her education through English textbooks. The informed narrator's story shows that at the same time as Tambu is escaping some of the hard work of the homestead by getting an education, her ideas about escape are influenced by this education. Thus Tambu recognizes escape not just in the absence of hours of farming but in the presence of English plants.

The young narrator highlights her escape against what she understands as her mother's entrapment which she calls the sufferings of 'being female and poor and uneducated and black.' (p. 89) When Tambu returns to her village after a year at the mission, she notices many things about the homestead and about her 'emancipation' from it.

> 'Why don't you clean the toilet any more?' I reproached my mother, annoyed with her for always reminding me, in the way that she was so thoroughly beaten and without self-respect, that escape was a burning necessity. (p. 123)

The young narrator sees her mother as totally trapped and sees nothing limiting Maiguru, because she defines being trapped as whatever can be left behind after gaining an education. Just as she considered Babamukuru's plants liberating not only because they weren't for food, but because they were English, she sees oppression when she sees her mother working in the fields to grow food, but sees liberation when she sees Maiguru serving tea and biscuits. (p. 73) In this instance, Maiguru does have less preparation work to do, but more importantly the food that she is preparing is distinctly marked as English.

Because the young narrator's understanding of her mother's entrapment is too simplistic, her ideas about escape through education are also too simplistic. The informed narrator sees that both educated and uneducated women can be trapped by gender and coloniality. She describes both Mainini and Maiguru as trapped in different ways, but unlike when she was younger, believes that they can have similar moments of resistance within their entrapment. The informed narrator no longer sees Mainini as totally squashed by 'being female and poor and uneducated and black,' but sees that her mother endures her life according to other people's decisions because her 'mind, belonging first to her father and then to her husband, had not been hers to make up.' (p. 153)

Mainini is trapped by the role which she plays in her family; her lack of choice about the role traps her as much as the role itself. Her role as a food producer and preparer is the location of some of her emotional struggles, but it is also the location of a moment of resistance. When Tambu decides, against her mother's will, to go to 'Young Ladies College of the Sacred Heart,' Mainini protests by withdrawing from her family role. She 'ate less and less and did less and less, until within days she could neither eat nor do anything, not even change the dress she wore. She did not go to Nyamarira to wash, or to the garden.' (p. 184) This protest is a combination of a conscious strategy and 'illness of [a] nature [which] is kept quiet and secret ... unlike a physical ailment of which everyone is told.' (p. 185) Her family is less worried about how Mainini treated herself than about how she met, or failed to meet, her duties to the family. Because her family cannot function without her, her resistance is effective, but for the same reason it is shortly recuperated. Lucia brings Mainini back to health by enforcing her responsibilities to her family and by showing her the respect that she can get from her role as mother. Lucia also incorporates the symbolic power of food into her healing; she insures that Mainini eats meat and milk which are usually served only to men during holidays.

Mainini is so upset about Tambu going to Sacred Heart school because she, like the informed narrator, sees the ambiguities in Tambu's escape plan. Tambu thinks that she needs an education to be well fed; Mainini points out what well fed means in this situation. She says to Tambu,

> If it is meat you want that I cannot provide for you, if you are so greedy you would betray your own mother for meat, then go to your Maiguru. She will give you meat. I will survive on vegetables as we all used to do. And we have survived, so what more do you want. (p. 141)

Again, it is apparent that what Tambu has set up as a contradiction between food and lack of food is much more problematic. She did have enough to eat when she was living in the village. Furthermore, Mainini is not totally conquered as Tambu thought. Mainini knows what Tambu is thinking and does not like it. Again she says directly to Tambu,

> Because [Maiguru] is rich and comes here and flashes her money around, you listen to her as though you want to eat the words that come out of her mouth. But me, I'm not educated am I? I'm just poor and ignorant, so you want me to keep quiet, you say I mustn't talk. (p. 140)

Tambu does want to eat the words right out of Maiguru's mouth. She observes that these educated words are what provide the meat which she wants to eat and she believes that these words liberate Maiguru.

The informed narrator sees that despite Maiguru's education which separates her from a subsistence culture, she too is trapped by her role in her family and in the colonial system. She is still in charge of preparing food and taking care of her family, and she still has little say in household affairs. Maiguru does not get to keep the money that she earns, despite her large role in providing money and food for her household. While Babamukuru gains authority and prestige in his family by bringing food and money to the homestead, Maiguru does not gain anything except more work. When Babamukuru brings a side of an ox to the homestead for Christmas, Maiguru says to him, 'When you provide so much food, then I end up slaving for everybody.' (p. 122) Her refusal to go to the village the next year and later her five days away from the mission are moments of resistance when she refuses to play her role. But her resistance is easily recuperated. Babamukuru needs her at home and brings her back to the mission from her parents' house. Nyasha understands that Maiguru is trying to escape from something broader than just Babamukuru, but when she realizes this she cannot even imagine what escape could look like. She says to Tambu,

> It's not really him you know. I mean not really the person. It's everything, it's everywhere. So where do you break out to? You're just one person and it's everywhere. So where do you break out to? ... So what do you do? I don't know. (p. 174)

Whatever Nyasha decides to do will be very important to Tambu. If education does not lead to escape as Maiguru's case seems to say, Tambu needs to find another path. Because Tambu has dedicated much of her life to her education, this need is urgent. At this point in the novel Tambu, who used to be very different from Nyasha, is quite similar to her. Nyasha, through her clothes, language, concern with weight, disrespect of her father, and her education has been marked as English in many of the same ways that Tambu's other symbols of liberation have been. But now these symbols are being shown to offer little hope of liberation. Nyasha rebels against the contradictions in her life with a 'nervous condition' that combines frenzied studying with disturbed eating.

Nyasha's extensive studying marks her refusal to fit a colonialist's definition of a 'good African.' By not studying at all, she would have compromised her father's position as a 'good African.' She could fail her exams and still get one of the few places in school because the government would make room for the headmaster's daughter. She sees that 'practising nepotistic ways of getting advantages would mean that Babamukuru would no longer qualify as good.' (p. 107) If she failed her

exams, Babamukuru would be torn between valuing his honesty and valuing his children's education, two mutually exclusive options, both of
which are important to a definition of good in English and African sets of
meanings. Nyasha threatens to fail, but instead decides to study incessantly so that she can contest the definition of herself as a good African. The
informed narrator understands that 'whites were indulgent' when it comes
to educating 'promising' African children as long as the 'promise' is 'a
grateful promise to accept whatever was handed out to them and not to
expect more.' (p. 106) She sees that the Babamukuru of her grandmother's
stories fits this definition. She understands that, '[the missionaries] thought
he was a good boy, cultivatable, in the way that land is, to yield harvests
that sustain the cultivator.' (p. 19) Nyasha studies so hard in order to
establish that she does not just accept whatever is handed to her; she
wants more. She uses her education not to benefit the 'cultivator' but to
criticize her 'cultivation'. She sees that the English have not only stolen
and cultivated the good land in Zimbabwe, but the 'good' minds. Nyasha
reads history so she can compare conditions in Southern Rhodesia to
apartheid in South Africa and so she can compare the labels 'freedom
fighter' with 'terrorist'. At the height of her nervous condition, she refuses
the colonial history she has been taught and tears her history book to
shreds.

At the same time as she rebels against a colonialist meaning of 'good
African,' Nyasha rebels against an African meaning of 'good daughter.'
Babamukuru wants his daughter to respect him and to treat him in the
way that the rest of his family does. Nyasha stays at school so long that
she is late for meals. She studies all night then does not go to breakfast.
Nyasha rebels by not eating or by eating and throwing up afterwards.
When she tries to avoid family meals, she affronts her father's authority.
He tries to regain it by commanding her:

> You will eat that food ... .Your mother and I are not killing ourselves working just
> for you to waste your time playing with boys and then come back and turn up
> your nose at what we offer. Sit and eat that food. I am telling you. Eat it! (p. 189)

Babamukuru does not regain his authority because Nyasha responds by
shovelling food into her mouth then rushing directly to the bathroom to
get rid of it.

Nyasha is working within two sets of cultural symbols to rebel against
restrictions of gender and coloniality. In 'Algeria Unveiled' Fanon explains
that Moroccan women worked within two systems of signification by
choosing one of their own symbols and altering it 'to exert a symbolic
pressure on the occupier.' (Fanon, p. 36) These women chose the symbol
of the veil as one that was already being noticed by the French. Even
though black had never been a symbol of mourning in their culture they
started wearing black veils to express mourning for the exile of their king.

Nyasha enacts a similar symbolic transformation when she has a nervous condition that is labelled as 'English.' She uses the symbol of food, which we have seen inscribed by neo-colonialist positions like *With These Hands* as a symbol of women's oppression in Africa. Nyasha's eating behaviour resembles what the English would diagnose as an 'eating disorder' in English girls. But by rebelling with food, she is not just acting anglicized, she is using symbols similar to those used by Mainini, Maiguru, and Tambu. Furthermore, Nyasha is not the only one to have a 'nervous condition.' Mainini's 'illness' (p. 185) when Tambu wants to go to Sacred Heart, and Tambu's illness when she refuses to go to her parents' wedding are also psychic and strategic moments of resistance.

The significance of a diagnosis of this 'Western disease' is important; a diagnosis means more than a description of Nyasha's eating behaviours. A diagnosis would show the English that she is not a 'grateful African' and that the rigid distinctions between African and English are permeable because she acts as 'English' as they do.[7] A diagnosis would force Babamukuru to treat her as westernized instead of expecting her to forget everything she learned in England. This diagnosis could work in the same way that Doris' money worked for Tambu; Tambu gained power both within her family by overriding her father's authority and within a colonial system by climbing a rank of its educational system. But where Tambu's methods appealed both to Doris' pity and to her parents' appreciation of her farming, Nyasha's methods appeal to neither the English doctor nor her father.

A diagnosis could offer Nyasha a place of symbolic power to which she could escape. However, she is unable to get this diagnosis, and receives only the corollary treatment of being hospitalized. For the doctors, the 'diagnosis' is tied to much more than eating disorders. The presence of her symptoms is not enough to prevent the first psychiatrist she sees from saying that she 'could not be ill .... .Africans did not suffer in [that] way ... .She was making a scene.'[8] This kind of statement belies the various kinds of nervous conditions that each of the female characters goes through; this psychiatrist, like *With These Hands*, suggests that African women might not have psyches at all. When the second psychiatrist hospitalizes her without a diagnosis, the idea that she was only making a scene is reinforced. Because Nyasha does not withdraw something which is needed by her family, her rebellion is not recuperated like Mainini's and Maiguru's are. But being pulled back into a family, and back into life, seem more successful, although less rebellious, than having her anger defined as a 'scene' while her psychological struggles destroy her body and her health.

Tambu worries about Nyasha out of concern about her cousin and out of fear about her own life. She wonders, 'If Nyasha who had everything could not make it, where could I expect to go?' (p. 202) Tambu is able to survive because her understanding of Nyasha changes. She understands that Nyasha does not have everything. This understanding involves perceiving her own role in food production as not totally oppressive and involves realizing the futility of relying on markers of 'Englishness' to liberate her. Importantly, her knowledge comes from the women's lives around her, more than from her classroom education. This understanding comes slowly. In the last episode that is narrated, Tambu is just beginning to question the role of her education in her life. The informed narrator tells that,

> Although I was not aware of it then, no longer could I accept Sacred Heart and what it represented as a sunrise on my horizon. Quietly, unobtrusively and extremely fitfully, something in my mind began to assert itself, to question things and refuse to be brainwashed, bringing me to this time when I can set down this story. (p. 204)

When Tambu tells this story she shows that she has found a way to escape, instead of the place to escape to that Nyasha sought. She can appreciate how she manipulated her skills at farming and Doris' pity to get money for her own education. She can include her 'nervous condition,' where by acting and feeling ill, she stood up to Babamukuru's ideas about Christian sin in her family and refused to go to her parents' wedding to act as a bridesmaid, food server and preparer. While Nyasha rebels against both English and African sets of meanings, Tambu works within both. Even her telling this story works within both systems: she uses the English language and the form of a novel to tell a story about her family, just as her grandmother used an oral tradition when she told stories of her family's past. Tambu has 'escaped' because she understands and can tell a story about the complicated ways that gender and coloniality are at work in her life and in the lives of the other women in her family.

## Notes

1. I am influenced by the methodology used by such critics as Carol Boyce Davies and Susan Andrade. Carol Boyce Davies, in 'Feminist Consciousness and African Literary Criticism,' expresses a view that an African feminist criticism needs to be 'both intertextual and contextual criticism: textual in that close reading of the texts using the literary establishment's critical tools is indicated; contextual as it realizes that analyzing a text without some consideration of the world with which it has a material relationship is of little social value.' Just as 'progressive African literary criticism grapples with decolonization and feminist criticism with the politics of male literary dominance,' an African feminist criticism explores these interconnected meanings in a text. (p. 12) Susan Andrade incorporates Davies' ideas among others in 'Rewriting History, Motherhood and Rebellion: Naming an African Women's Literary Tradition'. Andrade emphasizes the importance of recognizing who has written 'history' and how fiction can be seen as offering another narrative interpretation of history. By reading Flora Nwapa's *Efuru* and Buchi Emecheta's *Joys of Motherhood* with 'history' of the Igbo Women's War, she unravels how the radical potential of

Igbo women is 'not absent but silenced' (p. 105) at the same time as it resists silencing.

Davies, Carol Boyce. 'Introduction: Feminist Consciousness and African Literary Criticism', *Ngambika: Studies of Women in African Literature*, Edited by Carol Boyce Davies and Anne Adams Graves (Trenton: Africa World Press, 1986), p. 12.

Andrade, Susan. 'Rewriting History, Motherhood and Rebellion: Naming an African Women's Literary Criticism', *Research in African Literatures*, 21 (1990), pp. 91-109.

2. Spivak, Gayatri Chakravorty. 'Poststructuralism, Marginality, Postcoloniality and Value', *Literary Theory Today*, Edited by Arac and Johnson (Baltimore: Johns Hopkins University Press, 1991), p. 220.

3. Mohanty, Chandra. 'Under Western Eyes: Feminist Scholarship and Colonial Discourses', *Feminist Review* 30 (Autumn 1986), p. 68.

4. Fanon, Franz. 'Algeria Unveiled', *A Dying Colonialism* (New York: Grove Press, 1967), p. 38.

5. Dangarembga, Tsitsi. *Nervous Conditions: A Novel* (Seattle: The Seal Press, 1989), p. 1. All further references to this book are included in the text.

6. Some interesting examples of these kinds of coming of age stories can be seen in *Ambiguous Adventure*, by Hamidou Kane; *A Dakar Childhood*, by Nafissatou Diallo; *The River Between*, by Ngugi wa Thiongo; and *Miguel Street*, by V.S. Naipaul.

7. Again, I am influenced by Fanon's interpretation of the veil as symbol. In a footnote he writes, 'Certain unveiled Algerian women turn themselves into perfect Westerners with amazing rapidity and unsuspected ease. European women feel a certain uneasiness in the presence of these women ... not only is the satisfaction of supervising the evolution and correcting the mistakes of unveiled woman withdrawn from the European woman, but she feels herself challenged on the level of feminine charm, of elegance, and even sees a competitor in this novice metamorphosed into a professional, a neophyte transformed into a propagandist.' (p. 44).

8. It is interesting to note that a research article 'Anorexia Nervosa in a Black Zimbabwean' by T. Buchan and L.D. Gregory appeared in the *British Journal of Psychiatry* in 1984. I discuss it here to help elucidate issues of colonial and discursive authority involved in a 'diagnosis', not to help explain the 'disease'. In this study the diagnosis of an eating disorder erases how gender and colonialism might be operating in the 'patient's' life and psyche. Even though Buchan and Gregory do give a diagnosis, their assumptions are similar to the psychiatrist's in *Nervous Conditions*. Instead of saying Africans do not suffer in that way, they say 'this African is suffering in that way but only because she is not really very African at all.' The case history is disturbingly similar to Nyasha's story in *Nervous Conditions*: the 'patient' went to England as a child with parents who were both studying for master's degrees. There she started speaking English as her first language. When she returned to Zimbabwe she did well academically but poorly socially. She fought with her father and when she began her higher education in England she began to have 'psychological symptoms' including depression and compulsive eating and vomiting. With their reliance on psychological test scores and 'western' family dynamics theories, Buchan and Gregory do little to distinguish this case from an 'English case,' but they do a lot to distinguish her from other African women. They point to her life in England, her use of English, her educational level, and her nuclear instead of extended family. They emphasize the patient's 'feelings of loneliness' when she is in England; they say that these feelings are aggravated 'by her anxiety over the safety of her family who lived in an area where the guerrilla war situation was grave'. By focusing only on her feelings about her family, they ignore that this 'guerrilla war' might have broader meanings for

her, given that this war was fought for a Zimbabwe independent of both white settler rule and English colonialism. These meanings would be involved in her understandings of her British education and her life in England, as well as her relationships with her psychiatrists who were white settlers in Harare. By emphasizing her family and her examination anxiety, they erase the colonial situation in which she is living and studying. They also perpetrate a form of colonialism by blaming the sexism of Zimbabwean men for the patient's problems in the same way that With *These Hands* blames the sexism of African men. They repeatedly criticize her father and his Shona role as well as criticizing the two Zimbabwean men she dates, thus ignoring the agency that she might have had in her life, as well as exempting colonialism and themselves as settler psychiatrists from an oppressive role in her life.

It is also interesting that another article about 'eating disorders' in Zimbabwe has been published within a scientific discourse. 'Application of the Eating Disorders Inventory to a Sample of Black, White and Mixed Race Schoolgirls in Zimbabwe' finds that 'eating disordered behaviours' exist among all three groups. Its 'scientific' strategy of tests and charts does little to investigate meanings of this behaviour and operates with much the same framework as 'Anorexia Nervosa in a Black Zimbabwean. Hooper, Malcolm S. H., and Garner, David M. 'Application of the Eating Disorders Inventory to a Sample of Black, White, and Mixed Race Schoolgirls in Zimbabwe', *International Journal of Eating Disorders* 5 (Jan. 1986), pp. 161-168.

For an article which, in contrast to those discussed above, offers a useful method of understanding eating problems see 'A WAY OUTA NO WAY: Eating Problems among African-American, Latina, and White Women,' by Becky Wangsgaard Thompson. The name of the essay itself highlights many of the issues central to Nervous Conditions. The way Thompson explains disease does not focus on a scientific 'diagnosis' based on tests or family dynamics. She conducts interviews of 18 women and explores the interface of eating problems with sexual abuse, poverty, heterosexism, racism and class injuries. She concludes: 'Attending to the intricacies of race, class, sexuality, and gender pushes us to rethink the demeaning construction of middle-class femininity and establishes bulimia and anorexia as serious responses to injustices.' (p. 558) Buchan, T. and Gregory, L.D. 'Anorexia Nervosa in a Black Zimbabwean', *British Journal of Psychiatry*, 145 (1984), pp. 326-330; Thompson, Becky Wangsgaard. 'A WAY OUTA NO WAY': Eating Problems among African American, Latina and White Women', *Gender and Society* 6 (December 1992), pp. 546-561.

# KAREN KING-ARIBASALA

Guyanese-born Karen King-Aribisala, currently resides in Lagos, Nigeria, where she is a senior lecturer in the Department of English of the University of Lagos. She has travelled widely, having been educated in Guyana, Barbados, Italy, Nigeria and England. She has been writing fiction since the age of eight, and completed her first novel when she was thirteen. Many of her short stories and poems have been published in journals. *Our Wife* is her first complete published work of short stories.

KAREN KING-ARIBISALA

# Colours

My colour is pink. I do not like the colour pink. I have been made to choose this colour. The colour pink. It is too much a mixture of the red and the white. A watering down of the violence of the red which I have always favoured growing up and out.

I have always known my colours and painted for my true self, unhampered until now. In my paintings yellow is the colour of the sun. Green is the colour of grass. Blue is the colour of my sky. Black is the colour of my night. In the paintings which I paint of my native Lagos, I never mix the colours with white. I allow them life, my colours, their bold assurance bright. No watering down of the red – which is the colour of my blood – with white.

When I told him this so many months ago when first we met, he laughed with all his perfect teeth. All white. I let his tongue, long and red-wagging, like the butchered red stump of an animal's tail, wag me off my feet. I was paddled with the red long-beating stump of tongue into his pink-mouth-held arguments of precise sounding rational teeth all perfectly shaped and even-chiseled.

Inside his mouth was dark and pink and I looked up at the palette and touched the gums carefully to see if by touching alone his tender parts – I would touch him. But the gums were hard and moist for he had just spoken with the wetness of his red tongue and his white teeth in favour of pink.

My head was stifled, suffocating in his mouth. For although I was not yet with child my stomach protruding proclaiming another me perhaps-a-girl child, I was still too big at that time to comfortably be held in his mouth. My legs which protruded, kicked the air outside his mouth violently and my slippers tickled his mouthstache – a wide bristly hairy thing which my parents said I would get used to in time. After the wedding. And he, my husband-to-be, sneezed. I shot out of his mouth all wet and strangely chaste. I smoothed my hair which was damp with wet moistness from his pink roomed mouth.

At that time I preferred European dress to Nigerian wear and staunchly refused the geles, the bubas and wrappers which my husband-to-be preferred. He said he wanted a woman as wife who though an established painter, well-educated in foreign parts, would not neglect her roots, her tradition. My constant refusal to wear traditional African dress, my abhorrence of pink was causing him much pain.

And at that time, the time of his courting, I still had the body of will to laugh and to refuse the cavernous mouth of pink and I asked his mouth with white teeth and red tongue a simple 'Why?'

'Why go to my family and ask for my hand in marriage if all he wanted was a woman of pink persuasion?' I was not the woman for him.

These were his words spoken in English to woo from me pink-acceptance: 'My sweet honey love, my Mojoyin. Please be reasonable. You are after all an educated woman, a talented painter. You have to choose a colour for the motif of the traditional engagement ceremony, which may I remind you is more important here in Yoruba land than the Christian wedding.'

I sat numbly thinking of colour. Pure colours I liked. I did not like pink. It is not only the watering down of red. It was the colour which as a baby girl my mother had forced me into. 'Pink' she always said 'is the colour for baby girls and blue is the colour for baby boys.'

I was now a grown woman in my early twenties and I hated pink. 'See-ing as you're so ambivalent, I had better decide for us, for you. It must be all this time you've spent out of Nigeria. You have been brought home to marry me. Emi ni ni ayanmo Emu ni akunle yan e'

He translated the words just to be sure I understood their colour. 'I am your destiny.'

He fingered his mouthstache, twirling the tips with tongue-wet fingers. 'It is my duty as your husband to take care of you, make decisions for you. It is my responsibility.'

'Any colour, any colour but pink' I said wanly for I was feeling nauseous. He patted the stomach which held our child. 'Don't worry my dear. Everything will soon be settled. Ile oko nile eko...      A husband's house is a woman's true school' I shall be your education from now on my dear.'

Again I felt sick, the bile rising in my throat. The feeling must have come from my slight sojourn in his mouth, together with the early morning sickness from the child I was carrying for him. His wife, any wife he had decided to have, would have to prove her fertility, her capability of increasing the clan even before the engagement.

'Did your senior wife object to my choosing the colour of our engagement? No! I chose cream for her. For your sweet self I choose pink. I am now a pink and cream man.'

He laughed loudly. It was true. I had seen the photographs of their engagement ceremony in two hefty albums. Her bouquet was made up of cream roses. Her ashoke was cream and all well-wishers were dressed in well-wishing cream asoke and bubas.

All that occurred so long ago I cannot remember. I have been so sick with this child inside me I have not been able to think and to do much and to say much to my family or his. I am now dressed in pink. My gele, my buba, my wrapper, my bouquet of roses all pink. And my husband-to-be as soon as the night was over, the dark night black, is also wearing a heavy agbada with pink motifs decorating it.

The many guests are seated under tents in the garden of my husband's family compound and we ourselves sit in two throne-like chairs facing them. To the side of our chairs is the High Table; a long table with a white cloth covering it so. Attached to the cloth with sticky bits of cellotape are tiny paper pink rosettes and pink ribbons. The florist could not find fresh pink flowers at such short notice – my husband and I had debated the pink issue for too long – so he had arranged for a vase of pink plastic flowers, vigorously scrubbed, to be set in the centre of the table. A retinue of aged relatives on both sides of the family were drinking from pink plastic cups and eating from pink plastic dishes and idly thumbing the programmes of the proceedings, which of course had pink letterings on them. My husband to be said that he had had to pay an awful lot of money to have them done up in this way.

It was a fine afternoon, the colours exactly as I would have painted them. The sky blue. The grass green. The sun yellow. My unseen red blood beating in my body with another life. These colours in my palette's eye pulsed stronger than the pink and I smiled at my new husband. He was, after all, a good man and although twenty years older than myself we got along reasonably well. Both our families were quite sure it was a good match. And then there were so many presents which we had received. It would take months to open all of them.

Some were visible. The traditional gifts – Our families had supplied sacks of rice, huge tubers of yam, reams of material, some pink, some not. We received bottles and bottles of alcohol, pots of honey, along with the prayers for our happy married life. I had never attended such a wonderful engagement ceremony and the engagement ceremony was mine. The ceremony would be the talk of the town for weeks to come, months perhaps.

The dancing was in full swing. My husband had at my prompting, arranged for dancers from Calabar to perform for the wedding guests. And there they were, all dancing before us, his mouth, his teeth, his tongue lapping contentment as they swivelled their bodies on green grass, pretending to be boats.

'You see my dear. You can't say I always have my way, There are the Calabar dancers – dancing for you.' He twirled his mouthstache. 'And I've got another surprise for you.'

As I watched the Calabar dancers I was transported on their heaving boats, their hands grasping paddles, bottom-lurching on river green grass to the thudding sound of the drums of my red blood. They were bare to the waist; on their heads vigorous mountains of minature trees attempting to touch the sky. Their ankles and wrists jingled with a ringing clasp bell tinkle. On their hips wide accordion pleated sticking out circular skirts of red, blue, yellow, green, jaunty on their river-grass journey across green grass.

My husband had granted me this gift. After spending years abroad I had told him I had always wanted to see Calabar. The bright colours of their dancing. He had remembered. He had given me this gift.

Everyone was clapping and cheering and my husband laughed and looked at me, winking mischieviously. 'Did you see it?' he whispered through his mouthstache.

'The dancing? Thank you so much. I had no idea...'

'No. Not that. Did you see it?' he repeated.

I saw nothing more than what I had seen before, the dancers with colour in movement and sound bright; the tent, the crowd.

I looked up at the sky. Night was fast approaching and the sky was no longer the blue of my paintings. Stretched across the vanishing blue were pointing fingers of cream and rosy pink, the colours skein-threads of light unravelling.

'Did you see it?'

'What? Who?' I asked genuinely perplexed.

He pointed to the far side of the lawn which I hadn't seen because of all the dancing limbs. It was a goat. It was tied to a stake in the ground and it sported a pink ribbon around its neck and it wore a pink chiffon like material draped around its waist. As if it had been a human that is. As if it had had two legs. It had four legs as most goats do and began to defecate in round small black tidy pebbles the way that most goats do. I could not see its tail.

I was looking at the goat and everything seemed to disappear when I saw the goat.

'What is it?' I asked my husband.

'My dear are you alright?'

'What is it?'

'It is a goat. Your goat. My special gift to you.'

'Is it a female goat or a male? I can't tell from here.'

'Of course it's female my dear, are you sure you're feeling alright?' I wasn't. I had a sudden urge to go to the bathroom and excused myself. My husband, all husband, rushed to assist me

'My dear, is it the child? You're feeling ill. Don't worry, it will soon be over. Why, my first wife only suffered morning sickness for a week. Now she has three children and look at her.'

Disengaging myself from his hold I looked at my senior wife also sitting at the High Table. She was, of course, very healthy. She was eating some moin moin, although I couldn't be sure at that distance.

'In the pink!' said my husband pinching my arm. And although I could feel myself being dragged into his mouth-filled rational teeth and wondered if in my pregnant state I would still be able to be sucked into his mouth. I grabbed the stake to which the goat was tied to prevent myself from moving into the mouth of my now-husband. It wouldn't be right at a traditional ceremony to be inside my husband's mouth in front of all these important wedding guests. The spectacle would be indeed the talk of the town and I didn't want that at my wedding.

The goat had at the back of her a collection of tidy black pebble dung and the pink chiffon accordian of skirt ruffled slightly in the breeze. After a while I could not see any colour at all. In my nauseous state I had been dragged into the pink cavern of my husband's mouth after all. And after all even though the gele scratched the palette of my husband's mouth, I was firmly lodged inside the house of his mouth. I could not get out. I could hear the guests cheering. They clapped. They shouted 'What a good wife!' 'Iyawo!' 'She is now our wife!' 'What a lucky man. She has begun her education. Ile oko nile eko.' 'Your husband's home is your learning place.'

I could not see the night. The night of black. The black solid and pure as I paint and choose to paint with bright colour. The black. The night of black was grey.

# CARIBBEAN

# ERNA BRODBER

Erna Brodber was born in Jamaica in 1940. She is a respected sociologist and her published works include *Abandonment of Children in Jamaica* (1974), *A Study of Yards in the City of Kingston* (1975) and *Perceptions of Caribbean Women* (1982). She worked at the Institute of Social and Economic Research in Mona, Jamaica, from 1975 to 1983. She is at present a free-lance writer and researcher.

Erna Brodber also writes poetry, short stories and plays, some of which have been awarded prizes in Jamaica. Her first novel *Jane and Louisa Will Soon Come Home* (New Beacon Books, 1980) was greeted with critical acclaim. Her most recent novel *Myal* won the Commonwealth Writers Prize in 1989.

ERNA BRODBER

# Why I Write

As long as I can remember being, I have been shy. I am the one in the photograph who holds on to Mama's skirt hanging from the chair on which she sits and whose face is in her armpit. My sister whom I follow in birth order, correctly has her hand on Mama's shoulder, fingers just barely touching that shoulder, her head erect and her eyes front. My sister was the one who took the visiting Parson's white daughter around the church yard. What do you say to someone who looks like that? Blue and with straw hair. This was our first close-up view of a white child and there is my sister walking and talking with her as if she's known her all her life! I admired my conversationally capable sister. I continued through life to admire out-going people, an easy thing what with my ring-side seat, for my best friend was always one of that kind. My shyness did not mean that I didn't do my bit of public-speaking and drama. I was considered quite good at that, so people and I did get a chance to hear my voice but as we know reciting and acting are of set pieces and do not require the mental inventiveness, verbal agility and the ability to out-psyche the other that conversation requires. I lacked these.

My first job after high school required no ability to converse. I was a government temporary clerk, who, caught reading on the job, was exiled to the registry where I saw files and files. They don't ask you to talk and the people who want files simply scribble a code which you, the file clerk decipher quietly to yourself. I was rescued from this and helped to get a teaching job in Montego Bay, the tourist capital of the island of Jamaica. This is where change began. It moved slowly towards fruition ... Being one of three natives in a boarding house of twenty teachers required little change and this was my private and public life for three months. Then Marie came – my Jamaican Chinese-friend-to-be. Marie was a university graduate but seemed shy to me. She knew my sister, having been an undergraduate with her for two years on the same campus at the University of the West Indies, Mona, Jamaica. Marie must have thought that I shared my sister's conversational abilities. We hung together and to avoid what seemed to this sister to be unreasonably long minutes of silence, I felt constrained to talk.

It was the habit of young staff of the girl's school and of the boys' school to spend Saturday nights at the night club. I was young staff. It was on one of these occasions that I heard Marie making conversation, the butt of which was my conversational style, how we had walked for a mile and how I had talked the whole way. Fancy that. Me, a chatterbox. And there is the husband of a friend of mine who until now calls me 'Miss wide open spaces'. I had talked, he says, from Montego Bay to Kingston – three hours – about my love for 'wide open space'. Chatterbox, me. Conversing but without the mental inventiveness, verbal agility, etc. of good conversation. All that effort for nothing. I went back to conversational silence, and so totally, that on my first job after University – this was in Trinidad – a fellow paused in a conversation to say hello to me. I painfully opened my mouth and responded. 'Good,' he said, 'I just wanted to be sure you weren't dumb.'

I was so dumb in my three undergraduate years that even I believed I was dumb. I listened with awe as the out-going argued with this professor and that. Once more I was the friend of the most out-going and was totally amazed to see that without entering into the conversational frays, without being able to splice my speech with such beauties as 'ipso continuum', without being able to verbally tear apart a mate's presentation, I graduated close to the top of the class. That taught me a lesson. I could make my point without speaking. That was 1964.

I could make my point through writing but I still felt socially inept. Thank God the loquacious still sought my friendship and kindly filled all the spaces in any conversation at which I was as usual, the silent participant. How this that I am going to say, happened I can't remember but it is the fact that a couple of these bright persons whom I admired, started seeing in one to one settings and asking me questions. I heard my answers to them presented in new conversations and said to myself, 'If you have daag fi bark fi you, why should you bark for yourself.' I was conversationally lazy but no one need lose anything. Someone else will carry the message. Someone will find a way to me. And the message not the medium is the thing. But I was a university teacher by now. How do you sit quietly in a learned seminar or in a faculty meeting? I tried, felt odd, dropped out and was finally dropped out of the university scene.

So now my pen definitely is my tongue, for I am constitutionally poor at conversation and have accepted my lot. That's why I write.

ERNA BRODBER

# One Bubby Susan

This man here Cundal. Frank. Don't know if you know him. Used to work down at Institute way back when. Now this man now, write a book and say in there say Miss Susan is something some Arawak person carve into a cave. Man even have a photo in this book, of a lady standing in the mouth of this cave and looking for truth like as if is somebody really carve her. But I am here to tell you that nothing don't go so. Them long long time when Cundal writing, where them get camera to go take picture of Miss Susan? You no see something not too quite right? Is just these white people like come to people country, look round two time, take photo, measure this and measure that, no ask nobody no question, no sit down and meditate, and baps – them have answer. Same way. So this man now write it into book that Miss Susan is a Arawak carving and people believe. What in book is gospel so everybody go believe. Well is not so. I am sitting down quiet to myself when my ears start to tingle and I get a strong smell of that flowers that we used to string as bead. The smell so strong, I nearly faint and then the lady start to talk and she tell me.

Well Cundal right bout one thing. The place. Miss Susan really belongs to that place. To be exact, she feel she belong there. I already tell you she don't carve there. Now I telling you, she feel she belongs there. So the place is right. Dryland. Near to Woodside. In the parish of St. Mary. Now, you know Westmoreland? That is another parish. Now, look at the map of Jamaica. Right. Well you see how Westmoreland chack over the other side of the world from St. Mary. Well, forget that. Just them white people and them scribes again. Listen to this now. The world is not flat. Columbus done tell them that long time, so why them must draw the map flat out like a dry up goat skin with no goat, is something I can't see. Pay them no mind. Now, if you take that map and roll it a certain way, you will see that Westmoreland nearly to fit into St. Mary. Now listen again. If you go outside and take a long pole and push it down into the ground, you see that there is a whole world down there. Sea, earth, river. You can swim the sea and you can swim the river but you can't swim the earth. But the earth have many holes and you can walk upright. No need to swim, for those who never born with fin. You can walk under the earth from one side to the other. Anybody who know how the caves situate that is. Now why I telling you this? For you to know that for those who really know the land, it is nothing to get from Westmoreland to St. Mary. Look again in hour book and see if the people who really know the land was not doing the same thing in St Mary that the Westmoreland people was doing. Communication knowledge. That's what I call it.

Is a simple matter when you look at it. But simple as it seems to me now and to you now, I didn't find it out for myself. Is Miss Sue tell me. Say it was nothing to swips from Westmoreland to St. Mary. She used to do it all the time. Is Westmoreland she rightly come from, but she land up in a cave in St Mary. Not as a carving. And I coming to tell you how now. Miss Sue say, time for her to get married and she never want to married. She did like fly through cave and talk to rat-bat and climb tree and talk to bird and so on. She never want plant no maize and beat up nothing into mortar. Matter of fact all this bammy that her people so proud bout never mean one thing to her. Too dry. She could find fat grass to eat raw any day so why plant cassava and grater it and dry out the milk and cook it? Never make no sense to her and she couldn't bother with it. And that is what a wife suppose to do with all her time. Excuse me. Not true. Not all her time, for them used to play bato. I don't know what that is. Favour like soft ball to me when she describe it. She say big man and woman used to play it too. And regular. So it really wasn't mortar pestle all day long. But what sense thump ball when she coulda swing from tree to tree and whistle to the birds and be by herself But them insist say everybody must married. So Miss Sue say, she say, run way for her rather than this wife thing. And she do it sudden. Just get a vaps and leave. Tell no one. Now you know that Miss Sue wouldn't really have nothing to pack. The picture on the money is real. Ain't nothing but a little grass around the hips and grass was easy to come by. So she split. In one second.

I don't say she disappear into nothing. That would make it easy and as she tell me, it was not easy the way she reach to Dryland, though it was really close in a way, to her place. What happen now is this. Everybody know everybody. The whole place divide up among chiefs. You leave from one spot to the other, is a new chief. And no fussing or fighting. If they see you at one place long, they say you want to join them and they start same time to find out if you married and if you not married to marry you off and get you into this bammy-making, bato-playing thing all over again for married is all them know bout. No sense in that. So Susan decide she ain't go touch earth except at night when nobody not around to see her. So is pure cave she into all day. Now when she staying in this Dryland cave, a strange thing happen. Hard as she listen she couldn't hear a thing. No mortar pestle, no 'yeow, yeow' and bato playing. She say she say to herself 'Must be just a breed of backless dogs living in this place'. So little by little she start to come out to the cave front. She don't see nobody so she start to make it a habit. Both the staying in that cave and the sitting out at the front from time to time in the day.

Now Susan tell me how she used to sit down still and do this deep breathing, for with all the time she bound herself to spend in the cave, when she get air she did want to take in as much as she could take. Now I don't know if these Arawak Indians is any relative to the Indians in India but I swear to you, what Miss Susan show me that she was doing, was one of those yoga pose that make a person look like Buddha. Now what you would think if you come up to a cave and see a person who you never see yet in the small-small community that you live in, sitting down like a Buddha? Talk the truth. You'd think it was a duppy or a God. Exactly. Well somebody did come and somebody did think so. And this is the beginning of poor Miss Susan's sorrows.

Miss Sue did have it in her head that the quietness of the place was because those who did live there run way leave it and she say to herself 'This is mine. A gwine relax.' But it was not quite so. Man, woman and child – except for that lazy one, playing sick-gone off yes, but only for part day and on shift. Everybody wasn't there one time and when them come home, them so tired, them just drop asleep. Gone make clay pot and make them in abundance. Mr Christopher Columbus come with him red rags and all a-body and them breed of barkless dog now bartering pot for red rag. That's how come the place was so quiet and Miss Sue so alone. But the little boy come and see her and start coming back and seeing her in her Buddha pose and start to have nightmare and to blurt out that him see a god and to have people saying is sick him really sick.

Now you know them always say anybody who say them see God sick, and usually them leave you and your imagination to fight it out. Until they come to need a God. Like how you see AIDS now, it was syphilis that time that come with the tourist rags. People start dropping dead like flies. And the bad treatment was something else. Man used as target practice! It was bad enough that everybody was running off to Agualta Vale to mess around in clay and march down to close to Port Maria where the whitemen be and were in the bargain neglecting them ground and putting life out of kilter. Now married life was mashing up for the whitemen was putting their hands and all, where they should not be put and on top of that beating up the Arawak men and running their swords through them. It was time enough to need a God so when what lazy chap keep on saying that is a god him see, man and man start to make a trek, a few at first, to Miss Susan cave.

Now I have to stop to tell you that the lady's born name was not Susan. Many a time she tell me, but that Arawak name cannot stick in my head and since she don't really object and everybody know who I am talking about, let it remain 'Miss Susan'. Right? Right. So as I was telling you, people now start to come and peep at Miss Susan in her Buddha pose and to nod – 'Is God.' A funny thing was happening too, and to Miss Sue. When she take the pose, is like vibrations would come through her fingers from the air and she would know all sorts of things. When the first man come up and put a problem, Miss Sue find she just give him a answer straight out of her head and that she was right. She turn God now!

Miss Sue say she didn't mind the questions, for is not really she was answering, is just something or someone using her mouth, but what she did mind was the whole heap of thanksgiving. Up to now, she can't get rid of the smell of duppy chain out of her mind. So much garlands come make out of this thing and put round her neck. No more peace any more.

Can't even breathe. People cooking racoon and agote as sacrifice to her. People is something else though! It happens that she could really get into a deep meditation and she find the meditations getting longer and that those times she don't even feel like passing her business-there, but it would come by itself all the same. You know the people rush her push her down, take up this thing, say is gold from the gods, must be that the white man want! Push her away and scrape it up, say they going pay tribute with it! The thing get so ridiculous with no little bit of space for herself that Sue start to consider that it was just as cheap she did married and put up with the bammy-making and the bato. One thought lead to the other and the other to her usual rebellion and Miss Sue say to herself 'Not a blast' and decide that she not going to be no God with no privacy. She decide she gwine form dead and let them leave her.

How she going do this now? She stand up straight now, press herself against the cave wall and hold her breath yoga style. And people did believe that she was dead. And it vexed them. At the very time when the tourists eating out them life and they have no help but from this God, the God decide to strike! Is stones now. And they start to pelt her. You could say that they want to get her back to life, if is kind, you kind. But I know that is plain straightforward disappointment and vexation that make those stones come. Even when she drop, them still flinging. Even when she so weak, she drop off of the rock face altogether and long time drop into the sink hole, them still seeing her there and still stoning. Day after day. Is now them practice to try to see if, like the whiteman was doing with them, they could use her for target practice! Now them try to throw stones round what them think is the outline of her body! Go look at it yourself and see if you can't see how the flying stones lick the rock face and make the sink that form the image?

So is so the carving come. No man don't sit down and carve it. And is no real likeness of Miss Sue. Anyway, it is not the habit of that breed of Indians to carve? They mostly draw. So is just anger make that image. I don't know why Miss Sue want me to tell this story but I tell it. Perhaps want to set the record straight. Perhaps want to say something about freedom but if is that, I can't see the point for I can't see that running from hole to hole and being a people's God is any kind of freedom. Perhaps she want to say you must be careful how you give or how you stop giving. I don't know. People still flinging stone at that cave. They even lick off one of the breast that those before them make in anger and them now call the image *One Bubby Susan*. I don't know if is something she want to say about this woman's lib business like how she is a woman. Perhaps she want to say to women 'Make them call you angel but don't make them make you into no heavenly being, for that is so-so burden-bearing and the day name day you say you tired, them get vex and lick you down kill you.' I don't know but here is the story and I know that the man Cundal shoulda-eh study him head well before him go call Miss Sue this flesh-and-blood woman a carving.

Lorna Goodison was born in Kingston Jamaica. She is a major Jamaican poet. Her first book of poems *Tamarind Season* (Institute of Jamaica, 1980) was greeted with critical acclaim as was her first public appearance in London in 1985 for the International Poetry Festival in memory of Michael Smith and for the Fourth International Book Fair of Radical Black and Third World Books. Her second book of poetry *I Am Becoming My Mother* (New Beacon Books, 1986) confirmed her growing reputation and won the Americas Section of the British Airways Commonwealth Poetry Prize in 1986.

*Heartease* (New Beacon Books) is Lorna Goodison's third book of poetry. It continues and deepens her striving towards an organic perception, an intensity of vision drawing on a fountain of striking poetic imagery. The poems enact an essential engagement with the authentic, the boundary life of woman.

# Lorna Goodison

## THE WOMAN SPEAKS
## TO THE MAN WHO HAS EMPLOYED HER SON

Her son was first made known to her
as a sense of unease, a need to cry
for little reasons and a metallic tide
rising in her mouth each morning.
Such signs made her know
that she was not alone in her body.
She carried him full term
tight up under her heart.

She carried him like the poor
carry hope, hope you get a break
or a visa, hope one child go through
and remember you.  he had no father.
The man she made him with had more
like him, he was fair-minded
he treated all his children
with equal and absolute indifference.

She raised him twice, once as mother
then as father, set no ceiling
on what he could be doctor
earth healer, pilot take wings.
But now he tells her he is working
for you, that you value him so much
you give him one whole submachine gun
for him alone.

He says you are like a father to him
she is wondering what kind of father
would give a son, hot and exploding
death when he asks him for bread.
She went downtown and bought three
and one third yards of black cloth
And a deep crowned and veiled hat
for the day he draw his bloody salary.

She has no power over you and this
at the level of earth, what she has
are prayers and a mother's tears
and at knee city she uses them.
She says psalms for him
she reads psalms for you
she weeps for his soul
her eyewater covers you.

She is throwing a partner
with Judas Iscariot's mother
the thief on the left hand side
of the cross, his mother
is the banker, her draw though
is first and last for she still
throwing two hands as mother and father
she is prepared, she is done.  Absalom.


## RECOMMENDATION FOR AMBER

With her, you would have a guide
to the small nubians in the garden.
They live only under bushes
that have never known knives.

They come out at night
riding on seasonal cicadas
whose noise is a radar guide,
they have given her minute boxes

of see-in-space eye ointment.
A very little rubbed on the eyes
makes you see good duppies.
With her Mondays could be Sunday.

She would go to church on Monday
then stay indoors all afternoon
sleeping, because there is no
difference in days with Amber.

No matter how she tries she loses
things (she is not orderly)
But she will summon them back again
by invoking their names over and over.

So if you pass outside her window
and hear her repeating insistently
'keys' or 'comb', just know
that this is her strange ceremony

the finding of lost objects.
Invariably she finds what's missing
or if it's taken, in its place will come
something amazingly much better.

She is blessed with a remarkable nose
she can identify the ingredients
in perfumes just so, like she can
isolate the trail of the gentle tuberose

from beneath the more sensual oil slick
smell of the cat glands secreting civet.
She also knows the secret properties
of gemstones. Take amber itself her name.

Though neither rare, costly nor a gem
but the golden night sweat of a tree
compassionate and resilient, it's special
because it is self healing.

Despite her tendency to wearing her hair
wild and her slow egyptian eyes which are
fixed always above her employer's head
she has a good hand at plain cooking.

# OLIVE SENIOR

Olive Senior was born and brought up in Jamaica. She has worked in journalism both in Canada and Jamaica. Although *Gardening in the Tropics* is her first Canadian publication, she is the author of a previous book of poetry, *Talking of Trees*, two books of short stories, and non-fiction works, including *Working Miracles: Women's Lives in the English-Speaking Caribbean*. Her first book of short stories, *Summer Lightning*, won the Commonwealth Writers Prize in 1987. A new book of stories, *The Discerner of Hearts*, is scheduled for publication by McClelland & Stewart in early 1995. Olive Senior divides her time between Toronto and Jamaica.

OLIVE SENIOR

# Tell the Queen I'm Sorry

Every afternoon just before four o'clock, Uncle got ready to go out. Not that he needed much preparation. He had never taken off his three-piece suit since he got back from England so all he had to do was put on his bowler hat and take up his walking stick and gloves. But even these simple actions were imbued with great purpose and deliberation, as was everything that Uncle did. His hat set at the right angle, his gloves precisely delineated in his right hand in relation to his cane, he would set out.

'Good afternoon to you, Girlie,' he would call out in his deep melodious voice.

'Good afternoon, Uncle,' I would say, coming out of my bedroom where I was studying to watch him set off.

Ramrod stiff, Uncle would walk down the three concrete steps onto the path to the road, never missing a beat, behaving exactly, I am sure, as if he were going for a walk in Piccadilly Circus. The only difference is that here there was no pavement, in fact there wasn't much of a road, only a track covered with stones and marl with no drainage so the sides of the road were deeply rutted from the water which formed channels there every time it rained. It was a good thing there was so little traffic, because the only place to walk was in the middle of the road. None of this seemed to bother Uncle. He would step into the road swinging his cane, heedless of what the sharp rocks were doing to his highly polished English shoes or the dust from the marl was doing to his clothes. Stepping stiffly and precisely, he would walk the mile and a half to the square, lifting his hat in greeting to everyone he passed, smiling his smile that never wavered because it was fixed on his face, turned forever inward. At the square he would walk down one side, turn precisely at the corner, cross the road and come up the other side and head for home again, resisting with a slight inclination of his head the blandishments of the men inside the bar – Grampa's friends – to come in and have a drink. Uncle would simply smile his smile, nod and pass on; he never spoke to anyone on his walk.

Uncle didn't walk like anyone else; he held his body so stiffly, he was exactly like the little wind-up toy man I once had which moved with a mechanical jerk of its hands and feet. That's how Uncle walked. He held himself stiffly at all times, even when he was sitting down. I had never once seen him relax his posture, as none of us had ever seen him out of his three-piece suit.

For the first few days after Uncle came back from England, nobody thought too much about his behaviour. Everyone knew that he would need time to adjust to being back home after twenty years and expected that as soon as the stiffness and strangeness wore off, Uncle would start behaving like a normal person again. From the start though, Gran had tried to get him to take off his suit and his vest and his tie, she couldn't imagine how he wasn't boiling in those heavy black English woollen clothes, she said. She hadn't seen any other clothes, because although he came back with a trunk, he hadn't taken anything out except pyjamas and a robe, toilet articles and a fancy comb and brush set, and he kept it locked. She had offered to unpack his things, air out and hang up his clothes and iron what needed ironing.'No, thank you Mother,' he said and she was so awed by her son come home from England that she didn't press him. She did try again by offering him one of his father's cambric shirts and khaki pants to put on, as well as a pair of his shoes for they still wore the same size, thinking perhaps that he had no tropical clothing, but again he said,'No, thank you Mother,' and that was that. His voice was fruity and melodious, so cultured, so precise, I thought, as if he formed the words around a ripe plum in his mouth.'No, thank you' was all he ever said but even that I loved to hear him say.

'Take him a little time to unwind and get used to our ways again,' I heard Gran telling Grampa every night,'soon get back to normal.'

Grampa didn't answer. Grampa wasn't used to saying much except on Friday nights when he went down to Mr Ramsay's bar and drank white rum. Then he became loquacious enough, noisy even, and could sometimes be heard loudly disputing with his friend Mr Anderson as late at night, they both staggered up the road, drunk. Gran who would be lying in bed, listening, would sigh and shake her head, get up and turn up the lamp which she had left burning low and hurry back into bed and pretend to be asleep when Grampa came staggering in. She never said anything to him about Friday nights because other than that, he didn't give her much to complain about.'Not like when we were young, O boy,' she would say,'that man made me cry the living eye water every day.' But Grampa had mellowed with age and now hardly spoke at all. Uncle didn't speak either, unless he was spoken to. Then, no matter what was said or offered he would say,'No, thank you.'

I was the only one to whom Uncle said anything more and I never knew why. But Gran said he had been close to my mother before he went away and though she was dead now, I was the spitting image of her. Sometimes I wondered if Uncle thought I was the little sister he had left behind, for they called her Girlie too.

When Uncle first came back I was on Easter holidays and out of curiosity, I sometimes hung around the verandah where he sat, ramrod stiff, hoping he would say something to me. He sat on the chair all day long, smiling his secret smile, never relaxing his pose until Gran called him to the table for a meal. Then he would come and sit stiffly at the table and go through the pretence of eating, but hardly anything ever passed his lips. Even with all the clothes he wore, you could see that Uncle was very thin.

For a long time he never gave any indication that he noticed me at all. Then one afternoon as I was passing his door I was astonished to hear him call out,'Come here, Girlie, and listen to my heart.'

Feeling somewhat embarrassed, I went and pressed my ear to his chest. 'What do you hear?' he asked.

'It's beating, Uncle,' I said, for what else was there to say?

'No Girlie, you are wrong,' he said.'That's not my heart you hear beating. I don't have a heart any more. That's a mechanical contrivance they put inside of me. Ticking like a clock. They took my heart out when I went into the hospital there, the doctors attached some wires to my head and when I was unconscious they took my heart out and put in this machine.' I would have believed this astonishing news were true if he hadn't continued.'I never asked them to do that, Girlie. I never asked them. It was advantage-taking to the highest degree. I wrote to the Queen about it. Forty letters I wrote to the Queen. And you know what the Queen wrote me back to say?'

He was waiting for a response so I dutifully said,'No, Uncle.'

'The Queen, Girlie, wrote back to say it was none of her business. Can you countenance that? Isn't she supposed to be the Queen of us all down to the humblest? Don't we all walk with money in our pockets with her face on it? Millions and millions of people all over the world carrying her face in their pockets. And then to say it is none of her business that *her* doctors in *her* hospital – *Royal* it says in large letters outside for everyone to see – her doctors take away my heart and put a clock inside. You think that is right, Girlie? I have to be careful how I drink you know. For the rest of my life I have to be careful. For suppose the machine they put inside of me starts to rust? But I'll never give up Girlie. If I have to spend my whole life seeking justice, that I will do. One day I will show you my entire correspondence with the Queen.'

'Yes, Uncle,' I said.

Uncle pulled his watch out of his fob pocket, looked at it, and since it was precisely one minute to four he put his hat on his head, took up his gloves and walking stick.'Good afternoon to you, Girlie,' he said and he set off on his walk.

When I told Gran what Uncle said, Gran burst into tears.'Poor Sonny. Poor Sonny,' she said.'What a way life hard, eh?'

Grampa didn't want to talk about their son but Gran was always forcing him to. Grampa didn't say anything but we knew he was embarrassed. Wasn't this the son he had boasted about for twenty years? When he heard Uncle was finally coming home, hadn't he bought a round for everyone in the bar that Friday night? Hadn't they all bought him a round? Hadn't Grampa got so drunk from the celebration he had to be carried home?

Grampa was extraordinarily proud of his son because while everyone had sons or daughters overseas that they were always bragging about, his son was the one with the brains, he had been saying that for twenty years, the one who was always studying. Mark you, Grampa used to get a bit vague about the studying. Uncle had left to study medicine. Many many years he spent studying. Nobody knew what happened but nothing seemed to come of it. Next thing they knew, he was studying something else. Every time they heard, he was studying something different. After a while, Grampa and Gran never really knew what Uncle did, for he hardly ever wrote home. They didn't even know that Uncle had a wife and children until this strange woman named Clarissa wrote to say Uncle was ill and in hospital. She didn't specify the nature of the illness and the name of the hospital meant nothing to them. After that they heard from her occasionally though she never specifically replied to any of their letters; wrote more to express her feelings at any given point in time than to assuage theirs: he was in and out of hospital, she was having a hard time with the children, well poor Sonny was never much good for anything was he? Grampa and Gran didn't know what to make of that, so they pretended they hadn't read it.

All along, Grampa pretended; he was always announcing good news of his son, boasting of his grandchildren and their achievements. Everyone knew he was pretending since who got letters from abroad and who didn't was an open secret shared with all by Postmistress, but nobody ever let him know that they knew, for a lot of people with children overseas had had to resort to the same type of face-saving from time to time. It was just that Grampa had been doing it for longer than most. Over the years, he continued to make up news of his son to tell to his bar cronies. And they went and dutifully told their wives as if it were gospel truth, so then Gran had to end up lying as well. For the ladies would say to her after church.

'My my, Miss Margaret, I hear Sonny get another big job, eh?'

'Well yes, Miss Dorcas,' she'd say,'you can't keep a good man down.'

But Gran would try to hurry off before the discussion got too deep, because she never knew what news Grampa had manufactured about Uncle this time and she was afraid of getting it all wrong. She didn't quarrel with Grampa because a man had to have something to boast about and others in the district were always making them so angry, what with their children coming home or sending them gifts. Every day somebody would pass by on the road with something or other they had got from foreign, just to torment them it seemed. The boys would walk with their shirt sleeves rolled up to show off new wristwatches, the girls would wear their new high heel shoes, they'd walk with radios to their ears and that silly girl even tried to push her baby in a pram down the rocky road, sent by her equally silly sister from Birmingham. It was worse when new things came in: television sets (even before they had electricity, or indeed, a television station), refrigerators and stereograms. Not to mention all their fancy clothing, new curtains and bedspreads.

Grampa and Gran were embarrassed that they had never got anything from their son abroad. So when Uncle's wife wrote and said she was sending him home because she couldn't do any more, they went off to meet him still hoping against hope that he would bring them a truckload of gifts to make up for all the years of deprivation. It wasn't that they really *wanted* anything. It was a matter of principle; they needed things to show off with. Just like everybody else.

Before Uncle came home, Gran used to hold him up as an object lesson to me.'See there Girlie, see where you can reach if you study and apply yourself. Reach to England. Go all to university like your Uncle Sonny. You stick to the books there, girl.'

After Uncle returned with nothing but a trunk which he kept locked and they saw how he was, Gran changed her advice. I don't know at what stage Gran decided that Uncle was mad, though at first she never ever used that word. What she said was that Uncle was suffering from'brain strain' which everybody knew was caused from too much studying. So whereas before she was always urging me to study, was always checking on my progress, now she worried constantly that I was overdoing it, that I too would strain my brain.'Remember what happen to your uncle,' she would say from time to time,'you better pack up the books now and go to bed.'

At night though, when she talked to Grampa in their room beside mine and I listened through the wall, she was turning different theories over in her head, I could see that. Gran and Grampa hardly seemed to sleep and I would always be surprised to come awake and hear Gran talking in the middle of the night in her normal conversational voice.'Johnnie,' she would say to Grampa,'You think we did push Sonny too hard when he was little? You think we did ask too much of him? He really never have time to play like them other little boys around, you know. He was always a serious little fellow, serious from the day he was born.'

I settled down to listen to Gran, as if to keep her company, for even if Grampa were awake he would never answer her, except to grunt now and then or if she went on too long to angrily say,'Woman, why you don't shut up and let a man get his sleep?' Sometimes, it was as if Gran never heard him, she would continue to talk aloud for hours. I would try to stay awake and listen, in case Gran said something about my mother; my mother died when she had me so I never knew her, and Gran never liked to talk about her, so all I knew was what I heard Gran say when she thought nobody but Grampa was listening. But since Uncle came home, he was all she talked about.

'He wasn't even a year yet when Girlie born. But Sonny never give a day's trouble, he must have known his poor mother never had no time to fuss over him,' she would say.'That Girlie! She took up all my strength. The minute she get over one sickness she get another. Never know she would make it through her first two year. I never had time for that little Sonny, but I never see a child tough so. Sonny never cry. And from he was little he was helpful. Never a day's trouble. He was a perfect child.'

Gran would fall silent for a while, thinking, no doubt, of her two lost children, and I would be falling asleep again when her voice would rouse me back to wakefulness.

'But Johnnie, talk truth now. You don't think we did use him too hard from he was little, seeing how he was the one boy pickney? Remember how he used to get up from dew-fall to go to the spring for water? Then he had was to get rabbit feeding. Then he go look wood and tie out the goat. Then he walk the five mile to school for is clear to Ramble he had to go for no school was here those days and no bus neither. Then he come home and he running around again till night dark you have to say. Then he spend half the night studying. Remember Johnnie? And you was hard on him, you know. Used to beat him for blind for the slightest thing. Old man, your temper was well short those days.'

Grampa would groan loudly from his side of the bed as if he were being tortured but Gran would ignore him.'He did always want to succeed. From he was little he would tell me, "Mamie. I am going to be a doctor. I am going to be a big important man. Going to make you and Papa proud of me." And I would say, "Yes. Yes mi son. Be a doctor for you Mamie and Papa." I would sit up night after night with him beating the books there till he pass the scholarship to school. I was proud that I had such a serious boy. Never grinny-grinny and playey-playey like those other children around. Walk and hold himself straight from those days. Like a little soldier.'

'Lawd woman, is foreign mad him,' Grampa would finally snap out, goaded beyond endurance into speech.'What you want to go into all them old-time story for? What is past is past. The boy leave here good-good as you full well know. Don't is the two of we did walk with him to Number Two pier and watch him board the ship? The SS *Caroni. I* will never forget the day. We send off a good-good boy to England dress in him suit and tie, looking like a little Englishman before him even reach. Is them place there mash him up. People not suppose to go so far from home. It weaken yu constitution. You nuh see how much people round here gone mad from foreign?'

What Grampa said made me think. I started to think of all the people around we knew who had gone away and come back. And several that I could think of were what we would call 'not righted'. Miss Pringle's daughter Gloria came back from the States walking and talking to herself, acting like mad ants all day long until she went right off her head and the Black Maria had to come and take her in straightjacket to Bellevue. Bagman who was somebody's pickney as he often told us though everyone had forgotten whose, Bagman dressed in crocus bag clothes black and stiff with dirt and slept on the pavement outside Chin's hardware shop and didn't trouble a soul unless it was full moon when he went into the banana field behind the shop and brayed like a donkey. Bagman had gone to England to fight in the war and that's how he came back. Mr Robinson had a son in Bellevue who had also gone to England to study and Miss Mary's daughter had killed herself and her two babies in England after her husband left her for another lady. If I weren't so sleepy I'm sure I could remember others. So many of them it seemed, and they had all gone away somewhere. Was there something in the atmosphere of foreign that made people go mad, as Grampa was suggesting?

I was interested in the topic because I wanted to go away myself, wanted to go to England to study. But I had no intention of going mad though I could see myself learning to talk rich and fruity like Uncle. That was what I liked best about him. But I was also sorry for him. I truly wanted to know what had happened to make him act the way he did. I used to imagine from the way he walked that he was holding all his pain in, that if he could only talk about it, spill it all, his body would come all relaxed and plastic again. But Uncle never talked. And after a while, nobody talked to Uncle. Well, Grampa wasn't given to talking anyway, though when Uncle first came, he tried. But increasingly as Grampa realised that Uncle was mad, you could see him drawing up everything inside himself, the same way Uncle had done, for Grampa was ashamed. He was ashamed because Uncle wasn't keeping his madness at home. He would have felt better, he told Gran one night, if Uncle had the kind of madness that you could lock up, so nobody would know about it. But no one could keep Uncle off the road, he went parading his madness every day for all the world to see.

After only a few weeks, everyone in fact accepted that Uncle was mad. They stopped calling him 'Mister Sonny' and 'Doctor' and 'Sir' which they'd called him when he first came. Now he was plain 'Sonny' to everyone including the little children who would trail behind him mimicking his stiff-legged gait, his fixed smile. The adults were more tolerant, though they shouted out things good-humouredly as he passed. Then he became such a fixture that they no longer noticed him. Uncle after a few months had become a local 'character', like Bagman or Turnfoot Tiny.

But what Grampa found really unbearable was that his drinking buddies in the bar simply ceased referring to Uncle in his presence. They behaved as if the son he had talked about for twenty years had suddenly vanished from the face of the earth and their wives did likewise. Grampa was glad that nobody talked about Uncle but at the same time he felt ashamed, cheated and ashamed. Anything would be preferable to having a child afflicted with madness.

Gran and Grampa would become fearful for me sometimes. Aside from showing her nervousness about my studying too much, Gran would say,'Girlie dear, when you go away to high school you must never tell anybody that you have a mad uncle. Never. For they might think you tar with the same brush, you know. Madness can run in the family. Don't ever let anybody know your uncle mad.'

As if I had any intention of telling anyone! I was glad I had got a scholarship and was going away to boarding school, for having Uncle around in the district was hard enough. I had to put up with so much teasing from the children at school, had got into the first and only fist fights of my life because of Uncle. I was glad I was going far away from the problem.

Uncle began to bother me a lot because he brought into the house such discomfort. When it had been just me and Gran and Grampa, we all seemed to fit together so well. Now with Uncle there we all sat at mealtimes totally silent, nobody saying a word, all three of us pretending he wasn't there, but totally conscious of him nonetheless though his behaviour at table or through the day never varied, so there was really nothing to see. After his first day with us, everything Uncle did was predictable. He would delicately cut up his food and go through the motion of eating, but hardly anything passed his lips. I wondered how he stayed alive. And always the three-piece suit which was getting more ragged and dirty every day, the stiff posture, the fixed smile. I thought that perhaps if we tried to get Uncle to talk it would help, but both Gran and Grampa had withdrawn themselves from him; I could almost feel them pulling away. They became as distant and silent as Uncle was, and soon the house which had once seemed to be so warm, so full of love and caring, now seemed empty and cold, as if nobody lived there anymore.

When I went back home each time on holidays the house seemed emptier and emptier, the two old people and Uncle appeared to rattle around in it like dried peas in a pod, all shrinking in their separate spaces, deadlocked in their silences. The only thing that happened is that one day Uncle decided to show me his correspondence with the Queen. He called me into his room and told me to shut the door, and he unlocked the trunk. At last I was getting to see what was inside this mysterious trunk that held Uncle's darkest secrets. Over the years since he came, Gran and Grampa had discussed what he could possibly have inside it. They had probably never given up hope that it might contain some treasure, such as the foreign goods for which they so longed.

But when Uncle opened his trunk, all that he had inside it were papers; letters in envelopes going brown and brittle with age, the letters so creased from handling they were falling apart; hundreds of sheets of yellowing paper covered with what I took to be Uncle's tiny and precise handwriting. He was taking all the papers out as he talked and laying them on the table, but he never really gave me a chance to look at anything for as soon as he had emptied the trunk, he immediately started putting everything back in. And he talked nonstop during all this activity.

'Here Girlie, here are all my letters to the Queen,' he said, waving packages of paper at me.'And here are her replies. But this, Girlie,' he said, grabbing up a fistful of sheets,'this is my case. My case that I have been preparing for years now, all my life. Six million pounds in damages I am claiming. Don't you think I am owed compensation? I and my children and my children's children? I never wanted to go into that hospital, Girlie. They dragged me in there. Kidnapped me, you have to say. Inflicted indignity and disfigurement on my person. Took out my heart and put in a mechanical one. And you know why, Girlie?' Uncle thrust his face at me and for once his eyes seemed to focus as they bored into mine.

'No Uncle,' I said.

'Because those people only understand machines. That's what I found out about them. Want to turn us all into machines. So they can work us as they like and wear us down as they like and nobody can say one little thing. Because we are not human any more. But see here, Girlie. I am making my case. I want you to take it for me. Take it to England. Take it to the Queen. You can tell her I am sorry, if you want. Tell the Queen I'm sorry to discombobulate her. But it's a long time now I've been waiting for my settlement. And I can't wait any more.'

In between talking, Uncle was putting the papers back into the trunk, and as soon as he finished, he locked it, looked at his watch, and found it was time for him to go for his walk. As far as I know, he never opened the trunk to show anyone his papers again.

I eventually had to leave Gran and Grampa and Uncle in their empty space. I went off to England and I didn't come home again for a long time. In England, sometimes I understood a little of what might have happened to Uncle there. So many things every day that might have given him the final push. I always felt a little guilty about Uncle, guilty that I had never really come to grips with the enigma that he represented; guilty that I had never attempted to contact his wife and children when I was in England, but what would I have had to tell them?

When I went home the last time, both Gran and Grampa had died and Uncle was living by himself in the house. I went to visit him, bracing myself for the worst, but I was surprised to find that in some subtle and undefined way, the house no longer seemed as empty and cold as it had before. Uncle had changed in superficial ways; he no longer wore the suit, perhaps it had simply fallen apart; but he was still dressed formally enough, for with his short-sleeved shirt he wore braces and a tie. Before he died, Grampa had given a neighbour permission to farm the land, on condition that they looked after Uncle. All they did was put food in front of him and wash his clothes, but he didn't seem to need anything else. Uncle still appeared oblivious to everything around him, still wore on his face that secret inward turning smile. Still held himself stiff as a wind-up toy and went for walks at four in the afternoon regular as clockwork, swinging his cane and lifting what was now a soft felt hat to everyone that he passed.

I was astonished that he knew exactly who I was as soon as I stepped through the door. The house was dark and gloomy and looked as though it hadn't been dusted for years. But I saw at once that Uncle had at last opened the trunk and spread out his papers; every inch of every flat space in every room – floor, beds, tables, chairs, was covered with his papers letters, envelopes and the loose sheets with the minuscule, precise handwriting.

'Girlie,' he said in greeting,'it is almost ready. I have almost finished my case. I am getting ready to send it to the Queen.'

It seemed strange to me that the house even though it belonged to a madman and was falling apart no longer felt dry and rattling the way it had up to when I left. For me, the ghosts of Gran and Grampa were still there, and I felt sad that I would never see them again. But Uncle entertained no ghosts, for both he and the house seemed alive for the first time since he came. Behind the facade, behind the stiff soldierly gestures, a heart seemed to be beating steadily. It was as if when he finally found room to open the trunk and spread out his papers, he also, for the first time in his life, poured out his presence.

# CANADA

# CLAIRE HARRIS

Claire Harris settled in Calgary after coming to
Canada from Trinidad in 1966. She is the author of
five collections of poetry, including *Translating Into
Fiction* and *Travelling To Find A Remedy*, both from
Goose Lane Editions. In 1985, she received a
Commonwealth Prize for Poetry. Her most recent
book of poetry *Drawing Down a Daughter* (Goose
Lane) was a finalist in the 1993 Canadian Governor
General's Award).

CLAIRE HARRIS

# Why I Write

Because I can. Obviously, not the whole story, but important nevertheless. Perhaps if I were a fabulous blues singer I wouldn't write. And it isn't enough simply to write. For me the very look of the piece must declare a refusal to accept the boundaries. Refusal. That's the key word. I write, at least at this stage of my life, I write because the images of myself, of the world of women, of what I am supposed to value, of my society, the accepted 'common-sense' of dominant segments of the Western project and of the place it has constructed for me, as well as the 'me' it has tried to construct are unacceptable. More important, these notions hinder, perhaps even prevent the development of 'whole' persons, and simple decency.

The persons I am thinking of here, since I am perceived as a creature of the Western world, are white. But Western culture has been congratulating itself recently on having won the war of 'civilisation'. So I must accept that along with its suits, its languages, its attitude of total war, it has spread its construct of me and its diseased notions of racial hierarchy as fundamental to the human project.

The human project. The discovery of the possibilities, the freedoms, the terrors, and limitations of being human. In this space/time. Not original. But the confessional alternative – why me/why here – strikes me as not only ignoring the possibility of chance, but also of being altogether too self-centred for a species for which social stimulation is a developmental requirement ... and much too self-important.

From the beginning my work has been about putting people, mostly women, in impossible situations and seeing what happens. Most of these people are of the Americas. They are also poor and/or oppressed. Their poverty and/or oppression the essential result of Western, patriarchal hegemony. So it was I discovered how a man could use a baby as a football; how a woman could castrate a man; how any human being could take up arms. I suppose I discovered how I might be able to do these things. And in doing so, discovered the dominant other.

The problem of being black in the West is that one cannot avoid internalizing this dominant other. Therefore, of the generations of Africans forcefully stranded here, especially those born before 1960, the marvel is their physical and emotional survival and the rich variety of their contribution, scientific, artistic, economic, to the enterprise of which they form an integral, if largely unacknowledged part. I could not begin to write until I saw my particular job in all this as a kind of archaeology. I had to dig up myself.

Layer by layer the cultural sediment that makes me what I am. I have to know what is most narrowly genetic, familial, experimental, and what regardless of education, class, and place of birth, we Blacks hold in common. I have to know which strands of thought and practice are essential Africa; which strands are Europe; which are/were designed in the white hot cauldron of the Caribbean to ensure the survival of the human spirit. How did we come to the incredible, private, life-saving cynicism that enables us to watch the manoeuvres of the Euro-American Axis to ensure continued domination without turning to bombs? How is it so many of us wait with real calm for you? How easy, African in the West, to hold always the moral hill! What does that do to us? To you? This is the rocky ground of the writing I do.

Like almost every one writing today, I mean, of course, almost everyone black, I am obsessed with language, and the world it creates. So personal and political a tool. With the notion that language conceals as much as it reveals. With the difference between theory and the relatively actual. With the shifting ground between the two. With how one holds on. Life is so often 6.6 on the Richter scale ... if one pays attention. That's why I read detective fiction ... squalid, almost gothic, fairy tales for the twentieth century.

CLAIRE HARRIS

# Inside Passage

Only once in my whole life I travel a far distance by sea. Is when I make the voyage out from Trinidad to university in Ireland; from a way of seeing everything 'double': so one part you see the African-Trinidad way; the very same time you see story-book British. You cultured. A good word when you think what is milk culture. Thing so automatic, seem so necessary to respect you ain't even know you doing it, eh. Still it got this sour aftertaste. I move from that to seeing myself as 'other'. I telling you straight; was a singular experience. Take ten days or so from Trinidad to England. It begin a trip what carry me five hundred years. So when I hear the theme of this conference 'voyages', what come to mind is plunging seas, a grey ship, coming home. Talking my talk here today, it going be only about them seas. I dividing this into two: 1) How all them voyage I take, that emigration, how I suspect it shape what I writing; 2) That word, – **woman**, how it come too too clear aint no accident it mean what it mean. That also kneading the work.

Ever since I know myself, everybody take it for granted I going be a writer. So how come it take me 16 years to get start? I come from that class a West Indian what never really take this race thing serious. On the whole they behave like is somebody belch at table; they too polite to notice. I remember when I about eleven I tell them home about some Expat teaching at the convent. My father first he laugh, then he say the world full of fools why should she be different. Then he get serious and he say nobody what anybody really good leave England to come to a dot in the Caribbean. Is what I needed then and I grateful to him. But looking back from now, I see this ambivalence. Every body else live at the centre of they world but not us. Still my parents was fierce in they pride, so it take a while for me to accept that along with all the classist stuff I absorb, it have so much what bound to be racist.... I get to Ireland and pretty soon I want a language; I want Gods; I stop writing.

Now this culture thing: Is a real callaloo of myth, religion, language, ethics, economic pattern, science and art all bubbling together, you know. And we right down there in the pot bubbling along with it. We an everything else relate, an is all-a-we, an it aint have no way to escape. Body and mind you is what you culture is. It become a kind of seasoning the whole world taste of it; and the world aint have any other way to taste. Everybody else use water from they own well to make base. In these island, what ever we class or race, we using water for-so from a European well. Is so we ending up hand in hand with a culture what try to reduce we to nothing. Is so sometime, somewhere, we bound to find weself obozkee. Allyuh see this all all the time at these conference when all them ideological, them critical terms is always an everytime something other people come up with. Now is how any a we could think that European rules of organising ain't consciously or unconsciously going wipe we out, especially where topic and style ups an reflect what actually going down? On the other side we trap in a economic reality. Some of we, what want to eat, aint got no choice, cept irony.

But it have a worse thing: I cant imagine a writer what aint love language, but this language I love, aint sweet on me. No matter how you look at it the more real we be, we Africans in the Americas, the more we out there on the edge. It clear is time for we to start thinking for we self about we self in the world, laying down we own string and following it to the end. For those of we what cant eat in the Islands, and is more and more of we, is the most important thing. Because I telling you straight, out there where it aint have anything to hide behind, we got nothing to tell the children. They aint dumb; they see the ole talk aint working anywhere. Is time we reinterpret the signs. Otherwise is another generation we risking. And dont bother mamaguying yourself; it aint have nothing to do with class.

Any how, yes, my mother used was to say never play game by anybody else rule. Meaning if I aint play slave no body could play master. I begin to see I get a real opportunity here with this language thing/this interpretation thing ... it take awhile before I could use it.

Now it aint possible to write serious without choosing. People what born with a deep down proud, they can't Naipaul. In fact any kind of victim shuffle, it out. That only leave you with one choice and that is the choice to know for youself. Knowing for youself mean you have to know not only *who* you really is but *where* you really is. Now after Europe I aint know nothing that count except that one thing... (I better say right here eh, nobody beat me up; nobody spit on me; this landlady do me a real favour, tell me I in her house under false pretence: Claire Harris couldn't possibly be your real name.) After Jamaica I know a little more. Mostly what I aint going to do. In Trinidad, I realize nobody ready for me. (In 1965 I say I making a rule in my English class... unless youself white I aint marking no story with white hero. Them days, you read children story in those elite school and all the people have blue eye. Well is uproar in the staff room. They say I racist; I crushing chile.) Eventually I pick myself up an I leave. I did get a job in New Zealand but life take a turn in me skin and I end up in Canada.

Now is one thing to live in a country as student, is another thing to enter they market place. Is a worse thing when people see you propose to eat you food/drink you music/and dress you dress. I learn living there. 1) A

West Indian person living away got to decide for she one self what in the callaloo matter to she. 2) It aint have no way of being other than as member of you own group. And whether you like it or no you place in opposition. Now it have oppositional site an oppositional site. If you talk you private life, if you want to scream racism, that's fine. They custom to that. If you want to write about Trinidad that is fine too. Be real real careful if you start looking deep at the society; be even more careful if you start laughing. Though in true laugh is only a way of dealing with this looking business. This looking close is the hardest part; mostly what you find it terrifying. Anyway I start to read serious because I had was to find for myself the source of all them crazy ideas about Africans these societies have. And the even crazier ideas about themselves. I start traveling with me eyes open. I remember this idea lamblassing me that what I write have to be different. Still it have this whole cloud of dead white man complete with Austen, and Eliot hanging over one shoulder. They grow me up in a house full of books and female ancestor stories. Grandmother, Aunts, Great Aunts everybody proud for so and full of words. So this even more demanding cloud of dead black women on the other shoulder waiting to see what I go make with what they win for me. I was paralyze. Finally, I take a year off for Africa. Was 1974.

I only had was to land, three weeks later the dam burst. I start writing. So when I meet up with John Pepper Clark it had this sheaf of trembling poems clutch in my hand. He mentor me for long enough. Looking back, I did really need Africa. Them people aint have a clue what it mean to lose you self. And I find out I have a world view; and I find out just how much water it had in my wine. I'se a West Indian; I descend from people what had to create themself in the West, eh. For me it come clear. There aint no way to graft a Yoruba self onto the West Indian self; You got to surrender to Africa completely. By then I did have enough surrender; enough of other people culture. I finally free to begin finding the New World African. Of course I return to Canada full of Africa. And proud as hell. I soon see is contain I cant contain all that in 20 or 40 lines. Is so I begin journeying with the long poem. Is just fact that thousand mile of prairie, sky gone to forever out side my window make the outer landscape mirror the inner one.

I start myself up as a public poet. I want to say this is what it mean to be alive today. This is what it mean to be human. Everybody like they shock about what going on now they decolonise the rest of Europe. Aint no surprise to me. Is not the same thing happen in India, in Africa? Is not that civilisation what haul we here to lock we down in they stink all the way from Africa? Aint they wipe out whole peoples in the Caribbean, in Africa? God know where else! (And is guns I talking not disease.) Aint civilisation wipe out half the European Jews? Aint it the other half of those self-same European Jews what wiping out Palestinians? Aint half the world confuse technology with something special they call 'civilisation'.

My subject, it seem to me, this minute (notice all them weasel words I throwing at you) my subject is what different between that superior moral image, all that moral philosophy all them colonising societies fool themselves with. (And is all I really mean: the usual suspects, plus most of them in the Americas, Far/Near/Middle East, Ethiopia and all the rest of them in Africa, the Zulu and so) and how violent, how in truth it uncaring; how it anti-life. How it most primitive in it basic tribal insistence. And when I say primitive here I mean peoples what still think *any* woman/and the man over the hill aint fully human. Boil down what happening all over the 'developed' world that is what it truly is. That primitive. In such a space I ain't got nothing to lose. Cept myself. So I set up to counter all them image of Africans, all them image of women, all image of 'civilisation as we know it' what they re-colonizing the globe with, for image what a little closer to what I myself see really happening.

Now this feminism thing: is a matter of ownership. All over the world societies feel they owning they women. They think it natural as breathing. What difference, it only in degree. In the Americas is one in four have the subtlety of the fist.

It have judge what say a man could rape you, and you bound to carry he thing. It have judge what say domestic violence different; like domestic science I suppose is part of homemaking; It have judge what lock up woman to protect she foetus, but any man could damage he sperm: drink, drugs, chemicals, you got to carry it. It have politician talking 'family values', what they mean keep woman in the market place, preferably part time, that way you just don't bother with fair payment. That way as a langniappe you get control. It have politician what fraid to outlaw automatic weapon; so the next maniac could shoot 7 women engineers instead of fourteen. An I aint even going get started on Anita Hill; or on them so what raping they girl child.

Voyaging through these things what is one thing, what like the sea and can't divide, what is me/African/female/of the Americas, lead to charge my poetry overtly political. Is like saying I make poetry out of words. It have anybody who work aint political? Some of we overtly support the status-quo, and some of we don't. A more real point is me own participation in Canada, it hegenomic role. (After all what I doing is teaching people, who thinking I cant really influence, how to use the verbal tool like a boss. And I teach them because is live well I like to live well.) Some of this insinuate itself into the work.

If I could, is rupture I would want to rupture this world and make it back safe for all-a-we. But as I dont believe in omelette, so I trying to rupture the *idea* of limits, of expectation in form. I does always talk story; even so I write a layered kinda poetry. I like to fool around with words, I like even the way they line up, the way they look on the page. I like to see the way they different ways of meaning on the line support what I wanting to say deep inside, an still leave space for the reader to create she own thing. Is so I move in to the poem as a ship I buy for meself. I plant my flag where I feel like. And I take it over.

# ARITHA van HERK

Aritha van Herk was born in 1954 in the parkland region of central Alberta, to parents who immigrated to Canada from Holland in 1949. She attended the University of Alberta in Edmonton.

Her first novel, *Judith*, won the $50,000 Seal First Novel Award in 1978, and, following the publication of her second novel, *The Tent Peg*, in 1981, she was selected as one of Canada's ten most promising young writers in the 45 Below competition. *No Fixed Address: An Amorous Journey* confirmed her international reputation. It won her a nomination for the Governor General's Award for Fiction for 1986; and was awarded the Howard O'Hagan Prize for the best Alberta novel. In 1990 she published an experimental *geografictione, Places Far From Ellesmere*. Her collected crypto-fictions, hidden or secret messages ignited by the rubbing together of criticism and fiction, are published in the recent volume *In Visible Ink*. Aritha van Herk is also an editor and critic and she has contributed to such collections as *The Road Home* and *Alberta Bound*. Dangaroo Press has recently published *A Frozen Tongue*, a collection of her essays.

She is currently teaching at the University of Calgary.

ARITHA VAN HERK

# Why I Write

In a lifetime of composing excuses and their alternatives, I have algebraized many such excuses for my writing. Rage, frustration, the trepidation of answering the ancient litany of the repetitive male voice declaring itself agent, keeper, and writer of all valid and valued experience. Fear of failure, the containment of patriclinous inheritance, infects my joy, my pleasure in language. Fear and joy wrestle to control the addictive and crazy tenacity of my yearning to *language* Joan of Arc's burning and statutory rape, to *language* endive and gouda cheese and the bakery in Camrose that sold brownies, to *language* the tough-rooted buffalo beans that bloomed in the ditches of my childhood. Tenacity, for its own sake, clinging to words, and the joy/fear that keeps words rooted, like those tough-stemmed wildflowers that signalled the arousal of spring in my Canadian prairie. We could not pick them – they refused to succumb to jam jars or vases; but we could pluck a labial blossom and suck, from its thin stamen, a tinge of incipient honey. Waiting for the rotund school bus that would carry us into town, we stood at the end of the lane and suckled wild sugar, that invitation to the bees, from buffalo beans. And for a moment, our sadness would evaporate.

I have learned (the hard way) that writing is unwise. But wisdom has an interesting way of retreating to a time when it will combine with age and discretion. For now, tenacity will have to do. There is labour tied to that tenacity, hard and unremitting labour that fights its own transfusions, that insists on the carbuncles of resistance. Writing has never had any ease, any surety, for me. I cannot say, like Flannery O'Connor, that I write because I am good at it, because in my heart of hearts I do not believe I am good at it, even when others tell me that I am. I believe only that writing is my expiation, my gesture of defiance and rupture, my subversion of authority, and me the author about to be dismembered by the explosion I am planting. Writing, I feel again and again as if it is my own constructedness that I explode, my own safety that I must expose. Fearful, anxious, full of grief, I try to touch the page with the variations on pain and joy that I believe it is so essential to record, wanting to leave a thumb or fingerprint, however faint.

There is an abstractedness to talk *about* writing that is difficult to transcend. The writing act demands a strange immunity from the concrete world at the same time as it requires a tremulous complicity with that exactly mundane concrete world. Writing is speech, but silent speech, speech that requires a reader to unlock its door, to open its knowledge. I was never much interested in being a pale and oppressed poet, grateful to be obscure and unread; instead, I long, with every passionate longing possible, for the reader/lover, to complete my language act, to comfort me in my grief, and me in hers.

Tenacious, I write on, despite a continuing inarticulacy, the inarticulacy of someone whose early world was without privilege or the luxury of self-awareness. Survival was the mill that ground my childhood, heel-trodden shoes and boiled potatoes and patched clothes; it became what I wanted to escape, but escaping, ran toward. The survival that transcends physical well-being was the survival of my imagination, and escaping became its primary object. But there is always a cost, a ransom. The scutage I pay is risk, over and over again risk and its consequents, its strange habits of bereavement. From scraps I patch my stories and their declarations; I have lost my dictionary of saints and I seek in vain for a patron of women writers, writers like me, who are pushed to their knees and yet stagger up again and again.

So why do I write? To escape? To declare? To express grief and loss? Saint Agatha's breasts she carries on an offering platter, the king's reward for her refusal to marry him a sword through her flesh. This is the threat the woman writing faces. If she declares: 'No, I will not speak the king's story, live out his scenario, bear his literary children,' Io, she holds her words, her shapely shapes, bleeding on a platter.

In Egypt, at the temple of Isis on the island of Philae, the goddesses prowl and recline; they figure in graceful profile, full of pride and power. They bestow words, that much is clear from their upraised hands, from the gestures of their flexed thighs. At Philae, recovered now from the mouth of the Nile, the muddy waters that submerged the island, the temple is re-preserved, re-intacted. It is possible to visit Isis and her votaries there, to see the oldest of the old, the goddesses from whom all becoming arose.

Yes, her images are carved into the stone walls of the temple, have been there for thousands of years. Beautiful, terrible, she knows the mysteries of the stars, could, with a sweep of her arms, lay waste, or save. Scorpions are her servants. She personifies female creative power. The subsequent text of Roman and Christian oppression undid her mysteries. Her temple was flooded, her votaries killed; male gods overthrew her and took precedence over her. But stories are written over stories and that story too is inscribed on the temple.

Imagine this.

A Copt, a Christian, full of fanatical zeal, determined to eradicate Isis and her power, standing on a rickety branch ladder with a hammer and a chisel. How do you deface a goddess? You deface her. All her stone configurations, her particular femaleness, the turn of her powerful ankles, and the straight edge of her nose, have been defaced. Her nose, her breasts, her toes, chipped and chipped and chipped from their stone speech, the millions of chisel marks resisting her power as *the one who is all*. Stone effigies worked at for hundreds of years, marking her down. If the woman is erased she will be forgotten, no one will believe in her, pray to her, take refuge in her winged arms. The temple usurped, Isis and her images undone, disinscribed.

It was 1981. I was in Egypt. I was afraid, afraid, as always, of writing. I stood in the courtyard of that temple, and saw centuries of male hands with their furious chisels, trying to efface her feet, her breasts, her nose. The draperies of her clothing swung as richly as ever, her back was as straight, the throne, her horned crown, were there, untouched. Only her femaleness chipped away, relentlessly edited. Grief fell over my soul like a shadow, a grief I could not explain, relentlessly Calvinist myself, baptized and christened and raised up to believe in god the father, why should I grieve for the passing of a now eccentric Egyptian goddess?

There was courtyard within courtyard, all beautifully configured women, chipped into submission. I followed through, the enclosures of the temple smaller and smaller, until there was only one room left, the inner sanctuary, perhaps eight feet by ten, a dirt-packed floor, a thick wedge carved into the stone as a door, and within, total darkness. Dark darkness. Heavy and redolent, the kind of darkness that sends missionaries scurrying for bibles and cholera shots.

I lit a match.

There, within the sacred precincts, they must have felt that she was harmless if unseeable, for her images were untouched. No zealous convert had been conscripted to deface her woman's features. She paces the room, imperious, her woman's eyes and mouth seeing and speaking, etched as clearly as when she ruled over heaven and earth.

The match went out. I fell to my knees. She did not speak; there was no beam of light. But the deep sadness, the river of grief and fear, was, for a moment, lifted from my heart. And although the walls around me wrote tenacity, a fanatic determination to erase, they wrote more deeply the tenacity of resistance, patience, survival, and risk.

Why do I write? To stave off grief? To carve enchantments? To mourn the dead and injured? To taste again, for one fleeting moment, the exquisite and unbelievably erotic suggestion of honey before it becomes honey, savoured by a scab-kneed child in a ditch by the side of a gravel road. To celebrate the tough-stemmed signal of buffalo beans.

ARITHA VAN HERK

# Especially Jericho

It is a hot, still afternoon, and God (whatever that linguistic construct might occupy at the moment) is on the side of the Israelites. God is always on the side of the Israelites. He considers it to be his job, getting them together in the first place, sending them out into the desert to suffer and starve, burnt with hunger and devoured with burning heat. Moses is dead (has apparently died undiminished, his eyes still bright and his 'natural force' – does that mean his virility, his ability to get it up? – unabated, despite his one hundred and twenty years), and God is doling out territory, Canaan, the land that he promised, first to Abraham, then to Isaac, then to Jacob. The land stretches from Lebanon as far as the great river Euphrates, all the land of the Hittites to the land of the great sea. This land is already occupied, but God has promised it to the Israelites, under the command of Joshua, every place that the sole of his foot will tread. All arguments with God are pretty much the same; full of references to inheritance and loaded with bargain. 'If you do what I say, I'll be on your side; if you stick to my rules, you'll have "good success wherever you go" – just like Moses did.' But now Joshua is the recipient: of the mantle of power, of the insider intercourse, privileged discourse. Moses has 'laid hands upon him,' and God has fingered him, so Joshua is in command, of commands; he has become the link between knowledge and power. He is directed to cross over Jordan (another one of those tricks of the dry path through the middle of a flooding river) and to 'take possession', the imperative of an already occupied territory. Joshua relays his commands to the people, instructing them to prepare for siege, and reminding them that all dissenters will be put to death. Thus does he utilize his appropriative privilege: 'God has told me that this country will belong to us; I tell you to follow my instructions in order to fulfill these words.' What one says the other will enact. What one enacts, the other will say. Joshua's power is located in this relayed articulation.

But all this anointed stuff is an illusion. Joshua is a favourite of God's because he is a warrior, with a warrior's ways, smart enough to know that the country over Jordan is not likely to fall willingly into his rapacious hands. Secretly – (why? because the people will not think him infallible?) – he sends ahead two spies, saying, 'Go, view the land, especially Jericho.' Bring back information, look for holes in the habits of those about to be conquered and dispossessed.

The nature of a spy is to recognize the gaps in a language, and to enter a world through its absences. The two spies selected by Joshua hie themselves to Jericho and without much fuss, seemingly effortlessly, which points to some prior knowledge and experience, they lodge themselves with a woman who appears to represent a rift in the fabric of Jericho. How they know her or why they choose her is unexplained, or perhaps mere silent acquiescence. For Rahab is described quite simply, as a harlot.

Rahab is lucky: she lives in the wall, or at least the wall has been built as part of her house. The edges of cities are better propositions for commerce than their centres, Rahab has known this for some time. She is able, also, in the early mornings, her favourite hour, to look across the plain at the gathering light over Jordan, and to sing quietly to herself while she combs her long black hair. She is remarkably similar to Rapunzel, but she is unaware of this cross-contamination of mythologies – she does not, at this moment, anyway, feel herself to be locked up in a tower.

And then, on what is an otherwise normal day, these two dudes show up. Strangers, yes. Spies, sure enough: investigative men all look the same, they are indubitably recognizable, but what can you do if a pair of them walk through the door? Blow their cover? Far better to pretend that you are both blind and deaf, far better to speak judiciously. Although their whispered discussion is audible enough – and what they want is clearly different from what she is accustomed to providing. But each feels it necessary to enact the pretence of customary demand.

Well, strangers are visible, and spies are ubiquitous. More than one person on the streets of Jericho sees the two of them in their dark glasses and their slightly shiny suits waving her business card around. And it only requires their Jerichoan counterpart (one investigative agent implies his opposite) to report – quite rightly – their suspicious presence to the king, who has lately heard too many stories about the siege of Troy, which are keeping him awake nights. Although she is a Jericho citizen, that wouldn't have mattered a whit to Rahab, except that the strangers have occupied her patio for some hours by then, after easing their toes out of their too-tight shoes and clicking the ice in a pair of lime rickeys while they survey the view as it slips toward twilight. One FBI man is much like another, and when the Jericho contingent starts pounding on the door down at street level, Rahab wonders if she shouldn't just let them all loose on one another, slip out the back door, and the outcome be damned.

But threateningly muscled FBI or CSIS men pounding on your door – no matter how sturdily thick-planked it is – in the evening are never a civilized matter, and their sheer effrontery makes Rahab wild; they know the necessity of her business, and they really have no right to inflict their cold eyes on her establishment, no matter how they are supposed to represent state security. And the two strangers are such babies, like young

Mormons in their earnestness, desperate to get caught. So she goes down to lift the bar in her flannel nightgown, rubbing her eyes as if she has been aroused from sleep. Every gesture becomes part of a discourse, and she knows that the more she resembles their older sisters, the less likely they will be to harass her.

They are grunting with the effort of their hammering, and their shouts to open seem to prefigure the bellows that will tumble the walls of the city in only a few days, but Rahab has scant patience for déja vue, and assumes only that here is merely a repeated case of intransigent men.

'Yes?' She manages her question sleepily, but with enough edge so that they should read her annoyance at this interruption.

They have almost fallen into the opening door, and now they are busy smoothing back their hair and straightening their too narrow ties. 'Give them up,' they say, marvellously in unison.

'Who?'

'Those men who showed up this afternoon. The king wants them. They're spies.'

'Those guys?' She manages this with just enough derision to reveal that she doesn't think her visitors capable of the intelligence to be intelligent.

And the two intelligence in front of her, sneaking surreptitious looks over her shoulder into the rush-lit hallway, nod vigorously.

She holds the door farther open. 'I do not know where they came from. They were here all right, but they've gone. When the gate was to be closed, at dark, the men went out; I'm not sure which direction they went – if you hurry you can probably catch up with them.' This is such an old trick that she is sure the two federales in front of her will suspect it, so she fights to keep a straight face – all the while imagining a quick flash of late night *Gunsmoke* episodes.

They look properly disbelieving, but then, they are trained to disbelieve. So she holds the door farther open, and invites them inside for a quick search. She has taken the precaution of battening her naive visitors down under a great heap of flax stalks, rushes that the roofers just delivered; they will begin thatching tomorrow. She doesn't like to be caught in an outright lie; but she has to maintain her amoral integrity somehow. They're trying to count her customers already, trying to tell her that she has to charge G.S.T., which she resents, since she does not consider herself a *service* in any way. And mercifully, the visitors do not rustle and sneeze, but manage to pretend quite convincingly to be thatch. Later, she will remember their proficiency at concealment, and will berate herself silently for not having recognized then that something was dreadfully, dreadfully wrong. They looked as fresh as missionaries, but that too was a disguise. Still, she will answer herself, even if you had noticed, what would you have done? Even if you'd turned them over, would things be different now? Maybe they'd be worse and you'd be dead.

Rahab bargains out this scene with herself again and again; she tries on different courses of action, different words, in this incipient drama that has worn itself into her skin, that she now veritably wears as a costume. But no matter how many variations she introduces, she is still only able to see herself, in one way or another, losing. The only question, the only true variable, is which loss, which untenable resolution is the least acceptable. That she has never resolved. Not yet.

Oh, when the feds have gone, they come out from under her flax stalks and shower her with gratitude and promises. None of which she pays much attention to, listening with one ear to the sound of the noisy pursuit that sets out to the river ford, hearing the gate of the city slam shut with a mighty thump. Here, on the wall, she knows the city's life so intimately, so particularly, that she could tell the king a thing or two, if he weren't so eager to hire and to invest his ear in those oblivious and black-suited thugs. Odd, what kind of language a man will trust.

'You can sleep on the roof for a few hours,' she says. 'Then I'll get you out of here. But do me a favour and stay hidden, all right? I don't need any more trouble with those goons. I'm the one that will get arrested. You'll just get a reprimand.'

She descends to her private bedroom, her own room where no one intrudes, and brushing her hair again, thinks of all the rumours she has heard. Strange stories of the Red Sea drying up, of the two kings of the Amorites, so powerful and with such enormous armies, utterly destroyed. Jericho is a lazy city. If there is to be a siege, it will fall, for it relies on the strength of its walls for defence, and has no practice fighting an enemy. Later, she will think that she imagined the horrific scenes she sees enacted in front of her, she will refuse to believe her own déja vue, that she sees, in the light of her lamp, all the careful structures of her life crumbling beyond any intercourse she has ever undertaken in speech or in knowledge, even in rebellion.

Well, she has taken a risk.

She goes up to the roof, shakes them both awake. In the paler shade of moonlight, she can suddenly see how young they are, barely shaven, these fresh-faced boys. 'Listen,' she says. 'Something's making me nervous. If you're planning a massacre, then swear to me, by God, that you'll remember that I saved you from those gum-shoes. I've heard about you guys. I've heard you're pretty good at mass destruction. So, you give me a sign that you'll exempt me, and my father and my mother and my brothers and my sisters, and all their kids. Or I turn you in, right now.'

In the moonlight, she looks ten feet tall, Rahab, even though she is barefoot and bony. They are surprised at her language – they've only heard negotiation coming from the mouths of men, and it is disconcerting to hear her bargain as shrewdly as some of their leaders. Besides, they aren't exactly in a position to argue with her, there under the rushes of the roof. 'Okay, okay. Our lives for yours. If you don't talk about us, then we'll save you when we attack the city.'

'Not just me. My father and my mother and my sisters and my brothers and their kids. Got it?'

'Well,' says one doubtfully, 'how will we know -?'

'They'll be right here in this house with me. No excuses.'

'Sure,' says the second one. 'Just get us out of here in one piece.'

Rahab looks at the sky. Aside from everything else, she is a proficient astronomer. 'Two hours,' she says. 'The moon will go down. I'll be back.'

They huddle there on the roof and shiver in the damp of the night. 'Joshua isn't going to like this,' says the first one. 'He's going to give us shit for coming here, when we were supposed to gather our intelligence on the street.'

'They'd have noticed us. This city is pretty suspicious. I think she may have saved our asses.'

They are beginning to feel numb with the cold when she re-appears, a grey shape in the night that has grown increasingly overcast. Or she seems to loom out of the dimness behind a huge woven basket, her laundry basket, to be precise, but as two young men who have never done their own laundry, they haven't the means to conceptualize that.

She pulls open the round lid. 'Get in,' she says to the first one.

'What?'

'Get in. I'm going to let you down over the wall. You've got three hours until daylight. Head for the hills and hide for a few days until they've stopped looking for you. Then you can go your own way.'

'That thing looks awfully flimsy.'

'It's a woman's strongest vessel. Next to her body. Get in.'

They don't understand that, having no nose for irony or metaphor. But her tone is unbrookable, and first one, then the other curls himself into the strong willow basket and permits her strong arms to lower him down to the ground outside the city wall. Just before she puts the lid on the second, she leans over into its open mouth, so that her face looms large above his.

'Swear,' she hisses. 'My father and my mother and my brothers and my sisters and their children and me. Swear.'

Her eyes flare in the darkness and her hair around her head, if he had known any mythology at all, would have reminded him of Medusa. All he can do is pluck at a thread in his shirt, the fancy embroidery that his intended has so carefully stitched there, and pull it between his fingers. He dares not leave her anything more – she might use it against him as a promise, like the famous Tamar of Genesis who kept Judah's signet and his cord and his staff in order to force him to keep his familial promises. One can never trust a woman dressed as a harlot; she might turn out to be your sister, or your daughter-in-law, there is no telling.

But her face insists on an oath and its token. Otherwise, he suspects that the rope which is tied to the handles of the basket will simply unknot itself and he will thump to broken bones on the other side of the wall.

'My oath on it,' he says hoarsely. 'When we invade, tie this scarlet cord in your window, but make sure your family is all here in your house. If one of you goes out into the street we'll have no means of knowing and we'll spill his blood along with the rest. So long as you keep our business secret, we will respect this promise. But if you tell, all bets are off.'

Later, Rahab will puzzle over this moment, so short and quick, that later elongated itself in a long shadow over the rest of her life. In that moment, the moon lapsed from the sky and her bare feet cold on the rushes of the roof, she knows that her complicity, her self-effacement in this bargain, will be the nexus of her survival. Or at least, her family's survival. Strange that she bargains so hard for her family. She has little connection with them any more, and their relations are strained by their scorn for her occupation, however much she argues with them that it is hard to make her own way, that she wants to be a woman of independent means and without the stricture of a foul and greasy husband. Far better to service strangers that one can send out the door, dispatch without having to speak to the next morning.

Yes, later, Rahab will struggle to find a rationale for the events of this moment, but at this moment, all she can do is stare down at the boy/man, the potential killer doubled up in her laundry basket, and demand that he swear an oath to her.

And in return, swear herself, snatching the scarlet thread from his fingers. 'According to your words, so be it.' Wrapping the rope around a wooden post and slowly edging the basket down the height of wall, she thinks wildly of Cassandra, the Trojan prophetess, imprisoned in just such a basket for the madness (or was it foresight?) that the impregnable fortress of Troy and its incipient fall inspired.

She feels the basket reach the ground with a jar and then the weight within step away, so that if she had not held the scarlet thread in her hand, she could have imagined that she had only imagined those two cowboys, with their Bryllcreamed hair and their high-tone watches and sunglasses. She pulls her basket back up, then awkwardly dances it back to the washing room, and even though she knows the willow wands smell of sun and river, can catch a faint emanation of their malesmell, not sex or sweat but the distinctive spoor of bargaining, the metallic trade-off of escape. And she deliberately binds the thread in her window, visibly, as pretty as any seamstress's declaration.

She continues to imagine to herself that she has imagined everything, the men and their mission, her naive entrance into the game of hide and seek, her bargain with them – except of course for the gay red bow of the thread. And despite the bureau men who return three days later, hot and sweaty and not a little pissed off, insisting that she has misled them, and that those men were nowhere to be found, not a track, not even a burnt stick or a tree notched. But while they tear her house apart, systematic in their frustration, she points out that the gate has been kept shut – by royal decree – since they left on their search. The strange men obviously escaped *before* the posse; perhaps they were unusual enough to fly rather than walk. Which makes the older and larger of the several thick-set thugs crack her loom, eyes narrow on her face to see if she will protest. And she does, sharply and with considerable scorn for his childishness, which matters not a whit to him. He mutters something to the effect that she ought to be grateful that they are not breaking her bones.

Which ache with a kind of arthritic anxiety through the long days that follow, when the sun stands hotly in the centre of the sky and she is certain that she has made a fool of herself, there is no need to worry about the marauding Israelites and their infamous Joshua. Still, rumours fly around the city all that week, of people dancing behind a casket, of the river Jordan altering its flow, of stonehenges rising in the desert, and peculiarly superstitious rituals with men cutting off one another's foreskins with flint knives. Rahab is never sure if she hears these rumours as whispers on the streets or whether she dreams them, although later she will know them to be the discourse of invasion and attack, these tales incitement for the forty thousand armed warriors who encamp on the plains of Jericho, in visible view of the walls and the apoplexy of the king, now sending out promises of wealth and capitulation with wily ambassadors who never return but are only swallowed by that sprawling camp sweltering in the late summer sun. At last, they recognize that there is no hope of diplomatic resolution, and the city shuts its gates as tightly as a nutcracker's jaws, pretending invulnerability while it waits to see what kind of siege these strangers will mount.

The rumours on the streets are stories that Rahab can hardly credit; in her economy of listening they are neither received knowledge nor subjective knowledge nor procedural knowledge nor constructed knowledge, they are simply an echo to the great silence that she feels is threatening to engulf her city, her people, her home. She is careful not to dwell on the red cord in her window. It seems now like trumpery, even vanity.

But then, when the invasion comes, she is not surprised, can only watch in amazement as the entire army begins marching around the circumference of the city wall, the ark and the priests in a version of spectacular carnival, and the ram's horns trumpeting so loudly that you cannot hear yourself think. Well, this won't get them anywhere, she thinks, looking down at the flashing of helmets below her. They're going to have to get past the battlements or they'll be stuck on the plain forever. But every day it seems that the sound of the ram's horns grows louder until it is a din inside her inner ear and she cannot escape it, cannot find a silent spot anywhere in the house or town, can only hear the blast of those foul trumpets blaring over the heart of her nervous imagination. Around her, words rattle and the reports of the journalists are blasé and bored – they prefer the clash of weapons to the noise of fanfare. All the while Rahab is locked in a silent argument with herself about reason and rationality and knowledge as closure and even whether what she knows that she knows is negotiable, or whether she should pretend that she does not know what she knows.

So much for rationality, or instinct either. On the sixth day, she runs to her father's house early in the evening, and insists that they come to stay with her, that it is safer at the edge of the city, that they can escape over the wall if the city falls. Her sisters are nervous enough, by now, to want to stay with her, Rahab has always seemed the practical one, the survivor, and at least they will be able to see what is happening from her house, whereas at home all they can hear is the din. But her parents are adamant that they want to stay in their home, that the walls will never fall. Besides, they do not feel exactly right taking up residence in the house of a woman of ill repute, even if she is their daughter. Rahab has to shout at them, has to persuade them that she knows more than she knows, and her imagination helps, she manages to talk them into coming, for the night at least, with the fiction that they should be together as a family once in a while, they ought to spend a little more social time together.

And it is a curiously quiet night. Once that army stops tromping around the perimeter of the city, they have a quiet meal together, without squabbling, for the first time in years, and so relaxed are they that they manage to sleep late the next morning, hearing the din of the circling Israelites only vaguely. Until of course that final, hugely explosive shout, until the very walls of their impregnable city crumble beside them – with them, for Rahab's house is built into the wall – and the entire wall shudders and in a slow cinematographic dust, shivers down, only Rahab's house wall standing in its section, with that red cord suddenly brilliant in the early morning light.

Still, they are a Jericho family, and Rahab has to stand arms outflung in front of the door to keep them inside, to prevent them from running into the street. She does not explain the nature of her bargain, she only holds them there, physically, as if every articulate bone in her body speaks. Although later she will remember their looks, their barely-concealed anger at her, believing that she has betrayed this city, shown the enemy its weak spots, the inevitable decay in the fortress.

But true to the many oaths that were sworn in the laundry basket, they are spared. Joshua himself strides to the door in his sweaty leathers and his metal gauntlets and takes the scarlet thread between his fingers. His eyes gleam with a fanatical pleasure, and he waves a blood-stained sword at her terrified family. 'Are these all yours?'

'My family,' she says evenly, wondering herself at her own pre-constructed escape, her strange integration of so much knowledge that it feels as if she will stagger to her knees with the weight of it.

He laughs, hugely, the belly-laugh of a brutal victor. 'Is this her?' he asks of the two spies that she so recently hid under her thatch, panting up to the step beside their commander. They nod, barely, too afraid of him to squeak a reply. And after all, they have only just witnessed him shouting down the walls of this fortressed city, they have some reason to be speechless.

'Are you sure? All women look the same in the dark.'

She will never forgive him for that. All her life she will hold that remark against him, in her brooding reversioning of memory; in the tents of these people who have tumbled down her city, she will remember her cool and quiet house that somehow remained hers despite the men who came and went from her door.

'You beast,' she thinks, standing there on the doorstep with her family clustered behind her, while in the street she sees a thigh pumping blood, an arm sliced off, an eye run through. Her citizens are being slaughtered, the pavement is running black with their blood.

And they are ushered out, the harlot's bargain, past the wholesale deaths of their neighbours, they are helped over the rubble of the city walls and escorted to the edge of the camp of Israel, urged to sit down and drink some water while the city is burned with fire, the dead and maimed within it adding to the smoke, and only the gold and silver, the pitchers and the vessels of bronze and iron are brought out, tumbled into a great heap on the sour grass of the plain.

Rahab and her father and her mother and her brothers and her sisters and all their children now huddle together watching with wide eyes the final moments of their old and oh so proudly built city as it crumbles into a great pool of blood and smoke.

And at the end of a long, long day full of hoarse screams and the hiss of flame, Joshua stands in front of them again, blackened with the ash and smoke of the burning, legs spread in the balanced thrust of the victor, and makes his pronouncement. 'You, woman, hid my messengers. You and your family may live, but I warn you,' and he looks now at the men and the boys, as if the women simply do not hear him, 'Cursed before the Lord be the man that rises up and rebuilds this city, Jericho.'

They can only bow their heads before him in the submission of captives.

But they adjust, curiously well, this family, take on the habits and the rituals of their captors, even intermarry, and slowly forget their initial shame as the blood kin of a harlot. Only Rahab, sitting leather-faced in the door of her tent forty years later, continues to hate Joshua, continues to ponder that moment of her own tactful suicide, when, faced with a choice, she had no choice but to die by her own hand, to die or to die or to die in order to survive. In silence, for she has never liked the tongue of these invaders, she ponders the construction of her bargain then. How did she come to such a pass to seek permission from such monsters, how did she make such a trade-off?

She knew what she knew: she knows it still, nothing can erase the sting of her knowledge. And yet, she subverted herself and her knowledge, as much as declared complicity. And in the choices that were offered that night, in the bargain that she struck on behalf of survival, she knows full well that she self-murder wrote. Rahab does not comfort herself that her choices were no choices. In that moment when she arrived at the nexus between one agent and another, she should have offered them to each other, let them eat each other. She is alive, but still a suicide. She would be more alive if she had died within her city.

And so she sits in the door of her tent, watching the light in the eastern sky, and dreaming of her rooftop and her cool house within the long-since fallen wall of Jericho.

DOROTHY JONES

# Restoring the Temples:
# the Fiction of Aritha van Herk

> And women, we have no temples, they have been razed, the figures of our
> goddesses defaced, mutilated to resemble men, even Athena destroyed. Where do
> you worship when your temples are stolen, when your images are broken and
> erased, when there is only a pressure at the back of your brain to remind you that
> we once had a place to worship. Now lost, leaderless, no mothers, no sisters, we
> wander and search for something we can have no memory of.[1]

'Where do you worship when your temples are stolen?' Scourging out
usurers and usurpers may transform a den of thieves into a house of
prayer, but what if the place of worship and the divinity enshrined there
have been swallowed in oblivion? These are questions Aritha van Herk
addresses in each of her novels, *Judith* (1978), *The Tent Peg* (1981), *No Fixed
Address* (1986), where a young woman's efforts to establish her autonomy
are portrayed in terms of a spiritual quest. Luce Irigaray writes in her
essay 'Divine Women':

> To have a will, it is inescapable to have a goal. The most valuable of which is to
> *become*. Infinitely.[2]

She goes on to say, 'Becoming means to accomplish the plenitude of what
we can be', and continues:

> This is what we need to become: free, autonomous and sovereign. There has never
> been any construction of subjectivity, or of any human society, which has been
> worked through without the help of the divine.[3]

But such help is not readily available for women in a culture where God
has been constructed in man's image, and J.L., heroine of *The Tent Peg*,
castigates that arrogance which has compelled women to worship in
temples of male intellect: 'The forehead of a man is the seat of wisdom,
the place of being, the centre of thought' (p. 172). Irigaray points out that
the unique *masculine* God through whom man seeks to establish his
relationship to the infinite, is quite unsuited to figure the perfection of
*women's* subjectivity.[4]

> Only a God in the feminine can look after and hold for us this margin of liberty and power which would allow us to grow more, to affirm ourselves and to come to self-realisation for each of us and in community. This is our other still to be realised, our beyond and above of life, power, imagination, creation, our possibility of a present and a future.[5]

Aritha van Herk seeks to restore to women a sense of the numinous through reshaping traditional myths of female divinity. Drawing on both classical and biblical sources, she deploys the stories of Circe and Arachne together with legends of such heroic figures as Judith and Jael. An equally important myth underlying her fiction, however, is that of Demeter and Persephone which celebrates the relationship between two women, the desolation of its disruption and the joy of reunion. It figures most prominently in *Judith* but has a significant bearing on the other novels as well. Each heroine, Judith, J.L., Arachne, has a close friend, Mina, Deborah, Thena, who is vitally important to her development – although she contributes little to the narrative action – and an account of their initial meeting, or the moment when they first acknowledge their closeness, occurs mid-point in each novel. The friend, associated in some way with the maternal, becomes a mirror where the heroine discovers her essential self reflected, and their association strikes a divine spark necessary to the accomplishment of the heroic quest.

> Without the possibility, and indeed, the necessity, of a God incarnated in the feminine, through the mother and daughter and in their relation with one another, no substantial help can be given to a woman.[6]

In *Judith*, the quest is circular, as the heroine, striving to become her own woman, abandons life as a farm girl under her father's loving domination for secretarial work in the city, where she becomes the boss's mistress, returning again to the country after her parents' death to establish her own pig farm. In the Greek myth, Persephone, enticed by their beauty, plucks a clump of narcissus, opening up a pathway for Pluto's chariot.[7] Judith, driven from home by dissatisfaction with a life where 'all the women are housewives and all the men are country louts' is lured to the city through hopes of greater independence. But her love-affair, and all it represents, traps her within the routines of office life, forcing her into a standard mould of femininity where she commits 'acts of barbarity' on herself, 'plucking her sleek eyebrows, rolling her straight hair into curls, thrusting golden posts through the holes of her ears',[8] and restricts her bodily freedom by wearing fashionable shoes and dresses. The red M.G. Judith's lover forces upon her is a version of Pluto's chariot, and he himself is a wintry figure who takes her walking into 'the snow-driven wind' as a prelude to seduction. He remains anonymous, yet all-pervasive:

Even so, she saw him everywhere, in shaving-cream ads, in the dark-haired man
three seats down, in someone waiting at a corner for the light to change, briefcase
in hand and trench coat buttoned and precise. So common, she could not rid herself
of his recurring image. (p. 36)

City work offers only a poorly paid, subordinate position where Judith
must depend on her employer both for life's necessities and any available
luxuries, because Pluto, God of the underworld, is also the God of wealth.
    One festival honouring Demeter in ancient Greece, the Thesmophoria,
was celebrated solely by women to ensure the fertility of crops and their
own fecundity.

The casting of pigs sacred to Demeter into subterranean chasms during the course
of the rites, probably represented the descent of Kore into the nether regions of
Pluto, and the bringing up of the putrefied remains of those thrown in the previous
year, placing them on an altar and mixing them with seed-corn to secure a good
crop, was said to commemorate the swallowing up of the swineherd Eubuleus by
the earth when Kore was abducted, and the engulfing of his herd in the chasm. The
festival, therefore, was regarded as an annual commemoration of the Corn-maiden's
descent into the underworld.[9]

Judith takes up her farming enterprise around the beginning of November,
the time of year the Thesmophoria was held. The practical knowledge of
pig-farming gained in her youth, submerged and largely forgotten during
her city years, now revitalizes her life, a fertilizing agent like the pig-flesh
ritually dug out of the earth. Pigs in the ancient world were images both
of female sexuality and of the mother goddess: 'the goddesses are all
great, white, round maternal sows (Ishtar, Isis, Demeter, etc.)',[10] and in
*Judith* the pig-barn resembles a temple of female divinity:

...Judith entered the barn's loomy redolence eagerly. She was whole here, a part of
their tumescent sanctuary of female warmth. It was that, their femaleness, the subtle
scent that lifted from beneath their alert tails, surrounding her like a soothing
conspiracy. Expectant, they pressed forward against their fences, eyes glowing
under the naked light bulbs. Transformed and spellbinding they surrounded her
like priestesses of her creed. They had been waiting for her. (p. 48)

    The pigs exercise a magical transformation on Judith who herself
becomes an enchantress figure able to transform her own world. In
attempts to understand her metamorphosis, she scrutinizes herself from
time to time in the mirror, a symbol of that obsession with appearances
society induces in women and which Irigaray regards as yet another
barrier separating them from their own divinity.

...their duty to deck themselves out, to mask themselves, make-up etc. instead of
letting *their* physical, corporal beauty appear, their skin, her/their form(s), all this
is symptomatic of an absence, for them, of a feminine god who opens up for them
the perspective of a transfiguration of *their* flesh.[11]

Judith is alarmed to see her mother's face reflected in her own:

> Now her face was pale and colorless, hair short and ragged. More familiar than any image of herself, her mother's motion of passing her hand over her face, erasing something there. And it was her mother's face, smooth and younger, looking back at her from the mirror.
>
> 'Can I go outside now?' Her mother turned from the mirror on the wall, fingers pursing her lips, hand moving from brow to chin, wearily molding it back, back into place. She touched her hair nervously then sighed. 'Sweep the floor first, Judy.'
>
> And after she swept the floor she ran outside and held her face into the wind, knowing it would never be like her mother's, she would never try to smooth it clear like that, so desperate and exposed. (pp. 35-6)

Unlike Persephone, who is released from Pluto's clutches through Demeter's efforts, Judith must discover in herself the determination to escape her captivity, for her mother can reflect only the conventional role model of female subservience.

> We look at ourselves in the mirror in order to *please someone*. Rarely to interrogate the state of our body or 'soul', rarely for us, and with an eye to our becoming.[12]

One of the novel's epigrams comes from *Through the Looking Glass*, and Judith must learn to move through the mirror to discover on the other side a world where even 'pigs have wings'.

She finds her true reflection in Mina Stanby, wife of a neighbouring farmer. Their first meeting occurs the same night as the birth of the first piglets which promises the success of Judith's venture. Although Mina sometimes resembles Judith's now dead mother -'Just so her mother had stood' (p. 56) – she does not in her heart submit to the traditional female role: 'She moved as if she were the only woman in the house yet free from it' (p. 52). The bonds of friendship deepen so that Judith represents the daughter whom Mina, with three grown sons, never succeeded in having. On the afternoon Mina comes to the barn, watching as Judith helps another sow to farrow, the two acknowledge they are kindred spirits, each with an emotional stake in the farming enterprise which symbolises the assertion of female space, independence and autonomy.

> ...Judith slid over the fence again, bent to scrub her bloody hands with straw. She hesitated, then blindly thrust her right hand toward Mina. Eyes following relentlessly, the pigs saw Mina get to her feet, take Judith's hand in both her own and hold it there, the two of them caught together in the incantation of their joining. (pp. 93-4)

The handclasp, representing the embrace of Demeter and Persephone, is followed by a succession of butterfly images. Judith is in flight from the netherworld where the girls she worked with had resembled 'pretty grubs, white and dead' and her own body lying beneath her lover had seemed 'pale and grub-like'. Her emergence from the chrysalis is suggested by the paper on her bedroom wall, with its design of oriental butterflies, resembling a dress she had worn in childhood on which butterflies floated 'like exotic orchids that would surround her in undiscovered mysteries'. A richly sensual image, the butterflies also symbolise aspiration and transcendence. To achieve fulfilment, Judith must re-establish contact with her childhood self. As a child she ran downstairs with a 'movement so practised it was almost like flying', and the adult Judith lies down in the newly fallen snow, moving her arms and legs to make the pattern of a winged angel, just as when she was a little girl. The paradox by which she achieves her wings through pig-farming is alluded to in van Herk's choice of epigraphs.

'The time has come,' the Walrus said,
   'To talk of many things:
Of shoes – and ships – and sealing-wax –
   Of cabbages – and kings –
And why the sea is boiling hot –
   And whether pigs have wings.'
                    *Through the Looking Glass*
                    Lewis Carroll

There is a herb in father's garden,
Some calls it maidens' rue:
When pigs they do fly like swallows in the sky,
Then the young men they'll prove true.
                    An old English folk song

Although flying pigs traditionally signify impossibility, a determined and aspiring young woman might well become airborne. Butterflies are summer creatures, and the novel ends in spring with Judith and Mina watching Judith's newly acquired boar mount one of the sows as the cycle of regeneration begins yet again.

And together they laughed, those insane women, laughed at everything they could and as hard as they could as they danced about in the melting snow. (p. 178)

The story of Demeter and Persephone has accumulated a great wealth of literary association over the centuries, but until very recently, it has been mediated almost entirely through male culture. Some writers have focused on the image of female vulnerability. For Milton, Persephone is analogous to Eve in all her frailty:

...that fair field,
Of Enna, where Proserpin gathering flowers,
Herself a fairer flower, by gloomy Dis
Was gathered, which cost Ceres all that pain

To seek her through the world,...[13]

But Persephone, in her role as Queen of Death, also serves as an image of the *femme fatale* gathering helpless men within her dangerous embrace.

Pale beyond porch and portal,
Crowned with calm leaves she stands
Who gathers all things mortal
With cold immortal hands
Her languid lips are sweeter
Than love's who fears to greet her
To men that mix and meet her
From many times and lands.[14]

Sarah Pomeroy complains that in classical myth even goddesses are 'archetypal images of human females, as envisaged by males' - Athena, the asexual career woman, Aphrodite, the frivolous sex object, Hera, the respectable wife and mother. Not even a female divinity was considered sufficiently complex to combine all these capacities: 'A fully realized female tends to engender anxiety in the insecure male.'[15] Roland Barthes argues that myth has a depoliticizing function, 'purifying' representations of human relations so that artfully contrived social structures appear natural and eternal.[16] Although the Homeric Hymn to Demeter of the seventh century B.C. stresses the bond between mother and daughter, even suggesting that natural growth and fertility depend on its maintenance (since Demeter curses the earth with barrenness until Persephone is restored), it also implies that, just as all human beings inevitably die, so a young woman will naturally be caught up in a male embrace severing her from the world of women. It is perhaps significant that, even from a male point of view, wifehood should be equated with death! Mary Lefkowitz laments the very limited scope classical mythology allows to female experience. Once female figures in myth accomplish the *rite de passage* into adulthood, very few options are allowed them:

If they choose to marry, they may either die themselves or kill their husbands and/or children. If they choose to remain celibate, they must do men's work or become frozen in some aspect of their maiden state; for example they turn into trees. There are no other possibilities![17]

Lefkowitz concedes, however, that Persephone is something of an exception. She can survive marriage as an individual because she is, 'in a sense, recycled', spending only part of each year with her husband and living the rest of the time in Olympus with Demeter, becoming a maiden daughter again.[18] It is not surprising, therefore, that a number of modern feminist theorists and writers have sought to repoliticize this particular myth. Mary Daly and Adrienne Rich frequently focus on it in ways which suggest it could be a continuing symbol for women in contemporary society: '...every mother must have longed for the power of Demeter, the efficacy of her anger, the reconciliation with her lost self'.[19] The myth is valuable, not only because of its celebratory aspect, but because it also offers an opportunity to explore situations where women are divided from one another, their vital energies suppressed.

Aritha van Herk engages in such exploration in *The Tent Peg*, while at the same time exalting female strength and creativity. In *Judith* the Greek myth reflects a process of initiation. The action, both past and present, occurs almost entirely in the winter months and only at the end of the novel, when Judith's personal triumph is complete, do we emerge into spring. *The Tent Peg* is a summer narrative, even if it is a cold summer spent in 'The middle of the Wernecke mountains in an alpine valley that never feels summer, just varying shades of winter' (p. 42). Like Judith, the heroine, J.L., moves from city to country to work as cook in a geological survey camp in the Yukon, the only woman in a group of nine men. J.L. is more seasoned, more of an initiate, than Judith when she leaves her student existence in Edmonton, cynically dismissing a whole array of lovers. But she has also established a deep and sustaining friendship there with Deborah, a singer, to whom she confides in letters her sense of loss and alienation as she seeks to function within an entirely male world.

For the greater part of the novel J.L. resembles Demeter, the corn goddess, rather than Persephone. As cook, she assumes a traditional female role: 'we know the smoothest, most efficient way of making food and giving food and clearing up the remains of food, nourishers always' (p. 59). But cooking, like alchemy, involves transformation, and in the novel J.L. is endowed with transforming power. Her presence is the catalyst enabling Mackenzie, the team leader, to discover rich gold deposits in a survey area which proves deficient in the uranium the geologists were directed to search for. She effects her greatest transformation, however, among those she works with, evoking admiration, affection and even reverence from men who initially regard her with resentment, suspicion or amusement. The cook tent, a place of abundance filled with the 'rich, yeasty smell' of bread-making, becomes a sanctuary – comparable to the pig-barn in *Judith* – where J.L. presides as priestess, the meals she serves coming to resemble a eucharist. Like her biblical namesake Jael, who killed the Canaanite captain, Sisera, by driving a tent peg through his temple, nailing him to the ground as he slept, she also breaks open the sleeping temples, penetrating the complacency of her male companions to create new awareness and self-knowledge.[20] What in the old testament is a deed of savage cruelty becomes a redemptive act, essential to restoring those temples of female divinity whose destruction J.L. laments.

In both cookery and alchemy, fire is the agent of transformation, and just as the lighted torch was one of Demeter's traditional attributes,[21] so flame is a principal metaphor associated with J.L.: 'She holds enough anger inside her to burn a person right through'. Franklin, one of the geologists, regards her as 'A candle clear to fix my thoughts upon' (p. 80), while Milton, the young Menonite farm boy, illumined by a glimpse of J.L.'s naked body, compares her to a lamp: 'And her body is alight, it reflects a heat and radiance that I never thought bodies could possess. Luminous glass, perfectly turned' (p. 211). Mackenzie perceives her similarly: 'She turned herself inside my hands, with each movement the porcelain quality of her skin, more luminous, as if my hands could ignite a light within her' (p. 213). Fire is also a cleansing agent, and at J.L.'s instigation the men light a campfire each night where they burn the day's garbage. It draws them into a circle, helping fend off the outer darkness.

> Now, around the fire, we are one voice rising and falling, a group of men in unison with the bony shadow of a woman weaving a spell. (p. 152)

As Demeter, taking the role of nurse at Eleusis during her separation from Persephone, tries to render the princely child Demophoon immortal by thrusting him into the heart of the fire each night, so J.L. attempts to purge her companions of their arrogance, fear and insensitivity.

But she also knows how readily an assertive, visionary woman may herself be consigned to the flames like another Joan of Arc, and along with all women she carries on her back a bundle of faggots which could fuel her own immolation.

> I've tried to throw it off, fling it to the ground and abandon it, but although I sometimes lose a stick or two, the weight is still there, old myths and old lovers, old duties, my mother's warning voice, my infallible conscience. (p. 37)

Fending off the remorseless encroachments of the male world, J.L. struggles continually to preserve her sense of self intact. In the novel's central episode, a grizzly bear visits the camp with her cubs in tow and two of the crew watch in terror as J.L. stands only a few feet away apparently conversing with her. The sight of the creature, like a furious demonic power rising from the earth, fuses with memories of her friend Deborah, constantly under pressure because her beauty makes her so vulnerable to male predators. The encounter is an epiphany, comparable to the handclasp between Mina and Judith in the barn, for as J.L. faces the bear she recognizes that her love for Deborah is the primary source of strength in her own life, enabling her to endure her present situation. Once again, women friends re-enact the union of Demeter and Persephone. Deborah is identified with the maternal figure of the bear accompanied by her two cubs, which is, in turn, associated with Mackenzie's wife, Janice, who ten years earlier had taken their two

children and left him without any explanation in an act of desperate
self-assertion.

> She left for herself. You were a good man but you couldn't give that to her, it had
> nothing to do with you. It was herself she was after and the only way she could
> find that was by leaving. (p. 202)

Jancie's departure is also associated with the rockslide which occurs one
night as a substantial portion of the mountain above the camp collapses:
'it must have been like a rockslide to her, the suddenness, the enormity of
it. One small trickle of pebbles taking half a lifetime with it' (p. 130). J.L.
describes the earth as giving birth to herself (p. 137), and like the bear,
with which it is associated, the dangerous, shifting Yukon landscape
embodies a ferocious female energy, so that it becomes the dominant
maternal figure in the novel with which the various women characters are
identified as they discover sources of power within themselves.

In van Herk's use of the Greek myth, Demeter and Persephone are
interchangeable. Although J.L. is associated with Demeter, especially in
her yearning to see Deborah again, she has, like Persephone, emerged
from an underworld captivity where she had been fettered by 'the
growing chain of men who rattle and clink behind me' (p. 113). Hope of
release comes to her deep in the stacks of the University Library, although
the messenger of liberation is not Hermes, but Jamesie, a former lover
who complains in disgust: 'Why don't you go live in the Arctic? Who
would miss you?' (p. 24). J.L. recognizes that she and Deborah share a
common identity: 'Perhaps that's why they call us Siamese friends. The
one is wearing the other's costume, we are forever and irrevocably
intertwined' (p. 190). Because both confront the same problem of male
dominance, each must in turn provide strength and nurture for the other.
But Deborah is not just a friend in whom J.L. sees herself reflected, she is
also an artist: 'That voice could make shape of chaos, give tongue to every
unarticulated secret and intuition' (p. 11), and it is she who, in the words
of the biblical prophetess celebrating Jael's victory over Sisera, hymns
J.L.'s triumph over the camp bully, Jerome. Through her vision, the
woman artist creates the image of what women might be, holding up to
female recipients of her art a mirror reflecting their own potential. In this
respect the woman artist is Demeter, delivering the daughter she has
created out of the bondage of obscurity.

But the act of creation is never complete. J.L.'s triumph is substantial, yet
temporary, for as summer ends, she must move on still enclosed by the
framework of a patriarchal society designed to thwart every impulse to
self-determination. Nevertheless, she transforms the final bonfire on which
the survey team burn the remains of their camp into a celebratory ritual,
dancing on the kitchen table before it subsides into the flames. She rejects
the role of Joan of Arc, saint and martyr, to assume that of pagan

priestess, transforming the attendant circle of men as the summer burns
beneath her feet.

> For a moment I can pretend I am Deborah celebrating myself, victory, peace
> regained. And in their faces I see my transfiguration, themselves transformed, each
> one with the tent peg through the temple cherishing the knowledge garnered in
> sleep, in unwitting trust. (p. 226)

Demeter and Persephone, the artist and her creation, are identified in the
moment of triumph. Just as Judith's victorious emergence from the
underworld is associated with images of butterflies in flight, so J.L.
dancing among the flames resembles the immortal phoenix arising from
the funeral pyre she has ignited through the force of her own wings. The
immolating flames are now the refiner's fire in which a new spirit is
forged.

*Judith* and *The Tent Peg* transform a traditional myth into a container for
women's perception of who they are and what they might become. But
both heroines must continue to struggle in a hostile society to preserve
their victories and their vision of female friendship. Because the story of
Demeter and Persephone is a metaphor of seasonal change, joy in the
reunion of the two goddesses is tempered by knowledge that they must
part again. In *No Fixed Address*, however, Aritha van Herk, while still
asserting the image of female divinity, breaks the myth wide open to
release her heroine from a situation where achievement and loss alternate
so remorselessly. Arachne who 'has always hammered against the
impossible: fate, birth, life',[22] battles not only the male world, but pushes
against the constraints of human existence itself. The picaresque narrative
moves with an intricate, spiderwebbing motion through the heroine's past,
present and future, tracing the process by which she has emerged from
life as a tough, streetwise kid growing up in East Vancouver into the
prosperous new existence she enjoys in Calgary when she is first
introduced to the reader. She lives happily with Thomas, her 'Apocryphal
lover', so perceptive and accommodating he is almost too good to be true,
and she delights in her job as sales representative selling women's panties
to stores in the country towns of Alberta and Saskatchewan for a firm
called Ladies Comfort. But, despite this, Arachne remains restless, seeking
scope for greater self-development than even her present existence
permits.

This tension is reflected in the opening pages by images of
imprisonment and mortality which also point to the motif of Persephone
in the underworld. The novel is prefaced by a meditation on female
underwear throughout the centuries: 'It was for a long time taken for
granted that woman's body should be prisoner, taped and measured and
controlled' (p. 10). Now that underwear has been relegated 'to the casual
and unimportant' some measure of liberation has been attained, and the

narrative next focuses on Arachne, seller of underwear who wears none herself. Even though she purveys comfort to ladies – cool easy to care for cotton – together with imaginative stimulus and sensual enticement – bikinis in galvanic, fruit, peppermint and ice-cream colours – her work is linked with time and death. She must always carry the black 'midnight line', along with that other very popular item, the boxed set of coloured panties each embroidered with a different day of the week, and to do her job efficiently she must appear 'dead ordinary'. Early in the novel Arachne visits a cemetery where she meets Josef, an old Yugoslav immigrant. Persephone was swept down into the underworld through plucking a handful of flowers, and Arachne yearns to lie among flowers and merge with the earth: 'There is a field of rape down the road. Let the yellow close over her...' (p. 17).[23] Because of his great age (he is almost ninety) and the persistence with which he tracks down Arachne, it seems that Josef might be death's emissary, especially when, after their first meeting he seeks out her hotel room:

> He bends, slides one arm between her bare legs, the other around her shoulders, and picks her up, holding her above... in an iron embrace. (p. 29)

But, in reaching out to Arachne, Josef is holding fast to life, and through their passionate sexual encounters, the two establish an alliance against death. Instead of Pluto abducting Persephone, it is Arachne, defying propriety, law and reason, who eventually kidnaps Josef from the nursing home to which his relatives consign him. This bid for freedom inevitably fails; with the police on her tail, she flees westward, her flourishing Calgary life in ruins, and the novel gives no clear indication of Josef's ultimate fate.

Judith's spiritual journey moves in a circle from country childhood, to the city and back, and *The Tent Peg* implies J.L. will complete her circle by returning to Edmonton, although the novel suggests she may travel further. Arachne's return to the rain-filled streets of her Vancouver childhood, while concluding one cycle of existence, precipitates a further journey with no foreseen ending. Throughout the book, images of stasis and stickiness carry negative connotations. Escaping from Calgary's comfortable middle-class world which has her 'tied and tagged', Arachne finds herself temporarily trapped in Banf National Park: 'she has one of the famous yellow stickers with the miniature beaver looking at its tail stuck inside her wind shield distracting her vision; she has to stay, she has the sticker' (p. 241). The temptation to cease moving, which regularly assails her, is expressed in terms of subsiding underground into the male embrace of death, of taking her place within the traditional male-oriented myth. Leaving Banf, she falls in with a mildly satanic ex-coalminer, Dougal McKay, who tries to sell her a disused mine, entry into the netherworld: 'The foul reticent portal mouthing earth' (p. 267). Pluto-like, he helps her attain wealth, only to cheat her again, so she must later ambush him to repossess it. When, after an all night drinking session with McKay and his friend Frank, Arachne wakes in foetid darkness, locked between two drunken male bodies, it requires a mighty effort of resurrection to break out of this lightless burrow.

Constant movement is the keynote of Arachne's character and driving is her regular escape-route; the fat black 1959 Mercedes Type 300 she inherits in adolescence is a 'four-speed ticket to flight' (p. 161), symbolising control over her own life: 'She loves that car more than herself' (p. 315). Significantly, the description of receiving her inheritance, interwoven with an account of how she met her best friend Thena, comes mid-point in the novel. The two women come across each other in the garage which services the Mercedes, for female friendship is a driving force in women's search for autonomy. Although the Demeter and Persephone motif remains highly significant, mother/daughter relationships in *No Fixed Address* are presented as problematic. Thena's two teenage daughters reject her feminist values: 'They mince to school, they experiment with makeup, they are themselves' (p. 143), while Arachne maintains an armed truce with her own mother, Lanie, accepting her hostility and indifference because 'She and Lanie wanted the same thing' (p. 41). But although a patriarchal world divides women so that a daughter's mere existence may impede the mother's freedom, the identification between women characters is even more important than in van Herk's previous novels. Thena, 'a mirror for others' and the candle which illumines (p. 59), is the heroine's alter-ego, and Arachne's more outrageous exploits are sometimes tempered by recollections of her shrewd commonsense. Other women characters also reflect or project the female energy and aspiration embodied in the heroine. She hears a famous feminist, priestess and 'golden Amazon' (p. 251) address a women's conference, and meets a woman artist with eyes of different colours and hair half blonde, half brunette, who proves a figure of heroic confidence: 'I'm going to take up sculpture and chisel a statue of Isis out of Mount Lougheed' (p. 247). Arachne, hair now dyed blonde in an attempt at disguise, also meets her *doppelgänger*, a hitch-hiking sales representative who peddles snuff and claims to be a failed poet. Despite their different hair colour, each exactly mirrors the other, and together they correspond to the figure of the halved artist. Society may often drive women apart and subdue their inner being, but they can still hope to be made whole through discovering other women whose lives reflect what theirs might become

This pattern of women's lives echoing, reflecting or paralleling one another is important to the image of female divinity van Herk constructs within her novel. Despite their individual limitations, Lanie, Thena and Arachne together, three generations of women, represent the Great Goddess, venerated long before the establishment of the Greek pantheon, in her triple aspect of crone, child-bearing woman and virgin.[24] Thena's name links her to the goddess Athena, irreverently challenged in legend to a contest of skill by the cunning weaver, Arachne, whom she transformed into a spider for her presumption.[25] But van Herk's Arachne is also a manifestation of Athena, just as Persephone and Demeter are reflections one of the other, and her career also incorporates allusions to Christian myth. Lanie, exhausted after her daughter's birth, exclaims to her husband: 'Christ, Toto' (p. 84). Arachne's paternity is doubtful, and the mysterious visitor who effectively names her and bequeaths the car so necessary to fulfil her potential, is called Gabriel. She performs her ministry by selling panties for ladies' comfort and delight, and after leaving Calgary she undergoes more than one symbolic death and resurrection. In a Vancouver sushi bar she is served a eucharistic meal, a kind of last supper of sliced fish arranged on the plate to resemble a spider, and as she eats Arachne is released from all the worlds she has ever known, dying both to her blighted childhood and to the love and joy of her limited and limiting Calgary existence.

After three months of oblivion, she finds herself on a ferry crossing the Strait of Georgia. If Judith represents Kore, the maiden abducted by Pluto, and J.L. signifies Demeter, goddess of growth and fruition, then Arachne is Persephone, queen of the dead, for the dyad of mother and daughter forms part of the more ancient triad of the Great Goddess.[26] Arachne challenges mortality itself, piercing to the heart a man who tries to molest her on the ferry, representative of Charon transporting souls into the realm of death, and she continues her harrowing of Hell by summoning from the waters off Long Beach a drowned airman with whom she vigorously makes love. Female energy cannot yet find its full expression within the boundaries of existing society, and Arachne, her movement west halted by the sea, returns to the mainland and begins driving north into a frontier world where past, present and future merge – a visionary realm symbolised by the 'four-dimensional nothingness' of Canada's frozen north. What women may become is still unexplored and potentially dangerous territory. Arachne's narrative ends with her Ascension as a group of geologists she has met on the road bundle her into a helicopter, piloted by a woman. (Perhaps she is J.L. back in the Yukon fulfilling her ambition, hinted at in *The Tent Peg*, to become a professional flier?) When the road gives out, only flight is possible: 'She watches the roadless world below her, knowing she has arrived'.

Once again flight is a metaphor of female triumph, but it involves Arachne's departure from the everyday world, leaving the other women characters, like the feminist conference speaker who can 'lift worlds' with her eloquence, and the woman artist who portrays 'Revolution. Kitchens', to perpetuate her story and celebrate what she represents. The woman artist is a divided figure because she must reflect both Arachne and her *doppelgänger* – the possibility of brilliant achievement on the one hand, and on the other, the plodding endurance necessary to maintain independence and autonomy. Lanie and Thena are also artist figures. As a fortune-teller, Lanie employs literary skills of intuition and imagination, and Thena, the only person to whom Arachne speaks truly about herself, reads her friend so she can eventually tell her story: 'Every adventuress requires a teller of her tale, an armchair companion to complete the eventualities' (p. 146). The shadowy narrator figure whom we encounter throughout the novel is also dependent on Thena (to whom in some respects she corresponds) as a principal source of information about Arachne. Her research into the history and social implications of female underwear prompts her to seek the legendary seller of panties, and her reflections on the situation are expressed in italicized passages interpolated throughout the novel. She is yet another representative of the woman artist pursuing an ideal of female transcendence with which she cannot quite make contact, for she and Arachne never actually meet, and the novel concludes with her driving north following a never-ending trail of Ladies Comfort panties. For women confined within a restrictive society, Arachne represents inspiration and hope. She is the Comforter who sustains their endeavours, and whose possible second coming may inaugurate a new heaven and a new earth.

Just as in *The Tent Peg* Deborah the artist and J.L. the heroine she celebrates are twinned characters, each reflecting the other, so in *No Fixed Address* the fictional narrator, travelling the routes first traced by Arachne, is strongly identified with the complex directions of her life. The figure of Arachne, the picara, whose story inevitably assumes the form of a journey, has much in common with Luce Irigaray's view of the divine: 'A mode of self-completion without finality'.[27]

> Can we forego will without dying? It seems impossible. One has to want something. It is vitally, not morally, necessary to want something. It is the condition of our becoming. To have a will it is indispensable to have a goal. The most valuable of which is to *become*. Infinitely.[28]

Demeter's search for Persephone and their seasonal reunions are echoed by various incidents in *No Fixed Address*, but the search for the goddess, represented by the narrator's endless pursuit of Arachne, is also a framing device which serves as a metaphor of the novelist's activity. Through the power of imagination, the woman artist draws on myth and legend to recreate the image of female divinity which has been so long lost or suppressed. In doing so, she identifies with her creation, releasing the divinity within herself, a continuing process with no foreseeable conclusion: 'There is no end to the panties; there will be no end to this road' (p. 319).

Becoming means to accomplish the plenitude of what we can be. This trajectory is, of course, never achieved. Are we more perfect than we were in the past? It's not certain.[29]

In her novels, van Herk suggests women must continually struggle to free themselves from 'the norms, ideals and fantasies imposed on them by phallocentrism',[30] turning away from the mirror which sends back flat, superficial images: 'The mirror freezes our becoming through breath, our becoming through space'.[31] Only at those moments when a woman's life touches the lives of other women who share her aspirations will she discover a true reflection of what she herself can become, and it is at such moments the nature of female divinity is most potently revealed.

## Notes

1. Aritha van Herk, *The Tent Peg* (Toronto: McClelland and Stewart, 1981), pp. 172-3. Further references are incorporated in the text.
2. Luce Irigaray, *Divine Women*, tr. Stephen Muecke, Local Consumption, Occasional Paper 8 (Sydney: Local Consumption Press, 1986), p. 4. I am indebted to my colleague Dr Anne Cranny Francis for drawing my attention to this paper.
3. *Ibid.*, p. 4.
4. *Ibid.*, p. 6.
5. *Ibid.*, pp. 12-13.
6. *Ibid.*, p. 12.
7. See *The Homeric Hymns*, II, 'To Demeter', tr. Hugh G. Evelyn-White (London: Heineman, 1974), pp. 289 - 91.
8. Aritha van Herk, *Judith* (Toronto: McClelland and Steward, 1978), p. 166. Further references are incorporated in the text.
9. E.O.James, *The Ancient Gods* (N.Y.: Capricorn Books, 1964), p. 161. Persephone is sometimes referred to as Kore or Proserpine and Pluto as Dis.
10. Nor Hall, *The Moon and the Virgin* (London: Women's Press, 1980), p. 82. van Herk also draws on the Circe myth in *Judith*. For a discussion of this, see Dorothy Jones, 'A Kingdom and a Place of Exile': Women Writers and the World of Nature', *WLWE* (vol.24, no. 2, 1984), pp. 269-271.
11. Irigaray, *op. cit.*, p. 6.
12. *Ibid*, p. 7.
13. Milton, *Paradise Lost*, IV, ll. 269-272.
14. Algernon Charles Swinburne, 'The Garden of Proserpine', ll. 49-56.
15. Sarah B. Pomeroy, *Goddesses, Whores, Wives, and Slaves: Women in Classical Antiquity* (N.Y.: Schocken Books, 1975), p. 8.
16. Roland Barthes, *Mythologies*, trans. by Annette Lavers (St. Albans: Paladin, 1972), p. 143.
17. Mary R. Lefkowitz, *Heroines and Hysterics* (London: Duckworth, 1981), p. 42.
18. *Ibid.*, p. 43.
19. Adrienne Rich, *Of Woman Born* (N.Y.: Bantam Books, 1976), p. 243.
20. The story is found in *Judges*, chapters 4 and 5.
21. Erich Neumann, *The Great Mother*, tr. Ralph Mannheim (London: Routledge & Kegan Paul, 1955), p. 311.

22. Aritha van Herk, *No Fixed Address* (Toronto: McClelland and Stewart, 1986), p. 142. Further references are incorporated in the text.

23. Arachne's second meeting with Josef is also preceded by a visit to another cemetery where she picks a yellow buffalo bean to add to the pile of flowers on a new grave. (See *NFA*, p. 150).

24. The future Lanie predicts for Arachne is 'Pleasure, virtue, riches, virgin... watch the signs for what's emergin', (p. 49), since in the ancient world a goddess's virginity signified her independence and autonomy rather than abstention from sexuality. See Esther Harding, *Women's Mysteries* (London: Rider, 1982), pp. 103-4.

25. The principal classical source is Ovid's *Metamorphoses*, book six. For fuller discussion of van Herk's use of the Athena myth, see Dorothy Jones, 'The Spider and the Rose: Aritha van Herk's *No Fixed Address*', *WLWE* (vol. 27, no 1, 1987), pp. 50-55.

26. Neumann, *op. cit.*, p. 319.

27. Liz Gross, *Irigaray and the Divine*, Local Consumption, Occasional Paper 9, (Sydney: Local Consumption Press, 1986), p. 12.

28. Irigaray, *op. cit.*, p. 4.

29. *Ibid.*, p. 4.

30. Gross, *op. cit.*, p. 15.

31. Irigaray, *op. cit.*, p. 7.

ISABEL CARRERA

# *Caprice* and *No Fixed Address*: Playing with Gender and Genre.

Contemporary Canadian writing is rich in texts that break the boundaries of genre and gender. The postmodern character of many of these texts often accounts for the former, while the latter is almost inevitably linked to feminist awareness. Women's writing has explored the possibilities of trespassing, of crossing literary borders and of subverting conventions in many areas, but the insistence of feminist discourse has also produced its effects in male writing. This is exemplified by many of Robert Kroetsch's texts, for instance, which are relevant here as an intertext with the two novels we are about to discuss: Aritha van Herk's *No Fixed Address* (1986) and George Bowering's *Caprice* (1987).[1] These are only two of the travelling women who inhabit recent Canadian narrative, mapping out the country while exploring the limits of a particular fictional genre.

*Caprice* and *No Fixed Address* are novels in which a male-centred narrative genre is transformed and deconstructed by the presence of a female protagonist. Not surprisingly, as they are usurping a man's role, both protagonists are women of action. Caprice rides around the British Columbia interior and across the border seeking to revenge her dead brother, shot by (American) Frank Spencer. Arachne goes through successive episodes and jobs in her native Vancouver until we meet her as a sales rep, making good business out of selling women's underwear to stores all over Alberta, and keeping herself amused with the road-jockeys she encounters on her way. While the first enacts a tale of the western, the second is so clearly a picaresque hero that one (or certainly a Spanish 'one') wonders how some of van Herk's early reviewers managed to overlook the fact.

The similarities between the two texts immediately invite comparison. Both are dominated by the presence of the main, female, character, whose gender is enhanced by her subversive or incongruous incursion in male territory. The women's physique is correspondingly impressive and unconventional. Neither treads lightly on the ground: they beat it with their feet, they thump, and heads are turned. Their eyes are of unusual colours, green in one case, grey in the other. Arachne's gaze can pin one down, her body language is a challenge. Caprice has bright red hair and freckles, and her tallness is an imposing feature. The emblematic means of transport adds to their uniqueness: Caprice's Spanish-born black steed, *Cabayo*, and Arachne's black vintage Mercedes attract quite as much attention as their owners; it is, of course, their combination with a female that makes animal and vehicle so extraordinary. The uniqueness of the women is finally represented in their names, Caprice and Arachne Manteia.

The movement of these two women, criss-crossing the west of Canada, falls within the collective task of mapping and inscribing the area in literature, a task to which other Prairie and West-Coast authors have contributed in the past. Van Herk and Bowering's texts show signs of the common geographic and cultural ground inhabited by the authors. Theirs is a literary space whose roads often intersect – hence the intersection of their narratives, which share a parodic, self-conscious, intertextual approach which thoroughly enjoys the game of literature and assumes a reader who participates of the enjoyment. The narrator moves between the omniscience of the third person and the direct involvement of the reader/narratee in the second person. Both novels are writer-reader texts, making full use of the participants in the communicative chain, with concessions to the reader balanced out by the authors' own visitation of the text, Bowering including his own poems and his persona, G. Delsing; van Herk in her self-portrait as the woman artist towards the end of the novel, and possibly in the italicized section, ambiguously the reader/author's voice.

However, the emphasis on the combination of gender and genre remains the closest link between the novels. And yet it is precisely the tension between these two elements that separates them and makes the protagonists of the narratives (and the narratives themselves) more radically different than would appear at first sight. If Caprice and Arachne are to be true to the genre that each inhabits, their discourse (their selves) must differ; but perhaps more important is the fact that the gender of the author (implied or 'real'), and the gender of the *story-maker* embedded in their stories, have already conditioned the separation.

George Bowering's *Caprice* is a remodelling of the western, a genre which is not only male-centred in subject-matter but also the cliché of popular male reading. Its female counterpart is popular romance. The picaresque, in its traditional formula, contains examples of females, but their discourses are usually filtered through the moralizing voice of a male narrator or the exemplary outcome of their adventures, which are in any case limited by their gender. It is only in the 20th century that a few *pícaras* begin to speak freely. But even today, the genre in its modified form is strongly associated with mobile men, as shown in the fact that *No Fixed Address* was immediately compared to Kerouac's *On the Road* and, nearer home, Kroetsch's *The Studhorse Man*.

A panoramic study of the evolution of the picaresque[2] shows that the genre has slowly moved away from history towards romance. *No Fixed*

*Address* is subtitled *An Amorous Journey*, and the character Caprice is
defined in her own story as 'romance': 'It may be simply your room, as
far as you're concerned, Miss Caprice,' says the journalist of the
Austro-Hungarian Empire, 'but for the literate people of the empire it will
be legend. It will be history. Most important, perhaps, it will be romance'
(p. 171). While neither Bowering nor van Herk may have had in mind
popular romance in writing their novels, it is interesting to note a second
genre embedded in them both: a quest which touches on the various
definitions of romance, as if the attempt to make the western or the
picaresque female-centred, attracted such a subgenre.

The gendered author and reader expected of the western and of romance
would appear to be reflected in the authors and reviewers of these two
novels, as shown in their treatment of the main characters. Two Canadian
critics, writers themselves, seem to confirm expectations at the reception
end, and to sense them in the production: 'I love her [...]' writes Stan
Dragland of Caprice, 'and I think Bowering loves her too.' Constance
Rooke, on her part, says of Arachne 'I loved her, and I loved the writer's
fondness for her.'[3] The writers' presence is hard to resist in these novels.
Van Herk has spoken about her creation of strong female characters: 'I like
tough women, who can act. I'm also interested in the woman as a trickster
figure. [...] I'm interested in showing female characters that are images of
what women can do, the possibilities of the world. And I don't apologise
for them not being realistic.'[4] The statement underlines the suitability of
the picaresque to her purpose and her preference.

George Bowering, for his part, has explained the birth of the idea of
*Caprice*: 'I noticed two things about the western: one, that they were all
very male-centred, and, two, that it always has something to do with dry
land. [...] And so I said O.K., I want to make a western which is
female-centred. I would just turn everything around – that way it is not
just a parody, but an investigation of a western, putting it on trial,
almost.'[5] Thus his purpose relates firstly to genre, then to gender, although
a woman is essential (or perhaps instrumental) in the process. His own
fondness for his creation is perfectly credible, as we shall see, in terms of
fantasy.

Arachne and Caprice have been described by their reviewers as female
and male fantasies respectively, and their paperback (Canadian) editions
include commentary to this effect. One of the early male reviewers of *No
Fixed Address* declared, incensed at this 'feminist diatribe', that Arachne no
doubt fulfilled some women's fantasies like Mike Hammer fulfilled some
men's.[6] The back cover of the Penguin edition of *Caprice* quotes *The
Winnipeg Free Press*: 'Caprice herself seems to have galloped out of Mr
Bowering's sexual fantasies.' Allowing for some truth in the appreciation
of the characters as author-reader's fantasies, the above description would
make of Arachne the *subject* of a fantasy, with whom the female
author-reader may identify; the remark about Caprice, in contrast, makes

her the object of the fantasy of the author, thus pointing towards a crucial factor of differentiation between Caprice and Arachne.

Caprice's physical appearance is certainly suggestive of depictions of women in certain types of male fantasy literature. Larger than life, provided with loud boot heels and soft leather gloves, she sports a large whip and, as we are repeatedly told by various onlookers, her breasts *do not bounce*. Furthermore, her perfect thighs are 'not ruined by that lateral bulge of flesh that sometimes makes women's trousers look like breeches' (p. 119). A contemporary model of beauty indeed, riding on a horse and equipped, as said, with a whip. Bowering explains that he chose the whip as the singular weapon required by the genre because he 'did not want her to be a gunperson'.[7] One can see that such a symbolic inversion would be rather disturbing. This figure, out of yet another subgenre, male popular romance/comic magazine/pornography, is mostly silent, though she has the added attraction of a slight foreign accent (she comes from Quebec), and the must of contemporary intellectual fantasy; she is a beauty endowed with brains: a poet, a creator of wor(l)ds. This latter part of the fantasy is fittingly reserved for the narrator-author and reader, as she keeps it secret from the uncouth westerners she encounters.

Arachne's physique is equally striking, but in very different terms. It is mainly her face and its expression that is described, 'her dark hair and wide-set green eyes, wide cheeks, this strange pronouncement to her bones, a wide mouth, broad shoulders even'; a face that shows 'Rebellion. Dissention. Trouble' (p. 98). Her features are strong and solid. They reflect personality far more than sexuality, however explicit the text may be about the latter. Her body is, above all, solid; her expression rebellious. When Arachne looks back to her real self, she sees her in sneakers and jeans, and the dress that brings out her stunning beauty is a silk trouser suit which matches the colour of her eyes. For her eyes remain her characteristic feature. Eyes of 'needling insolence', eyes that defy those they encounter in a woman who *looks*, and annuls the male gaze.

The connection between Arachne and women's fantasies is undoubtedly a true one, though a far less simplistic one than the male reviewer seemed to have in mind. Nancy K. Miller[8] has challenged the Freudian assumption that female fantasies are reduced to the erotic while young men's include egoistic or ambitious wishes. Miller claimed that women writers' texts contain egoistic desires along with erotic ones, and that the repressed content which gives birth to the fantasy is 'not the erotic impulses, but an impulse to power: a fantasy of power that would revise the social grammar in which women are never defined as subjects' (p. 41). Later in the same essay she asserts that 'the plots of women's literature are not about "life" in any therapeutic sense, nor should they be. They are about the plots of literature itself, about the constraints [placed] on rendering a female life in fiction' (p. 46). It is the combination of these two things that makes of *No Fixed Address* a 'portrait of contemporary fantasies', as its back cover states. For Arachne fulfils the double fantasy of erotics and power, while escaping literary constraints. Arachne encompasses wishes well beyond sexual behaviour: wishes related to autonomy and to subjectivity.

Like popular romance fiction, No Fixed Address inverts the usual pattern in that it poses woman as subject, man as object.[9] As Alison Light has maintained,[10] the reasons for the attraction that women feel for popular romance go much deeper than has generally been acknowledged, even by feminist criticism. Starting from the psychoanalytical consideration of fictions as fantasies, she states that romance offers women, first, a dream of equality in heterosexual relationships, and second, an access to a subjectivity which operates within the field of pleasure. Once again, these are unmistakable characteristics of No Fixed Address. Arachne is very much the subject of her text. She is persistently the grammatical subject of the sentences, and it is her consciousness that is conveyed, directly and often painstakingly, through the third-person narrator; it is through her eyes, her mind, and her body that we perceive her sexual encounters, her attitudes and her desires. Although we occasionally are tuned in to the mind of other characters, notably that of her stable love, Thomas, Arachne remains the main focalizer of her story. Her sexuality is described from her own perceptions, as is Thomas's gentleness, the perfect touch of his hands, his knowledge of her body, his acceptance of herself as she is.

If Thomas appears 'too good to be true' as has been said, it is as well to remember that no realistic characters are intended in the novel, that we are moving in a genre of exaggeration (the picaresque) and of fantasy. Thomas is the female fantasy of a lover who 'knows what she wants before she wants it', and whose gentleness and understanding have long been a female sexual fantasy trying to assert itself against the male belief in the magic attribute of potency. Thomas also accepts Arachne's unrestricted freedom, an ungendered fantasy, here established as such. The wish-fulfilment in No Fixed Address is closely related to these elements, too often overlooked in discussions of the novel, and perhaps obscured by the more striking dimension of Arachne's unrepentant promiscuity, another literary barrier parodically broken by this picaresque female character ('You don't have to love them. You just come fast. Make sure you beat them end don't count on having time for more than one' [p. 34]).

The comparison with Caprice in the aspects of subjectivity, autonomy and female fantasy is revealing of gender and genre conditioning. Their very names, both exceptional, point towards differences in the conception of the two women, and of their function in the text. The mythical references of Arachne are clear, but whose caprice is Caprice? Her own? The narrator's? The author's? Caprice's beauty may fit some women's own subjective fantasies, and many would enjoy the idea of wiping molesters off the ground, with a whip or by any other means; travelling and writing are also desires of many women. But signs of Caprice's pleasure in her story are strangely absent, and her own consciousness is only vaguely conveyed. Presented as highly erotic to observers, there is only passing indication of her own desires or behaviour, except for brief reports of apparently satisfactory and faithful passion for her schoolteacher, baseball-player boyfriend, Roy Smith; a caring friend, but one who tries to coax her into marriage and into adopting his name (a rather insoluble inversion), who tries to make her forget her quest and settle down in his company. She is a puzzle to him as Arachne never is to Thomas, for Roy is acting here within the boundaries of genre, the faithful schoolteacher who hopes for the hero's reform.

The question of Caprice as subject/object is linked to the narrative process of the novel as a whole, and its insistence on *seeing*. Our focalizers vary, and we alternatively see (and are told we see) Caprice through 'ordinary English eyes', through American eyes, Indian eyes, male and female eyes, but we rarely see through her own. The reader is persistently put into the position of voyeur, watching Caprice, voyeurism in *mise-en-abyme*, as s/he, by reading, watches the watchers, interprets the interpreters, moves telescopically away from the two Indians on the hill watching/interpreting the stories that develop in the valley, to a close-up of Caprice's story. On one level, the desire to actually *see* her is strongly created; 'Lord, she was beautiful. You should have seen her' (p. 117). It is no wonder that Douglas Barbour states in his early review that he 'can't wait to see the paperback'. On another level, it arouses the desire to read her, to see through those eyes with which she surveys the terrain, but through which we very seldom are allowed to look. Her eyes, unlike Arachne's, do not challenge the male gaze.

But the ultimate difference between Caprice and Arachne is, as it should be, of a strictly narrative kind: it lies in their story-maker, their creator within the text. For while Arachne spins her own journey/tale, Caprice's story is being written for her in advance. Caprice has been tempted into the tale by Frank Spencer, murderer of her brother, conductor of her story of vengeance. Her limits are textual, of genre. Her repeated dialogue with Roy Smith is revealing: 'Will you give up this terrible adventure and come home with me. No. Why not. You know, you have read the things I have read. Those are just things to read. Then why did they get written. Why can't you just write it then. I am writing it, that is what I am doing' (p. 76). But her writing is preordained, she is dutifully writing an inescapable story; her fate. As the crucial moment of the showdown approaches, Caprice wonders where she is being led by Spencer and why she is going on: 'Why was she following this trail with no known destination? She recognized the feeling. She was writing because she was looking forward to the last stanza' (p. 226). Caprice, the poet, is acting out/writing a temporary tale of vengeance in the West, a tale pre-written for her by an American man. She is inhabiting a genre in which she is an outsider, in which language must be transformed to adjust to her ('I've got to do what

I ... a woman ... a sister,'[p. 175]), cast in a role which she performs reluctantly, looking forward to its end, to her return to Quebec and to writing poetry. Her adventure of the West reads like a parenthesis in a life meant otherwise. Her narrative is a displacement and once her vengeance is consummated, Caprice as we know her is dead.

By contrast, Arachne's genre is her essence from beginning to end, it is one with her trickster figure and her autonomy, relying as it does on episodic, open-ended structures and free-moving, amoral protagonists. Reaching a destination would defeat her object. She is 'infatuated with motion' (p. 68), has no wish to reach the last stanza. She is presented (as traditional pícaros are) as the creator of her own story, erasing when convenient, refusing to be tied down by anything or anyone, including author or reader, who must finally give up their search and abandon their 'Notebook on a missing person'. Her journey, her quest, has no end. She acts out all the phases of the necessary but impossible search for identity, all within the genre: she moves from a negative perception of self to a stable, successful social self, then to a deeper recognition in Josef and the Wild Woman, and from there unto the unknown, unexplored dimensions of personality, of life and death. There is no end to her road. She is not murdered, as Caprice was, by the ending of her story.

Thus the choice of genre conditions the stories, but so does the degree of centrality given to gender. The tighter plot of the western (hardly altered by the gender inversion) imposes the path on Caprice; or, alternatively, the predominance of genre over gender does so. The extent to which the western is put to trial is undermined by the fact that Caprice's presence causes such a commotion. Otherwise, the difficulties are more of language than of plot (Is she a cowgirl, a cowperson, a bullgirl?). Much of the humour and literary play of the book are born from the transformations of the western that are not gender-dependent, and from the comment on the literary creation of 'The West'. The title *Caprice* thus goes beyond reference to the protagonist.

The genre of the picaresque, for its part, having traditionally explored, in the first person, the life-story of its protagonist, leads easily into female subjectivity, and its openness and amorality permits an unorthodox view of femaleness without the constant reminder of intrusion. In this particular version, there is a possible female chain of subjectivity, moving from author to text/protagonist/storymaker and to the reader. In *Caprice* the connection as subjects is only possible between author and reader if the reader is male and Caprice is their common object of fantasy.

Despite the important differences in subject-position between these novels, it is hardly a coincidence that different genres and gendered authors have allowed the protagonists freedom from similar literary constraints. Both Arachne and Caprice are allowed to be *bad* (even though Caprice's only childhood wish was to be good, yet another sign of her reluctant participation in her story); they are free from the usual punishment inflicted on transgressors, and are equally free from the happy ending of marriage, despite serious temptations. In the western, genre dictates that marriage will not take place; traditional picaresque might dictate the opposite, but today's female narrative has long been writing beyond that ending. In her last reversal of convention, Caprice rides east into the sunrise, leaving the schoolteacher behind: true to dictates of genre, subversive in the norms of gender. Behind the novel itself is left a deconstruction of the myths of the West, and a (brief) incursion of femaleness into male language. Arachne disappears into the cosmos, leaving questions poised about her future – or her present - leaving behind a transgression of gender norms, a full appropriation of a genre, which can no longer be its male-centred self. For it has merged with the female subjectivity of romance to create a hybrid that combines subjectivity and autonomy, the best of both wor(l)ds.

## Notes

1. George Bowering, *Caprice* (Markham: Penguin, 1988); Aritha van Herk, *No Fixed Address* (Toronto: Seal Books, 1987). All subsequent references are to these two editions.
2. See Introduction in G. Pellón & L.J. Rodríguez, eds., *Upstarts, Wanderers or Swindlers. Anatomy of the Pícaro*, (Amsterdam: Rodopi, 1986).
3. Stan Dragland, 'Wise and Musical Instruction: George Bowering's *Caprice*', *West Coast Review*, vol. 23, no. 1, Spring 1988, p. 86; Constance Rooke, note in *The Malahat Review*, Sept. 1986.
4. Interview by Gyrid Jerve, in *Kunapipi*, vol. VIII, no. 3, 1986, p. 68.
5. Peter Quartermaine and Laurie Ricou, 'Extra Basis: An Interview with George Bowering,' *West Coast Review*, vol. 23, no. 1, Spring 1988, p. 62.
6. For an account of early reviews on *No Fixed Address*, see Stephen Scobie, 'Aritha van Herk On the Road: Arachne's progress,' *Brick*, no. 29, Winter 1987, pp. 37-40.
7. Quartermaine & Ricou, p. 62.
8. 'Emphasis added: Plots and Plausibilities in Women's Fiction', *PMLA*, vol. 96, no. 1, Jan. 1981, pp. 36-48 (page references in text).
9. For a discussion of this inversion, see Ann Barr Snitow 'Mass Market Romance: Pornography for Women is Different,' *Radical History Review*, no. 20, spring/summer 1979.
10. '"Returning to Manderley" – Romance Fiction, Female Sexuality and Class', *Feminist Review*, 16, 1984.

# —— JANICE KULYK KEEFER ——

Janice Kulyk Keefer was born into a Ukrainian-Polish family in Toronto, Canada on June 2, 1952. She was educated at the University of Toronto and the University of Sussex, from which she received her D.Phil. in 1983. She has lived in England, France and in Nova Scotia as well as Ontario, where she currently makes her home. The author of eight books of poetry, fiction and literary criticism, she has lectured on Canadian literature and given readings from her own work throughout Canada and Europe. She teaches Transcultural Canadian Literature and Creative Writing at the University of Guelph in Ontario.

JANICE KULYK KEEFER

# Why I Write

Because I'm in love with language, subject to that impossible eros whose desire leads to anguish and pleasure, both unspeakable, yet leaving their presences everywhere in the text, their long, narrow footprints tracing a choreography that is my only mark of who and what I am. And my way of signalling to that most intimate yet independent of partners, the reader, who will dance away from me with my text in her arms, making up her own pas de deux, turning my fictions, poems, words into her corps de ballet.

*A clumsy child, my knees forever encrusted with bandages covering the cuts I got by tripping over my own feet going to and from school. In ballet class I would keel over whenever we had to pirouette, lacking any sense of balance, or so my teacher lamented. In my Ukrainian folk-dancing classes, I was the one who veered to the left when everyone else turned smartly right; steps I had perfectly by memory scattering like wayward birds as soon as I had to translate them into body.*

It's my way of making the world real to me; making up the world, and thus making it mean, though the process has more to do with cloudiness than clarity. A way of exploring, digging up the packed earth of who and what I thought I was, making it friable, fractured and thus a seedbed for countless possibilities, only a minute fraction of which I will ever pursue into printed language. A way of connecting with, intersecting, overlapping with all those who are other than me, whether they are lover, friends, family, strangers – my maternal grandmother, whose love for me was the sky of my earliest emotional landscape or, in a story I have just finished, Maria Alexandrovna Ulyanova, Lenin's mother. *Or that friend of my mother's and mother of someone who was once my best friend, a woman whom I knew only as a child, and yet whose dying obsessed me until I could make a fiction from, not of it. Entering her dying and making of it a haunted house to be explored and ultimately evicted from.*

Out of a compulsion to retrieve, recuperate the stories, lives, people who would otherwise be lost – those lives we've made obscure by not looking or caring or remembering them.

*In this the particular preoccupation of the writer who's the child of immigrants, who can't help but look both ways – country of origin, country of adoption – before she crosses any fictive street? The stories I grew up on, in my swimming-pool-serene, west-end Toronto suburb, stories about a small village in Poland, the river edging my grandparent's fields, on the other side of which was Russia. My mother and my aunt dressing-up in rusty black veils and long, dragging skirts to play mourners at the funerals of all the young Polish men shot trying to cross that border into the Workers' Paradise. The twin babies buried in that village who would have been my aunt and uncle had they lived; all the stories I, growing up, made up about them, alternative selves in another world, another language, that language to which I've remained a stubborn – but not perfect – stranger.*

To know who I am; to construct myself, to slough off and slip on selves; to sustain *asacra conversazione* with self, others, language and world, however mediated, conflicted, impossible and desirable. To maintain myself on that site between a consuming belonging to and abject isolation from the community into which I was born. To be able to imagine communities other, fuller, better than what I no longer take as given.

Because it is, if not the greatest, then the most absorbing joy I know.

JANICE KULYK KEEFER

# Going over the Bars

*Breathe out, breathe in, breathe out, breathe in. In must always follow out for the whole business to go on at all. Even if it feels like rubbing your lungs back and forth along a grater, even if you have to throw yourself into the effort, the way you once threw yourself into an office assignment or a piece of housework. Out, in, breathe out, breathe in*

For a moment it feels as though she's swinging, abandoning her body to a plank of wood, ropes burning the palms of her hand – a surge of air. *Oh I do think it's the pleasantest thing/ Ever a child can do.* An old rhyme, misremembered. Once she knew it by heart, one she'd spent whole afternoons swinging at the park, hanging her head back till her hair swept the ground; the whole world upside down as she aimed her toes at the sky.

*Up in the air and over the trees/ Till I can see so far.* Words going back and forth, in and out of her head, as if she were eight years old and swinging so high she gets dizzy. Never so high that she'd lose control, and go sailing over the bars. Some mornings she'd find the ropes of the swings wound crazily around the crossbar – someone's gone over, she'd think, and back away, avoiding the swings for the rest of that day, and perhaps a whole week after. Byrd Ellen went widdershins around a church, and no one caught sight of her again on God's good earth. Going over the bars she'd fly right off, and never come back at all.

*Breathe out, breathe in, breathe out, breathe in.* Dizzy. It's because of the medicine, fraying the links between nerve and brain. But how can it stop her from feeling the scrape of their feet down the thinning tunnels of her blood, the way they jostle against her bones? Her bones, bitten to a coarse, harsh lace. There are holes under the scars which were her breasts, yet still they keep on, voracious, insatiable; racing from one watering hole to another. But they are nearly done for, those indefatigable travellers. Soon they'll find themselves without a destination, never mind a road to take them there. Her blood and bones will suddenly give out, like a bridge suspended over a gorge, swaying, snapping as they rush across. *Breathe out, breathe in, breathe out, breathe in*

Who decided it was best for them to bring her here? Her husband has arranged for her bed to face the window; he's arranged for the window to look out onto a garden, but when she does manage to open her eyes she can only stare at the ceiling. At home she'd look up to find rivers crackling an endless plain; the canals of Mars were there, and bruises from the Moon's sallow face. A map, a reassurance, like her doctor's jokes, the press of her husband's hand, the trusting incomprehension of her children. But here the ceiling is a mirror; bones that feel like lumps of powdered ivory, snagging bleached-out skin. The travellers themselves are white, devouring her with stiff, colourless lips. She thinks of plagues passing over the face of the land: locusts, sirocco winds. There is a drought inside her: arteries, veins turned into skeleton leaves, a fringe unravelling.

Trees, she thinks, have the best of death, their flesh compact, burning clear and dry. She remembers them in winter, black-haired skeletons against a blank of sky. Or well and truly dead: branches polished beyond all possibility of bud or leaf: petrified lightning against blue summer air. And the way the leaves slough off – the leathery smell, the not unpleasant sourness of their decay. Flesh is a nicer word than meat. Once she'd felt shamed by its sheer, sickened sprawl inside of her; now there is almost nothing left of it, they have worn it down with their rats' feet, rats' mouths, rats the size and speed of tigers. *Breathe out, breathe in.* It's this shifting an iron bar from one hand to the other, the weight of air that makes her lungs ache. It's the funeral scent of the flowers: iris clogged in its caul, tulips reeling on worm-soft stems. Today he's come in unexpectedly; he should be at work, he should be with the children. He's here, now, because he knows the flowers make it impossible for her to find her breath; to throw it out again, lift up her hands to catch it back.

He takes the flowers and the vase away. Now she won't have to hear the noise the tulips make as their petals distend; the hiss as the iris shrivels. Now she will be able to hear her breath coming in, going out, the slow, unsteady creak of a swing... It takes him a long time to get rid of the flowers and return to her bed; to his waiting. Once he'd waited for her at airports and hotels; waited for her to finish dressing the children or undressing herself. Now he waits for the moment when a line fine as a hair will sever his life from hers; her dying from death. *Out, in. Breathe in after out, out after in, or the swing will stop, altogether.*

*** 

Death may be an accomplishment of which we're all capable. Dying – at least, her kind of dying – is another matter. It is loss of control. Not surrender, but loss; progressive, irreversible; absolute. Out of an infinitude of cells all perfectly ordered and obedient, one becomes malignant: *disposed to rebel, disaffected, malcontent.* One cell deserting the ranks, changing itself, creating an other in its own likeness. And that other spawns another, and another. Functions not so dissimilar to her own: to eat, to reproduce. To journey: *metastasis.* Her body an unknown continent discovered, devoured by travellers who burn so many bridges that there's no road back, nothing to go on to. They trespass on the routes of her blood and brain; they tunnel her bones. And her body answers back by closing shop, boarding the windows, locking the doors of whatever's left unvisited. They call it failure – her kidneys are failing, her liver and spleen. Her body an examination paper with X's piling up.

At first she'd dismissed the disaffected and rebellious cells. 'I'm not giving an inch, not half an inch – you think you can do as you please, change as you will, but I'm not letting even one of you get your way.' Her friends had applauded her spirit: she was a fighter and a winner: she wouldn't walk but swagger through the shadow valley. But something – not her friends, not her family, not even her own bravado – let her down. She'd had to switch tactics, lecture them the way she might have lived to lecture her children in another ten years: 'What you're doing is stupid, useless – can't you understand? Like it or not, I'm the one in authority here – you have to play by my rules.' At last, she'd tried reason.: 'Don't you see that you're eating the hand that feeds you? If I'm gone how will you travel, where will you go? It's completely illogical – in nobody's interest, surely you must understand.'

And then she'd refused all parley – they were no longer rebels, but an invading army. *Exterminate all the brutes!* They had been scalped, torched, drowned with chemicals. Five, three, perhaps only one escaped the assaults that poisoned her, as well. Fleeing to undefended ground, pitching camp and recruiting forces, sending out vanguards to occupy still further reaches of a land lush, helpless as grass. That was the point at which her doctor had stopped joking, and her husband's hand had not seemed quite so firm when it grasped her own. Her children's clear and perfect faces became smudged when they looked at her: how could she help them, when she couldn't even save herself? She'd spoken one last time, not to rebels, or a victorious army, but to an unimaginable horde of travellers. 'I see, now. You're not invading me; my body sent you, it has even kindly provided you with an itinerary. You may not even know that you're destroying yourselves by killing me – you may not even care. It's not you who are making me die. My body's committing suicide, and I'm given nothing at all to say in the matter. My body has simply stopped talking to me.'

After the first operation he'd brought her home, put her in the spare bedroom, the one where they'd hung the old, bleached-out curtains with their tenuous patterns of gazebos, lovers and gardens. She was content: here she could rest; here she could save something from the wreckage, knit up the forces of something she could now call, with all formality, her soul. This was the occasion to read Dante, to listen to nothing but Bach. But the print scratched her eyes, the notes blurred into one inchoate adagio. Very well, she would shut eyes, shut ears, draw the curtains so that the lovers drowned in the muggy light that struggled through the lining. She would lie in a square white bed, enwomb herself, unfold the truth of everything she'd been taught, everything she'd wanted to be true. All the birthing and growing and coupling for which the cells first joined themselves: whipcord sperm, moon-faced egg – this counted for nothing. Only this malignant birth was real, parthenogenesis of rebel cells. Born to die, this was the truth her body uncovered under all its layers of skin, muscle, bone, grown fragile as tissue paper.

Yet it meant nothing. Knowing brought no peace, no certainty, no end of wanting. When her children came into her room she still stretched out her arms to hold them. Holding them too long, too tight, breathing in the bread-and-butter scents of their skin and hair. They were very good, they let her hold them – they were afraid of her. It was the truth, though her husband denied it. He wasn't concerned with what was true, only with the angles of belief, measured by love's geometry. He was quite clear, quite confident on this: he wasn't dying.

Everything she'd known and felt, watched and thought through; everything she'd expected to have to hand, a rod, a staff to keep her place, guarding whatever ground she'd gained – she'd lost it. And her dying brought no revelation, only confirmation of obscurity. But she wouldn't give in to it. If she'd lost control of what was happening to her body, and why, she could at least dictate the how and where. She would *not* be taken from her home, dragged over the border from pain to stupor, dumped into a gleaming terminal where strangers would speak to her only in charts and graphs, syringes, intravenous bags. But in the end she was taken, dragged and dumped. Then *she* was lectured to and reasoned with: *You need special drugs, special care. Your husband can't cope any more. It's become too hard on the children.* The ambulance attendants were angels, substandard issue: they lifted her as clumsily as if they'd been wings, not hands. She couldn't refuse them with her body, which had refused her orders for so long now; how could she refuse them with her mind, bumbling slow, soft circles round a wick of morphine.

*Once out of nature I will never take/ My bodily form from any living thing.* What made the poet think he'd be given any say in the matter? Metempsychosis, her soul sidling into the body of a dog, a cat, a rat, – or perhaps just such another one as she, a body that will suddenly, and for no reason whatsoever, turn on itself after thirty years of working perfectly, the cells unfathomably obedient, so many of them reciting their messages word for word, relaying the codes through blood and tissue and across placental seas. Her children carry her body inside them the way she once carried theirs. Her body, and its switch, the mind, but not her soul, psyche, *pneuma*, whatever it is that lifts her onto the wooden plank, pulls it back, back, and then releases her into an arc of air. *Breathe out, breathe in.*

Those who hold that the soul perishes with the body are consigned to fire, on the authority of a great poet. And yet she could never acquiesce to an eternity of bliss, that potpourri of rose and fire. She cannot even think of angels except as white cockatiels, talons and tail feathers clipped, twisting their heads to the side of short, arthritic necks and croaking *holy, holy, holy*. She has read about accidental Lazari, expiring momentarily on operating tables, pacing vestibules of foggy light before their lives click on again. Do we at least get the afterlife we desire? Or does it depend on whether we perform our deaths the way we should? She is as nervous about this as she was about piano recitals, passing exams, taking off her clothes for her first lover. And yet it seems so simple – all she has to do, when the time comes, is to assume transparency. Her soul will weigh no more than a scrap of cellophane, than breath on a mirror. It will float out of her body the way paper rushes up the flue of a chimney, the way children jump off a swing in full sail.

*Breathe in, breathe out...* Her husband visits after work, every day – he has stopped bringing the children; they are staying with their aunt in a different part of the city. He brings her their crayon drawings, stick figures drawn with the simplicity that certainty inspires: a circle and five lines = a body. Crayon lines cannot be erased, but only scratched away, and even if the colour's gone, a line will remain, like a cut that's bled dry. She has held her daughters, sung to them, bathed them, scolded them for their four and two years of life: they will remember her, at worst, as a stick-figure pinned to a square white bed; at best, as a temporary cradle of arms and breasts and lap. She told him, as soon as she knew, that he should remarry. They were drinking the bottle of *Liebfraumilch* he had bought on the way home from the doctor's (Chekhov's physician had ordered *him* champagne). 'A wife for you, a mother for the children' – she'd said she didn't want him to play Heathcliff to her Cathy. He'd made a face that was not even a passable imitation of Olivier.

*I am incomparably above and beyond you all.* These will be her last words, if she has voice enough to speak them, and if anyone happens to be there to hear. Such things happen – everyone dies alone, though some are fortunate enough to have an audience. For it will be a show – of confidence, or unconcern, of panic or simply transformed energies: the effort her body now expends in crumpling and uncrumpling the paper bags of her lungs, sending her blood on its sluggish rounds, dispensing endless hospitality to footsore, hungry tumours, will go into lighting sure, slow fires of decay. Malignant cells and healthy – *All are punished*.

*Breathe out, breathe in.* She'd thought to go about her dying with a certain style. At first she'd entertained illusions the way you do the kind of guest you're certain to impress. But it came to nothing. She remembered a film she once saw, an image of a large, moon-faced woman cradling a death's-head in a muslin bonnet. But no *magna mater* has come to offer her the breast. Death and the maiden? He's stood her up – she hasn't caught so much as a glimpse of his spindle-shanks, a twirl of his scythe. Perhaps because she has no flowers to give Him, having twice rolled the stone away to bring her children out. They haven't yet learned to mourn the death of a pet – now they will be marked for ever: 'Their mother died when they were very young.' A letter of introduction to *Herr Angst*.

Her husband holds her hands. They are an arrangement of bones – doesn't he fear they will fall apart in his hands, a game of pick-up sticks? Her husband pays his calls and she knows his presence in the way she knows that Saturn and Jupiter orbit the sun: invisibly, at an incalculable distance. *Breathe out, breathe in, swing up, swing down, hold tight to the ropes, hold tight* – He is holding her hands and bending his face towards her, eyes wide open, like the tulips she made him throw away. Murmurings, measurements, a trigger of morphine. Shaking out the long, fine hair she no longer has; running to the swings at the end of the park.

*Incomparably above and beyond.* He leans in over her, asking her what it is she wants, can he get her anything, is she in pain? How to tell him she feels nothing save the rush of air against her face as she swings higher, higher. She is somewhere between body and mind – it is too difficult to explain, and she has lost her voice, just as she's lost the ability to curl her fingers round even a child's hand, to return a pressure. *Breathe out, breathe in.* But she wants him to understand this being in-between. It is something like looking at colour transparencies whose outlines haven't quite meshed, so there's a gap between where the line is drawn and the colour begins. A gap. Not absence, and certainly not an abyss, but just an unexpected space to slip through. Like that possibility, high up on a swing, of pumping so hard you go up and over the bars.

She'd never been able to do it, as a child, and she'd forbidden her own children to try. Because they would break bones, smash skulls, end up in hospital. *Swing up, swing down, swing harder, higher.* She's been so stupid to have left it behind her, left it so long, as if it were shameful; a childish thing. When she'd taken her own children to the playground she'd avoided the swings, sitting instead on a corner of the sand-box, or patrolling the rim of the paddling pool, trying not to get splashed. Now she doesn't care if anyone sees her like this, alone and free, head down and her long hair brushing the ground. The world turned upside down, a sky of packed earth, with stones for stars.

Swinging back and forth, higher and higher till the bars creak and groan. *Over the wall, and up in the trees/Till I can see so far.* She can see everything now; the cracked ceiling over her head pulls back, like flesh from the sides of a wound. It shows whatever it is that lies in the gap between outline and colour. Dante, Bach, *Mehr Licht*, but all that fills her head now is a children's rhyme. *Out, in, out.* The swing comes up to its highest point; she's gripping the rope so tight it tears her hands. Something splits inside, a hairline crack; something firey, clear as glass spills out. *In, out. Out.*

Over the bars.

# BONNIE BURNARD

Bonnie Burnard grew up in Southwestern Ontario. She has lived in Northern Ontario and British Columbia and moved to Saskatchewan in 1974, where she now lives with her teen-aged children.

Her first collection of short stories, *Women of Influence*, received the Commonwealth Best First Book Award in 1989. Recent publications include a story in the anthology *Soho Square 111*, published by Bloomsbury, edited by Alberto Manguel and in *Canadian Short Stories*, published by Oxford, edited by Robert Weaver. She was the editor of *Old Dance*, a collection of love stories, published in 1986 by Coteau Books. One of the stories from *Women of Influence*, 'Music Lessons', was adapted by the writer and televised on the C.B.C. She is one of ten Saskatchewan writers profiled in the video series *Through The Eyes of a Writer*, produced by Gordon McLennan and has been an active supporter of literary art in Saskatchewan.

BONNIE BURNARD

# Why I Write

I am guilty of allowing myself to become distracted by issues about which I can do very little. The foremost of these issues is practical: the inability to make much money as a Canadian short story writer. Tied directly to this is the extraordinary amount of quiet time I need in order to write anything which holds my interest. By quiet time, I mean the kind of time where, for days and nights running, the world of the imagination takes hold. I would not want (would be afraid of) a life filled with this kind of time, but I do need substantial chunks of it to get to the place where I can make a piece of fiction. All of this is further complicated by a middle class determination to raise my children well (to accommodate their potential, creative and other) and to live in something other than squalor. In short, I want it all. I want enough money to service my middle class family needs and to free my imagination to write, but I need a full time job to get it; a full time job precludes writing. If I were young and beautiful I would marry for money. If I could water down my own puritanical literary code, I would write potboilers full of greed, lust and violence to subsidize the work I care about. The romantic concept of artistic struggle is pretty much lost on me.

In a country like Canada, I think it is absurd to tie an imaginative writer's income to royalties. Our most esteemed poets sell very few books (500 to 1000 is usual) and therefore make little income ($500 to $1000). Things are only marginally better for short story writers and novelists. Artists (and I take imaginative writers to be artists) are shackled to a free enterprise market system. Literary publishers, subsidized by government grants and still very conscious of the recent time when there were few Canadian literary books published, have limited their dreams to the publication of more and more books rather than to the possibility of offering decent payment (which could be as easily subsidized as the managing editor's salary) to the writers (literary artists) they do publish. There is a Writer's Union in Canada, but its membership is a mix of everyone who writes books; the Union is not likely to split its membership over this issue.

Grants for artists are available here in Canada, both from the federal government and the provincial government. We line up and go after this money, armed with our publication records and with the support of people interested in our work. Juries of peers decide who, among thirty, forty, or fifty worthy candidates, will get the ten grants. I've been lucky sometimes, but there is no reason to believe this will last; every time I get a grant, someone else whose work is equally good doesn't.

All of this is pretty much useless prattle. I don't expect change. And I am hampered by guilt: it's all relative. At least I have the freedom to imagine what I want to imagine and there are publishers. At least I have three healthy kids. People elsewhere are not so lucky. But the freedom to do something allows only possibility. Time and energy get the writing done. (Could this all be related to my being a single mother?)

The qualms about the actual writing are much more illusive. They hang around the periphery, gumming up the imaginative works.

I have been thoroughly conditioned by my time and place to be dazzled by the intellectually tough, the sophisticated and the worldly, by black humour and nihilistic vision; to be repelled by the sweet, the hopeful, the sentimental slop which  is the usual alternative to the aforementioned. And yet.

If the short story is about memory, and I think at its best it often is, then I am at cross purposes with myself. What I remember (from just last week, for instance), what moves me, what remains locked into my psyche, are small, sweet bits of hope, of strength or simple tenacity. Who the hell wants to read a book of stories full of small, sweet bits of hope, strength and tenacity? The bits have to be buried (as they are in reality), made almost invisible in a mundane and merciless chaos. It ain't easy.

I want to give evidence of what I suspect (need?) to be true, without trashing it. It is like wanting to touch something beautiful, knowing you could foul it with the touch.

BONNIE BURNARD

# Nipple Man

John McLarty's furniture, in his office in the History building, his old teak desk and the two extra chairs and the filing cabinets and the potted plants, had been placed in every conceivable configuration, and he'd changed the drapes, at his own expense, twice. He believed there was a perfect arrangement, something conducive to clear thought, to an overall peace of mind, for himself and everyone who entered his office. He'd had some help, initially from his reluctant wife, and then from the others and recently even his daughter had gone up with him on a Sunday afternoon. They'd shared a bottle of wine as they hauled things around and argued amicably about what looked good where.

His window, which was directly in front of him when he sat at his desk, overlooked the largest expanse of grass left on the campus since the building program of the seventies. The grass, a dozen kinds of green on any day of the week from April through November, was usually spotted with the small bodies of students wandering from one lecture to another. Few of them stayed on the narrow sidewalk. John's building was connected by this sidewalk to Talbot, further up the hill, where the economics people plied their trade. He'd never been there. Seventeen years on this campus and he'd never even thought to walk over. Everything he needed was on his own floor and the floors beneath him, colleagues, support staff, archives. He did, of course, use the main library at the base of the hill but none of the other faculties overlapped his own. Except socially, for those who could endure it. He wasn't one of those who could endure it.

They'd given their share of dinner parties, or Carol had, he'd simply been there to pour the scotch, when they'd first arrived and they'd continued for a few years to make appearances at the gatherings orchestrated by his fellows in the History Department. And then they'd eased out. Carol had eased them out. She'd said one spring evening, standing in her panty hose and camisole at the bathroom mirror, applying her blush, sucking in her tummy, that she couldn't go. He thought she was sick, or premenstrual, or maybe exhausted from the kids, who were just at the age when they had to be lifted and carried and fed and buckled up and wiped clean and tucked in, but she said no, she was fine, everybody else was sick. And she repeated some of the dirty, cynical gossip she'd heard exchanged by warm little groups in kitchens and she told him about the clammy hands tracing her funny little ass when they were crowded around pianos in living rooms and about the rigorous, nerve-wracking effort needed to keep the whole thing in perspective. And the clincher, which had been a whispered longing, expressed by a dull-witted Yank who had long since departed for greener academic pastures, to see her nipples. She said she'd wanted to strip off her blouse and bra right there at the Bar-B-Que and say there you go sweetie, and aren't they as plain as plain can be, and you will notice they are not erect under your gaze and there's not a snowball's chance in hell they ever will be and now will you please just pass me that jar of mustard beside you there.

You didn't say that, John said, plugging in his shaver, what did you say? And nothing, she said. I said nothing, nothing at all. I walked over to you and Jenny and interrupted some inane discussion you were having about a cactus.

They'd skipped the dinner party. They'd gone instead to a dismal Bergman film and seen Liv Ullmann's nipples, which, if he remembered correctly, and he did, were not as plain as plain can be. That night, when they climbed into bed, when he should have been his most attentive, he began, habitually, to cast his dreams to other women. He didn't remember doing it before that night, not habitually.

The marriage had lasted only four more fretful years and then she'd gone off with the kids and her nipples and her funny little ass to seek a better life. She finished her stalled degree at another university and was now teaching computer science. She was a respected member of one of the hottest faculties in the country, or so their old friends told him, whenever they could work it in. And she'd married a moderately successful architect. They lived with the kids who were still at home with her in a house overlooking the Pacific, which they'd built on a great slab of smooth brown rock. John had been welcomed there often, for the sake of the children. He'd never once manoeuvered the preposterous slope of the driveway without feeling like an impotent uncle, but he'd endured, he'd needed to hold his kids as they grew. And everyone understood. There were lots of books on this kind of stuff.

For a time, he'd attributed this disaster to the dull-witted Yank at the pork Bar-B-Que, but then he'd relented and recognized the surrounding difficulties, the dead-locked impossibilities, many of them his own. On really good days he was content simply that they'd made it as far as they had, and that the damage, if his accounting could be trusted, had been minimal. He'd never told her what he dreamed of, habitually, only that he dreamed. And she'd had the decency to keep the worst of her secrets to herself. He watched her keeping them.

He'd had to sell the house and take an apartment and he was no sooner into it and lonely than they started to show up in his office, the women from his dreams, with their nipples. Not the precise women, but very close. Those years, seven or eight of them, ran in his mind like a long raunchy film, one naked young bosom after another. Not that they weren't fine women, some of them. Occasionally, more than occasionally, he re-membered their fineness.

Most of them were simply young. They wore T-shirts and only T-shirts with their jeans. They expected him to make love to them with a wisdom he couldn't count on all night long and half the next day. They were en-thralled by nakedness and long stretches of time and their own capacity to enjoy skin and nerve endings and they lied to him about his virility, not huge lies, but lies just the same, and necessary. And they wouldn't eat anything, wouldn't cook or sit still to eat a decent dinner.

They installed in him a status which was false, though flattering beyond anything he'd ever known. They looked up to him, literally, with sweet smooth cheeks.

He consoled himself with the conviction that he'd freed them to go after what they wanted and most of them did. Some had returned to his office boasting degrees better than his own. And two had come back to show off babes in arms, and fuller hips, and leaking nipples. Given the chance, he would have set the infants on the floor beside his filing cabinets to nap in-side their downy sleepers while he jumped their still familiar mothers.

The victorious visits had more or less stopped when he found Marion. He was marching alone down the library steps one balmy Indian Summer evening, gazing up through the trees, and he might actually have fallen over her if she hadn't spoken. 'Careful,' she'd said, and he'd excused him-self, feeling clumsy. She sat near the bottom of the long flight with a pile of books piled beside her on the step, exposed by one of the high new lights installed for campus security. He noticed immediately that her cheeks were wet. She wasn't young. A young woman in tears on the library steps would not have slowed him down.

He assumed that a public display from a woman this age did not indi-cate anything personal, he guessed she was in some kind of physical dis-comfort, that she'd been hurt, and he was right. She said she was just back to work and was likely pushing herself too hard but she was so damned tired of waiting to feel herself again. She said she supposed she should get the books back inside and then get herself home and watch David Letter-man or something. He told her he didn't see that such drastic action was necessary and he began to load her books, economics texts, one Welty and one Hardy, into his briefcase and then into his arms.

'Can you stand?' he asked. 'My car is just over in the north lot. I'll bring it around and then I'll take you home.' And he hauled her books across the cool grass to the north lot. It didn't occur to him until he was back and helping her into his car to ask her who she was. She was Marion Alderson; she taught economics, had done so for three years on this cam-pus and for many other years on other campuses across the country. She was just getting over a little bit of surgery and she lived in one of the high rises on the other side of the bridge. Maid Marion he'd called her and she'd raised her eyebrows, smiling only slightly. He got her home, up the elevator and into her suite with her books settled on an elegant glass desk in her living room and he saw, when her back was turned, that she had a set of those perfect calves that actresses from the fifties used to have, with heavier thighs, he could read them under her dress as she walked. He accepted her graceful thanks and took his leave, feeling a little bit the hero, feeling decent and lively.

He didn't phone her, didn't even think of phoning her until two months later when he was marking a particularly fine paper on the Boer War. He found his directory and his finger hit the numbers to her office over in Talbot, just out of his sight line. He told her he wanted to know only if she was feeling herself yet and she said yes she was and thanks again for the gallant assistance and when he didn't take the conversation to its close she asked if she could buy him lunch in the Talbot cafeteria as a token of her gratitude. Sure she could, he said.

So they met, properly. And she was much better, much stronger. She wore an expensive shirtwaist, paisley, Carol had wanted such dresses when they couldn't afford them, and very fine leather shoes with narrow high heels. These, he knew, were to show off the legs. Her hair looked especially clean and full, it was a dark grey blonde and it swayed around her head as she talked. Only her eyes, a guarded deep brown, set off by rays of crow's feet, disappointed him. As he ate his grilled cheese he imagined her eyes bright, throwing off a phrase or two from the accumulated vocabulary of old eyes.

Now that she was well, her voice was clipped and businesslike and funny. She was one of those women who wear no rings but talk without apology about their grown-up children. Her breasts looked full and solid though he couldn't begin to find her nipples; they were lost under the swirling blue paisley. After two hours they counted between them, with some guilt, five students left waiting in the halls outside their offices.

He liked her, he decided he liked her tremendously and by the time he took their trays to the cafeteria window, standing in line with economics people he recognized but didn't know, he felt the need to be in love again. As he walked back across the grass to his office he very deliberately resurrected all he knew to be true and ridiculous and daunting about what he needed. He lined it all up, chose what he wanted to believe, and dumped the rest into the caverns long since dug at the back of his brain. He was going to get into her pants and he was going to fall in love, in whichever order was necessary. She could decide the order.

It didn't take him long to fall in love. She was available and game. They went to concerts in the city park put on by a youth orchestra and to a fall fair thirty miles out of the city and once to the horse races, where he lost forty dollars and she came away even, and smug. They talked about her husband and about Carol over caesar salad and beer and about books she'd had a chance to read that year and about economic theories he'd wanted to comprehend, and she said one evening, while putting down a twenty for her part of the dinner, that she had no credit cards. She said she thought unnecessary debt was very unwise and that night he'd stood in his kitchen in his gotch and cut his Visa card into pieces with his nail scissors. The next day he took enough money out of his savings to pay off every cent owed to everyone for everything.

They even had a short Sunday afternoon at her apartment with two of her children and one of his own, all gathered in the city for youthful, compelling reasons. The younger adults had thrown back beer nuts and pretzels, eyeing each other and circling their parents warily, as had been expected, though they gave brief, spontaneous lip service to companionship and fun, for anyone. The companionship line had come from his long-legged son, gratis, full of good cheer. Just drink your beer, he'd told him.

He expected by this time, quite rightly he thought, to be into her pants. She was friendly beyond bearing, she touched his arm or his back whenever there was even the mildest excuse to do so, but she'd said no twice to his offer to tuck her up and she kissed him chastely.

Because he knew no other way he asked her one night, over a late dinner after an economics lecture on the campus which he'd understood and agreed with, why they weren't making love. 'I want to bite those thighs,' he said. He didn't broach her nipples; he wasn't entirely without discipline.

She plopped sour cream over her baked potato and loaded it with chives. 'I'm forty-seven years old,' she said. 'I would bet you've never been with a forty-seven year old woman.'

'No,' he said, grinning.

'It's no joke,' she said.

He knew what had to be done. He was sure he could match her. He listened to her go on about Dostoyevsky over dessert and as soon as they were into the car in the parking lot he pulled up his shirt and let his stomach hang out over his belt, though it wasn't as obscene in the dark as he'd hoped. He took her hand and placed it on his thick, hairy flesh.

'There,' he said. 'Flat as a board.'

She took her hand away.

He hiked up his pant leg and pointed to a long lumpy vein just under his skin. He'd been watching its steady movement to the surface for a year.

'Look at this,' he said. 'Like an old log bobbing up.'

She watched his excitement calmly for a minute and then she lifted her bum off the seat and pulled her dress up to expose her thighs.

'Yes indeed,' he said. 'I'd recognize them anywhere.' He started the car and got them on their way, sticking to the passing lane of the main thoroughfare from the city core to the campus.

'There's more,' she said.

He turned off onto a quiet side street, continuing home at a steady sixty kilometers an hour. She had unbuttoned her shirtwaist, a soft green print, and was pulling her arms out of it as he drove. He saw, glancing as often as he could in the intermittent light from the street, what she wanted him to see. Her lacy black bra was filled with something other than flesh, something similar in texture and shape to the kids' old bean bags. She reached around and unhooked her bra, letting it fall heavily into her lap. He was looking at a war zone.

He slowed and pulled the car over to the side of the road.

As soon as his hands were free he turned and used them to cover the two nearly healed slices.

Her eyes were bright, finally, but not with the sulky passion he'd put there in his dreams. She looked empty, and raw.

His thumbs moved over the rough dark texture, up and down, up and down.

'They don't hurt much anymore,' she said.

He leaned over and buried his face in her. The scars felt strong and final on his cheek, as if the cells had said, this is it, don't ever cut here again. He was astounded by their warmth, scars as warm as flesh can be.

'You might have told me,' he said.

She put her hand into his thinning hair, lifted it between her fingers, watched it fall back into itself, soft and orderly. 'I'm telling you now.'

He could hear her heart, as clearly as he'd heard his own, when he'd been alone and listening for it.

'They're in my mind,' he said. 'Safe and sound.'

He took what he could into his mouth, the thick layers of tissue where the needle had gathered the skin, the tough ridges rising like a mountain chain where all other land had disappeared.

He knew escape would always be a possibility. There were ways. He'd had some practice. He could be bravely direct or clever, cowardly, subtle. It wouldn't matter much. She was braced for anything.

He could feel her fingers absently working their way through what was left of his hair. She was a million miles away.

'I've got them,' he said, bending quickly, sinking his teeth into a hard and shapely thigh.

# JOY KOGAWA

Joy Kogawa was born Joy Nozonie Nokayama in Vancouver, BC on June 6, 1935, a third generation Canadian of Japanese ancestry. Her father was an Anglican minister. In 1942, she and her family became victims of the Canadian Government's policy of internment and dispersal of Japanese-Canadians in response to the Second World War. 'Some 21,000 people of Japanese ancestry – 17,000 of whom were naturalized or Canadian-born citizens – were uprooted from their west coast homes' in 1942. Kogawa, now divorced with two children, lives in Ontario.

*Obasan*, published in 1981, is part-autobiography, part-exorcism and part-fiction. It became a focus for the Japanese-Canadian community's demands for restitution and brought a half-forgotten history back into the light of public attention. It has won several major awards: the 1981 Books in Canada First Novel Award, the Canadian Author's Association 1982 Book of the Year Award, the Periodical Distributors Paperback Award, and several literary awards in the United States.

# Joy Kogawa Interviewed by Jeanne Delbaere

Jeanne Delbaere interviewed Joy Kogawa in the Château de Colonster during the XIth Annual Conference on Commonwealth Literature and Language Studies in German-speaking countries (Aachen-Liège, 16-19 June 1988).

*Before* Obasan *appeared in 1981 you had written three volumes of poetry. The novel itself reads like a poem: did it grow out of your poetry?*

I had been writing poetry since 1964. I had never thought of writing a novel. Poetry was for me a kind of discipline of dreams, a search for whatever it was that was being born within myself. Because the ideal seemed to be unattainable I looked for an avenue out of the struggle and that was an act of entering the landscape of poetry. All the answers that appeared out of the dreamworld were the language of poetry.

*Does this mean that you were not aware of the political implications of your novel?*

No, I wasn't. The writing of *Obasan* was very unconscious. I was doing what I always did with poetry, i.e. struggling with something. I was therefore not conscious of any political act. The political reality was the background rather than the foreground of my book. I struggled to free something that wanted to be free. It was a journey towards some accurate point which kept receding, a weariness of the search and at the same time a compulsion to continue.

Obasan *does indeed give the impression of having been written out of a deep sense of personal compulsion but by splitting open the stone of silence (to use your beautiful image in the prologue), it also made audible the so far voiceless Japanese-Canadian community. With* Obasan *a whole piece of the Canadian mosaic was made visible.*

None of this was conscious during the writing of the book. A character in it may have said this kind of thing but it was not part of my search. It was not even a personal quest. It was more like breathing, an act of life. Writing is so automatic for me that I cannot not write.

*In the novel the narrator Naomi has two aunts: Obasan, the silent one and Emily, the speaker and warrior. Did you at the time identify with either of them?*

Yes, I identified with the silent aunt. She was more who I was as a human being, struggling as I did myself with this silence.

*Would you still identify with Obasan now?*

I don't think so. I feel much closer to the speaker now, so much so that I might call my new book *Aunt Emily* but I haven't yet made up my mind. It will depend on the quality of her struggle.

*Do I understand that your new book will be a sequence to* Obasan?

Yes, the story of *Obasan* began in 1972, went back to the 1940s and then again to 1972. My new novel begins in 1983, moves back to the 1950s and finally returns, past 1983, to the present. Naomi is still the narrator. A problem that troubles me with her is that I have always wanted to move her out of her spinsterhood but this is not easy because she is such a repressed person.

*From what you said about your present identification with Aunt Emily it is clear that the new book will also be more consciously political.*

Yes, I now feel that to struggle is important. The Japanese-Canadian community is only one small pebble on the beach of human experience but there is a universal element in our struggling political endeavour. We feel some sort of solidarity with the world's communities in their effort to speak. That is why I find this conference so interesting. Many of the papers I have heard dealt with oppressed or marginalized cultures. We need to honour our struggle for mutuality and plurality and our efforts to overcome the dominations. Wilson Harris talked about that marvellously well this morning.

*You feel that Canada will be a better country if ethnic differences are preserved?*

I think so. When you have strong constituencies you have a stronger whole. Besides, there is more human richness when there is more diversity. Our Japanese-Canadian community was fairly strong before the war. There were about twenty-two thousand people along the West Coast. In Vancouver we had our own newspapers, our own commercial areas, our own hospital, etc. Now we no longer exist as a geographic community. The dispersal has worked and assimilation has become a fact. Our people have spread across the country; their properties were taken away from them and they never went home again. Much of our distinctive character has been lost in the process, many of our specific values reified. But I do not think that what is vital for the soul has been lost. It is more that it has been transposed.

*Could you mention one of these specific values?*

Yes, tenderness towards the old, for instance. This was a cultural value from the East and it is tragic that it has very little corporate expression in the West and that is a great loss. But in the lives of individual Japanese families it still remains and of course tenderness will never be lost from the world. No matter how deeply it may be buried it will never be absent from the human condition and I believe that those who consciously keep it alive bring immeasurable power into the world.

*Do you see a link between your political struggle to redress the wrongs of the Japanese-Canadians and your position as a Canadian woman writer?*

I do. I came to the women's movement via the movements for minority rights and vice-versa. I feel that they feed each other because they are identical in so many ways. I see in the women's movement a great unifying force among cultures in conflict with one another, where there are real impasses like in Israel at the moment. Women can play a very positive role. One of the strongest hopes is in the women of the world becoming politically conscious and fighting with the women of other countries against oppression. There is a particular responsibility of women in oppressed cultures to educate women from oppressor cultures about the desperation of their plight and their need for the resources of the women's movement. There is also a responsibility for the women of the oppressor cultures to consciously and passionately don the role of the victimizer, however painful that may be, and to join in solidarity with their oppressed sisters. As a Canadian I have experienced both positions.

*The narrator of* Obasan *also has this dual position, being a victim who is identified by her fellow Canadians as a victimizer.*

You are right. This one-dimensional view of Japanese-Canadians resulted in their being severely victimized. Reality demands of all of us that we know the ways in which we are identified as both victims and victimizers. I think victimizers experience a one-dimensional identity of their own sense of victimization and therefore the corrective to this situation is for us all always to know we are both.

*Don't you fear that your new political commitment might affect the quality of your writing?*

It might. I have thought of it but it is what I am now and I cannot do anything against that. I now believe in the necessity of struggle. One is alive because one chooses to struggle.

*What is interesting is that the process of becoming conscious came to you after* Obasan *was written.*

Maybe it had been in me all the time but I didn't know it. The link between our unconscious and reality is mysterious. I'll tell you something that happened to me when I was writing *Naomi's Road,* a children's version of *Obasan* which I had been asked to do for Oxford University Press. Because it dealt with Naomi at a much younger age I had decided to expand on the friendship between her and Mitsi, a mean little girl mentioned only briefly in *Obasan.* The very day after I had written about the imaginary Mitsi I got a letter from the real one asking me whether I remembered her and giving me all sorts of details about her present life. The extraordinary thing was that almost all she said about herself in the letter had found its way into the chapter I had written the day before though I hadn't heard from her in over forty years.

*To be a writer in Canada as in any other post-colonial society often involves a complicated process of appropriation and subversion of European literary models. This does not seem to have been your case.*

No. Having had no university training I have never had a very strong sense of a tradition behind me. My reading has always been very sporadic. In a way I exist in a vacuum.

*This may be the secret of your originality. Your voice is unique. It does not resemble anything we know. What about your links with Japan?*

I feel strongly ambivalent towards things Japanese and also highly critical. My commitment is to Canada. My ties to Japan were severely destroyed by the experience of the Second World War. Being in Germany for this conference made me think a lot about the parallel between the Japanese history of war atrocities and Germany's struggle today with its past. Our corporate identity is built up of our stories and for us to be reconciled with the story of ourselves as evil requires an enormous courage, an almost superhuman effort towards reconciliation. We know we must not ever forget lest we repeat the evils of our ancestors, the evils of our grandparents perhaps – their lethargy, their blindness, their false innocence and in many cases their barbarism. To embrace that and to demand of ourselves a refusal to repeat that history is a great calling.

DIANA BRYDON

# *Obasan*: Joy Kogawa's 'Lament for a Nation'

In 1965 George Grant published *Lament for a Nation: The Defeat of Canadian Nationalism*,[1] a book asking Canadians whether they had 'the power and the desire to maintain some independence of the American empire' (p. vii). Underlying that question, Grant saw 'the deeper question of the fate of any particularity in the technological age' (p. ix). Grant's elegy looked backwards to Canada's origins in a vision of 'community which had a stronger sense of the common good and of public order than was possible under the individualism of the American capitalist dream' (p. x). By looking backward, he hoped to inspire Canadians to continue forward along a different route than that charted by American capitalism. Joy Kogawa's *Obasan*[2] recreates the anguish of one particular community facing the faceless bureaucratic destruction created by the homogenizing impulse Grant feared. *Obasan* is an elegy for lost particularity, and a plea that the value of the particular be recognized and reasserted by the fragments that have survived its sundering. Kogawa continues Grant's questioning of the future that we are building for ourselves through our increasing reliance on the spirit of technology to solve our immediate problems, while ignoring our eternal ones. More specifically, she extends Grant's questioning of the power and desire of Canadian nationalism to promote a vision of the common good through respecting difference.

In 'Storm Glass', an article appearing elsewhere in this issue, Coral Ann Howells perceptively describes *Obasan* as 'an elegy for a lost community'.[3] Kogawa implies that the loss of the West Coast Japanese-Canadian community weakens the entire Canadian and indeed human community in their resistance to the deadening homogenization of imperial technological culture, a culture that reached its apotheosis in the atomic bombs that destroyed Hiroshima and Nagasaki. Like Grant's *Lament for a Nation*, Kogawa's *Obasan* recreates the spirit whose loss it laments, in the hope of reviving the potential for a differently directed future. Like Grant, Kogawa believes that 'our private and public realities are coextensive, and that the accuracy of our actions is dependent on our being grounded in our spiritual resources'.[4] *Obasan* explores the limits and strengths of those resources.

*Obasan* grips our imaginations through its juxtaposition of a lyric intensity of longing for a renewed community against a documentary realism that charts its loss. But by rewriting history from the perspective of the dispersed and defeated, it retrieves the memory that it hopes can once again become future-oriented. It describes the Canadian nation at a time of great collective sickness, showing how the disease of racism infecting the body politic spreads to emerge as the tuberculosis that kills Naomi's father and cripples her brother. Naomi sees her Aunt Emily as 'one of the world's white blood cells, rushing from trouble spot to trouble spot with her medication pouring into wounds seen and not seen' (O, p. 34). Memory and resistance become the medication necessary for a cure. Through their very victimization, Naomi's people themselves have become part of the sickness to be cured, but paradoxically they will also be part of the cure. Their insistence on mattering, through silent demonstration and articulated affirmation, confirms the strength of the specific to resist dispersal and destruction, the command to disappear and the patronising welcoming back into the fold as 'our Japanese'. But this survival comes at a cost to the psyche few would choose – had they the choice to pay.

*Obasan* enacts a dialogue that is never resolved between those who confront injustice through adopting the strategy of silent endurance and those who would try to change the world for the better through 'lobbying and legislation, speech-making and story-telling' (O, p. 199). Implicitly, through its own story-telling, it moves from silence into voice, but paradoxically into a voicing that includes the enigma of silence. Kogawa ignores simplistic oppositions between speech and silence, exploring instead the potential for the creative use and abuse of power in each.

Obasan, a silent presence, and Naomi's mother, a silent absence, define the two poles of silence that structure the novel's exploration of loss. Obasan pulls Naomi inward, toward the reduced community of Uncle, Aunt and two children that deafens itself to the slurs of the world. Naomi's mother pulls her outward to recognise her solidarity, cemented through suffering, with the victims of Nagasaki and all other war atrocities. Appropriately, Naomi's mother's sister, her aunt Emily, the 'word warrior' (O, p. 32), also pulls Naomi outward from the potentially solipsistic world of Obasan's nuclear family, a bulwark that cannot defend its members from the encroaching public world. Yet there is a wisdom and integrity in Obasan that anchor Naomi, preventing her from the flight that she both envies and fears in Stephen.

*Obasan* teaches that you can't run away from your roots, but neither can you go home again. Naomi mourns the loss of innocent childhood security that she associates with home before her mother's own call home to attend a sick grandparent. Yet even in her nostalgia for that lost perfect past before racism disrupted all certainties, Naomi recognizes another memory that contradicts her nostalgia. Old Man Gower stands for the disruption of community that was always there. The confidence of unproblematic belonging is forever denied us. Naomi asks herself: 'Is it the lie that first introduces me to the darkness?' (O, p. 63). She links the loss of Eden with the speaking of a lie and with its silent acceptance by she who knew it to be false yet did not speak to affirm the truth. Her complicity in Old Man Gower's lie shattered her first secure sense of belonging completely to her mother's world. He introduced her to a troubling difference, her own capacity to make moral decisions as an individual, however flawed her child's judgement might be, however confused her apprehension of the issues at stake. He split the coherence of her childhood world by introducing a gap between what she knew to be true and what was said. In this moment she learned that both speech and silence can deceive. Truth is no longer self-evident. It has become elusive. Choice has become a possibility.

The lie represents the breaking of the trust on which our sense of community is founded. Old Man Gower's lie parallels the government's lies that follow. Both say that their exploitation is for their victims' own good. These lies must be exposed before reconciliation can follow. Betty Lambert's powerful play *Jennie's Story* shows Jennie literally swallowing the lye/lie which has shattered her home and her community in order to take upon herself the symbolic cleansing necessary for spiritual renewal. *Obasan* too accepts this mythic rite of symbolic sacrifice that enables communal renewal. Naomi's mother has not died in vain. Her death, once accepted and understood, enables Naomi to turn from her own personal hurt to confront the hurt done the fabric of her nation, as outlined in the Memorandum sent by the Co-operative Committee on Japanese Canadians. She had avoided this document on earlier occasions. *Obasan* ends with its words, as if Naomi can only now accept its message that the government's actions against Japanese Canadians undermined the entire Canadian community. Naomi forgives, but refuses to tolerate, the prejudice that has weakened both victim and victimizer. In 'Is There a Just Cause?',[5] Kogawa insists that 'as a Canadian I am embarrassed by my country's bureaucratic racism at home and its condemnation of racism in other countries...'. The lie must be repudiated: 'Let it not be said of our country that we preached democracy and practised racism until the very last Issei died' (p. 21). Consistency of word and deed, honesty and integrity are the individual values she wishes to see the nation validate, yet she knows how these very values may work against the acceptance of difference because of the challenge the particular always makes to the coherence of the whole.

*Obasan* reminds us of the complicating differences that nation, class and gender bring to the already problematic and culturally specific construction of race. It is not simply that the experience of racial oppression mirrors that of sexual oppression, but rather that the experience of racism changes the experiences of gender, nation and class. Richard Cavell argues that in insisting on the Canadianness of the

Japanese-Canadians, Aunt Emily's manuscript thrusts 'toward an assertation of sameness. Naomi, instead, is concerned with difference. She knows she is not Canadian because she is Japanese'.[6] I interpret Aunt Emily's arguments differently. When she goes through government documents crossing out the words 'Japanese race' and writing in 'Canadian citizen' (p. 33), she is refusing a societal representation of her identity that denies her the power of choice. She is not denying her Japanese race nor her Japanese culture, but she is insisting that race cannot be assumed to determine her communal loyalties. The community we choose through political affiliation supersedes that we are given through the accident of birth. We must create our own home, through the responsible practice of our citizenship.

Just as she rejects a racially-determined label, so Aunt Emily also rejects the idea of 'Canadian' as a homogeneous and fixed identity. In her opinion, 'the Canadian' must prove flexible enough to accommodate 'milk and Momotaro' (O, p. 57). To be Canadian is not to be the same as other Canadians; it is to contribute collectively to the composite idea of creative community that Canada ideally could be. Similarly, Aunt Emily also rejects the gender-specific label of 'old maid' (p. 8); she insists on defining her own difference in her own way. Naomi, in contrast, finds herself both intimidated and angered by the power of such definitions to shape her own experience of herself. Choosing, for her, is not possible. She feels trapped by others' needs and her own fears.

Nonetheless, I think it is a mistake to place *Obasan* within a pattern of women's fiction that argues that women must first construct a self and assert selfhood before they can question that construction.[7] *Obasan* shows that selfhood cannot be freely chosen; its constructions depend on the possibilities open to it. Naomi's community has been disrupted; without it as a nurturing context, she finds herself only as alienated and wounded. Her experience makes her distrustful of strength, and even of the sure conviction of the rightness of one's own actions. Paradoxically, she finds a different kind of strength in doubt, and in the ability to see and feel from several different perspectives. She experiences herself as both Little Bear and Goldilocks, intruded upon and intruder. She can give up neither identification without giving up an integral part of her growing self. She is uncomfortable with her role as teacher, knowing that her students have been conditioned to expect an authority that she will not exercise. Instead, she provides attentiveness to their difficulties and a tentativeness that implicitly questions traditional authority. She may feel a failure and remain consumed by doubt, but the novel implicitly endorses her decision to refuse the easy claiming of institu- tionalized authority open to her as a teacher. Similarly, she refuses the easy authority of the victim.

But this capacity for multiple imaginative identifications and its accompanying acknowledgement of the power relations implicit in the construction of identity do not lead to the suspension of values that Linda

Hutcheon believes characterizes postmodern fiction, and in particular what she calls historiographic metafiction. *Obasan*, like *Lament for a Nation*, is committed fiction. Its commitment avoids the Empire's sure belief in the rightness of its manifest destiny. Instead, it affirms a commitment to a wholeness that 'comes from joining and from sharing our brokenness'. Kogawa asserts that we 'need to remember the paradoxical power in mutual vulnerability'. For her, 'Life is a series of making and unmaking plans along a continuum of uncertainty ('Just Cause?', p. 20). Such statements define a post-colonial awareness that in Wilson Harris's words attempts 'to define a deeper participation in themes of responsibility through a diversity of associations, however perilous, rather than through an apparent unity that conforms and remains static in the end'.[8] The theme of responsibility is not abandoned but deepened and diversified.

Unlike Maxine Hong Kingston's *Woman Warrior*, *Obasan* is not about the growth of an individual girlchild into an acceptance of the doubleness of her ethnic American identity. Naomi's story is the story of her community. She defines herself through her relations to others. In *Obasan*, she probes the nature of her connection to her lost mother, and to Obasan, who both is and is not her mother. In the sequel, it appears that she will probe her relation to Stephen, the brother who seeks to deny his family connections. Constructing a self involves constructing a community that will enable a different conception of selfhood – as open rather than closed to the needs of others.

Francesco Loriggio argues that 'even a writer so obstinately deprecatory towards technology and modernization as George Grant failed to see that filiation and descent, the hereditary, the small, the local, the intra-national were, when set against homogenization, affiliation or consent, some of the pockets of resistance he was looking for'.[9] *Obasan* reaffirms Grant's vision of an alternative model of community to that offered by the 'technology of empire' but qualifies our understanding of the nature of that alternative. Instead of locating it in the inherited traditions of British conservatism, Kogawa shows that the future of Canadian difference depends on our openness to difference generally. *Obasan* does much more than record a forgotten and misunderstood episode in our past. It does more than introduce yet another 'ethnic' voice into the Canadian mosaic. Through its questioning of the problematics of how history gets written and ethnicity gets defined, it draws our attention to the power relations that structure our thinking about what is possible and what is desirable in contemporary Canada. It challenges all Canadians to rethink their vision of our society and its values.

## NOTES

1. George Grant, *Lament for a Nation: The Defeat of Canadian Nationalism* (1965; Toronto: McClelland & Stewart, Carleton Library No. 50, 1970).
2. Joy Kogawa. *Obasan* (1981; Harmondsworth: Penguin, 1983). All further references are to this edition and are included in the text.
3. Coral Ann Howells.
4. Joy Kogawa, 'The Enemy Within' in *The Writer and Human Rights*, ed. The Toronto Arts Group for Human Rights. (Toronto: Lester & Orpen Dennys, 1983), p. 209.
5. Joy Kogawa, 'Is There a Just Cause?' in *Canadian Forum*, March 1984, 20-21; 24.
6. Richard Anthony Cavell, 'The "Dialogue of Being": Dialogical Form in Klein, Kroetsch and Kogawa' in *Canada Ieri e Oggi*, ed. by Giovanni Bonanno. (Schena, 1986), p. 52.
7. Linda Hutcheon, *The Canadian Postmodern: A Study of Contemporary English-Canadian Fiction* (Toronto: Oxford University Press, 1988) p. 6.
8. Wilson Harris, *Tradition, The Writer and Society: Critical Essays* (London: New Beacon, 1967), note.
9. Francesco Loriggio, 'The Question of the Corpus: Ethnicity and Canadian Literature' in *Future Indicative: Literary Theory and Canadian Literature*, ed. by John Moss. (Ottawa: University of Ottawa Press, 1987), p. 64.

CORAL ANN HOWELLS

# Storm Glass: The Preservation and Transformation of History in *The Diviners, Obasan, My Lovely Enemy*

Margaret Laurence's *The Diviners,* Joy Kogawa's *Obasan,* and Rudy Wiebe's *My Lovely Enemy* all offer fictive reconstructions of the history of vanished people on the prairies.[1] *The Diviners* is concerned with nineteenth-century Scottish settlers around the Red River and with the indigenous Métis; *Obasan* records the experiences of Japanese-Canadians who underwent a peculiarly traumatic form of enforced resettlement in the western provinces during World War II; and *My Lovely Enemy* is concerned with prairie Indians in the early nineteenth century pre-European colonisation and with Mennonite settlers. These are all regional and historical fictions but curiously, when taken together, they disperse notions of regionalism in the sense of identifiable community, emphasising instead multiplicity and separateness within the geographical space of the prairie. It is true that the historical events they record occupy different time slots over the past one hundred and fifty years, but there is something very odd about western Canada in the way that the prairies 'island people and events in large spaces without swallowing them or synthesising them'.[2] These three narratives deal with mutually exclusive communities who are largely ignorant of the others who may previously have existed in the same places. Wiebe's narrator Professor James Dyck declares that 'the problem is, writing prairie Indian history' (p. 43); I suggest that the problem is, writing prairie history at all. It is a question of the difficulties of historical representation in a place of vast surfaces where there is very little sense of an accumulated stratified past (by contrast with e.g. Thomas Hardy's Wessex or Geoffrey Hill's *Mercian Hymns*). Prairie historical fiction focuses on gaps and vanishings, and part of the fascination of these novels lies in the different ways in which the prairie is figured as textual space.

In this paper about the problematics of prairie historical fiction I begin with an image from Jane Urquhart's short story 'Storm Glass'. That story is set in Ontario not on the prairie, but its image of a piece of broken glass tossed about for years in a lake and so robbed of its ability to cut, beautifully encapsulates the idea of relics, their preservation and transformation:

What had once been a shattered dangerous substance now lay upon the beach, harmless, inert and beautiful after being tossed and rubbed by the real weather of the world. It had, with time, become a pastel memory of a useful vessel, to be carried, perhaps in a back pocket, and brought out and examined now and then. It was a relic of that special moment when the memory and the edge of the break softened and combined in order to allow preservation.[3]

This looks as if it might be a useful metaphor for historical facts and inheritance. Indeed, historical evidence occurs as *objets trouvés* in all these texts – talismans, letters, documents, photographs, a prehistoric Medicine Wheel – and because such evidence is always incomplete and fragmented, historical 'truth' is already blurred at the edges like the piece of glass. As Linda Hutcheon says in her excellent essay, 'History and/as Intertext', 'The past *was* real, but it is lost or at least displaced, only to be reinstated as the referent of art, the relic or trace of the real.'[4] Yet Hutcheon's comment suggests that the storm glass image as analogy for historical facts raises problems, for these *objets trouvés* are not static like pieces of glass; they may be misted over and dulled by time, but precisely because of this process and the fragmentary nature of the evidence, historical representation always remains provisional and 'susceptible to infinite revision'.[5] It is at the point of engagement with historical fiction that the storm glass image breaks down/breaks apart. Interestingly both Kogawa and Wiebe emphasise the need to split open/to shatter received orthodox histories and conceptualisations of the past; it is only Laurence who seems to be able to accommodate the past without radical upsets, and she does this by creating a romance of origins which allows her narrator a 'homecoming'.

Any historical novel insists on a combination of different kinds of textual evidence – documentary plus imaginative response and fictive invention – creating the multiple codes of a discontinuous text which has plural significances but no single meaning. *The Diviners* with its mixture of personal history, pioneer narratives and legends preserved by Scots and Métis oral tradition registers the pluralism of Canadian prairie history, with its sense of slippage from historical origins together with the urge to reinvent the past in order to feel at home. Yet the dominant image of the novel remains a very fluid one, that of the river which flows both ways. *My Lovely Enemy* presents powerful images of opposition between fragmentation and unity, while recognising that such a desire for unity is utopian. *Obasan* is a chronicle of fragmentation, where even remembered family unity is an illusion in a community where Japanese-Canadians were always under threat.[6] It is a story of absences told in the absence of loved ones, and its central enigma is solved in the absence of the mother through the 'slippery pages' of a letter which has to be translated. And what is made here? Not unity, but an open mesh of language. And what is telling? Not wholeness, but a splitting open of the stone of silence. Edges that seemed softened by time have their ability to cut dangerously restored in all these novels through their narrators' intense imaginative engagement with the 'facts' of the past. I believe that any historical novel is engaged in the process of 'figuratively speaking' (as Joseph Conrad described his writing of *Nostromo* in his Author's Note to that historical novel), where factuality is displaced into fiction at the same time as the relation between the present and the past is revitalised. This fiction-making effort is really the opposite process to that of the preservation of relics that may be 'brought out and examined now and then'.

The three novels I have chosen constitute very different kinds of historical fiction; through them one may consider both the formal properties of narrative and the appropriateness of particular narrative forms for historical exploration/explanation. My project is very much influenced by Hayden White's readings of 'the historical text as literary artefact' and his focus on the rhetorical strategies within historical narratives. The proposition that it is not possible to make a naïve binary opposition between historical fact and historical fiction because any historical record is already textualised/contextualised/interpreted when we inherit it, liberates historical representation into a condition of perpetual revision 'in the light of new evidence or more sophisticated conceptualisations of problems'.[7] When White proceeds to show that histories follow identifiable fabular or mythic patterns like that of the Quest or the tragic plot of Decline and Fall, when he emphasises the fictive component of all historical narrative, we have arrived at the borderline between history and historical fiction. That borderline is blurred and almost dissolved by correspondences between the two kinds of narrative: 'Although historians and writers of fiction may be interested in different kinds of events [those which can be assigned specific time locations and those which are invented] both the forms of their respective discourses and the aims in writing are often the same.'[8] What White highlights about historical narrative is the point of view from which events are told, for it is this which conditions the kind of narrative configuration or plot structure which emerges. His remarks find a striking correspondence in Wiebe's description of his own fiction as 'looking at the actual stuff of history from a slightly different angle'.[9] History is both ancestor worship and the demystifying of unfamiliar threatening events, and the rhetorical strategies of writing history have to do with the way that historical narratives may be made accessible to readers within a particular culture.

Historical fictions participate in this cultural process/processing, and they take questions of narrative configuration a stage further along the line of 'history from a different angle' as they move from the social function of history towards subjectivity and imaginative reconstruction. The question we need to ask is, What is the imperative encoded in the particular narrative forms of the three novels I have chosen? It is partly a subjective imperative (peculiar to the individual narrator) and it is partly an imperative inherent within the chosen language and literary conventions

employed in every novel. *My Lovely Enemy* registers the subjective imperative behind historical narratives in several ways. There is the character-
isation of Professor James Dyck with his desire to 'see truly differently'
(p. 63) i.e. to restructure perceptions of history by adopting a visionary
mode; there is the description of Sir George Simpson's nineteenth-century
exploration narrative as 'imperialist' (p. 37); there is also Gillian Overton's
creative view of history as 'personality' (p. 88) in a world always 'under
construction'. So, history in *My Lovely Enemy* is not only the unearthing of
personality through Dyck's quest for the heroic figure of the vanished
Cree chieftain Maskepetoon, but it also becomes the celebration of the historian's personality as Dyck establishes a shadowy parallel between himself and Maskepetoon, affirming their correspondence through the shared
image of a body slowly turning in prairie space (p. 57 and p. 167). The
vision of history in *My Lovely Enemy* is partly a personal religious vision
designed to heal difference; but it is also impersonal, a product of the
postmodernist fictional form which Wiebe has chosen with its shifts
between realism and fantasy generating multiple ways of apprehending
reality while paying attention to what is on the margins. Decentralisation,
dissolution and through that 'unimagined discovery' hover as possibilities.
A different combination of personal/impersonal imperatives operates in
*The Diviners*, where the subjective imperative is enacted in Morag Gunn's
imaginative effort to reinvent her lost ancestry and so come into her
inheritance, 'convinced that fiction was more true than fact. Or that fact
was in fact fiction' (p. 25). And Morag does come home, though to a different place from where she started, returning to the house in Ontario, 'to
write the remaining private and fictional words, and to set down her title'
(p. 453). There is also an impersonal urge here inherent within the rather
old-fashioned modernist narrative that Laurence has chosen, and this is
the modernist urge towards moments of transcendence beyond fragmentation. These epiphanies are represented for Morag and Jules Tonnerre by
'objective correlatives', in relics like the Scottish plaid pin and the Métis
hunting knife. It is in their exchange of talismans as much as through the
living presence of their daughter Pique that Laurence's narrative effects
the reconciliation between two cultures and so confirms her prairie history
as a romance of origins.

*Obasan* combines personal and impersonal imperatives in yet another
kind of negotiation with the past, which is intimately related to the point
of view from which the narrative is told. Naomi Nakane is telling the
story of the Japanese-Canadian experience of dispersal and dispossession
during the second World War and she is telling it in 1972 while still living
on the prairies, having never gone back to Vancouver from which she was
banished in her childhood. Naomi is herself one of the dispossessed, and
her quest is a coming to terms with loss and absence as she searches for
a language to re-establish her own psychic wholeness out of the tragic
history of the Japanese-Canadian community. This is an intensely sub-

jective quest narrative that works through strategies of silence and enigma towards revelation. There are also impersonal imperatives at work here urging connections across fragmentations of story and structure, and these are the imperatives of lyric poetry. The fragmented form of Naomi's first person narrative includes letters, diaries, newspaper clippings speaking in multiple voices, as it also contains shifts from place to place, and the crucial absence of her mother. Yet connections are made in this narrative through its being assimilated into the forms of lyric poetry. In an interview in which she described the writing of the novel Kogawa said,

> The first draft was more like a very long poem than anything else – a lot of imagery, a lot less connectedness between things [i.e. the discursive connections of prose narrative]. Up till then all I'd done was write poetry, and everything else seemed boring to me... Yes, I was basically writing poetry at this point, even if it was very, very long.[10]

What remains in the finished novel are the urgent lyrical imperatives of metaphor, by which I mean that while recognising difference and separations there is also a mesh of images which invent likeness or connections between things and so shadow an imaginable coherence. I think this best describes Kogawa's way towards reconciliation of the present and the past, as Naomi recognises herself as an inheritor: she has to learn to listen to her mother's silence when her mother comes to her as a ghost in dreams. For Naomi, through all the gaps and contradictions in her experience, the one categorical assertion is that love cannot be doubted, and Kogawa's narrative like Wiebe's recognises the importance of the unconscious as a medium for the divine power, for love, for inspiration. Naomi learns to embrace the mystery of her mother's love in absence, accepting incompleteness within herself just as she accepts her dual inheritance from her aunts. In telling her story Naomi has been guided by Aunt Emily whose way has always been that of the Woman Warrior, and she tells it in the oblique manner of Obasan. As Kogawa said in the interview quoted previously, 'I think that the day of Aunt Emily is always today; Obasan has tomorrow and yesterday in her hands. I think we need them both' (p. 148). It would be simple-minded to see *Obasan* as a historical novel confirming optimistic Canadian social myths about multiculturalism and multiethnicity, for this is really an elegy for a lost community and the ending is not about integration though it is about forgiveness. Naomi has rehabilitated herself as a speaking subject and the story ends on fragile promise for the future, but Naomi is silent and alone in a secret place on the Alberta coulee.

The question remains of how the prairie is figured in *Obasan* and in the other two novels. One might begin by making the point that in *Obasan* the prairie is presented as alien space in what is a twentieth-century version of a nineteenth-century settlement narrative about wilderness. To Naomi as a child, coming to Lethbridge Alberta is 'coming to the edge of the world, a place of angry air' (p. 191), and the beetfields provide a landscape of nightmare. Such space can only be robbed of its threat by metaphor and simile with their affirmations of resemblance to other known loved places. The novel told by the adult Naomi begins on the coulee with the sound of a fisherman's voice:

> 'Umi no yo,' Uncle says, pointing to the grass. 'It's like the sea.'
> The hill surface, as if responding to a command from Uncle's outstretched hand, undulates suddenly in a breeze, with ripple after ripple of grass shadows, rhythmical as ocean waves. We wade through the dry surf, the flecks of grass hitting us like spray. (p. 1)

As Naomi remarks after her uncle's funeral, 'Perhaps some genealogist of the future will come across this patch of bones, and wonder why so many fishermen died on the prairies' (p. 225). Naomi's final reconciliation takes place on that coulee, which has become for her a secret wild garden, the place where the underground stream 'seeps' through the earth. Gaps between present and past are fused by the image of this underground stream, for it relates the topography of prairie place to Naomi's psychic landscape through which memories and dreams have seeped into waking life, making secret and restorative connections as 'soundless as breath' (p. 247). [11]

In *The Diviners* prairie spaces are not as important as the prairie town, or rather its edges like the Nuisance Grounds or the wilderness beside the Manwaka River, for Morag's journey is from a condition of marginality towards a homecoming. It is a homecoming which does not however mean a return to the prairies but to McConnell's Landing in Ontario, her inheritance 'by adoption'. The romance of ancestral place hovers on the periphery for Morag and Jules's daughter Pique who is planning to go back to her Métis uncle's farm at Galloping Mountain in Manitoba, but hers is a different story from her mother's. Morag's own story is really about displacement and resettlement, a version of the pioneer homemaker's family romance, for which the Upper Canada settler Mrs Parr Traill, Morag's 'sainted Catherine', provides an irritating if very appropriate model.

*My Lovely Enemy* is the novel most intimately connected with prairie place, transformed by Wiebe's mythologising imagination into fictional space. For Wiebe the land is still the locus of power as it had been for nineteenth-century white settlers and for the indigenous Cree and Blackfoot. Wiebe is seeking 'to uninvent the grammar of history' which dispossessed the Indians and to restore through his fictions the Indian sense of the spiritual power of prairie places. [12] Working by a logic of the emotions, Wiebe takes his direction here from Jorge Luis Borges's story, 'Tlön, Uqbar, Orbis Tertius', for that fantasy of invented worlds offers multiple possibilities for the reinterpretation of history.[13] However, Borges's time fantasy lacks the very element which Wiebe's novel foregrounds – the element of place – for in *My Lovely Enemy* the prairie itself is the very ground of continuity, the place where transformations of history happen. As his narrator says, 'On the prairie the only graspable image for time is the movement of a body in space; consequently, the only image for a person's outlook on humanity is direction' (p. 156). In a novel like this, the gaps within history may be bridged when images of time are converted into images of place, and revisions of history take place on the prairie reimagined as textual space.

The innocuous image of storm glass smoothed by time has been shattered in this study of the multiplicities and discontinuities within prairie fiction. I would like to end with the suggestion that the efforts of fictive historical narrative, enmeshed as they are with the narrator's subjectivity, are directed less towards the preservation of history than towards creating what Hayden White calls 'a congenial imaginary relationship which the subject bears towards his/her own social and cultural situation'.[14]

NOTES

1. Margaret Laurence, *The Diviners* (1974); rpt. Toronto: McClelland & Stewart, New Canadian Library, 1978); Joy Kogawa, *Obasan* (1981; rpt. Harmondsworth: Penguin, 1983); Rudy Wiebe, *My Lovely Enemy* (Toronto: McClelland & Stewart, 1983). All page references will be to these editions and included in the text.
2. J.J. Healy, 'Literature, Power and the Refusals of Big Bear: Reflections on the treatment of the Indian and of the Aborigine', in R. McDougall & G. Whitlock, ed., *Australian/Canadian Literatures in English: Comparative Perspectives* (Sydney: Methuen, 1987), p. 80.
3. Jane Urquhart, 'Storm Glass', in *Storm Glass* (Erin, Ontario: The Porcupine's Quill, 1987), p. 39.
4. L. Hutcheon, 'History and/as Intertext', in J. Moss, ed., *Future Indicative: Literary Theory and Canadian Literature* (Ottawa: University of Ottawa Press, 1987), p. 173.
5. Hayden White, 'The Historical Text as Literary Artefact', in *Tropics of Discourse* (Baltimore: Johns Hopkins University Press, 1978), p. 82.
6. For a socio-historical account to supplement Kogawa's fiction, see Ann Gomer Sunahara, *The Politics of Racism: The Uprooting of Japanese-Canadians during the Second World War* (Toronto: Lorimer, 1981).
7. H. White, 'The Historical Text as Literary Artefact', p. 82.
8. H. White, 'The Fictions of Factual Representation', in *Tropics of Discourse*, p. 121.
9. S. Newman, 'Unearthing Language: An Interview with Rudy Wiebe and Robert Kroetsch', in W.J. Keith, ed., *A Voice in the Land* (Edmonton: NeWest, 1981), p. 230.
10. 'Joy Kogawa', in A. Garrod, ed., *Speaking for Myself: Canadian Writers in Interview* (St John's, Newfoundland: Breakwater, 1986), p. 150.
11. For a fuller discussion of the language of *Obasan*, see C.A. Howells, *Private and Fictional Words: Canadian Women Novelists of the 1970s and 80s* (London: Methuen, 1987), pp. 125-9.
12. See J.J. Healy, p. 80.

13. Jorge Luis Borges, 'Tlön, Uqbar, Orbis Tertius' (1961; rpt. in *Labyrinths*, Harmondsworth: Penguin, 1982).
14. H. White's concluding essay in *The Content of the Form: Narrative Discourse and Historical Representation* (Baltimore: Johns Hopkins University Press, 1987). My reference is taken from S. Bann's review, 'Hayden White and History', *London Review of Books*, 17 September 1987, 17-18.

# JOAN CRATE

Joan Crate was born in Yellowknife, and she has lived in the Northwest Territories, British Columbia, Alberta and Saskatchewan. Although she dropped out of high school, she now has an M.A. in Creative Writing from the University of Calgary. Her first novel, *Breathing Water*, was published in 1989. She has also published a book of poetry, *Pale as Red Ladies* (Brick). Her work has also been published in several Canadian journals and anthologies and aired on CBC radio. Joan Crate is presently teaching English at Red Deer College. This selection is from a novel in progress entitled *Night Terrors*, to be published by NeWest.

JOAN CRATE

# Why I Write

I have met writers who have told me that they 'have' to write, that writing to them is almost as necessary as breathing, an involuntary, undeniable compulsion. Frequently I have wished to be like those writers. Nevertheless, I'm not. I write because writing interests me. I can't say it's always 'fun', although sometimes that is the case. Generally, though, I find it a serious act, even when I p/lay with the mus(e)/ic of words.

Maybe that's it. Maybe the feat of writing is like a sexual act, an encounter on sheets. Who knows what may happen, what might be created? There's always the possibility of surprise, of conceit, extended metaphor, rising action, climax. Or intense frustration.

Certainly writing requires not just a little passion, and there's the seduction of form, of abstract and concrete images, their ap/peals to the ears, all the senses: taste, touch, smell, shape, colour ('so much depends/upon//a red wheel/barrow').

The 'creative' urge is perhaps pro/creative. After having four children, I may still be attempting the impossible goal of achieving proficient parenthood. I continue producing works that are difficult to conceive, that prove to be unpredictable and disobedient in their infancy, words that never come when they're called, no matter by what name, what genre.

Or maybe writing provides me with an excuse for ignoring even the most basic rules of cooking, of cleaning.

JOAN CRATE

# Going Back

Eileen walks down a street wrapped in a white cape. It's the cape she bought not long before she was admitted to the hospital, when she let Terri take her shopping.

'There's this fabulous little consignment store. You've got to see it,' Terri had prattled. 'Good quality stuff and cheap. They have some dresses and suits I think yer gonna like. You've got to get some new clothes, ya know. No one can find you in the old ones and you can't wear that one skirt and pair of pants that fit you forever.'

So Eileen had conceded, and during lunch hour they had driven to the consignment shop in Terri's Firebird since it had the advantage of signal lights and tyres with visible tread.

Once inside the dingy store, Terri swept fram rack to rack like 'Employee of the Month' on amphetamines, calling Eileen's attention to a number of dresses and suits in 5's and 7's, sizes Eileen hadn't worn since she was a kid. Terri clutched hemlines, pinched waists, demanded that Eileen examine seams, linings, the frayed tabs that gave cleaning instructions. Although Eileen tried valiantly to share Terri's enthusiasm, she was unable to. How heavy the garments looked, their fabrics rough and thick. Eileen couldn't bear the thought of them scouring her skin, pressing down her shoulders, binding her limbs, her lungs.

'No,' she said, 'I don't like them.'

And then her eyes ascended from the teal cotton, the grey corduroy, the black and burgundy wool blends that Terri had spread out before her like a dreadful smorgasbord, to a billow of pure light. The white cape.

Now she walks in it, chilled to the bone, yet light, full of air.

Eileen was unprepared for just how cold it is, and she draws the white wool closer to her skin.

Just when it seemed that Spring was here to stay, when buds appeared on trees and birds in the sky, when the bank had tacked up their 'The early bird gets to earn' bulletins for a new type of term deposit, and 'Invest in Endless Summers' posters suggesting short-term loans; just when she had started to peer hesitantly into future seasons, to talk of summer heat and possible vacations; the snow fell. The previous afternoon a frozen north wind dispensed it like a clump of bad news.

The face of the city has been changed, all sharpness erased, all colour bled. Everything: the street, traffic lights, sidewalks, cars, buildings and the sky reflect the snow's blank stare.

It's difficult to see Eileen walking in her white cape. She knows this. White against white, and she has pulled up her hood to conceal her dark hair, her face.

It's just before twelve. Mr. Mason was in a meeting, and this enabled Eileen to slip out of the office early to drive downtown. She parked the car – somewhere, she really can't remember – and caught the train into the city centre.

The traffic on the street is heavy, yet enveloped in a blanket of ice-fog it sounds and feels a great distance away. In another city perhaps, or another time. Clouds have fallen into the streets, isolating the people from the place, feet from the sidewalks, cars from asphalt. Eileen is encased in cloud, has become cloud with edges difficult to define.

She lids her eyes. The slur of traffic immediately dulls and Eileen wonders what happened, feels she has been eclipsed by weather. Suddenly there are no more cars and people, no colour at all. She has disappeared. Did anyone notice? Eileen has disappeared.

When she opens her eyes, the sky has darkened and nothing can be seen but Eileen's white cape, and emerging from it, her long fingers clasped together for warmth. She blinks. So very dark, yet now a yellowish light flickers, a candle flame, and another, and another. A head emerges below her, hair a silver rope down her back, eyes lowered, and a veined brown hand lights candle after candle. 'Blessed are thee among women.'

The woman's body does not exist, is merely a shadow, unless she is wearing black, all black in the blackness. The heavy wooden cross at her thin neck suggests shoulders, a torso.

The woman falls – to her invisible knees Eileen supposes – and clutches her hands together. Her face lifts, eyes travel. Up. Up over Eileen's white thighs, her white breasts, her face emerging from the white hood.

The woman shrieks. She jerks her head around as if searching for someone else to share her vision, to confirm it.

'No, it's here, she's really here! A miracle! Mother Mary!' But there is no one to witness Sophie's revelation.

'I'm not worthy,' the woman gasps. Her fingers have found the hem of Eileen's white cape. They grope. They bring the material to her crumpled lips, kiss, kiss again and again.

'Mother,' Eileen interjects.

Below Eileen the dark eyes ignite, flicker wildly over Eileen's features. The face stretches open in terror, then amazement, shudders in and out of a frantic range of emotions. Her hands pull from the hemline, convulse, and the wooden cross bobs frantically.

Eileen hopes this is not the onset of a heart attack. She does not want to witness her Mother's death, much less be the cause of it. She wants nothing at all to do with the crazy woman who was raised by the nuns in their school, ruined by the nuns. The woman who ruined her. She crouches down, dips her fingers into shadow and touches the quivering bones of her mother's shoulder. 'Calm down.'

'Yes,' Mother gasps. 'Calm down.'

Eileen watches her mother, so tiny below her, eyes a torch fuelled with hope, and also fear – always present when Mother looks at Eileen. This fear in Mother's eyes spills out, splashes her daughter even now, as she stands over the woman, out of another time, invulnerable. She should be invulnerable, yet Mother's fear seeps through Eileen's white cape, soils her skin. This small, mad woman.

'Lord have mercy,' the old woman whispers.

How *can* she be here at the altar of the Virgin Mary, with Mother kneeling before her. How is it possible? The woman is convinced she is witnessing a miracle.

At dinner time she will clutch her hands together, eyes wild, and babble of her vision to the sisters, the priest. And Mother, frantic mother, will not be believed.

'For God's sake Mother, it's me, Eileen!'

The woman straightens, peels her lips from Eileen's hem, and looks up to her. Eileen shivers.

Who would have thought after all these years that she would still be incensed by Mother, afraid of Mother, that she would still sting with the memory of words the woman had flung at Eileen in the middle of some cold night so long ago.

'Unholy,' she had screamed, pointing at her daughter, who was terrified by waking up standing next to the woodstove, not knowing how she got there, why her feet were cut from shards of the crockery soup pot, her legs scalded, who did not know why Mother pointed at her, why she uttered those words Eileen has tried a lifetime to forget, the words she can't forget, 'Possessed, possessed!'

'Nightmares, Sophie. Just nightmares,' Pop had insisted, patting Mother's shoulder. But she shook him off. No, she would not believe him. 'Evil!' she cried, still pointing at Eileen. 'God help us,' her eyes blazing. 'Cast out the demons with a word,' she hissed.

Eileen remembers. Eileen can neither forget nor forgive.

Mother believed it. For most of Eileen's life, Mother believed that her daughter was possessed by the devil, by demons, by an unclean spirit; she named them all; and for oh, such a long time, Eileen will not admit how long, she believed it too. Part of her believed it, though it was not logical, not reasonable. Forever she had believed it, though for a time when her children were babies, when she was a young wife who pictured her future as a tree-lined street, sunny and well travelled, this belief was reduced to a small doubt that nibbled behind her eyes only when she was tired or when the children cried in the night, or her husband stalked out of the house announcing, 'It's closing in on me. I need more space!'

'Forgive me, Eileen,' Mother grunts, her eyes bright as beer bottle glass. 'Please, please forgive me!'

Behind Mother the sky bleaches. Snow falls into her grey hair, flickers over her face. She grips Eileen's hem tighter, feels it dissipate in her fingers. 'No! Don't go!' she beseeches her daughter turning to mist. 'I have sinned.'

'You sure as hell have,' Eileen tells her, melting into a diferent land-scape.

She inhales icy air, welcomes the chill in her lungs. She wonders what time it is, and if she's late for work. Just how long did she leave for? How long was she with Mother? Who begged her forgiveness. Who needs her forgiveness.

Eileen looks around her. She is alone on the street in Calgary with the snow, the present, and the traffic. And Mother's final plea.

Poor Mother.

# ISABEL HUGGAN

Isabel Huggan was born in Ontario, Canada, in 1943,
and spent her life in that province until 1987 when,
with her husband and daughter, she moved to
Kenya, and then to France, where she now lives. A
writer of short stories whose work appears in
magazines and anthologies, and a teacher of creative
writing, Isabel also writes occasional book reviews
and a regular newspaper column. She happily
confesses that her daughter has *never* been a
Brownie. *The Elizabeth Stories* was published in 1984
in Canada by Oberon Press, and in 1987 in the USA
and Britain by Viking-Penguin, and in 1990 in France
(as *L'Echappée Belle*) by Gallimard. It won the 1987
Book-of-the-Month Club 'New Voice' Award. Her
most recent book is *You Never Know*, published in
Canada by Alfred A. Knopf and in the USA by
Viking-Penguin.

ISABEL HUGGAN

# Why I Write

I started with stones. Smooth stones heavy to my eight-year-old hands and shining black with the cold water of Lake Huron still dripping through my fingers. Wet, the stones gave up their fossil-secrets more easily – back home dry and dull, in bushel baskets stacked behind the furnace, they mumbled and murmured, mysterious and vague, until I spit on them and brought to life those ancient fragments of shell and half-remembered fern. Rubbing my saliva on the stones I would feel sad, for although I loved keeping these stone treasures I didn't know what to do with them. I simply needed to have them.

Real fossils are time's shorthand, abbreviated geology, the world contracted, something to hold in the hand – compact, concrete. Memory compounded, knowledge condensed into this – the texture of wet stone beneath the tracing fingers of a child.

Around the time I was so enamoured of fossils, some adult friend of the family gave me another rock, a small chunk of iron pyrite. Fool's gold. I am holding it now and it sits like a dense gleaming toad in my palm, its jagged metallic surfaces catching the light – but it doesn't shine like real gold, does it? (Me, innocent, worrying I might be taken for a fool by all that glitters.)

Now, no longer naive but still sifting through words to find the real ones, on the lookout for those which seem, even for a moment, like something else. Corners of my brains stacked with baskets of words, treasures to be lingered over and examined, lessons to be learned.

The face of a stranger in an underground train passing mine in the station, the flash of what? who? it could have been, it might well be ... the beginning of a story not true until it's written, not real until it's read. Grasping the quick moments, making them into something else more lasting...

I have always been a loyal sentry and merchant of nostalgia, setting up my souvenir stall on the road to the wharf by the River Styx. 'Here now, madam, a little something to take with you? A line of poetry smooth as a pebble, a phrase bright as an insect's wing, a sweet clause shed as easily as a snakeskin in the grass. Embrace my words, madam, and keep them, even as you go into the final darkness. You cannot take your fossils, you cannot take your jewels ... but read my pages before you get in the boat and you'll carry them across to the other side. You'll have this world forever.'

Me, I never followed the oral tradition, have never been a troubadour, can't play the guitar. Singing stories has to do with plot, who did what to whom and why, and then the chorus again to make sure we remember. No, I belong to the other tribe who painted dreams on the walls of caves, who stacked up stones on the tops of hills, who left behind things to mark their passing.

I am one of them, putting things into words, writing the pictures, writing the smell and feel of the wind. The stench of blood, the sound of marching feet, the shadow of passing clouds. The born baby, the dead hope, the crazy kiss...

'Get it down,' my credo. 'Make it real' my anthem. This thing made of words is what I have made of myself ... and as soon as I have made it, I let it go.

And let it sink like a stone, let it build like a stone in the hands of men making walls, let it sing like stone beneath feet in the streets. Let it lie in your hand like a stone from the deep. Here, let me give it to you to hold for a while.

'Fossil!'

ISABEL HUGGAN

# Starting with the Chair

My son is balancing on the edge of a rocking chair in the corner of my study with a thick red anthology of English Literature on his knee, and he is telling me that these sonnets of Shakespeare's are really very good, especially the satisfying couplets at the end. I am sitting at my desk, where I had been writing a letter until he knocked at the door, and am trying not to show my pleasure, for at his age my approval annoys him as much as he desires it.

A small scene, infinitely expandable, endlessly rich in possibility. Lives ready to be unfurled from any point in the room, histories waiting to be explicated like unfolding Chinese boxes. Start anywhere.

Start with my son Oliver – his dark curls, so like his father's, falling down his forehead as he bends intently over the page, in love with English itself. He reads two sonnets aloud to prove how good they are, and he rolls the words around in his mouth as if they were large, sweet grapes. Those Italian ones, pale green and tasting of honey – we used to pick them from the vineyard ourselves the year we spent in Tuscany on Daniel's sabbatical. Oliver was only a toddler then.

Or the book from which he reads – my university text 25 years ago when I was studying English literature, believing absolutely that someday I would be a poet. A real poet. Along the margins of the pages are now-obscure references, silly drawings, brief but suggestive messages written to a young man who sat beside me in that first-year survey class. (His name, apparently, was Jeffrey.) From the look of these pages it is clear that I paid little attention to the text...my interest was not in someone else's poems but in my own.

Oliver at 16 shows much greater respect for what the past can offer, and he seems to have a genuine love of the printed word – but his real concern lies elsewhere: he wants to be a doctor, he says. A psychiatrist. That's probably the result of his seeing one – only a therapist, really, but we decided it was essential during these last few months since Daniel and I finally divorced. Oliver has transferred most of his affection and filial allegiance to the doctor, who explains to Daniel and me that this is a necessary process he must go through to heal his legitimate hurt and anger at having his life disrupted. I feel wounded by 'legitimate' as if he too is subtly blaming us... But in fact, he is a kindly man, and only wants to see our son through this difficult time as well as he can. It will pass, the doctor promises. All things shall pass.

Or the room in which we sit – where, outside the window, several enormous clumps of lavender are falling over themselves with fragrant blossoms: but the latch on the window is closed and we cannot catch the scent. We can only imagine it, as we do as soon as we so much as think the word lavender. Which comes first to mind, Oliver and I asked each other over supper last week, the colour of lavender or the smell? We could not agree, but it took us through the breaded turkey right past salad to dessert. It is hard, sometimes, to find a topic of conversation to keep us from staring at our plates as we eat in silence, both of us deep in our dark and private thoughts. Neither of us speaks of missing Daniel but we are aware of his absence, there is still hurt radiating from the void where he was. We are an amputated family suffering phantom pain.

Or the desk at which I am seated, its surface cluttered with papers and small objects, each one able to transform moment into memory. These things I carry from place to place, talismans against my own oblivion – the empty enamelled box, the Ojibway sweet-grass basket full of shells and calling cards, or the small clay god, mouth puckered in a round O as if ready to whistle, whose eternal task it is to banish depression. (So Daniel was told by an old lady in a Guatemalan market from whom he also bought a jade pendant to ward against indigestion; the stone left green marks on my clothes when I wore it on a chain around my neck.)

Or the rocking chair on which my son sits. Yes, I like the idea of a chair as means of transportation and of entry. The chair as engine, the chair as door, the chair as key. Start with this chair...

The padded seat is covered with floral needlepoint, giving the chair a more elegant appearance than it had when first I got it from my mother's sister, Auntie Glad. Its covering then had been drab fabric in a geometric design unsuitable for an old-fashioned chair. It was obviously a scrap of material brought home by Gladys from the textile factory where she used to buy remnants for next to nothing. Her house filled itself over the years with homemade pillows and slip covers and curtains in odd patterns and clashing colours: nothing matched, and that was as she liked it. She was an expansive, happy woman who took delight in a motley life – the unforeseen pleasures, the unexpected bargains.

My aunt kept the old chair in her home for more than two decades because, although it had been left to my mother in my grandmother's will, it was not allowed in our house by my father, who detested rocking chairs. It was old, so old it was possibly valuable, but no one knew exactly from where it had come or where it had been made – there was some talk it'd been brought over from Britain but I think more likely it was from one of those small towns in Ontario where you see empty furniture factories nowadays. It had belonged to my great-grandmother who died on the family farm near Belleville at the beginning of this century and that, rather than its status as an antique, gave the chair legendary rank in our genealogy: the matriarch who founded our Canadian line had died in its arms.

The chair is big, with such a wide berth it takes up a lot of room as it rocks: my father's major argument against it was always its size whenever the subject came up. Which it didn't often, since my mother always favoured harmony over strife, and allowed as how it was far more sensible to keep the chair at Glad's (who lived only an hour away) where she could sit in it from time to time. In her eyes, there had been a nice compromise: in mine, the chair always meant my father had won and she had lost.

My mother remembered spending happy hours as a child curled on the padded seat, which was large enough for her to pull her legs up underneath as she read. Whenever she described this scene, she portrayed herself with a novel in one hand and an apple in the other. It was a picture which intrigued me, because it seemed as if my mother was Jo in *Little Women*, who was, of course, who I wanted to be. It was curiously unsettling to have both Jo and my mother in mind at once.

Although the chair is sufficiently broad for a child's body to sprawl comfortably, no adult locked within its encasing arms can do anything but sit very straight against its firm back. Slouching and slumping are out of the question. Which is how the chair tells us about the character of the Welsh-born lady who died in it: she must have had her spine rigid against the wooden back even as she drew her last breath, for when they found her she was sitting with hands folded in her lap, as stiffly upright in death as she'd been in life.

Actually, it wasn't 'they' who found her, it was Janet, the young hired girl she'd employed only that spring (my great-grandmother died in November). Janet came from a Scottish family on a neighbouring farm down the concession, and had taken good care of the old woman all through the summer, quietly watching her stubborn grasp on life weaken. Janet never let on what she thought to any of her employer's children or grandchildren when they came to visit – that soon she'd be out of a job.

The day my great-grandmother passed on had been a busy one for Janet, baking raisin bread and lemon pie and two kinds of cake to serve when Norma Walpole, wife of the Methodist minister, came to spend her regular Tuesday afternoon 'keeping company'. Mrs. Walpole was a good-hearted, stout soul who liked a little something with her tea, and Janet always obliged. That day the Reverend's wife had spent her hours in sociable silence, as the elderly are wont to do, sitting by the parlour wood stove and crocheting a little. Simply being present.

Janet saw Mrs. Walpole to the front door just as the clock in the hall struck five, and after clearing the tea-things she'd come into the room to stoke up the waning fire in the stove. Then had pulled the heavy drapes against the night, noting there was a thin line of cold blue light still on the horizon: it made her think of all the months of winter darkness yet ahead, she said.

After she'd done that, still chattering (as she did continually to fill the still rooms with the sound of a voice), she'd gone over to arrange a woollen shawl around those frail and ailing shoulders. It was normal for my great-grandmother to sit wordlessly, dreaming by the fire, and so that didn't trouble Janet, she kept on talking as always: it was only when her hand brushed the silent woman's wrinkled neck that she cried out in fright, for the feel of the skin was like ice.

Janet was inconsolable, blaming herself for not being with her mistress at the moment of departure from this world, for having let her die alone in the room. 'All alone, with never another soul to see her out.' She wept and howled and it seemed would never be comforted: luckily, my great-uncle Howard, still single at forty and youngest of the deceased's five living children, arrived late that night from town where he was a senior partner in a small law firm, and took it upon himself to offer solace to Janet in the pantry while the rest of the family were organizing things in the parlour.

When, some months later, it became evident that Uncle Howard's charitable efforts would bear fruit, he and young Janet were married by Reverend Walpole and Janet became my mother's favourite aunt. I remember her as a very old lady, speckled all over like a wild bird's egg, and with a sharp little face which always looked slightly injured and put-out. She was not well-educated and in a family such as ours where pride was taken in academic accomplishments – it was how one left the farm, after all – poor Janet was forever scorned and until her dying day referred to, behind her back, as 'the help'. Howard progressed in life in spite of Janet, his sisters and brothers and their children all said, and only my mother liked her and stuck up for her and claimed that it was entirely on her account that he eventually became a judge.

It was from Janet that the story about the chair originally came, and it may have been because of fondness for her aunt that my mother felt such strong sentiment about a piece of furniture. She would tell and retell Janet's tale as if it were her own, as it were she herself who had found her dead grandmother. My mother's mother – Howard's sister – had been left the chair because she was the eldest of the five, and when she died, they found she'd written on a slip of paper, stuck in the corner of her dressing table mirror, that her daughter Gwen was to have 'the old padded rocker'.

And then my mother Gwen died, unexpectedly and far too young, and Auntie Glad said to me at her funeral, 'Now child, you're the eldest, you'll have her chair.' No longer a child – I'd been married for two years and was pregnant with Oliver at the time – I couldn't think for a moment what she meant until she made the movement of rocking back and forth. 'It'll be a grand place to suckle the baby,' she added, looking pointedly at my rounded abdomen. 'That straight back'll give you good support, and the arms are the right height too, mark my words. You and that husband of yours come and get it soon as you can.'

Unlike my father, Daniel is a man of loosely held opinion, letting notions run carelessly through his life like glass beads through an Arab trader's fingers. If I liked the big chair and wanted it in our house, it was all the same to him...personally, he thought it grotesque, he said, but maybe a change of covering would help.

Life was always like that with Daniel during our years of marriage: his slight removal from, and disavowal of, whatever I liked or wanted, but passive acceptance. Yes, have it, by all means. I'd never prevent you, what sort of guy do you think I am, anyway? Easy-going laughter, acquiescence, and what I believed for too many years must be love.

Of course I did nurse Oliver in the chair, for Gladys had been correct, the enclosure of the back and arms provided a firm frame within which to experience that new, strange sensation of his tiny sweet mouth pulling fiercely at my nipple. Sometimes it would be so sharp I'd feel as if my entire body were about to splinter itself around the room, and it was only the old chair holding me together that prevented me from flying apart. From the joy of motherhood or from the pain? Who knows.

Oliver is our only child, Daniel's and mine. I feel as if I have let my mother's family down by not having a daughter to whom to pass the chair, and I am glad that big jolly Aunt Glad and little freckled Great-Aunt Janet are dead and gone so that they don't have to know our line is dwindling out. Of course, neither of them would ever have said a word to make me feel bad, but they would have felt quietly sad. I know it, and I still grieve on their account as well as mine.

But the way things have turned out, it's been better having only one kid to call himself – ruefully, and with some humour – the 'product of a broken home'. Oliver divides his heart evenly between us, us and the doctor, that is. I understand – I've been to a therapist too, although not the same one. It was a few years ago, around the time Daniel brought back the small clay god, hoping with that gesture to make me smile, to force me to forgive him for having gone to Guatemala in the first place.

We both acted as if what had happened was a quarrel over principles – I disagreed with his doing business in that country and he, typically, said that his deals (importing native crafts to Toronto) were nothing to do with politics. As if money could change hands in Guatemala in the 1980s without that being a political act! In truth, I had been increasingly depressed about how little we understood each other well before his trip, and I found myself sinking deeper into gloom with each new event which proved me right.

But the clay god did make me laugh, and I was genuinely touched by his wanting me to feel better, to be myself again: I would sit in the old rocking chair, enclosed and safe, trying to remember how we had fallen in love, hoping that if I could figure that out we could manage to keep on going. I wanted to stay married at the same time as I was clearly, and increasingly, miserable. When I was feeling especially low, I would think of my great-grandmother, wishing that I too could simply give up the ghost as I rocked. Nothing overtly suicidal, you understand, just that total giving up which is deeper than apathy, worse than anger. And which eventually passed.

Oliver and I have lived here without Daniel since last year and the new arrangement suits me well: I am nearly finished the book of poems I began years ago, and with luck it will be published later this fall. My contract is with a small regional press, never going to make me famous but at least respectable, acceptable, a real poet after all this time... Naturally, being a perfectionist, I am still fine-tuning some of the poems and it's an interminable process, for I am always capable of finding another word to alter or remove.

The problem is usually Daniel – not his direct interference of course, or even his name, but a word here or a phrase there which evokes his face, the sound of his voice, the way he would lean back when he was listening which meant he wasn't really listening at all. The intensity of his pale blue eyes seems to crop up everywhere: in one poem the sky, in another (about a young girl running away from home), the colour of a passing car. Somehow, his physical presence makes its way unbidden into all my poetry... No matter that I want these poems to be pure, or believe myself to be creating them from language undefiled by remembrance, I find Daniel emerging and taking over.

You see here, for example. All sources flow to the same end as all rivers run into the sea. No matter which object in the room I might have chosen, I have only one story to tell and there is only one end to the story.

One day our marriage came apart as Daniel, sitting on the edge of the bed pulling on his socks, said that I must believe it was nothing personal, but it was finished. It, whatever it had been that was us. 'Honestly, nothing personal,' he said again. I was stricken, not with shock or sadness, but with rage -- rage at myself for having tried too long to stay in love with him, and rage that it was Daniel, ever the slippery prevaricator, the laid-back procrastinator, Daniel who had dared first to speak the truth.

My son leans back now in the rocking chair with a sigh of deep satisfaction, having read the last two lines of Sonnet 30. The chair makes a gaspy, creaking sound and then the room is suddenly very still, as if every object in it had drawn breath, and I look down at the letter (an impersonal letter dealing with a forgotten insurance policy) I've been writing to Daniel, and tears come to my eyes. Oliver will be entirely fed up if he thinks his recitation has made me emotional, and so I keep my head down for a long time, as if contemplating Shakespeare's genius. My inky words before me on the ivory-coloured paper swim and blur, and I pull myself together only by thinking of the old rocking chair, which leads me to plucky little Janet, her back firmly wedged against the corner of the pantry shelf, lifting her skirts for Howard. A spunky survivor, that Janet. There's a lesson there.

Oliver rises from the chair, and closes the old red textbook with a snap. 'What would have happened if you'd gone off with this Jeffrey?' he says, and in his awkward, adolescent way puts his hand on my hair in a comradely pat. 'This person you wrote notes to in the margins,' he adds.

'Ah, he was never a serious candidate,' I say, raising my head again and ready to banter in the way we've developed between us these past months. 'He was only marginal, Oliver.'

But nothing is marginal, is it? Not the book nor the old rocking chair, nor the letter to the father of my son, nor the sound of sonnets being read aloud as the sun is streaming through the window. Nor the lavender outside, strung all over with bees. It is all history, and it is all here in every present moment.

There is nothing in our lives that doesn't fit.

# UNITED KINGDOM

# JO SHAPCOTT

Jo Shapcott came to prominence when she won first prize in the National Poetry Competition in 1986. Her first collection, *Electroplating the Baby*, published in 1988 by Bloodaxe Books, was awarded a Commonwealth Prize. She is the first person to have won the National Poetry Competition twice – it was awarded again in 1991 for the widely acclaimed poem, 'Phrase Book'. Shapcott has won several other awards and prizes for her poetry including the *New Statesman's* Prudence Farmer Award. In 1991 she was the Judith E Wilson Senior Visiting Fellow at Cambridge University. Her second volume of poems, *Phrase Book*, published by OUP in 1992, was a Poetry Book Society Choice.

# Jo Shapcott

## BO PEEP SAVES THE WORLD

Sheep are self-sacrificing,
though not many people know it.
You can set a flock to eat up
the smog, to nibble at the nitrate
slime on the field and suck
the effluent from the river.

Best of all, their farts are full of ozone
and they do their utmost as they
huddle under trees against the storms
to send enough into the atmosphere
for mending the holes in the sky
over the Antarctic and the Arctic.

They can stand a season or two
of this work, remaining strong and clean
and even lambing, though they won't have twins.
Then the heart goes out of them
and they crumble one by one over a few days,
little heaps of spoiled wool dotting the field
too dangerous to touch.

## RHINOCEROS

What else to do
but nourish the rhinoceros
inside me, feed him up with good hay,

cream his rough hide
with almond oil
until it gleams,

polish the two horns
on his face with beeswax
until he gets surprising glimpses,

rinse his scaley feet
in rosewater.
Once prepared let him

find the deepest pit
of mud within my heart
and let him roll, roll, roll.


## THE MAD COW IN SPACE

Down there is little England, London, a flash
of crazy vision showing me a row
of heads on spikes outside the Tower. Still rotten,
still beautiful but ruined for me now
I've seen stars with no atmosphere in the way.
Millions are on the Underground, going to work.
I can see them too, teeming just under
the Earth's crust. I'm weightless. Couldn't
fall over if you pushed me for a year.
The silence is an uproar and I write
with a special pen in which the ink can flow
without gravity to drag it onto the page.
I'm trying to escape the pull myself:
don't want to look back at the Earth or send
more messages down to base about the way
it looks from here. Believe me, every smash,
every shot, every crack and blast is visible
and going right to plan but I can't stand
the Earth's screams as the blood touches her prissy skirt.


## LIFE

My life as a bat
is for hearing
the world.

If I pitch it right
I can hear
just where you are.

If I pitch it right
I can hear inside your body:

the state of your health,
and more, I can hear
into your mind.

Bat death is not listening.

My life as a frog
is for touching
other things.

I'm very moist
so I don't get stuck
in the water.

I'm very moist
so I can cling
onto your back
for three days and nights.

Frog death is separation.

My life as an iguana
is for tasting
everything.

My tongue is very fast
because the flavour
of the air
is so subtle.

It's long enough
to surprise
the smallest piece of you
from extremely far away.

Iguana death is a closed mouth.

## LITTLE REQUIEM

One, two.
My mother's head's so bad she isn't sure
Three, four.
That she can count to ten, so I count with her.
Five, six.
A little spasm at her eyelid, 'No.'
Seven.
An angry flap of fingers, 'I just want,'
Eight.
  'To know,' Nine.
     'How,' Ten.
       'To take,' Ten.
         'The last,' Ten.
'Breath.'

# MARINA WARNER

Marina Warner was born in London of an Italian mother and an English father. She has written five novels including *Indigo* and *Mermaids in the Basement*. *The Lost Father* (1988) was a Regional Prize Winner of the Commonwealth Writer's Prize. She also writes history and criticism, focusing mainly on female symbolism (*Alone of All Her Sex: the Myth and the Cult of the Virgin Mary; Joan of Arc; Monuments and Maidens*), and her study of fairytales, *From the Beast to the Blonde*, will be published in October 1994.

Marina Warner lives in London with her husband, the artist John Dewe Mathews, and one son.

MARINA WARNER

# Why I Write

I was a bookworm as a child, because I liked entering other worlds through stories. Above all, I liked stories which imagined secret or hidden or hitherto unapprehended worlds: *The Secret Garden* by Frances Hodgson Burnett and myths about the underworld (or the empyrean). I had an Edwardian illustrated book by a man called Guerber, *The Myths of the Greeks and Romans*, and the stories it told, about Persephone abducted while she was picking flowers to become queen of hell and Ariadne helping Theseus enter the labyrinth to kill the Minotaur and Icarus falling after his wings melted made a permanent impression on me. I also liked Enid Blyton and the children's adventures she described – passing behind a waterfall to find treasure, and I especially wanted to be a tomboy like her character George in the *Famous Five*. So I think that writing was linked with refusing the limits of my state, and with voyaging – with leaving the space of home, school and my given circumstances (a clumsy, plump girl child lacking in courage), and in many ways it still is. I do a lot of research so that I can carry myself off to other worlds and inhabit them imaginatively.

But the other worlds are also alternatives, possibilities, strategies of redress. Both in the historical studies I've written and in the fiction, I go on the attack – sometimes of what I cherish – to redraw its limits and its promises. I am now finishing a study of fairy tales, and the reason I was attracted to them, not only as an avid reader of them since childhood, but as a critical writer, lies with their utopian defiance – their 'heroic optimism', in Angela Carter's phrase. The Czech dissidents' maxim used to be 'Live as if the freedoms you want are yours already'; in a way, writing is one way of living the freedoms you want.

MARINA WARNER

# Salvage

(After Tiepolo's *The Finding of Moses: Exodus* 2: 4-9)

The only other woman living in the hotel besides Kate wasn't a guest, but the hotelier's girlfriend, and she waited on him with quiet ceremony each night as he presided over the restaurant from the corner of the dark inner room behind the bar. A *pied-noir*, he'd come out to this corner of the colonies with the first strangers' army a long time ago, and he too had kept the flowery manners of the past, and a formal mode of speech. She never sat down with him, but now and then disappeared behind a curtain, where, it was said, she also fixed pipes for him to smoke, later. The ropes standing out on the backs of his hands betrayed how the circulation of his blood had slowed right down.

There were a few other women, younger than Kate, who frequented the veranda of the hotel; they weren't admitted into the dining room, or to the hotel's inner courtyard. It was easy, once inside, to forget that a war was going on, as a broad-leafed frangipani tree spread scented shade on the tables set out underneath and dropped waxy flowers on to the undiminished fine linen of earlier days, while croissants were brought warm from the oven by the cook; he, too, had learned his trade from the former power. The other women were kept outside. They waited for customers at the *gueridons* on the veranda, with fizzy drinks from bottles with famous American brand names. You could tell from the cap, which was stamped off-register by hand, that they weren't the real thing.

Kate was shown the difference during the first days of her stay in the city, and she soon learned on her own account how everything was used more than once, passed from hand to hand, leaving a tiny doit of wealth behind as it went. Imitation wasn't really the word. Nor was fake, or cheat. It was more that things were adapted. Taken, named, made to resemble, to belong to a family of other things that offered them hospitality and added value. Salvaged.

She'd arrived in the final spasm of the counter-insurgents' offensive and she was to stay to within a few days of their success; she'd come because the man she'd recently married was reporting there for a London paper, and seeing the news of mounting catastrophe after he'd left had made her so frightened for his safety, she chose to join him. Passing the billboards made her imagine worse terrors than she would ever come across in reality – she was right in some ways. But it had been a risk, less on account of the danger the war presented than the nuisance she might become to him, as indeed it turned out. Her female presence undercut his heroic witness to the general savagery, the regime's reprisals, the horror of the rebels' attacks. Though the city would fall, it was at that time still the most protected fortress of the whole country, out of range of the rebel army's artillery, under strict curfew from dusk to dawn and seething with soldiers of the allied armies come to help save the incumbent government. She loved her husband much more than he requited, and because she was young and girlish with it, she felt that life had dealt her a hand with undue generosity. So she liked to provoke his cold impatience and prove her devotion by forgiving it and loving him the more.

One of the other journalists in the hotel played go-between on her behalf; after that, she befriended two of the bargirls, learned their first names, Solange and Noelle, and went to eat with them off formica and steel tables, bowls of spicy soup and dishes of fried fish after – sometimes, for it was the rainy season – plunging knee deep through the monsoon flood that swelled with tidal power in the streets every evening, to reach the place down some  alley the girls knew was cheap and good. Kate paid, it was the least she could do. She would see Solange and Noelle separately, and she never sat with them on the veranda for fear of causing embarrassment: a soldier might think she was turning a trick as well, and as she was white, she offered unfair competition – though in her own country she was considered a young woman with pleasant features, but certainly no siren. Solange giggled when they walked along side by side, for Kate soon outstripped her and then had to stop to let her draw level again; Kate was wearing cotton trousers and sandals in the heat, and her usual gait was a stride, whereas Solange wore the country's traditional costume, silk, tight-fitting, and she had tiny beaded sandals with gilt high heels, so that she furled and unfurled when she moved like the kite-tails that streamed from some of the yards in the city where children cut out relief agency ricebags and stitched them to a frame of jetsam. This was another of their reclamations, another secondary use, another salvage, transforming the foreign into the native.

The journalist who had effected Kate's introduction to Solange – it was necessary because she could have been an official, a medical worker, a missionary, intent on stopping her practise her trade – pointed out to her that even the bras in vogue in the country had been colonised: 'They're all uplift and points like the nose of mortar shells – the style that went out at home with hula hoops!'

When Kate went to the room where Solange lived, she expected something like the brothels of Amsterdam: a pallet spread with a white sheet, a bidet on a stand, a towel, a mirror, a curtain, a calendar with a photograph of a Swiss chalet or a Cotswold lane. She travelled there alongside her in a different cyclo; through the swirling putty water her wrinkled old driver pedalled. The cyclo drivers were either too old or too young to be conscripted, and as this meant a pensioner or a child, Kate sat back helplessly pricked by the sight of the man's chicken calves as she was drawn through the muddy torrent and the hooting, kerosene fog of traffic by someone for whom she'd give up her seat on the tube if she was at home. 'What else can you do?' Richard said to her when she moped about it. 'Don't be silly. They need the money, your hire puts bread on their plate, rice in their ricebowl. There are quite enough beggars round the place without your helping to create more by refusing to ride the cyclos. Come on.'

It turned out that Solange lived in a small wooden cabin on legs, polished and plain and flat-bottomed, like the cobles built for easy beaching Kate had known as a child on summer holidays in Yorkshire, but stranded here under a canopy of banana and some flowering trees, with her mother and two children, one who looked about five, the other a baby, an infant, but mute with the slate-blank eyes she knew from other children in the city streets. Solange showed her a photograph of the elder child's father, resorted to bargirl slang to describe their sweet and eternal love: 'You are my number one baby, my oochy poochy sweetiepie,' she chanted, quoting him. 'Solange, my honeypot, you're good enough to lick all over.' He was about twenty in the army snapshot, with a moustache, a white GI with an Italian name. He had been going to volunteer for a second tour; he'd promised to send money for Tony Junior; she was still waiting, still hoping, though it had clearly been years. Oh, it was so bloody typical, such utter stale buns, Kate could have slapped Solange. She had hoped that she was making it up, that she didn't know who the father was, she'd rather her life was a racket, wanton anarchy, ferocious, cynical chaos, than have her duped and asking for more. Yet wanting to hit her, Kate saw, was the invitation her swaying sweet baby-talking presence issued, the drowned kitten seductiveness she'd learned.

Meanwhile, Solange's mother, in black pyjamas, was squealing and flapping at the child until he went outside again holding the baby and stopped gawping at the roundeye woman with their mother. When had she started work again after this infant? Kate saw a gash, imagined tender walls, sore breasts, and firmly set such thoughts aside.

'I no want im fight. Not like other kids,' said Solange. 'Soon he go to army, get killed.' She pointed at the child who was now holding the baby in his arms. 'Junior eight years old now.' It was less hot in her hut than outside, but her lip was pearled, and she wiped her face with a towel, then handed the aluminium waterpot to her mother to fill from the standpipe in the street outside.

Kate was large for the room; she became aware of her heft as she sat on the stool Solange indicated, and waited while the pot began to rattle on the primus lit on the step outside. The boy was now playing under the eave of the hut's floor; looking for ants, for spiders. He'd left the baby lying on the ground on a mat in the shade of the wall. Solange said, 'She sleep now.'

The bed was in the corner; there was a curtain, a picture, of a Filippino Lippi Madonna. Solange was clearly better off than some of the other girls, who worked the alleys and were firmly kept from even the veranda of the hotel. She still had her teeth, for one thing. 'The blowjob experts have them pulled,' one of the other guests in the hotel had informed her one night. 'When they're kids. The earlier the better. Soldiers don't like taking those kind of risks.'

At Solange's she was drinking tea from a cup with a dragon pattern on it like the set her parents had in Hebden Bridge; it was a different shape, however, more like an eggcup. She wondered what Solange did on the bed in the corner; she thought about her mother and the children in the room with her. She had seen families, all curled up together, kindle-like, using one another's legs and backs for pillows, sometimes out by the traffic on the pavement where it was cooler than under the tin roofs of the shanties. They could sleep through a lot; they had learned to sleep through the mortar explosions since the shelters had been flooded out and the attacks were gradually closing in, the centre of the  city coming into range.

'You take him home with you, Kate. You call up Tony. Then Tony Junior go to college, go with you.'

'I live in England.'

'England, America, same, same. Yes? You rich. You take him when you go England. Him learn quick.'

Tony Junior had come in again, encumbered by the baby, who clung to him like a growth.

Kate nodded, but said, 'I can't, Solange. It isn't possible. I'm sorry.'

When she left, she gave her $20, two, three tricks' worth, maybe more. The boy ran for a cyclo. Solange smoothed the note between her pale slender fingers and smiled. She tapped a tooth, gold, as was fashionable. 'I sell this, bribe officials, stop him go army.'

The city was full of business; though there were shortages, there was also surplus, and bartering was brisk on the pavements. Medicines beyond their due date lay on rush mats in neat piles like towers of toy bricks, beside varied anatomies of hardware and dead soldiers' paraphernalia – contraband watches, radios, hi-fis, compasses, electrical parts and bicycle parts, recharged batteries, boots, coats, wallets, belts – as well as rebottled Dewar's and Black Label and Jim Crow and Kentucky sour mash with the wrong screwtops. Their minders were mostly children, boys. With small, lithe hands, the vendors would clutch at her arm, and screech at her, begging her to buy. If she didn't want anything from their display of wares, they had plenty more stuff elsewhere they could fetch, they had anything she might want. This was the world of the jokes she overheard,

'You want my little sister? No? You want my little brother? You want nice big smack- cheap, cheap? You like sucky sucky?'

Girl children were not so visible; they were indoors, she supposed, under protection or already conducting curtained business of their own. In the market, the slimy, fetid, sprawling down-town market in the Chinese quarter of the city, there was still plenty of food for sale, much strangling of various fowl and gutting of fish, crabs lumbering in wicker cages and jackfruit splitting at the seams and ripely adding to the mixed perfumes in the contrived darkness. The first time Kate went, she was attracted by the toys, the heaps of paper boats and houses, horses and mobiles, figures of men and women made of indigo- and cochineal-dyed rice paper stitched by hand. She bought a rider on a stiff-legged steed, a pagoda, and a bundle of paper money in brilliant scarlet with gold-leaf stamps on it, while the market women roared with laughter at her, calling out names. Later she was told, 'They were shouting "Peasant" – because of your hat.' (She had taken to wearing a tribal straw hat against the sun.) She also learned, from another informant, that her toys were funerary offerings: 'The gooks burn them on the pyre, so that the dead can take that stuff to heaven with them. It's symbolism, far-out Budhist symbolism.' Kate took them  up to her hotel room, still loyal to their delicate craft, though she realised they wouldn't travel well.

Solange's boy was the first child Kate was offered. There were no babies arranged on the rush mats and no booths at the market which dangled them for sale. But as goods, babies came her way, along with other things she could have tried if she had a fancy to. She was never offered a girl baby, however. Her own singular state remained intact, if anything became deeper. When she commented to Richard, after the third child she was asked to take, that she was surprised they were all boys, he said, 'It stands to reason. They don't want them to be called up. It's a good story. I should write it. But it's Human Interest, and the paper wants War Games – the Allied Strategy, the Body Count, the Weapon Stockpile, the odds on a ceasefire, etc. Why don't you do it? It'd keep you busy.'

'I've never written an article,' she said.

'You write law reports, you brief barristers. You know how to string your thoughts together on paper.'

She began to listen in on the talk in the hotel.

'Where can you get contraception in the city?' she asked.

One of the wire men answered, after a mock display of shock, 'Anywhere and everywhere. They're free at the PX; they're in every bar that's got a john, and the girls have got them on them.'

'So why's the birth rate so high?'

Then she met Jinty, and found comfort in the company of another woman. Jinty was short and plump and solid like a riding mistress; her hair clasped her head closely as if used to a hard hat. She came from

Surrey, and lived in Cobham when she was at home, among gorse bushes and pines. But she specialised in children in crisis, famine relief, and the administration of foreign aid. The charity organisation called Sangrail had sent her to this war, to see if there was any way through the political deadlock; the charities' money to the government was routinely siphoned off, money to the rebels was against UN rules; the counter-insurgents were holed up in villages badly needing supplies of all kinds, but officially they did not exist, so it was not possible even to put into gear any means of helping civilians in the territory they held. After a month of impasse with officials, when Kate met her at a function in the Canadian envoy's villa Jinty was concentrating her attention on the city's orphanages. 'I'm practical,' she told her. 'Wrangling with colonels isn't my cup of tea at all. I don't want to waste time wittering, though the Lord knows I still have to do a heck of a lot of it. '

The next day, Kate went with her to a children's hospital, down the side streets heavy with kerosene and churning with cyclos, to the old European quarter of the city, where three Belgian nuns in a convent founded in the last century were nursing foundlings, some of whom had been left on their doorstep, while others had been brought in from the war, from burned villages, from the evacuated rebel-held countryside.

'It doesn't interest me, who wins,' Jinty was saying. 'Does it you? No? Good. Let the generals argue the toss with one another. There's plenty to be done while they chinwag.'

They were at the door of the infirmary. In Italy, at the Innocenti hospital in one of the northern towns, Kate had once seen the special compartment in the door, where the babies used to be put. It was like a night safe in a bank's outer wall – the packet was passed through without one party seeing the other. But here there was no sign of the place's purpose, of the bundled children delivered to the step, as she had half expected. The nun who came to open the door to them wasn't a foreigner, but a native, wearing a grey veil and pearl-headed pins to secure it to the white wimple that covered her ears and neck. She kissed Jinty, and left one hand on her shoulder with lingering tenderness; they exchanged words in French, and Kate recognised in the missionary's voice the West African accent of fellow students from her days at Gray's Inn.

'Soeur Philippe,' the nun introduced herself. The skin of her palm was dry and hard. 'Come and see our children.' She had that way of smiling nuns catch from statues: beatific, and without a trace of laughter.

This first infirmary gave model treatment, compared to other establishments Kate was to visit. At first she thought she was doing as Richard said, and gathering material for an article on the plight of the abandoned children and orphans of the war, but soon she found that without consciously embarking on helping Jinty, she was running errands and carrying out certain tasks for her. There was, as Jinty had said, plenty to do. In the Belgian nuns' hospital the children lay two to a cot, one at each end, on a sheet, with a nappy on and a bottle each tied to a strut in the cot's side near their mouth; most of them were far too weak to reach the teat even if they were developed enough to roll or otherwise make a move towards it. So someone had to go round and try to fit the babies' mouths to their feed and stimulate them to suck. There wasn't time to pick a child up and nurse him – or her – individually; there were far too many in need. Starvation had turned their clocks back; they looked like medical photographs of gestating embryos, with huge frontal lobes and tiny sperm-like limbs. She could have scooped one of them into the palms of her hands like a frog.

'You see, they are frequently born premature. The mothers are not eating enough, in their bodies they are – how shall I say – not healthy... Their way of life ...' Soeur Philippe joined her hands over her habit as if praying. 'They do not leave their children to die. No, they abandon them so that they have a chance to survive. Somewhere else. Here, or, if possible, in Europe, America. They dream... but, you know ...' She put out her hand and touched a baby's face; the open eyes, huge as an owl's, did not flicker. 'On fait de son mieux.'

Jinty was examining the register: 'I need to make a copy of the figures, to send to London. We must have facts. It's not to be believed otherwise.'

The nun shook her head. 'The register is out of date, it is hard to keep it up. We pray at the burials, of course, we remember all of them in our prayers. But the record – we don't have time for the record.' Jinty handed Kate the book, where in theory each child was to be entered – case history, weight, race, symptoms, treatment, outcome (discharge to another orphanage, or death). 'Make a few copies anyway – and come back.'

Kate took the ledger; she tried various shops with photocopiers, but none was working – contraband toner was harder to fake than bourbon and Coke – so eventually she went round to the daily briefing centre and used the journalists' office facilities, thinking how stupid she was not to have thought of that immediately. She was confused, the children had confused her, they made her feel lewd in her healthiness and her strength. The smell of them was still in her nostrils, the leaky milk-and-piss sickliness of their feeble hold on life.

That night in the hotel she spoke up, from the table where she was sitting on her own – Richard had again gone up-country with a general to write up the regime's supposed progress – and she addressed the room, over the head of the Agence France Presse rep who was also dining on his own, directing her comments to the group of wire service journalists and other papers' stringers who were eating together. 'I saw about two hundred babies today,' she began. 'They've been abandoned in the last few months, since the offensive started. Most of them looked as if they were dying. They're mostly half black and half white. The mothers are all bargirls, apparently.'

'Yeah,' said one newspaperman. 'The whole fucking country's one big brothel. That's our present to the people: we teach the women how to fuck. That's freedom. That's a law of the free market.'

'Who's going to use a rubber when his life is on the line? It's tough.' This was another man, joining the conversation. 'Those guys, they want to leave something of themselves behind.' The veteran newspaperman, famous for hard-hitting coverage, spread his hands and shrugged.

Another put in, 'Two hundred? That's a lot of children. I reckon they're telling us something about what's happening out there. Nobody wants to get caught with anything incriminating on them when the end comes, now do they? And what would be more incriminating than a little roundeye babba with funny-coloured skin?'

The most famous reporter of all nodded at Kate and called out, 'It's like we wrote at the start of the war, it's still the same story. "You gotta destroy the village in order to save it." You gotta leave your fucking child if you want him to stay alive. The only safe place to be is elsewhere.'

The next day, Kate joined Jinty in a different orphanage, this one for babies and children who could feed themselves and obey their minder's order to sit in line on potties and perform. Many of these did not have foreign fathers, but had lost their parents, either through death during a raid or through dispersal, as they took flight from a village under attack or were scattered as they stole into the city at night for safety. The authorities in this establishment were secular, and local: The Good Fortune and Long Life Prudential Society.

'You should watch out,' one reporter said when she'd finished telling them. 'They'll bleed you for all you're worth, that little lot. It's Madam So-and-so's outfit, isn't it? Her good works, my ass. It's just a cover for far more important business. She's using it to launder – you take a little look at the books, little lady, and you see if you can make head or tail of the finances of the Good Fortune and Long Life Prudential Society – if they've got any books they'll let you see.'

When she brought it up with Jinty, the older woman replied, 'Journalists like plots. I'm not interested in plots, and the people aren't characters to me, they're not pieces on some almighty chessboard. Close your mind to them. If you think about who you're helping you'll never do a thing. There'll always be a good reason to sit on your bottom and do nothing.'

That day they also went to a city shelter for disabled children. These were orphans of all ages, and their handicaps were in some cases the results of wounds bombs, shrapnel, gas – but in other cases congenital or the result of neglect, of malnutrition. When Kate arrived in the former warehouse, the reek of disinfectant was overwhelming. It was dark inside, and though this at least helped keep down the temperature under the metal roof, the lack of windows made the atmosphere inside asphyxiating. First she noticed that the walls were dripping and the dirt floor was covered in a film of water tinged with the blue-grey bubbles of some toilet cleansing fluid; then she saw that the children were soaking too, lying nappy-less on rubber sheets draped on iron bedsteads or on the floor, where ammoniac puddles had also collected.

'They hose them down in the morning,' Jinty told her. 'It's the quickest way to clean up the ones who are incontinent, and restore some level of hygiene to the premises.' She looked round the room, as Kate swallowed, and went on, 'Boys and girls are all mixed in together, so we can't vouch for another sort of hygiene.'

Jinty had commandeered a team of allied soldiers to plumb in showers and basins, linked to the standpipe in the street outside; Kate had accompanied her to the army depot and watched her rustling up the equipment, the parts and the fittings, from the sergeant on duty. They began moving the children from one side of their dark quarters to the other, to separate the boys from the girls. To the ones with power in their arms, Kate gave piggy-backs; their heads on her shoulders like stones, their breath distempered by starvation. One girl patted her hair, and said something softly, twisting her head around to smile in her eyes. She was admiring it, Kate realised, admiring it for its difference from her own, in lightness of colour and fluffiness of texture.

She helped put up a partition, to give some privacy to the older girls who had started to menstruate. It was built of tough cartons that had delivered something marked Fragile to the assisting army; they'd been salvaged from one of the many public dumps before someone else could take them to turn them into a whole  family's shelter. Jinty, with a male army nurse she had also commandeered, was washing some of the children and covering them in clothing they had brought. On examination close up, many of their bodies were terribly damaged, but there were no dressings available, and only bleach for disinfectant. A softish, wadded parcel from England had miraculously passed through the thieving hands of customs and other authorities; it proved to be full of teddy bears.

Trying to tend the children, Kate was reminded of the heaps of rubbish behind the foreigners' haunts and near other places of abundance, like the market, where the natives swarmed to pick over the fruit and vegetables, the burst packaging, the rags and debris. The little boy lying prone on the rubber sheeting whom she began swabbing looked as if he had fallen from a tree on to stones where wasps and worms had feasted on the tears in his flesh. She clenched her teeth to stop herself gagging, her repugnance increased by shame that she should feel disgust at all.

Jinty noticed, and told her, kindly, 'Listen, old girl, no need to linger. You need time to get used to this sort of thing. Go on, have a breath of fresh air outside. If you can find some.'

Richard came back from his expedition to the counter-insurgents' territory. He was frustrated in his attempts to file, because the government censors had picked up his denunciations of the three-cornered civil war; he was furious. In the hotel, the number of pressmen had grown; from the corner of the dining room where he was waited on by his companion, the proprietor now rewrote the hotel charges on a nightly basis as prices rose; the wines drunk improved in labels and vintage as he dug deeper into the last of the cellar. There was a trade in passports and visas at the bar; in other things as well. Contractors arrived and were busy; the beggars at the hotel door grew bolder, as did the rats, sometimes making an appearance before the dining room was empty to snatch at fallen scraps. The embassies notified their nationals to leave. 'You're to get out, Kate, there's no two ways about it,' said Richard. 'It's the end, and I've got to stay as long as I can. But you ...'

She tried to make love to him that night. She saw the children's bodies in her mind's eye, their gaze shadowless, like the moon in eclipse. She wanted the sap and the kick of sex to move this darkness and lift the heavy bodies of the orphans where they were lodged in her, torpid and undigested. But Richard wouldn't, he too lay leaden, a reproach to her, as if he were saying in his unresponsiveness, How could you at a time like this? She was half-thinking to herself, We should have a child ourselves, a strapping, crowing, pink-and-white child who knows how to express hunger and discomfort and ask for everything, not like these inert lumps of flesh in their silence and their stink. All the time she'd been with Jinty trying to help her with the orphans she'd never shed a tear. It had left her as numb and cold as if she were made of ten-day-old suet, and she hated herself for it and for not being able to get through to Richard: he was out there on the front line, fighting, even when he was in bed with her, and women had no place there, no, nor love either. So she wept now for herself, lying naked in the stifling room, hearing the distant boom and crackle of the mortars and the scratch of the rats in the walls.

*I watch the big English who come one day see my mother drink tea with her I follow her offer her cigarettes the man gave me sell sell. She say no cigarettes but she give me two quarters an tell me no smoke myself have something eat she no recognise me I go with her she go to sisters' infirmary where they take babies she ask why you follow me I tell her you pretty woman you kind woman she laugh she say go away home I say please I come see you again tomorrow she say no no I say please again she gets angry shoo shoo little boy I no have more money I say please she no say name of hotel but I know where she stay (she no realise I know) but she say tomorrow she come one more time say goodbye she leaving she sad this country number one people in it so sweet and never complain she say. I find my mother home she sick now an I tell her and she say, Take Theresa so I take my sister mother give us money for cyclo, I only ride cyclo one time before and I tell driver go sisters' infirmary, he go and I leave Theresa in basket with blanket and other things on the step*

*first nobody come and I hidin by door nearby an waitin an watchin hopin big English come like she say an then I see her she hot she puff she stop an make little cry when she see basket and baby then she pick up Theresa and hug Theresa an look in basket I wait see what she do then if she ring bell give Theresa to door sister she do she go in with sister they talk talk high voices big English I hear she cry again*

*my mother burn many offering she light candle though she sick she walk to church to make special prayer for Theresa The big English no want to take me I too grownup take care of things here now so mother pray she take Theresa and we all be leaving soon soon for to find Tony*

After the fall of the city later that year, and the establishment of the new regime, Kate returned there to join Jinty, who had remained throughout, and to complete the adoption process of the child she had finally chosen when she found her lying on the steps of the Belgian nuns' infirmary on her last day in the city, just before she left because Richard – and the British government representatives too, to be fair to him insisted that she did. Jinty helped her with the paperwork; by the end, she'd spent some $10,000, she reckoned, acquiring her daughter. But it was a small price to pay for Theresa, of course. That was her given name: it was written on a paper and plastic bracelet which must have been borrowed from a hospital and left in the basket, alongside one or two other tokens. Just like a fairytale, and the child did feel to her like a fairy boon, she had to admit. Theresa, who had lain there in her way as if predestined, who had put her arms around her neck confidingly when she picked her up that first time as if she knew her and understood that she could care for her, that she would care for her. She had turned over inside at her touch: Theresa was like the spark in flint and she lit Kate back to life.

Jinty said, 'A lot of people bleat about uprooting children from their culture and whatever. Culture? When you haven't got enough to eat? When you'll be on the streets by the age of ten? Oh, they're dear, clever little things, and they might manage to survive, but what kind of a life will it be? Don't let the doubters and the purists torment you, you go ahead, Kate, give Theresa an English life, give her pony clubs, ballet classes, meat and two veg, Beefeaters, the battle of Trafalgar, the lot. Hell's bells, one has to believe in something. Besides, she's half-and-half anyway – her father could have been God knows what.'

When Theresa was six and began going to school all day, Kate took on full-time work for Sangrail as an expert on refugees, specialising in adoption and immigration law. Richard was usually travelling, still avoiding the conjunction of marriage, still covering the hot spots (but for another paper now – his old one had been taken over and now, in the interest of profits, used only news agencies' reports). So Kate decided she couldn't manage with only part-time help any longer, and began to employ a housekeeper. She picked her first from the large population of boat people whom she was helping to get the right papers for the country of their eventual choice; Kate knew her way through the red tape –

refugee law, immigration law, political asylum – and how to finger exactly the right subsection of the right bill for her client. Canada was very popular, and so were some of the Caribbean countries. It became her special field of expertise, and a trickle of women from Theresa's birthplace – and sometimes their husbands – had passed through her house and lived for a time in the basement flat. It wasn't an ideal relationship, of course. She would have preferred not to be an employer at all, a 'mistress', a 'madam'.

Kate sometimes thought of Solange and Noelle and wondered what had happened to them; how badly they had been punished for fraternisation, how well they had survived the new regime's 'lustration' programmes. She once or twice asked her contacts for news, but it was very difficult to trace someone when all you knew about her was that she had been a bargirl with a child or two, information which would not be the most helpful way to identify her, given the character of the new government.

One day a refugee liaison centre Kate worked with telephoned her about a case: an economics exchange student in Paris had applied for his mother to leave and join him. She wanted to work in England, she had a little English. He was making approaches-to transfer his scholarship to LSE, in order to continue his studies. He was bright, and he was resolved, at present, to return to his country; he had prospects and he was not seeking residency or citizenship for himself. As for his mother, he had specifically given them Kate's name as a possible sponsor. Would she take up the case?

Madame Ng's first name was Phong; she arrived to start her post as housekeeper in the summer holidays of Theresa's eleventh year (or what was thought to be her eleventh year, on the basis of a conjectured age of three months when she was found). Kate interviewed her beforehand; she asked her how she and her son had known about her. Phong smiled: she had heard about Kate in the city, everyone had. Kate was straining to catch something that seemed familiar in Phong's face, something that sounded familiar in her voice, but every time she thought she caught a flicker, it passed. It was like trying to remember a name; it's on the tip of your tongue but it just won't form itself. She dismissed the fleeting resemblance as fantasy, stirred up by a yearning for reparation, a sense of loss, of the page irrevocably turned. Kate thought then that she might never be able to stop feeling this ... interconnectedness with the women in the city who had lived those lives and had the babies – it wasn't guilt, exactly, but something shared, as if when she was holding Theresa she wanted to turn into one of them and look in the mirror and find herself changed to match her daughter.

Phong looked so much older than Solange would have been, with her hair cut short and straight and her torso slightly bent – an abdominal operation had left a lumpy scar, so she listed forward as she walked as if to shield her vulnerable tissue from bumps and angles. Kate sometimes found herself scanning her, wondering about Theresa's real mother, and her imagination would begin to whirr and she'd have to tell herself to stop it, stop it. That way madness lies: a hall of mirrors and no end to the reflections.

Phong was very proud of her son, quite rightly; and the new regime's debriefing about America had impressed her deeply. She didn't want to emigrate there, unlike some of her predecessors, but to stay in London and work for Kate. That was what she said, what she insisted she wanted. It was hard to get work papers for her, but Kate promised to do her best (though she also pointed out to her that housekeeper/ nanny wasn't the best-paid job in the world, especially at the wages Kate could afford, nor the most rewarding in other ways).

Theresa soon outstripped her new nanny in height – in spite of her puny size in the first year of life, she'd since been nourished on muesli and kiwi and other vitamin-rich foodstuffs and had grown rangy in limb, with a light sheen on her skin like a hazelnut. Moving with the quicksilver energy of childhood, she tended to be impatient with her refugee minders, especially with their lack of English and their timorous ways of negotiating London transport systems, and Kate would have to scold her and teach her to make allowances for newcomers. But from the start Phong seemed to dust off the little girl's prickliness. 'I love Mummy best, this much,' Theresa would say, stretching her arms wide. 'Then Daddy, this much' – bringing them in a little – 'And then you, Phong, this much!' She'd then stretch them out again, hooting. One time, playing this game, her mouth was full of spring rolls Phong had cooked for her, and Kate stood in the doorway, watching her at the kitchen table as Phong dished up another. 'You eat now, Theresa, and don't chit-chat so much,' responded Phong, already busy scouring the pan at the sink.

Kate felt a tweak of jealousy, but she squashed it. It would be stupid to mind that Theresa at last had a nanny she really seemed to like. She had always wanted her to feel something in common with the people she came from. And after all, it was the dream of every working mother to find someone who could stand in for her, when she couldn't be there all the time to take care of her child herself.

CHANTAL ZABUS

# Spinning a Yarn with Marina Warner

*We are here meeting within the context of 'Antwerp 93' in Belgium. From what I understand, this country is not alien to you?*

I was here from the ages of six to twelve. For the first three years, I was at school at Les Dames de Marie in Brussels, which is where I learned French. It was quite an extraordinary experience – the atmosphere was very different from anything I had known before and I didn't speak a word of French when I first went there. It was a convent, with all the walls painted with enormous frescoes representing great moments in Belgian history and the lives of the saints. Quite a big school and an intensive drill which I had never been used to: we were all marched in line and we all sang songs together and we learned everything by heart. I learned a bit of Flemish. And it was all a great novelty.

*And who sent you there?*

After the war my father opened an English bookshop in Cairo, and it had been burnt down during the first wave of anti-British riots in 1952 – I hope one day to write about this, something to do with the colonial situation and growing nationalism. His shop was picked out because the books he sold were in English and French and were a symbol of cultural imperialism. My father thought Egypt was an extraordinary place, a very cosmopolitan place. And then in the war he met people who owned Smith's, the book chain; they had made friends. He was very bookish, and he thought it would be a good idea to serve the international community in Cairo.

*Your father is English but your mother is Italian?*

She's from Puglia – Ninfania in *The Lost Father*. My mother was called Terzulli and she was the youngest of four daughters. The book is very carefully faithful to the structure and chronology of my mother's life. I wanted to use that as a kind of armature. It's like taking the sonnet form and working with it: it gives you boundaries, a framework within which to explore the themes; it sets aside extraneous inventions because you have givens of the historical record. What was interesting to me as I began researching the Italian background of fascism in the South and the immigration to America and all that was that I found that my mother's family were completely typical: the exact time that they attempted to emigrate to America, the time they came back, the time they went again, all these were peaks on the graph, so that in a sense they were very symptomatic of the social upheavals of the time.

*Sicily comes up in* In a Dark Wood.

That does not come from my mother's life; that arose from my own interest. I used to love going to Sicily (and I will probably go back at some point). Sicily is quite different from Puglia, though they do share a lot in common, with the Normans and the Greeks – and that is not immaterial. One of the things I was concerned about in *The Lost Father* was the way southern Italy was seen as a benighted place of poverty and cruelty and and a kind of emptiness. And I wanted to reverse that and show that it is one of the most ancient parts of Europe and that it is very deep, with problematic aspects like the machismo they all suffer from. In the novel both the men and the women suffer from the cult of the strong man.

*You said somewhere that, given that Europe was first raped by Zeus, one should remember the feminine origin of Europe.*

I tend not to think of these things as fixed.It is not so much that Europe is feminine in origin; it is that half its history must have been feminine at some point and that there are both secrets and stratagems within that feminine side which we forget or ignore at our cost, our great cost. The exchange of fictions, the exchange of dreams and fantasies are very ancient forms of survival. Of course, it can work both ways. Unfortunately, what we are seeing now with the growing number of states is a nationalistic use of folklore in an aggressive, nationalistic, ethnic-pure way, and we must be aware of that. But at the same time there is a cultivating of common history through story-telling and the exchange of ideas which does cut across borders and frontiers while maintaining differences, because of course, all stories are told with local variations. In a way the story is a site of both particularity and a medium to universal experience and a sort of universal communicability.

*And stories seem to be passed on from woman on to woman.*

Of course, that is something very important, something that I have been working a lot on in the new book that will come out next year about fairy tales. It is a critical study of fairy tales, and it is particularly about how human voices, especially women's, are at work in the fairy tale.

*You explored that aspect – the feminine side of history or her-story – in the fairy tales in* Indigo. *Feeny retrieves Ariel's story.*

In fact *Indigo* grew out of my work on fairy tales. I really wanted to write the book on fairy tales but I stopped *From the Beast to the Blonde* and wrote *Indigo* instead. The idea for *Indigo* grew so strongly that I couldn't keep it at bay. I couldn't finish the fairy tale book: I had to write *Indigo*. A lot of the ideas in the fairy tale book are worked out in fictional form in *Indigo*. And what is sad but part of the human condition is that Feeny tells the story of Ariel as she has been told it.

*But you ultimately retrieve it and set the record right, as it were.*

In a way, what the novel perhaps suggests is that Feeny weaves another story within that story -the 'Beauty and the Beast' story. In that one, she's free of the historical burden. She teaches Miranda to rethink the world; she herself can't do it because she's a colonized subject: she loves the Everard family, she has been their nurse, she loves Anthony. In a sense she has been incorporated and colonized; she's an island that has been taken over. But at the same time, through her possibilities of rethinking her lot and distributing rewards and punishments, she stands for me as the exemplary fiction writer who can be colonized and still speak. Another example would be an African writer writing in English. The Anglophone writer is in a position to reach more people, so that out of the colonized position, he or she addresses a larger audience and then reinvents the experience that audience has received historically. Maxine Hong Kingston is a very good example – the Chinese American writer: in the way she takes the Chinese baggage of superstitions, the weight of the Chinese past, and she tells it in a new way, she recasts it as an American, if you like.

*There's a Chinese background too in* In a Dark Wood *and you told* The Guardian *that you always wanted to learn Chinese. Why China?*

I think it came from a comic strip, actually. In Rupert Bear, there's a character – a Chinese emperor, I think – who flies around on a carpet. And this made me feel that China was the most wonderful place. It was a dream of the Other when I was growing up. It was *the* fabulous country. It was moot between Arabia and China, really: I could have chosen *The Arabian Nights* but I just went a bit further. My dream of the Other was China. I suppose it came from my father; he was so interested in history. China's antiquity made it seem magical and the Chinese value-system appealed to me because they valued the poet, the writer over the soldier. They practised writing as a sort of magic art, divination by writing. It appealed to me as a child, as a civilization. It was different from the Romans, you know, marching across the world in straight lines of roads built with slaves. What the reality of China is and was is a different matter: it is a horrendous place of oppression.

*And you could have talked about another 'Other', if I may say so. You talk about 'a touch of the tar brush'. What does that mean? Do you have a Creole background?*

The thing is, you see, we never knew that we had it. My sister and I - at the period when I was in love with China - had no idea that our family was connected to the Caribbean, no more idea than we might be Chinese. Nobody was more British than my father and his family. Partly because my grandfather was this quintessential English thing: he was the captain of the English cricket team. In those days, the captain of a cricket team was the alternative to the King of England. It was the national game, highly structured in social terms, very much Gentlemen vs. Players. There was such a hierarchy in the game itself. Cricket epitomizes the British view of its own colonialism – mannerly, courteous, calm and effective. It crystallizes in itself the British view of themselves as colonizers. They were not Goths or Huns; they came in with cricket, the civilizing art of cricket. C.L.R. James wrote *The Black Jacobins* and *Beyond the Boundary*, in which he talks about race and power, class and cricket to show how they are absolutely bound together in the former power which the British exercised.

So my grandfather belonged to that world. Nationality laws were recently passed in England: my father wouldn't qualify today as a British citizen because his grandfather was born in the West Indies and his greatgrandfather and so forth, for many generations, had been born in Trinidad or Antigua. So he would have been excluded.It was strange to me that he could be so completely British and yet not British.

When my father went back to Trinidad for the first time, he discovered lots of Warner cousins, some of whom were black. Now there are three possible reasons: one is that in the present some have intermarried. But before that either they were called Warner (because slaves took the names of their owners) or they were actual children.

There's a story with which I started *Indigo* and then did not write – I don't plan my novels very strictly. The kernel of the *Indigo* novel is really the story of Ariel; baby Roucou. In the seventeenth century, Thomas Warner, who was the first settler of the island of St. Kitts in 1623, and was made Governor of the West Indies by the King of England, was married to a local woman. By that marriage he had a son who was known by the name of Indian Warner; he was appointed by the British Governor of Antigua. Thomas Warner's white son (by his English wife) inherited the Governorship of St. Kitts when his father died. The two brothers fought a very bitter battle, in the course of which the white Philip Warner tricked Indian Warner and massacred him and his entire crew, on a boat where they were having a peace talk. And for this Philip Warner was actually brought back to England and tried in the Tower of London and found guilty. He wasn't beheaded but he lost his governorship. So, way back in the seventeenth century, there was already intermarriage. But the story of intermarriage in the early colonies is never told. Because by the time the empire was established as the Raj, as in Africa and so forth, at much later stages, you get severe segregation, and a different kind of imperial culture, more like apartheid, more like South Africa, more regimentation and hierarchy.

*In that respect, do you feel close to someone like Jean Rhys, in* Wide Sargasso Sea? *Because there is a brief mention of 'her hapless waifs' in* The Skating Party *(p. 73).*

*Wide Sargasso Sea* is a book that I absolutely loved when I read it. She is a writer I read a lot twenty years ago. When I thought of *Indigo*, I did not actually go back and read *Wide Sargasso Sea* because I was worried about its influencing me. If there are overlaps, that would be because the work is deep in my unconscious.

*What about Virginia Woolf,* The Voyage Out? *Was that somehow at the back of your mind?*

I also felt a sort of kinship with her. She is somebody I read when I was young like Jean Rhys and she meant a great deal to me. *The Waves* was a revelation. I haven't yet written a book as truly experimental as that.

*Are you looking for, let's say, a woman sentence? Do you feel that linguistically you are searching for a feminine way of saying things?*

One of the things that makes me want to write fiction is that it's very hard to write non-fiction from that side of the mind. People have tried to make autobiographical criticism, some people successfully but it's not as satisfying as the fictional enterprise. One of the things that I'm pleased about in the reception of *Indigo*, and even more strongly in the response to *Mermaids in the Basement* is that after all these years of writing I seem to have won a little bit of ground, that people accept what they used to criticize before terribly: they used to say that my writing was lyrical, flowery, old-fashioned.

*What about the use of colours in your work? There are touches of colours here and there as if you were dipping in bowls of colour. In* Indigo, *of course, it is completely structural. But also Paula in* In a Dark Wood *mentions 'rolls of rainbow-coloured skeins or ranges in sequence of colours.' It comes up again and again, as well as dyeing and weaving.*

Well, it's traditional female work and I'm keen to write it. We English have this metaphor of spinning a yarn for telling a story. A lot of early records of story-telling have to do with weaving. In the *Iliad*, for instance, Helen is weaving her own story; and when Paris comes back, he sees that in her loom she is weaving the story of the Trojan war. She's actually a figure in her own story, the story is unfolding as she weaves. That's a very real metaphor for female creativity.

I'm actually interested in limits of language and of course colour is one of the areas where there's a difficulty. The eye perceives more than language can tell. Consider, for example, the colour of one's eyes. Language cannot follow the complexity of human perception. So in a way, to some extent, the whole task of writing is to try and catch perception, to make a record of it, to capture its fleeting impulses. Consciousness is filled with minute impulses. And of course emotions are also very difficult to capture. Besides, there's a sensuous side to it: I do like looking at pictures a lot.

*Talking about which, you mention painting quite a bit. Paula in* In a Dark Wood *paints; there is the 'Judgment of Cambyses', Gerard David's diptych in Bruges, which is mentioned in* The Skating Party. *So you are interested in painting and other forms of art. And talking about female figures. Would you agree with Paula who says in* In a Dark Wood, *remarking on 'the hatred of women which constantly turns up in the stories', as in the stories of Ariadne (and you take up the story again in* Mermaids in the Basement), *Adromeda, Amazon and about Hercules and Dejanira she says 'Yet another piece of sexist trash.' Would you tend to agree with Paula's somewhat feminist statement?*

I had no idea that the problem bothered me as long ago as that! That's what my book on Fairy Tales is about. I was worried: if these stories are told by women, if women are relating their history and then striving for survival, if these memories are carried by them, why are there so many dead mothers, wicked sisters, wicked mothers, murderers, ...?

*Is that why Miranda is such a key figure in* Indigo? *It is to some extent a rewriting of* The Tempest, *but you seem to focus on Sycorax and Ariel and Miranda as if it was like some sort of unholy matriarchal trinity.*

Yes, it was meant to be the converse. Shakespeare was writing the father's plot. Prospero works out the plot for his daughter. Prospero's wife is conspicuously absent. The only woman is Miranda, the others are off-scene, but also obscene (like Sycorax). So I tried to write the daughter's plot, to take the story from the other side and show how the daughter extricates herself from the father's plot.

*What about a recent reworking of* The Tempest *by Greenaway in* Prospero's Books?

I saw the film after I'd written my book. I didn't want to be influenced, to find his images in my head. And in fact some people have said to me that when they read *Indigo* they see his film. But this is completely wrong. Greenaway is very sadistic to bodies, both male and female, and he's addicted to spectacle. The play is very empty, very unpeopled, eerie. I think Shakespeare advisedly moved the drama to this 'cell', the idea of the enclosed watery space. The film's crowdedness completely flouts the spirit of the play. The other things I didn't like about it was the extraordinary, somnambulist, spellbound condition of Miranda. Also, it's almost disgraceful how little thinking had gone into the Caliban part; when you consider how extraordinarily interesting and pregnant with meaning this figure has become for our time, it's shameful to have there a sort of baboon, with hanging red testicles. Greenaway pretends to be intellectual, to be interested in current thinking about issues such as violence and racism, yet he allows a very fine dancer, Michael Clark, to interpret Caliban in this simplistic, brutish way. I'm sure he could have been inspired to do it differently. Sycorax is a completely conventional hag from hell. Of course, I was in a way pleased that he hadn't thought of the play in another kind of light.

*I'd like to move to another issue, the way you talk about human sexuality. There are overt sexual accounts in* The Lost Father *if you recall (Tomasso 'jerking off') with vivid details. Do you feel that sexuality should be straightforward? Because that is certainly not lyrical, if you have been accused (rightly or wrongly) of lyricism. I would not expect that almost macho writing. There's a masturbation scene in 'Full Fathom Five' in* Mermaids *with Noah and also the rape in Suzanna's story.*

There are violent scenes in *Indigo* too. Well, the masturbation scene comes from direct personal memories because I am a pre-pill child. So all my early experiences of sex had to do with male masturbation. Writers magnify little things that have happened in their lives. Some of these stories could take place in contemporary settings, in bed-sitting-rooms, but for some reason I need to put them in some imaginative distance from myself. But certainly a lot of them happened to me. I'm quite sensitive to explicit sexual writing in other writers. I'm not very keen on it, I find it difficult to read. So I'm surprised when I seem to do it myself. It's not something I particularly identify myself with.

*What about gay relationships, lesbianism? You do incorporate some of these elements in the short stories, possibly also in the novels. Are you trying to make a statement when you talk for instance about retreat for women only? Is that harking back to your experience in convents or is it a commitment to gay rights?*

I read aloud the 'Ariadne after Naxos' story the other day, one of the early stories in the collection, – I wrote it in 1981 – and it was interesting to see how much it had dated in terms of sexual politics. The convent of women was a fairly recognizable representation of a certain sort of feminist position which was not particularly lesbian. That is what has changed and it shows how polarized feminism has become. If you had to set a story now in a convent where women lived alone, the place would probably have to be doctrinally lesbian. Sexual politics would be part of the retreat, whereas in 1981, when I wrote it, it was perfectly plausible for women to separate themselves from male society, but not because of their sexual preferences. I may be backward in that; in America it had happened by the 70s already. People like Kate Millett were already writing about the Lesbian Nation in the 70s. We were behind in England, but it was plausible. Whereas I could see it would have to be changed now. Ariadne would have to experiment with lesbianism and then decide that she was bisexual and that it was not for her.

*Are you perceived as a feminist (whatever that means now) in England?*

I am seen as a feminist by the enemies of feminism, seen in that light by journalists or spectators who like to sneer at feminism of any kind. But feminists don't see me as a feminist. I am sort of caught in between. That isn't true of all feminists, but I am perhaps not socially and politically active enough, more literary and cultural. I think the fairy tale book is very feminist, but I'm not sure it will be seen as that. British feminism is a strange, multi-facetted creature, some of it deeply psycho-analytical in French style. People like Jacqueline Rose (author of *The Haunting of Sylvia Plath*) at one extreme. I can identify with her, her work is very cultural and literary. She has a strong engagement with Lacan and she has quite a following. That's one pole. Then there's the strong historical pole, working on the experiences, the economics of working women past and present; practical historical feminism. I don't really fit into either of these groups, I'm rather a hybrid. But I would like to be identified with the movement. Sometimes I feel rejected.

*Are you perceived as a postmodern writer or as a post-colonial writer. Have any of these labels been applied to you?*

Well, one or two people since *Indigo* have thought of me as such. In fact I'm rather pleased because I have been invited to take part in the Black Writers' Convention which is happening in mid-November, and I'm one of the very few white writers. So I'm very honoured that they think I can take part. And I think that it's because *Indigo* rewrites experience in a post-colonial way, and of course I acknowledge freely that my influences include that kind of writing, some of my earliest loves. Jamaica Kincaid was a writer I loved when she first started publishing. And Caribbean lyricism has always interested me a lot. I like Derek Walcott, whereas a lot of English critics find his work too lyrical, too flowery, too orotund, too sort of easy; they want the acerbity of Larkin or Auden. I like Aimé Césaire as well and George Lamming. I've always felt a great kinship with that richness of language and this heightened register of feeling.

*Do you feel any kinship now with contemporary English writers like (Nigerian-born) Ben Okri? Which brings me to ask you about English literature and the way it is heading. Kazuo Ishiguro is considered an English writer ...*

There's a new phenomenon: writing in the English language that is not American (we have to take American out of it because the rhythm and pitch are so different). 'Commonwealth Literature' is one of its misnomers. It suggests something rather cosily universal. Besides, Kazuo Ishiguro doesn't come into it that sense.

*It is better to say 'New Literatures in English' or 'Literatures in English' where English is a new lingua franca.*

Yes, we can consider the case of Ian Burnma, who wrote an interesting novel about cricket, called *Playing the Game.* It's worth looking at. It's about masks and identity, about an Indian cricketer who becomes an Englishman through cricket. Ian Burnma interprets it for himself, as a Dutchman, who has become an Englishman. So he's writing in English even though he's Dutch: this cannot be Commonwealth literature. I admire Ishiguro a lot, but he's a very elliptical, chaste, austere, spare writer. I don't identify with him. Besides irony isn't my main mode.

*Do you like Margaret Drabble? John Fowles? Any other contemporary writer?*

I haven't read her for a while. I'm not quite sure why not because I like her very much. I feel disloyal. I loved *Possession,* of course: it's wonderful, marvellously witty, a great achievement. I liked Ben Okri's *The Famished Road* a lot. I read it before it won the Booker Prize; so I was able to read it with an open mind and I was able to enjoy it free of its glory, which can spoil a reading really. I thought it had marvellous visionary elements in it. I used to like John Fowles but I haven't read him for a long time. His fiction is more nineteenth-century, ample. I don't see myself as writing ample books, but they come out longer than I think. I expect them to be fragmentary and then they turn out more monumental than I intend.

*Do you see yourself writing both critically and creatively? Because you do seem to alternate.*

Partly because I like pursuing a dual search, at several levels of inquiry, historical and imaginative. It is like a treasure hunt. I had a lot of fun with the book which will be called *From the Beast to the Blonde.*

*What about the Legs of the Queen of Sheba? Because there is a short story in there. There is also the children's opera which was performed two Christmases ago.*

They did it terribly well. The idea also turns up in *The Lost Father.* But the short story came first. It's a story which obviously obsesses me because I've done it in different forms, treated also in my theoretical essays. She enters medieval folklore as a wise queen, but as an anonymous outsider figure, which has to do with her blackness: she's identified with Ethiopia and becomes the mother of Menelek, founder of the Ethiopian royal house. This is all legend, but because of that, she's identified in the folklore as an outsider. I was interested in the idea that the outsider holds the secret of the story, that she knows the riddles. She presents a forerunner of the story-teller, the Mother Goose figure.

*You like to retrace the ancestry of things -like that of St Cunera and Snow White. Do you see yourself somehow writing more about women?*

Yes. People are asking me why I am not writing about men for a change. I feel there's more to explore with women.

*Do you feel somehow history has to be supplemented?*

Yes. More has to be uncovered. There are many purloined letters; many aspects of female experience have not yet been handled even though a lot of work has been done on the hidden voices of women in history. That's the enriching part of feminism. You're right, history does have to be supplemented. Angela Carter, for whom I have a huge admiration, took a lot of traditional material, like music hall jokes about women, and she speaks against it, in high spirits, in a sort of comic vein. I really admire that. It's another strategy which people can use. I've just reviewed the new Margaret Atwood, *The Robber Bride.* I enjoyed it, it's very entertaining. She's a master of narration. She also takes misogynistic themes, but she tends to retain them without inversion and she's not merciful. She lacks Angela Carter's tonic good nature, her belief in prosperity, laughter and love, not in a tender or soapy way but with robust, ironical colouring. There are images of tragedy too in Atwood, but in the novel I am talking about Atwood is straightforward about the hatreds of women for one another. The figure of the Robber bride herself is a fairly conventional destructive femme fatale.

*We have spoken about female writers. Anyone you feel kinship with in Africa?*

From Africa, Lessing and Gordimer. Doris Lessing had a huge influence on me many years ago, in her sense of immediacy and her direct style. Maybe I learnt something from her.

*So you have many ancestors.*

I am afraid so – No, I'm glad it's so.

# JACKIE KAY

Jackie Kay was born in 1961 and brought up in Scotland. Her poetry has appeared in various anthologies including: *A Dangerous Knowing* (Sheba), *Beautiful Barbarians* (Onlywomen Press), *Black Woman Talk Poetry* (Blackwoman Talk), and *Dancing the Tightrope* (The Women's Press). She has written a couple of plays. *Chiaroscuro* is published by Methuen in Lesbian Plays, and *Twice Over*. At the moment she is living and writing in London. She has written three collections of poems, *The Adoption Papers, Two's Company*, and *Other Lovers*, all from Bloodaxe. The poems reprinted here from *The Adoption Papers* were read at a conference in Aachen/Liege in 1988.

JACKIE KAY

# Let It Be Told

Precise beginnings are always hard to find. I could say I started taking my writing seriously when I was twelve years old and had my first poem published in *The Morning Star*. That was certainly a starting-point: I remember my sheer excitement at the seriousness of the printed word. It looked so proper! But, I can't really say that I took my writing very seriously then. Even now, I'm struggling with, 'But who wants to hear about why *you* write anyway? How many "epics" have you written?'

So, I pick up my pen, after picking it up and putting it down for ages now. I am well behind my deadline. (The impact of 'deadlines' on my life has been one thing that's forced me to take something seriously – somebody wants/needs it, fast.) What finally motivates me, apart from my promise, is all the pieces I've read in various books by women writers telling of their inspiration, reason, and motive for writing. I've chewed over such articles endlessly, commenting to myself, 'Oh, that's interesting', or 'That explains such and such...' It adds another dimension to what you have already observed.

Another starting-point: I remember, at sixteen or so, my English teacher telling me I should go and see the then writer in residence of Glasgow University, Alasdair Gray. I took her advice, and she sent him some of my poems. I remember his flat vividly; it fascinated me. Strewn with paints, canvas, books, papers, it looked as if a war of creativity was going on there. He had a hard job finding me a coffee mug. As he let me in, he said: 'Well, there's no doubt about it at all, in my mind, you are a writer.' I repeated that sentence of his. But I didn't properly believe him, or rather I didn't really believe in myself. I was appreciative of the encouragement though. Chuffed. And I told my parents.

'A Writer.' There was something about the word that just didn't fit me. Writers were eccentric white men who could be as crazy as they wanted and get away with it; writers were not within my reach. I used to imagine them walking among the daffodils until they happened upon an inspiration. Later I saw that they need not necessarily be in the countryside, or roaming the clifftops, but they were still usually white and mostly male. The ones we were taught at school – that lot, they were the 'Writers'. 'Poet' had the same kind of not-me ring to it. Poets didn't ever seem to me like ordinary people. Even Rabbie Burns, who surely was as ordinary as they came and poor with it, was made extraordinary by immortality. Immortality isn't after all an everyday occurrence. It's hard to trace back where all these ideas came from.

On reflection, I think they came from an absence rather than what was actually there. I never knew of many black writers at school. In fact the first time that I can remember actually reading something by a black person was when I was fifteen years old. It was a poem called 'Telephone Conversation' by Wole Soyinka. Not surprisingly, being the only black kid in my class, I was the only one who understood what the poem was actually about. It made a huge impact on me; and I think it was one of the first things I ever read that taught me you can laugh and feel extreme pain at the same time.

But Wole was a drop in the ocean; one poem, however powerful, was not enough for me to conjure up even several black writers, let alone a whole community. I didn't even know then that Wole Soyinka was a poet, novelist and playwright. These things have to change. You can teach an awful lot by not teaching. In other words, you can say that Frances Harper, Alice Walker, Tony Morrison, Audre Lorde, Flora Nwapa, Gwendolyn Brooks, and the work of countless others does not matter, that it is not significant by not teaching it. You can go one step further; you can deny their existence. And that is what I believed: 'serious black women writers' did not exist. So how on earth could I call myself one?

It is a struggle to say the words and actually believe in them. I still cannot say 'I am a writer,' without my tongue being right inside my cheek or my cheeks flushing. It takes time. Time to come to terms with memories like this one. Nine years old in primary school. One of the two black kids in the school – the other was my brother. A woman is carrying out some kind of pronunciation test. Big words. At the end of it, she says, 'My, my, you can pronounce some of those words better than me!' Shock horror – she didn't expect me to, evidently. Other people's assumptions of you, whether you want them to or not, do interfere with your own image of yourself. At least until you get older and can put certain assumptions into a context. As Audre Lorde says in *Zami*, you don't have words for racism when you are a child, but you experience it.

Another problem I had with the idea of being a 'writer' was my own fear that writers were selfish, self-indulgent depressives who sat up through the night sacrificing sleep in order to create morbid images that would frighten sleep away from their readers! I'm exaggerating, but you must be familiar with the image. The poems that I wrote in my early teens always concerned broad political issues such as apartheid and poverty and inequality and starvation. I never thought it was important to write about me particularly. Then one day I got a very nice rejection letter from this Scottish Arts magazine which told me to write less about world struggle and more about myself, because 'I' wasn't in my poems.

The slogan 'the personal is political' had not yet made an impact on my life. I still couldn't write about me, or write obviously from my own point of view without feeling somehow that it was not worthy. My writing was more 'real' when it was as far away from my own experience as possible. That seems ironic, but I don't think I was alone in that. And, it is not really all that surprising considering we live in a society that continues to devalue the opinions of young black girls.

When I was thirteen I started to write a novel called 'One person: Two Names' about a 'black' (I said 'brown' then) girl and a white girl who were on the run in Los Angeles. (I even had to have the location as far away as possible to emphasize that it had nothing to do with me; it was purely creative.) I sat in my bedroom poring over the atlas. It didn't seem to matter that I had never been there. I watched the telly, didn't I? I filled eighty jotter pages in my neatest handwriting and kept 'my book' under my bed in a tiny black suitcase. Occasionally, I brought it out and read it to my school pals in lunch hours. I even got my pal Gillian to design a cover for it. So we covered it in brown wrapping paper and she drew on top of it. It gave me a huge kick, that cover. But it was also like one great joke, as if there was something supremely funny in being able to take myself seriously enough to get my friend to design my jotter cover! Big ideas!

Joke or not, I must have really needed to write to spend so much of my time manically scribbling away. It was not until I was about nineteen or so that I recognized the urgency of my need. I was down in London in the summer of 1981 – a memorable summer of SWAMP 81 and resistance in Brixton. I was staying in a squat in Vauxhall, not far from Brixton, where the police were relentless in their breaking in to black people's homes and smashing up their belongings. I was working in Westminster Hospital as a porter, the only woman porter in the entire hospital. One of my jobs was to sell the newspapers in the mornings. It was dreadful. Pushing the power of the media on a hospital trolley from ward to ward. Selling it! I felt like a traitor. All those headlines. The white patients would buy their papers, read the headlines, shake their heads and talk among themselves about how the country was going to the dogs; suppressing the urge to say 'Send Them All Back Home' in the presence of any black nurse or hospital worker. Because they were after all lying sick in bed, and that is a pretty vulnerable position! You could feel the place bubbling with resentment. And the way in which the papers reported the 'RIOTS' endorsed every white person's racism and gave them a right to it.

That was the summer that I joined my first writing group, a black women's writing group. It gave me so much validation being around other black women who wrote, and getting feedback on my stuff and giving opinions on the writing of the others. I think this kind of support is crucial because writing is a very isolating activity. I read a lot that summer too. I discovered Tony Morrison and devoured *The Bluest Eye*. I read Audre Lorde's *The Black Unicorn*. Both of these books had a momentous effect on me. They reiterated the feeling that I got from the group, that I was not alone. I totally identified with Pecola's desire to have blue eyes, though I can't say I ever wanted blue eyes exactly, I just wanted to be white; a pair of brown or hazel eyes would have been all right as long as my skin wasn't the colour it was! But her belief in her own ugliness, the sad intensity of the need to be something she wasn't, all recalled the girl I used to be. The knowledge that the desire to negate yourself was not unique to me came as such a relief. Sometimes I feel ashamed of ever having wanted to be white, now that I am very happy to be black. But being brought up in a very white society, by white parents, and never knowing that the words *positive* and *black* could come together made it very difficult to be delighted about it. This is something that I consistently want to bring out in my writing: that when you literally do not know, because you have not seen, any positive black images, then in isolation it is virtually impossible to conjure them up on your own.

Reading *The Black Unicorn* filled me with such joy and relief. I was amazed at how much company these poems could keep. Here at last was a woman who wrote, without shrinking, about her love of other women. I had never ever read anything by a black woman who was also a lesbian. I was so excited by Audre Lorde's poems, her images, the clarity of her vision. They were so, so different from anything I was reading at university. She gave me a name. In print. She told me I was not alone. Her poems taught me to acknowledge fear and get on with life; and not to be terrified of need. I could feel the need in her poems:

> I am
> the sun and moon and forever hungry
> the sharpened edge
> where day and night shall meet
> and not be
> one
>             ('From the House of Yemanja', *The Black Unicorn*, Audre Lorde.)

After that hot summer, I returned to Stirling where I was doing a degree in English. I felt so isolated – all the support and validation I'd felt from being around other black lesbians was not in my day-to-day life any more. As far as I knew I was the only black lesbian in the whole of Scotland. I didn't meet any others. So I put my head down and worked. I wrote loads of essays about other people's work, few of whom were black and rarely women. The writing didn't seem relevant any more although I could get something from it intellectually. I felt I could not afford to forgo a degree, so I stayed on, writing letters to the women I'd met and made friends with, and waiting eagerly for the replies. I continued writing my own poems whose main theme was isolation. It struck me then how important it is to be in an environment where you do not feel an outsider, where you have so few reflections of yourself. Conversely, it is often exactly this feeling of intense isolation that produces writing. There is nowhere else to take these feelings except on to paper. So much of the writing that means something to me has been born of a sense of aloneness, a feeling of being marginalized.

Our dreams were never meant to be mapped. White people did not even want us to read and write, didn't want our stories passed down, tried to wipe out our history. Published feminist writers, who in the seventies were mostly white apart from one or two exceptions, perpetuated the exclusion of black women in their discussions of how men had wiped out women's history. Nobody seemed to want to even note our existence. I remember just how disappointed I was as I read one book after another without a single mention of a black woman. We just weren't in the picture. All of this – what surrounded me and what I read – made me realize the absolute necessity of writing, of creating definitions, of breaking that dangerous silence. I wanted to read what black British women had to say, so maybe some other woman would get something from what I had to say.

Whatever form of writing you choose, day-to-day realities of where we can go, where we live, who has insulted us that day, who has held us that day, must in some way, however obscure, feed into what we write. To this extent, I see writing as a sort of up-to-date history – a writing of the present that in the future will stand as a document for the past. Presumably, as Britain's black population grows, the black Scottish population will increase so there might not be the reaction of this woman in my poem, 'So you think I'm a Mule?'

'Where do you come from?'
'I'm from Glasgow.'
'Glasgow?'
'Uh huh. Glasgow.'
The white face hesitates
the eyebrows raise
the mouth opens
then snaps shut
incredulous
yet too polite to say outright
liar
she tries another manoeuvre
'And your parents?'
('So you think I'm a Mule?', *A Dangerous Knowing: Four Black Women poets*)

Perhaps in another fifty years' time, black Scottish people might not be considered a contradiction. This, to me, is another thing that writing is all about, being able to embrace contradictions, acknowledge them. I think we have to acknowledge them because they have destroyed so many people. At first when I really began to acknowledge my blackness, I wanted to deny my Scottishness, because I felt ashamed at being so old without knowing any kind of black culture. Now I feel I can do both. I wrote a poem recently about acknowledging all that I am called, 'Kail and Callalou':

> what is an Afro-Scot anyway
> Mibbe she dan dance a reel and a salsa
> remember Fannie Lou Hamer and Robert Burns
> and still see Tam O'Shanter peeking into that barn
> – what did you think of pair Meg's tail coming off like that?
> mibbe they wear kilts and wraps
> and know that Ymoja
> offered yams and fowls
> and Corra could prophesize

I am a firm believer in recording our contradictions. I think that we learn from the past in the stories that are passed down, the pieces that we read. Even fables have contradictions; many of them are held together by their contradictions – the poor girl in a castle; the rich girl in a cottage. Passing down stories is tradition, is history, is learning, is experience. The power of the story is in the handing down. Something that could have died is still living. Struggle itself is immortal.

Robert Burns's poetry is still powerfully relevant – we still live in a world where the rich get richer and the poor get poorer, for a' that. And I've been influenced by all that. I was brought up on Burns Suppers and kailies. I was steeped in Scottish tradition which is rich with myth and imagery. I am glad I was brought up in a culture, a strong one. From an early age, I was conscious of the value of creative work – poems, plays, novels, paintings, and how creativity could tell history. In the work of every black writer I've ever read, I've found the theme of the past, the importance of it; and, alongside that, the terror of no past, of the past being wiped out. Paule Marshall, Gayl Jones, Barbara Burford and countless others all acknowledge the ancestors, both the ones we know of and the ones we don't.

For me writing is a constant challenge – to write to satisfy myself and hopefully to satisfy readers or listeners, to *give* something so that people can relate to what you are saying. When someone, particularly another black woman, reads, or listens to a poem or story of mine and says that she can identify with it, that she's felt the same, the validation that gives me is enormous. It enables me to keep challenging, to feel that there is some point in what I'm doing.

It is important for me to challenge structures and stereotypes not just in the content of what I'm saying but in the style. The discovery that poems need not rhyme, that stories need not have a definite beginning, middle and end, that plays do not need to be all dialogue, was like a liberation in itself. I think that writing with a political motive must also include a challenge to traditional styles. That is also part of the politics. Finding a new language to complement radical ideas.

In 1985 *Theatre of Black Women* asked me to write them a play. I would never have thought about writing a play because I thought you had to have special technical skills to write plays. Just as I used to think I couldn't be a poet, I felt I couldn't be a playwright. I feel extremely pleased that *Theatre of Black Women* provided me with an opportunity to do something that I might not otherwise have done, certainly not for a good few years. Writing *Chiaroscuro* was a whole new experience for me. I never wanted to write an ordinary naturalistic drama. I wanted to combine poetry dialogue and stories in the one piece. I wrote an initial first draft which did not have enough dramatic conflict nor solid enough characters. The company organized a period of four-week workshops to assist me with the rewrite. Joan-Ann Maynard directed these workshops. For me this was an exciting experience. Other women were creating on top of my foundation, improvising, building backgrounds, interacting. Joan-Ann understood precisely what I was trying to say in the play. It was so different to writing on your own in your bedroom, working with all these women. I kept feeling like it was a dream come true. It took the lonely feeling of writing away and gave me inspiration and ideas to feed back into the writing. The play could never have been the same without all of these women. I find the idea of people working on a project collaboratively really satisfying. In the rehearsal period, I had to let go and let the director bring it to life. Joan-Ann worked with Pamela Lofton, who choreographed, and Gail Ann Dorsey, who wrote music to my lyrics. All of this was so exhilarating to have people using their own particular skill and inspiration on the one piece of work.

The whole process taught me a lot. I learnt how to let go. Never before had I even had anyone else perform my work. I've always read my own poems. It was amazing how much the meaning could change depending on the emphasis and the interpretation. I learnt how to create in a complementary way with other women.

Now that I've seen *Chiaroscuro* several times, I feel that there is much room for improvement, and if I were to write another play, or rewrite this one, I would change things. But you can only learn through making mistakes. Part of being a public writer is being able to take the risk of making mistakes. That's often very frightening; at least in some other types of work you can make mistakes in private! I think it is this that stops many women from publishing or performing their work. The fear of criticism, the fear that it really is not good enough and somebody, maybe everybody, is going to tell you how far from good it is. Writing is risking. It is making yourself publicly vulnerable and you have to learn to deal with that if you choose to be public. You have to learn to be accountable and responsible for your own words. And that is not easy.

Every writer who looks over work she has done a while before would want to change something about it. Every writer can, after publication or performance, see flaws. It is the ability to see flaws and not lie down and die that keeps you on your toes, keeps you changing and challenging. Even although being 'public' is frightening, it also has a huge number of benefits. You can hear directly what people think, you can respond to suggestions, you can see that people are actually getting *something*, and that in itself is thrilling. I remember the first poetry reading I ever gave at Southall. I was bowled over by the appreciation. It gave me strength to go on and write some more. It made writing seem less isolating. Writing is after all about communication, but you can often feel as if you are communicating with nobody except yourself! So, seeing attentive faces, hearing laughter, seeing tears even, all give you something back. It is a relationship. You see just how much of a relationship it is in the theatre where the audience can literally change a play by the way they respond to it. Writing is all about developing relationships both within the work itself and outside of it.

*Chiaroscuro* is about four different black women and their relationship to themselves, each other, their colour, their sexuality. It is about communication, the ways they find to relate to each other, the ways they don't find. One of the themes that runs through the play is naming and namelessness. The play opens with each woman – Aisha, Beth, Opal and Yomi – telling the audience how she came to get her name. It is also about how you can invent names if you have no tales of generation after generation. How you can make your own definitions, invent you own past. How to name the nameless.

It is of paramount importance to name ourselves, to put ourselves on the map so that we cannot be lost. To make a record of our existence and our struggle. The chorus of the last song is:

> If we should die in the wilderness
> let the child that finds us
> know our name and story
> know our name and story

We rarely see any positive black characters on television or in the theatre. Only in the last couple of years have publishers wanted to publish black writers' work, have theatre companies wished to commission black playwrights, have television researchers hunted for black scriptwriters. Despite this recent interest, there is still a huge absence. A play from a black British point of view is still too much of a rarity. The creation out of this void, this absence, is in itself a political activity: it says, 'I refuse to have my sisters' and brothers' existence denied. Here we are.' Of course it is not enough simply to create what you see as being positive black characters; we can often stereotype ourselves, or believe certain lies that we were fed in our childhood. The fact that we live in a racist and sexist society can often inadvertently be reflected in what we write. And society can attempt to tokenize black writers just as they can anybody else, to set up a hero or two to assuage the complexities of racist guilt. Black writers have to be alert to the current search to find, for example, a British version of Alice Walker. We must keep our own vigilant standards. That's why I think constructive criticism is so crucial. I know I have an awful lot to learn from other people and I appreciate it when people take time to tell me what they think of my work, what criticism they have of it, but of course I cannot take the 'let me rip you apart' kind of criticism.

Strangely enough, I find criticism hard to take for another reason. It sometimes embarrasses me because people are treating my work seriously enough to criticize it. There is something very positive about that.

Everything I write is influenced by all of my contradictions and all of my experience. It cannot be otherwise now. I am a woman. I write as a woman. I am black. I write from a black point of view, even if I'm creating a white character, I'm still creating her from a black point of view. I am a lesbian. I write from a lesbian's perspective. I believe somewhere that I have something to say and I will say it.

SO YOU THINK I'M A MULE?

'Where do you come from?'
'I'm from Glasgow.'
'Glasgow?'
'Uh huh. Glasgow.'
The white face hesitates
the eyebrows raise
the mouth opens
then snaps shut
incredulous
yet too polite to say outright
liar
she tries another manoeuvre
'And your parents?'
'Glasgow and Fife.'
'Oh?'
'Yes. Oh.'
Snookered she wonders where she should go
from here –
'Ah, but you're not pure?'
'Pure? Pure what
Pure white? Ugh. What a plight
Pure, Sure I'm pure
I'm rare...'
'Well, that's not exactly what I mean,
I mean ... you're a mulatto, just look at...'
'Listen. My original father was Nigerian
to help with your confusion
But hold on right there
If you Dare mutter mulatto
hover around hybrid

hobble on half-caste
and intellectualize on the
"Mixed race problem",
I have to tell you:
take your beady eyes offa my skin;
don't concern yourself with
the "dialectics of mixtures";
don't pull that strange blood crap
on me Great White Mother.
Say I'm no mating of a she-ass and a stallion
no half of this and half of that
to put it plainly purely
I am black
My blood flows evenly, powerfully
and when they shout "Nigger"
and you shout "Shame"
ain't nobody debating my blackness.
You see that fine African nose of mine,
my lips, my hair. You see lady
I'm not mixed up about it.
So take your questions, your interest,
your patronage. Run along.
Just leave me.
I'm going to my Black sisters
to women who nourish each other
on belonging
There's a lot of us
Black women struggling to define
just who we are
where we belong
and if we know no home
we know one thing;
we are Black
we're at home with that.'
'Well, that's very well, but ...'
'No But. Good bye.'

# Jackie Kay

## THE MOTHER POEM 2

I always wanted to give birth
do that incredible natural thing
that women do – I nearly broke down
when I heard we couldn't
and then my man said to me
well there's always adoption (we didn't have
test tubes and the rest then) and well
even in the early sixties there was something
scandalous about adopting
telling the world your secret failure
bringing up an alien child
who knew what it would turn out to be?

but I wanted a baby badly
didn't need to come from my womb
or his seed for me to love it did it
and I had sisters who looked like me
didn't need carbon copy features
blueprints for generations
it was a baby a baby a baby I wanted

so I watched my child grow
always the first to hear her in the night
all this umbilical knot business is
nonsense – the men can afford deeper sleeps
that's all. I listened to hear her talk
and when she did I heard my voice under hers
and now some of her mannerisms
crack me up

all them stories could have really had me
believing unless you are breast
fed you'll never be close and the rest
my daughter's warmth spills over me

leaves a gap
when she's gone
I think of her mother

She remembers how I read her
all those magazine and newspaper
cuttings about adoption
she says her head's an encyclopedia
of sob stories – the ones that were never
told and committed suicide on their wedding nights

I always believed in the telling anyhow
you can't keep something like that secret
I wanted her to think of her other mother
out there thinking that child I had will be
eight today nine today all the way up to
god knows when I told my daughter
I bet your mother's never missed your birthday
how could she?

now when people say ah but
it's not like having your own child is it
I say of course it is what else is it
she's my child I've brought her up
told her stories wept at her losses
laughed at her pleasures. She is mine.

yes well maybe that's why I don't
like all this talk about her being Black
I brought her up as my own
as I would any other child
colour matters to the nutters
but she says my daughter says
it matters to her

I suppose there would have been things
I couldn't understand with any child
we knew she was coloured
they told us they had no babies at first
and I chanced to say it didn't matter
what colour it was and then they said
oh well are you sure in that case
we have a baby for you
to think she wasn't even thought of as a baby!
my baby my baby

## THE TWEED HAT DREAM


Her mother just turns up at the door.
With a tweed hat on. I thinks
she doesn't suit tweed, she's too young.
In all these months I've never put a face to her
that looks like my daughter – so picture me
when I see those lips!
In fact she looks a dead spit
except she's white lightning white.
She says in a soft well-spoken  voice
Can you let me see her? I know I shouldn't
but can you? What could I do?
She comes in swift as wind in a storm
rushes up the stairs as if she knows the house
already, picks up my baby
and strokes her cheeks endlessly
till I get tired and say I'll be downstairs.
I put the kettle on, maybe
hot tea will redden those white cheeks,
arrange a plate of biscuits which keep
sliding onto the floor.
*She's been up there helluva long*
I don't know where the thought comes from
but suddenly I'm pounding the stairs like thunder.
Her tweed hat is in the cot. That is all.


## THE MEETING DREAM


*If I picture it like this it hurts less*

We are both shy
though our eyes are not
they pierce below skin
we are not as we imagined
I am smaller, fatter, darker
she is taller, thinner
(and I'd always imagined her hair dark brown
not grey) I can see my chin in hers
that is all, though no doubt
my mum will say when she looks at the photo

*she's your double she really is*

There is no sentiment in this living room
a plain wood table and a few books
we don't cuddle or even shake hands
though we smile sudden as a fire blazing
then die down
her hands play with her wedding ring
I've started smoking again

We don't ask big questions even later by the shore
we walk slow, tentative as crabs
No *so what have you been doing the past 26 years?*
Just *what are you working at?* Stuff like that

Ages later I pick up a speckled stone
and hurl it into the sea
*is this how you imagined it to be?*
I never imagined it.
*Oh.* I hear the muffled splash.
It would have driven me mad imagining
26 years is a long time

Inside once more I sip hot tea
notice one wood framed photo
the air is as old as the sea
I stare at her chin till she makes me look down
her hands are awkward as rocks
my eyes are stones washed over and over

*If I picture it like this it hurts less*

One dream cuts another open like a gutted fish
nothing is what it was
she is too many imaginings to be flesh and blood.
There is nothing left to say;
neither of us mentions meeting again

# JOAN RILEY

Joan Riley was born in St Mary, Jamaica, and now lives in Britain. Her most recent novel is *A Kindness to the Children*. Her other novels, *The Unbelonging* (1985), *Waiting in the Twilight* (1987) and *Romance* (1988), are all published by The Women's Press.

JOAN RILEY

# Writing Reality in a Hostile Environment

Race might seem like a strange concept with which to start a paper on literature. But it is also appropriate to the context in which many non-indigenous people live and work and survive throughout Europe.

In Britain as in the rest of Europe, the so-called *race question* goes deep into the fabric of society, not race in its biological and innocuous meaning, but as an emotive and infinitely manipulable form.

Manipulation of public opinion, however politically or socially shaded depersonalises black peoples and creates acceptance of a set of *truths* which has nothing to do with race. This is a historical phenomena, which meant recent black immigration into Europe, found societies where racism and its resultant prejudices, were totally integrated into existing cultural and social norms.

A great deal of Europe's creative energies in the past few centuries has gone into expunging collective guilt. It was necessary to justify atrocities committed on non-white peoples for economic gain, by creating the myth of inferiority and a sliding scale of humanity.

So when black and Asian peoples started arriving in any numbers, they were already marked...not only by skin colour, but with the stigma of slavery, indentureship and subordinate colonial status.

As immigrants they were convenient scapegoats who were linked in the public mind to undesirable behaviour such as mugging and with social problems such as urban decay.

It was in this climate that creative self-expression struggled to flourish.

*The Reality of Existence and Gender.*

The development of an indigenous literature based on the experience of black people in Britain is a relatively recent phenomena. Although there are notable exceptions, i.e. Buchi Emecheta's *Second Class Citizen* and *In the Ditch*, the black experience in Britain was usually interpreted by 'white' usually sociological parameters.

The practical result of this, has been a tendency to attempt a frame of reference that tied closest to white perceptions and expectations of black

lives, based as it is on the old colonial definitions of superiority and black
non-humanity and inferiority.

For Afro-Caribbeans, due to a whole series of historical, economical and
political necessities which could not adequately be dealt with here, this
has meant being locked into the position of underclass.

There is a saying, that if you want to know a people you should read
their literature. If that had been the test of existence, black people and
Asians in Britain would have been non-people. Literature was constantly
imposed from without and the effort to separate them from their history
went on in schools, colleges and society in general.

In the case of Afro-Caribbeans in particular it was almost like the genesis
of a new people. Part of a new white created and imposed definition of
black, with a forty year existence and no past. Even within this limited
definition women came out nowhere. The community was defined in
terms of men, and the notorizing of the 'youth'. The idea seemed to be,
that men faced oppression, and it was a woman's duty to be
understanding. This was of course not unique to Britain. Certainly it was
an extension and continuation of the situation brought from the
Caribbean. If Afro-Caribbean men had little space for expression in Britain;
women seemed to have no place in the black experience. Men defined the
black experience, and women were expected to actively work for male
freedom before staking a claim for their own.

When I was a young undergraduate, accepted definitions of black
women, came out of the perceptions of black men. The works of Afro-
American and Caribbean men were often cited as authoritative sources of
information about black women, their lives and character. After all, they
were black they should know. No one seem to notice the irony. There was
little doubt cast on the impartiality of men coming from rigidly patriarchal
systems, full of macho stereotypes, yet having to cope with women forced
to strength through economic and social necessity. The so-called hierarchy
of oppression, in the making then, became more entrenched and accepted
and in the following decade.

Allied to this situation was the popular attitude in Britain that the
pattern of racial 'co-existence' in the United States was one that any
situation of black and white would undergo. There seemed to be an
attitude in Britain that the black dimension to available literature was
already covered. For what was coming out of America would eventually
be true of any western industrial country with a black presence.

That this might be a stereotype never seemed to be a matter of even
passing consideration; despite the fact that no one would consider
comparing the situation of say, Tamils in Sri Lanka with the Protestants
in Northern Ireland. The fact that Afro-Americans were present at the
inception of annexion was brushed aside as irrelevant.

There has always been a tendency to confuse, rather than link, the
historical developments within the Caribbean basin with that which exist

in the United States. This has been foisted by the common experience of slavery and the traditional migratory tendencies of Caribbean peoples towards the United States. It has also been a comfortable cushioning reality with overtones of inevitability taking away responsibility for a range of injustices from the shoulders of the host community.

The writer of the black reality in Britain must of necessity challenge this perception. This very challenge creates a hostility that pre-disposes towards suppression and condemnation of a literature that creates pain.

*The Writer and Responsibility.*

As a writer I am responsible only to myself and my conscience. This is a truth which has taken me many years to finally accept. I write from my own perception, and makes no pretence that it is on behalf of anyone. Writing on issues considered to be controversial, means that once published it's too late to apologise for the work, and to justify is to devalue it. Trying to satisfy everyone is to please no one and one becomes very much like the farmer and the donkey in the fable; with a whole series of imposed opinions riding on your back.

Nevertheless, with the the paucity of literature geared to the black experience in Britain, there is a tendency on all sides, to load onto writers' shoulders the responsibility for the collective conscience of a community. Rejection of this role often lead to hostility and the claim that a writer has turned her back on her *roots* or *sold out*. Yet acceptance could put you in an equally untenable position, where ownership of your own thought process is subject to community approval.

To be a black person and a woman, writing in Britain is to tread a thin line. Coming from the Caribbean, yet choosing to write about the lives of ordinary black women in Britain creates certain ambiguities. For many British-born black people it is seen as a marked failure, that much of what is written as a representation of their environment comes from what they would consider non-indigenous people.

Choosing to write about women considered *losers* raises other questions of hostility...both from radical black men, seeing themselves as scapegoated by an unholy alliance of black women and white feminist, and from black feminists, unable to accept the portrayal of weakness as well as strength in black women as an integral part of their essential humanness.

Many in the black community perceive themselves as under siege. They see the negative portrayal of black people, in all media forms, and routinely in formalised social responses. The reaction is to close ranks, to be afraid of frank examination, even if this resistance indirectly aids the process of de-personalisation, which creates lesser values for black lives. The idea of black people portrayed in certain adverse situations, is considered appalling, however disturbing and effective it might be, in challenging the non-person stereotype. Equally too is the idea of black people portrayed as incorporating bad traits as well as good. Understandable though this resistance is, it creates a difficult climate in certain situations for the writer to find manoeuvring space.

Hostility from the white community is twofold: from white feminists angered that racism is given precedence over what they see as the more important gender issues notably sexism and from the white people in general, because the content of the literature strikes too close to home. It not only points a finger at their unacknowledged and systematic discrimination; but also challenges their comfortable world view.

Of course certain things were difficult to accept, by people of all political persuasions. For instance, the prevalence of racism in Britain, although partially acknowledged has never been acted on as a central factor in combatting the way black children progress through the school system or why and how black people in general are positioned in the socio-economic framework of society. Instead, the success of a small minority is used as the exception, to prove the very opposite of this concept... In this way the oppressed is made to take full blame and responsibility for her/his oppression. For many black writers, this is the first *truth* that they stumble across early in the exposure of their creative output.

Colour like poverty seem to have become more and more another facility for the rich. In the same way as one would go to the theatre, and give to charity, one could also take on anti-racism; without varying perception or behaviour one iota.

Everybody read the black American writers and were moved, *but at least it couldn't happen in Britain. Issues around the Caribbean and African could be taken aboard.* After all these were independent places, and their problems were because of their own incompetence, (not the legacy of centuries of exploitation) and so Britain was left with clean hands.

It's hardly surprising that the only authors writing in Britain, deemed worthy of notice, were those who concentrated on *elsewhere*, or wrote in the terms of the transient. One wonders if this might not be due to the British reluctance to come to terms with the existence of a settled permanent black presence. Racism against black people could be coped with, when not articulated, or so long as it came over that it was an extreme minority, and the majority were benevolent and tolerant.

Literature from the Caribbean is considered *safe*; but still by and large irrelevant to the real lives of black children growing up in Britain. Accepted wisdom is that, they live in Britain so they should accept and learn about Britain forgetting that this is what they've been doing in Caribbean schools for generations. The idea seems to be that Afro-Caribbean children must learn to co-exist so long as this means the erradication of who they are and the history which has brought them to where they are.

Images of the Caribbean, despite a rich body of literature to the contrary remain that of a rural, 'backward' place, full of ignorant easy-going and illiterate people, with little ambition and less morals.

Education policy seemed to consider it necessary to separate (what was termed) the British black from any comparison with the media defined quaint backwardness and simplicity of the Caribbean and bumbling savagery of Africa. This happened at a time, when black American writers were beginning to enjoy a great deal of popularity in Britain and the parallels with the American ghettos were immediately obvious. The fact that differences might also have existed, was something that was never taken on board; for a part of British perception of black as negative - whether it be in the role of victim, sly criminal or savage destroyer - had been shaped by the way urban black communities in America were portrayed in both print and electronic media. So long as it did not challenge this perception, black literature was a comfortable *right on* thing to read. It was only when black writing was about the British backyard, that it started to get uncomfortable.

*The Dilemma.*

Many black writers often feel trapped between a variety of warring factions. There is constant pressure to justify and apologise for the written text; and equally 'to conform' the next book, the next story the next time. The creative process becomes a constant struggle, not to shy away from honest opinion in the interest of approval. The role of the writer in society is an ever present topic, obscuring issues, which I would consider crucial. These include issues such as the lack of an independent and representative black critique, one which surveys black works in its own context and on its own terms. This is not, I hasten to add, a plea for dual standards of literature, only one where adherence to eurocentric values are not a precondition for the label, *excellent*.

Too often good works are stifled from view, because the reviewer is unable to step outside narrow prejudices and cultural confines. Others because sadly, the critical appraisal lacks the open honesty of the work in question; and hides behind platitudes such as impartiality, and the equally absurd idea that art can be divorced from cultural and social contexts. In many cases, criticisms show a lack of familiarity with the content of the book, doing little credit to either the author or reviewer.

*Finally: The Ending.*

In my own creative process, there is an ongoing struggle to create a breathing space. It is important to represent my perceptions as clearly and honestly as I can. Yet I would be dishonest if I did not admit to being disturbed by the levels of hostility I have often received from certain quarters.

My initial reaction to hostility, apart from disbelief, was to withdraw as fast as possible into privacy. This was followed by a long process of self-examination, and a struggle to understand what was expected of me, and more importantly, if I, as a writer, really had a burden of responsibility to all these various factions; many of whom, I hadn't even know existed. Creating is a private process, and like many writers without a literary background, I was ill-prepared and resentful of the glare of public scrutiny which followed it. It is a dilemma I have seen time and again in writers, presented in many forms, and it is one which is intensified by the complex, secretive nature of guilt in British social life.

I have long come to terms with the expectation that my work will be criticised for the sake of criticism with one theme in the book, elevated out of context to provide fuel for unconstructive, and destructive attacks, on both book and author. This is by no means a unique experience. Black writing remains a novelty, and black writing without a happy ending raises issues of guilt and resentment.

My own perception of what my work sets out to do often mitigates against any kind of happy ending. This is not because I am an unremittingly gloomy individual; quite the contrary in fact.

On the other hand my view of creativity demands a high level of involvement. As a result I feel happy endings in much of my work, would be a betrayal of the community of women who give unstintingly of their lives to flesh my creative world. A sop to the, *I'm alright generation*, who make up so much of the readership of works like mine.

At the end of the day, for someone to close the book on conflicts resolved, is for them to close out the world of endless struggle, disappointments, bad housing, raw deals, that continue to be the daily lives of many millions of people. It is also for me to be providing, from the struggle of a community, a voyeur's view, safe, tidy and packaged as just another digestable, environmentally polluting commodity, to go with the television dinners and no deposit bottles. To allow my readers to retreat back to their comfortable world and not accept their collective part in solving the issues that did not go away with the final full stop would be to have failed in achieving the purpose of the work.

Writing a reality out of step with perception carries a high emotional and intellectual price. Yet not to do so is to deny the possibility that eventually, perceptions and reality can move closer together. As a writer I do not claim to be able to change society. Certainly, I have never pretended to have any answers or possibilities for resolving the human condition. Granted there are questions, uncomfortable questions. But questions which create debate, however hostile, keep a normally hidden reality uncovered and raises the possibility of change.

# SUJATA BHATT

Sujata Bhatt was born in 1956 in Ahmedabad, India and raised in Pune, India. She has lived, studied and worked in the United States, and is a graduate of the Writers' Workshop at the University of Iowa, Iowa City. She has published two collections of poetry with Carcanet Press, England and Penguin Books, India: *Brunizem* (1988) won the Alice Hunt Bartlett Prize and the Commonwealth Poetry Prize (Asia). And *Monkey Shadows* (1991) was a Poetry Book Society Recommendation. She received a Cholmondeley Award in 1991. In Spring 1992 she was the Lansdowne Visiting Writer/Professor at the University of Victoria, British Columbia, Canada. She now lives in Bremen with her husband, the German writer Michael Augustin, and their daughter. Sujata Bhatt works as a freelance writer and has translated Gujarati poetry into English for the *Penguin Anthology of Contemporary Indian Women Poets*. Her work has appeared in various British, Irish, American and Canadian journals and her poems have been widely anthologized and have also been broadcast on British, German and Dutch Radio. Her new collection *The Stinking Rose* is due from Carcanet in February 1995.

SUJATA BHATT

# Why I Write

Recently, I've been a frequent visitor to the U.K. and Ireland, and I do read a great deal of the poetry that has been written and is being written here. My publisher is based in Manchester, so I feel directly involved in this poetry scene although my observations are those of an outsider. As an Indian who studied and lived in the U.S. for some time, now lives in Germany, and is today writing these lines from Spain, I wonder whether the role of poetry today is really very different in all of the above mentioned countries.

What indeed is the current role of poetry? To provide some relief from the stupefying noise of the media; to provide another means of communication than that used by 'our' politicians. Poetry should say something valuable without resorting to the jargon-laden language increasingly used by many lawyers, economists, sociologists, anthropologists, let alone literary critics and other professional recipients of our craft. Poetry creates a quietness in the language, a silence that allows time for all the intricacies of slowly unfolding words. Poetry gives back patience, tolerance and a certain dignity to the language. This is not to imply that poetry should remain a solemn affair. On the contrary, poetry is a very spontaneous and vigorous *play* with words that stretches language to its true limits. Poetry can reveal absurdity and joy in breathtaking forms. Ultimately, poetry exposes a layer of being and a view of reality that ordinary speech cannot encompass.

In the last decade of the twentieth century, I see the poet as an ecologist conserving not only a vital dimension of language but also the human bonds connected with such language.

Throughout the world, however, poetry affects the lives of very few people. It is a voice without amplifiers. The role of the poet is like that of a Greenpeace crusader in a tiny boat challenging a supertanker filled with chemical waste. And although the waste continues to be dumped in the seas, at least a few people are made aware of it. Ten years ago only a handful of people with a green chip on their shoulder seemed to care about our environment. Nowadays, significantly more people are seriously concerned about the problems of pollution, and the first steps are being taken to prevent greater catastrophes.

Why, then, should the poet not hope that at the *fin de siecle* more people will realise how vital poetry is?

# Sujata Bhatt

## NINNIKU

1.

*Ninniku, ninniku*
the Japanese said
as they examined the Buddhist
monks. *To hear insults*
*with patience* on the way to Nirvana.

The Buddhist mind
is strengthened by the sharp
light of garlic.

White... White... is the flame of garlic
the heat of garlic.

Then Queen Maya, Siddhartha's mother
dreamt that a white elephant
entered her womb.

White –

And that was the colour of the swan
Siddhartha rushed to save.

White –

And that was the colour
of Kanthak, the horse he once rode.

White –

And that was the colour
of the elephant he once rode.

The Japanese met Buddhism
and *ninniku* sprouted
along with the lotus.

*om mani padma hum*
the monks whispered
ever sleepless, ever vigilant,
every day they walked for miles –

for the body must be able
to bear the Truth,
for without the body the mind cannot
climb the steep path of right mindfulness.

*om mani padma hum*
the monks whispered
with garlic on their breath.


2.


*Ninniku:*
To bear insults with patience.
That's what they have to do,
those immigrants
from the garlic-eating regions.
Some travel north
and some travel west
but they all learn to keep their distance.

Sometimes the women
   in desperation
douse themselves with perfume –
musky jasmine
   husky rose –
later on the bus, humid
vapours mingle with garlic
on their skin and clothes; only sharpen
the luminous
homesickness
in the whites of their eyes.


Note: When Buddhism came to Japan in the 6th century AD, the Japanese adopted a new word for garlic, *ninniku* the characters for which mean 'to bear insults with patience". Buddhist monks are permitted to use garlic for its medicinal properties. The Japanese have never been enthusiastic garlic eaters. This information from: *Garlic: Nature's Original Remedy* by Stephen Fulder and John Blackwood, Healing Arts Press, Vermont, U.S.A., 1991.

## NOTHING IS BLACK, REALLY NOTHING

1.

*nada es negro, realmente nada*
So Frida Kahlo wrote
one day in her diary.

But Frida, how black you could paint
your pulled-back hair, your braids,
and the little dark hairs above your lips –
How black your eyes
your eyebrows;
how black the hairs of your monkey
especially in *Fulang-Chang and I.*

But nothing is black.
True black that breathes
must shine with blue light,
green shadows – some say
a reddish glow means
the colour isn't black enough.

2.

Then there was *elephantinum,*
elephant-tusk-black.
For Plinius records the tale
of Appelles, born around 350 BC he was
Alexander the Great's blue-blooded court painter –
he was the first
to create the colour black called *elephantinum*
from fired ivory.

Dry distilled from tusks,
the fat fired out
from the elephant tusks...
and in the end black powder extracted,
distilled,
dry, dry...

And you can extract black
out of grape seeds.

And you can extract black
out of wood or gas
or out of that oil hidden deep within
the earth.

How black do you want
your paint?


3.

I do not want
to consult the dictionary
for words about black.
I know those one-sided words
already: a black heart, a black mood,
a black day, a blunt blackjack –

I keep brooding instead
over my daughter's love for black –

How when she was not quite three
and the blond children teased her
for having brown hair,
she was only angered by their inaccuracy.
'This is not brown!' she screamed,
holding up a fistful of her hair.
'It's black!
My hair is black, black –
Not brown!'

As if to say
she knew her colours well.
She no longer confused orange with red,
indigo with violet,
or brown with black.
She could understand light green, dark green,
yellow, blue, she learned
        the names so quickly.


4.

Now I keep turning back to you Frida –
Nothing is black

but how you loved your black hair
that's not really black
and how many different black strokes
you found (when nothing is black)
to pull out every shade
        of blackness
from your hair, your self –


## SHARDA

After all these years
my mother has forgotten her name –
the name of the girl
she most admired –
the girl who lived across the street
when my mother was little.

So I tell her
it must've been Sharda.
Sharda:
A mature name, full of dignity.
Sharda, who is the lute: Veena –
light sun-notes flicker
transparent across blood-dark
heavy tones – Sharda who is both
Sarasvati and Durga –
dragonfly wings
shimmer, curious above the drowned squirrel –
How can one name
contain so much?

'Sharda, Sharda!' I can see
her mother calling her.

Sharda was a serious girl.
She wore silk *chanya choli:*
that is, a long full skirt and a tight
bodice-blouse – she sparkled.
She was nine-years-old.
She knew many prayers.
She sat alone
in the *puja* room –
she was doing *arti*

she was ringing the small brass
prayer bell with one hand
and holding a small flame
also brass cupped in her other
hand – when she slipped
and the *ghee* spilled across
her silk clothes and the wick
spit fire over her fingertips.

Maybe there was a gust of wind –
      something fluky
so even the huge crows fled
with their elbow-wings.

Why was there nobody
   at home that day?
Why was there no one
   who heard her cry?

'Such things happen.'
My mother says.
I suspect Sharda's elders.
Did she have too many sisters?
'No, no! It wasn't like that.'
My mother shakes her head.

Still, we can agree about how
she spun, hopping around
      and around
trying to escape the flames.

Then she was sucked in –
it was like a sudden wave
a wall
with a sharp undertow –
A fire-wave
almost silent
compared to water.

'Sharda, Sharda!'
My mother must have called
for a long time
even after they found her.

# ELLEKE BOEHMER

Elleke Boehmer was born in Durban, South Africa, of Netherlands parents, and is now resident in Britain. Her first novel *Screens Against the Sky*, which was described as an 'astonishing debut ... expertly told' by *The Sunday Times*, was shortlisted for the 1990 David Higham Award. She teaches in the School of English at the University of Leeds and also writes about issues of postcoloniality in the new English literatures. Her second novel, *An Immaculate Figure*, is published by Bloomsbury.

ELLEKE BOEHMER

# Why I Write

Once I met a man who though he loved novels, he mistrusted them. He said he believed in reality. He didn't want his attention to stray from reality. But it did. He was a compulsive reader.

Making things up is what human beings do. We are story-making creatures, though we make these stories in different ways. We fantasize, we create different plots for ourselves out of randomness. Writing is the way I have chosen of making stories. I know if I didn't write, things might get dangerous. An event takes a particular shape, but I am aware of other shapes it could have taken. There was a time when I couldn't distinguish between them. Now I channel invention into novels. Why I write.

I write about tainting. I am interested in error and the consequences of error. The way people bear, or refuse to bear, the burdens of the past. One thing leads to another, in story as in life, but this isn't always admitted. The person I curse today may tomorrow tend my best friend's wound. I am intrigued by the ordinariness of wrong. Error is often very banal. No doubt South Africa, where I grew up, gave me these concerns. *Screens Against the Sky* was a domestic tale. But it was also about national claustrophobia. In my latest novel, *An Immaculate Figure*, the heroine Rosandra White, a beauty queen and girl-next-door, believes she can strip off various roles as she finishes with them. She doesn't see herself as part of a plot – a plot that could move towards dangerous conclusions.

Is there escape from all this, from consequences? An evasion of nemesis? Lately restlessness, and release, have started to preoccupy me. I would like to write about Britain, which has been my migrant home for years. British writing like British society is full of structures. People know their place inside these structures. I want to create some space around this fixity. I want to write a travel tale about a forbidden passion, set in England.

ELLEKE BOEHMER

# Fado in Lissabon

What he told her. Usually, that his heart was no good. Sometimes, how he missed the sea.

She takes the yellow-painted motor launch across the river and on the other side has salted cod, sweet lemonade. The air here is brackish. The waitress's mouth is painted brick-red. At the far end of the wharf men are bringing in jelly fish. The black nets filled with blubbery white.

Lissabon, he said the name in his own language, touching it musically. He did not usually sing, not aloud. He silently mouthed the songs of the woman with the black eyes who featured on every one of his album covers. He played these records late at night and early in the morning, when the rest of the family was asleep. He played them softly. He said, I love to hear that voice. It contains everything, the whole world.

The churches she discovers in side streets are quiet. They are dusty buildings clogged with wrought iron and marble bric-à-brac. In them something is missing. He would have avoided the churches, of course. He avoided holy vessels of memory and spirit. He liked to burn his photographs from time to time. There were pictures of his youth, the tall house in Rotterdam, the years spent in the navy, Queen Wilhelmina in white lace shaking his hand. He used old letters for kindling. The last time, he added his navy epaulettes to the blaze.

One church she visits is damaged by fire. Pigeons are nesting behind the altar. A woman with a Pentax tells her, what a pity, such beautiful monuments in this country and they don't take care of them.

When he came home that day, knowing what he had suspected all along, he played his music at noon for the first time. Song after song the woman's voice was rich and strong and without hope. In a corner stood two children in summer dresses giggling. The man rocked from side to side at the record player, mouthing the words.

The area with the fado bars confuses her. The bars look alike. Each pumps songs of immense sorrow onto the street. She chooses at random. The man at the door takes her coat and seats her beside the cigarette machine. On the table is a bottle of Dao and a vanilla pudding in a wine glass. She and the two other customers make a short row at the edge of an empty raft of tables. Perched on the bar is an albino canary in a cage.

But after all, he did not make it here. He said one day, laughing, I'll get there though I die in the attempt. I have to make it, it's fated. I, a sea-faring man from a sea-faring nation. Having sailed the routes of the old explorers. The Arabian Sea and the Indian Ocean. It was '43, '44, about then. Patrolling around Aden and Jakarta, liberating East Timor. And then having not made it into Lissabon.

His attention wandered when he thought of these things. He hummed to himself. Out of that great city, he would add, sailed the white man bearing the astrolabe, influenza, unfinished maps of the world, the telephone. Up that river he came again weighed down with the heaviness of his ambition. Returning to a city which an earthquake had ground to dust.

The singer here is not comfortable. A few minutes ago she was laughing melodiously with the guitarist behind a wooden screen. On the dias she is unhappy. The edge of her red shawl dusts the floor. She croons a little and stands still, stout on black stilettos. The other two customers have struck up a conversation in English.

'You should take a vacation,' says one. 'You'll get used to it.'

Then, soon after he'd heard what he had to hear, he stopped playing his fado records. He stayed in bed. They put the pile of records within reach beside the bed. The album covers boasting of the woman with the black eyes and brick-red lips. He took no notice. He murmured the names of distant cities. Trust them, he said. After the earthquake they rebuilt all of Lissabon by careful design. However I'm told they got it wrong, the streets aren't symmetrical. It's hard to believe. I must go to see it some day.

She is joined by a Mocambiquan, a fourth customer, who smells of lemon soap. He is wearing a checked blue and red shirt and a cap. He says he is a student. Can he sit with her?

On the wall behind the Mocambiquan's head she notices a signed and framed photograph of her father's singer. The signature has run into the complicated embroidery of her gown. The singer's eyebrows are straight and black, she is not smiling.

The Mocambiquan tells her he comes here every weekend for fado. The singer must be made drunk, is his opinion. The music is African really, and she is not, she doesn't feel it. He orders two bottles of Dao, he gives one to the musicians behind the wooden screen. On the table he spreads red and black pamphlets, and pens and a notebook. He adds an extra vase of flowers taken from an empty table.

She thinks she hears him say the singer behind the screen was once his lover. Then he is explaining the pamphlets. The place has very quickly become loud. The singer is suddenly singing with great power and steadiness. The Mocambiquan points to a small button on his shirt, then jabs at the title of his pamphlets. These say, Free East Timor. She shakes her head, she is having trouble hearing him. He says, mouthing the words, take bus route 25. She realises he is asking her to join him tomorrow on the beach, at the old Coke kiosk. There, the surf is good.

But vinyl does not burn easily, they discovered. The album covers and the photograph of his destroyer did. He laughed to see the flames dance in the big metal waste bin. He laughed also when he broke the photograph frame on the floor. He added to the bin rubbing alcohol, old letters and a yellowed journal, his navy epaulettes, and the broken photograph frame. But he had his children light the matches. Two matches. Hers was the second. She saw the red lips of the woman leap into flame. Then they watched him laughing and retching into his pillow, and laughing again, and beating a silent tune with both hands on the mattress.

The Mocambiquan draws a map to make clearer the route to the beach. The singer has come to sit at their table. She looks at him with an expression of deep hopelessness. She watches him draw. Then she speaks, he translates. This is a difficult city for a stranger to find their way and feel happy, he says slowly, watching her lips. Because it was rebuilt askew. It is a city full of junk, and bad singers, and aging dictators, he adds, built askew.

# SOUTH AFRICA
### (Reactions to Freedom)

# LAURETTA NGCOBO

Lauretta Ngcobo is a South African by birth. She left South Africa twenty-nine years ago and went into political exile. She spent the first six years of her exile in different countries in Africa and then came to live in Britain. Initially she had left her children in South Africa with her mother. Later they were able to join her, as was her husband, and once that happened, it was possible for all of them to live together as a family for the first time in Britain. Lauretta was a teacher by profession, and worked as such until a year ago when she retired. She has published two novels, *Cross of Gold* (Longman, 1981) and *And They Didn't Die* (Virago, 1990), as well as several essays on the subject of African women and their concerns. She has also edited an anthology of writing by black women, *Let it be Told*.

LAURETTA NGCOBO

# Now That We're Free

This month I voted for the first time to choose my own government in South Africa. The exercise of this belated right, when it came, left me numb. Throughout that day I experienced a pause, both of mind and feeling. I have lived in exile for 31 years. Years charged with a restlessness that would not leave me; preoccupied variously with a sense of loss; a loss of country, of friends and relations, of language, and to some degree, a loss of self. So, on the 26th of April 1994, I paused to look back on the years spent in deficiency. However, this could not last for long, for the occasion did not belong to the past, but to the future. The next few days flowed like glue as the whole world waited with baited breath for the results, even though it was a foregone conclusion that the ANC would win. I waited with the world, tense and fearful that the worst, in the form of internecine violence, might yet follow the elections. When South Africa and the world could not wait any longer, the results were declared anyhow. And no one complained about the drawing board results. On the contrary, everyone was satisfied. Well, that is, if you overlooked all the irregularities. Nobody does things quite like South Africans.

Then joy exploded and filled the whole country. The fizz still continues now after a month of the momentous elections, cascading waves of exultations from the street parties, the swearing in of the elected members, the inauguration, the opening of Parliament. Everything, as in a dream state, has swept the whole country into the new South Africa. Mandela spoke endlessly of unity, of peace, of reconciliation, as if to make every person in the whole country *believe* that this was possible, that it was happening, that there was now at last, one country and one people. *'The time for the healing of the wounds has come. The moment to bridge the chasms that divide us has come. The time to build is upon us... Let there be work, bread, water and salt for all... Today we celebrate not a victory for a party but a victory for all the people of South Africa... South Africans might have their differences, but they are one people with a common destiny in a rich variety of cultures...'*

If the people in the street have not fallen back into the routine of cold reality, I doubt if this can be said of Mandela and his new government. A cold shiver went through those in the know when it was reported, a few days after the new government took over that the Nationalist Government had blown 55 billion rand in their last year. It seemed unreal that this could be the expression of the goodwill they professed. What squandermania must have possessed them, in the midst of so much need and poverty. It seems clear that while in the pre-election days, Africans were busily engaged in the steamy hot frenzy of Black-kill-Black, the Nationalists were looting the national coffers. What Apartheid debts? And such fat pension provisions for the fat cats of Apartheid! Well, one can't help wondering if the highly vaunted reconciliation hymn is not all sung on one side of the old divide. The African paying the victory tax! Some of us were filled with foreboding when we heard that 'men of stature' like Pik Botha, let alone their underlings, were not that ready to vacate their offices. Well, it makes one wonder. It does not require a particularly astute politician to surmise that the freedom we have just won is only half the coin. It is political, and not economic. That's another battle to be won. The ANC has given up so much in the name of compromise and economic realism. In the face of the many pressures, can Mandela's government legislate against economic domination where that economy and the general know-how are safely in the hands of the private sector. No. Neither are we suggesting that they do. It depends very much on the White South Africans themselves now. If they have truly renounced Apartheid, they must show it in their willingness to share their economic might and skills. If the majority of Africans have been magnanimous in political victory, the white sector must concede much more than they seem willing to do so far.

There is another victory yet to be won, if South Africa must be restored to her space in Africa. The cultural battle. There is no other place in the continent which is less African than South Africa. We have not only lost our heritage, we sometimes betray a sense of shame about our identity. If ever there was one moment that dampened my euphoria on that day of days, Mandela's finest hour, the day of his inauguration, it was when he was sworn in. The Afrikaner who swore in F.W. de Klerk, flew against the trend of the occasion by using Afrikaans. But, for Mandela, it was English. I sincerely feel that in a country where three quarters of his people could not understand English, Mandela should have used his own language, perhaps in addition to English. And I am certain that all other groups would have felt included in that all-embracing moment. Otherwise, the overwhelming taste of victory still lingers in my mind.

# ZOË WICOMB

Zoë Wicomb was born 1948 in the Cape Province of South Africa. Spent 18 years in Britain studying and teaching English. Returned to South Africa in 1990 where she teaches English Language and literature at the University of the Western Cape.

*You Can't Get Lost in Capetown* was published by Virago.

ZOË WICOMB

# Why I Write

At first it was easy to answer this question. I said that I wrote because I could not speak (a curious answer from a garrulous person) – because as a black person, an outsider in Britain, I somehow did not have the right to speak. When health visitors or shopkeepers spoke to me in pidgin they constructed for me the choice of silence, of replying in their pidgin, or of replying in a caricatured voice of Her Majesty. Never in my own. My license to speak as a teacher or to speak in the domestic domain never transferred to that of the public, to the arena outside the immediate classroom or the home. This silence rendered me ineffective within institutions, marked me as an outsider and writing seemed to offer a way out of it. I have always tried to write, as a child and as a student but never sustained it. There is a huge leap between having the potential to write – most literate people do – and actually producing a text, an act which also always depends on material conditions. I managed it and the terror of speaking has not diminished, but at least I now face myself to do so, even if it is always under the threat of aphasia. What this suggests is that writing for me has become an act of self-validation, something about which I feel uneasy. I ought to have felt validated by being an effective teacher, a job which I believe to be more important than writing. But I suppose since the world does not agree, I have unwittingly, to my own disappointment and in spite of my claims, somehow absorbed its values – another instance of the operation of ideology.

Nowadays I genuinely cannot answer the question. Since I find writing so difficult, such torture really – and I am a painfully slow writer – I don't know why I persist. Academic writing, or my homespun brand of academic writing, is no easier for me. I am driven by outrage at the inequities and injustices that abound in my immediate world and beyond, but why I choose to write I do not know. Teaching, which can deal with issues more directly, is in so many ways more effective as a means of changing attitudes. I am suspicious of those who say that they write for the liberation of their country. All writing is, of course, political and we shouldn't underestimate the importance of literature in the reproduction of ideology; nevertheless it seems dishonest to claim that you write in order to bring about political change. There are other shorter and more effective routes to that end. The notion of the message in effective writing seems to me to be a foolish one since it never includes an investigation of the elocutionary force of that message. I would certainly send messages if the receivers promised to act upon them, but since no one will do as I say, messages, as used in the Northern British variety of English, are best got at supermarkets.

It strikes me that the question of why you write is as strange as the question of why you like chocolate. It is impossible to 'explain' the vagaries of your palate and perhaps the only sensible thing you can say is that it is marked by ambivalence. You like chocolate because it gives you pleasure but you also know that it is bad for you. I have always liked language, messing about with words, arranging them this way and that, just as others might like messing around with numbers. These activities do not seem qualitatively different; but our culture has given them different values, based, I suspect, on commodification or the marketability of an end product. Perhaps I can only respond to the question by recasting it in terms of why writing is given such particular value in our society and also why social attitudes towards writing or art in general, are so profoundly ambivalent. On the one hand there is absurd veneration and on the other the kind of contempt which sees writers as being engaged in a somewhat unseemly activity, like shitting in public, or as foolish crackpots who deserve no better than to live in poverty. The analogy with the position of women in society is striking: the consecration of women as virgins or mothers or other fetishsation of Woman which at the same time allows women as human beings to be treated with contempt. The oppositional is also, of course, to be found right there in the business of writing: the intensely private which through the very act of committing it to language becomes intensely social; the known which in our attempts to represent in language, turns out to be about what we had not known, what we discover. And so, it seems, having started with no reply to the question, I have replied after all which only goes to show how you can write yourself out of or into anything.

ZOË WICOMB

# Comment on Return to South Africa

I thought unequivocally of my return to South Africa, as many years of absence, as going home. The years spent in xenophobic Britain seemed entirely negligible and being at home is about a special sense of belonging, a confidence that makes terrifying things like driving a motorcar or speaking to the bank manager less than intimidating. But the experience, as any teenager anywhere in the world would have known, has thrown up the knowledge that home is an ambiguous site where you belong and feel comfortable but where you also encounter revulsion or horror, perhaps the most revolting aspect of horror is that it is comfortable in the home. I discovered that I had to some extent grown up in Britain and that deracination or hybridity need not be pathologised in the interest of what Paul Gilroy calls ethnic absolutism; indeed, they are conditions that are essentially me and must be accepted and embraced as such. One can also be an outsider at home, speak a different language at times, which is what psychoanalytic theory has been saying all along about subjectivity and multiple identities.

And yet, and yet, when I found myself away during the elections, when I cast my lonely vote in Glasgow, I was beside myself with longing to be home. I cursed myself for embracing fashionable theories of 'nation as imagined community' for not recognising in myself the need to participate in the celebrations with my family and friends, the need to know through witnessing and thus to be able to bear witness of the event. All my theories displaced by a desire for the politically 'vulgar' and toyi-toying notions of comradeship. But alas, being on unpaid leave, I could not afford the trip back. My distress was no doubt linked to the shame of the Coloured vote in the Western Cape, a shame that so many of us had always felt in relation to our ethnic grouping. It was, I remembered, precisely the politicals of a *national* liberation that allowed us to shake off the shame of Colouredness with its history of collaboration with Apartheid, to reshape our identity and rid ourselves of the very name. The vote has reestablished that name, reinserted it into our culture thus producing a fissure in the very notion of national liberation and demanding a closer study of racial politics.

It is nevertheless impossible not to feel a tremendous sense of optimism, not least because of the way in which ordinary people have conducted themselves in the process of voting. And the election has in a sense demonstrated that violence is essentially a condition of Apartheid; it has also restored the notion of 'ordinary South African people' (which we will no doubt later wish to contest) who stand in the queues and chat and scratch themselves in the head after the totalising media construction of warring, rampaging, ululating folk.And I must confess to an embarrassing pride ( embarrassing because is national/racial – a notion which I have always disavowed) in Nelson Mandela who is indeed, in Simon During's words, the most charismatic living figure of the enlightenment.

However, I also fear for our fragile democracy. How will military values acquired during the struggle be converted to civic values and why does no one address this crucial aspect of reconstruction? Is the military not over represented in the new cabinet and why is this so? What future for writing with the discredited 'Mother of the Nation' in a key role as 'Mother of Arts and Culture'? Why is the obscenity of the Apartheid government reproduced in the fantastic salaries drawn by our new Members of Parliament while our streets are filled with homeless beggars? How long can we expect 'ordinary South African people' to wait patiently for a better life? It is worth remembering Western capitalist commentators on the dangers of the ANC getting more than 66% of the vote, the underlying presupposition being that no one could be expected to invest in South Africa without the safeguard of white power-sharing. In other words, the ANC's failure to gain an overwhelming majority is paradoxically what gives it the remotest chance of being a successful government. But with the firm commitment to mass education and raising levels of literacy, which is after all the first raw material for writers, one can only be optimistic about another generation of readers and writers who will be attentive to the central position of irony and paradox in all aspects of our culture.

Emma Mashinini was born in Johannesburg. She began her career as a factory worker before founding the Catering and Commercial Allied Workers' Union of South Africa (CCAWUSA) in 1975. In 1986 she became Director of the Division of Justice and Reconciliation for the Church of the Province of Southern Africa. She is currently Deputy Chairperson of the National Manpower Commission. Emma Mashinini is the author of *Strikes have followed me all my life* (The Women's Press, 1989) and has won numerous awards for her activities on behalf of the trade union movement.

# I Speak as a Woman Person: Geoffrey Davis Interviews Emma Mashinini

*Emma, let me begin by saying what a great privilege it is for me to meet you here in Geneva. Having read your book* Strikes have followed me all my life[1] *one cannot but be excited at the opportunity to talk to someone who has experienced in her own life so much of what it has meant to be a South African during the decades of apartheid and who has been so consistently involved in the struggle to bring about change. You lived in Sophiatown before it was demolished, you were at the Congress of the People where the Freedom Charter was passed, you have been associated with so many of those who carried forward the freedom struggle over the years, some of whom gave their lives for it, like David Webster and Neil Aggett. Above all, you have devoted much of your life to the Trade Union movement which pioneered fundamental change inside the country, and now – at last – you are experiencing the transition to a post-apartheid society. I should therefore like to talk to you about the whole course of your career, focusing specifically on women's issues and ending with some questions about where you see yourself and the country in these momentous times.*

*I'd like to begin with your earlier career, because for someone from outside the country it would be fascinating to learn something about Sophiatown. So many people have written about that legendary place – Don Mattera, Can Themba, Trevor Huddleston among others – and, of course, there was the Junction Avenue Theatre Company's highly successful show at the Market Theatre.[2] How do you see Sophiatown looking back at it now? Do you think it has been over-romanticised perhaps?*

I don't think it is over-romanticised at all. It was so wonderful when we had Trevor Huddleston, who had come to South Africa and had gone back to Sophiatown.[3] I wasn't in his company, but I saw it on telly, especially when he went to visit a home, which is called St. Joseph's Home for Children, who are deserted by their parents. As they drove to that centre, they drove past my home, because it was in Toby Street. So these memories always come back. I've only been to Sophiatown once. I had also visited that home, because it happened to be an Anglican home for children who needed care. What really touches you is that certain things may have changed, but the layout of Sophiatown is still Sophiatown and the names of the streets are still the same names which were there. The first street was Toby Street, the next one was Bertha Street, then

Gerty Street, and so on. So it's those memories which we can never forget in this government of national unity and reconciliation. Sophiatown will always be our home.

*Another of your memories of the South Africa of the 1950s must be the Congress of the People in 1955 which, of course, is one of the great dates in the history of the liberation struggle before the political movements involved like the ANC were actually banned – and you were there?*

I was there in Kliptown. I was still a young woman who was still having babies. I'm sure I would have got prizes for bringing children into the world! I had one in the back and one here, and was expectant of another one, but I was there in that wonderful congress. And not so long ago during these very sad times of our country, there was a train massacre which had happened in Kliptown. And afterwards, as after the congress, we took a train with all our bishops from the church just to give solidarity to their people. And it was very interesting when I said to the people: This is where the congress was, in Kliptown. It seemed as though it was something very new for many of them to know that square was where the People's Congress was. Now it's like a flea-market, they sell everything there, vegetables, chickens, it's a very busy square now, the People's Congress Square.

*In your book you trace your own politicisation back to that period of your life.*

Yes, my life changed, because I sat there, and I was listening to all the speakers. And, you know, it came back to me to say: why am I in this congested township? Kliptown itself was a slum. It was a real slum. And only then did I get the exposure of saying, why am I in a slum and other people are not in slums? So this is how you get this thing. No one tells you, your situation around you just tells you that: Hey, you'd better get up and do something.

*While we are talking about your early political development, I also want to ask you about the Black Consciousness Movement. In your book you talk a lot in terms of human dignity, identity, black identity. Would it be true to describe your own development as moving from a predominantly black consciousness notion of recapturing black identity towards the present phase of non-racialism, that you celebrate in your contribution to a* Book of Hope?[4]

Definitely, one can never run down anything about Black Consciousness. I think Black Consciousness made us, and we must always be conscious that we are black. We can speak of non-racialism, but for the development of the black person – that I will always stand up for, because we need to find that equality with other people as black persons. Most of our leaders today came from the Black Consciousness movement, especially when they were still students at the university during the time of Steve Biko. That did not mean exclusion of other people, but it just said: Black man, black person, black woman, wake up, stand up for yourselves, and know who you are. That I still live for. And this is where it comes in now. Our ministers are mainly black, and you cannot be dependent, you've got to be self-sufficient as a black person.

*I feel that the values of which you are speaking were perhaps those which informed your early trade union activity, too. Is was in the mid-70s, wasn't it, when you became a union organizer?*

Yes. Many people misunderstood me and it did not make me very popular in certain quarters. But I was fighting to say that we need to be self-sufficient. If I ever forgot that I was black, I would have been so dependant of other people and never have made my own way through. This is what I did not want to be recognized in an umbrella of any other person, because I have my own human dignity, which I need to present.

*And did you think that your activity in the trade union essentially changed that status of underling?*

Yes, it did. It did in a number of ways, because we were one of the trade unions which said, we want to work side by side with the white trade unions, with the other trade unions, not to be a cut off them but to work on *equal* terms. We worked very peacefully and very wonderfully together.

*In those days it wouldn't have been possible to have been a member of a multi-racial trade union though, would it?*

It would not. You could not have been, but you could have been what at the time they called a sister union, or something less than a sister union.

*How did you first get interested and involved in the trade union movement yourself?*

I was a garment worker and I became a shop steward. I stated in my first book that it was the time when black people were treated like slaves. You kept quiet until you could keep quiet no longer. And then the workers elected me to be their shop steward. That was my first involvement with the trade union.

*How did you view your early collaboration with white trade-unionists like Morris Kagan of the National Union of Distributive Workers? They were instrumental in really getting you going. Rather like an early non-racialist practice, I suppose?*

In fact I would say that. It was at meetings when I was a shop steward in the Garment Workers' Union that we met. Maybe I was a bit outspoken. This was a meeting where all the Morris Kagans were present. When there was a need for a black trade union in the commercial distributive trade, they must have connived among themselves to say, we think that woman would be the right person to come and start this union.

*What did you set out to achieve?*

That was not the first approach. I had been approached to work for other unions in other industries before.At that particular time I was holding quite a senior position in the garment industry and that slightly made me not want to leave, you know, and for no earthly reason. It wasn't even a paying thing, but it was the status. I've always pushed for status, to say I must be recognized for what I am and who I am. But when this approach came, I gave in and said, I think I will give it a go – and it worked out. Coming from the garment industry to the commercial distributive trade was very different. It was like night and day, and again it was Morris Kagan who really assisted me. It was like my university for the first time, because he gave me so many statutes, so many books, and said, read and if you don't understand, come and ask me. Luckily I came across someone who was almost like myself. He didn't say: If you can't do it I'll do it for you. He said: If you can't do it, come and ask me how to do it. That was a development. That's why I like him. So with my black consciousness you can say I owe much to working very closely with other people.

*Were you very much a lone woman organiser in the trade union movement? What role did you see for women in the movement at that time?*

You mean in the Garment Workers' Union? That was a women's union, and we had a leader who had kept the home fires burning in the trade union movement for a long time, Lucy Mvubelo, who was the General Secretary. There was Johanna Cornelius who was white, and Anna Scheepers and others, who were also working alongside this union. And the women were very vocal.

*When you founded the Catering and Commercial Allied Workers' Union of South Africa (CCAWUSA) that was no longer solely a women's union, was it?*

No, it wasn't just a women's union. Neither was the Garment Workers Union just women, but the majority were. Then I moved into the Commercial Catering and Allied Workers Union. The reason why we started this union was the shop workers; firstly there were no shop-assistants who were black because of job reservation. So I think the reason why the white union saw the need that there must be a black union was two ways: It is because they were undercutting them by employing many black shop assistants who were paid at a lower rate than the white shop assistants. So it was good to have them organized, to bring them in par with the other shop workers, so that it should not just overpower the other union.

*What do you regard as he essential achievements of your union?*

It really is such a pride to see that, firstly, I have been a human rights pusher and not necessarily a women's rights fighter in my life, but we achieved so many things for women's rights within the union itself. I mean, just the maternity benefits which we achieved were extended from the black union to the white workers, because we had achieved that. We were not saying, whatever we have achieved is strictly for the black workers; we said it was for the workers in that particular industry. And that was very great. Even nursing of the babies after you have had your maternity leave, time off to go and nurse your baby – that was very important as well. And the working conditions for every other worker, be it man or woman

*Was maternity leave something that white women workers could expect to be granted for, say, a year and a black woman not? What was the situation?*

Well, if the agreement did not extend to cover them, we don't know what they would have done, but you know they have been so complacent that I don't think they would have reacted. It would have been some talking which was going to happen, but they would not have reacted as we would have reacted. It had to be the other way round.

*One thing which impresses me about* Strikes have followed me all my life *was not least that marvellous picture of yourself and your friend Joyce Seroke confronting police and police-dogs during a demonstration protesting against the conferring of the Freedom of Soweto on a government minister, Dr. Piet Koornhof. How did you manage to overcome your initial anxiety at being arrested for your trade union activities?*

Those were the days when you really had to do something for your people, you know, for yourselves. We just did not have to give in to all those threats about policemen coming to our townships, just because someone is coming to be given the right of the township, when we are suffering in the township – and then we are threatened with dogs. It was very good that it happened. I didn't even know there was someone taking a picture of it which reached the whole world, and people started coming up about what was happening in South Africa.

As we talk I'm going to come to a point to say: I am here representing the government now. And I still find it so difficult because I come from the resistance movement. And now I must speak in another language and I'm so used to fighting against that which is not right. So I would do it again.

*Your own life history does reflect that astonishing transition black people have gone through in South Africa recently – from opposition to government – doesn't it?*

Yes, definitely it has that. In fact when people were standing up to be parliamentarians it was not anything which would really have struck me to say I would stand up for. I thought I had done my work. It has come to the end of the road, let the other people go. But I want to say that I will always hero-worship the trade unions in South Africa because they have the greatest respect for history. I am here today representing government in the International Labour Organization. It is something that I would not have done had it not been for the trade unions.

*Would you say that in a sense the trade unions functioned as a liberation movement inside the country at a time when the political organisations were banned and in exile?*

Oh yes, definitely. It is the trade unions that played the leading role. I stated in my book that I am proud that I've worked for two organisations which have contributed very heavily for the liberation of South Africa. My present boss is Desmond Tutu, you know. Coming from the trade unions to the church, the work that I did in the church was in the department of human rights – and again it was nothing but fighting for the liberation of the people. The trade unions have made a great contribution to the liberation that we have today. We owe it to the trade unions.

*But, of course, from the 1970s to the present the trade unions did themselves have a great struggle to gain recognition for black unions, didn't they? I was wondering whether when you applied to register your union after the Wiehahn Commission of Inquiry's report you didn't feel that the Commission had in effect placed you in a somewhat compromising situation, where you were having virtually to comply with apartheid structures in order to finally get the unions off the ground?*[5]

In fact I was elected to be the spokesperson of the trade unions during the Wiehahn Commission, and in this position I'm holding now I meet with people who were part of the Wiehahn Commission, who remind me that when Wiehahn asked me, 'Do you think trade unions need to be involved in politics?' and I was very adamant to say: 'Yes, Trade Unions have to be involved in politics' they say now, 'What do you think now? What should the situation be?' They are hitting me back with what I said at the time. I see it's different now, because now we have politicians back on the ground, but the trade unions will always keep a vigilant eye to see what is happening with the politicians.

*That reminds me of what your present boss, Desmond Tutu, himself said about the church – that when the liberation movements were unbanned, he would go back to being a full-time churchman...*

And he did in fact. He became very on the quiet side, but that does not mean that even if we have this government of the people in place, the church and the trade unions are going to take everything rosily. We must see the implementation of what they promised would happen. So we will still be a vigilant eye.

*Yes, I'm very sure of that. Let me go on now to ask you about the setting up of the Congress of South African Trade Unions (COSATU) in 1985, because, of course, that was a huge step forward for the trade union movement, wasn't it? You were involved in that, weren't you?*

Yes, we were an independent union. There were three other unions that were independent, too. While there were two federations, we did not belong to either of the two. So these independent unions came together and saw that here was a need to have one federation for the country. This is how the whole thing came about, we started unity talks which eventually gave birth to COSATU.

*The present situation of transition to a new society in South Africa must be changing the role of the trade unions in some senses. What do you see as essential challenges facing the trade union movement in the interim five-year period we have before us now?*

Interestingly, as it is right now, we have two federations, COSATU and NACTU, the National Council of Trade Unions. They are working so closely together now that Jay Naidoo has gone to Parliament and Sam Shilowa has taken his place. On the other side, it is Cunningham Ngcukana, who is the General Secretary of NACTU. We've brought a very large team from South Africa to the ILO for the first time. I think there were about 12 trade unions, from the employers even more, and then about the same number from the government. Because the COSATU General Secretary was not available, the NACTU General Secretary is the leader of the trade unions. It does not matter which camp you come from. For me this is so significant that I am very certain that if they can start new unity talks we will end up with one federation for the country which will make us – I keep on saying *us*, and I'm supposed to be the government! – it should make *them* very powerful. I really hope it comes to that stage. The unions really haven't softened up because of having the government that we are having. They really are trade unions who are still very strong.

*Do you see the trade unions fighting for worker's rights just as effectively as before, even with the new government, which will presumably be more sympathetic to their aims?*

Yes, I think they will. I'm sure of that. They will even have more time to fight for worker rights on the shop floor, because they are not spread on politics and other things. So I think that in the world of work, management has got to be ready for even more powerful and stronger trade unions. They will need a bit of time of adjustment to the future role they must be playing. Once they have got to that, I think they will be very strong on collective bargaining, more than ever before. That heavy emphasis on liberation of the woman or liberation of the man; it was liberation of the nation. Now that we have achieved that, there has got to be a special focus on strengthening the recognition of women. The time has come that we should move even further from decision-making to power. Women must be seen to have power, women must see themselves and know they have power. They demonstrated this very clearly during the elections. I think that women were the majority in the queues for voting. And we had the strongest vote as women. So that shows that woman have power.

*How strong is the representation of women in the present parliament, though?*

It's thirty three and a third percent. I believe that in the past South Africa was rated 130th in the world concerning the representation of women. We have now moved to the tenth place. The Speaker of the House is a woman, Frene Ginwala.

*She's an excellent choice.*

Yes. She was President of the Coalition of the Women. We are not very excited, but we have two Cabinet Ministers and three Deputy Cabinet Ministers. We haven't done very well in that position. Neither have we done well when it comes to the Premiers in the provincial legislatures. We have not done well there. But now we have thirty three and a third percent at a first go we must get ready for better things.

*It's a significant start, isn't it?*

Yes, a start.

*Coming to your book now, I think for any reader certainly the most moving part of the work must be your account of your period in solitary confinement, and especially the psychological trauma in the aftermath of detention. I know you suffered very greatly from that experience, and so it seems almost impertinent to ask you about it. I would, however, just like to ask you very briefly what do you think it was that sustained you, that gave you the strength to cope with an ordeal which for those of us who've never had to go through it is almost impossible to imagine?*

I really think that my sustenance comes from not sitting back, and going on, and on, and on, and on. And I want to thank my father for that. When I came out of prison I was badly tortured, as you know, and I was very exhausted. And he pushed me and said: 'You must go to work. Even if you can go to work just for a few months. So that the people who wanted to destroy you must not get credit of it. Go to work!' And I went to work, and from there I gathered my strength and I went on, and on, and on, and on.

When Anna Rutherford called me from Denmark, 1 think I would not have easily been excited or ready to make a call to any other country for someone I don't know. But because it was Denmark, I just thought I must call this person. Denmark for me is very important, because of the treatment they gave me. So I just honour anything that comes that way in my life.

*You went to the Rehabilitation Centre for Torture Victims in Denmark, didn't you?*

Yes. It's run by Inge Genefke. She set up that clinic. I'd gone back to Denmark once on a church mission. I could not speak to her, but it was enlarged, it was a very big clinic from the time when was there in 1982. I think it did a lot of good service. I remember I was there with a huge number of people from Chile, at the time of their problems, and it really was very helpful. A nurse who used to work in that clinic has visited South Africa twice now and each time she comes, we meet and have dinner together. So it's been wonderful.

*Good. How do you view the experience and its significance for you in your life, particularly in the context of your later work? I'm thinking especially of your work with the division of Justice and Reconciliation, set up by the Church of the Province of Southern Africa?*

It has been very good in the sense that there are a lot of contributions which have been made by the church. You know that our church is part of the South African Council of Churches and there is a lot of work on justice and peace in South Africa. The peace accord comes initially from the churches who brought in business and the politicians. That was a contribution which has led us to where we are today, we had to fight all the injustices which were causing violence. The church was very much involved in all the crisis committees, in all the areas where there was a lot of violence. We had monitors coming from all over the world, coming via the church to be monitors or observers during the violence even before the voting time.

Maybe something which you do not know is that I am now holding a very senior position in what was called the National Manpower Commission. I am the Deputy Chair of that, even though my new minister does not like the word 'Manpower Commission.' Now it's going to be National Labour Commission, we are going to change the name. That has been a very significant position, and I was put into this position. Jay Naidoo called me at home and said: 'Emma, I'm in a meeting here with a number of unions. We just want to know: can you please agree that we nominate you to go and serve on this committee?' And I said: 'Jay, I don't know what that is, but because it is Labour and it is Trade Union, I'm ready to do it.' And I will learn as I go.

*What are your duties in this new capacity?*

In this new capacity we are making all the legislation, which is actually taken to the Cabinet before it goes to Parliament. In the world of work and especially the Industrial Relations Commission itself, they all come from the National Manpower Commission. And I am the Deputy Chairperson there.

*Do you have a special responsibility for the rights of women in the work-place, for instance?*

Yes, we do have an Equal Opportunities Committee, which is a subcommittee of our Human Resources Committee, and I am the Chairperson of Human Resources, and then comes the subcommittee and the equal opportunities fall within that. May I just elaborate?

*Yes, please.*

In fact I arrived here before the whole delegation, because there was a Women's Forum, which took place from the 1st to the 3rd of June here in Geneva, and which also focused on women's issues in the new era. That particular conference is going to come out with a document which is going to be presented at the Beijing World Conference of Women next year in 1995. So there is a lot which I learned out of this particular meeting like the migration of women. When we speak about migrant workers in South Africa, our focus is always thinking about men going to the mines. Yet there are so many migrant workers who are women, who have come to South Africa because they have followed their husbands and for a number of other reasons. There is not much legislation for the women, but there is for the men. So because we are receiving so many migrant workers, this has opened my eyes to see that we need to do a lot for the women when we go back.

*The migrant labour system has existed in South Africa since the discovery of diamonds in the last century hasn't it? The compound system has always prejudiced the situation of women. Do you see the change as bringing, shall we say, a restoration of family life with the dismantling, at least partially, of the migrant labour system in the new South Africa? Or is the migrant labour system going to carry on as it has before? There is a lot of talk about reorganising and reconstructing the single-sex hostels as family accommodation, isn't there?*

I think that just in a human way those things ought to have been done away with long time ago. We would not have had most of the problems that we are having in South Africa - when it come to violence - if we were having home and family life in order. The hostel, the compound system, the migrant worker system all have divided our families, and the government is going to do everything in their power to see that the single-sex hostels are done away with. There is no responsibility that can come out of any kind of unity of that nature. I mean every home needs a head of a family, even though in South Africa you find that in most homes women are mainly the heads of the households. You need to be a family and you need to live as a unit.

*I was very impressed by the theme of family solidarity running through your book. Your family were very supportive to you when you were in prison. And also in the* Book of Hope, *you place a very strong emphasis on the role of the family in society.*
*I was going to go on and talk about women's issues in South Africa, but some of the suggestions I was going to put to you have already been answered by implication. I was going, for instance, to ask you whether you still felt that you were a token woman. You used the phrase in your book to describe your first moving into the labour movement, when you sometimes felt that you were a token woman in a male-dominated preserve.*

Maybe it's in my making, you know, that in many of those positions or in most of my involvement I find that I am surrounded by men. And when defining tokenism at one time with a friend I was feeling bad and said: 'Why is it that I'm always about the only woman or before other women come in, once I get in there I make sure that other women come in?' And she said: 'How do you get there?' Usually you are not nominated, you are elected to that position, so that takes away the tokenism, because you are elected to that position.

My position in the church is mainly working with bishops, you know, and when I came in the women themselves were not ordained to the priesthood. From my Department of Justice we saw that as an injustice.

*It is indeed. It reminded me very much of reading about the situation in England, where, of course, the ordination of women has led to something of a division within the Church of England. Did you encounter a great deal of opposition on that issue in South Africa?*

In fact we gave the lead, we got the ordination of women ahead of the Church of England, and we had about 90% support for that. Those who were not supportive of it did not react negatively. They had to work around it and but remained within the church. After we got it, the women in the Church of England kept saying: 'If South Africa can get it, we are sure we shall get it.' So it was South Africa that led the way.

*Another issue which has always been very important in the lives of black women in South Africa has been the situation of domestic workers. I read that you had been involved in campaign towards the unionisation, the labour representation of domestic workers.*

Yes, we are now having very strong unions, organizing the domestic workers to a point where that exploitation which used to be where one domestic worker would be a general worker and look after the children has been minimised quite A lot. It has created problems for either the domestic worker or the mother, because now the domestic workers are aware that they have got to work for so many hours. They are making more money because now they work part-time for this employer and part-time for that one. For the first time the other woman has to do some house chores as well! So it was development for both the women, the madam and the domestic worker. Yes, it was development for both of them.

*Presumably the law that prohibited a domestic worker being accommodated in the house in which she was working has been abolished as well?*

Yes, it has been abolished, but...

*That doesn't mean the practice has been abolished.*

No, the practice has not been abolished at all. Up to now the legislation does not cover the domestic workers. It is just for one area, the farm workers, who are now covered by the Labour Relations Act. The domestic workers are not as yet covered. With the dismantling of the homelands – certain homelands had had legislation for domestic workers - the National Manpower Commission has now got to work on harmonising industrial relations for one South Africa, not a fragmented South Africa. So this is going to push the government to make up its mind and legislate for the domestic workers.

*The transitional constitution which is now in force in the country instructs Parliament to create a commission on gender equality. Has this already been created? What do you see as its tasks and opportunities?*

I said that during the TEC there was a subcommittee, which was focusing on gender issues. I am sure that is going to go on. I haven't as yet come across what it is that they are going to be giving some preference to in that particular committee. But being a worker, there is something I am going to insist on and that is that the committee should look at a social clause and how it affects us as women.

*What do you see as the essential problem facing women, the essential issues to be dealt with affecting black women in the townships and in the rural areas of South Africa at the moment?*

There are many, especially homelessness. There is a lot of homelessness. Our country has developed and grown so fast, people are living in shack areas instead of homes. Women are badly affected by being homeless, and that goes for the rural areas as well. People are struggling with no water and long distances to walk to work. If there is no good education for the children, the first person who is affected is the woman. Mothers are badly affected if there is no progress in anything. So they are very special, and it is very important for then that there should be progress with homes, there should be progress in education, and they have got to be made as comfortable as possible. Hospitalisation is becoming a private institution. Even though we never had old age homes, at times some of the elderly people could go to hospital. Now that cannot be afforded. Again it is the woman who is going to have to look after the elderly and the sick. So the role of the woman is growing day by day. From babyhood to adulthood the woman is involved.

*Can we perhaps now come to your writing? What was the impetus that made a writer of you when before you had been a factory worker, a labour leader and a trade union organiser, all sorts of things in fact, but you hadn't in your earlier career been a writer? What motivated you to put pen to paper, to write it all down and provide us with a record?*

There are certain things I am grateful to apartheid for and this is one of them! Had it not been for apartheid, had they not put me into prison, had they not tortured me, I would never have known that I can be a writer. A friend convinced me by saying, 'you have been to all the hospitals, you have attended so many other treatments, but you know what is good for you? It is to put it on paper'. It is very therapeutic for you, you must write about what has happened in your life, it is very therapeutic, because it is like a session each time when you get it out of your body and put it on paper. That's what made me a writer.

*How do you actually go about writing? Do you write by hand and then edit over and over again? Do you dictate? How do you proceed?*

It started as we are doing now. Because it was a friend pushing me to do this, she used to interview me every time we met, at any meeting, in any country, in South Africa, overseas, anywhere. And we discovered that there were repetitions. I wouldn't know what I had said the last time and we were repeating what we did all the time! It had to be transcribed, I read it and made certain alterations, and I had someone help me edit. But I ended up scribbling and writing and this is where I am with the *Book of Hope*. I never taped, I was always writing myself.

*Do you regard your earlier procedure as more like the African tradition of story-telling, of passing the story on to the younger generation in oral rather than in written form?*

Yes, yes, it definitely was. And at the time for me it was not very significant how I did it and why I did it. But now that we are where we are in South Africa I seem to value my book very much - to see that many a person is going to read it some years after today and will know that there was apartheid and this is what apartheid was all about.

*It does constitute a historical record of a very important phase in the history of your country, doesn't it, apart from the creative aspect of the writing, but simply as a historical document? It is important that works such as yours be there for coming generations to find out what it was all like in those forty years.*

Yes. I have grand-daughters. My life is all surrounded by daughters, so I speak as a woman person. They insist, please write again, you must write. We sit down and argue about what I've got to write about. I think they got their inspiration from the first book, so that just shows how much it means to the younger generation itself.

In South Africa, you know, we each have several names. I'm Emma Mashinini, but I'm also known as Tiny. You find that there are other children who are my children's age group who just know me as Coqo Tiny, which means Granny Tiny. One was at Wits University busy writing a piece about this Emma Mashinini, and she did not know that this Emma Mashinini was the same as Coqo. When I went to her home, she looked at the picture in the book and became very excited. So I really think it means a lot to the younger generation and I encourage so many people now to say: Please document.

*You mention in your book that you had participated in a film called* Mama, I'm crying. *I confess I know nothing about the film, nor about your participation in it, so I'd like to ask you about that.*

Yes. It was Betty Wolpert and Joyce Seroke. They were making a film called *Mama, I'm crying.* They had discovered after about 50 years, now that they are friends, that they lived in the same area. They didn't know one another because of apartheid, because they could not play together. This woman then moved to Europe, but she remembered a nanny in South Africa who had brought her up, who had been like a mama to her, a mother to her. She went to South Africa to look for this woman and she found the children of that woman. Their mother had died and her mother had died, and they regard one another as sisters now. It was called *Mama, I'm crying,* because once their mother was nursing her and she wondered who had brought them up. So *Mama, I'm crying* was a very important story.

*And you played a role in the film?*

Yes, I was asked to come and play a role in the film.

*Strikes have followed me all my life was published in England by the Women's Press wasn't it? And I see it has now been published in the States as well. Did you feel that this deprived you of the real readership, namely the people of South Africa who didn't have access to it? Is the book being reprinted in South Africa? Is it available in South Africa now?*

Now it is available. It could not have been printed in South Africa because of the State of Emergency. Yes, it did deprive the South African readership of the book. It is mainly the universities and some of the intellectuals, who would have access to the book, unlike in England and in the US. I think the trade unions made a great fuss about my book. The TUC in Britain and the trade unions in the US, they really made a very big fuss about my book and it had a lot of readership. In the US in fact they actually even produced a hardcover, and they are using it in the universities very much.

*What has been the reader response to it, as far as you can judge?*

Well, I think that it has exposed them to quite a number of things. Their response is many times that nobody thinks anybody can forget the name of their child. It breaks their hearts and it exposes them to a number of things. I think it has been read.

*It seems to me in a sense that your book can he placed within two traditions of South African literature. The one is, of course, the tradition of prison literature. I'm thinking of works by Albie Sachs, by Ruth First, by Breyten Breytenbach.[6] The other is the writing of life histories by women. One thinks of Ellen Kuzwayo, Sindiwe Magona and, of course, of Helen Joseph and Mary Benson.[7] Are you aware of their writings? Would you place yourself in these two traditions?*

Yes. I know all the people you have quoted quite well. In fact, I'm going to England to spend a few days with Mary. I have spent some time with Sindiwe Magona. She has already written her second book, you know.[8] She is going ahead quite a lot. I need to work hard to be rated with them. It was not a best-seller, my book, when it came out in South Africa, so I wouldn't easily say that I rate myself with them. But because there are not sufficient women writing I'm very proud of that. I need to work very hard and spend more time. And I will have that time, because maybe I will be retiring before long.

*You were saying that Sindiwe Magona has now written a second book. Many people who write a first book must be tempted to write a second one, and I understand you are doing just that as well? How are you getting on with your own second project? Is it finished yet?*

No. It's not finished, and I've had very little time to do it. It will be only by 1995 that I'm going to concentrate a lot of time on it. It is going to focus on women as women, their involvement, their contribution. And maybe it's a good thing that I have waited until now, because I can say a lot of praise about the role women have played up to the time of going to the elections. And then there is the experiences of the various countries I have gone to. It would never have been easy for me to say things about what I have seen in Cambodia, in Mozambique, how other countries are struggling during the governments of apartheid, because they always want to say, 'You are better than other countries.' And we've never been ready to accept that. The book is the exposure of some of the struggles, and I want to write about women. As a writer you know that things always come when you start writing.

*Will you be writing about the experiences of women internationally, of Cambodian women, for instance, as well? What occasioned your visit to Cambodia, a country which, I imagine, very few South Africans have ever been to?*

Yes, it was very unusual. Many people were very scared on my behalf to say why am I going to Cambodia. It was when I came here for the publishing of the book. Three people were elected to go to Cambodia to speak to the people, to give them hope, to say: don't think that this is the end of the world. There is hope after everything. They wanted people who have been survivors. One was a survivor from Palestine, the other one was a survivor from Germany, and I was a survivor of apartheid. So the aim was to go and give hope to the people of that country, to say that if I could do it, you can do it as well. So I think it was a very good journey.

*The Jew and the Palestinian you just referred to are presumably those that you mention in your contribution to the* Book of Hope, *who in a sense give you so much hope for a reconciliation in South Africa too between people who were once on different sides.*

They could travel together now because they had reconciled. After all that they had gone through, they could still reconcile. And in South Africa this has been demonstrated too. We see our President Nelson Mandela and Mr. de Klerk. They can sit and talk, and differ, and agree to differ. That is what reconciliation is all about. I never thought that I will reconcile very easily, but you are just forced by circumstances to say, you need to reconcile. South Africa is now at a very interesting stage where people are speaking about a Commission of Truth to encourage reconciliation. There should be Commission of Truth, where people should confess what they had done, and then the transition of reconciliation will be strengthened. It seems to be encouraged by the politicians and by the churches. I saw my archbishop also as very supportive of it.

*How did you experience the recent elections?*

Ah! You know, at the opening of my book I'm sure I'm going to say that on the day of elections for me it was a three-generation election. Why three? It was myself, my daughter, and my grand-daughter. Can you imagine how long I've waited to vote that I had to go and vote with my third generation?! And there was so much joy in that, on that day, standing in lines, I did not want to go and vote on a special day when they were saying, people of a certain age should go and vote. I didn't want a hand-out of a vote. I had worked hard for it, and I had to stand in the queue to go to vote.

*That's wonderful. You conclude your book* Strikes have followed me all my life, *with the lines: 'when liberation is achieved, then, I must say, I am prepared. I've lived a hard life, but I have always wanted to see the day of liberation. And when we get there, as a coward, perhaps, I am prepared to die, to say: I've lived and struggled for all these years. Now that we've achieved justice - now that we've attained that - now may I not rest in peace?' (p. 135) Now that the day has indeed arrived and you have seen it, you don't seem to be resting in peace, you seem to be as busy as you ever were!*

Writers are never honest people. Somewhere I think I said, the day when Nelson Mandela comes out of prison I'm ready to die. He's been out of prison for some time now. He reminded me about that when he saw me and he said: 'I think those people in prison were very busy, you know, they know so much about what was happening. I hope you are not going to die because we see that we still need you.' Now the day of liberation has come I want to see the implementation of what we were fighting for. The reconciliation, reconstruction and development which we want to see in our country. It will be a joy to see that, you know, to see people having homes, to see children going back to school. Just to have a home and family life for people. I think that's the time when I will be ready to die.

*Can I ask you one final question, which I imagine will also perhaps reflect something of your own career in the transition to a post-apartheid society? What has brought you back to Geneva this time?*

I'm here in Switzerland with a tripartite group from South Africa, a group from the employers from the workers and from the government. We have come to the International Labour Organisation and South Africa has just become a member again after 30 years of absence from the international world of labour. Luckily I was here in November with Jay Naidoo and others when we were pleading with them that we needed this recognition. We knew that we were going to win the elections and that we would join and become members of this important organisation. I am here with my minister of labour, Tito Mboweni, and I am the next delegate. It's two delegates for the government, one for the employers and one for the union. So I'm one of the two delegates of government. I never thought that day would ever come.

*Times have changed. Congratulations.*

Thank you, thank you.

(Note: I should like to thank our student Corinna Wohlfarth for transcribing this text. GVD)

Notes

1. Emma Mashinini, *Strikes have followed me all my life. A South African Autobiography* (London: The Women's Press, 1989); (New York: Routledge 1991).
2. Don Mattera, *Memory is the Weapon* (Johannesburg: Ravan Press, 1987); (London: Zed Press, 1987) (under the title: *Gone with the Twilight: A Story of Sophiatown.* Can Themba, 'Requiem for Sophiatown.' Trevor Huddleston, *Naught for Your Comfort* (London and Glasgow: Collins, 1956).
3. Trevor Huddleston, *Return to South Africa: The Agony and the Ecstasy* (London: Harper-Collins, 1991).
4. *A Book of Hope* (Claremont: David Philip, 1992).
5. The Wiehahn Commission was appointed under the administration of P.W. Botha to inquire into industrial relations in South Africa. Pursuant to its recommendations, black unions were allowed to register and to negotiate labour agreements on an official basis.
6. Albie Sachs, *The Jail Diary of Albie Sachs* (London: Harvill Press, 1966); (Cape Town: DaviD Philips, 1990). Ruth First, *117 Days. An Account of Confinement and Interrogation under the South African 90-day Law* (Harmondsworth: Penguin, 1965). Breyten Breytenbach, *The True Confessions of an Albino Terrorist* (London: Faber, 1984).
7. Ellen Kuzwayo, *Call Me a Woman* (London: The Women's Press, 1985). Sindiwe Magona, *To My Children's Children* (Cape Town: David Philips, 1990); (London: The Women's Press, 1991). Helen Joseph, *Side by Side* (London: Zed Press, 1986); (Parklands: Donker, 1993). Mary Benson, *A Far Cry: the Making of a South African* (London, New York: Penguin, 1989).
8. Sindiwe Magona, *Forced to Grow* (London: The Women's Press, 1992).

# OVERVIEWS

GILLIAN WHITLOCK

# Contemporary Australian Women's Writing: An Overview.

Elizabeth Jolley has dubbed the 1980s a 'moment of glory' for the woman writer in Australia, a phase in the national literary history when women writers and readers entered the mainstream. Thea Astley takes a more general view when she typifies the 80s as a 'decade of the minorities'. The traditional oppositions and centres which have organised Australian literary production have been displaced to allow space not only for the experience of women but also a marked sense of regional, ethnic and class-based difference.

The prominence of women's writing in the 80s was such that the WACM (as Elizabeth Webby dubs the white Anglo-Celtic male who has been the icon of Australian literary traditions and patronage) has suffered considerable anxiety. It is striking that, as we look to previews of the decade, we find little in the way of precursors for this surge. For example in her review of Australian women's novels of the 1970s in the first edition of Carole Ferrier's *Gender, Politics and Fiction*, Margaret Smith ruefully concludes that, whereas some of the earlier twentieth century literature by women can be seen as the product of first wave feminism, 'as yet in Australia there has not been a groundswell fully emerging with the second-wave.' Smith's overview stands now as a marker of how rapidly the reading of women's writing in Australia is changing, and how prolific Australian women writers have been in the past two decades. In the early 80s it was the work of Helen Garner, Thea Astley, Nene Gare and Glen Tomasetti that occupied Smith's attention, and it is noticeable that at that stage a sense of a female tradition of Australian women's writing has not yet emerged. *Wacvie* and *Karobran* are noted as examples of Black writing; and three significant lesbian novels, *All That False Instruction, Palomino*, and *Alone*, which focus on 'the doomed quality of Australian lesbian relationships', are mentioned. Smith concludes that there is still no conscious attempt to come to terms with the history of women and a female tradition in literature here.

Now, ten years on, the contours of the groundswell in women's writing related to second wave feminism are clearly evident. Although the more generous arts-funding policies begun by the Labor federal government in the early 70s in the first instance did not foster women's writing in particular, there was a flourishing feminist culture which was the seedbed for women's writing. Work by Australian writers such as Christina Stead, Henry Handel Richardson and Katherine Sussanah Prichard were included in the women's studies courses which got underway in a number of Australian universities by the mid-70s. Reviews of early second-wave fiction (such as Helen Garner's *Monkey Grip* and Jean Bedford's *Country Girl*) were unfavourable. However a more receptive and feminised literary culture emerged in magazines and journals associated with the women's movement, such as *Hecate, Lip, Scarlet Woman, Refractory Girl*, and *Sibyl*. These journals generated a polemical feminist criticism. By the 80s a number of important feminist critical works challenged the traditional constructions of Australian cultural and literary studies: Kay Schaffer's *Women and the Bush*, Drusilla Modjeska's *Exiles at*

*Home,* Susan Sheridan's *Grafts: Feminist Cultural Criticism,* and Ferrier's *Gender, Politics and Fiction.* Bibliographies by Debra Adelaide (*Australian Women Writers. A Bibliographic Guide*) and Margaret Murphy (*Women Writers and Australia*) facilitated revisions and excavations of a tradition of women's writing in Australia, bringing into new light (and re-publication) nineteenth-century writers such as Mary Gaunt, Rosa Praed, and Ada Cambridge.

In one of a number of anthologies of Australian women's writing published late in the 80s, *Eight Voices of the Eighties,* I selected work from those writers who have been typified as the 'crest' of the current wave of women's writing here: Helen Garner, Thea Astley, Jessica Anderson, Barbara Hanrahan, Olga Masters, Kate Grenville, Elizabeth Jolley and Beverley Farmer. I made this selection rather self-consciously, aware of the promotion of women writers in a 'star' system and the way that this group of writers are all part of the dominant, white Anglo Celtic culture in Australia. An anthology by Sneja Gunew and Jan Mahyuddin also published in 1989, *Beyond the Echo: Multicultural Women's Writing,* reminds us that the surge in women's writing has produced a new constellation of writers: Inez Baranay, Lily Brett, Ania Walwicz, Rosa Cappiello, Sara Dowse, Beth Yahp, Antigone Kefala, Angelika Fremd, Lolo Houbein are the best known of a much larger group of writers who write from a diversity of non-Anglo Celtic backgrounds. As Gunew and Mahyuddin argue in the preface to their anthology, these writers offer new 'Australias'; for many women writing from multicultural, non-English-speaking backgrounds, places from which to speak have been absent, or subsumed in an often common assumption that such places are, and have always been, universally available to any member of a society.

Anthologies, overviews and critical appraisals allow us to take cross sections of perceptions of Australian literary culture cross the past decade or so. As we have seen, Margaret Smith in 1980 viewed nothing like the complex and diverse women's culture which editors of anthologies scanned in 1989. The recent re-publication of Ferrier's *Gender, Politics and Fiction,* a second edition with some revisions, is another opportunity for gauging the 'state of the art', as it were. Like Ferrier, I tend to think that Thea Astley was slightly premature in identifying the 80s as the 'decade of the minorities'. New chapters in Ferrier's book address Aboriginal women's writing, erotic and lesbian writing, and the erosion of traditional generic distinctions in current writing. It may well be that an array of different perspectives is emerging more fully now, in the wake of the incursions made by women writers in the 80s. Aboriginal women's narratives by writers such as Monica Clare, Labumore, Mum Shirl, Ella Simon, Sally Morgan, Ruby Langford, Glenyse Ward, Eva Johnson, Doris Pilkington and Mabel Edmund are increasingly recognised as distinctive and complex narratives, worthy of recognition as literature (rather than the conventional acceptance as history or sociology). Of course Sally Morgan's *My Place* is one of the best known Australian novels of the 80s. What is less often remarked upon is the recent emergence of a significant number of autobiographical writings by Aboriginal women. Ferrier's reading of these novels identifies strategies of resistance which are mobilised in these texts as markers of a different aesthetic, an intervention which challenges the conventional generic boundaries of English literature.

Bronwen Levy's chapter on women's erotic writing reminds us that the changed configuration of women's literary production in Australia and elsewhere is due to both the development of a market for women's writing and the more sophisticated and diverse ways of reading women's writing in terms of issues of gender and sexuality. So Levy's reading of erotic writing (that field which, you will recall, Smith identified as marked by 'doom') recognises the place of Mary Fallon's *Working Hot* (1989) as an Australian version of *The Lesbian Body,* and as one of the most interesting recent Australian fictions. Yet she also re-reads earlier writers, such as Zora Cross and Lesbia

Harford, so elucidating a long-standing tradition of erotic (and anti-erotic) writing previously obscured.

The developments in writing, publishing and criticism I have glossed here are both a pleasure and a danger for the woman writer and critic. Australian women writers have in the past decade found a market and an intelligentsia sensitive to issues of gender and sexuality to an unprecedented extent. However critics have begun to express concern about the current mainstreaming and apparent domestication of women's writing. Bronwen Levy has argued from a marxist perspective, for example, that mainstream women's writing is relatively apolitical, the emphasis on domestic and personal issues can be absorbed into the masculinist literary tradition as a kind of women's version of Australian nationalism. In the past few years a number of feminist small presses and magazines have either closed or been incorporated. Writers such as Anna Couani have expressed concern at the current forms of production and marketing of women's writing in Australia; 'now that we have so many more women in print and multinational corporations catering to the women's market, we are faced with the structuring of our women's writing world brought about by marketing executives, arts bureaucrats, etc., but not necessarily by feminists and rarely by people/institutions which are independent of "market forces"'. The concerns I am drawing attention to here are, of course, not particular to the Australian scene; my point is that in tracking the course of women's writing here and elsewhere we need to look beyond the boundaries of texts themselves to the institutions within which they are produced, circulated, promoted and read. How we choose to read the shift of women's writing and criticism away from the periphery and the activist base of an organised feminist movement towards the mainstream concerns of publishers, academics and the market will depend upon our political and personal agendas. 'Feminisation' has amounted to an increased visibility of women in publishing, reviewing and academia. Has it also validated a certain kind of writing (generally the expressive realist mode) and the movement of a benign feminism into the mainstream? Can writings accorded coffee table status function in opposition?

These questions and our responses to them will be critical in determining the future development and reception of women's writing in Australia. Recently there have been a number of feature articles on high profile women in Australia, many of these (Hilary McPhee, Lyndall Crisp, Louise Adler, Ita Buttrose among them) have their power base in the publishing industry. Louise Adler, director of Heinemann Australia, is particularly proud of having 'won over' Thea Astley from her longtime publisher, Penguin, in 1990. 'I have relaunched Thea. She had become part of that Penguin image of contemporary Australian writers. I think she is one of the best Australia has, and I wanted to market her very individually.' (*Weekend Review*, 23-24/1/93) Adler claims to have sold 'two to three times as many as most of Astley's books with Penguin.' This claim has immediately been contested by the Penguin General Manager, neverthless this clash of the Titans must amuse Thea Astley, whose work remained neglected for many years until the emergence of a readership for women's writing in the late 70s. That Astley's work is now, twenty years on, the object of power plays and counter claims between Australia's publishing supremos is indeed ironic. That her work finds a wide readership is sweet reward towards the end of a long and frequently neglected career as a writer. However this clash also reminds us that the rules of the game have changed little now women are in the driver's seat. It is now more likely that there will be a number of women writers in any anthology, collection or overview of 'Australian writing'. However the demise of so many of the small publishers and journals which fuelled the proliferation of women's writing in the past decades, and the likely cut back of Arts funding through the Australia Council suggest that in the next decade the minorities will be in 'a time of hard'.

JANET WILSON

# Contemporary Women's Writing in New Zealand

New Zealand women's writing, gathering momentum since the late '70s, shows no sign of abating. Pre-eminent is Janet Frame, 70 this year, doyen of New Zealand letters since the publication of *Living in the Maniototo* (1979) and *Carpathians* (1988) and her autobiography. Frame's contemporaries and co-survivors of pre-feminist Aoteara like poet and children's writer Ruth Dallas, and novelist Ruth Park have also published their autobiographies. Most distinctive is that by Lauris Edmond, known also for her prodigious output: ten volumes of poetry, two plays and a novel since 1975. Edmond came to writing late in life and so did novelist and short story writer Barbera Anderson, whose prose, since her first publication in 1989, has been widely praised for its Flaubertian elegance. Still flourishing are novelist Joy Cowley who now writes short fiction including acclaimed stories for children, poet Fleur Adcock, whose continued attachment to New Zealand, despite living in London, makes her somewhat more than an ex-patriate, and Elizabeth Smither, whose poetry is admired for its linguistic precision and enigmatic flavour, qualities which her recent short stories also display.

Women no longer have the same anxieties about publishing and status that pervaded the more restrictive social climate of the '50s and '60s. Culturally and ethically sensitive anthologists like Cathie Dunsford (*Me and Marilyn Monroe*, 1994), and Wendy Harrex (New Women's Press) and the 1985 and 1989 Penguin anthologies of *Contemporary New Zealand Poetry* which include both English and Maori, have increased publishing opportunities. Relaxation of formal constraints in literary practice since the 1960s has allowed women to be more assertive, to experiment with fictional techniques, and develop more informal relationships with readers. Crucial to this transition has been the biculturalism of Maori writers such as Keri Hulme, whose *The bone people* is a quasi-nostalgic revisioning of Maori-Pakeha relationships, and Patricia Grace, whose short stories and novels (*Potiki, Cousins*) about the tangata whenua use the dualities of biculturalism to explore the condition of marginality generally. The political nuances of gender and ethnicity constitute the ideology of dramatist Renee, whose classic, minimalist dramas of working-class life (*Pass It On, Jeannie Once*) are now recognised as a distinct subgenre. But the full implications of the Maori Renaissance will emerge only in time.

Poetry thrives both in oral and in written forms, and the preoccupations of women poets have contributed significantly to post-'60s revisions of the canon. Michelle Leggott, influenced by the American poet Zukofsky, inscribes an indigenous post-modernism, a position shared in a less technically adventurous, but more sexually and culturally enigmatic way by Janet Charman. Others like Dinah Hawken and Jenny Bornholdt have variously adapted their ideas and world views to contemporary literary fashions. Cilla McQueen delivers a distinctive style of performance poetry, blending image and synaesthesia into a tonal aesthetic, while Bernadette Hall specialises in the deft turn of phrase and the protean image. Anne French, whose *All Cretans Are Liars*

(1987) was a prizewinning debut, combines realism with linguistic innuendo and technical innovation.

Most exciting, however, is the upsurge in fiction and especially in the short story. For the new writers today a short story collection almost inevitably precedes writing in other genres, whereas previously only established novelists – Joy Cowley, Margaret Sutherland, Fiona Kidman, Patricia Grace, Yvonne du Fresne – produced collections. A proliferation of anthologies has enhanced women's visibility, given the genre greater status, and provided outlets for newer writers like Margaret Blay. Among the finest practitioners today are Barbara Anderson, Joy Cowley, Shonagh Koea, Stephanie Johnson, Fiona Farrell, Anne Kennedy, Kate Flannery, Sheridan Keith, and Sarah Delahunty. Ranging from naturalism, to fantasy, to postmodern fictiveness, and conscious of the genre's potential for self reflexiveness, social satire, comedy, ellipsis and teasing puzzles, they uniformly avoid the domestic realism of the '50s and '60s. Also healthy is the novella or long short story, a potent form for women ever since Katherine Mansfield. Jean Watson writes consistently in this genre and Elizabeth Knox's fictionalised recreations of her childhood (*Paremata, Pomare*) have demarcated new territory. But the biggest explosion in women's writing today is undoubtedly in children's literature. The classic stories of Margaret Mahy, recognised internationally before they were in New Zealand, remain unsurpassed. Young teenage fiction is also developing an attentive readership due to the very considerable accomplishment of writers like Tessa Duder, Diana Noonan, Caroline McDonald, Joan de Hamel, writer of children's adventure fiction since 1973 and, most recently, Paula Boock.

Perhaps because the short story now approaches the novel in stature and is an acceptable outlet for experimental writing, women's fiction since *The Bone People* (1983) has been diverse rather than sensational. Output since 1990 has increased by almost half again with many new writers. Yet recent novelists like Christine Johnston, Barbara Anderson, Anne Kennedy, Fiona Farrell, Patricia Grace, Renee, Stephanie Johnson, Gaelyn Gordon are usually better known for short fiction or drama. Among significant publications are Elizabeth Knox's *After Z-Hour* (1987), Fiona Farrell's *The Skinny Louie Book* (1991), Colleen Reilly's *Christine* (1988), Sue McCauley's *Other Halves* (1982), poet Rachel Alpine's *Farewell Speech* (1990), Christine Johnston's *Blessed Art Thou Among Women* (1991) and those by Australian-based Rosie Scott: *Glory Days* (1988), *Feral City* (1992), *Lives on Fire* (1993). Established novelists like Marilyn Duckworth and Fiona Kidman have consolidated their reputations for conventional social realism by thematising contemporary issues rather than transforming them into metafictional games or linguistic conundrums as Janet Frame does.

Contemporary New Zealand women writers are in general more experimental, witty and urbane than their predecessors. Borrowing from diverse models for their literary practices, they reveal hidden dimensions in familiar genres, and revitalise those which previously had limited indigenous representation: Maori literature, children's fiction, the novella, autobiography.

KOH TAI ANN

# The Sun in Her Eyes: Writing in English by Singapore Women

Singapore writing in English goes back a mere forty-five years, and the work of the women writers is of even more recent provenance.[1] From the forties to the mid-sixties, anglophone literary works were mostly by male authors as far fewer women than men in Singapore had formal education (let alone an education in English, the language of government and of professional advancement and when during the colonial and immediately post-colonial days primary education was not universal even for males).

Furthermore, it was tertiary education which played a crucial, enabling role in literary production for it was not till after the post-war establishment of the University of Malaya in Singapore in 1948 and the appearance of undergraduate magazines that local literary work began to be published in earnest. It followed also that the first anthologies of these early poems and short stories were produced and sponsored, too, by male undergraduates, graduates and male-dominant graduate institutions.[2]

Expectedly, like the male writers, the earliest published women writers were university graduates. However, up till the seventies few women went on to establish themselves as writers.[3] The most inclusive local anthology of the poetry in English to date, *The Second Tongue: an Anthology of Poetry from Malaysia and Singapore*, published in 1976, almost twenty years after the appearance of the first anthology of local verse in English,[4] features the poems of only eleven women as compared to that by twenty-seven men. The disproportion is actually greater if the ratio is measured according to number of poems rather than number of poets included. By then, too, twelve of the men had each published at least one volume of poems, some more; but only five of the women had published or were to go on to publish one volume or more. These were the Malaysians Shirley Lim and Hilary Tham and the Singaporeans Wong May, Lee Tzu Pheng and Geraldine Heng, who, all except for Heng, began publishing their poems in the sixties. Since the late sixties, however, Tham, Lim and Wong have lived abroad or emigrated and all three have had volumes of verse published outside Malaysia or Singapore. Heng has hardly published any poetry after her first volume. Of the Singaporean women who began publishing in the late sixties, only Lee Tzu Pheng has continued to bring out subsequent volumes – in her case, three. Chung Yee Chong, a promising woman poet of the early seventies, appeared in a joint collection with four male poets;[5] another, Angeline Yap who began publishing in a school poetry magazine 'collected' her mostly juvenile poems in a first volume; but neither seems to have published any poetry since. Other women – Rosaly Puthucheary, Nalla Tan, Kamala Nesamoni, Sakina Kagda, Bessie Lee, Lin Hsin-hsin and most recently, Catherine Lim (who is better known for her short stories) have also published a volume or more each. But unlike earlier women poets such as Wong May and Lee Tzu Pheng, these other poets have been either little noticed or like Tan and Puthucheary, have received mostly negative reviews. Among other women poets who have published poetry or short fiction regularly in magazines, but not collected their work are Ho Poh Fun and Heng Siok Tian, the latter a promising young writer who has also had her plays staged.[6]

That the early 'serious' literary energies of women writers went into poetry indicated, too, the lead established by the men. The poem was both the preferred and up till the seventies, the prestigious literary form, an importance reinforced partly by its pioneering status in the writing in English, and partly by its having been represented by its practitioners and literary critics (often synonymous) as an important expression of the English-educated elite's participation in the nationalist anti-colonial struggle in the fifties for political and cultural independence from the British, its determination to establish an autonomous literary voice.

The critical stance, the engagement with social, political and cultural issues – indeed, these were almost its *raison d'etre* – set the agenda, too, for the poetry in English by Singaporean women poets. Such 'commitment', the making of poetry 'out of one's inner life' which simultaneously registered 'the forces at work in society' (to quote the creed and practice of 'pioneering poet', dominant male literary figure and patriarch of the local literary scene, Edwin Thumboo),[7] privileged and universalised the poetry in English as the expressive vehicle of national consciousness and identity.

Significantly, Lee Tzu Pheng's best-known, most-quoted poem is '"My Country and My People"' – despite the irony lent to the title by its being hedged by quote marks (marks often omitted by careless readers who have missed the poem's quietly interrogatory spirit, apparent right from the opening lines):

My country and my people
are neither here nor there, nor
in the comfort of my preferences,
if I could even choose.[8]

Lee's basic inclinations as her later work shows, lean however, towards the private, personal world. Like most of the women poets, she prefers to write of love, family, friendships, relationships, suffering, and female selfhood. Lee's woman tries particularly to hold on to the tangible and despairs at the immateriality of words and intellectual production:

being woman
what would I want
with mind-children

these hands
only can hold
formed flesh

words
against my mouth
dry silent[9]

'Prospect of a Drowning' the bleak title poem of her first volume characteristically focuses on a despairing 'insufficiency' while her second volume, *Against the Next Wave*, its stoic title derived from a line in the earlier poem, tries to salvage at least something from pain: 'strange how suffering propels us/ to new insight'.[10] Betrayal and disillusionment are increasingly countervailed however, in both this and her third, latest volume *The Brink of an Amen* by a sustaining courage inspired by a new-found Christian faith.

Men also took the lead in the publication of prose fiction. The first local anthology of short stories in English, *The Compact*[11] in 1959 and the first Singapore novels in English which appeared in 1972 were all male efforts.[12] But by 1976, Geraldine Heng was able to put together a collection of short stories, *The Sun in Her Eyes* 'by Singapore women', two of whom (Rebecca Chua and Nalla Tan) went on to publish a collection each of their short stories.

As the first anthology and subsequent anthologies of short stories by Singaporean and Malayan/Malaysian writers show,[13] this form was also male-dominated – until the appearance of Catherine Lim, Singapore's first short-story writer proper. Before her, no male Singapore writer has ever and none of the women writers to date has had the popular success that she has enjoyed since her first short story collection *Little Ironies: Stories of Singapore* quietly appeared in 1979. *Or Else, the Lightning God* quickly followed in 1980. Both volumes sold steadily, even going into several more printings, although her work has attracted little local critical attention.[14] Her novel, *The Serpent's Tooth*, an expansion of her short story 'Or Else the Lightning God', has been less successful with readers although it is typical of her short stories in general in its representations of the clash between generations, the conflict of the old ways and the new. Here too, are found her accurate renderings of Chinese custom and ritual, contemporary manners or mores, and recognizable Singaporean types – the strong-willed, ambitious English-educated daughter-in-law, the old matriarch and mother-in-law, members of the upwardly mobile English-educated class, its family relationships, preoccupations, 'life style', values and so on. She tells her stories well, relying much on surprise turns in the plot or exploitation of her Singaporean characters' self-delusions to produce what has become a standard feature of her stories, the ironic twist at the end.[15]

Universal education since Singapore's achievement of independence in 1965 with almost the entire school population since the late seventies being educated in English, growing affluence, rapid modernisation and urbanisation accompanied by inevitable socio-cultural changes have produced a growing reading public for local English writing which fictionally represents and/or examines these developments. Lim's short stories showed there was much local material ready for literary record and treatment while the rise in feminist consciousness among Singaporeans has both fueled her later works (such as *The Woman's Book of Superlatives*) and encouraged more women to express themselves, chiefly through fiction and drama which focus on feminist themes. Her success however, seems to have thrown into the shade other serious, perhaps more experimental women short story writers who have not her eye for telling detail and her sheer ability to tell a story. Among these others are Rebecca Chua, Wong Swee Hoon and Claire Tham, the last-named being the youngest and most recently published. A lawyer by profession, Tham's short stories focus on the lives of comfortably-off, usually middle-class types, the obviously conforming being set against or contrasted with the overtly or covertly rebellious members of this largely Western-educated group.

The only Singapore woman novelist proper (in the sense that she has published more than one novel and consistently published others over a period of time) is Su-chen Christine Lim whose most recent novel, *A Fistful of Colours,* was awarded the newly-instituted Singapore Literature Prize for best unpublished fiction manuscript. She is also the most consistently 'serious' novelist, choosing plots, characters, themes or issues which depict Singapore society at a particular stage of its development as experienced by representative women characters. She is serious too, in the thought she gives to her narratives, each novel adopting (albeit not necessarily successfully) a different narrative form in an attempt to give force to different perspectives. Her main women characters range from the liberated ex-novice, radical student activist, Marie Wang of *Rice Bowl*, to the traditionally-oppressed Yoke-lin, heroine of her daughter Yen-ti's journal which *Gift from the Gods* purports to be and to the three modern Singaporean women whose chequered marriages, relationships and life-stories make up *A Fistful of Colours.*

The other novelist who is akin to Christine Lim in seriousness is Minfong Ho. Her reputation as a young people's novelist has been largely established in the U.S. mainly through her sensitive, vivid portrayals of the lives of adolescent or teenaged girls caught in turbulent social and political conditions in Southeast Asian societies familiar to Americans such as those in Thailand (*Sing to the Dawn; Rice Without Rain*) and Cambodia (*The Clay Marble*). She is also a short story writer of considerable skill and penetrating observation, but has yet to bring out a collection of her short fiction.

Of the other women, most of whom so far have published only one novel, Ovidia Yu and S. Kon are the most serious and productive. Both, especially S. Kon are better known, however, for their plays, a few of which have been successfully staged, while Yu has also published some short stories including one prize-winning effort. Yu's *Miss Moorthy Investigates* is a skilfully told and entertaining 'who-dun-it' with a feminist slant, while Kon's *The Scholar and the Dragon*, like Christine Lim's *Gift of the Gods*, features characters of the generation of immigrant Chinese who lived in Singapore in the nineteenth and first half of the twentieth century. Other first novels, published most recently by women writers in obvious response to the current hunger for local writing in English by the English-educated Singaporean reading public, are the 'semi-autobiographical' *The Lotus Blossoms* and its sequel, *China My Love* by San; *Women in Men's Houses* by Wee Kiat and *Treachery is the Game* by Shirley Lau. San's 'semi-autobiographical' novels set in Singapore, Hong Kong, Europe and China depict through the life and loves of its heroine, Lienhwa (Lotus Blossom), the cultural clash of East and West, Capitalism and Chinese communism in a way reminiscent of the fiction of Han Suyin. Less melodramatically, Wee Kiat attempts to exemplify in the lives of three women who are close, mutually supportive friends, the triple oppression of Chinese women summed up by the Confucian saying 'that a woman obeys three masters in her life – her Father, her Husband and her Son'. But the novel's content and prose-style do not move much beyond that of the standard fiction which used to be a mainstay of old-style women's magazines and which still mark feature articles found in their successors today such as Singapore's *Her World* and *Female* magazines. Lau's novel owes more of its style and preoccupations to pulp fiction, but unlike Wee Kiat's novel, without any pretensions to move beyond and above the formulaic intrigues and doings of the rich and powerful who operate in a world of boardroom or office politics, ambitious, egoistic husbands, bored wives, adultery and expensive life-styles.

Apart from the growing thirst for fiction in English among a reading public increasingly English-educated, there is also a current boom in the writing and staging of local plays in English. Professional theatre groups have emerged and so have women playwrights – Ovidia Yu and S. Kon as mentioned earlier, Eng Wee Ling, Eleanor Wong and others whose plays although staged, exist still in unpublished form. As theatre flourishes along with theatre studies newly introduced at the two local universities to cater to this growing interest, more plays including those by women are likely to be published in the future.

Notes

1. This account does not include women writers in the other main Singapore official languages of Malay and Chinese. For reference to these and their work, see the section on Malaysia and Singapore in the chapter on Southeast Asia, and individual author and title entries in *The Bloomsbury Guide to Women's Literature*, ed. Claire Buck, (London: Bloomsbury Publishing, 1992), pp. 228-30.
2. For fuller detailed accounts, see Edwin Thumboo, Introduction, *The Second Tongue: an Anthology of Poetry from Malaysia and Singapore* (Singapore: Heinemann Educa-

tional Books, 1976), and my 'Singapore Writing in English: the Literary Tradition and Cultural Identity', in *Essays on Literature and Society in Southeast Asia: Political and Sociological Perspectives*, ed. Tham Seong Chee (Singapore: Singapore University Press, 1981), pp. 160-185.

3. According to Thumboo, 'Before the mid-sixties, very few women wrote creatively; there were no women among the pioneer poets.' (Introduction, *The Second Tongue*, p. xxxii).

4. *Litmus One: Selected University Verse, 1949-1957* (Singapore: Raffles Soceity, University of Malaya, 1958).

5. *Five Takes* (Singapore: University of Singapore Society, 1974).

6. Heng Siok Tian's first volume of poems, *Crossing Your Chopsticks* (Singapore: Unipress) is in press and is expected to appear in 1993.

7. Evident, for instance, in his praise of Lee – that her 'most notable poem to date, 'My Country and My People' (sic) brings together personal and public history with candour' (Introduction, *The Second Tongue*, p. xxx1).

8. *Prospect of a Drowning*, p. 51.

9. 'Orphans', (*Prospect of a Drowning*, p. 5).

10. 'In Sight' (*Against the Next Wave*, p.14).

11. Sub-titled '(a Selection of University of Malaya Short Stories 1953-1959)', Herman Hochstadt, ed. (Singapore: Raffles Society, University of Malaya in Singapore, 1959).

12. Goh Poh Seng, *If We Dream Too Long* (Singapore: Island Press); Kirpal Singh (the lawyer), *China Affair* (Singapore: University Education Press).

13. See *Twenty-two Malaysian Short Stories: an anthology of writing in English* (Singapore: Heinemann Educational Books, 1968) and *Malaysian Short Stories* (Singapore: Heinemann Asia, 1981) both compiled and edited by Lloyd Fernando; and *Singapore Short Stories*, Vols. 1 and 2, (Singapore: Heinemann Educational Books, 1978), ed. Robert Yeo.

14. Lim's popularity was confirmed first by *Or Else the Lightning God* being made a local lower secondary school literature textbook and then in the late eighties by *Little Ironies* being selected as a Commonwealth-wide Cambridge 'O' Level examinations textbook (to which Anne Brewster and Kirpal Singh have provided a students' guide). Peter Wicks, an Australian, writes regularly about her and her work (eg. 'Of Family and Irony: Catherine Lim and *The Serpent's Tooth*', *Commentary: Journal of the National University of Singapore Society*, 7, 2 & 3 (1987), pp. 97-102.

15. Her latest novel, *Meet Me on the Queen Elizabeth 2!* about 'a predatory Chinese female intent on advancing her interests among solitary, unsuspecting gentlemen on board a luxury cruise ship' (Author's Preface) appeared in July, 1993.

## Bibliography of Singapore Women's Writing *

Chua, Rebecca: *The newspaper editor and other stories* (Singapore: Heinemann Asia, 1981)

Chung, Yee Chong: *Five takes*, poems by Chung Yee Chong and others (Singapore: University of Singapore Society, 1974)

Eng, Wee Ling: *Confessions of three unmarried women and other plays* (Singapore: EPB Publishers, 1989)

Gay, Jenny: *Sweet and sour Singapore* (Singapore: Angsana Books, 1992)

Han May (Hon, Joan): *Star sapphire* (Singapore: Times Books International, 1985)

Heng, Geraldine, ed.: *The sun in her eyes: stories by Singapore women* (Singapore: Woodrose Publications, 1976)

Heng, Geraldine, ed.: *Whitedreams: poems* (Singapore: Woodrose Publications, 1976)

Heng, Siok Tian: *Crossing your chopsticks and other poems* (Singapore: Unipress, 1993)

Ho, Minfong: *Rice without rain* (London: Andre Deutsch, 1986; New York: Lothrop, Lee and Shepard, 1986; Singapore: Times Books International, 1986)

Ho, Minfong: *Sing to the dawn* (New York: Lothrop, Lee and Shephard, 1975; Singapore: Times Books International, 1985)

Ho, Minfong: 'Tanjong Rhu', in *Tanjong Rhu and other stories*, ed. Ban Kah Choon (Singapore: Federal Publications, 1986)

Ho, Minfong: *The clay marble* (New York: Farrar Straus Giroux, 1991)

Kagda, Sakina: *Fragrant journeys; poems of travel* (Singapore: Intellectual Publishing, 1987)

Khoo, Catherine: *Love notes* (Singapore: Heinemann Asia, 1990)

Kon, S. (Stella Kon): *The emporium and other plays* (Singapore: Heinemann Educational Books, 1977)

Kon, S. (Stella Kon): *The immigrant and other plays* (Singapore: Heinemann Educational Books, 1977)

Kon, S. (Stella Kon): *The scholar and the dragon* (Singapore: Federal Publications, 1986)

Kon, S. (Stella Kon): 'Trial' in *Trial and other plays*, ed. Max Le Blond (Singapore: Federal Publications, 1986)

Kon, S. (Stella Kon): *Emily of Emerald Hill; a monodrama* (London: Macmillan Publishers, 1989)

Lau, Shirley: *Treachery is the game* (Singapore: Times Books International, 1993)

Lee, Tzu Pheng: *Prospect of a drowning* (Singapore: Heinemann Educational Books, 1980)

Lee, Tzu Pheng: *Against the next wave* (Singapore: Times Books International, 1988)

Lee, Tzu Pheng: *The brink of an amen* (Singapore: Times Editions, 1990)

Lee, Bessie: *In love a sweetness ready: a book of poems* (Singapore: B. Lee, 1982)

Leong, Margaret: *The air above the tamarinds: a collection of poems* (Singapore: Eastern Universities Press, 1957)

Leong, Margaret: *Rivers to Senang* (Singapore: Eastern Universities Press, 1959)

Leong, Margaret: *The air above the tamarinds*; second edition with new poems, intended to be 'companion volume to *Rivers to Senang*' (Singapore: Eastern Universities Press, 1959)

Lim, Catherine: *Little ironies; stories of Singapore* (Heinemann Educational Books, 1978)

Lim, Catherine: *Or else, the lightning god and other stories* (Singapore: Heinemann Asia, 1980)

Lim, Catherine: *The serpent's tooth* (Singapore: Times Books International, 1982)

Lim, Catherine: *They do return; but gently lead them back* (Singapore: Times Books International, 1983)

Lim, Catherine: *The shadow of a shadow of a dream; love stories of Singapore* (Singapore: Heinemann Asia, 1987)

Lim, Catherine: *O Singapore! stories in celebration* (Singapore: Times Books International, 1989)

Lim, Catherine: *Love's lonely impulses* (Singapore: Heinemann Asia, 1992)

Lim, Catherine: *Deadline for love and other stories* (Singapore: Heinemann Asia, 1992)

Lim, Catherine: *The woman's book of superlatives* (Singapore: Times Books International, 1993)

Lim, Catherine: *Meet me on the Queen Elizabeth 2!* (Singapore: Heinemann Asia, 1993)

Li, Lien Fung: *The sword has two edges: a play* (Singapore: Times Books International, 1979)

Lim, Su-chen Christine: *Rice bowl* (Singapore: Times Books International, 1984)

Lim, Su-chen Christine: *Gift from the gods* (Singapore: Graham Brash, 1990)

Lim, Su-chen Christine: *A fistful of colours* (Singapore: EPB Publishers, 1993)

Lin, Hsin-hsin: *Take a word for a walk* (Singapore: Select Books, 1989)

Lin, Hsin-hsin: *From time to time* (Singapore: Select Books, 1991)

Lin, Hsin-hsin: *Love and 1st BYTE* (Singapore: World Scientific Publishing, 1992)

Nesamoni, Kamala: *Sound of waves* (Singapore: Asia Pacific Press, 1975)
Parrish, Cecile: *Poems* (Singapore: Renee Parrish, 1966)
Puthucheary, Rosaly: *The fragmented ego* (Singapore: Woodrose Publications, 1978)
Puthucheary, Rosaly: *Pillow your dreams* (Singapore: Woodrose Publications, 1978)
Puthucheary, Rosaly: *Dance on his doorstep* (Singapore:Crescent Design Associates, 1992)
San (Liao, San): *The lotus blossoms* (Singapore: Times Books International, 1991)
San (Liao, San): *China my love* (Singapore: Times Books International,1992)
Tan, Nalla: *Emerald autumn and other poems* (Singapore: N. Tan, 1976)
Tan, Nalla: *The gift and other poems* (Singapore: Federal Publications, 1978)
Tan, Nalla: *Hearts and Crosses* (Singapore: Heinemann Asia, 1989)
Tham, Claire: *Fascist rock; stories of rebellion* (Singapore: Times Books International, 1990)
Tham, Claire: *Saving the rainforest and other stories* (Singapore:Times Books International, 1993)
Wang, Anna: *A-musings 69* (Singapore: Anna Wang, 1991)
Wee, Kiat: *Women in men's houses* (Singapore: Landmark Books, 1992)
Wong, May: *A bad girl's book of animals* (New York: Harcourt Brace and World, 1969)
Wong, May: *Reports* (New York: Harcourt Brace Jovanovich, 1972)
Wong, May: *Superstitions; poems* (New York: Harcourt Brace Jovanovich, 1978)
Wong, Swee Hoon: *The landlord* (Singapore: Federal Publications, 1984)
Wong, Swee Hoon: *The phoenix and other stories* (Singapore: Heinemann Asia, 1985)
Wong, Swee Hoon: *A dying breed* (Singapore: Heinemann Asia, 1991)
Yap, Angeline: *Collected poems* (Singapore: National University of Singapore Department of English Language and Literature Shell Literary Series, 1986)
Yeoh, Soh Choo: 'Cell-city' in *Trial and other plays*, ed. Max LeBlond (Singapore: Federal Publications, 1986)
Yu, Ovidia: 'A Dream of China' (First Prize Winner, Asiaweek Short Story Competition, 1985). *Asiaweek*, 18 January, 1985.
Yu, Ovidia: *Miss Moorthy Investigates* (Singapore: Landmark/Hotspot Books,1989)
Yu, Ovidia: *Mistress and other creative takeoffs* (Singapore: Landmark Books, 1990) (with Desmond Sim and Kwuan Loh.)

*This is an inclusive not a select bibliography.

### Studies and Essays*

Brewster, Anne: 'Singaporean and Malaysian Women Poets, Local and Expatriate [Lee Tzu Pheng, Shirley Lim and Wong May]', *The Writer's Sense of the Contemporary*, ed. Bennet, Ee and Shephard (Nedlands: University of Western Australia, 1982)
Lau, Yoke Ching: *Speaking as women: a study of four poets writing in English from Singapore and Malaysia*. Unpublished M.A.thesis, National University of Singapore, March, 1989. [The four poets are Wong May, Shirley Lim, Lee Tzu Pheng and Geraldine Heng.]
Leong, Liew Geok: 'The Poetics of History: Three Women's Perspectives', unpublished paper delivered at Association of Commonwealth Literature and Language Studies 7th Triennial conference, Singapore, 16-21 June, 1986.
Koh, Tai Ann: '"Sing to the Dawn": Novels by Singapore Women', in Thelma Kintanar, ed.,*Women Novelists of Southeast Asia* (forthcoming).
Su, Elizabeth: 'Wong May: an introduction', *Commentary* 4, 2, 1980, p.53 - 55.

* The occasional book review has been so far the more usual form of critical response.

## LILAMANI de SILVA

# Sri Lankan Women Writers In English 1983-1994

For years, Lankan writers were locating the moral impetus for their writing in the theatre of rural and urban life, in scenarios of poverty, class/caste inequity, and, of course, like every one else, in the entrances and exits of Eros and Thanatos. That traditional stage has not been abandoned by contemporary Sri Lankan women writing in English. Given the macabre events of the last decade, writers have also faced a far more demanding scene and script, which some have boldly confronted. That confrontation is hardly safe, but it is played out in the words and works of some of our women writers.

Jean Arasanayagam, who has had fame and made a name in the last ten years with over a dozen publications in poetry and fiction, says that her 'major preoccupation has been with the vast, immeasurable tragedy of a country at war.' As the decade moved on, her poetry gained in strength and legitimacy by the incorporation of Lankan forms and consideration of serious Lankan concerns. Some of the titles of her collections – *Apocalypse '83* (1984), *Trial by Terror* (1987), *Reddened Water Flows Clear* (1991) – testify to her commitment to meet the challenges of her time and space. *A Colonial Inheritance* (1985) and *Out of Our Prisons We Emerge* (1987) are other collections of poetry produced in the last few years. Arasanayagam's work offers an intellectual challenge to the reader, but demonstrates, also, her delightful capacity for nuanced wit as she writes of her passage in an alien milieu, as 'Daughter-in-Law' in a Sri Lankan Hindu household or foreign visitor on an Indian tour. She also has to her credit two collections of short stories, *Fragments of a Journey* (1992), which has to do with the search for identity, and *The Cry of the Kite* (1984), offering vignettes of village-life in Jaffna, the now war-ravaged zone in the north.

Another poet, Kamala Wijeratne, has produced four collections of her poems since the first, *The Smell of Araliya*, in 1983. The consequences of Lankan political strife are germane to her concerns in poetry. Many of the poems in *A House Divided* (1985), *Disinherited* (1986), *That one Talent* (1988), and *The White Saree and Other Poems* (1994), are articulations of grief, pleas for compassion, and messages of hope issuing from the voice of a stricken mother figure. These imply the problematic notion that national unity is possible through individual acts of caring. Wijeratne's rhetorical question, 'Shall I trumpet men's wrongs/ And drum their acts of shame/ And raise a clamour to reach the stars...?' is indicative of the pointedness of her poetic enterprise. Also dealing with the problems of violence and national unity are Eva Ranaweera's *Selected Poems*, which is a medley of complex voices of many politically oppressed and embattled peoples of our time, and Manuka Wijesinghe-Vallenda's *Silouhettes for Justice* (1994), which is a record of history's liberation struggles that have used violence as a medium and culminated in betrayal and failure. Both works are symptomatic of the compulsion of poets to provoke reader response to the issues of our time.

One of our established poets, Anne Ranasinghe, has several publications to her credit, including *Plead Mercy*, and *Of Charred Wood, Midnight Fear* (with English and German versions of the poems). In 1985, she brought out *Against Eternity and Darkness*, and in

1991 *At What Dark Point* and *Not Even Shadows*. Poems of life in the land of her marriage, of family growing up, leaving home, and traumas of aging are the stuff of her poetry. The enabling ground for her creative energy is the sense of always being an exile in an alien land and memories of the holocaust. These haunt Ranasinghe's writing even now, many decades after her flight from Nazi Germany. Ranasinghe also writes short stories and radio plays and her work has been broadcast in several countries and translated into several languages.

Yet another collection of interesting poetry on personal themes published in the last decade is *The Unpredictable Blood* (1988) by Alfreda de Silva. She writes for 'A day she has put by/ Like a squirrel's winter hoard/ Knowing what harsh hungers/ rage in the unpredictable blood/ in a lean season.'

A lively and culturally enriching bilingual book of poems for children, entitled *A Little Bit of Poetry* (1992) by Leila Ekanayake is, perhaps, the only one of its kind. The illustrated Sinhala and English versions of the poems stand side by side. *A Little Bit of Poetry* is well written in both languages. Also in the category of Children's literature is Padma Edirisinghe's *Child and the Earth* (1990). The title reveals an educational objective, but the text incorporates fantasy, history, and folklore.

In the genre of fiction, Sita Kulatunga's *Dari. The Third Wife* is a sensitive portrayal of a Nigerian marriage, and, because of that sensitivity, the novel almost legitimizes polygamy, or so its critics would say. *Dari* was a contender for the prestigious Gratiaen Prize.

Maureen Seneviratne, who has a dozen books to her name, is an essayist, biographer, and short story writer. The two collections of short stories, *Mists On a Lake* (1984) and *The Fleeting Emptiness* (1986), display her skill in weaving into little stories the crises of contemporary life. Her latest collection of short stories is *Leaves from As'vattha* (1991).

Lalitha K. Witanachchi depicts the conflict of values and interests confronting Lankan communities forced to choose between traditional and progressive ways of life. *The Paddy Bird* is a story set in the Dumbara valley where the advent of technology for the survival of the agrarian community means sacrificing the beautiful valley and village to the waters of the new reservoir. Witanachchi's later collection, *The Wind Blows Over the Hills* (1993) is a variation upon the above theme and is as pleasing as the earlier work; it was a joint-winner of the Gratiaen prize awarded earlier this year.

From short-story writer Suvimalee Karunaratna we have a novel *Lake Marsh* (1993). The title functions as a proleptic metaphor for this novel that shows Lankan society sinking steadily under the mire of corruption, exploitation, and political unrest.

Other noteworthy works are Lolita Subasinghe's *The Twins and Other Stories*, Nafeela Muktha's first work *The Unique Pilgrimage* (1993), and Vijita Fernando's collection *Eleven Stories* (1988).

One of our illustrious novelists, Punyakante Wijenaike, who broke ground in the sixties and seventies with such novels as *The Third Woman, The Waiting Earth*, and *Giraya*, produced a recent work titled *Yukthi and Other Stories* (1991). The stories are set in 1987-89 – a violent time-frame in Lankan events. The account 'The Gun and the Poster' is particularly successful. Written with ironic humour, it depicts a people's resilience amidst confusing state rule.

A spate of family sagas (some of which we now call 'faction') visited the Lankan literary scene with Michael Ondatjee's *Running in the Family*. The genre receives enthusiastic reception, not least, for the vantage point it affords our class, caste, linguistic, ethnic and other struggles. Belonging in this category, *A Way of Life* (1987), also by Punyakante Wijenaike, is narrated from the perspective of a child, who records the life style in her grandparents' home, representative of affluent Sinhala households: 'a mixture of east and west.' Also included in this genre is Yasmine Gooneratne's *Relative Merits*. So too is *Pagoda House: Recollections of Childhood* (1990) by Alfreda de

Silva. It is a reminiscence of key events from the point of view of a curious and energetic youngster growing up in her grandmother's home. These sketches of 'Ceylon' life convey the essence of what, in retrospect, seems a halcyon era in our history.

The question of translation is receiving a great deal of discussion in academic circles right now. Lakshmi de Silva and Ranjini Obeyesekere are two women writers who have translated significant Sinhala literature into English. De Silva has translated into English two of the most popular plays in Sri Lanka, E.R. Sarachchandra's *Sinhabahu* and *Maname*. Obeyesekere's most recent effort is *Jewels of the Doctrine* (1994) and in 1987 she edited the special issue of the *Journal of South Asian Literature* on the subject 'Sinhala and Tamil Writing from Sri Lanka.'

Women have not been as prolific in creative writing and drama. Nedra Vittachchi and Indu Dharmasena persisted in this regard, but the present seems a fallow season. We saw, however, in translation, successful productions of the work of Wole Soyinka and Ngugi Wa Thiong'o by Somalatha Subasinghe and Neloufer de Mel.

In criticism, although women writers published a number of journal articles, no major texts have appeared yet, except from Yasmine Gooneratne residing in Australia. Gooneratne is, undoubtedly, the best known and most published contemporary Lankan scholar in literature. The latest of her critical texts is *Silence, Exile, and Cunning: The Fiction of Ruth Prawer Jhabvala* (1983). She is also the author of the acclaimed novel *A Change of Skies* (1991).

From Chitra Fernando, also living in Australia, we have *A Garland of Stories*, a collection of tales for children. Fernando's three other works of fiction have the lives of Lankan women characters as the main focus: *Three Women* (1984), *The Golden Bird and Other Stories* (1987) and *Between Worlds* (1988). Chandani Lokuge also lives in Australia; she published *Moth and Other Stories* in 1992.

In 1991 Eva Ranaweera compiled *Some Literary Women of Sri Lanka*, which is based on a survey of fifteen women writers who use English as their medium. As Ranaweera points out, Lankan women writers in English belong to a class that enables them to have the freedom, exposure, and the economic independence necessary to write. However, in spite of that few Lankan women can claim to be earning their living by writing. As Punyakante Wijenaike said in her 'Why I Write', the 'financial rewards are small and limited'.

RANJANA SIDHANTA ASH

# Indian Women's Writing in English

Indian writing in English over the last ten years – 1984-1994 – has been plentiful though of uneven quality. A brief personal selection has to make several omissions and the major gap here is the exclusion of women writers of the South Asian diaspora, such as Meena Alexander, Sujata Bharati Mukherjee, Suniti Namjoshi. What follows is a strictly geographic choice, restricted to women who write in English and live in India. With the mobility now fashionable in literary circles there is a tendency of some writers to gravitate between the motherland and the West, especially the USA. However, the work of the writers mentioned here continues to be India-based and not unduly coloured by what might be described as the double vision of migrancy literature, that is, viewing India and things Indian from a foreign perspective.

Probably the dominant note in much of the decade's fiction and poetry – the two genres under discussion – is that of 'womanism', to use Alice Walker's term. It is writing that celebrates women, mainly Indian woman and roughly of the writer's own class and community. Boundaries are crossed rarely and mainly by the older generation – Anita Desai, Nayantara Sahgal in fiction, or a cosmopolitan academic like the new poet, Rukmini Bhaya Nair. Male characters are often of secondary importance, and the central narrative or poetic voice is that of a woman whose consciousness directs her relationships. This female-centred writing received new encouragement when India's first feminist book publishing house, Kali for Women, was established in 1984. Its decade of publishing helped to promote an intellectual milieu in which Indian feminist thought has produced its own interpretations of India's past, the colonial legacy, the impact of Indian and third-world nationalism, and the fact of social and economic development. The publication of *Recasting Women: Essays in Colonial History* edited by Kumkum Sangari and Sudesh Vaid (Kali for Women, Delhi, 1989) marks a significant landmark in Indian feminist perceptions within academia similar to the tremendous influence exerted by the establishment of India's premier feminist journal, *Manushi*.

Kali for Women's anthologies of short stories by Indian women embody this new note of celebrating womanism. The stories do not always end on a note of female liberation. Lesbianism is scarcely touched on and the absence of working-class and peasant women disappointing. However, the stories reveal a new concern with women's sexuality, desires and interesting variations on the theme of motherhood. *Truth Tales* (1986) and *Slate of Life* (1990) were mainly stories translated from Indic regional languages, whereas the most recent collection, *In Other Words* (1992), has 14 stories written in English. Some of the writers are well known, like Vishwapriya Iyengar, Shema Futehally: others include Githa Hariharan, a newcomer who has received almost instant acclamation with the publication of her first novel and a collection of short stories.

The Iyengar story, 'No Letter from Mother', encapsulates the still problematic place of English within Indian society and literature. The girl in a boarding school longs to hear from her mother rather than to receive letters from her father but the mother's poor knowledge of English can only produce a few lines. It has been a decade also of fulminations by Indian women academics and others against the imposition of English and English literature on India by the British and by the post-colonial Indian establishment. (see, for example, Gauri Vishwanathan, *Masks of Conquest*, New York, 1989; Svati Joshi, ed., *Rethinking English*, Delhi, 1991; Rajeshwari Sunder Rajan, ed., *The Lie of the Land*, Delhi, 1992). Nevertheless, English has become more entrenched in the capitalist development of the subcontinent and an avenue of upward mobility into the world of privilege.

Among the ramifications of this Indianisation of English are two that affect women's writing. There is a shift to English to gain a wider and foreign readership by those hitherto hostile to the language. Mrinal Pande, a major Hindi writer and editor, has recently had a semi-autobiographical novel in English published in London (*Daughter's Daughter*, Mantra, 1993). More marked is the effect of most women's bilingualism and multilingualism on the kind of English they write. In one of the short stories in the latest Kali collection, an entire paragraph has a third of the words borrowed from the writer's mother tongue while most others have incorporated regional languages. Whereas Anand had to create very meticulously a pasticho of Panjabi in his 1930s novels, today's women writers slip into an easy flow of an Indianised version of English, translating freely oral and religious verse from regional languages and from Sanskrit. Shashi Deshpande makes use of her native Kannada and the Sanskrit she learnt at school as central features in her recent novels – *That Long Silence*, (London,

1988) and *The Bending Vine* (London, 1993). Githa Hariharan's first novel, *The Thousand Faces of Night* (Delhi, 1992), contains some of the most luminous translations to be found of Sanskrit scripture and a recreation of Sanskrit descriptions of the many manifestations of the great goddess, Devi.

The decade's writing by Indian women has broken with the alleged homogenised culture of the upper classes of India, pursuing similar life styles in club bars and five-star hotel bedrooms, that tended to colour Indian English writing. There is a greater emphasis, for example, on regionalism. This could have had a negative result considering the rise of religious fundamentalism in India over the decade and the threats it posed to the country's secularist policy and a much-treasured cultural synthesis of Sanskritic and Indo-Persian inheritance. Fortunately writers like Deshpande and Hariharan who create their narratives from within their known communities - high caste Hindus, generally Brahmins – are also feminists who use Hindu custom and scripture to subvert tradition, and to underline their injunctions to liberate women.

It is the old guard that maintains in their writing the earlier broad vision that characterised Indian writing of the 1930s and 1940s, and the even earlier humanism of Tagore. Anita Desai's last two novels have not only moved away from her earlier fictional world of neurotic privileged women imprisoned in domesticity but they have also begun to explore political issues especially in the field of communal tension and conflict. *In Custody* (London, 1984) continues her engagement with Urdu and Urdu poetry first evident in *Clear Light of Day* (London, 1980). It is the story of the neglect and death of a major Urdu poet symbolising the fate of the language in an ever-growing Hinduised India which regards Urdu merely as the language of Muslims and not worthy of protection.

It is also a novel where she discards a woman's perspective writing very skilfully from the viewpoint of a man, a Hindu college lecturer devoted to Urdu poetry. Her latest novel to date goes further into contemporary politics and the meeting of cultures as circumstances force people out of their protected ethnic identities into the turbulence of refugee life. *Baumgartner's Bombay* (London, 1988) depicts the life of a German Jew cast out of Nazi Germany and finding refuge in India. It reveals a Desai who can create a world of moral decay and urban squalor with the same confidence as she did with her earlier settings in gardens and boudoirs.

Nayantara Sahgal, always concerned with macropolitics through her journalism and family upbringing, had made only marginal references to the larger world of Indian political and economic development in her earlier work. Her last three novels, however, have made politics a pivotal to the narrative. *Rich Like Us* (London, 1985) dealt with Indira Gandhi's Emergency, which suspended India's democratic rights and civil liberties for several years, and its impact on the lives of three sets of characters. *Plans for Departure* (London, 1986) is that rare Indian-English novel with a European woman as its central character. In this Sahgal links western feminism in the phase of suffragette activity with Indian nationalism pre-World War I. Her last novel to date *Mistaken Identity* (London, 1989) is an allegory of the cultural synthesis of Hindu and Muslim traditions and heritage in the 1920s and 1930s. Sahgal's established position as a major political novelist in English, similar to Mahasveta Devi's in Bengali writing, has recently been given a new dimension. The publication of a correspondence with her partner, now her husband, of extracts from letters written over three years in their relationship connects her two concerns – commitment to a better democratic state and equal rights across gender and class, as well as providing Indian women's writing with a new genre of personal letters. *(Relationships: Extracts from a Correspondence*, by Nayantara Sahgal and E.N.Mangat Rai, Kali for Women, 1994).

Poetry by Indian women writing in English is prolific. A fourth of a new anthology of women poets is in English, the rest being translations though many of the poets,

Meena Alexander, Shanta Acharya, Sujata Bhatt, Ketaki Kushari Dyson and Suniti Namjoshi are part of the South Asian diaspora. (Arlene Zide, ed., *The Penguin Anthology of Contemporary Indian Women Poets*, Delhi, 1993). Perhaps it lacks the sensuality and musicality of the oral poetry Indian women have been composing at work and in enjoyment. Sarojini Naidu was able to capture some of the rhythm and colour in her English poetry written at the turn of the century but that is now decried in today's love of the unadorned and low-keyed. However, when the unadorned is compressed with many layers of meaning, suggestion and allusion, as in Alexander and Bhatt, the poem gains a new strength.

The big names of the past have not had new volumes published in the decade. Kamala Das's self-published first volume of collected poems contains her best work from the 1960s and 1970s. Gauri Deshpande's poems appear regularly. Since her much acclaimed first collection, Eunice de Souza has published two others, *Women in Dutch Painting* (Bombay, 1988) and *Ways of Belonging* (Edinburgh, 1990). They contain some of her best work in an ironic style spiced with her acerbic wit. She has explained her poetic credo as validating the stuff of women's lives as it is, not transcending it. In these volumes that stuff is drawn from Dutch paintings, Goan Catholicism, Greek mythology and Konkani villages.

Among the newcomers the common thread is the desire for freedom, especially in the exploration of heterosexual desire and an exposure of the hypocrisy of institutionalised religion and tradition. Tara Patel's persona in her first collection, *Single Women* (Calcutta, 1991) is caught between the desire of being free – wanting out of being someone's daughter or wife – and to experience sexual fulfilment. 'Even a one-night stand is luxury', she writes in the title poem. She wonders how her mother reacted to sex and whether she turned to religion, to Rama and Krishna, imagining herself to be Sita and Radha, their consorts, while her husband was becoming an alcoholic.

Imtiaz Dharker's *Purdah* (Delhi, 1989) crosses cultural frontiers as the poet, born a Muslim in Pakistan, raised in Britain and returning to India through her marriage to a Hindu, writes of women ambivalent about traditional morality and mores. The purdah, for example, protects and secures a woman in her privacy but it also imprisons her and, with time, becomes her shroud. She goes to the mosque for peace and 'the grace of light through marble' only to hear the mullah's wrath and some woman's 'defilement'.

Rukmini Bhaya Nair, a cosmopolitan academic, writes of her experiences at Cambridge, California and various countries of South and Southeast Asia in a very sophisticated first collection – *The Hyoid Bone* (Delhi, 1992). She is a meticulous poet whose craft is subtle and varied. She can write with a sense of mischievous fun about a clay horse from Bankura in West Bengal, as well as forge complex links between the illusory deer in the *Ramayana* which lured Sita into the clutches of Ravana and real deer being hunted down by sportsmen in the redwood forests of California. She uses her knowledge of several languages and her professional expertise as a professor of Linguistics in Delhi to construct interesting stanzaic patterns as in a poem called 'Genderole'.

It is their multilingual skills that one looks forward to among new developments in Indian women's poetry in English. Ruth Vanita, for example, with her first collection due out shortly, is both a lecturer in English at Delhi University and a translator from Hindi for *Manushi*. It is the combination of such talents that makes the 1990s appear promising.

JANE BRYCE

# Writing as Power in the Narratives of African Women

'I could speak until tomorrow.'
(Utterance by a woman performer, used by Karin Barber as the title of her book on Oriki.)[1]


'You know women's conversation never ends.'
(From Idu by Flora Nwapa.)[2]


There we dreamt about
the tall, black and handsome
like Heathcliff. Was he
African to us? Did he look
like the men we knew?
like our fathers and brothers?

Or we thrilled to blonde
blue-eyed dreams, identified
with white winner-masters,
who strode through Edgar Wallace,
Rider Haggard, and Joseph Conrad.

There would be no more polygamy
in our world, no more pain,
for we were special ...
Polygamy was for natives, illiterates and all such creatures. Our men would come
a-gliding, clouds of snow behind them,
moving phantomly to the sounds of violins,
looking like Tony Curtis, Fred Astaire and the Duke of Edinburgh!

They will lead us away, they will,
To monogamous havens
And True Romance Bliss.

(From 'When Father Experience Hits With His Hammer (Song for the Middle Class
African Woman)', Molara Ogundipe-Leslie.)[3]


We are all mothers,
and we have that fire within us,

of powerful women
whose spirits are so angry
we can laugh beauty into life
and still make you taste
the salt tears of our knowledge –
For we are not tortured
anymore;
we have seen beyond your lies and disguises,
and we have mastered the language of words,
we have mastered speech.

(From 'Liberation' by Abena Busia)[4]

The situation of African women's writing as indicated by these four excerpts, is one of a self-conscious disjunction. Yet it may be that very condition which provides the ground for creativity, which elicits the specific response of a need and a desire to write. At first glance, it is possible to read the excerpts as illustrating a decisive rupture, between a past ('traditional' or pre-colonial) in which women owned and were confident of their powers of expression; and a present characterised above all by anxiety, an all-pervasive ontological insecurity brought about by the intervention of colonial education, missionary values, western consumer capitalism and cultural imperialism.

But such a reading is instantly rendered inadequate by its false binary opposition of then and now, pre-and post, oral and written. To begin with, both the 'oral' utterances have come to us through print. Karin Barber, moreover, demonstrates through *oriki*, the unending capacity of oral culture to adapt itself to new circumstances, to reshape and reform itself in response to contemporary pressures and requirements. Orature, by this reading, is less the fossilised domain of anthropology than alive and contiguous to current forms of cultural expression. The rupture so seductively sung by proponents of a nostalgic purity enshrined in the African past now appears, in the light of a post-Négritude, post-colonial reading of culture, itself a little *passé*. Rather than a definitive closure constituting a decisive break with tradition, it may be more appropriate to see African women's writing as a process, with both historical and innovative dimensions. This may well be the truer significance of Idu's 'You know women's conversation never ends.' For both Ogundipe-Leslie and Busia's poems are situated within a perceived community, suggesting less the anguish of the isolated modernist self than a dialogue, with shared points of reference.

But, you will say, it's obvious to anyone that the dominant tone of these two textual fragments is, indeed, anguish. They speak above all a highly wrought self-consciousness, a far cry from the confident, celebratory embrace of *excess* in the 'oral' quotations. Neither irony, in Ogundipe-Leslie's case, nor defiance, in Busia's, can obscure the pain, the violence accompanying the accession to writing. The colonial school system, whose project it was to undermine custom, paint polygamy as immoral and elevate virginity above fertility as the index of a woman's value, offered instead a fantasy of romantic love and monogamous marriage. Not only that, but the cultural representations in whose image schoolgirls were invited to construct themselves were classics of imperialism. Jane Eyre, we know by now, only got her Rochester at the expense of the silencing, suppression and death of the colonial Other, Rochester's first bride. The crossing of the Sargasso Sea, in reality or fiction, necessitates a psychic dislocation. The mirror of colonial education invites its privileged subject to see herself as – white: the fainting heroine in the arms of the hero on the True Romance covers. Which, of course, is impossible, as experience shows, forcibly, hammering home a different reality.

Meanwhile, the counter-discourse to colonialism, the 'adversarial resistance' (Said) of liberation, necessitates another kind of dislocation, a violent repudiation of that internalised false consciousness, an unpicking and stripping 'naked piece by piece' of that constructed self. But this is not an individualist project, to be undertaken as a lonely quest by the tortured sensibility of the artist. 'For we are not tortured/anymore', having wilfully and collectively performed that transition from helplessness to responsibility. The question at issue in the discussion here is *how*. The answer, I think, is in the evocation of the oral heritage, the framing by Ogundipe-Leslie of her satirical statement as a Song. It is a 'Song for the Middle Class African Woman', whose experience is demonstrably different from that of the village *oriki* singer or the rural trader of Nwapa's fictional world, but is inextricably linked to it by powerful bonds of history, heritage and association. In the discourse of the literature of Empire to which Ogundipe-Leslie refers, such women are 'natives, illiterates', unreconstructed by western education, impervious to its civilising influence. Yet both these poems demonstrate the inability of that discourse to eradicate and silence the previously-existing discourse of orature as empowerment.

For the fact is, that orature is not just a convenient literary metaphor of origin, it is a concrete and visible daily expression of a specific relationship to history, to form, to language, to an aesthetics fundamental to a particular world view. From the women *oriki* singers of Karin Barber's Yoruba town, to the nightclubs of Lagos, Accra, Nairobi, Harare, Abidjan, Dakar, to the battlefields of Mozambique, Zimbabwe, Angola, orature is alive and doing its work of cultural definition and celebration. From popular music to the poetry of resistance, from 'gossip' and children's games to marriage and naming rituals, something functions which is stronger than any liberation rhetoric. It is that communal sense of self-recognition, the counter to the colonial mirror, which finds expression in these poets in their use of the collective 'we'. In her address to the 'Middle Class African Woman', Ogundipe-Leslie includes herself. In Busia's words, 'We are all mothers,' with the power and potential to create, once 'your' lies and disguises have been recognised for what they are, and 'our' speech reclaimed for our own use.

It is not too great a leap from this point to the proposition that women in Africa, the educated, middle-class women of whom we speak who have been obliged to undergo this process of self-conscious decolonisation – in other words, writers – have adopted narrative as their favoured tool- Edward Said contends that narrative is a fundamental trope 'an activity in which politics, tradition, and interpretation converge.'[5] He proposes that the great master narratives of western civilisation, emancipation and enlightenment, unable to face the challenge of the Imperial Other, have been replaced by multiple narratives which privilege the representation of the Imperial relationship. The narratives of African women have emerged within this post-colonial context, where the emphasis is not on a naive return to origin, but on retrieval, rediscovery and reinvention.

For Busia a primary focus of African women writers is 'on the significance of narration as the control of the meaning of 'one's own life'.[6] Control and empowerment reside even in the paradoxical decision to write in the colonial language. As W.D. Ashcroft argues in an essay on the relationship between post-colonialism and feminism, both are marked by a concern with language, the 'master tongue', as a means of control. He suggests that the way out of an essentialist notion of 'women's language' is to view all 'authenticity' as constructed, and to focus on the speaker. 'Language is a process rather than a system – something people do.'[7] Hence, for Mariama Ba writing in French or Ama Ata Aidoo in English, their use of the colonial language may be seen as an implicit assertion of distance from the nostalgia for origins, a recognition of the need for a revisioning of culture and their relationship to it from a post-colonial perspective. What results is, in Ashcroft's term, an 'intersection of ontologies': 'woman', 'African', 'post-colonial', 'feminist'. These terms, especially the first two, are becoming increasingly problematised as the body of women's writing grows. For too long it has been our project as readers and critics to validate whatever goes in the name of 'African women's writing' without interrogating those very terms. Looking back, we can see the necessity of this response as a strategy akin to the rhetoric of post-independence nationalism. Without in any way meaning to belittle the usefulness and timeliness of a text like *Ngambika* when it appeared on the scene in 1986, it is not possible now to overlook the prescriptive and homogenising tendency of its (albeit brave) attempt to define an 'African' feminism. Its editors situated their text at the point of transition from 'the early identification of biases in male writers to an exploration of the works of women writers who have remained outside of the purview of literary criticism.'[8] What this irresistibly suggests is our arrival at another point of transition, led there, inevitably, by the proliferation in textual strategies offered by the accumulation of African women writers' narratives. The work of reclamation, of forcibly shifting the perspective which marginalises and excludes whatever is not amenable to the dominant discourse, is valuable, essential and ongoing. But. recent readings of African women's writing in the light of post-colonial theories of language and cultural syncretism, have pointed the way to a possible new perspective, privileging diversity and heterogeneity.[9] The benefits of this to all of us who practise the business of post-colonial literature is obvious. Criticism is the ground on which creative writing either thrives or shrivels. As Biodun Jeyifo puts it, the relationship of theory to African Literature is one of discursive power, the power to police language (Eagleton), to define and relegate and hierarchise and marginalise. It is 'your lies and disguises' versus the power' of 'our' narratives, or, as Jeyifo puts it: '...the question of an African critical discourse which is self-constituted and self-constituting in line with the forces acting on the production of African literature is intimately connected with the fate of that literature.'[10]

The most immediate obvious stumbling block for critics of African women's writing is the fact that so many of us do not live on the continent. In this sense, the postcolonial discourse of marginality and displacement is given a new and ironic dimension by the continual tug away from the geographical site of the narratives towards the metropolitan centres. Jeyifo points out the very real effects on scholarship in Africa of material problems such as a lack of resources, a crumbling educational infrastructure, lack of access to and the expense of books, difficulties of communication, and so on. We deceive ourselves if we overlook the way in which the enormously disproportionate resources available in the west, particularly North America, weight the whole discussion. Which texts and authors are known, which are written about, who gets invited to international conferences, has access to multinational publishers, publicity and foreign audiences, are all decided by criteria which may be as arbitrary as personal encounter.

The question of publishing is crucial. Those who are best known – Flora Nwapa, Mariama Ba, Ama Ata Aidoo, Buchi Emecheta, Bessie Head – are those whose books are available abroad because published by foreign-based presses. In the anglophone world, Heinemann, Longman and Macmillan dominate. The close economic and cultural ties between France and its ex-colonies mean that, while the leading francophone African publishers are based in Dakar and Abidjan (Nouvelles Editions Africaines) and Yaounde (les Editions CLE), their products are also distributed in France. It is however only those who have been translated into English (Mariama Ba, Aminata Sow Fall, Nafissatou Diallo) whose works tend to be included in discussions by anglophone critics. This inevitably has an unbalancing effect, in turn, on readers' perceptions. African women writing in African languages, like Asenath Bole Odaga in Luo, Colette Mutangadora, Jane Chifamba, Bertha Msora and Katina Muringanise in Shona, or

Barbara Makhalisa in Ndebele, remain unknown and unrecognised outside their own countries. Those writers who, for ideological or practical reasons, write in the metropolitan language but publish with indigenous publishers have to face the fact that they will thereby be confined to a local audience. Despite the efforts of African publishers at co-publishing and distributing in other African countries, import controls and taxation are such as to limit the movement of books across borders. The problem is being addressed by such strategies as the Oxford-based African publishers' co-operative set up by Hans Zell, to bring African published books to Britain, and by the determination of African publishers to succeed in a market dominated by the multinationals. Zimbabwe, which at Independence in 1980 had only Zimbabwe Publishing House (ZPH) and Mambo, now has Nehanda, Baobab and Anvil, and ZPH is in serious competition with Longman and Macmillan for the lucrative educational market. Yet, according to a ZPH editor, very few (perhaps 1 in 10) manuscripts submitted are by women. Tsitsi Dangarembga is the only internationally acknowledged Zimbabwean woman writer, and this is at least partly a result of the fact that her novel, *Nervous Conditions*, was published by the British-based Women's Press (1988). The recently established Ghanaian publisher Woelie is proud of having scooped many of the leading names in contemporary Ghanaian writing - Kofi Anyidoho, Kofi Awoonor and others – yet Ama Ata Aidoo, a Ghanaian based in Zimbabwe, similarly elected to publish her latest novel, *Changes*, with the Women's Press (1991).

There is obviously a need for an African-based feminist publishing house, yet none exists. Individual women have established presses: Flora Nwapa's Tana, Buchi Emecheta's Ogugwu Afor, Asenath Bole Odaga's Lake Publishers, Aminata Sow Fall's Caec (Centre d'Animations et des Echanges Culturelles), but apart from the last one, these publish mainly the author's own works, and do not exist primarily to encourage other women. Women writers are thus at the mercy of a publishing establishment which has tended to apply male-defined criteria of what is acceptable in a literary text. By this I mean that the consensus which has grown up, primarily within the universities, of what constitutes an appropriate form and content for African fiction, has been shaped first by a New Critical colonial heritage and subsequently by the ideologies of nationalism and decolonisation. Neither of these is fertile terrain for the otherness of women's writing, with its tendency towards redefinition of cherished cultural and political norms and its relocation of the centre of interest in the domestic, the personal, or the oppositional.

One area of publishing that women on some parts of the continent have been able to appropriate and use to their own ends is the undervalued one of mass-market romantic fiction. Here the Macmillan Pacesetter Series, aimed at a younger/less literate audience, has been particularly useful, and more women appear as authors in its list than the more 'serious', and therefore prestigious, Heinemann and Longman's Lists. Writers like Helen Ovbiagele, Yemi Sikuade, Rosina Umelo, Yemi Lucilda Hunter and Christine Botchwey have both used and subverted the romance vehicle, adapting the 'formula' so familiar to African readers from the ubiquitous Mills and Boon, indigenising and altering it in subtle and significant ways. That the romance formula has something to offer African women writers and readers is evident too from its use by more recognised writers publishing with Longman, for example, Zaynab Alkali or, most notably, Ama Ata Aidoo's *Changes*. This author's deliberate decision to write a love story set in Accra (for which she tenders an ironic 'apology') is in itself a subversive act, for by now she is recognised as being part of the 'canon', however reluctantly on the part of a male-dominated critical establishment.

It is not only in romantic fiction but in the more ephemeral media of women's magazines, women's pages in the newspapers, television and radio, that women's narratives may be found. The invisibility of women's writing is all too often a function of a depressed economy and scarcity of outlets. Ghana is a case in point. To discover women's cultural production in Ghana, one needs to look beyond print, in the formal sense of books, to a magazine like *Obaa Sima*, run single handedly by its editor, Kate Abbam. Despite paper and ink shortages, delays and low sales at times of economic crisis, she has kept the magazine coming out for over 20 years, since 1971. Back issues offer a startling store of popular romantic fiction, by women and men, in the form of stories and serials, including Kate Abbam's own romantic novel, *Beloved Twin*, serialised in 1972. Women writers find outlets too in the less formal and structured field of radio scripts, television and journalism, though the press in Ghana (unlike in Nigeria) offers few opportunities for creative writing. One well-known journalist, Ajoa Afari, has published a collection of her pieces for the *Mirror* 1976-1986, *Thoughts of a Native Daughter* (1988) and a collection of short stories: *A Sound of Pestles* with a local publisher, Afram (1992). Apart from this, a decade of economic decline has caused many women to sublimate their creativity in religious activities, including writing, and the religious publisher Asempa encourages creative writing with a religious message. Women are active as performers of *abibidwom*, a form of prayer in the Methodist Church using a traditional Fanti song form. The Asante and Ewe traditional cultures, too, render up women as contemporary secular performers and composers. The conclusion is obvious: though the view from the metropolitan centres will be that there is very little in the way of women's narratives emerging from Ghana, and while this is true in terms of published texts, there is a stream of creativity flowing invisible to the outside eye.[11]

Women in African countries are, needless to say, evolving their own strategies for dealing with the problems of economic depression, material scarcity and invisibility. In Kenya, in 1991, a group of university and publishing women organised the first ever women's writing workshop, away from the capital, in Nakuru. Women, canvassed from all the language groups, were invited to write on the theme of 'Our Secret Lives.' Those not able to write or speak English spoke their stories onto tape for later translation. The outcome was two volumes of short stories, many of them openly autobiographical, *Our Secret Lives* (Phoenix, 1992) and *They Have Destroyed the Temple* (Longman). Untutored as these narratives are in any formal, literary sense, they do, nonetheless, represent a collective assumption of power, a counter-discourse to the dominant Kenyan patriarchal dictum that 'Women have no secrets.'[12]

A similar phenomenon has been brought about in Zimbabwe by the Zimbabwe Women Writers group, formed in 1990. The group is remarkable for including in its membership 'well-known' writers like Ama Ata Aidoo and Micere Mugo, both non-Zimbabweans, the South African activist Norma Kitson and numerous white and black educated Zimbabwean women, and yet avoiding the pitfalls of elitism. It has carried out its declared commitment to 'grassroots' women by establishing a countryside network of writers' groups, and by running a workshop in the rural area of Rushinga, where again indigenous language speakers were encouraged to tape their stories. Starting with a cheaply produced publication of selections of its members' writing, ZWW are intending to publish more as resources become available. Such activities as these bespeak a political awareness and understanding of the potential of collective action which runs directly counter to the individualistic, elitist, capitalist ethic represented by the multinational publishers.

I am aware that by choosing to address these other strains and strata of women's writing in Africa, I have excluded many writers whose work, if only because it is more accessible to the readers of this paper, cries out to be mentioned. I have, besides, side-stepped many important issues that need to be taken up and looked at by post-colonial feminist critics. How, for example, do we place the work of a writer like Marjorie Oludhe-Macgoye, whose novels, over a period of decades, have examined the situation of women in Kenya, in different social and cultural contexts. Deeply influenced by the work of Acoli poet, Okot p'Bitek, in reclaiming for written literature the oral aesthetic tradition of the Luo culture into which she married, Oludhe Macgoye is by origin white and British. To return to an earlier point in this paper, issues of authenticity, ethnic essentialism versus cultural hybridity, coalesce around this author's narratives. If the criteria for assessing post-colonial women's writing are to be, as Ashcroft suggests, empowerment, revisioning and reinvention across the frontiers of race, birth, language and geography, then this writer occupies a significant space in Kenya's literary scene. By the same criteria, how are we to place a writer like Buchi Emecheta, whose worldwide reputation and acknowledgement by the western women's movement as an important Black Woman Writer have arisen in a context of displacement, distance from her fictive territory, and alienation from its contemporary social practices. Who is more 'African'? The expatriate who embraces Africa or the African who embraces the West?

It seems the question of what constitutes 'African women's writing' is one that generates a multiplicity of further questions. Without attempting to effect a closure on the subject, I will deflect a conclusion with yet another textual fragment:

Look for me in the silence.


I creep among you, putting shame to your
conceit
You, whose attention is turned away to the sky –
shout
You do not see the chameleon mocking your fear.
If you still seek me, turn your hearts to the
silence,
alert to the forest.[13]


Notes

1. Karin Barber: *I Could Speak Until Tomorrow: Oriki, women and the past in a Yoruba town* (Edinburgh, 1991).
2. Flora Nwapa: *Idu* (London: Heinemann, 1970), p. 97.
3. Molara Ogundipe-Leslie: 'When Father Experience Hits With His Hammer,' *Sew the Old Days* (Evans, Ibadan, 1985), p. 30.
4. Abena Busia, 'Liberation,' *A Double Colonisation*, eds. Kirsten Holst Petersen and Anna Rutherford, (Sydney: Dangaroo, 1986), p. 121.
5. Edward Said, 'Representing the Colonised: Anthropology's Interlocutors'; in *Critical Inquiry*, 1989, Winter; 15 (2), pp. 205-25.
6. Abena Busia, 'Rebellious Women: Fictional Biographies – Nawal el Sa'adawi's *Woman at Point Zero* and Mariama Ba's *So Long A Letter,*' in *Motherlands*, ed. S. Nasta (Women's Press, 1991).
7. W.D. Ashcroft, 'Intersecting Marginalities: Post-colonialism and Feminism,' in *Kunapipi*, Vol XI, no. 2, 1989, p .26.
8. Eds. C. Boyce Davies and A. Adams Graves: *Ngambika* (African World Press, Inc, 1986), p. 6.
9. Particularly inspiring to me have been the essays by Elleke Boehmer, Judie Newman and Lyn Innes in *Motherlands* (op. cit.), and by Florence Stratton, Biodun Jeyifo and Susan Andrade in *Research in African Literatures*, 1990, vol. 21, no.1.
10. Biodun Jeyifo, 'The Nature of Things: Arrested Decolonisation and Critical Theory,' in *RAL* (*op.cit.*).

11. I am grateful to the cultural researcher, Esi Sutherland – Addy, whom I interviewed, for this information on women's activities in the churches and as performers drawing on Ghananian cultural traditions.
12. In Kenya, Muthoni Karega of Phoenix publishers, a participant, and Dr. Wanjiku Kabira of Nairobi University, organiser of the women's workshop, talked to me about its aims and the way it was conducted.
13. Marjorie Oludhe-Macgoye: 'Mathenge,' *The Heinemann Book of African Poetry in English*, selected by A. Maja-Pearce (Heinemann, 1990), p. 19.

DENISE deCAIRES NARAIN and
EVELYN O'CALLAGHAN

# Anglophone Caribbean Women Writers.

'Of Course When They Ask for Poems About the
"Realities" of
Black Women'

What they really want
at times
is a specimen
whose heart is in the dust

A mother-of-sufferer
trampled, oppressed          (Grace Nichols)

Since women have been producing literature in the Caribbean for centuries, the 'emergence of the Caribbean woman's voice' has less to do with a sudden manifestation of talent than with the politics of publishing and the current 'marketability' of this writing. In the last two decades publishing houses in Britain and North America, no doubt influenced by the Women's Movement (and the relative increase in women's purchasing power) as well as growing interest in black and post-colonial literatures, have recognized both the existence and 'bankability' of women's writing from the Caribbean and have hurried to provide access to this writing via print. Sometimes, in the rush to catch this trend, material which needs further development and crafting has been published.

The very term 'Caribbean women's writing' is problematic, considering the diversity of the work and of the writers. Cynically, one could suggest that the collective label is a handy marketing device. A glance at the covers of a few recent anthologies of Caribbean women's poetry which feature the image of a strong, stoical, black woman, raise interesting questions in relation to *the* Caribbean woman. This image functions as visual short-hand for the archetypal, long-suffering, strong, black Caribbean matriarch

– a representation of *the* Caribbean woman which has circulated in regional literary texts from the very early days (witness Edith Clarke's/Lamming's much-quoted phrase, 'My mother who fathered me'). In these collections (*Jamaica Woman, Watchers and Seekers, Creation Fire*), the ethnic diversity of the contributors belies the representativeness of this image. This privileging of the black, working-class woman, while being 'politically correct' tends to homogenize writing by regional women, encouraging fixed agendas of appropriate subjects and setting limits on just who actually qualifies to be considered 'Caribbean'.

It raises the question, too, of the role played by various metropolitan feminist publishing houses in setting such limited parameters: are some black women's texts published as part of a 'numbers game' in which Western publishing houses seek to disprove the charge of Eurocentrism? The problem with this of course, is that in attempting to 'give' the 'Third World woman' a 'voice' and to celebrate it, critical questions about how/what this 'voice' is saying are seldom asked.

A related issue is the thorny question of quality, since volumes like *Creation Fire* include very finely crafted poems as well as several which require substantial editing; what the unevenness of the work included suggests is that simply *naming* one's experience and oppression as a Caribbean woman is enough to ensure publication. A willingness to raise uncomfortable critical questions is one of the refreshing features of another anthology, this time of Trinbagonian women, *Washer Woman Hangs Her Poems in the Sun*. Margaret Watts in her preface asks: 'Why women? Why these women poets? Why washerwoman?'; she then goes on to raise the issue of 'quality', to state just how Trinbagonian is being defined and to suggest why women are being anthologised separately. This kind of questioning is important in that it keeps the category 'Caribbean woman writer' in flux and reminds us that, to quote Grace Nichols, '...there ain't no easy-belly category/ for a black woman/ or a white woman...'

The editors of the two recently published prose anthologies, *Her True True Name* and *Green Cane and Juicy Flotsam*, take pains to note the difficulty of balancing representationality and selectivity along with their underlying desire to publish as wide a sample of Caribbean women writers as constraints allow. In this 'overview' we would also stress the need to move away from totalising representations of Caribbean women's writing while at the same time asserting that it *is* politically expedient to consider women writers of the region in one category, given the fact that writing of the region has tended to be dominated by male writers which, in turn, has resulted in the circulation of limited/limiting representations of Caribbean women. What follows, then, is an outline of some of the thematic and formal similarities in the work of Caribbean women writers which link them under one 'label' – though we stress that this label must be flexible.

One of the narrative perspectives used by many of the prose writers is that of the girl-child/adolescent, often detailing the alienating nature of adult/child relationships: *Crick Crack Monkey* by Merle Hodge; *Annie John* by Jamaica Kincaid; a fair number of Olive Senior's short stories; and Zee Edgell's *Beka Lamb* are cases in point. More specifically, West Indian women writers focus on 'mothering' (by biological *or* non-biological mother figures). Their treatment of the mother is, more often than not, ambivalent; by contrast grandmothers feature much less problematically for the young protagonists. Among the poets, mothers and motherhood are also recurrent themes with Lorna Goodison's volume, *I Am Becoming My Mother* being the most sustained exploration. Her poem, 'For My Mother, May I Inherit Half Her Strength' is a powerful praisesong for the (stereotypical) strong black, Caribbean woman but it also painstakingly catalogues the *cost* of that stereotyping. In addition, connections between mother and 'motherland' are explored as the sense of 'home' and place are gendered in much of the writing.

Ambivalence informs the treatment of the journey to and the love/hate relationship with the 'Mother Country'. While authorial affirmation tends to be firmly behind the *Caribbean* as motherland, since many West Indian women writers now live away from 'home', either temporarily or permanently, the migration experience has consequently become an important theme in their writing. The novels of Jamaica Kincaid, Elean Thomas, Michele Cliff and Joan Riley all deal with opposing pulls of 'motherland' and 'Mother Country'.

This sense of 'unbelonging' and nostalgia for the Caribbean is also explored in the poetry of Grace Nichols, Amryl Johnson and, more recently, Merle Collins (all of whom are now based in Britain), and problematized in Joan Riley's *A Kindness To the Children* and Vernella Fuller's *Going back Home*. Perhaps more work needs to be done on the differences in representation of the Caribbean as 'home', in the texts of writers based in the region and those residing outside. Marlene Nourbese Philip, based in Canada, focuses on the issue of language and the lost/suppressed 'mothertongue' in her quest for a sense of cultural belonging. Philip explores the crucial role of patriarchal/colonial discourses in suppressing the mother tongue – associated, historically, in the Caribbean context with the suppression of African and Creole languages – and in *Looking For Livingstone* she 'reads' the silence 'beneath' the narratives of empire.

Discussions of poetry in the Caribbean have always tended to be dominated by the two male heavyweights, Brathwaite and Walcott (which poses role model problems for the would-be woman poet), but in much nationalist and 'protest' poetry the emphasis has been on the need for a vigorous and forceful (read, 'phallic') language with which to challenge the colonizer: as Bongo Jerry puts it, 'MAN must use MEN language/ to carry dis message.' The macho thrust of much nationalist poetry perhaps helps to account for the relative dearth of women poets in the early pre- and post-independence period. In the 1980s and 1990s women writers generally have asserted their ability to function as more than symbolic keepers of culture/nurturers of Creole and are experimenting with the Caribbean language continuum in interesting and innovative ways. Lorna Goodison, in her 'Heartease' poems, uses an impressively polyphonic voice, drawing on a range of discourses and seamlessly weaving linguistic registers (Jamaican Creole, Rasta idiom, Standard English, Biblical phraseology) in the 'body' of her texts to represent the body politic or 'the nation'.

Among the prose writers, language may not be as obvious an issue but experimentation is evident in the strategies used to render the authorial voice less authoritarian/more democratic; in Olive Senior's 'Ballad', Miss Rilla's story is narrated by Lenora, a young Creole speaker whose own story is told in the telling of Miss Rilla's and the process of story telling is itself also a focus of the text.

Brodber, Collins, Pollard and Senior also use a multiplicity of narrative voices within texts which eschew the hegemony of the omniscient narrator by articulating a variety of voices from the Creole community. The increasing number of female-authored short story collections should be noted too, since this form easily accommodates such a diversity of perspectives. Multiplicity of narrative voice facilitates the representation of a world of fluid boundaries (between self/other, living/dead, mad/sane, dream-/reality). This refusal of closure, of boundaries, of single truths, now designated 'postmodernist', is notable in Rhys's *Wide Sargasso Sea* and continues in the writing of Brodber, Kincaid and Nourbese Philip. Some of the most interesting writing by anglophone Caribbean women evidences a move away from linear, 'realistic' narrative and a willingness to challenge conventional generic boundaries.

This experimentation with language and 'voice' in Caribbean women's poetry and prose links into larger, thematic questions of (quests for) 'identity', a holistic sense of self, which have always been central to Caribbean literature. Obviously, they resurface in West Indian women's literary investigation of how sociopolitical hierarchies of race and class, the legacy of slavery and colonialism, impact upon female protagonists. Grace Nichols's *i is a long memoried woman*, for example, is a sustained poetic mapping of the violently damaging effects of slavery on the contemporary black Caribbean woman's attempt to construct a relatively stable identity. Janice Shinebourne's *Timepiece*, Merle Collins's *Angel*, and *Beka Lamb* also demonstrate the ways in which socialization into gender roles are crucially informed by race and class expectations.

The conflicting demands of such socialization are often shown to be potentially damaging to female self-awareness, dividing instead of uniting women (Tia and Antoinette in *Wide Sargasso Sea*, for example). The resulting isolation and alienation are taken further in texts like *Jane and Louisa Will Soon Come Home* and *Beka Lamb* which offer studies of protagonists exhibiting severe 'ontological insecurity', resulting in nervous breakdown, 'madness' and self-destructive impulses.

Among the poets, Christine Craig's 'Crow Poem', Olive Senior's 'To the Madwoman in My Yard' and Jean Binta Breeze's poem, 'Riddym Ravings' all deal with the theme of women and 'madness'. Mahadai Das, an Indian-Guyanese poet, focuses on the exploration of psychic landscapes in her most recent volume, *Bones*, pointing an accusing finger both at limiting 'feminine' roles in causing fragmentation and dislocation of self, and at capitalist exploitation of the 'Third World Woman' which reduces the woman to body parts: hands and feet. Another 'version' of ontological insecurity may be read into the way the poets, moreso than the prose writers, often focus on the process of writing itself and express anxiety about their 'right' to write, so that the writing of poetry is associated with the delicate balancing skills of the trapeze artist, with pain (sometimes with the pain of childbirth), or with a sense of poetry as an invasion of their 'personhood'.

A frequent target in West Indian literature has been the alienating effects of colonial education, usually buttressed by the teachings of an authoritarian Christianity. Again, by foregrounding a female protagonist, women writers demonstrate how restrictive gender roles are enshrined in colonial ideology. Works like Michele Cliff's *No Telephone To Heaven*, Olive Senior's stories and her poem 'Colonial Girl's School', *Crick Crack Monkey* and *Annie John* dramatize how effectively this insidious conditioning operates. Furthermore, in these and other texts, older women *within* the community are indicted for their role in socializing girls to become 'young ladies'. This oppressive 'ladyhood' is associated with Christian and Victorian strictures as to respectability and morality with their attendant taboo on the expression of female sexuality. Many writers point to the association of sexuality with shame, defilement and the forced renunciation of childhood freedom (with its relative androgyny).

The women poets of the region are more explicit in treating the issue of female sexuality positively; Marlene Nourbese Philip and Grace Nichols, for example, suggest that the body and the erotic can be used as a source of power. Philip, uses female 'body language' to destabilize patriarchal discourses while Nichols attempts to reclaim and celebrate the woman's body, specifically the black woman's body, by offering alternative definitions of beauty to challenge dominant Eurocentric paradigms of femininity. Interestingly, this focus on the body (always a contested site in feminist analyses of patriarchy) has been instrumental in Nichols receiving sustained critical attention in Britain to the point where she is often perceived as the archetypal Caribbean *woman* poet.

Much of the writing is, implicitly or explicitly, committed to sociopolitical change; this also has implications for the critical reception of such texts in that we, as critics, may need to rethink the kind of criteria used in interpreting these texts so that we can attempt to factor in this issue of 'consciousness raising' in the literature by women of the region.

Appropriately, women writers challenge limited definitions of *the* Caribbean woman which operate in society but which have also circulated in male-authored texts (stereotypes such as strong matriarch, tragic mulatto, virgin or whore). Increasingly too, this challenge to stereotypical representations is coming from women writers from a variety of ethnic groups who have to date been either underrepresented or 'misrepresented'. Ramabai Espinet and Rajandaye Ramkissoon-Chen, for example, are two new poetic voices that attempt to portray Indian Caribbean experience from the *inside*, attending to the tensions between ethnic and gender roles. Mahadai Das's work (mentioned above) also contributes to complexifying the trite stereotype of the Indian woman in the Caribbean as 'passive'; so does Olive Senior's story, 'The Arrival of the Snake Woman'. The image of the 'white' woman as insipid, asexual 'mistress' is also interrogated in the writing of Michele Cliff and Pauline Melville, and a new interest is being taken in the white West Indian writer Phyllis Shand Allfrey, who (like Rhys, to some extent) has often been considered not 'Caribbean enough'.

The literature generally suggests authorial endorsement of relational interaction, especially in terms of mutual female support – although this is not to assert a facile affirmation of sisterhood – even as it depicts sterile and confrontational interpersonal situations, particularly between men and woman. Riley's *The Unbelonging* and Goodison's 'Ceremony For the Banishment of the King of Swords' are two extreme examples of the latter. To date, there have been few explicit portrayals of lesbianism apart from the poetry of Dionne Brand and sections of Nourbese Philip's *Looking For Livingstone*. However, many texts deal unselfconsciously with the physicality of women's relationships with each other – one thinks of the sensuous evocation of the mother-daughter ritual baths in *Annie John*.

West Indian fiction by women tends to emphasize affinity with natural landscape, which sustains (as in Brodber's *Myal*, *Wide Sargasso Sea*, *The Orchid House*) and can engender what Goodison calls 'Heartease'. For her, as for several other writers, the natural world is seen to provide access to the realm of the spirits, the magical, the supernatural, coexisting with the everyday without incongruity. Brodber's two novels, *Annie John*, several stories by Senior, Pollard and Adisa, as well as the work of Nourbese Philip, all demonstrate this juxtaposition.

This sense of rootedness informs the ease with which the writing manipulates the whole range of language registers, and confidently negotiates the supposed gap between oral and scribal forms. In the fiction, writers freely draw on such diverse features of orality as proverb, songs (of all provenance), folk and fairy tale, and Biblical rhetoric. In poetry, the most striking appropriation of the oral tradition has been manifested in 'dub poetry', as practised by male performers such as Mutabaruka, Linton Kwesi Johnson and Mikey Smith. As Jean Binta Breeze points out, the form presents particular problems for the woman who attempts to enter this field, since female sexuality has not, until recently, been perceived as having a place in the identity of the 'radical dub poetry'. In fact, even in the revolutionary challenge which 'dub poetry' presents to the conventional hierarchy of literary discourses (which privileges poetry) the dominance of the male voice continues.

Merle Collins and Amryl Johnson, in their most recent collections of poetry, point to other possibilities for the incorporation of orality in the *sounding* of their poems; as with the fiction, the poetry utilises song, refrains from children's games and calypso rhythms, and in some cases is sung rather than simply read (indeed, Johnson's *Gorgons* was released on cassette prior to publication). Such poetry insists women *will* be seen *and* heard.

Finally, Caribbean women writers, in common with women writers worldwide, frequently use the autobiographical mode; however, 'confessional' or intimate narratives tend to be as much explorations of national and political as of personal concerns, as in

*Beka Lamb* and *Angel*. The political also informs the use of comedy, which tends to be playfully subversive, and is usually at the expense of hypocrisy, assumed or pompous patriarchal authority, and self-aggrandizement of all types. This applies to both the fiction (Melville, Senior, and Pollard) and the poetry (Nichols, Johnson, and Goodison).

While stressing the necessarily partial scope of this overview, we would wish to highlight the striking variety of Anglophone Caribbean women's writing. Like the culture from which it springs, this writing epitomizes the features of the creolization process: inclusivity, polyphony, syncreticity and hybridity; imposing any totalizing label on the literature would be to ignore its deconstructive thrust which seeks to undo simplistic binary oppositions of any kind. It is this fracturing of hierarchised ways of reading the Caribbean, that is particularly liberating in regional women's writing.

**Bibliography of works cited**

Poetry Anthologies:

Pamela Mordecai & Mervyn Morris, eds.: *Jamaica Woman* (London: Heinemann, 1980).
Rhonda Cobham & Merle Collins, eds.: *Watchers and Seekers* (London: The Women's Press, 1987).
Ramabai Espinet, ed.: *Creation Fire* (Toronto: Sister Vision Press, 1990).
Watts, Margaret, ed.: *Washer Woman Hangs her Poems in the Sun* (Trinidad: Gloria V. Ferguson Ltd., 1990).

Prose Anthologies:

Carmen C. Esteves & Lizabeth Paravisini-Gebert, eds.: *Green Cane and Juicy Flotsam: Short Stories By Caribbean Women* (Rutgers, 1991).
Pamela Mordecai & Betty Wilson, eds.: *Her True-True Name* (London: Heinemann, 1989).

Prose Works Cited:

Opal Palmer Adisa: *Bake Face and Other Guava Stories* (Kelsey Street Press, Berkley; 1986).
Phyllis Shand Allfrey: *The Orchid House* (Constable, 1953). Reprinted by Virago.
Erna Brodber: *Jane and Louisa Will Soon Come Home* (London: New Beacon, 1980).
Erna Brodber: *Myal* (London: New Beacon, 1988).
Michele Cliff: *No Telephone To Heaven* (Dutton, 1987).
Merle Collins: *Angel* (London: The Women's Press 1988).
Zee Edgell: *Beka Lamb* (London: Heinemann, 1982).
Vernella Fuller: *Going Back Home* (London: Virago, 1992).
Merle Hodge: *Crick Crack Monkey* (London: Heinemann, 1981).
Jamaica Kincaid: *Annie John* (London: Picador, 1982).
Paule Marshall: *Brown Girl, Brownstones* (New York: The Feminist Press, 1981).
Pauline Melville: *Shapeshifter* (London: The Women's Press, 1990).
Grace Nichols: *Whole Of A Morning Sky* (London: Virago, 1986).
Velma Pollard: *Considering Woman* (london: The Women's Press, 1989).
Jean Rhys: *Wide Sargasso Sea* (Hammondsworth: Penguin, 1968).
Joan Riley: *The Unbelonging* (London: The Women's Press, 1985).
Joan Riley: *A Kindness To The Children* (London: The Women's Press, 1992).
Olive Senior: *Summer Lightning and Other Stories* (London: Longman, 1986).
Olive Senior: *Arrival of the Snake Woman and Other Stories* (London: Longman 1989).
Janice Shinebourne: *Timepiece* (Leeds: Peepal Tree Press, 1986).

Elean Thomas: *The Last Room* (London: Virago, 1991).

Works of Poetry Cited:

Dionne Brand: *No Language Is Neutral* (Toronto: Coach House Press, 1990).
Jean Binta Breeze: *Riddym Ravings And Other Poems* (London: Race Today Publications, 1988).
Merle Collins: *Rotten Pomerac* (London: Virago, 1992).
Christine Craig: *Quadrille For Tigers* (Mina Press, 1984).
Mahadai Das: *Bones* (Peepal Tree Press, 1988).
Lorna Goodison: *I Am Becoming My Mother* (London: New Beacon, 1986).
Lorna Goodison: *Heartease* (London: New Beacon, 1988).
Amryl Johnson: *Gorgons* (Coventry: Cofa Press, 1992).
Grace Nichols: *i is a long memoried woman* (London: Karnak House, 1983).
Grace Nichols: *Lazy Thoughts of a Lazy Woman* (London: Virago, 1989).
Marlene Nourbese Philip: *She Tries Her Tongue, Her Silence Softly Breaks* (Charlottetown: Ragweed Press, 1989).
Marlene Nourbese Philip: *Looking For Livingstone* (Toronto: Mercury, 1991).
Velma Pollard: *Crown Point and Other Poems* (Leeds: Peepal Tree Press, 1988).
Olive Senior: *Talking of Trees* (Kingston: Calabash, 1985).

DONNA PALMATEER PENNEE

# Canadian Women's Literary Discourse in English, 1982-92

For those of us who take seriously the various and imbricated post-isms that underwrite and overdetermine our critical utterances, the task of writing literary history, even in as narrow a fragment as that demarcated by my title (and imposed by the word-limit of this forum), is both exciting and daunting. Competing claims and imperatives – to be as thorough as possible in coverage (and of what?) or to make strategic choices for the sake of a coherent narrative? to speak in lists or to historicize the scene(s) of writing? – mark my task in such ways as to signal at once the discursive richness and methodological fraughtness of contemporary literary critical gestures, the demands and rewards of an increasing attention to the multiple imbrications of the literary and the social (in their broadest senses). Committing the critical self to text and to limited text, is, for me, enormously difficult, and the difficulty is compounded by the object of this survey – the most explosive, prolific, and diverse decade in the history of women's writing in English in Canada.

My title signals a recognition that in Canadian literature in general, the distance between what we used to call the primary and secondary works, never very great even in the early history of CanLit, has diminished further in the last decade, not so much because of a belated (and misunderstood?) Barthesian sense of the death of the author (though the rise of the masculinist scriptor, especially in the Canadian West cannot be discounted), but in part because of the (at least) doubled position(ing) of so many of

Canada's women writers as both 'authors' and 'critics' (e.g., Lola Lemire Tostevin, Daphne Marlatt, Aritha van Herk, Janice Kulyk Keefer, Jane Rule, Margaret Atwood, Donna E. Smyth, Dionne Brand, Claire Harris, Makeda Silvera, Smaro Kamboureli, Himani Bannerji, Di Brandt, et al.), but also because of the collective and collaborative nature of the production and reception of women's literary discourse (creative and critical) in Canada. The women and words/*les femmes et les mots* conference (Vancouver, B.C., 1983, published as *in the feminine* [Longspoon, 1985]) and the Imag(in)ing Women conference (U of Alberta, 1990) superbly exemplify the diversity (in linguistic, ethnic, racial, erotic, class, and formal/generic constituents) of women's (uses of) 'literary' words. The beginning of traditional bibliographical compilation and codification of Canadian women's literature in *Gynocritics/gynocritiques*, edited and introduced by Barbara Godard (ECW, 1987), has rapidly been overtaken by the diversity and sheer proliferation of women's literary voices; conferences and journals have become extremely important forums for the production and reception of women's literary discourse.

A few books can be cited, however, as signs of the interrelatedness of the creative and the critical in women's literary discourse in Canada, for example, *A Mazing Space: Writing Canadian Women Writing*, edited by Shirley Neuman and Smaro Kamboureli (Longspoon/NeWest, 1986), and *Language in Her Eye: Writing and Gender: Views by Canadian Women Writing in English*, edited by Libby Scheier, Sarah Sheard and Eleanor Wachtel (Coach House, 1990), which contains pieces by writers of fiction, poetry, drama, journalism, and literary criticism. The cross-genre and cross-cultural representation in *Language in Her Eye*, the remarkably playful and 'irreverent' reshaping of 'academic' discourse instantiated by/in *A Mazing Space*, and the (often fractious) recognition of multiple constituents of women's subjectivities in an anthology such as *Telling It: Women and Language Across Cultures* (proceedings and commentary from a 1988 Women's Studies conference at Simon Fraser University, edited by Sky Lee, Lee Maracle and Betsy Warland; Press Gang, 1990), together are indicative of prevalent modes and issues of women's literary discourse in Canada. Journals such as *Room of One's Own, Tessera, Atlantis, Fireweed* (all devoted solely to women's writing), and *Toronto South Asian Review* and *Fuse* (devoted to transcultural discourse in Canada, and keenly aware of the intersections of gender, colonialism, and other constituents of reading and writing), are significant participants in women's literary discourse in Canada in the last decade.

Several of the above examples are not only indicative of the persistent crossings of traditional genre boundaries in Canadian women's writing, they also contain both anglo- and francophone texts; but bilingualism often occurs *within* texts as well, a register of how french feminist theorizing (Continental and québécoise) often informs contemporary (anglo)feminist writing. Examples might include Lola Lemire Tostevin's poetry which foregrounds and enacts the linguistic and bodied construction of women (e.g., *Color of Her Speech* [Coach House, 1982], *Gynotext* [Underwhich, 1983], and *Double Standards* [Longspoon, 1985]); Daphne Marlatt's collection of free verse/journal fragments *Touch to My Tongue* (Longspoon, 1984) which signals her break with the (mostly male) west coast phenomenologists, a break adumbrated in the matrilineal journal/autography/poetry of *How Hug a Stone* (Turnstone, 1983) and made clear once and for all in her much awaited ('poetic'/ fragmented) novel, *Ana Historic* (Coach House, 1988); here, the excavation of private family history parallels the excavation of a more public colonial history, and enables the discovery of a lesbian identity amidst the past and present obstacles to finding/establishing a women's continuum. The frequent bilingual intertexture of Canadian women's writing also registers how women's position in patriarchy figures as analogous to Quebec's position within Canada (as in, for example, Anne [McLean] Diamond's prose poem, *A Nun's Diary* [Vehicule, 1984; 1989] and short stories in *Snakebite* [Cormorant, 1989], or Gail Scott's experimental/poetic novel *Heroine* [Coach House, 1987] and her essays *Spaces Like Stairs*

[Women's Press, 1989], or Carole Corbeil's more accessible novel of middle class family relations, *Voice-Over* [Stoddart, 1992]).

The analogy between women in patriarchy and Canada's position vis-à-vis empire (whether it is the high cultural empire of England or the capitalist culture of American imperialism) is not as much of an issue as it was in women's writing in the 1970s (in the work of Margaret Atwood, Margaret Laurence, and Marian Engel, for example), although Atwood's novels *The Handmaid's Tale* (McClelland & Stewart, 1985) and *Cat's Eye* (1988) (more obviously the former) continue to thematize parallels between gender and colonial issues, as does Susan Swan's novel *The Biggest Modern Woman of the World* (Lester Orpen & Dennys, 1983) in which the story of the commercial (and gendered) exploitation of the historical giantess, Anna Swan, also tells a story of exploitative American-Canadian and familial relations. Donna E. Smyth's novel *Subversive Elements* (Women's Press, 1986), a fusion of environmentalist manifesto and handbook, earthmother primer, scholarly treatise, autobiography, regional history, and fictional romance, makes explicit the links between the exploitation of women and natural resources, and the marginalization of women's concerns in politics and history, of the maritime provinces in Canada, and of Canada in the American   technomilitary complex. Kristjana Gunnars' novel (a series of highly lyrical autobiographical and metafictional meditations) *The Prowler* (Red Deer College, 1989), also concerns exploitative political relations as they surface in her family's history and in the history of successive imperialisms of and forced migrations into Iceland. Similarly, though the protagonist of Sarah Murphy's novel *The Measure of Miranda* (NeWest, 1987), if such experimentally dense prose can be said to contain anything so conventional as a protagonist, is Canadian, she is preoccupied with the political horrors of Central America, and through them becomes increasingly conscious of gender(ed) horrors within the politics of family, professional, and national life.

Such texts as these, though they by no means represent the mainstream in publication or in criticism, are indicative of an increasingly complex creative and critical literary engagement with women's (and nations') multiple subjectivities. A formerly unidirectional awareness of gender and colonialism has been exploded in part by an interrogation of degrees of complicity in various forms of colonization of others, but in greater part by the proliferation of the voices of indigenous women (for example, Jeanette Armstrong, Beth Brant, Lee Maracle, Joan Crate, Beth Cuthand, J. B. Joe, Anne Cameron, Beatrice Culleton, and many others), and the voices of lesbians, women of colour and of immigrant or nonanglo backgrounds (for example, Dionne Brand, Claire Harris, Marlene Nourbese Philip, Himani Bannerji, Ayanna Black, Gay Allison, Betsy Warland, Sky Lee, Joy Kogawa, Yeshim Ternar, and many, many others) in whose work the intersections and imbrications of class, ethnicity, race, erotic preference, nation(s), and language(s) defy univocality and categorization of women's experience in general and of Canadian women's experience in particular. Very local, very specific but also very international women's concerns have come to characterize a significant portion of (anglo)literary discourse in Canada in the last decade. The work of Dionne Brand, for example (in her poetry, *Primitive Offensive* [Williams-Wallace, 1982], *Winter Epigrams and Epigrams to Ernesto Cardenal in Defense of Claudia* [1983], *Chronicles of a Hostile Sun* [1984], and *No Language is Neutral* [Coach House, 1990], her short stories, collected in *Sans Souci* [Williams-Wallace, 1988], and her criticism and film documentary work on racism and women's political activism), ranges from personal excavations of her birthplace (Trinidad) and lesbian identity to larger excavations of race and racism (whether in the context of the history of slavery or a train trip from Toronto to Montreal), to elegies on persecution wherever women commit themselves to political activism and discursive change (whether in a suburb in Toronto or in government offices and jails in Grenada).

But not all women's writing in Canada in the past decade is feminist or otherwise activist (*Language in Her Eye*, for example, represents both highly theorized/politicized statements and complaints that 'theory' and theoretically-inflected feminism function as censors). And not all women write (or continue to write – witness Audrey Thomas's most recent collection of short stories, *The Wild Blue Yonder* [Penguin, 1991]) in linguistically self-conscious and genre-transgressive forms. Apart from Alice Munro and Atwood's work (her most recent title of ten in the last decade is *Good Bones* [Coach House, 1992]), much of the bestselling fiction, of such accomplished stylists and prolific writers as Carol Shields, Jane Urquhart, Constance Beresford-Howe, Janice Kulyk Keefer, and Janette Turner Hospital, is written, by and large, in a recognizable tradition of realism and unified subjectivity (which isn't to say that it will or must be consumed as such). Similarly, regional (and again, for the most part realist) fiction continues to constitute an important vein of (anglo)Canadian writing (e.g., Sandra Birdsell, Gertrude Story, Rosemary Nixon, Lois Braun, Pat Krause, Bonnie Burnard, Edna Alford, and Sharon Butala of the various western provinces). The short story remains by far one of our most prolific and accomplished forms: Rosemary Sullivan has edited two anthologies for Oxford University Press (*Stories* and *More Stories by Canadian Women* [1984, 1987], but other indicative surveys include *Imagining Women* (Women's Press, 1988) and *Frictions* (Second Story Press, 1989); and several new writers whose work is as quirky in content as it is superbly crafted, have collections of their own (for example, Terry Griggs, Barbara Gowdy, Eliza Clark, Cynthia Flood, and Diane Schoemperlen). Likewise, the lyric and imagist impulses in poetry remain strong, though often pulled by a narrative impulse into prose lyric as well (e.g., Anne Michaels, Mary di Michele, Janice Kulyk Keefer, Roo Borson, Diana Hartog, Jan Horner, Patricia Young, and many others, and, the best of an earlier generation of women poets, P. K. Page and Phyllis Webb).

And finally, not all women's writing situates itself in relation to or is interested in other women's writing: the documentary and long poem traditions in Canadian writing continue to draw the interests of, for example, Sharon Thesen, Paulette Jiles, and Judith Fitzgerald (this poetry is strongly influenced by the formalist concerns of such poets as George Bowering, Robert Kroetsch, and Stephen Scobie), just as Aritha van Herk's fiction and criticism (see especially her 'cryptofrictions,' *In Visible Ink* [NeWest, 1991]), however feminist-inflected, has become increasingly 'cerebral' (which isn't to say that we can't have cerebral *and* bodied writing, for we do – witness the poetry of Bronwen Wallace, Erin Mouré and Lorna Crozier, for example, or van Herk's own novels).

As varied and polyglossic as the decade has been, it has also been a period of great loss, with the deaths of Marian Engel (1984), Margaret Laurence (1987), Gwendolyn MacEwan (1987), Bronwen Wallace (1989), and Adele Wiseman (1992), but a volume of Wallace's poems has been published posthumously (*Keep That Candle Burning Bright and Other Poems*, Coach House, 1991), and a collection of Engel's short stories (*Tattooed Woman*, Penguin, 1985). We have also been treated to the publication of previously unreleased material from earlier generations of women writers. Sheila Watson, for example, finally published her 1930s manuscript *Deep Hollow Creek* (McClelland & Stewart, 1992), the novel which preceded *The Double Hook* but seemed able to surface only after the feminist excavation of a specifically gendered and colonial history, suppressed for so long by a virile modernism. Likewise, Elizabeth Smart's stories, letters, drawings, poems, and autobiographical fragments have been published, as have 'new' stories of L. M. Montgomery, reissued stories of Sara Jeannette Duncan, new and collected poetry by Margaret Avison and Dorothy Livesay, and collected essays from Adele Wiseman and Miriam Waddington. And the critical anthology, *Re(Dis)covering Our Foremothers: Nineteenth-Century Canadian Women Writers*, edited by Lorraine McMullen (U of Ottawa, 1990), both resurrects once- or little-known writers and resituates the known. Women from myriad pasts (not just those of anglo ancestry) have come into speech in myriad ways in this most recent and rich decade in women's literary discourse in English in Canada.

# NOTES ON CONTRIBUTORS

RANJANA ASH is an Associate Fellow of the Centre for Research on Asian Migration at the University of Warwick and an editor/consultant for the Heinemann Asian Writers' Series.

MELISSA BOYDE and AMANDA LAWSON are post-graduate students at the University of Wollongong, NSW, Australia.

ANNE BREWSTER teaches at Curtin University, Western Australia.

JANE BRYCE teaches at the University of the West Indies, Barbados.

DIANA BRYDON is Professor at the University of Guelph, Canada.

ISABEL CARRERA teaches at the University of Oviedo, Spain.

SHIRLEY CHEW is Professor of Commonwealth literature at the University of Leeds.

HEIDE CREAMER lives in Massachusetts and researches on feminist writing and theory.

GEOFFREY DAVIS teaches at the University of Aachen, Germany.

NELOUFER DE MEL teaches at the University of Colombo, Sri Lanka.

LILAMANI DE SILVA teaches at the University of Peradeniya, Sri Lanka.

JEANNE DELBAERE is Professor at the Free University of Brussels, Belgium.

CORAL ANN HOWELLS is Professor of Canadian literature at Reading University, U.K.

LARS JENSEN is a graduate of Aarhus University and a post-graduate student at the University of Leeds, U.K.

DOROTHY JONES is Professor at the University of Wollongong, Australia.

JOAN KIRKBY is Professor at Macquarie University, Sydney, Australia.

KOH TAI ANN is Dean of Humanities at Nanyang University, Singapore.

ELAINE LINDSAY is completing her doctorate on several Australian women writers and does freelance reviewing for major Australian papers and magazines.

DENISE deCAIRES NARAIN teaches at the University of Sussex.

EVELYN O'CALLAGHAN teaches at the University of the West Indies, Barbados.

DONNA PALMATEER PENNEE teaches at Guelph University, Canada.

KIRSTEN HOLST PETERSEN teaches at Roskilde University, Denmark.

XAVIER PONS is Professor at the University of Toulouse, France.

ANNA RUTHERFORD teaches post-colonial literature at the University of Aarhus and is editor of *Kunapipi* and director of Dangaroo Press.

MARYLYNN SCOTT lives in Toronto, Canada.

GERRY TURCOTTE teaches at the University of Wollongong, NSW, Australia.

GILLIAN WHITLOCK teaches at Griffith University, Queensland, Australia.

JANET WILSON teaches at the University of Otago, New Zealand.

CHANTAL ZABUS is Professor at the University of Louvain, Belgium.


# PHOTOGRAPHY CREDITS

*Ama Ata Aidoo* p. 338 by Diana Van Maasdjik
*Sujata Bhatt* p. 554 by Jutta Golda
*Elleke Boehmer* p. 562 by Gillman & Soame
*Erna Brodber* p. 370 by Julian Stapleton
*Bonnie Burnard* p.450 by Dave Traynor
*Joan Crate* p.480 by Evan Taylor
*Tsitsi Dangarembga* p.344 by Anna Rutherford
*Shashi Deshpande* p. 270 by Anna Rutherford
*Diane Fahey* p. 102 by Gai Wilson
*Kathleen Mary Fallon* p. 110 by Corrie Ancone
*Beverley Farmer* p. 64 Philip Talihmandis
*Kate Grenville* p. 140 by William Yang
*Githa Hariharan* p. 280 by Jytte Bjerregård
*Janette Turner Hospital* p. 126 University of Sydney News
*Isabel Huggan* p. 486 by R. D. Huggan
*Jackie Kay* p. 530 by Suzanne Roden
*Joy Kogawa* p. 460 by Anna Rutherford
*Janice Kulyk Keefer* p. 440 by Susan Gilbert Tileston
*Bharati Mukherjee* p. 310 by Tom Victor
*Lauretta Ngcobo* p. 568 by Anna Rutherford
*Oodgeroo* p. 2 by Reece Scannell
*Joan Riley* p. 546 by Anna Rutherford
*Olive Senior* p. 382 by Victor Chang
*Jo Shapcott* p. 498 by David Hunter